Women, Fire, and Dangerous Things

George Lakoff

Women, Fire, and Dangerous Things

What Categories Reveal about the Mind

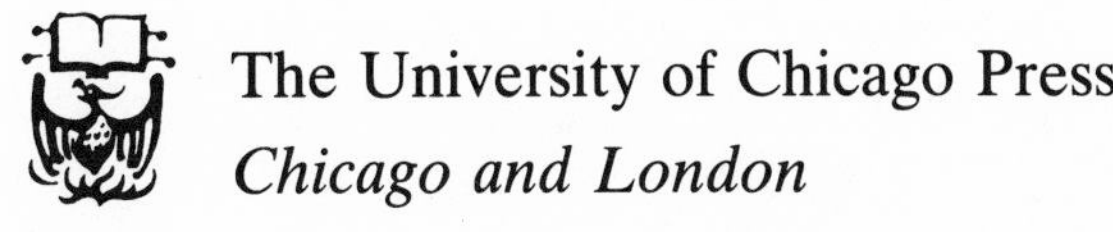

The University of Chicago Press
Chicago and London

George Lakoff is professor of linguistics at the University of California, Berkeley. He is the coauthor, with Mark Johnson, of *Metaphors We Live By*, also published by the University of Chicago Press, and the author of *Irregularity in Syntax*.

The University of Chicago Press, Chicago 60637
The University of Chicago Press, Ltd., London

Printed in the United States of America
97 96 95 94 93 92 91 90 89 88 65432

Library of Congress Cataloging-in-Publication Data

Lakoff, George.
Women, fire, and dangerous things.

Bibliography: p.
Includes index.
1. Psycholinguistics. 2. Categorization (Psychology).
3. Cognition. 4. Thought and thinking. 5. Reason.
I. Title.
P37.L344 1986 401.'9 86-19136
ISBN 0-226-46803-8

To Claudia

Contents

Book II: Case Studies

Acknowledgments

This book is very much a product of the incredibly stimulating and open intellectual environment of the University of California at Berkeley, where I have been privileged to work for the past thirteen years. I could not have done this work anywhere else. Much of what I have learned during this period has come through interactions with remarkable colleagues, especially Brent Berlin, Hubert Dreyfus, Charles Fillmore, Jim Greeno, Paul Kay, Eleanor Rosch, Dan Slobin, Eve Sweetser, Len Talmy, Robert Wilensky, and Lotfi Zadeh. I have also been blessed with remarkable students, especially Claudia Brugman, Pamela Downing, Michele Emanatian, Rob MacLaury, Chad McDaniel, and Jeanne van Oosten, and much of this book reflects what I have learned from them. Case study 2 is an extension and elaboration of part of Brugman's 1981 master's thesis. Case study 1 was done jointly with Zoltán Kövecses, whose stay at Berkeley during the 1982–83 academic year was funded by the American Council of Learned Societies. Without their insight, their diligence, and their generosity, this book would be much the poorer.

I have also been fortunate to be part of a widespread network of cognitive scientists whose research complements my own and who have been unsparingly generous in keeping me informed of their research and in commenting on mine:

Alton L. Becker, at the University of Michigan
Dwight Bolinger, emeritus from Harvard, now living in Palo Alto
Gilles Fauconnier, of the University of Paris at St. Denis
Dedre Gentner, at the University of Illinois at Urbana
Mark Johnson, at Southern Illinois University
Zoltán Kövecses, at Eotvos Lóránd University in Budapest
Ronald Langacker, at the University of California at San Diego
Susan Lindner, in Palo Alto
James D. McCawley, at the University of Chicago

David McNeill, at the University of Chicago
Hilary Putnam, at Harvard University
Naomi Quinn, at Duke University
John Robert Ross, at the Massachusetts Institute of Technology
David Zubin, at the State University of New York at Buffalo

I would also like to thank R. M. W. Dixon and Annette Schmidt of the Australian National University for providing me with a lengthy discussion of their research on Dyirbal categorization, as well as Pamela Downing and Haruo Aoki, who provided me with details about Japanese classifiers. Mark Johnson and Hilary Putnam have been extremely helpful in discussing philosophical issues, especially their recent work. The philosophical views put forth here have been worked out in collaboration with Johnson over many years. Robert Solovay and Saunders Mac Lane provided enormously useful discussions of the foundations of mathematics. Extensive comments on drafts of the manuscript have been provided by Jay Atlas, Lawrence Barsalou, Claudia Brugman, Michele Emanatian, Charles Fillmore, Jim Greeno, Mark Johnson, Paul Kay, Zoltán Kövecses, Robert McCauley, James D. McCawley, Carolyn Mervis, Ulric Neisser, Eleanor Rosch, Edward Smith, Robert Wilensky. Sustenance of extraordinary quality was provided by Cafe Fanny in Berkeley.

This research would not have been possible without grants from the National Science Foundation (grant no. BNS-8310445), the Sloan Foundation, and the Committee on Research of the University of California at Berkeley. I would especially like to thank Paul Chapin at NSF and Eric Wanner at Sloan.

Large projects like this cannot be completed without enormous sacrifices on the home front. Claudia Brugman and Andy Lakoff have put up with my unavailability for longer than I would like to think. I thank them for their patience and perseverance with all my heart.

Berkeley, California
July, 1985

Preface

Cognitive science is a new field that brings together what is known about the mind from many academic disciplines: psychology, linguistics, anthropology, philosophy, and computer science. It seeks detailed answers to such questions as: What is reason? How do we make sense of our experience? What is a conceptual system and how is it organized? Do all people use the same conceptual system? If so, what is that system? If not, exactly what is there that is common to the way all human beings think? The questions aren't new, but some recent answers are.

This book is about the traditional answers to these questions and about recent research that suggests new answers. On the traditional view, reason is abstract and disembodied. On the new view, reason has a bodily basis. The traditional view sees reason as literal, as primarily about propositions that can be objectively either true or false. The new view takes imaginative aspects of reason—metaphor, metonymy, and mental imagery—as central to reason, rather than as a peripheral and inconsequential adjunct to the literal.

The traditional account claims that the capacity for meaningful thought and for reason is abstract and not necessarily embodied in any organism. Thus, meaningful concepts and rationality are *transcendental*, in the sense that they transcend, or go beyond, the physical limitations of any organism. Meaningful concepts and abstract reason may happen to be embodied in human beings, or in machines, or in other organisms—but they exist abstractly, independent of any particular embodiment. In the new view, meaning is a matter of what is meaningful to thinking, functioning beings. The nature of the thinking organism and the way it functions in its environment are of central concern to the study of reason.

Both views take categorization as the main way that we make sense of experience. Categories on the traditional view are characterized solely by the properties shared by their members. That is, they are characterized (*a*) independently of the bodily nature of the beings doing the categorizing and (*b*) literally, with no imaginative mechanisms (metaphor, metonymy, and imagery) entering into the nature of categories. In the new view, our bodily experience and the way we use imaginative mechanisms are central to how we construct categories to make sense of experience.

Cognitive science is now in transition. The traditional view is hanging on, although the new view is beginning to take hold. Categorization is a central issue. The traditional view is tied to the classical theory that categories are defined in terms of common properties of their members. But a wealth of new data on categorization appears to contradict the traditional view of categories. In its place there is a new view of categories, what Eleanor Rosch has termed *the theory of prototypes and basic-level categories*. We will be surveying that data and its implications.

The traditional view is a philosophical one. It has come out of two thousand years of philosophizing about the nature of reason. It is still widely believed despite overwhelming empirical evidence against it. There are two reasons. The first is simply that it is traditional. The accumulated weight of two thousand years of philosophy does not go away overnight. We have all been educated to think in those terms. The second reason is that there has been, until recently, nothing approaching a well-worked-out alternative that preserves what was correct in the traditional view while modifying it to account for newly discovered data. This book will also be concerned with describing such an alternative.

We will be calling the traditional view *objectivism* for the following reason: Modern attempts to make it work assume that rational thought consists of the manipulation of abstract symbols and that these symbols get their meaning via a correspondence with the world, *objectively construed*, that is, independent of the understanding of any organism. A collection of symbols placed in correspondence with an objectively structured world is viewed as a *representation* of reality. On the objectivist view, *all* rational thought involves the manipulation of abstract symbols which are given meaning only via conventional correspondences with things in the external world.

Among the more specific objectivist views are the following:

- Thought is the mechanical manipulation of abstract symbols.
- The mind is an abstract machine, manipulating symbols essentially in the way a computer does, that is, by algorithmic computation.
- Symbols (e.g., words and mental representations) get their meaning via correspondences to things in the external world. All meaning is of this character.

- Symbols that correspond to the external world are *internal representations of external reality.*
- Abstract symbols may stand in correspondence to things in the world independent of the peculiar properties of any organisms.
- Since the human mind makes use of internal representations of external reality, the mind is *a mirror of nature*, and correct reason mirrors the logic of the external world.
- It is thus incidental to the nature of meaningful concepts and reason that human beings have the bodies they have and function in their environment in the way they do. Human bodies may play a role in *choosing* which concepts and which modes of transcendental reason human beings actually employ, but they play no essential role in *characterizing* what constitutes a concept and what constitutes reason.
- Thought is *abstract* and *disembodied*, since it is independent of any limitations of the human body, the human perceptual system, and the human nervous system.
- Machines that do no more than mechanically manipulate symbols that correspond to things in the world are capable of meaningful thought and reason.
- Thought is *atomistic*, in that it can be completely broken down into simple "building blocks"—the symbols used in thought—which are combined into complexes and manipulated by rule.
- Thought is *logical* in the narrow technical sense used by philosophical logicians; that is, it can be modeled accurately by systems of the sort used in mathematical logic. These are abstract symbol systems defined by general principles of symbol manipulation and mechanisms for interpreting such symbols in terms of "models of the world."

Though such views are by no means shared by all cognitive scientists, they are nevertheless widespread, and in fact so common that many of them are often assumed to be true without question or comment. Many, perhaps even most, contemporary discussions of the mind as a computing machine take such views for granted.

The idea of a *category* is central to such views. The reason is that most symbols (i.e., words and mental representations) do not designate particular things or individuals in the world (e.g., Rickey Henderson or the Golden Gate Bridge). Most of our words and concepts designate categories. Some of these are categories of things or beings in the physical world—chairs and zebras, for example. Others are categories of activities and abstract things—singing and songs, voting and governments, etc. To a very large extent, the objectivist view of language and thought rests on the nature of categories. On the objectivist view, things are in the same category if and only if they have certain properties in common. Those properties are necessary and sufficient conditions for defining the category.

On the objectivist view of meaning, the symbols used in thought get their meaning via their correspondence with things—particular things or categories of things—in the world. Since categories, rather than individuals, matter most in thought and reason, a category must be the sort of thing that can fit the objectivist view of mind in general. All conceptual categories must be symbols (or symbolic structures) that can designate categories in the real world, or in some possible world. And the world must come divided up into categories of the right kind so that symbols and symbolic structures can refer to them. "Categories of the right kind" are classical categories, categories defined by the properties common to all their members.

In recent years, conceptual categories have been studied intensively and in great detail in a number of the cognitive sciences—especially anthropology, linguistics, and psychology. The evidence that has accumulated is in conflict with the objectivist view of mind. Conceptual categories are, on the whole, very different from what the objectivist view requires of them. That evidence suggests a very different view, not only of categories, but of human reason in general:

- Thought is *embodied*, that is, the structures used to put together our conceptual systems grow out of bodily experience and make sense in terms of it; moreover, the core of our conceptual systems is directly grounded in perception, body movement, and experience of a physical and social character.
- Thought is *imaginative*, in that those concepts which are not directly grounded in experience employ metaphor, metonymy, and mental imagery—all of which go beyond the literal mirroring, or *representation*, of external reality. It is this imaginative capacity that allows for "abstract" thought and takes the mind beyond what we can see and feel. The imaginative capacity is also embodied—indirectly—since the metaphors, metonymies, and images are based on experience, often bodily experience. Thought is also imaginative in a less obvious way: every time we categorize something in a way that does not mirror nature, we are using general human imaginative capacities.
- Thought has *gestalt properties* and is thus not atomistic; concepts have an overall structure that goes beyond merely putting together conceptual "building blocks" by general rules.
- Thought has an *ecological structure.* The efficiency of cognitive pro-

cessing, as in learning and memory, depends on the overall structure of the conceptual system and on what the concepts mean. Thought is thus more than just the mechanical manipulation of abstract symbols.
- Conceptual structure can be described using *cognitive models* that have the above properties.
- The theory of cognitive models incorporates what was right about the traditional view of categorization, meaning, and reason, while accounting for the empirical data on categorization and fitting the new view overall.

I will refer to the new view as *experiential realism* or alternatively as *experientialism.* The term *experiential realism* emphasizes what experientialism shares with objectivism: (*a*) a commitment to the existence of the real world, (*b*) a recognition that reality places constraints on concepts, (*c*) a conception of truth that goes beyond mere internal coherence, and (*d*) a commitment to the existence of stable knowledge of the world.

Both names reflect the idea that thought fundamentally grows out of embodiment. "Experience" here is taken in a broad rather than a narrow sense. It includes everything that goes to make up actual or potential experiences of either individual organisms or communities of organisms —not merely perception, motor movement, etc., but *especially* the internal genetically acquired makeup of the organism and the nature of its interactions in both its physical and its social environments.

Experientialism is thus defined in contrast with objectivism, which holds that the characteristics of the organism have nothing essential to do with concepts or with the nature of reason. On the objectivist view, human reason is just a limited form of transcendental reason. The only roles accorded to the body are (*a*) to provide access to abstract concepts, (*b*) to provide "wetware," that is, a biological means of mimicking patterns of transcendental reason, and (*c*) to place limitations on possible concepts and forms of reason. On the experientialist view, reason is made possible by the body—that includes abstract and creative reason, as well as reasoning about concrete things. Human reason is not an instantiation of transcendental reason; it grows out of the nature of the organism and all that contributes to its individual and collective experience: its genetic inheritance, the nature of the environment it lives in, the way it functions in that environment, the nature of its social functioning, and the like.

The issue is this:

> Do meaningful thought and reason concern merely the manipulation of abstract symbols and their correspondence to an objective reality, independent of any embodiment (except, perhaps, for limitations imposed by the organism)?

> Or do meaningful thought and reason essentially concern the nature of the organism doing the thinking—including the nature of its body, its interactions in its environment, its social character, and so on?

Though these are highly abstract questions, there does exist a body of evidence that suggests that the answer to the first question is no and the answer to the second is yes. That is a significant part of what this book is about.

Why does all this matter? It matters for our understanding of who we are as human beings and for all that follows from that understanding. The capacity to reason is usually taken as defining what human beings are and as distinguishing us from other things that are alive. If we understand reason as being disembodied, then our bodies are only incidental to what we are. If we understand reason as mechanical—the sort of thing a computer can do—then we will devalue human intelligence as computers get more efficient. If we understand rationality as the capacity to mirror the world external to human beings, then we will devalue those aspects of the mind that can do infinitely more than that. If we understand reason as merely literal, we will devalue art.

How we understand the mind matters in all these ways and more. It matters for what we value in ourselves and others—for education, for research, for the way we set up human institutions, and most important for what counts as a humane way to live and act. If we understand reason as embodied, then we will want to understand the relationship between the mind and the body and to find out how to cultivate the embodied aspects of reason. If we fully appreciate the role of the imaginative aspects of reason, we will give them full value, investigate them more thoroughly, and provide better education in using them. Our ideas about what people can learn and should be learning, as well as what they should be doing with what they learn, depend on our concept of learning itself. It is important that we have discovered that learning for the most part is neither rote learning nor the learning of mechanical procedures. It is important that we have discovered that rational thought goes well beyond the literal and the mechanical. It is important because our ideas about how human minds should be employed depend on our ideas of what a human mind is.

It also matters in a narrower but no less important way. Our understanding of what reason is guides our current research on the nature of reason. At present, that research is expanding faster than at any time in history. The research choices made now by the community of cognitive scientists will shape our view of mind for a long time to come. We are at present at an important turning point in the history of the study of the mind. It is vital that the mistaken views about the mind that have been with us for two thousand years be corrected.

This book attempts to bring together some of the evidence for the view that reason is embodied and imaginative—in particular, the evidence that comes from the study of the way people categorize. Conceptual systems are organized in terms of categories, and most if not all of our thought involves those categories. The objectivist view rests on a theory of categories that goes back to the ancient Greeks and that even today is taken for granted as being not merely true, but obviously and unquestionably true. Yet contemporary studies of the way human beings actually categorize things suggest that categorization is a rather different and more complex matter.

What is most interesting to me about these studies is that they seem to provide evidence for the experientialist view of human reason and against the objectivist view. Taken one by one, such studies are things only scholars could care about, but taken as a whole, they have something magnificent about them: evidence that the mind is more than a mere mirror of nature or a processor of symbols, that it is not incidental to the mind that we have bodies, and that the capacity for understanding and meaningful thought goes beyond what any machine can do.

BOOK I

The Mind beyond the Machine

PART I

Categories and Cognitive Models

CHAPTER 1

The Importance of Categorization

Many readers, I suspect, will take the title of this book as suggesting that women, fire, and dangerous things have something in common—say, that women are fiery and dangerous. Most feminists I've mentioned it to have loved the title for that reason, though some have hated it for the same reason. But the chain of inference—from conjunction to categorization to commonality—is the norm. The inference is based on the common idea of what it means to be in the same category: things are categorized together on the basis of what they have in common. The idea that categories are defined by common properties is not only our everyday folk theory of what a category is, it is also the principal technical theory—one that has been with us for more than two thousand years.

The classical view that categories are based on shared properties is not entirely wrong. We often do categorize things on that basis. But that is only a small part of the story. In recent years it has become clear that categorization is far more complex than that. A new theory of categorization, called *prototype theory*, has emerged. It shows that human categorization is based on principles that extend far beyond those envisioned in the classical theory. One of our goals is to survey the complexities of the way people really categorize. For example, the title of this book was inspired by the Australian aboriginal language Dyirbal, which has a category, *balan*, that actually includes women, fire, and dangerous things. It also includes birds that are *not* dangerous, as well as exceptional animals, such as the platypus, bandicoot, and echidna. This is not simply a matter of categorization by common properties, as we shall see when we discuss Dyirbal classification in detail.

Categorization is not a matter to be taken lightly. There is nothing more basic than categorization to our thought, perception, action, and speech. Every time we see something as a *kind* of thing, for example, a tree, we are categorizing. Whenever we reason about *kinds* of things—chairs, nations, illnesses, emotions, any kind of thing at all—we are employing categories. Whenever we intentionally perform any *kind* of action, say something as mundane as writing with a pencil, hammering with a hammer, or ironing clothes, we are using categories. The particular action we perform on that occasion is a *kind* of motor activity (e.g., writing, hammering, ironing), that is, it is in a particular category of motor actions. They are never done in exactly the same way, yet despite the differences in particular movements, they are all movements of a kind, and we know how to make movements of that kind. And any time we either produce or understand any utterance of any reasonable length, we are employing dozens if not hundreds of categories: categories of speech sounds, of words, of phrases and clauses, as well as conceptual categories. Without the ability to categorize, we could not function at all, either in the physical world or in our social and intellectual lives. An understanding of how we categorize is central to any understanding of how we think and how we function, and therefore central to an understanding of what makes us human.

Most categorization is automatic and unconscious, and if we become aware of it at all, it is only in problematic cases. In moving about the world, we automatically categorize people, animals, and physical objects, both natural and man-made. This sometimes leads to the impression that we just categorize things as they are, that things come in natural kinds, and that our categories of mind naturally fit the kinds of things there are in the world. But a large proportion of our categories are not categories of *things*; they are categories of abstract entities. We categorize events, actions, emotions, spatial relationships, social relationships, and abstract entities of an enormous range: governments, illnesses, and entities in both scientific and folk theories, like electrons and colds. Any adequate account of human thought must provide an accurate theory for *all* our categories, both concrete and abstract.

From the time of Aristotle to the later work of Wittgenstein, categories were thought be well understood and unproblematic. They were assumed to be abstract containers, with things either inside or outside the category. Things were assumed to be in the same category if and only if they had certain properties in common. And the properties they had in common were taken as defining the category.

This classical theory was not the result of empirical study. It was not even a subject of major debate. It was a philosophical position arrived at on the basis of a priori speculation. Over the centuries it simply became part of the background assumptions taken for granted in most scholarly disciplines. In fact, until very recently, the classical theory of categories was not even thought of as a *theory*. It was taught in most disciplines not as an empirical hypothesis but as an unquestionable, definitional truth.

In a remarkably short time, all that has changed. Categorization has moved from the background to center stage because of empirical studies in a wide range of disciplines. Within cognitive psychology, categorization has become a major field of study, thanks primarily to the pioneering work of Eleanor Rosch, who made categorization an issue. She focused on two implications of the classical theory:

> First, if categories are defined only by properties that all members share, then no members should be better examples of the category than any other members.
>
> Second, if categories are defined only by properties inherent in the members, then categories should be independent of the peculiarities of any beings doing the categorizing; that is, they should not involve such matters as human neurophysiology, human body movement, and specific human capacities to perceive, to form mental images, to learn and remember, to organize the things learned, and to communicate efficiently.

Rosch observed that studies by herself and others demonstrated that categories, in general, have best examples (called "prototypes") and that all of the specifically human capacities just mentioned do play a role in categorization.

In retrospect, such results should not have been all that surprising. Yet the specific details sent shock waves throughout the cognitive sciences, and many of the reverberations are still to be felt. Prototype theory, as it is evolving, is changing our idea of the most fundamental of human capacities—the capacity to categorize—and with it, our idea of what the human mind and human reason are like. Reason, in the West, has long been assumed to be disembodied and abstract—distinct on the one hand from perception and the body and culture, and on the other hand from the mechanisms of imagination, for example, metaphor and mental imagery.

In this century, reason has been understood by many philosophers, psychologists, and others as roughly fitting the model of formal deductive logic:

> Reason is the mechanical manipulation of abstract symbols which are meaningless in themselves, but can be given meaning by virtue of their capacity to refer to things either in the actual world or in possible states of the world.

Since the digital computer works by symbol manipulation and since its symbols can be interpreted in terms of a data base, which is often viewed as a partial model of reality, the computer has been taken by many as essentially possessing the capacity to reason. This is the basis of the contemporary mind-as-computer metaphor, which has spread from computer science and cognitive psychology to the culture at large.

Since we reason not just about individual things or people but about categories of things and people, categorization is crucial to every view of reason. Every view of reason must have an associated account of categorization. The view of reason as the *disembodied* manipulation of abstract symbols comes with an implicit theory of categorization. It is a version of the classical theory in which categories are represented by sets, which are in turn defined by the properties shared by their members.

There is a good reason why the view of reason as disembodied symbol-manipulation makes use of the classical theory of categories. If symbols in general can get their meaning only through their capacity to correspond to things, then *category* symbols can get their meaning only through a capacity to correspond to *categories* in the world (the real world or some possible world). Since the symbol-to-object correspondence that defines meaning in general must be independent of the peculiarities of the human mind and body, it follows that the symbol-to-category correspondence that defines meaning for category symbols must also be independent of the peculiarities of the human mind and body. To accomplish this, categories must be seen as existing in the world independent of people and defined only by the characteristics of their members and not in terms of any characteristics of the human. The classical theory is just what is needed, since it defines categories only in terms of shared properties of the *members* and not in terms of the peculiarities of human understanding.

To question the classical view of categories in a fundamental way is thus to question the view of reason as disembodied symbol-manipulation and correspondingly to question the most popular version of the mind-as-computer metaphor. Contemporary prototype theory does just that—through detailed empirical research in anthropology, linguistics, and psychology.

The approach to prototype theory that we will be presenting here suggests that human categorization is essentially a matter of both human experience and imagination—of perception, motor activity, and culture on the one hand, and of metaphor, metonymy, and mental imagery on the other. As a consequence, human reason crucially depends on the same factors, and therefore cannot be characterized merely in terms of the manipulation of abstract symbols. Of course, certain aspects of human reason can be isolated artificially and modeled by abstract symbol-manipulation, just as some part of human categorization does fit the classical theory. But we are interested not merely in some artificially isolatable subpart of the human capacity to categorize and reason, but in the full range of that capacity. As we shall see, those aspects of categorization that do fit the classical theory are special cases of a general theory of cognitive models, one that permits us to characterize the experiential and imaginative aspects of reason as well.

To change the very concept of a category is to change not only our concept of the mind, but also our understanding of the world. Categories are categories *of* things. Since we understand the world not only in terms of individual things but also in terms of *categories* of things, we tend to attribute a real existence to those categories. We have categories for biological species, physical substances, artifacts, colors, kinsmen, and emotions and even categories of sentences, words, and meanings. We have categories for everything we can think about. To change the concept of *category* itself is to change our understanding of the world. At stake is our understanding of everything from what a biological species is (see chap. 12) to what a word is (see case study 2).

The evidence we will be considering suggests a shift from classical categories to prototype-based categories defined by cognitive models. It is a change that implies other changes: changes in the concepts of truth, knowledge, meaning, rationality—even grammar. A number of familiar ideas will fall by the wayside. Here are some that will have to be left behind:

- Meaning is based on truth and reference; it concerns the relationship between symbols and things in the world.
- Biological species are natural kinds, defined by common essential properties.
- The mind is separate from, and independent of, the body.
- Emotion has no conceptual content.
- Grammar is a matter of pure form.
- Reason is transcendental, in that it transcends—goes beyond—the way human beings, or any other kinds of beings, happen to think. It concerns the inferential relationships among all possible concepts in this universe or any other. Mathematics is a form of transcendental reason.
- There is a correct, God's eye view of the world—a single correct way of understanding what is and is not true.
- All people think using the same conceptual system.

These ideas have been part of the superstructure of Western intellectual life for two thousand years. They are tied, in one way or another, to the classical concept of a category. When that concept is left behind, the others will be too. They need to be replaced by ideas that are not only more accurate, but more humane.

Many of the ideas we will be arguing against, on empirical grounds, have been taken as part of what *defines* science. One consequence of this study will be that certain common views of science will seem too narrow. Consider, for example, scientific rigor. There is a narrow view of science that considers as rigorous only hypotheses framed in first-order predicate calculus with a standard model-theoretic interpretation, or some equivalent system, say a computer program using primitives that are taken as corresponding to an external reality. Let us call this the predicate calculus (or "PC") view of scientific theorizing. The PC view characterizes explanations only in terms of deductions from hypotheses, or correspondingly, in terms of computations. Such a methodology not only claims to be rigorous in itself, it also claims that no other approach can be sufficiently precise to be called scientific. The PC view is prevalent in certain communities of linguists and cognitive psychologists and enters into many investigations in the cognitive sciences.

Such a view of science has long been discredited among philosophers of science (for example, see Hanson 1961, Hesse 1963, Kuhn 1970, 1977, and Feyerabend 1975). As we will see (chaps. 11–20), the PC view is especially inappropriate in the cognitive sciences since it *assumes* an a priori view of categorization, namely, the classical theory that categories are sets defined by common properties of objects. Such an assumption makes it impossible to ask, as an empirical question, whether the classical view of categorization is correct. The classical view is assumed to be correct, because it is built into classical logic, and hence into the PC view. Thus, we sometimes find circular arguments about the nature of categorization that are of the following form:

Premise (often hidden): The PC view of scientific rigor is correct.

. . .

. . .

. . .

Conclusion: Categories are classical.

The conclusion is, of course, presupposed by the premise. To avoid vacuity, the empirical study of categorization cannot take the PC view of scientific rigor for granted.

A central goal of cognitive science is to discover what reason is like and, correspondingly, what categories are like. It is therefore especially important for the study of cognitive science not to assume the PC view, which presupposes an a priori answer to such empirical questions. This, of course, does not mean that one cannot be rigorous or precise. It only means that rigor and precision must be characterized in another way—a way that does not stifle the empirical study of the mind. We will suggest such a way in chapter 17.

The PC view of rigor leads to rigor mortis in the study of categorization. It leads to a view of the sort proposed by Osherson and Smith (1981) and Armstrong, Gleitman, and Gleitman (1983) and discussed in chapter 9 below, namely, that the classical view of categorization is correct and the enormous number of phenomena that do not accord with it are either due to an "identification" mechanism that has nothing to do with reason or are minor "recalcitrant" phenomena. As we go through this book, we will see that there seem to be more so-called recalcitrant phenomena than there are phenomena that work by the classical view.

This book surveys a wide variety of rigorous empirical studies of the nature of human categorization. In concluding that categorization is not classical, the book implicitly suggests that the PC view of scientific rigor is itself not scientifically valid. The result is not chaos, but an expanded perspective on human reason, one which by no means requires imprecision or vagueness in scientific inquiry. The studies cited, for example, those by Berlin, Kay, Ekman, Rosch, Tversky, Dixon, and many others, more than meet the prevailing standards of scientific rigor and accuracy, while challenging the conception of categories presupposed by the PC view of rigor. In addition, the case studies presented below in Book II are intended as examples of empirical research that meet or exceed the prevailing standards. In correcting the classical view of categorization, such studies serve to raise the general standards of scientific accuracy in the cognitive sciences.

The view of categorization that I will be presenting has not arisen all at once. It has developed through a number of intermediate stages that lead up to the cognitive model approach. An account of those intermediate steps begins with the later philosophy of Ludwig Wittgenstein and goes up through the psychological research of Eleanor Rosch and her associates.

CHAPTER 2

From Wittgenstein to Rosch

The short history I am about to give is not intended to be exhaustive. Its purpose, instead, is to give some sense of the development of the major themes I will be discussing. Here are some of those themes.

Family resemblances: The idea that members of a category may be related to one another without all members having any properties in common that define the category.

Centrality: The idea that some members of a category may be "better examples" of that category than others.

Polysemy as categorization: The idea that related meanings of words form categories and that the meanings bear family resemblances to one another.

Generativity as a prototype phenomenon: This idea concerns categories that are defined by a generator (a particular member or subcategory) plus rules (or a general principle such as similarity). In such cases, the generator has the status of a central, or "prototypical," category member.

Membership gradience: The idea that at least some categories have degrees of membership and no clear boundaries.

Centrality gradience: The idea that members (or subcategories) which are clearly within the category boundaries may still be more or less central.

Conceptual embodiment: The idea that the properties of certain categories are a consequence of the nature of human biological capacities and of the experience of functioning in a physical and social environment. It is contrasted with the idea that concepts exist independent of the bodily nature of any thinking beings and independent of their experience.

Functional embodiment: The idea that certain concepts are not merely *understood intellectually;* rather, they are *used* automatically, unconsciously, and without noticeable effort as part of normal functioning. Concepts used in this way have a different, and more important, psychological status than those that are only thought about consciously.

Basic-level categorization: The idea that categories are not merely organized in a hierarchy from the most general to the most specific, but are also organized so that the categories that are cognitively basic are "in the middle" of a general-to-specific hierarchy. Generalization proceeds "upward" from the basic level and specialization proceeds "downward."

Basic-level primacy: The idea that basic-level categories are functionally and epistemologically primary with respect to the following factors: gestalt perception, image formation, motor movement, knowledge organization, ease of cognitive processing (learning, recognition, memory, etc.), and ease of linguistic expression.

Reference-point, or "metonymic," reasoning: The idea that a part of a category (that is, a member or subcategory) can stand for the whole category in certain reasoning processes.

What unites these themes is the idea of a cognitive model:

- Cognitive models are directly *embodied* with respect to their content, or else they are systematically linked to directly embodied models. Cognitive models structure thought and are used in forming categories and in reasoning. Concepts characterized by cognitive models are understood via the embodiment of the models.
- Most cognitive models are embodied with respect to use. Those that are not are only used consciously and with noticeable effort.
- The nature of conceptual embodiment leads to *basic-level categorization* and *basic-level primacy.*
- Cognitive models are used in *reference-point, or "metonymic," reasoning.*
- *Membership gradience* arises when the cognitive model characterizing a concept contains a scale.
- *Centrality gradience* arises through the interaction of cognitive models.
- *Family resemblances* involve resemblances among models.
- *Polysemy* arises from the fact that there are systematic relationships between different cognitive models and between elements of the same model. The same word is often used for elements that stand in such cognitive relations to one another.

Thus it is the concept of a cognitive model, which we will discuss in the remainder of the book, that ties together the themes of this section.

The scholars we will be discussing in this section are those I take to be most representative of the development of these themes:

– Ludwig Wittgenstein is associated with the ideas of family resemblance, centrality, and gradience.
– J. L. Austin's views on the relationships among meanings of words are both a crystalization of earlier ideas in lexicography and historical semantics and a precursor of the contemporary view of polysemy as involving family resemblances among meanings.
– Lotfi Zadeh began the technical study of categories with fuzzy boundaries by conceiving of a theory of fuzzy sets as a generalization of standard set theory.
– Floyd Lounsbury's generative analysis of kinship categories is an important link between the idea that a category can be generated by a generator plus rules and the idea that a category has central members (and subcategories).
– Brent Berlin and Paul Kay are perhaps best known for their research on color categories, which empirically established the ideas of centrality and gradience.
– Paul Kay and Chad McDaniel put together color research from anthropology and neurophysiology and established the importance of the embodiment of concepts and the role that embodiment plays in determining centrality.
– Roger Brown began the study of what later became known as "basic-level categories." He observed that there is a "first level" at which children learn object categories and name objects, which is neither the most general nor most specific level. This level is characterized by distinctive actions, as well as by shorter and more frequently used names. He saw this level of categorization as "natural," whereas he viewed higher-level and lower-level categorization as "achievements of the imagination."
– Brent Berlin and his associates, in research on plant and animal naming, empirically established for these domains many of the fundamental ideas associated with basic-level categorization and basic-level primacy. They thereby demonstrated that embodiment determines some of the most significant properties of human categories.
– Paul Ekman and his co-workers have shown that there are universal basic human emotions that have physical correlates in facial expressions and the autonomic nervous system. He thereby confirmed such ideas as basic-level concepts, basic-level primacy, and centrality while demonstrating that emotional concepts are embodied.

– Eleanor Rosch saw the generalizations behind such studies of particular cases and proposed that thought in general is organized in terms of prototypes and basic-level structures. It was Rosch who saw categorization itself as one of the most important issues in cognition. Together with Carolyn Mervis and other co-workers, Rosch established research paradigms in cognitive psychology for demonstrating centrality, family resemblance, basic-level categorization, basic-level primacy, and reference-point reasoning, as well as certain kinds of embodiment. Rosch is perhaps best known for developing experimental paradigms for determining subjects' ratings of how good an example of a category a member is judged to be. Rosch ultimately realized that these ratings do not in themselves constitute models for representing category structure. They are effects that are inconsistent with the classical theory and that place significant constraints on what an adequate account of categorization must be.

These scholars all played a significant role in the history of the paradigm we will be presenting. The theory of cognitive models, which we will discuss later, attempts to bring their contributions into a coherent paradigm.

There are some notable omissions from our short survey. Since graded categories will be of only passing interest to us, I will not be mentioning much of the excellent work in that area. Graded categories are real. To my knowledge, the most detailed empirical study of graded categories is Kempton's thoroughly documented book on cognitive prototypes with graded extensions (Kempton 1981). It is based on field research in Mexico on the categorization of pottery. I refer the interested reader to that superb work, as well as to Labov's classic 1973 paper. I will also have relatively little to say about fuzzy set theory, since it is also tangential to our concerns here. Readers interested in the extensive literature that has developed on the theory of fuzzy sets and systems should consult (Dubois and Prade 1980). There is also a tradition of research in cognitive psychology that will not be surveyed here. Despite Rosch's ultimate refusal to interpret her goodness-of-example ratings as constituting a representation of category structure, other psychologists have taken that path and have given what I call an EFFECTS = STRUCTURE INTERPRETATION to Rosch's results. Smith and Medin (1980) have done an excellent survey of research in cognitive psychology that is based on this interpretation. In chapter 9 below, I will argue that the EFFECTS = STRUCTURE INTERPRETATION is in general inadequate.

Let us now turn to our survey.

Wittgenstein

Family Resemblances

The first major crack in the classical theory is generally acknowledged to have been noticed by Wittgenstein (1953, 1:66–71). The classical category has *clear boundaries,* which are defined by *common properties.* Wittgenstein pointed out that a category like *game* does not fit the classical mold, since there are no common properties shared by all games. Some games involve mere amusement, like ring-around-the-rosy. Here there is no competition—no winning or losing—though in other games there is. Some games involve luck, like board games where a throw of the dice determines each move. Others, like chess, involve skill. Still others, like gin rummy, involve both.

Though there is no single collection of properties that all games share, the category of games is united by what Wittgenstein calls *family resemblances.* Members of a family resemble one another in various ways: they may share the same build or the same facial features, the same hair color, eye color, or temperament, and the like. But there need be no single collection of properties shared by everyone in a family. Games, in this respect, are like families. Chess and go both involve competition, skill, and the use of long-term strategies. Chess and poker both involve competition. Poker and old maid are both card games. In short, games, like family members, are similar to one another in a wide variety of ways. That, and not a single, well-defined collection of common properties, is what makes *game* a category.

Extendable Boundaries

Wittgenstein also observed that there was no fixed boundary to the category *game.* The category could be extended and new kinds of games introduced, provided that they resembled previous games in appropriate ways. The introduction of video games in the 1970s was a recent case in history where the boundaries of the *game* category were extended on a large scale. One can always impose an artificial boundary for some purpose; what is important for his point is that extensions are possible, as well as artificial limitations. Wittgenstein cites the example of the category *number.* Historically, numbers were first taken to be integers and were then extended successively to rational numbers, real numbers, complex numbers, transfinite numbers, and all sorts of other kinds of numbers invented by mathematicians. One can for some purpose limit the category *number* to integers only, or rational numbers only, or real numbers only. But the category *number* is not bounded in any natural way, and it can be limited or extended depending on one's purposes.

In mathematics, intuitive human concepts like *number* must receive precise definitions. Wittgenstein's point is that different mathematicians give different precise definitions, depending on their goals. One can define *number* to include or exclude transfinite numbers, infinitesimals, inaccessible ordinals, and the like. The same is true of the concept of a *polyhedron*. Lakatos (1976) describes a long history of disputes within mathematics about the properties of polyhedra, beginning with Euler's conjecture that the number of vertices minus the number of edges plus the number of faces equals two. Mathematicians over the years have come up with counterexamples to Euler's conjecture, only to have other mathematicians claim that they had used the "wrong" definition of *polyhedron*. Mathematicians have defined and redefined *polyhedron* repeatedly to fit their goals. The point again is that there is no single well-defined intuitive category *polyhedron* that includes tetrahedra and cubes and some fixed range of other constructs. The category *polyhedron* can be given precise boundaries in many ways, but the intuitive concept is not limited in any of those ways; rather, it is open to both limitations and extensions.

Central and Noncentral Members

According to the classical theory, categories are uniform in the following respect: they are defined by a collection of properties that the category members share. Thus, no members should be more central than other members. Yet Wittgenstein's example of *number* suggests that integers are central, that they have a status as numbers that, say, complex numbers or transfinite numbers do not have. Every precise definition of *number* must include the integers; not every definition must include transfinite numbers. If anything is a number, the integers are numbers; that is not true of transfinite numbers. Similarly, any definition of polyhedra had better include tetrahedra and cubes. The more exotic polyhedra can be included or excluded, depending on your purposes. Wittgenstein suggests that the same is true of games. "Someone says to me: 'Show the children a game.' I teach them gaming with dice, and the other says 'I didn't mean that sort of game' " (1:70). Dice is just not a very good example of a game. The fact that there can be good and bad examples of a category does not follow from the classical theory. Somehow the goodness-of-example structure needs to be accounted for.

Austin

Wittgenstein assumed that there is a single category named by the word *game*, and he proposed that that category and other categories are structured by family resemblances and good and bad examples. Philosopher J. L. Austin extended this sort of analysis to the study of words themselves. In his celebrated paper, "The Meaning of a Word," written in 1940 and published in 1961, Austin asked, "Why do we call different [kinds of] things by the same name?" The traditional answer is that the kinds of things named are similar, where "similar" means "partially identical." This answer relies on the classical theory of categories. If there are common properties, those properties form a classical category, and the name applies to this category. Austin argued that this account is not accurate. He cited several classes of cases. As we will see in the remainder of this book, Austin's analysis prefigured much of contemporary cognitive semantics—especially the application of prototype theory to the study of word meaning.

If we translate Austin's remarks into contemporary terms, we can see the relationship between Austin's observation and Wittgenstein's: the senses of a word can be seen as forming a category, with each sense being a member of that category. Since the senses often do not have properties in common, there is no classical category of senses that the word could be naming. However, the senses can be viewed as forming a category of the kind Wittgenstein described. There are central senses and noncentral senses. The senses may not be similar (in the sense of sharing properties), but instead are related to one another in other specifiable ways. It is such relationships among the senses that enable those senses to be viewed as constituting a single category: the relationships provide an explanation of why a single word is used to express those particular senses. This idea is far from new. Part of the job of traditional historical semanticists, as well as lexicographers, has been to speculate on such relationships. Recent research has taken up this question again in a systematic way. The most detailed contemporary study along these lines has been done by Brugman (1981), and it will be discussed below in case study 2.

Let us now turn to Austin's examples:

> The adjective 'healthy': when I talk of a healthy body, and again of a healthy complexion, of healthy exercise: the word is *not* just being used *equivocally* . . . there is what we may call a *primary nuclear sense* of 'healthy': the sense in which 'healthy' is used of a healthy body: I call this *nuclear* because it is 'contained as a part' in the other two senses which may be set out as 'productive of healthy bodies' and 'resulting from a healthy body'. . . . Now are we content to say that the exercise, the complexion, and the body are all called 'healthy' because they are similar? Such a remark cannot fail to be misleading. Why make it? (P. 71)

Austin's *primary nuclear sense* corresponds to what contemporary linguists call *central* or *prototypical* senses. The contained-as-a-part relationship is an instance of what we will refer to below as metonymy—where the part stands for the whole. Thus, given the relationships "productive of" and "resulting from," Austin's examples can be viewed in the following way:

Exercise of type *B* is productive of bodies of type *A*.
Complexion of type *C* results from bodies of type *A*.
The word *healthy* names *A*.
With respect to naming, *A* stands for *B*. (Metonymy)
With respect to naming, *A* stands for *C*. (Metonymy)

Thus, the word "healthy" has senses *A, B*, and *C. A, B*, and *C* form a category whose members are related in the above way. *A* is the central member of this category of senses (Austin's *primary nuclear sense*). *B* and *C* are extended senses, where metonymy is the principle of extension.

I am interpreting Austin as making an implicit psychological claim about categorization. In the very act of pointing out and analyzing the *differences* among the senses, Austin is presupposing that these senses form a natural collection for speakers—so natural that the senses have to be differentiated by an analyst. No such analysis would be needed for true homonyms, say, *bank* (where you put your money) and *bank* (of a river), which are not part of a natural collection (or category) of senses. In pointing out the existence of a small number of mechanisms by which senses are related to one another, Austin is implicitly suggesting that those mechanisms are psychologically real (rather than being just the arbitrary machinations of a clever analyst). He is, after all, trying to explain why people naturally use the same words for different senses. His implicit claim is that these mechanisms are *principles* which provide a "good reason" for grouping the senses together by the use of the same word. What I have referred to as "metonymy" is just one such mechanism.

From metonymy, Austin turns to what Johnson and I (Lakoff and Johnson 1980) refer to as metaphor, but which Austin, following Aristotle, terms "analogy."

> When *A*:*B*::*X*:*Y* then *A* and *X* are often called by the same name, e.g., the foot of a mountain and the foot of a list. Here there is a good reason for calling the things both "feet" but are we to say they are "similar"? Not in any ordinary sense. We may say that the relations in which they stand to *B* and *Y* are similar relations. Well and good: but *A* and *X* are not the relations in which they stand. (Pp. 71–72)

Austin isn't explicit here, but what seems to be going on is that both mountains and lists are being structured in terms of a metaphorical projection of the human body onto them. Expanding somewhat on Austin's analysis and translating it into contemporary terminology, we have:

A is the bottom-most part of the body.
X is the bottom-most part of the mountain.
X′ is the bottom-most part of a list.
Body is projected onto mountain, with *A* projected onto *X*. (Metaphor)
Body is projected onto list, with *A* projected onto *X′*. (Metaphor)
The word "foot" names *A*.
A, X, and *X′* form a category, with *A* as central member. *X* and *X′* are noncentral members related to *A* by metaphor.

Austin also notes examples of what we will refer to below as *chaining* within a category.

> Another case is where I call *B* by the same name as *A*, because it resembles *A*, *C* by the same name because it resembles *B*, *D* . . . and so on. But ultimately *A* and, say *D* do not resemble each other in any recognizable sense at all. This is a very common case: and the dangers are obvious when we search for something 'identical' in all of them! (P. 72)

Here A is the *primary nuclear sense*, and *B, C*, and *D* are extended senses forming a chain. *A, B, C*, and *D* are all members of the same category of senses, with A as the central member.

> Take a word like 'fascist': this originally connotes a great many characteristics at once: say, *x, y*, and *z*. Now we will use 'fascist' subsequently of things which possess only *one* of these striking characteristics. So that things called 'fascist' in these senses, which we may call 'incomplete' senses, need not be similar at all to each other. (P. 72)

This example is very much like one Fillmore (1982*a*) has recently given in support of the use of prototype theory in lexical semantics. Fillmore takes the verb *climb*, as in

– John climbed the ladder.

Here, "climbing" includes both motion upward and the use of the hands to grasp onto the thing climbed. However, climbing can involve just motion upwards and no use of the hands, as in

– The airplane climbed to 20,000 feet.

Or the motion upward may be eliminated if there is grasping of the appropriate sort, as in

– He climbed out onto the ledge.

Such contemporary semantic analyses using prototype theory are very much in the spirit of Austin.

Fillmore's frame semantics is also prefigured by Austin.

> Take the sense in which I talk of a cricket bat and a cricket ball and a cricket umpire. The reason that all are called by the same name is perhaps that each has its part —its *own special* part—to play in the activity called cricketing: it is no good to say that *cricket* means simply 'used in cricket': for we cannot explain what we mean by 'cricket' *except* by explaining the special parts played in cricketing by the bat, ball, etc. (P. 73)

Austin here is discussing a holistic structure—a gestalt—governing our understanding of activities like cricket. Such activities are structured by what we call a cognitive model, an overall structure which is more than merely a composite of its parts. A modifier like *cricket* in *cricket bat, cricket ball, cricket umpire,* and so on does not pick out any common property or similarity shared by bats, balls, and umpires. It refers to the structured activity as a whole. And the nouns that *cricket* can modify form a category, but not a category based on shared properties. Rather it is a category based on the structure of the activity of cricket and on those things that are part of the activity. The entities characterized by the cognitive model of cricket are those that are in the category. What defines the category is our structured understanding of the activity.

Cognitive psychologists have recently begun to study categories based on such holistically structured activities. Barsalou (1983, 1984) has studied such categories as *things to take on a camping trip, foods not to eat on a diet, clothes to wear in the snow*, and the like. Such categories, among their other properties, do not show family resemblances among their members.

Like Wittgenstein, Austin was dedicated to showing the inadequacies of traditional philosophical views of language and mind—views that are still widely held. His contribution to prototype theory was to notice for words the kinds of things that Wittgenstein noticed for conceptual categories. Language is, after all, an aspect of cognition. Following Austin's lead, we will try to show how prototype theory generalizes to the linguistic as well as the nonlinguistic aspects of mind.

Zadeh

Some categories do not have gradations of membership, while others do. The category *U.S. Senator* is well defined. One either is or is not a senator. On the other hand, categories like *rich people* or *tall men* are graded, simply because there are gradations of richness and tallness. Lotfi Zadeh (1965) devised a form of set theory to model graded categories. He called it *fuzzy set theory.* In a classical set, everything is either in the set (has membership value 1) or is outside the set (has membership value 0). In a fuzzy set, as Zadeh defined it, additional values are allowed between 0 and 1. This corresponds to Zadeh's intuition that some men are neither clearly tall nor clearly short, but rather in the middle—tall to some degree.

In the original version of fuzzy set theory, operations on fuzzy sets are simple generalizations of operations on ordinary sets:

Suppose element x has membership value v in fuzzy set A and membership value w in fuzzy set B.
Intersection: The value of x in $A \cap B$ is the minimum of v and w.
Union: The value of x in $A \cup B$ is the maximum of v and w.
Complement: The value of x in the complement of A is $1 - v$.

It is a natural and ingenious extension of the classical theory of sets.

Since Zadeh's original paper, other definitions for union and intersection have been suggested. For an example, see Goguen 1969. The best discussion of attempts to apply fuzzy logic to natural language is in McCawley 1981.

Lounsbury

Cognitive anthropology has had an important effect on the development of prototype theory, beginning with Floyd Lounsbury's (1964) studies of American Indian kinship systems. Take the example of Fox, in which the word *nehcihsähA* is used not only to refer to one's maternal uncle—that is, one's mother's mother's son—but also to one's mother's mother's son's son, one's mother's mother's father's son's son, one's mother's brother's son, one's mother's brother's son's son, and a host of other relatives. The same sort of treatment also occurs for other kinship categories. There are categories of "fathers," "mothers," sons," and "daughters" with just as diverse a membership.

The Fox can, of course, distinguish uncles from great-uncles from nephews. But they are all part of the same kinship category, and thus are named the same. Lounsbury discovered that such categories were structured in terms of a "focal member" and a small set of general rules extending each category to nonfocal members. The same rules apply across all the categories. The rules applying in Fox are what Lounsbury called the "Omaha type":

Skewing rule: Anyone's father's sister, as a linking relative, is equivalent to that person's sister.

Merging rule: Any person's sibling of the same sex, as a linking relative, is equivalent to that person himself.

Half-sibling rule: Any child of one of one's parents is one's sibling.

The condition "as a linking relative" is to prevent the rule from applying directly; instead, there must be an intermediate relative between ego (the reference point) and the person being described. For example, the skewing rule does not say that a person's paternal aunt is equivalent to his sister. But it does say, for example, that his father's paternal aunt is equivalent to his father's sister. In this case, the intermediate relative is the father.

These rules have corollaries. For example,

Skewing corollary: The brother's child of any female linking relative is equivalent to the sibling of that female linking relative. (For example, a mother's brother's daughter is equivalent to a mother's sister.)

Lounsbury illustrates how such rules would work for the Fox maternal uncle category. We will use the following abbreviations: M: mother, F: father, B: brother, S: sister, d: daughter, s: son. Let us consider the following examples of the *nehcihsähA* (mother's brother) category, and the equivalence rules that make them part of this category. Lounsbury's point in these examples is to take a very distant relative and show precisely how the same general rules place that relative in the MB (mother's brother) category. Incidentally, all the intermediate relatives in the following cases are also in the MB category—e.g., MMSs, that is, mother's mother's sister's son, etc. Let "→" stand for "is equivalent to."

1. Mother's mother's father's sister's son: MMFSs
   MMFSs → MMSs [by the skewing rule]
   MMSs → MMs [by the merging rule]
   MMs → MB [by the half-sibling rule]
2. Mother's mother's sister's son's son: MMSss
   MMSss → MMss [by the merging rule]
   MMss → MBs [by the half-sibling rule]
   MBs → MB [by the skewing corollary]
3. Mother's brother's son's son's son: MBsss
   MBsss → MBss [by the skewing corollary]
   MBss → MBs [by the skewing corollary]
   MBs → MB [by the skewing corollary]

Similarly, the other "uncles" in Fox are equivalent to MB.

Not all conceptual systems for categorizing kinsmen have the same skewing rules. Lounsbury also cites the Crow version of the skewing rule:

Skewing rule: Any woman's brother, as a linking relative, is equivalent to that woman's son, as a linking relative.

Skewing corollary: The sister of any male linking relative is equivalent to the mother of that male linking relative.

These rules are responsible for some remarkable categorizations. One's paternal aunt's son is classified as one's "father." But one's paternal aunt's daughter is classified as one's "grandmother"! Here are the derivations:

Father's sister's son: FSs

FSs	→	FMs	[by skewing corrollary]
FMs	→	FB	[by half-sibling rule]
FB	→	F	[by merging rule]

Father's sister's daughter: FSd

FSd	→	FMd	[by skewing corollary]
FMd	→	FS	[by half-sibling rule]
FS	→	FM	[by skewing corollary]

Moreover, Lounsbury observed that these categories were not mere matters of naming. Such things as inheritance and social responsibilities follow category lines.

Categories of this sort—with a central member plus general rules—are by no means the norm in language, as we shall see. Yet they do occur. We will refer to such a category as a *generative* category and to its central member as a *generator.* A generative category is characterized by at least one generator plus something else: it is the "something else" that takes the generator as input and yields the entire category as output. It may be either a general principle like similarity or general rules that apply elsewhere in the system or specific rules that apply only in that category. In Lounsbury's cases, the "something else" is a set of rules that apply throughout the kinship system. The generator plus the rules generate the category.

In such a category, the generator has a special status. It is the best example of the category, the model on which the category as a whole is built. It is a special case of a prototype.

Berlin and Kay

The next major contribution of cognitive anthropology to prototype theory was the color research of Brent Berlin and Paul Kay. In their classic, *Basic Color Terms* (Berlin and Kay 1969), they took on the traditional view that different languages could carve up the color spectrum in arbitrary ways. The first regularity they found was in what they called *basic color terms.* For a color term to be basic,

- It must consist of only one morpheme, like *green*, rather than more than one, as in *dark green* or *grass-colored.*
- The color referred to by the term must not be contained within another color. *Scarlet* is, for example, contained within *red.*
- It must not be restricted to a small number of objects. *Blond*, for example, is restricted to hair, wood, and perhaps a few other things.
- It must be common and generally known, like *yellow* as opposed to *saffron.*

Once one distinguishes basic from nonbasic color terms, generalizations appear.

- Basic color terms name basic color *categories*, whose central members are the same universally. For example, there is always a psychologically real category RED, with focal red as the best, or "purest," example.
- The color categories that basic color *terms* can attach to are the equivalents of the English color categories named by the terms *black, white, red, yellow, green, blue, brown, purple, pink, orange* and *gray.*
- Although people can *conceptually* differentiate all these color categories, it is not the case that all languages make all of those differentiations. Many languages have fewer basic categories. Those categories include *unions* of the basic categories; for example, BLUE + GREEN, RED + ORANGE + YELLOW, etc. When there are fewer than eleven basic color terms in a language, one basic term, or more, names such a union.
- Languages form a hierarchy based on the number of basic color terms they have and the color categories those terms refer to.

Some languages, like English, use all eleven, while others use as few as two. When a language has only two basic color terms, they are *black* and *white*—which might more appropriately be called *cool* (covering black, blue, green, and gray) and *warm* (covering white, yellow, orange, and red). When a language has three basic color terms, they are *black, white*, and *red.* When a language has four basic color terms, the fourth is one of the following: *yellow, blue*, or *green.* The possibilities for four-color-term languages are thus: *black, white, red, yellow; black, white, red, blue*; and *black, white, red, green.* And so on, down the following hierarchy:

black, white
red
yellow, blue, green
brown
purple, pink, orange, gray

What made it possible for Berlin and Kay to find these regularities was their discovery of *focal colors.* If one simply asks speakers around the world to pick out the portions of the spectrum that their basic color terms refer to, there seem to be no significant regularities. The boundaries between the color ranges differ from language to language. The regularities appear only when one asks for the *best example* of a basic color term given a standardized chart of 320 small color chips. Virtually the same best examples are chosen for the basic color terms by speakers in language after language. For example, in languages that have a basic term for colors in the blue range, the best example is the same focal blue for all speakers no matter what language they speak. Suppose a language has a basic color term that covers the range of both *blue* and *green*; let us call that color *grue.* The best example of grue, they claim, will not be turquoise, which is in the middle of the blue-to-green spectrum. Instead the best example of grue will be either focal blue or focal green. The focal colors therefore allow for comparison of terms across languages.

The existence of focal colors shows that color categories are not uniform. Some members of the category RED are better examples of the category than others. Focal red is the best example. Color categories thus have central members. There is no general principle, however, for predicting the boundaries from the central members. They seem to vary, somewhat arbitrarily, from language to language.

Kay and McDaniel

The Berlin-Kay color research raised questions that were left unanswered. What determines the collection of universal focal colors? Why should the basic color terms pick out just those colors? Kay and McDaniel (1978) provided an answer to these questions that depended jointly on research on the neurophysiology of color vision by DeValois and his associates and on a slightly revised version of Zadeh's fuzzy set theory.

DeValois and his associates (DeValois, Abramov, and Jacobs 1966; DeValois and Jacobs 1968) had investigated the neurophysiology of color vision in the macaque, a monkey with a visual system similar to man's. Their research concentrated on the neural pathways between the eye and the brain. They found six types of cell. Four of these, called *opponent response cells*, determine hue, while the other two determine brightness. The opponent response cells are grouped into two pairs, one having to do with the perception of blue and yellow, the other having to do with the perception of red and green. Each opponent response cell has a spontaneous rate of firing—a base response rate that it maintains without any external stimulation. There are two types of blue-yellow cells. The +B−Y cells fire above their base rate in response to a blue stimulus, and below their base rate in response to a yellow stimulus. The + Y − B cells do the reverse: they fire above their base rate in response to yellow and below their base rate in response to blue. Similarly, there are two types of red-green cells: + G − R cells fire above their base rate in response to green and below in response to red, while + R − G cells fire above in response to red and below in response to green. The two types of blue-yellow cells jointly determine a blue-yellow response, while the two kinds of red-green cells jointly determine a red-green response.

Focal blue is perceived when the blue-yellow cells show a blue response and when the red-green cells are firing at the neutral base rate. Purple is a combination of blue and red; it is perceived when the blue-yellow cells show a blue response and the red-green cells show a red response. Turquoise is perceived when the blue-yellow cells show a blue response and the red-green cells show a green response. Pure primary colors—blue, yellow, red, and green—are perceived when either the blue-yellow or red-green cells are firing at their neutral base rates. Nonprimary colors correspond to cases where no opponent cells are firing at neutral base rates.

The remaining two kinds of cells are light-sensitive and darkness-sensitive. Pure black, white, and gray are perceived when the blue-yellow and red-green cells are all firing at their neutral base rates and making no color contribution. Pure black occurs when the darkness-sensitive cells are firing at their maximum rate and the light-sensitive cells are firing at their minimum rates. Pure white is the reverse.

Given these results from neurophysiological studies, Kay and McDaniel apply a version of fuzzy set theory to make sense of the Kay-Berlin results. For example, they define degree of membership in the category *blue* as the proportion of blue response on the part of the blue-yellow cells. Pure blue (degree of membership = 1) occurs when the red-green response is neutral. Blues in the direction of purple or green or white have an intermediate degree of membership in the blue category. Corresponding definitions are given for other primary colors. The accompanying dia-

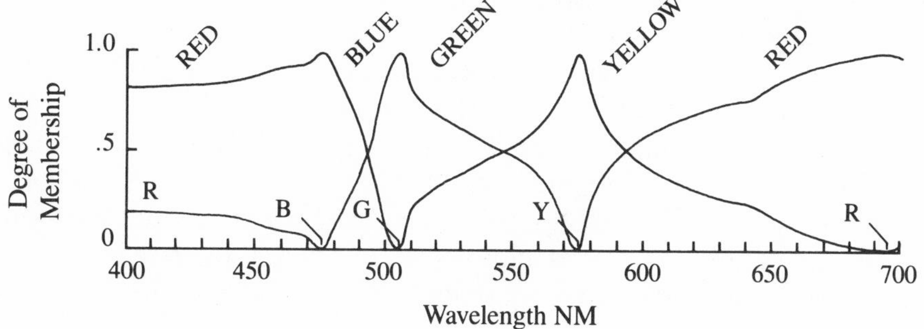

grams give curves that correlate degree of membership in color categories with wavelengths in nanometers for hues and percentage of reflectance for black and white.

The neurophysiological account only characterizes the primary colors: black, white, red, yellow, blue, and green. What allows us to "see" other colors as being members of color categories? What about orange, brown,

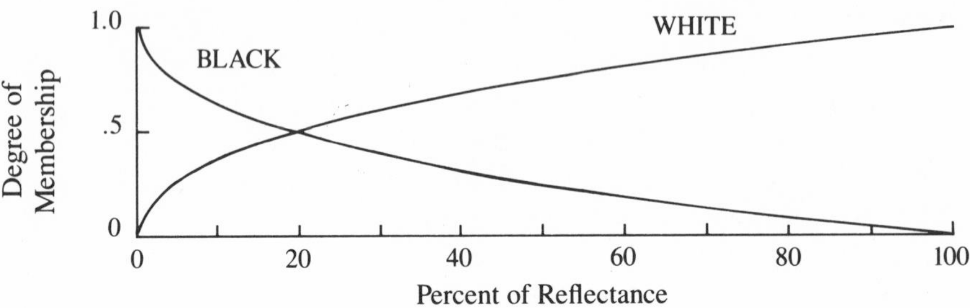

purple, etc.? Some cognitive mechanism in addition to the neurophysiology is needed to account for those. Kay and McDaniel suggested that such a mechanism would make use of something akin to fuzzy set theory.

The postulation of a cognitive mechanism that has some of the effects of fuzzy set theory enables Kay and McDaniel to do two things that the neurophysiological account alone could not do. First, it enables them to characterize focal nonprimary colors (orange, purple, pink, brown, gray, etc.) in the following intuitive way:

ORANGE = RED and YELLOW
PURPLE = BLUE and RED
PINK = RED and WHITE
BROWN = BLACK and YELLOW
GRAY = BLACK and WHITE

Thus, ORANGE is characterized in terms of the fuzzy set intersection of the RED and YELLOW curves. (Actually, for technical reasons the definition is twice the fuzzy-set intersection value. See Kay and McDaniel 1978, pp. 634–35, for details.) Correspondingly, PURPLE is defined in terms of the fuzzy set intersection of BLUE and RED, and GRAY in terms of the fuzzy set intersection for BLACK and WHITE. PINK and BROWN require somewhat different functions based on fuzzy set intersections.

The second advantage of fuzzy set theory is that it permits an intuitive account of basic color categories that include more than one focal color. Dani, for example, has only two basic color terms: *mili* contains black and all the cool colors, the greens and blues; *mola* contains white and all the warm colors, the reds, oranges, yellows, pinks, and red-purples. Some languages have basic color categories containing both blues and greens, while others have basic color categories containing both reds and yellows. Such cases can be accounted for intuitively by using fuzzy set union.

DARK-COOL = BLACK or GREEN or BLUE
LIGHT-WARM = WHITE or RED or YELLOW
COOL = GREEN or BLUE
WARM = RED or YELLOW

Thus, Kay and McDaniel make the claim that basic color categories are a product of both neurophysiology and cognitively real operations that can be partially modelled by fuzzy set intersection and union.

At present, this is the only plausible account we have of why the facts of basic color categories should be as they are. The Kay-McDaniel theory has important consequences for human categorization in general. It claims that colors are not objectively "out there in the world" independent of any beings. Color concepts are *embodied* in that focal colors are partly determined by human biology. Color categorization makes use of human biology, but color categories are more than merely a consequence of the nature of the world plus human biology. Color categories result from the world plus human biology plus a cognitive mechanism that has some of the characteristics of fuzzy set theory plus a culture-specific choice of which basic color categories there are.

The Kay-McDaniel theory seems to work well for characterizing the focal colors corresponding to basic color categories. But it does not work as well at the boundaries between colors. According to the Kay-McDaniel account, the boundaries, as well as the focal colors, should be uniform across languages. But this is simply not the case. The most detailed work on the detailed mapping of color categories, especially in nonfocal areas, has been done by MacLaury (in preparation). Among the test cases for the Kay-McDaniel theory are cases where a language does not have a separate color category for nonprimary focal colors, like purple and orange, colors that, in the Kay-McDaniel account, are "computed" on the basis of fuzzy set theory plus the response curves for the primary colors. The Kay-McDaniel theory predicts that colors like purple and orange should be treated uniformly across languages and that they should always be on the boundaries between basic color categories in languages that do not have separate categories for them.

But MacLaury has found cases where purple is entirely within the cool color range (a single color with focal points at blue and green) and other cases where purple is on the boundary between cool and red. He has also found cases where brown is subsumed by yellow and other cases where it is subsumed by black. That is, what we call "brown" falls within the range of a category with a center at pure yellow in some languages, and it falls within the range of a category with a center at pure black in other languages.

In Kay-McDaniel terms, this means that the fuzzy-set-theoretical functions that compute conjunctions and disjunctions for color categories are not exactly the same for all people; rather they vary in their boundary conditions from culture to culture. They are thus at least partly conventional, and not completely a matter of universal neurophysiology and cognition. What this requires is a revision of the Kay-McDaniel theory to permit conceptual systems for color to vary at the boundaries, by having the exact nature of the disjunction function be somewhat different in different systems. Such differences may not only be at the boundaries but at the focal peaks. Kay and McDaniel's theory implied that each binary disjunctive color category (e.g., COOL = BLUE or GREEN) should have two focal peaks (e.g., both focal blue and focal green). MacLaury has found cases where there is a cool category covering blue and green, but where there is a skewing effect such that the center of the category is at pure green alone or pure blue alone. Thus, in Kay-McDaniel terms, conceptual systems seem to have disjunction functions that take the blue and green response curves as input and yield an output curve with only one focal center. This would require a cognitive mechanism with more than just something akin to the operation of union in fuzzy set theory.

Color categories, thus, are generative categories in the same sense in which kinship categories characterized by Lounsbury are. They have generators plus something else. The generators are the neurophysiologically determined distribution functions, which have peaks where the primary colors are pure: black, white, red, yellow, blue, and green. These generators are universal; they are part of human neurophysiology. The "something else" needed to generate a system of basic color categories consists of a complex cognitive mechamism incorporating some of the characteristics of fuzzy set theory union and intersection. This cognitive mechanism has a small number of parameters that may take on different values in different cultures.

It is important to bear in mind that it is not just the names for colors that vary. The color names do not just attach to the neurophysiologically determined distribution functions directly. Cognitive mechanisms of the sort described above must be postulated in addition. There are general characteristics of the cognitive mechanisms, for example, the use of something like fuzzy set theory union and intersection. But, as MacLaury shows, color cognition is by no means all the same across cultures. Nor is it by any means arbitrarily different across cultures. The possible color ranges depend upon limited parameters within the cognitive mechanism.

Brown and Berlin: Glimpses of the Basic Level

The study of basic-level categories is usually traced to Roger Brown's classic paper, "How Shall a Thing Be Called?" (1958), and his textbook, *Social Psychology* (1965, pp. 317–21).

Brown observed that objects have many names: "The dime in my pocket is not only a *dime.* It is also *money*, a *metal object*, a *thing*, and, moving to subordinates, it is a 1952 dime, in fact, a *particular 1952 dime* with a unique pattern of scratches, discolorations, and smooth places. The dog on the lawn is not only a *dog* but is also a *boxer*, a *quadruped*, an *animate being*" (Brown 1958, p. 14). Brown also observed that of all the possible names for something in a category hierarchy, a particular name, at a particular level of categorization, "has a superior status." "While a dime *can* be called a *coin* or *money* or *a 1952 dime*, we somehow feel that *dime* is its real name. The other categorizations seem like achievements of the imagination" (Brown 1965, p. 320). Such "real names," Brown observed, seem to be shorter and to be used more frequently. They also seem to correlate with nonlinguistic actions.

> When Lewis' son first looked upon the yellow jonquils in a bowl and heard them named flowers he was also enjoined to smell them and we may guess that his mother leaned over and did just that. When a ball is named *ball* it is also likely to be bounced. When a cat is named *kitty* it is also likely to be petted. Smelling and bouncing and petting are actions distinctively linked to certain categories. We can be sure they are distinctive because they are able to function as symbols of these categories. In a game of charades one might symbolize *cat* by stroking the air at a suitable height in a certain fashion, or symbolize *flower* by inclining forward and sniffing.
>
> . . . .
>
> Flowers are marked by sniffing actions, but there are no actions that distinguish one species of flower from another. The first names given to things fall at the level of distinctive action but names go on to code the world at every level; non-linguistic actions do not.
>
> . . . .
>
> When something is categorized it is regarded as equivalent to certain other things. For what purposes equivalent? How are all dimes equivalent or all flowers or all cats? . . . Dimes are equivalent in that they can be exchanged for certain newspapers or cigars or ice cream cones or for any two nickels. In fact, they are equivalent for all purposes of economic exchange. Flowers are equivalent in that they are agreeable to smell and are pickable. Cats are equivalent in that they are to be petted, but gently, so that they do not claw. (Brown 1965, pp. 318–19)

The picture Brown gives is that categorization, for a child, begins "at the level of distinctive action," the level of flowers and cats and dimes, and then proceeds upward to superordinate categories (like *plant* and *animal*) and downward to subordinate categories (like *jonquil* and *Siamese*) by "achievements of the imagination." "For these latter categories there seem to be no characterizing actions" (Brown 1965, p. 321). This "first level" of categorization was seen by Brown as having the following converging properties:

- It is the level of distinctive actions.
- It is the level which is learned earliest and at which things are first named.
- It is the level at which names are shortest and used most frequently.
- It is a natural level of categorization, as opposed to a level created by "achievements of the imagination."

The next important impetus to the study of basic-level categories came from the work of Brent Berlin and his associates. Berlin's research can be viewed as a response to the classical philosophical view that THE CATEGORIES OF MIND FIT THE CATEGORIES OF THE WORLD, and to a linguistic version of this, THE DOCTRINE OF NATURAL KIND TERMS. That doctrine states that the world consists very largely of natural kinds of things and that natural languages contain names (called "natural kind terms") that fit those natural kinds. Typical examples of natural kinds are cows, dogs, tigers, gold, silver, water, etc.

Berlin takes these philosophical doctrines as empirically testable issues and asks: To what extent do the categories of mind (as expressed in language) fit the categories of the world? In particular, Berlin considers domains in which there *are* natural kinds of things: the domains of plants and animals. Moreover, botany and zoology can reasonably be taken to have determined to a high degree of scientific accuracy just what kinds of plants and animals there are. Since Berlin is an anthropologist who studies people who live close to nature and who know an awful lot about plants and animals, he is in an excellent position to test such philosophical doctrines empirically.

Berlin and his students and associates have studied folk classification of plants and animals in incredibly minute detail and compared those classifications with scientific classifications. Most of the research has been carried out with speakers of Tzeltal living in Tenejapa in the Chiapas region of Mexico. This enormous undertaking has been documented meticulously in *Principles of Tzeltal Plant Classification* (Berlin, Breedlove, and Raven 1974), *Tzeltal Folk Zoology* (Hunn 1977), and "Language Acquisition by Tenejapa Tzeltal Children" (Stross 1969). The results to date have been surprising and have formed the basis for the psychological research on basic-level categorization.

What Berlin and his co-workers discovered was that a single level of classification—the genus—was for Tzeltal speakers psychologically basic in a certain number of ways. Examples of plants and animals at the genus level are *oak, maple, rabbit, raccoon*, etc. The first way that the priority of the genus manifested itself was in a simple naming task. Berlin went out into the jungle with a native consultant, stopped on the path, and asked the consultant to name the plants he could see. The consultant could easily name forty or fifty, but he tended to name them at the level of the genus (oak, maple, etc.) instead of the level of the species (sugar maple, live oak), even though further study showed he could distinguish the species and had names for them. Nor did he name them at the level of the life form (tree), nor at an intermediate level (needle-bearing tree). The level of the genus is, incidentally, "in the middle" of the folk classification hierarchy, the levels being:

UNIQUE BEGINNER (plant, animal)
LIFE FORM (tree, bush, bird, fish)
INTERMEDIATE (leaf-bearing tree, needle-bearing tree)
GENUS (oak, maple)
SPECIES (sugar maple, white oak)
VARIETY (cutleaf staghorn sumac)

Further study revealed that this was no accident and that the level of the genus (what Berlin called the "folk-generic level") seems to be a psychologically basic level in the following respects:

- People name things more readily at that level.
- Languages have simpler names for things at that level.
- Categories at that level have greater cultural significance.
- Things are remembered more readily at that level.
- At that level, things are perceived holistically, as a single gestalt, while for identification at a lower level, specific details (called *distinctive features*) have to be picked out to distinguish, for example, among the kinds of oak.

In addition, Stross (1969), in a study of Tzeltal language acquisition, discovered that "the bulk of the child's first-learned plant names are generic names and that from this starting point he continues to differentiate nomenclaturally, while cognitively he continues to differentiate and generalize plants simultaneously." In other words, the basic-level (or generic) categories, which are in the middle of the taxonomic hierarchy, are learned first; then children work up the hierarchy generalizing, and down the hierarchy specializing. Thus, we can add the finding:

- Children learn the names for things at that level earlier.

But perhaps the most remarkable finding of all was this:

- Folk categories correspond to scientific categories extremely accurately at this level, but not very accurately at other levels.

This says something very remarkable about THE DOCTRINE OF NATURAL KIND TERMS: For the Tzeltal, this doctrine works very well at the level of the genus, but not very well at other levels of classification, e.g., the intermediate, the species, and the variety levels.

But now if one considers philosophical discussions of natural kinds, it turns out that this is not such a surprising result after all. In the literature on natural kinds, one finds that the usual examples of natural kinds are animals like *dog, cow, tiger*, and substances like *gold* and *water*. As it happens, they are all basic-level categories! In short, the examples on which the doctrine of natural kinds was based were all basic level, which is the level of the genus among plants and animals. At least for the Tzeltal, the doctrine works well for the kinds of examples that philosophers had in mind when they espoused the doctrine. For other kinds of examples, it does not work very well.

But if THE DOCTRINE OF NATURAL KIND TERMS fits well for the Tzeltal at even one level of categorization, it still seems to be quite a remarkable result. It suggests that there is one psychologically relevant level at which THE CATEGORIES OF THE MIND FIT THE CATEGORIES OF THE WORLD. However, Berlin's research into the history of biological classification shows this result to be much less remarkable. Scientific classification in biology grew out of folk classification. And when Linnaeus classified the living things of the world, he specifically made use of psychological criteria in establishing the level of the genus. This comes across particularly clearly in A. J. Cain's 1958 essay "Logic and Memory in Linnaeus's System of Taxonomy" (1958). The heart of the Linnaean system was the genus, not the species. It is the genus that gives the *general* characteristics and the species that is defined in terms of differentiating characteristics. But what is a *general* characteristic? As Cain observes, "The *Essential Character* of a genus is that which gives some characteristic peculiar to it, if there is one such, which will instantly serve to distinguish it from all others in the natural order" (p. 148). This is a psychologically defined notion of an "essential character"; which characteristics can be instantly distinguished depends on the perceptual systems of the beings doing the distinguishing. As Linnaeus's son writes,

> My Father's secret art of determining (delimiting) genera in such a way the Species should not become genera? This was no other than his practice in knowing a plant from its external appearance (externa facie). Therefore he often deviated from his own principles in such a way that variation as to the number of parts . . . did not disturb him, if only the character of the genus . . . could be preserved. Foreigners don't do so, but as soon as a plant has a different splitting (cleavage) of the corolla and calyx, or if the number of stamens and pistils . . . varies, they make a new genus. . . . If possible he [Linnaeus] tried to build the character genericus on the cleavage of the fruit so that all species that constitute a genus should have the same shape of their fruit. (Cain, p. 159)

Why did Linnaeus use the shape of the fruit as a basis for defining the genus? As Cain observes, "The characters chosen from the fructification were clearly marked, readily appreciated, easily described in words, and usually determinable on herbarium specimens" (p. 152). In other words, the shape of the fruit was easy to perceive and describe. Genera, as Linnaeus conceived of them, were "practical units of classification" upon which all biologists should be able to agree; it was important that they should "not become confused and indistinct in the mind" (Cain, p. 156). Most of Linnaeus's rules of nomenclature "follow directly from [the] requirement that the botanist must know and remember all genera" (Cain, p. 162)—again a psychological requirement. "Linnaeus states explicitly and repeatedly that the botanist . . . [and] the zoologist too must know all genera and commit their names to memory" (Cain, p. 156). Linnaeus also assumed, of course, that this practical system would also be "natural," in short, a convergence between nature and psychology could be taken for granted at this level.

In short, the genus was established as that level of biological discontinuity at which human beings could most easily perceive, agree on, learn, remember, and name the discontinuities. The genus, as a scientific level of classification, was set up because it was the most psychologically basic level for the purposes of the study of taxonomic biology by human beings. It was assumed that this would also fit certain real discontinuities in nature. Berlin found that there is a close fit at this level between the categories of Linnaean biology and basic-level categories in folk biology. This fit follows in part from the criteria used to set up the level of the genus in Linnaean biology; those criteria correspond to the psychological criteria that characterize the basic level in folk biology.

At the level of the genus, the categories of mind of the biologists who set up the level of the genus correspond closely to the basic-level categories of mind of Tzeltal speakers. But this is not merely a fact about psychology. It is a fact about both psychology and biology. Here is the reason: Within scientific biology, the genus is one level above the species—the level defined by interbreeding possibilities: two populations that are members of the same species can breed and produce fertile offspring. Typically, members of two populations that can interbreed have pretty much the same overall shape. In the course of evolution, two populations of the same species may change sufficiently so that interbreeding is no longer possible. At the point at which they cease to be able to interbreed, they become different species. But at this point they may still have pretty much the same overall shape. They will no longer be members of the same species, but they will be members of the same genus—the category one level up. Thus, one level up from the species in scientific biology, it is common to find certain general shape similarities. It may not always happen, but it is common.

Now overall shape is a major determinant of the basic level in folk biology. The basic level is primarily characterized by gestalt perception (the perception of overall shape), by imaging capacity (which depends on overall shape), and by motor interaction (the possibilities for which are also determined by overall shape). It is anything but an accident that the level of the genus in scientific biology should correspond so well to the basic level in folk biology.

Moreover, given the experience of people like the Tzeltal, who are indigenous to a circumscribed geographical area, there is a good reason why divisions in nature at the level of the genus should be particularly striking. In the course of evolution, the species that survive in a particular geographical region are those that adapt most successfuly to the local environment. Thus, for each genus, it is common for there to be only one species representing the genus locally. This does not always happen, but it does happen frequently. Thus, there tend to be genus-sized gaps among the *species* that occur locally—and these are very striking and perceptible gaps. Thus, divisions at the basic level in folk biology correspond to very striking discontinuities in nature for people in a circumscribed geographical area.

In summary, ethnobiological research has established that there is, at least for biological categories, a basic level of categorization. Among the Tzeltal, who have an intimate familiarity with a large range of plants and animals, the categories of the mind fit discontinuities in the world very well at the level of the genus, though not very well at other levels. The reason for this is partly because the level of the genus, as a fundamental level used in scientific biology, is a psychologically based level of categorization. But there are equally important biological reasons.

Basic-level categorization depends upon experiential aspects of human psychology: gestalt perception, mental imagery, motor activities, social function, and memory. (What I call "memory" here is the ability of a subject in a psychological test to recall on demand particular presented instances of the category.) To what extent is basic-level categorization universal? If we assume that human physiology and psychology are pretty much the same around the world, then any variation would most likely be due to culture and context. But how much variation would there be and what kind would it be?

Berlin has suggested (personal communication) that a distinction be made between a general human capacity for basic-level categorization (due to general physiological and psychological factors) and functional basic-level categorization, which adds in factors having to do with culture and specialized training. Berlin suggests that a given culture may underutilize certain human capacities used in basic-level categorization, for example, the capacity for gestalt perception. Thus, in urban cultures, people may treat the category *tree* as basic level. Such cases have been documented by Dougherty (1978). Moreover, there may be subpopulations of specialists in a culture who, through training, may achieve a more finely honed gestalt perception for a limited range of domains, e.g., breeds of horses, types of cars, etc. But this should be possible only in a limited number of domains, even for trained specialists. Berlin thus hypothesizes two kinds of nonuniversality: (*a*) one kind due to cultural underutilization of general human capacities, with the result that certain higher-level categories (e.g., tree) may be treated as basic, and (*b*) another kind due to special training, limited to subpopulations of experts who may treat a slightly more specific level as basic in some domains of expertise.

Berlin's hypothesis makes the following prediction: People from, say, an urban culture that treats trees as basic level should still have the general human capacity for gestalt perception and should thus be capable of learning to discriminate among trees readily at the level of the genus, but not so readily at the level of the species or variety. Berlin's hypothesis also predicts that there will be no whole cultures that will treat the level of the species or variety as basic, but that individuals may have a capacity for expertise in a limited range of domains and thus may be able to treat a small number of more specific categories as basic.

Berlin also predicts that there will be no culture where all the levels of categorization are different from ours or from the Tzeltal. In most domains, levels of categorization will be the same for all human beings, simply because human beings share the same general capacities for gestalt perception and for holistic motor movement. It is these capacities that have the major role in determining basic-level categorization.

Basicness in categorization has to do with matters of human psychology: ease of perception, memory, learning, naming, and use. Basicness of level has no objective status external to human beings. It is constant only to the extent that the relevant human capacities are utilized in the same way. Basicness varies when those capacities either are underutilized in a culture or are specially developed to a level of expertise.

As we shall see below, Berlin's results have a special philosophical importance. Berlin showed that human categorizations based on interactions with the environment are extremely accurate at the basic level. Basic-level interactions thus provide a crucial link between cognitive structure and real knowledge of the world. We will argue in chapter 17 that basic-level interactions can therefore form the basis of an epistemology for a philosophy of mind and language that is consistent with the results of prototype theory.

Ekman

In research spanning more than two decades, Paul Ekman and his associates have studied in detail the physiological correlates of emotions (Ekman 1971; Ekman, Friesen, and Ellsworth 1972). In a major crosscultural study of facial gestures expressing emotion, Ekman and his associates discovered that there were basic emotions that seem to correlate universally with facial gestures: happiness, sadness, anger, fear, surprise, and interest. Of all the subtle emotions that people feel and have words and concepts for around the world, only these have consistent correlates in facial expressions across cultures.

Although Ekman was by no means a prototype theorist, his research fits prototype research in the following way. The seven basic emotions appear to have prototype status. There are many shades and varieties of happiness, sadness, anger, etc. These form categories of emotions. Rage and annoyance, for example, are in the anger category. Basic happiness, anger, etc.—the emotions that correlate with the universal facial gestures—seem to function as central members of those categories. These emotions also appear to have basic-level status. They are readily recognizable by gestalt perception around the world. We have facial images and motor movements for them that represent the entire emotional category.

As we will see below in case study 1, emotional concepts are embodied, in that the physiology corresponding to each emotion has a great deal to do with how the emotion is conceptualized. We will see, for example, that anger is metaphorically understood in terms of heat and internal pressure. Ekman, Levenson, and Friesen (1983) have shown that there is autonomic nervous system (ANS) activity that corresponds to the basic emotions. The ANS activity that corresponds to anger is an increase in skin temperature and an increase in heart rate (experienced as internal pressure).

The experiments that demonstrated this involved two tasks. In the first, subjects were instructed to change their facial expressions, muscle by muscle, until their expressions matched the facial prototypes of emotions. In the second, subjects were asked to relive emotional experiences. Heart rate and left- and right-finger temperatures were recorded.

Two findings were consistent across tasks:

> (i) Heart rate increased more in anger (mean calculated across tasks ± standard error, +8.0 ± 1.8 beats per minute) and fear (+8.0 ± 1.6 beats per minute) than in happiness (+2.6 ± 1.0 beat per minute).
> (ii) Left- and right-finger temperatures increased more in anger (left, +0.10°C ±0.009°; right, +0.08° ± 0.008°C) than in happiness (left, −0.07°C ± 0.002°; right, −0.03° ± 0.002°). (Ekman, Levenson, and Friesen 1983, p. 1209)

Thus the metaphorical conceptualization of anger that we will explore in case study 1 is actually embodied in the autonomic nervous system, in that it is motivated by ANS activity that corresponds to the emotions as felt.

Rosch

The studies cited above are all special cases. It was Eleanor Rosch who first provided a general perspective on all these problems. She developed what has since come to be called "the theory of prototypes and basic-level categories," or "prototype theory." In doing so, she provided a full-scale challenge to the classical theory and did more than anyone else to establish categorization as a subfield of cognitive psychology. Before her work, the classical theory was taken for granted, not only in psychology, but in linguistics, anthropology, and philosophy, as well as other disciplines. In a series of electrifying papers, Rosch and her associates presented an overwhelming array of empirical studies that challenged the classical view.

The experimental contributions of Rosch and her associates are generally and justly recognized by cognitive psychologists as having revolutionized the study of categorization within experimental psychology. Rosch's experimental results fall into two categories: prototype effects, which extend the Berlin-Kay color research, and basic-level effects, which generalize Brown's observations and Berlin's results.

Prototype Effects

If the classical theory were both correct and complete, no member of a category would have any special status. The reason is that, in the classical theory, the properties defining the category are shared by all members, and so all members have equal status as category members. Rosch's research on prototype effects has been aimed at showing asymmetries among category members and asymmetric structures within categories. Since the classical theory does not predict such asymmetries, either something more or something different must be going on.

Rosch's early studies were on color. She learned of the Berlin-Kay color research midway through her own research and found that their results meshed with her own work on Dani, a New Guinea language that has only two basic color categories: *mili* (dark-cool, including black, green, and blue) and *mola* (light-warm, including white, red, yellow). Berlin and Kay had shown that focal colors had a special status within color categoraies—that of the best example of the category. Rosch found that Dani speakers, when asked for the best examples of their two color categories, chose focal colors, for example, white, red, or yellow for *mola* with different speakers making different choices.

In a remarkable set of experiments, Rosch set out to show that primary color categories were psychologically real for speakers of Dani, even though they were not named. She set out to challenge one of Whorf's hypotheses, namely, that language determines one's conceptual system. If Whorf were right on this matter, the Dani's two *words* for colors would determine two and only two *conceptual categories* of colors. Rosch reasoned that if it was language alone that determined color categorization, then the Dani should have equal difficulty learning new words for colors, no matter whether the color ranges had a primary color at the center or a nonprimary color. She then went about studying how Dani speakers would learn new, made-up color terms. One group was taught arbitrary names for eight focal colors, and another group, arbitrary names for eight nonfocal colors (Rosch 1973). The names for focal colors were learned more easily. Dani speakers were also found (like English speakers) to be able to remember focal colors better than nonfocal colors (Heider 1972). In an experiment in which speakers judged color similarity, the Dani were shown to represent colors in memory the same way English speakers do (Heider and Olivier 1972). Rosch's color research also extended to children. When three-year-olds were presented with an array of color chips, and the experimenter turned her back and said "Show me a color," the children picked focal colors overwhelmingly over nonfocal colors (Heider 1971). And when four-year-olds were given a color chip and asked to pick from an assortment of chips the one that matched best, the children did best with focal colors.

Focal colors correspond to what Rosch in her later research called *cognitive reference points* and *prototypes*—subcategories or category members that have a special cognitive status—that of being a "best example." Rosch showed that a variety of experimental techniques involving learning, matching, memory, and judgments of similarity converged on cognitive reference points. And she extended the results from colors to other categories, primarily categories of physical objects. She developed other experimental paradigms for investigating categories of physical objects. In each case, asymmetries (called *prototype effects*) were found: subjects judged certain members of the categories as being more representative of the category than other members. For example, robins are judged to be more representative of the category BIRD than are chickens, penguins, and ostriches, and desk chairs are judged to be more representative of the category CHAIR than are rocking chairs, barber chairs, beanbag chairs, or electric chairs. The most representative members of a category are called "prototypical" members. Here are some of the experimental paradigms used in studying categories of physical objects. Subjects give consistent goodness-of-example ratings across these experimental paradigms.

Direct rating: Subjects are asked to rate, say on a scale from one to seven, how good an example of a category (e.g., BIRD) various members are (e.g., a robin, a chicken, etc.).

Reaction time: Subjects are asked to press a button to indicate true or false in response to a statement of the form "An [example] is a [category name]" (e.g., "A chicken is a bird"). Response times are shorter for representative examples.

Production of examples: When asked to list or draw examples of category members, subjects were more likely to list or draw more representative examples.

Asymmetry in similarity ratings: Less representative examples are often considered to be more similar to more representative examples than the converse. Not surprisingly, Americans consider the United States to be a highly representative example of a country. In experiments where subjects were asked to give similarity ratings for pairs of countries, the following asymmetry arose. Subjects considered Mexico to be more similar to the United States than the United States is to Mexico. See Rosch 1975*a* and Tversky and Gati 1978.

Asymmetry in generalization: New information about a representative category member is more likely to be generalized to nonrepresentative members than the reverse. For example, it was shown that subjects believed that a disease was more likely to spread from robins to ducks on an island, than from ducks to robins. (This result is from Rips 1975.)

Family resemblances: Wittgenstein had speculated that categories were structured by what he called "family resemblances." Rosch showed that what philosophers took as a matter for a priori speculation could be demonstrated empirically. Characterizing "family resemblances" as perceived similarities between representative and nonrepresentative members of categories, Rosch showed that there was a correlation between family resemblances and numerical ratings of best examples derived from the above experiments. (See Rosch and Mervis 1975 and Rosch, Simpson, and Miller 1976.)

Such studies have been replicated often by other experimenters. There is no doubt that prototype effects of this sort are real. However, there have been some misunderstandings and debates concerning the interpretation of these results. Some of the debates will be discussed in detail below. But before we go on, we ought to clear up some of the common misunderstandings.

Rosch's genius has two aspects: she both launched a general challenge to the classical theory and devised, with her co-workers, replicable experiments demonstrating prototype effects, as well as basic-level effects. These experiments demonstrate the inadequacy of the classical theory; the classical theory cannot account for such results. But prototype effects, in themselves, do not provide any specific alternative theory of mental representation. And, as a responsible experimenter, Rosch has consistently distinguished between what her experimental results show and any theories that might account for those results.

Rosch went through three phases in her thinking about categorization.

- Phase I (late 1960s to early 1970s): Because she was studying color, shape, and emotions, she assumed prototypes were primarily a matter of (*a*) perceptual salience, or which things are most readily noticed by people; (*b*) memorability, or which things are easiest for people to remember; and (*c*) stimulus generalization, or the ability of people to generalize from one thing to something else that is physically similar to it. As she says (Rosch, in press): "Suppose that there are perceptually salient colors which more readily attract attention and are more easily remembered than other colors. When category names are learned, they tend to become attached first to the salient stimuli; then, by means of the principle of stimulus generalization, they generalize to other, physically similar instances."

- Phase II (early to mid 1970s): Under the influence of information-processing psychology, Rosch considered the possibility that prototype effects, as operationalized by the experiments cited above, might provide a characterization of the internal structure of the category. Thus, for example, the goodness-of-example ratings might directly reflect the internal structure of the category in mental representation. Two natural questions arose:
  1. Do the EFFECTS, defined operationally, characterize the STRUCTURE of the category as it is represented in the mind?
  2. Do the PROTOTYPES constitute mental REPRESENTATIONS?

  Given the assumptions of information-processing psychology, the experimental data can be interpreted most straightforwardly by answering yes to both questions. Rosch (1975*b*) initially interpreted her data in just this way.
- Phase III (late 1970s): Rosch eventually gave up on these interpretations of her experimental results. Such interpretations were artifacts of an overly narrow view of information-processing psychology. She came to the conclusion that prototype effects, defined operationally by experiment, underdetermined mental representations. The effects constrained the possibilities for what representations might be, but there was no one-to-one correspondence between the effects and mental representations. The effects had "sources," but one could not determine the sources given the effects. As she says of the research in Phase II (Rosch, in press): "The type of conclusions generated by this approach were, however, very general; e.g., that the representation evoked by the category name was more like good examples than poor examples of the category; that it was in a form more general than either words or pictures, etc. On the whole other information-processing researchers have considered the concepts of prototypes and typicality functions underspecified and have provided a variety of precise models, mini-models, and distinctions to be tested."

It is often the case that positions taken early in one's career tend to be associated with a researcher long after he or she has given up those positions. Many of those who read Rosch's early works did not read her later works, where she gave up on her early interpretations of the experimental results. Consequently, it is not widely known that Rosch abandoned the ideas that prototype effects directly mirror category structure and that prototypes constitute representations of categories. Because of this,

Rosch has had to provide explicit admonitions against overly simplistic interpretations of prototype effects—interpretations of the sort that she herself made in Phase II of her research. For example, she states:

> The pervasiveness of prototypes in real-world categories and of prototypicality as a variable indicates that prototypes must have some place in psychological theories of representation, processing, and learning. However, prototypes themselves do not constitute any particular model of processes, representations, or learning. This point is so often misunderstood that it requires discussion:
>
> 1. To speak of a *prototype* at all is simply a convenient grammatical fiction; what is really referred to are judgments of degree of prototypicality. . . . For natural-language categories, to speak of a single entity that is the prototype is either a gross misunderstanding of the empirical data or a covert theory of mental representation.
>
> 2. Prototypes do not constitute any particular processing model for categories. . . . What facts about prototypicality do contribute to processing notions is a constraint—processing models should not be inconsistent with the known facts about prototypes. For example, a model should not be such as to predict equal verification times for good and bad examples of categories nor predict completely random search through a category.
>
> 3. Prototypes do not constitute a theory of representation for categories. . . . Prototypes can be represented either by propositional or image systems. . . . As with processing models, the facts about prototypes can only constrain, but do not determine, models of representation. A representation of categories in terms of conjoined necessary and sufficient attributes alone would probably be incapable of handling all of the presently known facts, but there are many representations other than necessary and sufficient attributes that are possible.
>
> 4. Although prototypes must be learned, they do not constitute any particular theory of category learning. (Rosch 1978, pp. 40–41)

Despite Rosch's admonitions to the contrary, and despite her minimal theorizing concerning the sources of prototype effects, her results on prototype effects are still sometimes interpreted as constituting a prima facie theory of representation of category structure, as she thought was possible during Phase II of her research.

For example, take her results showing prototype effects within the category *bird*. Her experimental ranking shows that subjects view robins and sparrows as the best examples of birds, with owls and eagles lower down in the rankings and ostriches, emus, and penguins among the worst examples. In the early to mid 1970s, during Phase II of Rosch's research, such empirical goodness-of-example ratings were commonly taken as constituting a claim to the effect that membership in the category *bird* is graded and that owls and penguins are less members of the *bird* category than robins. (See Lakoff 1972 for a typical example.) It later became clear that that was a mistaken interpretation of the data. Rosch's ratings make no such claim; they are just ratings and do not make any claims at all. They are consistent with the interpretation that the category *bird* has strict boundaries and that robins, owls, and penguins are all 100 percent members of that category. However, that category must have additional internal structure of some sort that produces these goodness-of-example ratings. Moreover, that internal structure must be part of our concept of what a bird is, since it results in asymmetric inferences of the sort discussed above, described by Rips (1975).

This point is extremely important. Category structure plays a role in reasoning. In many cases, prototypes act as *cognitive reference points* of various sorts and form the basis for inferences (Rosch 1975*a*, 1981). The study of human inference is part of the study of human reasoning and conceptual structure; hence, those prototypes used in making inferences must be part of conceptual structure.

It is important to bear in mind that prototype effects are superficial. They may result from many factors. In the case of a graded category like *tall man*, which is fuzzy and does not have rigid boundaries, prototype effects may result from degree of category membership, while in the case of *bird*, which does have rigid boundaries, the prototype effects must result from some other aspect of internal category structure.

One of the goals of this book is to outline a general approach to the theory of categorization and to sketch the range of sources for superficial prototype effects. We will undertake this in chapters 4 through 6, where we discuss cognitive models. Our basic claim will be that prototype effects result from the nature of cognitive models, which can be viewed as "theories" of some subject matter.

One of the most interesting confirmations of this hypothesis has come through the work of Barsalou (1983, 1984). Barsalou has studied what he calls "ad hoc categories"—categories that are not conventional or fixed, but rather are made up on the fly for some immediate purpose. Such categories must be constructed on the basis of one's cognitive models of the subject matter under consideration. Examples of such categories are *things to take from one's home during a fire, what to get for a birthday present, what to do for entertainment on a weekend*, etc. Barsalou observes that such categories have prototype structure—structure that does not exist in advance, since the category is not conventional and does not exist in advance. Barsalou argues that in such cases, the nature of the category is principally determined by goals and that such goal structure is a function of one's cognitive models. Such a view has also been advocated by Murphy and Medin (1984).

Basic-Level Effects

The classical theory of categories gives no special importance to categories in the middle of a taxonomic hierarchy. Yet, as Berlin (Berlin, Breedlove, Raven 1974) and Hunn (1977) have shown for Tzeltal plant and animal taxonomies, the level of the biological genus is psychologically basic. The genus stands in the middle of the hierarchy that goes from UNIQUE BEGINNER to LIFE FORM to INTERMEDIATE to GENUS to SPECIES to VARIETY. Their results show a discrepancy between the classical theory of categories and a cognitively adequate theory of categories.

Rosch and her associates have extended the study of basic-level effects from cognitive anthropology to the experimental paradigm of cognitive psychology. Like Berlin, they found that the psychologically most basic level was in the middle of the taxonomic hierarchies:

SUPERORDINATE	ANIMAL	FURNITURE
BASIC LEVEL	DOG	CHAIR
SUBORDINATE	RETRIEVER	ROCKER

Just as Hunn (1975) argued that the basic level for animal categories is the only level at which categorization is determined by overall gestalt perception (without distinctive feature analysis), so Rosch and others (1976) have found that the basic level is:

- The highest level at which category members have similarly perceived overall shapes.
- The highest level at which a single mental image can reflect the entire category.
- The highest level at which a person uses similar motor actions for interacting with category members.
- The level at which subjects are fastest at identifying category members.
- The level with the most commonly used labels for category members.
- The first level named and understood by children.
- The first level to enter the lexicon of a language.
- The level with the shortest primary lexemes.
- The level at which terms are used in neutral contexts. For example, *There's a dog on the porch* can be used in a neutral context, whereas special contexts are needed for *There's a mammal on the porch* or *There's a wire-haired terrier on the porch.* (See Cruse 1977.)
- The level at which most of our knowledge is organized.

Thus basic-level categories are basic in four respects:

Perception: Overall perceived shape; single mental image; fast identification.
Function: General motor program.
Communication: Shortest, most commonly used and contextually neutral words, first learned by children and first to enter the lexicon.
Knowledge Organization: Most attributes of category members are stored at this level.

The fact that knowledge is mainly organized at the basic level is determined in the following way: When subjects are asked to list attributes of categories, they list very few attributes of category members at the superordinate level (furniture, vehicle, mammal); they list most of what they know at the basic level (chair, car, dog); and at the subordinate level (rocking chair, sports car, retriever) there is virtually no increase in knowledge over the basic level.

Why should most information be organized at a single conceptual level and why should it be this level in particular? To me, the most convincing hypothesis to date comes from the research of Tversky and Hemenway (1984). Berlin (Berlin, Breedlove, Raven 1974) and Hunn (1977) had suggested that gestalt perception—perception of overall part-whole configuration—is the fundamental determinant of the basic level. The experimental evidence accumulated by Tversky and Hemenway supports the Berlin-Hunn hypothesis. Their basic observation is that the basic level is distinguished from other levels on the basis of the type of attributes people associate with a category at that level, in particular, attributes concerned with *parts*. Our knowledge at the basic level is mainly organized around part-whole divisions. The reason is that the way an object is divided into parts determines many things. First, parts are usually correlated with functions, and hence our knowledge about functions is usually associated with knowledge about parts. Second, parts determine shape, and hence the way that an object will be perceived and imaged. Third, we usually interact with things via their parts, and hence part-whole divisions play a major role in determining what motor programs we can use to interact with an object. Thus, a handle is not just long and thin, but it can be grasped by the human hand. As Tversky and Hemenway say, "We sit on the *seat* of a chair and lean against the *back*, we remove the *peel* of a banana and eat the *pulp*."

Tversky and Hemenway also suggest that we impose part-whole structure on events and that our knowledge of event categories is structured very much the way our knowledge of physical object categories is. Their suggestion is in the same spirit as Lakoff and Johnson (1980), where it is suggested that event categories and other abstract categories are structured metaphorically on the basis of structures from the realm of physical experience.

Acquisition

One of the most striking results about basic-level categorization concerns the acquisition of concepts by children. If the classical theory of categorization were correct, then there should be no more to categorization than what one finds in the logic of classes: hierarchical categorization based on shared properties of the members of the categories. Before the work of Rosch and Mervis (Rosch et al. 1976), research on child development had not been informed by the idea of basic-level categorization. It had been concluded that, for example, three-year-old children had not mastered categorization, which was taken to be taxonomic categorization defined by the logic of classes. This conclusion was based on the performance of children in "sorting tasks," where subjects are asked to "put together the things that go together." Rosch and her associates observed that such studies tended to involve categorization at the *superordinate* level.

> The stimuli used in sorting tasks have tended to be of two types: If abstract (e.g., geometric forms varying in dimensions such as form, color, and size), they are typically presented in a set which has no structure (e.g., each attribute occurs with all combinations of all others); if representational (e.g., toy versions or pictures of real-world objects), the arrays are such that they can be grouped taxonomically only at the superordinate level. Thus, the representational stimuli used in sorting tasks are such that if the child were to sort the objects into those of like taxonomic category, he would have to put together such items as socks and shirt, dog and cow. Children do not seem to have been asked to sort together objects belonging to the same basic level category (e.g., several shoes or several dogs). We suspect this results from the fact that basic objects are so obviously the "same object" to adults that a task does not seem to be a problem of categorization to an adult experimenter unless objects are taken from different basic level categories. (Rosch et al. 1976, pp. 414–15)

Rosch and Mervis then compared sorting tasks for basic-level and superordinate categories. Basic-level sorting required being able to put together pictures of two different kinds of cows (compared to an airplane, say) or two different kinds of cars (compared to, say, a dog). Superordinate sorting required, for example, being able to put together a cow and a dog (compared to an airplane), or a motorcycle and an airplane (compared to a cow). At all age levels, from three years old up, subjects were virtually perfect on basic-level sorting. But, as had been well-known, the three-year-olds had trouble with superordinate sorting. They were only 55 percent correct, while the four-year-olds were 96 percent correct.

It is not true that three-year-olds have not mastered categorization. They have mastered *basic-level* categorization perfectly. It is *superordinate* categorization that is not mastered till later. The ability to categorize at the basic level comes first; the general logic of classes is learned later. Learning to categorize is thus something rather different from learning to use the logic of classes. Therefore, categorization itself is not merely the use of classical taxonomies.

It is important to bear these results in mind throughout the remainder of the book. The reason is this: It is sometimes claimed that basic-level categorization is merely classical taxonomic classification with additional constraints on cognitive processing added (e.g., perceptual and motor constraints). The Rosch-Mervis acquisition results show that this is not the case. Basic-level categories develop prior to classical taxonomic categories. They therefore cannot be the result of classical taxonomic categories *plus* something of a sensory-motor nature. Basic-level categories have an integrity of their own. They are our earliest and most natural form of categorization. Classical taxonomic categories are later "achievements of the imagination," in Roger Brown's words.

As Rosch and her co-workers observe, basic-level distinctions are "the generally most useful distinctions to make in the world," since they are characterized by overall shape and motor interaction and are at the most general level at which one can form a mental image. Basic-level categorization is mastered by the age of three. But what about children at earlier ages? It is known, for example, that two-year-olds have different categories from adults. Lions and tigers as well as cats are commonly called "kitty" by two-year-olds. Round candles and banks are commonly called "ball." And some things that we call "chair" may not be chairs for two-year-olds, e.g., beanbag chairs. The categories of two-year-olds may be broader than adult categories, or narrower, or overlapping. Does this mean that two-year-olds have not mastered the ability to form basic-level categories?

Not at all. Mervis (1984) has shown that although two-year-olds may have different categories than adults have, those categories are determined by the same principles that determine adult basic-level categories. In short, two-year-olds have mastered basic-level categorization, but have come up with different categories than adults—for very good reasons.

The difference is determined by three factors:

1. The child may not know about culturally significant attributes. Thus, not knowing that a bank is used for storing money, the child may attend to its round shape and classify it as a *ball.*

2. The salience of particular attributes may be different for a child than for an adult. Thus, a child may know that a bank is for storing money, but may attend to its round shape more than to the slot and keyhole, and still call it a ball. Or the child may attend to both and classify it as both a *bank* and a *ball.*

3. The child may include false attributes in the decision process. Thus, if the child thinks a leopard says "meow," he or she may classify leopards as *kitties.*

The point is that the level of categorization is not independent of who is doing the categorizing and on what basis. Though the same principles may determine the basic level, the circumstances under which those principles are employed determine what system of categories results.

Clusters of Interactional Properties

What determines basic-level structure is a matter of correlations: the overall perceived part-whole structure of an object correlates with our motor interaction with that object and with the functions of the parts (and our knowledge of those functions). It is important to realize that these are not purely objective and "in the world"; rather they have to do with the world as we interact with it: as we perceive it, image it, affect it with our bodies, and gain knowledge about it.

This is, again, a matter which has often been misunderstood, and Rosch has written at length on the nature of the misunderstanding. "It should be emphasized that we are talking about a perceived world and not a metaphysical world without a knower" (Rosch 1978, p. 29). She continues:

> When research on basic objects and their prototypes was initially conceived (Rosch et al. 1976), I thought of such attributes as inherent in the real world. Thus, given an organism that had sensory equipment capable of perceiving attributes such as wings and feathers, it was a fact in the real world that wings and feathers co-occurred. The state of knowledge of a person might be ignorant of (or indifferent or inattentive to) the attributes or might know the attributes but be ignorant concerning their correlation. Conversely, a person might know of the attributes and their correlational structure but exaggerate that structure, turning partial into complete correlations (as when attributes true of only many members of a category are thought of as true of all members). However, the environment was thought to constrain categorizations in that human knowledge could not provide correlational structure where there was none at all. For purposes of the basic object

> experiments, perceived attributes were operationally defined as those attributes listed by our subjects. Shape was defined as measured by our computer programs. We thus seemed to have our system grounded comfortably in the real world.
>
> On contemplation of the nature of many of our attributes listed by our subjects, however, it appeared that three types of attributes presented a problem for such a realistic view: (1) some attributes, such as "seat" for the object "chair," appeared to have names that showed them not to be meaningful prior to the knowledge of the object as chair; (2) some attributes such as "large" for the object "piano" seemed to have meaning only in relation to categorization of the object in terms of a superordinate category—piano is large for furniture but small for other kinds of objects such as buildings; (3) some attributes such as "you eat on it" for the object "table" were functional attributes that seemed to require knowledge about humans, their activities, and the real world in order to be understood. That is, it appeared that the analysis of objects into attributes was a rather sophisticated activity that our subjects (and indeed a system of cultural knowledge) might be considered to be able to impose only *after* the development of a system of categories. (Rosch 1978, pp. 41–42)

Thus the relevant notion of a "property" is not something objectively in the world independent of any being; it is rather what we will refer to as an *interactional property*—the result of our interactions as part of our physical and cultural environments given our bodies and our cognitive apparatus. Such interactional properties form *clusters* in our experience, and prototype and basic-level structure can reflect such clusterings.

As Berlin has observed, interactional properties and the categories they determine seem objective in the case of properties of basic-level categories—categories like *chair, elephant*, and *water.* The reason is that, given our bodies, we perceive certain aspects of our external environment very accurately at the basic level, though not so accurately at other levels. As long as we are talking about properties of basic-level objects, interactional properties will seem objective.

Perhaps the best way of thinking about basic-level categories is that they are "human-sized." They depend not on objects themselves, independent of people, but on the way people interact with objects: the way they perceive them, image them, organize information about them, and behave toward them with their bodies. The relevant properties clustering together to define such categories are not inherent to the objects, but are interactional properties, having to do with the way people interact with objects.

Basic-level categories thus have different properties than superordinate categories. For example, superordinate categories seem not to be characterized by images or motor actions. For example, we have mental images of chairs—abstract images that don't fit any particular chair—and we have general motor actions for sitting in chairs. But if we go from the basic-level category CHAIR to the superordinate category FURNITURE, a difference emerges. We have no abstract mental images of furniture that are not images of basic-level objects like chairs, tables, beds, etc. Try to imagine a piece of furniture that doesn't look like a chair, or table, or bed, etc., but is more abstract. People seem not to be able to do so. Moreover, we do not have motor actions for interacting with furniture in general that are not motor actions for interacting with some basic-level object—chairs, tables, beds, etc. But superordinate categories do have other human-based attributes—like purposes and functions.

In addition, the complements of basic-level categories are not basic level. They do not have the kinds of properties that basic-level categories have. For example, consider nonchairs, that is, those things that are not chairs. What do they look like? Do you have a mental image of a general or an abstract nonchair? People seem not to. How do you interact with a nonchair? Is there some general motor action one performs with nonchairs? Apparently not. What is a nonchair used for? Do nonchairs have general functions? Apparently not.

In the classical theory, the complement of a set that is defined by necessary and sufficient conditions is another set that is defined by necessary and sufficient conditions. But the complement of a basic-level category is not itself a basic-level category.

Cue Validity

One of the ideas that Rosch has regularly stressed is that categories occur in systems, and such systems include contrasting categories. Categorization depends to a large extent on the nature of the system in which a category is embedded. For example, within the superordinate category of things-to-sit-on, *chair* contrasts with *stool, sofa, bench*, etc. *Chair* would no doubt cover a very different range if one of the contrasting categories, say, *stool* or *sofa*, were not present.

Rosch has made use of contrasting categories in trying to give a theory of basic-level categorization. At the basic level, Rosch has claimed, categories are maximally distinct—that is, they maximize perceived similarity among category members and minimize perceived similarities across contrasting categories. Rosch and others (1976) attempted to capture this intuition by means of a quantitative measure of what they called *category cue validity*.

Cue validity is the conditional probability that an object is in a particular category given its possession of some feature (or "cue"). The best cues are those that work all of the time for categories at a given level. For example, if you see a living thing with gills, you can be certain it is a fish. *Gills* thus has a cue validity of 1.0 for the category *fish*, and a cue validity of 0 for other categories. Rosch and her associates suggested that one could extend this definition of cue validity to characterize basic-level categories. They defined *category cue validity* as the sum of all the individual cue validities of the features associated with a category.

The highest cue validities in a taxonomic hierarchy, they reasoned, should occur at the basic level. For example, subordinate categories like *kitchen chair* should have a low category cue validity because most of the attributes of kitchen chairs would be shared with other kinds of chairs and only a few attributes would differentiate kitchen chairs from other chairs. The individual attributes shared across categories would have low cue validities for the kitchen chair category; thus, seeing a chair with a back doesn't give you much reason for thinking it's a kitchen chair rather than some other kind of chair. Since most of the individual cue validities for attributes would be low, the sum should be low.

Correspondingly, they reasoned that category cue validity would be low for superordinate categories like *furniture*, since they would have few or no common attributes. Since basic-level categories have many properties in common among their members and few across categories, their category cue validities should be highest.

This idea was put forth during the earlier phase of Rosch's career when she still believed that the relevant attributes for characterizing basic-level categories were objectively existing attributes "in the world." Murphy (1982) has shown, however, that if category cue validity is defined for objectively existing attributes, then that measure cannot pick out basic-level categories. Murphy observes that individual cue validities for a superordinate category are always greater than or equal to those for a basic-level category; the same must be true for their sums. For example,

> (a) If people know that some trucks [basic-level] have air brakes, they know that having air brakes is a possible cue for being a vehicle [superordinate].
> (b) People know that some animals [superordinate] have beaks, but that fish [basic-level] do not (thereby giving *animal* a valid cue that the basic category does not have). (Murphy 1982, p. 176)

Murphy observes that his objection could be gotten around under the assumption that most attributes are not directly linked to superordinate categories in memory. This would be true, for example, given Tversky and Hemenway's characterization of the basic level as that level at which most knowledge is organized. But this would require a psychological definition of attribute (equivalent to our *interactional properties*), not a notion of attributes as existing objectively in the external world. But such a notion would presuppose a prior characterization of basic-level category—that level at which most knowledge is organized. Category cue validity defined for such psychological (or interactional) attributes might *correlate* with basic-level categorization, but it would not *pick out* basic-level categories; they would already have to have been picked out in order to apply the definition of category cue validity so that there was such a correlation. Thus, it seems reasonable to conclude that basic-level categories are, in fact, most differentiated in people's minds; but they are most differentiated because of their other properties, especially because most knowledge is organized at that level.

Clustering and Causation

Two of the themes that emerge from the research just discussed are the clustering of properties and the nonobjective, or interactional, character of properties relevant to human categorization. One of the most interesting of human categories from a philosophical point of view is the category of causes. Causation is represented in the grammar of most languages—and usually not just one kind of causation, but a variety of kinds. I have suggested elsewhere (Lakoff 1977) that the category of kinds of causation shows prototype effects in the ways that they are represented in natural languages. These effects are relatively uniform across languages.

We can account for these effects if we assume that prototypical causation is understood in terms of a cluster of interactional properties. This hypothesis appears to account best for the relation between language and conceptual structure, as well as for the relationships among the varieties of causation. The cluster seems to define a prototypical causation, and nonprototypical varieties of causation seem to be best characterizable in terms of deviations from that cluster.

Prototypical causation appears to be direct manipulation, which is characterized most typically by the following cluster of interactional properties:

1. There is an agent that does something.
2. There is a patient that undergoes a change to a new state.
3. Properties 1 and 2 constitute a single event; they overlap in time and space; the agent comes in contact with the patient.
4. Part of what the agent does (either the motion or the exercise of will) precedes the change in the patient.
5. The agent is the energy source; the patient is the energy goal; there is a transfer of energy from agent to patient.
6. There is a single definite agent and a single definite patient.

7. The agent is human.
8. a. The agent wills his action.
   b. The agent is in control of his action.
   c. The agent bears primary responsibility for both his action and the change.
9. The agent uses his hands, body, or some instrument.
10. The agent is looking at the patient, the change in the patient is perceptible, and the agent perceives the change.

The most representative examples of humanly relevant causation have all ten of these properties. This is the case in the most typical kinds of examples in the linguistics literature: Max broke the window, Brutus killed Caesar, etc. Billiard-ball causation, of the kind most discussed in the natural sciences, has properties 1 through 6. Indirect causation is not prototypical, since it fails in number 3, and possibly other conditions. According to this account, indirect causes are less representative examples of causation than direct causes. Multiple causes are less representative than single causes. Involuntary causation is less representative than voluntary causation. Many languages of the world meet the following generalization: The more direct the causation, the closer the morphemes expressing the cause and the result. This accounts for the distinction between *kill* and *cause to die. Kill* expresses direct causation, with cause and result expressed in a single morpheme—the closest possible connection. When would anyone ever say "cause to die"? In general, when there is no direct causation, when there is causation at a distance or accidental causation. Hinton (1982) gives a similar case from Mixtec, an Otomanguean language of Mexico. Mixtec has three causative morphemes: the word *sáʔà*, and the prefixes *sá-* and *s-*. The longest of these corresponds to the most indirect causation, and the shortest to the most direct causation. An explanation of this fact about the linguistic expression of kinds of causation is provided by Lakoff and Johnson (1980, chap. 20).

What is particularly interesting about this state of affairs is that the best example of the *conceptual category* of causation is typically marked by a grammatical construction or a morpheme and that the word *cause* is reserved for noncentral members of the conceptual category. There is a good reason for this. The concept of causation—prototypical causation—is one of the most fundamental of human concepts. It is a concept that people around the world use in thought. It is used spontaneously, automatically, effortlessly, and often. Such concepts are usually coded right into the grammar of languages—either via grammatical constructions or grammatical morphemes. For this reason, the prototypical concept of causation is built into the grammar of the language, and the word *cause* is relegated to characterizing noncentral causation.

Summary

The basic results of prototype theory leading up to the cognitive models approach can be summarized as follows:

- Some categories, like *tall man* or *red*, are graded; that is, they have inherent degrees of membership, fuzzy boundaries, and central members whose degree of membership (on a scale from zero to one) is one.
- Other categories, like *bird*, have clear boundaries; but within those boundaries there are graded prototype effects—some category members are better examples of the category than others.
- Categories are not organized just in terms of simple taxonomic hierarchies. Instead, categories "in the middle" of a hierarchy are the most *basic*, relative to a variety of psychological criteria: gestalt perception, the ability to form a mental image, motor interactions, and ease of learning, remembering, and use. Most knowledge is organized at this level.
- The basic level depends upon perceived part-whole structure and corresponding knowledge about how the parts function relative to the whole.
- Categories are organized into systems with contrasting elements.
- Human categories are not objectively "in the world," external to human beings. At least some categories are *embodied.* Color categories, for example, are determined jointly by the external physical world, human biology, the human mind, plus cultural considerations. Basic-level structure depends on human perception, imaging capacity, motor capabilities, etc.
- The properties relevant to the description of categories are *interactional properties*, properties characterizable only in terms of the interaction of human beings as part of their environment. Prototypical members of categories are sometimes describable in terms of *clusters* of such interactional properties. These clusters act as gestalts: the cluster as a whole is psychologically simpler than its parts.
- Prototype effects, that is, asymmetries among category members such as goodness-of-example judgments, are superficial phenomena which may have many sources.

The cognitive models approach to categorization is an attempt to make sense of all these observations. It is motivated by

- a need to understand what kinds of prototype effects there are and what their sources are

- a need to account for categorization not merely for physical objects but in abstract conceptual domains—emotions, spatial relations, social relationships, language, etc.
- a need for empirical study of the nature of cognitive models
- a need for appropriate theoretical and philosophical underpinnings for prototype theory.

These needs will be addressed below. But before we begin, it is important to see that prototype effects occur not only in nonlinguistic conceptual structure, but in linguistic structure as well. The reason is that linguistic structure makes use of general cognitive apparatus, such as category structure. Linguistic categories are kinds of cognitive categories.

CHAPTER 3

Prototype Effects in Language

One of the principal claims of this book is that language makes use of our general cognitive apparatus. If this claim is correct, two things follow:

- Linguistic categories should be of the same type as other categories in our conceptual system. In particular, they should show prototype and basic-level effects.
- Evidence about the nature of linguistic categories should contribute to a general understanding of cognitive categories in general. Because language has such a rich category structure and because linguistic evidence is so abundant, the study of linguistic categorization should be one of the prime sources of evidence for the nature of category structure in general.

Thus, we need to ask the general question: What evidence is there that language shows prototype and basic-level effects?

The issue is a profound one, because it is by no means obvious that the language makes use of our general cognitive apparatus. In fact, the most widely accepted views of language within both linguistics and the philosophy of language make the opposite assumption: that language is a separate "modular" system *independent* of the rest of cognition. The independence of grammar from the rest of cognition is perhaps the most fundamental assumption on which Noam Chomsky's theory of language rests. As we shall see in chapter 14, the very idea that language is a "formal system." (in the technical mathematical sense used by Chomsky and many other linguistic theorists) requires the assumption that language is independent of the rest of cognition. That formal-system view also embodies the implicit assumption that categories are classical (and hence can be characterized by distinctive features). Such views are also the norm in the philosophy of language, especially in the work of Richard Montague, Donald Davidson, David Lewis, Saul Kripke, and many others.

Thus, the question of what linguistic categories are like is important in two ways.

> First, it affects our understanding of what language is. Does language make use of general cognitive mechanisms? Or is it something separate and independent, using only mechanisms of its own? How this question is answered will determine the course of the future study of language. Entirely different questions will be asked and theories proposed depending on the answer.
>
> Second, the answer will affect the study of cognition, since it will determine whether linguistic evidence is admissible in the study of the mind in general.

It is for these reasons that it is important to look closely at studies that have revealed the existence of prototype effects in language.

There are actually two bodies of relevant studies. One is a body of research based on Phases I and II of Rosch's research on prototype theory. It is concerned with demonstrating the existence of prototype effects in language. The second body of research focuses on the cognitive model interpretation of prototype effects that we will be discussing below. The present chapter is a survey of the first body of results, which show little more than the existence of prototype effects in language. Chapters 4 through 8 and the three case studies at the end of the book will survey the second body of results, which focus more on the nature of the effects.

Prototype Effects in Linguistic Categories

The study of prototype effects has a long tradition in linguistics. The kinds of effects that have been studied the most are asymmetries within categories and gradations away from a best example.

Markedness

The study of certain types of asymmetries within categories is known within linguistics as the study of *markedness*. The term *markedness* arises from the fact that some morphological categories have a "mark" and others are "unmarked." Take the category of number in English. Plural number has a "mark," the morpheme *-s*, as in *boys*, while singular number lacks any overt "mark," as in *boy*. The singular is thus the unmarked member of the morphological category *number* in English. Thus, singular and plural—the two members of the *number* category—show an asymmetry; they are not treated the same in English, since singular has no overt mark. The intuition that goes along with this is that singular is, somehow, cognitively simpler than plural and that its cognitive simplicity is reflected in its shorter form. The idea here is that simplicity in cognition is reflected in simplicity of form. Zero-marking for a morpheme is one kind of simplicity.

In phonology, markedness is often understood in terms of some notion of relative ease of articulation. For example, the consonants *p, t,* and *k* are voiceless, that is, they do not involve the vibration of the vocal chords, while the minimally contrasting voiced consonants *b, d,* and *g* do involve vocal cord vibration. Thus, one can understand voicing as a "mark" added to voiceless consonants to yield voiced consonants, except between vowels where the vocal cords are vibrating to produce the vowels. In that situation, the voiced consonants are unmarked and the voiceless consonants are marked. Thus, there is an asymmetry in terms of relative ease of articulation. Voiced and voiceless consonants also show an asymmetry in the way they pattern in the sound systems of languages. For example, many languages do not have both voiced and voiceless consonants. If voicing and voicelessness were symmetric, one might expect an equal number of languages to have only voiceless or only voiced consonants. But in such a situation, the norm is for such a language to have voiceless consonants. Similarly, within a language, there are environments where it is impossible to have both voiced and voiceless consonants. For example, in English, after initial *s*-, there is no contrast between voiced and voiceless consonants. Only voiceless consonants may occur. English has words like *spot*, but no contrasting words like *sbot.* Similarly, at the end of words in German, there is no contrast between voiced and voiceless stop consonants. Only the voiceless consonants can occur. Thus, for example, /d/ is pronounced as [t]. In general, where the contrast is neutralized (that is, only one member of the pair can occur), the one which occurs is "unmarked" in that environment.

Neutralization of contrasts can also occur in semantics. Consider contrasts like *tall-short, happy-sad*, etc. These pairs are not completely symmetric. For example, if one asks *How tall is Harry?* one is not suggesting that Harry is tall, but if one asks *How short is Harry?* one is suggesting that Harry is short. Only one member of the pair *tall-short* can be used with a neutral meaning, namely, *tall.* Since it occurs in cases where the contrast is neutralized, *tall* is referred to as the "unmarked" member of the *tall-short* contrast set. Correspondingly, it is assumed that tallness is cognitively more basic than shortness and the word marking the cognitively basic dimension occurs in neutral contexts.

In general, markedness is a term used by linguists to describe a kind of prototype effect—an asymmetry in a category, where one member or subcategory is taken to be somehow more basic than the other (or others). Correspondingly, the unmarked member is the default value—the member of the category that occurs when only one member of the category can occur and all other things are equal.

Other Prototype Effects

Prototype effects have shown up in all areas of language—phonology, morphology, syntax, and semantics. In all cases, they are inconsistent with the classical theory of categories and are in conflict with current orthodoxies in the field which assume the correctness of the classical theory. Here is a sampling of studies which have shown prototype effects.

Phonology

There is no more fundamental distinction in linguistics than the distinction between a *phone* and a *phoneme.* A phone is a unit of speech sound, while a phoneme is a cognitive element understood as occurring "at a higher level" and usually represented by a phone. For example, English has a phoneme /k/ (sometimes spelled with the letter *c* in English orthography) which occurs in the words *cool, keel, key, school*, and *flak.* If attention is payed to details of pronunciation, it turns out that /k/ is pronounced differently in these words: aspirated velar [k^h] in *cool*, aspirated palatal [k'^h] in *keel*, unaspirated velar [k] in *school*, and unaspirated palatal [k′] in *ski.* English speakers perceive these, despite their differences in pronunciation, as being instances of the same phoneme /k/. However, there are other languages in which [k^h] and [k] are instances of different phonemes, and others still in which [k′] and [k] are instances of different phonemes.

Jeri Jaeger (1980) has replicated Rosch's experiments in the domain of phonology. She suggests, on the basis of experimental evidence, that phonemes are prototype-based categories of phones. Thus, the phoneme /k/ in English is the category consisting of the phones [k], [k^h], [k′], and [k'^h] with [k] as the prototypical member. Phonemic categories in general are understood in terms of their prototypical members. The nonprototypical phones are related to the prototype by phonological rules. Jaeger's results, if correct, indicate that phonological categorization, like other cognitive categorization, shows prototype effects. Her results contradict most contemporary phonological theories, which take the classical theory of categorization for granted. They point in the direction of a unification of phonology and other aspects of cognition.

Jaeger's other experimental results show:

- In English, the [k] after word-initial [s] is part of the /k/ phoneme and not either the /g/ phoneme or some velar archiphoneme.

- In English, the affricates [tš] and [dž] are unitary phonemes from a cognitive point of view.
- English speakers consider the following vowel pairs to belong together in a psychologically unified set: [ey-ae], [i-ɛ], [ow-a], [u-Λ]. The source of the speaker's knowledge about this set of alternations is the orthographic system of English.
- Phonetic features in general have psychological reality, but not all the features proposed in various theories do. [Continuant], [sonorant], and [voice] are confirmed as real by the experiments, but [anterior] is brought into question.
- Phonetic features are not binary, but consist of a dimension along which segments can have varying values.
- A psychologically real theory must allow for the possibility of more than one correct feature assignment for a segment.

The application of Rosch's experimental techniques to phonology is a real innovation that requires a thorough reevaluation of phonological theory.

Morphology

Bybee and Moder (1983) have shown that English strong verbs like *string/strung* form a morphological category that displays prototype effects. They argue that verbs that form their past tense with Λ (spelled *u* in English orthography) form a prototype-based category. The verbs include: *spin, win, cling, fling, sling, sting, string, swing, wring, hang, stick, strike, slink, stick, sneak, dig*, and some others that have recently developed similar past tense forms in certain dialects, e.g., *bring, shake.* On the basis of experimental results, they argue that the category has a prototype with the following properties:

It begins with *s* followed by one or two consonants: sC(C)-.
It ends with the velar nasal: /ŋ/.
It has a lax high front vowel: *I*.

Although the verbs in the category cannot be defined by common features, they all bear family resemblances to this prototype. *String, sling, swing*, and *sting* fit it exactly. The following have what Bybee and Moder analyze as "one" difference from the prototype: *cling, fling*, and *bring* have two initial consonants, but no *s*; *spin* and *stick* have the right initial consonant cluster and vowel, but differ from the final consonant by one phonological property each—*spin* has a dental instead of a velar nasal and *stick* has a velar stop instead of a velar nasal. *Win* has two minimal differences: no initial *s* and a final dental nasal instead of a velar. *Strike* also has two differences: a nonnasal final consonant and a different vowel.

This category can be categorized by a central member plus something else. In this case the "something else" is a characterization of "minimal" phonological differences: the lack of an initial *s*, the lack of nasalization, a different vowel, the difference between a velar and a dental consonant, etc. Bybee and Moder have investigated this case only and do not claim that these "minimal" differences will always count as minimal, either in English or in all languages. Without a theory of what counts as a minimal difference for morphological categorization, Bybee and Moder simply have a list of relevant differences that hold in this case. It would be interesting to see if a more general theory could be developed.

Syntax

In a number of studies ranging widely over English syntax, John Robert Ross (1972, 1973*a, b*, 1974, 1981) has shown that just about every syntactic category in the language shows prototype effects. These include categories like noun, verb, adjective, clause, preposition, noun phrase, verb phrase, etc. Ross has also demonstrated that syntactic constructions in English show prototype effects, for example, passive, relative WH-preposing, question WH-preposing, topicalization, conjunction, etc.

Let us consider one of Ross's examples: nouns. Ross's basic insight is that normal nouns undergo a large range of grammatical processes in English, while less nouny nouns do not undergo the full range of processes that apply to nouns in general. Moreover, even nouns that, in most constructions, are excellent examples of nouns may be less good examples in special constructions. Consider the nouns *toe, breath, way*, and *time*, as they occur in the expressions:

to stub one's toe
to hold one's breath
to lose one's way
to take one's time

These all look superficially as if they have the same structure. But, as Ross demonstrates, within these expressions *toe* is nounier than *breath*, which is nounier than *way*, which is nounier than *time*. Ross (1981) gives three syntactic environments that demonstrate the hierarchy. Starred sentences indicate ill-formedness.

I. Modification by a passive participle
A stubbed toe can be very painful.
**Held breath* is usually fetid when released.
**A lost way* has been the cause of many a missed appointment.
**Taken time* might tend to irritate your boss.

II. Gapping
I stubbed my toe, and she hers.
I held my breath, and she hers.
*I lost my way, and she hers.
*I took my time, and she hers.

III. Pluralization
Betty and Sue stubbed their toes.
*Betty and Sue stubbed their toe.

Betty and Sue held their breaths.
Betty and Sue held their breath.

*Betty and Sue lost their ways.
Betty and Sue lost their way.

*Betty and Sue took their times.
Betty and Sue took their time.

Ross's tests do not differentiate *way* and *time.* Here is a further test environment that confirms Ross's judgment:

IV. Pronominalization
I stubbed my toe, but didn't hurt *it.*
Sam held his breath for a few seconds and then released *it.*
Harry lost his way, but found *it* again.
*Harry took his time, but wasted *it.*

In each of these cases, the nounier nouns follow the general rule (that is, they behave the way one would expect nouns to behave), while the less nouny nouns do not follow the rule. As the sentences indicate, there is a hierarchy of nouniness among the examples given. Rules differ as to how nouny a noun they require. As Ross has repeatedly demonstrated, examples like these are rampant in English syntax.

More recently, Hopper and Thompson (1984) have proposed that the prototypical members of the syntactic categories *noun* and *verb* can be defined in terms of semantic and discourse functions. They provide an account with examples from a wide range of languages that indicate that nouns and verbs have prototypical functions in discourses.

Subject, Agent, and Topic

Bates and MacWhinney (1982) proposed on the basis of language acquisition data that prototype theory can be used to characterize the grammatical relation SUBJECT in the following way:

– A prototypical SUBJECT is both AGENT and TOPIC.

Van Oosten (1984) has found a wide range of evidence in English substantiating this hypothesis and expanding it to include the following:

- AGENT and TOPIC are both natural categories centering around prototypes.
- Membership in the category SUBJECT cannot be completely predicted from the properties of agents and topics.

As usual in prototype-based categories, things that are very close to prototypical members will most likely be in the category and be relatively good examples. And as expected, the boundary areas will differ from language to language. Category membership will be motivated by (though not predicted from) family resemblances to prototypical members.

- Noun phrases that are neither prototypical agents nor prototypical topics can be subjects—and relatively good examples of subjects—providing that they have important agent and topic properties.
- This permits what we might call a "prototype-based universal." SUBJECT IS A CATEGORY WHOSE CENTRAL MEMBERS ARE BOTH PROTOTYPICAL AGENTS AND PROTOTYPICAL TOPICS.

This characterization of subject is semantically based, but not in the usual sense; that is, it does not attempt to predict all subjects from semantic and pragmatic properties. But it does define the prototype of the category in semantic and pragmatic terms. Noncentral cases will differ according to language-particular conventions. The subject category is thus what we will refer to in chapter 6 as a *radial category*. In this case, the center, or prototype, of the category is predictable. And while the noncentral members are not predictable from the central member, they are "motivated" by it, in the sense that they bear family resemblances to it. *Motivation* in this sense will be discussed in great detail below.

Perhaps the most striking confirmation of the Bates-MacWhinney hypothesis comes from Van Oosten's study of the uses of the passive in English. Van Oosten picked out passive sentences as they occurred in transcribed conversation and compiled a list of all the uses. The list seemed random. She then compared her list of uses of the passive with her list of the properties of prototypical agents and topics. What she noticed was a remarkable correlation. According to the Bates-MacWhinney hypothesis, the subjects of simple active sentences should be capable of displaying all the properties of agents and topics. We can view this as a conjunction of the following form, where each P_i is either an agent property or a topic property:

P_1 & P_2 & . . . & P_n.

Passive sentences are used for various reasons—whenever no single noun phrase has all the agent and topic properties. Thus, passives (on the Bates-MacWhinney hypothesis) should occur when the subject of the passive sentence *fails* to have one of the prototypical agent or topic properties. Thus, the uses of the passive should be a disjunction of the form:

not P_1 or not P_2 or . . . or not P_n.

This was in fact just the list of uses of the passive that Van Oosten had compiled in her empirical study!

For example, among the agent properties are volition (call it P_1) and primary responsibility for the action (call it P_2). Correspondingly, passives can be used to indicate that an action was accidental (not P_1) or to avoid placing responsibility on the person performing the action (not P_2). Similarly, one of the topic properties of a prototypical simple active sentence is that the actor is already under discussion in the discourse (call this P_3). Correspondingly, a passive may be used to introduce (not P_3) the actor into the discourse, by placing the actor in the *by*-phrase. In this way, prototype theory enables Van Oosten to explain why the passive is used as it is. Van Oosten's analysis also provides evidence that supports the conception of subject as a category whose prototypical subcategory is predictable from semantic and pragmatic considerations.

Basic Clause Types

Just about all of the considerable number of contemporary theories of grammar recognize an asymmetry among types of clauses in a given language. In certain clauses, there is a "natural" or "direct" relationship between the meaning of the clause and the grammar of the clause. In English, for example, simple active declarative sentences—*Sam ate a peach, Max is in the kitchen, Harry drives a sports car, That fact is odd*, etc.—are usually taken as examples of that natural (or direct) relationship. Other kinds of clause types are usually considered as deviations from the basic clause type. Here is a handful of standard examples of such "deviations":

Passive: The peach was eaten by Sam.
Existential *There*-sentences: There is a man in the kitchen.
Patient subject sentences: This car drives easily.
Extrapositions: It is odd that Maxine eats pears.
WH-questions: What did Sam eat?

Different theories of grammar treat such basic clause types by different theoretical means. Harris (1957) hypothesized "kernel sentences." Chomsky (1965) hypothesized "deep structures." And virtually every theory of grammar since then has made some such distinction. What is of interest in this context is the asymmetry. The basic clauses show a privileged relationship between meaning and grammar; the nonbasic clause types do not show that relationship. Within the category of clause types in a language, the subcategory of basic clause types has a privileged status. This asymmetry between basic clause types and other clause types is a kind of prototype effect. Within the theory of grammatical constructions, described in case study 3 below, such prototype effects in grammar are characterized in the same way as other prototype effects, using the general theory of cognitive models, which is set out in the remainder of this book.

Summary

Linguistic categories, like conceptual categories, show prototype effects. Such effects occur at every level of language, from phonology to morphology to syntax to the lexicon. I take the existence of such effects as prima facie evidence that linguistic categories have the same character as other conceptual categories. At this point I will adopt it as a working hypothesis that language does make use of general cognitive mechanisms—at least categorization mechanisms. Under this working hypothesis, we will use linguistic evidence to study the cognitive apparatus used in categorization. On the basis of all of the available evidence, I will argue in chapters 9–17 that our working hypothesis is indeed correct and that as a result our understanding of both language and cognition in general must be changed considerably.

CHAPTER 4

Idealized Cognitive Models

Sources of Prototype Effects

The main thesis of this book is that we organize our knowledge by means of structures called *idealized cognitive models*, or ICMs, and that category structures and prototype effects are by-products of that organization. The ideas about cognitive models that we will be making use of have developed within cognitive linguistics and come from four sources: Fillmore's frame semantics (Fillmore 1982*b*), Lakoff and Johnson's theory of metaphor and metonymy (Lakoff and Johnson 1980), Langacker's cognitive grammar (Langacker 1986), and Fauconnier's theory of mental spaces (Fauconnier 1985). Fillmore's frame semantics is similar in many ways to schema theory (Rumelhart 1975), scripts (Schank and Abelson 1977), and frames with defaults (Minsky 1975). Each ICM is a complex structured whole, a gestalt, which uses four kinds of structuring principles:

- propositional structure, as in Fillmore's frames
- image-schematic structure, as in Langacker's cognitive grammar
- metaphoric mappings, as described by Lakoff and Johnson
- metonymic mappings, as described by Lakoff and Johnson

Each ICM, as used, structures a mental space, as described by Fauconnier.

Probably the best way to provide an idea of what ICMs are and how they work in categorization is to go through examples. Let us begin with Fillmore's concept of a *frame*. Take the English word *Tuesday*. *Tuesday* can be defined only relative to an idealized model that includes the natural cycle defined by the movement of the sun, the standard means of characterizing the end of one day and the beginning of the next, and a larger seven-day calendric cycle—the week. In the idealized model, the week is a whole with seven parts organized in a linear sequence; each part is called a *day*, and the third is *Tuesday*. Similarly, the concept *weekend* requires a notion of a *work week* of five days followed by a break of two days, superimposed on the seven-day calendar.

Our model of a week is idealized. Seven-day weeks do not exist objectively in nature. They are created by human beings. In fact, not all cultures have the same kinds of weeks. Consider, for example, the Balinese calendric system:

> The two calendars which the Balinese employ are a lunar-solar one and one built around the interaction of independent cycles of day-names, which I shall call "permutational." The permutational calendar is by far the most important. It consists of ten different cycles of day-names, following one another in a fixed order, after which the first day-name appears and the cycle starts over. Similarly, there are nine, eight, seven, six, five, four, three, two, and even—the ultimate of a "contemporized" view of time—one day-name cycles. The names in each cycle are also different, and the cycles run concurrently. That is to say, any given day has, at least in theory, ten different names simultaneously applied to it, one from each of the ten cycles. Of the ten cycles, only those containing five, six, and seven day-names are of major cultural significance. . . . The outcome of all this wheels-within-wheels computation is a view of time as consisting of ordered sets of thirty, thirty-five, forty-two and two hundred and ten quantum units ("days"). . . . To identify a day in the forty-two-day set—and thus assess its practical and/or religious significance—one needs to determine its place, that is, its name in the six-name cycle (say *Ariang*) and in the seven-day cycle (say *Boda*): the day is Boda-Ariang, and one shapes one's actions accordingly. To identify a day in the thirty-five day set, one needs its place and name in the five-name cycle (for example, *Klion*) and in the seven-: for example, *Boda-Klion*. . . . For the two-hundred-and-ten-day set, unique determination demands names from all three weeks: for example, *Boda-Ariang-Klion*, which, it so happens, is the day on which the most important Balinese holiday, Galungan, is celebrated. (Geertz 1973, pp. 392–93)

Thus, a characterization of *Galungan* in Balinese requires a complex ICM which superimposes three week-structures—one five-day, one six-day, and one seven-day. In the cultures of the world, such idealized cognitive models can be quite complex.

The Simplest Prototype Effects

In general, any element of a cognitive model can correspond to a conceptual category. To be more specific, suppose schema theory in the sense of Rumelhart (1975) were taken as characterizing propositional models. Each schema is a network of nodes and links. Every node in a schema would then correspond to a conceptual category. The properties of the category would depend on many factors: the role of that node in the given schema, its relationship to other nodes in the schema, the relationship of that schema to other schemas, and the overall interaction of that schema with other aspects of the conceptual system. As we will see, there is more to ICMs than can be represented in schema theory. But at least those complexities do arise. What is particularly interesting is that even if one set up schema theory as one's theory of ICMs, and even if the categories defined in those schemas were classical categories, there would still be prototype effects—effects that would arise from the interaction of the given schema with other schemas in the system.

A clear example of this has been given by Fillmore (1982*a*). The example is a classic: the category defined by the English word *bachelor.*

> The noun *bachelor* can be defined as an unmarried adult man, but the noun clearly exists as a motivated device for categorizing people only in the context of a human society in which certain expectations about marriage and marriageable age obtain. Male participants in long-term unmarried couplings would not ordinarily be described as bachelors; a boy abandoned in the jungle and grown to maturity away from contact with human society would not be called a bachelor; John Paul II is not properly thought of as a bachelor.

In other words, *bachelor* is defined with respect to an ICM in which there is a human society with (typically monogamous) marriage, and a typical marriageable age. The idealized model says nothing about the existence of priests, "long-term unmarried couplings," homosexuality, Moslems who are permitted four wives and only have three, etc. With respect to this idealized cognitive model, a *bachelor* is simply an unmarried adult man.

This idealized model, however, does not fit the world very precisely. It is oversimplified in its background assumptions. There are some segments of society where the idealized model fits reasonably well, and when an unmarried adult man might well be called a bachelor. But the ICM does not fit the case of the pope or people abandoned in the jungle, like Tarzan. In such cases, unmarried adult males are certainly not representative members of the category of bachelors.

The theory of ICMs would account for such prototype effects of the category *bachelor* in the following way: An idealized cognitive model may fit one's understanding of the world either perfectly, very well, pretty well, somewhat well, pretty badly, badly, or not at all. If the ICM in which *bachelor* is defined fits a situation perfectly and the person referred to by the term is unequivocally an unmarried adult male, then he qualifies as a member of the category *bachelor.* The person referred to deviates from prototypical bachelorhood if either the ICM fails to fit the world perfectly or the person referred to deviates from being an unmarried adult male.

Under this account *bachelor* is not a graded category. It is an all-or-none concept relative to the appropriate ICM. The ICM characterizes representative bachelors. One kind of gradience arises from the degree to which the ungraded ICM fits our knowledge (or assumptions) about the world.

This account is irreducibly cognitive. It depends on being able to take two cognitive models—one for *bachelor* and one characterizing one's knowledge about an individual, say the pope—and compare them, noting the ways in which they overlap and the ways in which they differ. One needs the concept of "fitting" one's ICMs to one's understanding of a given situation and keeping track of the respects in which the fit is imperfect.

This kind of explanation cannot be given in a noncognitive theory—one in which a concept either fits the world as it is or not. The background conditions of the *bachelor* ICM rarely make a perfect seamless fit with the world as we know it. Still we can apply the concept with some degree of accuracy to situations where the background conditions don't quite mesh with our knowledge. And the worse the fit between the background conditions of the ICM and our knowledge, the less appropriate it is for us to apply the concept. The result is a gradience—a simple kind of prototype effect.

Lie

A case similar to Fillmore's *bachelor* example, but considerably more complex, has been discussed by Sweetser (1984). It is the category defined by the English word *lie.* Sweetser's analysis is based on experimental results by Coleman and Kay (1981) on the use of the verb *lie.* Coleman and Kay found that their informants did not appear to have necessary and sufficient conditions characterizing the meaning of *lie.* Instead they found a cluster of three conditions, no one of which was necessary and all of which varied in relative importance:

> A consistent pattern was found: falsity of belief is the most important element of the prototype of *lie*, intended deception the next most important element, and factual falsity is the least important. Informants fairly easily and reliably assign the word *lie* to reported speech acts in a more-or-less, rather than all-or-none, fashion, . . . [and] . . . informants agree fairly generally on the relative weights of the elements in the semantic prototype of *lie.*

Thus, there is agreement that if you steal something and then claim you didn't, that's a good example of a lie. A less representative example of a lie is when you tell the hostess "That was a great party!" when you were bored stiff. Or if you say something true but irrelevant, like "I'm going to the candy store, Ma" when you're really going to the pool hall, but will be stopping by the candy store on the way.

An important anomaly did, however, turn up in the Coleman-Kay study. When informants were asked to define a *lie*, they consistently said it was a false statement, even though actual falsity turned out consistently to be the least important element by far in the cluster of conditions. Sweetser has observed that the theory of ICMs provides an elegant way out of this anomaly. She points out that, in most everyday language use, we take for granted an idealized cognitive model of social and linguistic interaction. Here is my revised and somewhat oversimplified version of the ICM Sweetser proposes:

THE MAXIM OF HELPFULNESS

People intend to help one another.

This is a version of Grice's cooperative principle.

THE ICM OF ORDINARY COMMUNICATION

(*a*) If people say something, they're intending to help if and only if they believe it.

(*b*) People intend to deceive if and only if they don't intend to help.

THE ICM OF JUSTIFIED BELIEF

(*c*) People have adequate reasons for their beliefs.

(*d*) What people have adequate reason to believe is true.

These two ICMs and the maxim of helpfulness govern a great deal of what we consider ordinary conversation, that is, conversation not constrained by special circumstances. For example, if I told you I just saw a mutual friend, under ordinary circumstances you'd probably assume I was being helpful, that I wasn't trying to deceive you, that I believed I had seen the friend, and that I did in fact see the friend. That is, unless you have reason to believe that the maxim of helpfulness is not applying or that one of these idealized models is not applicable, you would simply take them for granted.

These ICMs provide an explanation of why speakers will define a lie as a false statement, when falsity is by far the least important of the three factors discovered by the Kay-Coleman study. These two ICMs each have an internal logic and when they are taken together, they yield some interesting inferences. For example, it follows from (*c*) and (*d*) that if a person believes something, he has adequate reasons for his beliefs, and if he has adequate reasons for believing the proposition, then it is true. Thus, in the idealized world of these ICMs if X believes a proposition P, then P is true. Conversely, if P is false, then X doesn't believe P. Thus, falsity entails lack of belief.

In this idealized situation, falsity also entails an intent to deceive. As we have seen, falsity entails a lack of belief. By (*a*), someone who says something is intending to help if and only if he believes it. If he doesn't believe it, then he isn't intending to help. And by (*b*), someone who isn't intending to help in giving information is intending to deceive. Thus, in these ICMs, falsity entails both lack of belief and intent to deceive. Thus, from the definition of a lie as a false statement, the other properties of lying follow as consequences. Thus, the definition of *lie* does not need to list all these attributes. If *lie* is defined relative to these ICMs, then lack of belief and intent to deceive follow from falsity.

As Sweetser points out, the relative importance of these conditions is a consequence of their logical relations given these ICMs. Belief follows from a lack of intent to deceive and truth follows from belief. Truth is of the least concern since it is a consequence of the other conditions. Conversely, falsity is the most informative of the conditions in the idealized model, since falsity entails both intent to deceive and lack of belief. It is thus falsity that is the defining characteristic of a lie.

Sweetser's analysis provides both a simple, intuitive definition of *lie* and an explanation of all of the Coleman-Kay findings. The ICMs used are not made up just to account for *lie*. Rather they govern our everyday common sense reasoning. These results are possible because the ICMs have an internal logic. It is the *structure* of the ICMs that explains the Coleman-Kay findings.

Coleman and Kay discovered prototype effects for the category *lie*—situations where subjects gave uniform rankings of how good an example of a lie a given statement was. Sweetser's analysis explains these rankings on the basis of her ICM analysis, even though her ICM fits the classical theory! Nonprototypical cases are accounted for by imperfect fits of the lying ICM to knowledge about the situation at hand. For example, white lies and social lies occur in situations where condition (*b*) does not hold. A white lie is a case where deceit is not harmful, and a social lie is a case where deceit is helpful. In general, expressions such as *social lie, white lie, exaggeration, joke, kidding, oversimplification, tall tale, fiction, fib, mistake*, etc. can be accounted for in terms of systematic deviations from the above ICMs.

Although neither Sweetser nor anyone else has attempted to give a theory of complex concepts in terms of the theory of ICMs, it is worth considering what would be involved in doing so. As should be obvious, adjective-noun expressions like *social lie* do not work according to traditional theories. The category of social lies is not the intersection of the set of social things and the set of lies. The term *social* places one in a domain of experience characterized by an ICM that says that being polite is more important than telling the truth. This conflicts with condition (*b*), that intent to deceive is not helpful, and it overrides this condition. Saying "That was a great party!" when you were bored stiff is a case where deception is helpful to all concerned. It is a prototypical social lie, though it is not a prototypical lie. The concept *social lie* is therefore represented by an ICM that overlaps in some respects with the lying ICM, but is different in an important way. The question that needs to be answered is whether the addition of the modifier *social* can account for this difference systematically. Any general account of complex concepts like *social lie* in terms of ICMs will have to indicate how the ICM evoked by *social* can cancel one condition of the ICM evoked by *lie*, while retaining the other conditions. An obvious suggestion would be that in conflicts between modifiers and heads, the modifiers win out. This would follow from the general cognitive principle that special cases take precedence over general cases.

Cluster Models: A Second Source of Prototype Effects

It commonly happens that a number of cognitive models combine to form a complex cluster that is psychologically more basic than the models taken individually. We will refer to these as *cluster models.*

Mother

An example is the concept *mother*. According to the classical theory, it should be possible to give clear necessary and sufficient conditions for *mother* that will fit all the cases and apply equally to all of them. Such a definition might be something like: *a woman who has given birth to a child.* But as we will see, no such definition will cover the full range of cases. *Mother* is a concept that is based on a complex model in which a number of individual cognitive models combine, forming a cluster model. The models in the cluster are:

- The birth model: The person who gives birth is the *mother.*

The birth model is usually accompanied by a genetic model, although since the development of egg and embryo implants, they do not always coincide.

- The genetic model: The female who contributes the genetic material is the *mother*.
- The nurturance model: The female adult who nurtures and raises a child is the *mother* of that child.
- The marital model: The wife of the father is the *mother.*
- The genealogical model: The closest female ancestor is the *mother.*

The concept *mother* normally involves a complex model in which all of these individual models combine to form a cluster model. There have always been divergences from this cluster; stepmothers have been around for a long time. But because of the complexities of modern life, the models in the cluster have come to diverge more and more. Still, many people feel the pressure to pick one model as being the right one, the one that "really" defines what a mother is. But although one might try to argue that only one of these characterizes the "real" concept of *mother*, the linguistic evidence does not bear this out. As the following sentences indicate, there is more than one criterion for "real" motherhood:

- I was adopted and I don't know who my real mother is.
- I am not a nurturant person, so I don't think I could ever be a real mother to any child.
- My real mother died when I was an embryo, and I was frozen and later implanted in the womb of the woman who gave birth to me.
- I had a genetic mother who contributed the egg that was planted in the womb of my real mother, who gave birth to me and raised me.
- By genetic engineering, the genes in the egg my father's sperm fertilized were spliced together from genes in the eggs of twenty different women. I wouldn't call any of them my real mother. My real mother is the woman who bore and raised me, even though I don't have any single genetic mother.

In short, more than one of these models contributes to the characterization of a *real mother*, and any one of them may be absent from such a characterization. Still, the very idea that there is such a thing as a *real mother* seems to require a choice among models where they diverge. It would be bizarre for someone to say:

- I have four real mothers: the woman who contributed my genes, the woman who gave birth to me, the woman who raised me, and my father's current wife.

When the cluster of models that jointly characterize a concept diverge, there is still a strong pull to view one as the most important. This is reflected in the institution of dictionaries. Each dictionary, by historical convention, must list a primary meaning when a word has more than one. Not surprisingly, the human beings who write dictionaries vary in their choices. Dr. Johnson chose the birth model as primary, and many of the applied linguists who work for the publishers of dictionaries, as is so often the case, have simply played it safe and copied him. But not all. *Funk and Wagnall's Standard* chose the nurturance model as primary, while the *American College Dictionary* chose the genealogical model. Though choices made by dictionary-makers are of no scientific importance, they do reflect the fact that, even among people who construct definitions for a living, there is no single, generally accepted cognitive model for such a common concept as "mother."

When the situation is such that the models for *mother* do not pick out a single individual, we get compound expressions like *stepmother, surrogate mother, adoptive mother, foster mother, biological mother, donor mother*, etc. Such compounds, of course, do not represent simple subcategories, that is, kinds of ordinary mothers. Rather, they describe cases where there is a lack of convergence of the various models.

And, not surprisingly, different models are used as the basis of different extended senses of *mother*. For example, the birth model is the basis of the metaphorical sense in

– Necessity is the mother of invention.

while the nurturance model is basis for the derived verb in

– He wants his girlfriend to mother him.

The genealogical model is the basis for the metaphorical extension of *mother* and *daughter* used in the description of the tree diagrams that linguists use to describe sentence structure. If node *A* is immediately above node *B* in a tree, *A* is called the *mother* and *B*, the *daughter*. Even in the case of metaphorical extensions, there is no single privileged model for *mother* on which the extensions are based. This accords with the evidence cited above which indicates that the concept *mother* is defined by a cluster model.

This phenomenon is beyond the scope of the classical theory. The concept *mother* is not clearly defined, once and for all, in terms of common necessary and sufficient conditions. There need be no necessary and sufficient conditions for motherhood shared by normal biological mothers, donor mothers (who donate an egg), surrogate mothers (who bear the child, but may not have donated the egg), adoptive mothers, unwed mothers who give their children up for adoption, and stepmothers. They are all mothers by virtue of their relation to the ideal case, where the models converge. That ideal case is one of the many kinds of cases that give rise to prototype effects.

CHAPTER 5

Metonymic Models

Metonymy is one of the basic characteristics of cognition. It is extremely common for people to take one well-understood or easy-to-perceive aspect of something and use it to stand either for the thing as a whole or for some other aspect or part of it. The best-known cases are those like the following:

- One waitress says to another, "The ham sandwich just spilled beer all over himself."

Here *the ham sandwich* is standing for the person eating the sandwich. Another well-known example is the slogan:

- Don't let El Salvador become another Vietnam.

Here the place is standing for the events that occurred at that place. As Lakoff and Johnson (1980, chap. 8) showed, such examples are instances of general principles; they do not just occur one by one. For example, English has a general principle by which a place may stand for an institution located at that place:

- The White House isn't saying anything.
- Washington is insensitive to the needs of ordinary people.
- The Kremlin threated to boycott the next round of talks.
- Paris is introducing shorter skirts this season.
- Hollywood isn't what it used to be.
- Wall Street is in a panic.

In each of these cases, a place like *The Kremlin* is standing for an institution located at that place, like the Soviet government. Moreover, the principle applies to an open-ended class of cases, not to any fixed list. For example, suppose that I am running a company that has many branch offices, including one in Cleveland, and I have asked each branch to send in a report on how it is doing. Upon failure to receive a report from the branch in Cleveland, I could say:

– Cleveland hasn't reported.

The point is that a general principle is needed because one cannot list all the examples. Since such general principles are not the same in all languages, one cannot simply say that anything can stand for anything else in the right context. One needs to distinguish which principles work for which languages.

Such principles take the following form: Given an ICM with some background condition (e.g., institutions are located in places), there is a "stands for" relation that may hold between two elements *A* and *B*, such that one element of the ICM, *B*, may stand for another element *A*. In this case, B = the place and A = the institution. We will refer to such ICMs containing stands-for relations as *metonymic models*.

A particularly interesting case of metonymy occurs in giving answers to questions. It is common to give an answer that evokes the information requested, and there seem to be language-particular metonymic models used to do so. Take, for example, the case described by Rhodes (1977), a linguist who does fieldwork on Ojibwa, a Native American language of central Canada. As part of his fieldwork, he asked speakers of Ojibwa who had come to a party how they got there. He got answers like the following (translated into English):

– I started to come.
– I stepped into a canoe.
– I got into a car.

He figured out what was going on when he read Schank and Abelson's *Scripts, Plans, Goals, and Understanding* (1977). Going somewhere in a vehicle involves a structured scenario (or in our terms, an ICM):

Precondition: You have (or have access to) the vehicle.
Embarcation: You get into the vehicle and start it up.
Center: You drive (row, fly, etc.) to your destination.
Finish: You park and get out.
End point: You are at your destination.

What Rhodes found was that in Ojibwa it is conventional to use the embarcation point of an ICM of this sort to evoke the whole ICM. That is, in answering questions, part of an ICM is used to stand for the whole. In Ojibwa, that part is the embarcation point.

Ojibwa does not look particularly strange when one considers English from the same point of view. What are possible normal answers to a question such as "How did you get to the party?"

- I drove. (Center stands for whole ICM.)
- I have a car. (Precondition stands for whole ICM.)
- I borrowed my brother's car. (This entails the precondition, which in turn stands for the whole ICM.)

English even has special cases that look something like Ojibwa.

- I hopped on a bus. (Embarcation stands for whole ICM.)
- I just stuck out my thumb. (Embarcation stands for whole ICM.)

In short, English can use the embarcation metonymically to stand for the whole ICM, just in case there is no further effort involved, as in taking a bus or hitchhiking.

There are many metonymic models in a rich conceptual system, and they are used for a wide variety of purposes. The kind of most interest for our present purposes are those in which a member or subcategory can stand metonymically for the whole category for the purpose of making inferences or judgments.

Metonymic Sources of Prototype Effects

As Rosch (1978) observed, prototype effects are surface phenomena. A major source of such effects is metonymy—a situation in which some subcategory or member or submodel is used (often for some limited and immediate purpose) to comprehend the category as a whole. In other words, these are cases where a part (a subcategory or member or submodel) stands for the whole category—in reasoning, recognition, etc. Within the theory of cognitive models, such cases are represented by metonymic models.

The Housewife Stereotype

We have seen how the clustering of cognitive models for *mother* results in prototype effects. However, an additional level of prototype effects occurs in the *mother* category. The source of these effects is the stereotype of the mother as housewife. Social stereotypes are cases of metonymy—where a subcategory has a socially recognized status as standing for the category as a whole, usually for the purpose of making quick judgments about people. The housewife-mother subcategory, though unnamed, exists. It defines cultural expectations about what a mother is supposed to be. And because of this, it yields prototype effects. On the whole in our culture, housewife-mothers are taken as better examples of mothers than nonhousewife-mothers.

Such goodness-of-example judgments are a kind of prototype effect. But this effect is not due to the clustering of models, but rather to the case of a metonymic model in which one subcategory, the housewife-mother, stands for the whole category in defining cultural expectations of mothers. Other kinds of metonymic models will be discussed below.

Working Mothers

A *working mother* is not simply a mother who happens to be working. The category *working mother* is defined in contrast to the stereotypical housewife-mother. The housewife-mother stereotype arises from a stereotypical view of nurturance, which is associated with the nurturance model. According to the stereotypical view, mothers who do not stay at home all day with their children cannot properly nurture them. There is also a stereotypical view of work, according to which it is done away from the home, and housework and child-rearing don't count. This is the stereotype that the bumpersticker "Every Mother Is a Working Mother" is meant to counter.

The housewife-mother stereotype is therefore defined relative to the nurturance model of motherhood. This may be obvious, but it is not a trivial fact. It shows that metonymic models like stereotypes are not necessarily defined with respect to an entire cluster. In this case, the metonymic model is characterized relative to only one of the models in the cluster—the nurturance model. Here is some rather subtle evidence to prove the point:

> Consider an unwed mother who gives up her child for adoption and then goes out and gets a job. She is still a mother, by virtue of the birth model, and she is working—but she is not a *working mother*!

The reason is that it is the nurturance model, not the birth model, that is relevant. Thus, a biological mother who is not responsible for nurturance cannot be a working mother, though an adoptive mother, of course, can be one.

This example shows the following:

- A social stereotype (e.g., the housewife-mother) may be defined with respect to only one of the base models of an experiential cluster (e.g., the nurturance model).
- Thus, a metonymic model where a subcategory stands for the whole

category may be defined relative to only one model in a complex cluster.
- A subcategory (e.g., working mother) may be defined in contrast with a stereotype (e.g., the housewife-mother).
- When this occurs, it is only the relevant cognitive model (e.g., the nurturance model) that is used as a background for defining the subcategory (e.g., working mother).

Thus, only those mothers for whom nurturance is an issue can be so categorized. Stepmothers and adoptive mothers may also be working mothers, but biological mothers who have given up their children for adoption and surrogate mothers (who have only had a child for someone else) are not working mothers—even though they may happen to be holding down a job.

Such models of stereotypes are important for a theory of conceptual structure in a number of ways. First, as we have seen, they may be used to motivate and define a contrasting subcategory like *working mother*. This is important because, according to the classical theory, such cases should not exist. In the classical theory, social stereotypes, by definition, play no role in defining category structure, because they are not part of any necessary and sufficient conditions for category membership! In the classical theory, only necessary and sufficient conditions can have a real cognitive function in defining category membership. For this reason, the classical theory permits no cognitive function at all for social stereotypes. But the fact that the conceptual category *working mother* is defined by contrast with the housewife-mother stereotype indicates that stereotypes do have a role in characterizing concepts.

The second way in which stereotypes are important for conceptual structure is that they define normal expectations. Normal expectations play an important role in cognition, and they are required in order to characterize the meanings of certain words. For example, the word *but* in English is used to mark a situation which is in contrast to some model that serves as a norm. Stereotypic models may serve as such a norm:

Normal: She is a mother, but she isn't a housewife.
Strange: She is a mother, but she's a housewife.

The latter sentence could only be used if stereotypical mothers were not housewives. Conversely, a category defined in contrast to a stereotype has the opposite properties.

Normal: She is a mother, but she has a job.
Strange: She is a mother, but she doesn't have a job.

Similar complexities arise for *unwed mother.* An unwed mother is not simply a mother who is not married. For example, an adoptive mother who is not married is not a unwed mother. And we would normally not use the term *unwed mother* for a millionaire actress who chose to have a child out of wedlock. *Unwed mother* is defined relative to the birth model. Hence, adoptive mothers, foster mothers, egg donors, etc. don't count. In the stereotypical case, the unwed mother did not choose to get pregnant, and she has difficulty supporting the child.

The term *daddy* is defined relative to a nurturance model, not just a birth model. Thus, one may ask of an unmarried pregnant woman *Who is the child's father?* but not *Who is the child's daddy?* One may be called a father before one may be called a daddy.

In summary, we have seen two kinds of models for *mother*:

- a cluster of converging cognitive models
- a stereotypic model, which is a metonymic model in which the housewife-mother subcategory stands for the category as whole and serves the purpose of defining cultural expectations

Both models give rise to prototype effects, but in different ways. Together, they form a structure with a composite prototype: the best example of a mother is a biological mother who is a housewife principally concerned with nurturance, not working at a paid position, and married to the child's father. This composite prototype imposes what is called a *representativeness structure* on the category: the closer an individual is to the prototype, the more representative a mother she is.

Representativeness structures are linear. They concern nothing but closeness to the prototypical case, and thus they hide most of the richness of structure that exists in the cognitive models that characterize the category. Representativeness structures, though real, are mere shadows of cognitive models.

It is important to bear this in mind, since prototype theory is sometimes thought of as involving only such linear representativeness structures and not cognitive models.

The study of representativeness structures has played an important role in the history of prototype theory—largely in demonstrating that prototypes do exist and in making a bare first approximation to finding out what they are and what properties they have. But a full study of category structure must go well beyond just isolating a prototype and giving a linear ranking of how close nonprototypical cases are. At the very least, it must provide an account of the details of the cognitive models that give rise to the representativeness structure.

Radial Structures

Here are some kinds of mothers:

- The central case, where all the models converge, includes a mother who is and always has been female, and who gave birth to the child, supplied her half of the child's genes, nurtured the child, is married to the father, is one generation older than the child, and is the child's legal guardian.
- Stepmother: She didn't give birth or supply the genes, but she is currently married to the father.
- Adoptive mother: She didn't give birth or supply the genes, but she is the legal guardian and has the obligation to provide nurturance.
- Birth mother: This is defined in contrast to *adoptive mother*; given an adoption ICM, the woman who gives birth and puts the child up for adoption is called the *birth mother*.
- Natural mother: This was once the term used to contrast with *adoptive mother*, but it has been given up because of the unsavory inference that adoptive mothers were, by contrast, "unnatural." This term has been replaced by *birth mother*.
- Foster mother: She did not give birth to the child, and is being paid by the state to provide nurturance.
- Biological mother: She gave birth to the child, but is not raising it and there is someone else who is and who qualifies to be called a mother of some sort.
- Surrogate mother: She has contracted to give birth and that's all. She may or may not have provided the genes, and she is not married to the father and is not obligated to provide nurturance. And she has contractually given up the right to be legal guardian.
- Unwed mother: She is not married at the time she gives birth.
- Genetic mother: This is a term I have seen used for a woman who supplies an egg to be planted in someone else's womb and has nothing else whatever to do with the child. It has not yet to my knowledge become conventional.

These subcategories of mother are all understood as deviations from the central case. But not all possible variations on the central case exist as categories. There is no category of mothers who are legal guardians but who don't personally supply nurturance, but hire someone else to do it. There is no category of transsexuals who gave birth but have since had a sex-change operation. Moreover, some of the above categories are products of the twentieth century and simply did not exist before. The point is that the central case does not productively generate all these subcategories. Instead, the subcategories are defined by convention as variations on the central case. There is no general rule for generating kinds of mothers. They are culturally defined and have to be learned. They are by no means the same in all cultures. In the Trobriands, a woman who gives birth often gives the child to an old woman to raise. In traditional Japanese society, it was common for a woman to give her child to her sister to raise. Both of these are cases of kinds of mothers that we don't have an exact equivalent of.

The category of *mother* in this culture has what we will call a *radial structure.* A radial structure is one where there is a central case and conventionalized variations on it which cannot be predicted by general rules. Categories that are generated by central cases plus general principles—say, the natural numbers or Lounsbury's account of the category *maternal uncle* in Fox—are not radial structures, as we are defining the term. We are limiting radial structures only to cases where the variations are conventionalized and have to be learned. We are also ruling out cases where the central case is just more general than the noncentral case—that is, where the noncentral cases just have more properties than the central case, but no different ones. Radial structures are extremely common, and we will discuss them in very great detail below.

Some Kinds of Metonymic Models

So far, we have looked at one case of a metonymic model: the housewife-mother stereotype. It defines a subcategory that is used to stand for the entire category of mothers in defining social expectations. Any time a subcategory (or an individual member of a category) is used for some purpose to stand for the category as a whole, it is a potential source of prototype effects. For this reason, metonymic models play an important role in prototype theory. Let us look at them a bit more closely.

In general, a metonymic model has the following characteristics:

- There is a "target" concept *A* to be understood for some purpose in some context.
- There is a conceptual structure containing both *A* and another concept *B*.
- *B* is either part of *A* or closely associated with it in that conceptual structure. Typically, a choice of *B* will uniquely determine *A*, within that conceptual structure.
- Compared to *A*, *B* is either easier to understand, easier to remember, easier to recognize, or more immediately useful for the given purpose in the given context.

- A metonymic model is a model of how *A* and *B* are related in a conceptual structure; the relationship is specified by a function from *B* to *A*.

When such a conventional metonymic model exists as part of a conceptual system, *B* may be used to stand, metonymically, for *A*. If *A* is a category, the result is a metonymic model of the category, and prototype effects commonly arise.

Most metonymic models are, in fact, *not* models of categories; they are models of individuals. Lakoff and Johnson (1980, chap. 8) have shown that there are many types of metonymic models for individuals. There are also many types of metonymic models for categories; each type is a different *kind* of source for prototype effects. There are as many types of metonymic prototype effects as there are kinds of metonymic models for categories. Here are some of the types I have come across so far.

Social Stereotypes

As we saw in the case of the housewife-mother, social stereotypes can be used to stand for a category as a whole. Social stereotypes are usually conscious and are often the subject of public discussion. They are subject to change over time, and they may become public issues. Since they define cultural expectations, they are used in reasoning and especially in what is called "jumping to conclusions." However, they are usually recognized as not being accurate, and their use in reasoning may be overtly challenged.

Here are some examples of contemporary American stereotypes:

- The stereotypical politician is conniving, egotistical, and dishonest.
- The stereotypical bachelor is macho, dates a lot of different women, is interested in sexual conquest, hangs out in singles bars, etc.
- The stereotypical Japanese is industrious, polite, and clever.

Since social stereotypes are commonly used to characterize cultural expectations, they tend to be exploited in advertising and in most forms of popular entertainment.

Incidentally, the *bachelor* stereotype provides a second level of prototype effects in addition to those that are a consequence of the *bachelor* ICM not fitting certain situations. Let us take a situation where the background conditions of the *bachelor* ICM do fit, a situation in which there are no cases that the concept was not defined to deal with: no priests, no gays, no Moslems with only three wives, no Tarzans. In these situations, there can still be prototype effects, but the effects will arise *within the clear boundaries of the category*. In such cases, the social stereotype of a *bachelor* will characterize the best examples, and those undisputed bachelors who don't fit the social stereotype will be less good examples.

A bachelor who is macho, promiscuous, and nondomestic fits the stereotype of *bachelor* better than, say, a nonmacho man who likes to take care of children, prefers a stable relationship with one person, is not interested in sexual conquest, loves housework and does it well, etc. Stereotypes are used in certain situations to define expectations, make judgments, and draw inferences. Thus, for example, if all one knew about someone was that he was a bachelor, one might be surprised to find that he loves housework and does it well, likes to care for children, etc. Thus, even though the *bachelor* ICM is defined within the classical theory and has clear boundaries in situations that conform to the background assumptions, prototype effects may still occur *internal* to the category boundaries, because of the presence of a social stereotype.

Incidentally, we often have names for stereotypes, for example, Uncle Tom, Jewish princess, stud, etc. These are categories that function as stereotypes for other categories. An understanding of such categories requires an understanding of their role as stereotypes.

Typical Examples

Typical examples include cases like the following:

Robins and sparrows are typical birds.
Apples and oranges are typical fruits.
Saws and hammers are typical tools.

Social stereotypes are usually conscious and subject to public discussion—and may even have names. However, the use of typical category members is usually unconscious and automatic. Typical examples are not the subject of public discussion, and they seem not to change noticeably during a person's lifetime. They are not used to define cultural expectations. They are used in reasoning, as Rips (1975) showed, in the case where subjects inferred that if the robins on a certain island got a disease, then the ducks would, but not the converse. Such examples are common. It is normal for us to make inferences from typical to nontypical examples. If a typical man has hair on his head, we infer that atypical men (all other things being equal) will have hair on their heads. Moreover, a man may be considered atypical by virtue of not having hair on his head. There is nothing mysterious about this. An enormous amount of our knowledge about categories of things is organized in terms of typical cases. We constantly draw inferences on the basis of that kind of knowledge. And we do it so regularly and automatically that we are rarely aware that we are doing it.

Reasoning on the basis of typical cases is a major aspect of human reason. Our vast knowledge of typical cases leads to prototype effects. The reason is that there is an asymmetry between typical and nontypical cases. Knowledge about typical cases is generalized to nontypical cases, but not conversely.

Ideals

Many categories are understood in terms of abstract ideal cases—which may be neither typical nor stereotypical. For example,

- The ideal husband is a good provider, faithful, strong, respected, attractive.
- The stereotypical husband is bumbling, dull, pot-bellied.

Naomi Quinn (personal communication) has observed, based on extensive research on American conceptions of marriage, that there are many kinds of ideal models for a marriage: *successful* marriages, *good* marriages, *strong* marriages, etc. *Successful* marriages are those where the goals of the spouses are fulfilled. *Good* marriages are those where both partners find the marriage beneficial. *Strong* marriages are those that are likely to last. Such types of ideals seem to be of great importance in culturally significant categories—categories where making judgments of quality and making plans are important.

A lot of cultural knowledge is organized in terms of ideals. We have cultural knowledge about ideal homes, ideal families, ideal mates, ideal jobs, ideal bosses, ideal workers, etc. Cultural knowledge about ideals leads to prototype effects. There is an asymmetry between ideal and nonideal cases: we make judgments of quality and set goals for the future in terms of ideal cases, rather than nonideal cases. This asymmetry is a consequence of a pattern of inference that we use with ideals. Ideals are assumed to have all the good qualities that nonideal cases have, but nonideal cases are not assumed to have all the good qualities of ideal cases.

Paragons

We also comprehend categories in terms of individual members who represent either an ideal or its opposite. Thus, we have institutions like the ten-best and ten-worst lists, the Hall of Fame, Academy Awards, *The Guinness Book of World Records*, etc. We have baseball paragons: Babe Ruth, Willie Mays, Sandy Koufax, etc. Paragons are made use of in constructions in the language: *a regular Babe Ruth, another Willie Mays, the Cadillac of vacuum cleaners*, etc. Scientific paradigms are also characterized by paragons. Thus, for example, the Michaelson-Morley experiment is the paragon of physics experiments—and is used by many people to comprehend what a great experiment in physics is.

A great many of our actions have to do with paragons. We try to emulate them. We are interested in the life stories of great men and women. We use paragons as models to base our actions on. We have a great deal of interest in experiencing paragons—we watch the All-Star game, go to Academy Award–winning movies, travel to the Seven Wonders of the World, and seek to own the paragons of consumer goods. We are constantly acquiring knowledge of paragons and regularly base our actions on that knowledge. Incidentally, we also commonly base inferences on a folk theory that people who are paragons in some domain are paragons *as people*. Thus, people are shocked to find great baseball players or powerful politicians engaging in normal rotten human behavior.

Generators

There are cases where the members of a category are defined, or "generated," by the central members plus some general rules. We saw this in the case of Lounsbury's analysis of the *maternal uncle* in Fox. But the natural numbers are perhaps the best-known example. The natural numbers are, for most people, characterized by the integers between zero and nine, plus addition and multiplication tables and rules of arithmetic. The single-digit numbers are central members of the category *natural number*; they generate the entire category, given general arithmetic principles. In our system of numerical representation, single-digit numbers are employed in comprehending natural numbers in general. Any natural number can be written as a sequence of single-digit numbers. The properties of large numbers are understood in terms of the properties of smaller numbers and ultimately in terms of the properties of single-digit numbers.

The single-digit numbers, together with addition and multiplication tables and rules of arithmetic, constitute a model that both generates the natural numbers and is metonymic in our sense: the category as a whole is comprehended in terms of a small subcategory.

The natural numbers, in addition, have other models that subdivide the numbers according to certain properties—odd and even, prime and nonprime, etc. Such models are not metonymic. They work by classical Aristotelian principles. But they only define *subcategories* of the natural numbers. The category as a whole is defined metonymically and generatively by the single-digit numbers plus rules of arithmetic.

To make matters more complicated, other kinds of numbers are also defined by metonymic generative models: the rationals, the reals, the imaginaries, the transfinite cardinals, etc. Thus rational numbers are understood as ratios of natural numbers, and real numbers are understood as infinite sequences of natural numbers. In other words, the rationals and the reals are understood metonymically in terms of the natural numbers—a subcategory used to generate the larger categories.

Submodels

Another way to comprehend a category is via a submodel. Take the category of natural numbers again. The most common submodel used is the subcategory of powers of ten: ten, a hundred, a thousand, etc. We use this submodel to comprehend the relative size of numbers. The members of such a submodel are among what Rosch (1975*a*) refers to as "cognitive reference points," which have a special place in reasoning, especially in making approximations and estimating size. Cognitive reference points within a submodel show prototype effects of the following sort: Subjects will judge statements like *98 is approximately 100* as being true more readily than statements like *100 is approximately 98*. This, of course, is context-dependent. For example, in discussing fevers, where normal body temperature is 98.6° Fahrenheit, it would be quite normal to say that *99 is approximately 98.6*. The reason, of course, is that 98.6 is a cognitive reference point where fever is concerned. (See Sadock 1977 for examples.)

Some submodels have a biological basis: the primary colors, the basic emotions, etc. Others are culturally stipulated, e.g., the Seven Deadly Sins.

Salient Examples

It is common for people to use familiar, memorable, or otherwise salient examples to comprehend categories. For example, if your best friend is a vegetarian and you don't know any others well, you will tend to generalize from your friend to other vegetarians. After a widely publicized DC-10 crash in Chicago, many people refused to fly DC-10s, choosing other types of planes despite the fact that they had overall worse safety records than DC-10s. Such people used the salient example of the DC-10 that crashed to stand metonymically for the entire category of DC-10s with respect to safety judgments.

Similarly, California earthquakes are salient examples of natural disasters. A. Tversky and Kahneman (1983) demonstrated that people use such salient examples in making probability judgments about the category of natural disasters. The reasoning used is what Tversky and Kahneman refer to as the "conjunction fallacy." We know from probability theory that the probability of two events, *A* and *B*, occurring is always less than the probability of just one of the events, say *B*. Thus the probability of coins *A* and *B* both coming down heads is less than the probability of just *B* coming down heads.

The theory of probability is defined for events *A* and *B*, which are not related to one another. Cognitive models may, however, relate events in our minds that are unrelated in the external world. What Tversky and Kahneman (1983) found was that when we have a salient cognitive model relating events *A* and *B*, it affects our judgments of the probability of *A* and *B* both occurring.

The following is a typical example of the kind Tversky and Kahneman used. One group of subjects was asked to rate the probability of:

> A massive flood somewhere in North America in 1983, in which more than 1000 people drown.

A second group was asked to rate the probability of

> An earthquake in California sometime in 1983, causing a flood in which more than 1000 people drown.

The estimates of the conjunction of earthquake and flood were considerably higher than the estimates of the flood. Tversky and Kahneman conclude:

> The attempts to predict the uncertain future, like the attempts to reconstruct the uncertain past, which is the domain of history and criminal law, are commonly based on the construction of hypothetical scenarios. These scenarios, or "best guesses," tend to be specific, coherent, and representative of our mental model of the relevant worlds.

In short, a cognitive model may function to allow a salient example to stand metonymically for a whole category. In such cases, our probability judgments about the category are affected.

To summarize, we have seen the following kinds of metonymic models: social stereotypes, typical examples, ideal cases, paragons, generators, submodels, and salient examples. They have a cognitive status, that is, they are used in reasoning. And they all yield prototype effects of some sort.

CHAPTER 6

Radial Categories

The category *mother*, as we saw above, is structured radially with respect to a number of its subcategories: there is a *central* subcategory, defined by a cluster of converging cognitive models (the birth model, the nurturance model, etc.); in addition, there are *noncentral extensions* which are not specialized instances of the central subcategory, but rather are variants of it (*adoptive mother, birth mother, foster mother, surrogate mother*, etc.). These variants are not generated from the central model by general rules; instead, they are extended by convention and must be learned one by one. But the extensions are by no means random. The central model determines the possibilities for extensions, together with the possible relations between the central model and the extension models. We will describe the extensions of a central model as being *motivated* by the central model plus certain general principles of extension. Much of the rest of this volume will be concerned with the concept of *motivation* and with the kinds of general principles of extension that govern the structure of radial categories.

As we saw in the case of *mother*, radial structure within a category is another source of prototype effects. Within radial categories in general, less central subcategories are understood as variants of more central categories. Thus, *birth mother* and *foster mother* are not understood purely on their own terms; they are comprehended via their relationship to the central model of *mother.*

Grammaticized Categories

It is common for the grammars of languages to mark certain conceptual categories. Inasmuch as language is a part of cognition in general—and a major part at that—conceptual categories marked by the grammars of languages are important in understanding the nature of cognitive categories in general. Classifier languages—languages where nouns are marked as being members of certain categories—are among the richest sources of data that we have concerning the structure of conceptual categories as they are revealed through language. Let us now turn to two examples of conceptual categories that are radially structured and that are marked by classifiers.

Women, Fire, and Dangerous Things

Borges attributes the following taxonomy of the animal kingdom to an ancient Chinese encyclopedia entitled the *Celestial Emporium of Benevolent Knowledge.*

> On those remote pages it is written that animals are divided into (a) those that belong to the Emperor, (b) embalmed ones, (c) those that are trained, (d) suckling pigs, (e) mermaids, (f) fabulous ones, (g) stray dogs, (h) those that are included in this classification, (i) those that tremble as if they were mad, (j) innumerable ones, (k) those drawn with a very fine camel's hair brush, (l) others, (m) those that have just broken a flower vase, (n) those that resemble flies from a distance. (Borges 1966, p. 108)

Borges, of course, deals with the fantastic. These not only are not natural human categories—they could not be natural human categories. But part of what makes this passage art, rather than mere fantasy, is that it comes close to the impression a Western reader gets when reading descriptions of nonwestern languages and cultures. The fact is that people around the world categorize things in ways that both boggle the Western mind and stump Western linguists and anthropologists. More often than not, the linguist or anthropologist just throws up his hands and resorts to giving a list—a list that one would not be surprised to find in the writings of Borges.

An excellent example is the classification of things in the world that occurs in traditional Dyirbal, an aboriginal language of Australia. The classification is built into the language, as is common in the world's languages. Whenever a Dyirbal speaker uses a noun in a sentence, the noun must be preceded by a variant of one of four words: *bayi, balan, balam, bala.* These words classify all objects in the Dyirbal universe, and to speak Dyirbal correctly one must use the right classifier before each noun. Here is a brief version of the Dyirbal classification of objects in the universe, as described by R. M. W. Dixon (1982):

I. *Bayi:* men, kangaroos, possums, bats, most snakes, most fishes, some birds, most insects, the moon, storms, rainbows, boomerangs, some spears, etc.

II. *Balan:* women, bandicoots, dogs, platypus, echidna, some snakes, some fishes, most birds, fireflies, scorpions, crickets, the hairy mary grub, anything connected with water or fire, sun and stars, shields, some spears, some trees, etc.

III. *Balam:* all edible fruit and the plants that bear them, tubers, ferns, honey, cigarettes, wine, cake

IV. *Bala:* parts of the body, meat, bees, wind, yamsticks, some spears, most trees, grass, mud, stones, noises and language, etc.

It is a list that any Borges fan would take delight in.

But Dixon did not stop with a list. He was determined to learn what made these categories of the human mind, categories that made sense to Dyirbal speakers—that they could learn uniformly and use unconsciously and automatically. In the course of his fieldwork, Dixon observed that speakers do not learn category members one by one, but operate in terms of some general principles. According to Dixon's analysis, there is a basic, productive, and fairly simple general schema that operates unless some specialized principle takes precedence. Dixon's proposed basic schema is this:

I. *Bayi:* (human) males; animals

II. *Balan:* (human) females; water; fire; fighting

III. *Balam:* nonflesh food

IV. *Bala:* everything not in the other classes

Here are some cases that fit this schema: Men, being human males, are in class I. Kangaroos and possums, being animals, are in class I. Women are in class II, since they are human females. Rivers and swamps, being bodies of water, are in class II. Fire is in class II. Wild figs are in class III. Tubers are in class III. Trees that don't bear fruit are in class IV. Rocks are in class IV. Language is in class IV.

The cases of particular interest are those that Dixon found to follow certain general principles beyond the basic cases given above. Perhaps the most general principle, which Dixon takes for granted and doesn't even bother to state explicitly, is what I will call the domain-of-experience principle:

> If there is a basic domain of experience associated with *A*, then it is natural for entities in that domain to be in the same category as *A*.

For example, fish are in class I, since they are animate. Fishing implements (fishing spears, fishing line, etc.) are also in class I, even though they might be expected to be in class IV, since they are neither animate nor a form of food. Similarly, plants that have edible fruit are in class III with the fruit they yield. One would otherwise expect fruit trees to be in class IV with the other trees. And in fact, if one is specifically referring to the wood of a fruit tree, say in reference to firewood or making an implement, then the classifier *bala* of class IV is used. Light and the stars, which are in the same domain of experience as fire, are in class II with fire. Fighting implements (e.g., fighting spears) and fighting ground are in the same domain of experience as fighting, and so are in class II with fighting.

Perhaps the most striking of Dixon's discoveries, and the one that accounts for most of the apparently aberrant cases, is what I will refer to as the myth-and-belief principle:

> If some noun has characteristic *X* (on the basis of which its class membership is expected to be decided) but is, through belief or myth, connected with characteristic *Y*, then generally it will belong to the class corresponding to *Y* and not that corresponding to *X*.

Though birds are animate, they are not in class I with other animate beings. Birds are believed to be the spirits of dead human females, and so are in class II. In the so-called mother-in-law language of Dyirbal (used to speak to tabooed relatives of the opposite sex), there is only one word, *balan muguyngan*, for both female spirits and birds. Certain birds are exceptions to this. Three species of willy-wagtails are believed to be mythical men, and so are in class I with men. The spangled drongo is in myth the bringer of fire (from the clutches of the rainbow snake); thus, the spangled drongo is in class II with fire. (Dixon claims that there are a number of other cases of this sort.) In myth, crickets are "old ladies," and so are in class II. According to myth, the moon and the sun are husband and wife; consequently the moon is in class I with other husbands, while the sun is in class II with other wives. The hairy mary grub, whose sting is said to feel like sunburn, is in class II with the sun. Wind is in class IV, but storms and the rainbow are believed to be mythical men and are in class I.

Dixon suggests one further principle, the important-property principle:

> If a subset of nouns has some particular important property that the rest of the set does not have, then the members of the subset may be assigned to a different class from the rest of the set to "mark" this property; the important property is most often 'harmfulness'.

Fishes are mostly in class I with other animate beings, but the stone fish and gar fish are harmful and so are in class II. These two fish are not included under the generic grouping for fish; thus, the generic term *bayi jabu* 'fish' cannot be used to refer to these two types of fish. Trees, bushes, vines, and grasses with no edible parts are in class IV. But two stinging trees and a stinging nettle vine are in class II with harmful things. Hawks might be expected to be in class II with other birds, but since they are harmful, their harmfulness is marked by placing them in another category—class I.

These principles largely account for the classification of loan words. Fruit, flour, cake (made from flour), and wine (made from fruit) are in class III. White man is in class I, and white woman is in class II. Matches and pipes (concerned with fire) are in class II with fire, but cigarettes (leaves which are consumed) are in class III.

Dixon does not, however, claim that *all* Dyirbal classification works by his principles. He cites a small number of exceptions for which he could find no explanation and for which there may be none—or for which an explanation may have previously existed and been lost. For example, it is not known why dog, bandicoot, platypus, and echidna are in class II instead of class I. Among loan words, money (unlike anything previously in Dyirbal culture) is unpredictably in class I. But the number of these exceptions is small.

Dixon's achievement is remarkable. He has shown that what might look superficially, to the Western eye, as a fantastic classification out of Borges, is from the perspective of the people doing the classifying a relatively regular and principled way to classify things.

In the process, Dixon has provided a superb example of how human cognition works. Though the details of categorization may be unique to Dyirbal, the general principles at work in the Dyirbal system show up again and again in systems of human categorization. They are:

Centrality: What we have called the basic members of the category are central. Willy wagtails and the moon are less central members of category I than are men. Stinging vines, gar fish and the hairy mary grub are less central members of category II than are women.

Chaining: Complex categories are structured by chaining; central members are linked to other members, which are linked to other members, and so on. For example, women are linked to the sun, which is linked to sunburn, which is linked to the hairy mary grub. It is by virtue of such a chain that the hairy mary grub is in the same category as women.

Experiential Domains: There are basic domains of experience, which may be culture-specific. These can characterize links in category chains.

Idealized Models: There are idealized models of the world—myths and beliefs among them—that can characterize links in category chains.

Specific Knowledge: Specific knowledge (for example, knowledge of mythology) overrides general knowledge.

The Other: Borges was right about this. Conceptual systems can have an "everything else" category. It, of course, does not have central members, chaining, etc.

No Common Properties: Categories on the whole need not be defined by common properties. There is no reason to believe that the Dyirbal find anything in common among women, fire, dangerous things, etc. Nor do they assume, so far as is known, that there is anything feminine about fire or danger, or anything fiery or dangerous about women. On the other hand, common properties seem to play a role in characterizing the basic schemas within a given category (edible plant, human male, human female).

Motivation: The general principles given make sense of Dyirbal classification, but they do not predict exactly what the categories will be.

Of these principles, motivation is perhaps the least obvious and is worth some discussion. There is a big difference between giving principles that *motivate*, or *make sense* of, a system, and giving principles that *generate*, or *predict*, the system. Dixon's analysis explains why the Dyirbal system is the kind of system that human beings can function with. It does not predict exactly what the system will be. For example, one must learn which domains of experience are relevant to categorization and which are not. Thus, fish live in water, and fish are in class I, but that does not make water class I with fish, nor does it make fish class II with water. The domain of habitation is simply not important for Dyirbal classification. Dyirbal speakers simply must learn which domains of experience matter for classification and which myths and beliefs matter.

What *is* predicted is that systems of classification tend to be structured in this way, that is, that there tends to be centrality, chaining, etc. The theory of categorization makes predictions about what human category systems can and cannot be like. It does not predict exactly what will be in a given category in a given culture or language.

Evidence from Language Death

Dixon's analysis on the whole makes sense of the Dyirbal system. But how do we know that it is right? Couldn't this just be some arbitrary analysis imposed by an outside analyst? Couldn't it simply be akin to an analysis of a literary work imposed by a critic? How do we know that there is anything psychologically real about Dixon's analysis?

In the first place, Dixon's analysis was not his own. The explanations he gives are just those that native speakers told him about. They are the accounts given by the Dyirbal themselves to explain those parts of their classification system for which they had a conscious explanation.

In addition, there is some indirect evidence that Dixon's analysis was basically correct. It comes from an unfortunate source. Dixon did his initial field research in 1963. At that time, English-speaking Australian culture had not yet impinged much on the Dyirbal community. But in the the years since 1963, the impact of white Australian society has been greater because of compulsory schooling in English and exposure to radio and television. As of 1983, only twenty years later, Dyirbal culture and the Dyirbal language are dying. Young people in the Dyirbal community grow up speaking English primarily, and learn only an extremely oversimplified version of traditional Dyirbal. Their experiences are very different from those of their parents and they either don't learn the myths or find that the myths don't mean much in their lives.

As one might expect, this has resulted in a drastic change of the categorization system. This has been documented by Annette Schmidt in a remarkable study, *Young People's Dyirbal: An Example of Language Death from Australia* (Schmidt 1985). Dyirbals who are roughly 45 or older speak traditional Dyirbal. Speakers who are under 35 speak some more simplified form of the language. Schmidt's study of the overall demise of Dyirbal included two degenerate stages of the categorization system: an intermediate stage (from five fluent speakers from an intermediate generation) and a very simple system (from much younger speakers). These two degenerate stages provide evidence that the analysis given above, or something close to it, is correct for traditional Dyirbal.

The intermediate stage shows the radial structure in the process of breaking down. The five speakers surveyed each showed a somewhat different loss of an aspect of radial structure. But the systems of these speakers only make sense in terms of the breaking-off of some radial links in the traditional Dyirbal system. In other words, each intermediate system lacks some of the hypothesized links that allow things that are not males and females to be categorized in classes I and II.

All of the intermediate speakers surveyed shared the following characteristics:

– The mythic links are kept: the moon, storms, and rainbows are still in class I with men and animals. The sun, stars, and birds are still in class II with women.

- Fire is still in class II with women, except that one speaker has fireflies going into class I with other animates.
- Fishing is lost as a domain relevant to categorization. Though fish are in class I with other animates, fishing spears and fishing lines have gone into class IV with other inanimate objects.
- Water is still in class II with women.
- Platypuses and echidnas are still exceptional animals in class II.

There were, however, variations among the speakers of the sort one would expect in a rapidly changing system.

- One speaker lost the danger link entirely; one speaker kept the danger link intact. All speakers kept dangerous things connected with fighting intact, such as fighting spears and shields. One speaker lost the natural-danger link entirely from class II, with stonefish and garfish going to class I with other animates and stinging nettles going to class IV (the "other" class, which has trees, shrubs, etc.). Two other speakers each lost one natural danger from class II—the stonefish and garfish.
- Two speakers lost the dog and bandicoot as exceptional animals in class II; they went into class I with other animals. One additional speaker lost the dog from class II.

In general, this pattern of what is retained and lost supports a radial analysis of the traditional system of the sort proposed by Dixon.

In the simple stage of the youngest speakers, the system has broken down almost completely and only the central cases of classes I and II survive, while class III is lost completely. Here is the simple system:

I. *Bayi:* human males and nonhuman animates

II. *Balan:* human females

III. *Bala:* everything else

There are two possible explanations for this resultant system. The first comes from language interference. These speakers have grown up with English, and this system is similar to the English pronominal system. It is also conceivable that this system preserves only the most central members of classes I and II and that human males and females are the most central members in all stages of Dyirbal. However, there is not enough data from other intermediate stages at this time to verify this.

Some Speculations

The analysis given above was based on what Dixon's informants told him about their categorization system. They told him nothing about why animals were categorized with human males, nor why fire, water, and fighting were categorized in class II with human females. I would like to make some speculations about why I think the system is structured that way. But before I do, I would like to make a suggestion concerning Dixon's principles.

It seems to me that the myth-and-belief principle and the important-property principle amount pretty much to the same thing as the domain-of-experience principle. The domain-of-experience principle says that there are certain domains of experience that are significant for Dyirbal categorization. They have to be listed: fishing, fire, etc. These provide links in category chains. Thus, if fish are in class I, fishing implements are also in class I. One way to look at the myth-and-belief principle is that it is a special case of the domain-of-experience principle. It says that myths and beliefs are domains of experience that are relevant for categorization. Dixon's important-property principle can be looked at in this way as well. It was set up primarily to handle harmful or dangerous things. That is the only important property it works for. One could equally say that danger is an important domain of experience for Dyirbal categorization and that it is on the same list of relevant domains as fishing, fire, and myths. Thus, all we would need to know is which domains of experience are relevant for categorization and then we would need specific knowledge of the domains.

Continuing this speculation, we could account for Dyirbal categorization in the following way:
The basic divisions are:

I. *Bayi:* human males
II. *Balan:* human females
III. *Balam:* edible plants
IV. *Bala:* everything else

Classes I and II would be in minimal contrast—male versus female—a standard contrast in categorization systems around the world. According to Dixon's analysis, classes I and II are not in minimal contrast, any more than I and III or II and III are. The importance of this will become clear shortly.

The domain-of-experience principle would then list those domains of experience relevant for categorization: fishing, fire, myths, beliefs, danger. This would have the following consequences:

- Since fish are in class I, fishing implements are in class I.
- Since storms and the rainbow are believed to be mythic men, they are in class I.

- Since birds are believed to be female spirits, birds are in class II, except for those three species of willy-wagtails who are believed to be mythical men and are therefore in class I.
- Since crickets are believed to be "old ladies," they are in class II.
- Since the moon is believed to be the husband of the sun, the moon is in class I and the sun is in class II.
- Since fire is in the same domain of experience as the sun, fire is in class II with the sun.
- Those things that are believed to be instances of fire are in the same domain as fire: the stars, hot coals, matches, etc.

What we have done is suggest that the domain-of-experience principle is responsible for fire being in the same category as women. The links are: women (via myth) to the sun (via relevant domain of experience) to fire. By the same means, we can link danger and water. Fire is dangerous, and thus dangerous things are in the same category as fire. Water, which extinguishes fire, is in the same domain of experience as fire, and hence in the same category.

It should be borne in mind that these are speculations of an outside analyst. Speakers of Dyirbal told Dixon nothing like this, neither pro nor con. Native speakers of a language are only sometimes aware of the principles that structure their language. Either this analysis is wrong, or the speakers aren't conscious of these structuring principles, or Dixon didn't ask the right questions. It is, at least in principle, an empirical issue, since this analysis makes somewhat different claims than Dixon's. This analysis suggests that fighting spears, stinging nettles, gar fish, and matches should be less central members of category II than girls. Tests have been developed by Eleanor Rosch and others (Rosch 1977) to measure relative centrality of members in a category. However, it is not clear that such tests can be applied in any sensible way to older members of an aborigine tribe. Still, the speculation is more than idle speculation. It is an empirical matter. The issue can be stated as follows:

Are women, fire, and dangerous things all equally central members of class II, with no motivating links among them?

Or are women central members of the category, linked in some fashion to the more peripheral fire and danger?

Schmidt's data on the breakdown of the system favor the latter hypothesis. But, in addition, Schmidt found one direct piece of evidence—a speaker who consciously linked fire and danger to women:

> buni [fire] is a lady. ban buni [class II fire]. You never say bayi buni [class I fire]. It's a lady. Woman is a destroyer. 'e destroys anything. A woman is a fire. [BM, 33 years, aboriginal male, Jambun]

Several things should be borne in mind about this statement. This is not a speaker of traditional Dyirbal; it is a younger member of the community, still fluent in the old language, but brought up primarily speaking English. There is no evidence one way or the other whether older speakers of the traditional language held such a belief. All it shows is that, for this speaker, there is a conceptual link of some kind between the presence of women in the category and the presence of fire and danger.

Our analysis makes another prediction as well. As the system breaks down one might expect distant links of the chain to break off. Schmidt cites one example where the entire fishing link breaks off and another where the entire danger link breaks off for a single speaker, while for other speakers the natural dangers branch alone breaks off. Under Dixon's analysis, in which human females and fighting (or harmfulness) are equally central, one might equally well expect human females to be assigned to another category. The analysis I suggest has as a consequence that the central subcategory—human females—would be the last to go. This, too, is an empirical question. There may well be speakers with intermediate systems which have kept everything in *balan* except human females. But given the end point of the change, with *balan* containing only human females, that is unlikely.

Under the analysis I am suggesting, human males and females would be central members of categories I and II, which would place these categories in a minimal contrast. This would explain some interesting subregularities. Under such an analysis one would expect exceptions to class I to go into class II—the minimally contrasting category. And conversely, one would expect exceptions to class II to go into class I. One would not expect exceptions in these categories to go into classes III or IV. This is exactly what happens. Animals are in class I, but exceptional animals (dogs, platypuses, bandicoots, echidnas) are in class II. Snakes are in class I, but chicken snakes and water pythons are in class II. Birds are in class II, as are dangerous things. Since dangerous things have to be marked by special categorization, dangerous birds (hawks) are marked as exceptional by being placed in class I. Given this analysis, one can even find a regularity in the exceptions.

One thing we have not addressed is why animals are for the most part in class I with human males. Dixon observes that there are no separate words for male versus female animals; that is, there is a word for kangaroo, and no separate word for female kangaroo. Kangaroo (*bayi yuri*) is in class I with most animals; if one wants to specify that a kangaroo is female, one must use the class II classifier (*balan yuri*). The reverse is true for exceptional animals. Dog is in class II (*balan guda*). If one wants to indicate that a certain dog is male, one must use the class I classifier (*bayi guda*). All this amounts to saying that animal names are unmarked for gender. The categorization system seems to be humans (male and female) versus edible plants versus inanimates. It seems to be a reasonable guess that if animals are going to go anywhere in a system like this, it will be with the humans rather than with the edible plants. And it would make sense that if the animals are unmarked for gender, they would be categorized with the unmarked human category, if there is one. In most languages that have classification by gender, the male category is unmarked. On the basis of such universal tendencies, it is not a surprise to find the animals categorized with the human males. However, all this is speculation. Dixon was unable to find any evidence that category I is unmarked relative to category II. It may be, but there is at present no positive evidence. Dixon did not want to speculate beyond his evidence, so he listed human males and animals as equally basic members of class I. According to his analysis, bats are no more central to this category than are boys. This is, at least in principle a testable matter. If I had to make a bet (a small bet) I would bet that boys are more central than bats.

I have made these speculations to show that the kinds of regularities Dixon uncovered can, at least in principle, be extended even further and to show that these questions are empirical questions. Questions like these need to be asked by students of classifier languages.

Tentative Conclusions

The analysis of the Dyirbal classifier system is shown in the accompanying diagram. Here the universe is divided up into four clearly defined mutually exclusive domains, represented by the boxes. These form what we will be calling a *base model.* All the base model tells us is that there are four distinctions. Three of them have an internal structure, with elements at the center. The centers are indicated by squares in the diagram. The fourth, being made up of what is left over from the first three, has no internal structure. The centers of the domains in the base model are also structured, by what we will call a *basic opposition model*:

human males vs. human females, or center of class I vs. center of class II

people vs. edible plants, or centers of classes I and II vs. center of class III

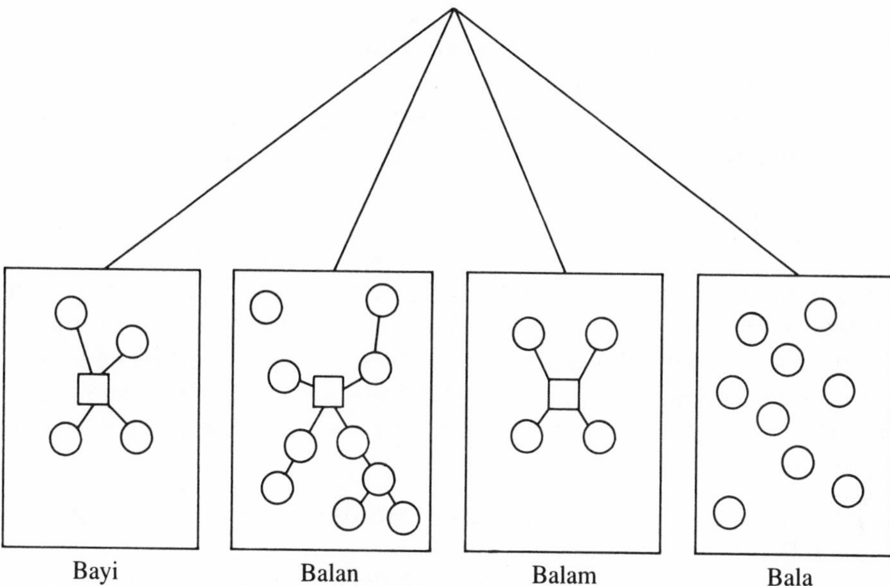

Finally, and perhaps most significant, there is the chaining structure inside the base model.

The clearly defined mutually exclusive domains of the base model are consistent with the classical theory of categories. But that does not make it a classical system. This system differs from the classical theory in that it does not have any defining characteristics that are shared by the members of the categories.

To describe this system, we need

- a *base model*, which in this case is very simple. It specifies that there are four distinct mutually exclusive categories, and that the fourth is made up of what is not in the first three.
- a specification of which subcategories are central, or *most typical*, of the first three categories.
- a basic opposition model, which structures the centers with respect to one another; e.g., male contrasts with female.
- a specification of chaining principles, in this case the domain-of-experience principle together with a list of domains relevant for categorization; among such domains are myth, fishing, danger, etc.
- a short list of exceptions, which are distributed according to the basic opposition model; for example, exceptions that would otherwise go in the male-centered category go in the female-centered category, and conversely.

The Dyirbal classifier system exhibits certain of the basic mechanisms used in human categorization. I would now like to turn to another case that exhibits other fundamental mechanisms used in categorization. This example is based on field research done by Pamela Downing (1984) and on conversations with my colleague Professor H. Aoki.

Japanese *Hon*

The Japanese classifier *hon*, in its most common use, classifies long, thin objects: sticks, canes, pencils, candles, trees, ropes, hair, etc. Of these, the rigid long, thin objects are the best examples. Not surprisingly, *hon* can be used to classify dead snakes and dried fish, both of which are long and thin. But *hon* can be extended to what are presumably less representative cases:

- martial arts contests, with staffs or swords (which are long, thin, and rigid)
- hits (and sometimes pitches) in baseball (straight trajectories, formed by the forceful motion of a solid object, associated with baseball bat, which is long, thin, and rigid)
- shots in basketball, serves in volleyball, and rallies in ping pong
- judo matches (a martial arts contest, but without a staff or sword)
- a contest between a Zen master and student, in which each attempts to stump the other with Zen koans
- rolls of tape (which unrolled are long and thin)
- telephone calls (which come over wires and which are instances of the CONDUIT metaphor as described by Reddy 1979 and Lakoff and Johnson 1980)
- radio and TV programs (like telephone calls, but without the wires)
- letters (another instance of communication; moreover, in traditional Japan, letters were scrolls and hence sticklike)
- movies (like radio and TV; moreover, they come in reels like rolls of tape)
- medical injections (done with a needle, which is long and thin)

To get a feel for this phenomenon, let us consider a few examples of noncentral cases where *hon* is used. (The form *ppon* is a variant of *hon*.)

Telephone calls:

denwa-no	*i-ppon*-gurai	kakete-kite-mo	ii no ni
telephone-GEN	*i-hon*-APPROX	attach-come-even	good although

'Although it wouldn't hurt to give (me) a phone call'

Baseball:

saisyo-ni	utta	*zyuu-yon-hon-no*	hoomuran-wa
first	hit	*14-hon*-GEN	home run-TOPIC

'The first 14 home runs hit'

Pingpong:

rarii-ga	*zyu-ppon*	izyoo	tuzuku mono
rally-NOM	*10-hon*	above	continue people

'People who can keep up 10 rallies'

Such cases, though not predictable from the central sense of *hon*, are nonetheless not arbitrary. They do not all have something in common with long, thin objects, but it *makes sense* that they might be classified with long, thin objects. Let us ask exactly what kind of sense it makes.

We will begin with martial arts contests using staffs or swords. Staffs and swords are long, thin, rigid objects, which are classified by *hon.* They are also the principal functional objects in these matches. A win in such a match can also be classified by *hon.* That is, the principal goal in this domain of experience is in the same category as the principal functional object.

Baseball bats are central members of the *hon* category. They are one of the two most salient functional objects in the game, the other being the ball. Baseball is centered on a contest between the pitcher and the batter. The batter's principal goal is to get a hit. When a baseball is hit solidly, it forms a trajectory—that is, it traces a long, thin path along which a solid object travels quickly and with force. The image traced by the path of the ball is a *hon* image—long and thin.

The extension of the *hon* category from bats to hits is another case of an extension from a principal functional object to a principal goal. It is also an extension from one principal functional object with a *hon* shape to a *hon*-shaped path formed by the other principal functional object. Incidentally, in the small amount of research done on *hon* to date, it appears that while base hits and home runs are categorized with *hon*, foul balls, pop flies, ground balls, and bunts are not. This is not surprising, since these are not principal goals of hitting, nor do their trajectories form a *hon* shape.

The relationship between the shape of the bat and the trajectory formed by the batted ball—between a long, thin thing and a trajectory—is a common relationship between image schemas that forms the basis for the extension of a category from a central to a noncentral case. Let us consider some examples from English.

- The man ran into the woods.
- The road ran into the woods.

In the first case, *run* is used for a case where there is a (long, thin) trajectory. In the second case, *run* is used for a long, thin object, a road.

- The bird flew over the yard.
- The telephone line stretched over the yard.

In the first case, *over* is used for a (long, thin) trajectory. In the second case, *over* is used for a long, thin object, a telephone line.

- The rocket shot up.
- The lamp was standing up.

In the first case, *up* is used for a trajectory. In the second case, *up* is used for a long, thin object, a standing lamp.

Such relationships are common and suggest that there exists what might be called an *image-schema transformation* of the following sort:

TRAJECTORY SCHEMA ↔ LONG, THIN OBJECT SCHEMA

This image-schema transformation is one of the many kinds of cognitive relationships that can form a basis for the extension of a category.

Some speakers of Japanese extend the *hon* category to baseball pitches as well as hits—again on the basis of such an image-schema relationship within the same domain of experience. Some speakers extend *hon* to pitches using both the trajectory and the contest-perspective, in which the hitter and pitcher are engaged in a contest. These speakers use *hon* only for pitches seen from the point of view of the hitter. There are also speakers who classify pitches with *hon* only if they achieve the principal goal of pitching. Since getting strikes is the principal goal of pitching, such speakers can classify strikes, but not balls, with *hon*. No speakers have been found who use *hon* to classify balls but not strikes. Similarly, no speakers have been found who classify bunts and foul balls with *hon*, but not home runs and base hits.

There are similar motivations behind the extensions of *hon* to other concepts in sports. Thus, *hon* can classify shots and free throws in basketball, but not passes. And it can classify serves in volleyball and rallies in ping pong. These are cases where there is both a trajectory and a possibility of scoring (achieving a principal goal).

There are several morals to be drawn from these examples:

First, what are taken to be the central cases for the application of *hon* appear to be concrete basic-level objects: sticks, pencils, bamboo staffs, baseball bats, etc. The direction of extension appears to go from concrete basic-level objects to other things, like hits and pitches.

Second, a theory of motivations for the extension of a category is required. Among the things we need in such a theory are image-schema transformations and conceptual metonymies, that is, cases where a principal object like a staff or bat can stand for a principal goal like a win or hit.

Third, hits in baseball and long, thin objects do not have anything objective in common. The relationship between the bat and the hit is given by an image-schema transformation and a metonymy. Hence, the classical theory, which requires that categorization be based on common properties, is inadequate.

Fourth, the application of *hon* to hits in baseball may make sense, but it is not predictable. It is a matter of convention—not an arbitrary convention, but a *motivated* convention. Thus, the traditional generative view that everything must be either predictable or arbitrary is inadequate here. There is a third choice: motivation. In this case, the independently needed image-schema transformation and the object-for-goal metonymy provide the motivation.

Ideally, each instance of the use of a classifier outside the central sense should have a motivation. The motivation cannot be ad hoc—one cannot just make up a metonymy or image schema just to handle that case. It must be justified on the basis of other cases. This imposes a criterion of adequacy on the analysis of classifier languages.

Some investigators have suggested that such a criterion of adequacy is too strong; they have claimed that some classifications simply are arbitrary and that no non–ad hoc motivation exists. That is an empirical question, and the facts are by no means all in. But arbitrariness is a last resort. Even if there are some completely unmotivated cases, one can still apply a slightly weakened criterion of adequacy. Find out which extensions "make sense" to speakers and which extensions seem "senseless," and account for those that make sense. Each sensible extension of a category needs to be independently motivated. It is important in a description of a language to distinguish those cases that are unrelated homonyms—that happen to have the same linguistic form, but for no good reason—from those cases which have the same linguistic form for a reason. No analysis of a classifier system is complete until this is done.

So far, we have seen that metonymies and image-schema transformations can provide motivation for the extension of a category. Another important kind of motivation comes from conventional mental images. Take the example of a roll of tape, which can be classified by *hon*. We know what rolls of tape look like, both when they are rolled up and when they are being unrolled. That is, we have conventional mental images of tape, both when it is in storage form and when it is being put to use. We also know that we unroll tape when we are about to use it and that the tape is functional when it is unrolled. A conventional image of tape being unrolled has two parts—the rolled part and the unrolled, functional part. The image of the unrolled, functional part fits the long, thin object image schema associated with the central sense of *hon*. The image of the nonfunctional rolled part does not fit the central *hon* image-schema. Metonymy is involved here; the functional part of the conventional image is standing for the whole image, for the sake of categorization. The functional part fits the *hon* schema. This is, presumably, the motivation for the use of *hon* to classify rolls of tape. Again, we cannot predict the use of *hon* for rolls of tape, but we can do something that is extremely important—we can show why it makes sense. Making sense of categorization is no small matter. And doing so in a manner that shows in detail how basic cognitive mechanisms apply is anything but trivial. If the cognitive aspects of categorization are to be understood, it will require attention to detail at this level. For example, *hon* can be used to classify medical injections. Why does this make sense?

Medical injections are another case where the principal functional object (the needle) is long and thin; the needles can be classified with *hon* and, by metonymy, so can the injections.

So far we have seen how image-schema transformations, conventional mental images, and metonymy all enter into categorization by a classifier. Let us turn to a case that involves all of these plus metaphor. Recall that *hon* can be used to classify telephone calls. The conventional image of engaging in a telephone call involves using the most functional part of the telephone, the receiver, which is a long, thin, rigid object that fits the central image-schema for *hon*. The other principal conventional image related to telephone calls involves telephone wires. These are understood as playing a principal functional role in telephone communication. These fit the long, thin object image schema. They also fit the CONDUIT of the CONDUIT metaphor—the principal metaphor for communication. In short, there are two related but different motivations for the use of *hon* for telephone calls. That is, there are two ways in which this use of *hon* fits the conceptual system, and where motivation is concerned, the more kinds of motivation, the better. Thus, it is not a matter of finding which is right; both can be right simultaneously.

So far, we have seen that extended senses of *hon* can be based on the central sense of *hon*. But extended senses may themselves serve as the basis for further extensions via category chaining. Recall that letters are classified with *hon*. There are a number of considerations that motivate such a categorization. First, letters were originally in the form of scrolls, often wound around long thin wooden cylinders. They have been categorized with *hon* ever since, and that image remains very much alive in Japanese culture through paintings and the tradition of calligraphy. Second, the conventional image of writing a letter involves the use of a pen, which plays a principal functional role and is also a long, thin object. Third, letters are a form of communication and therefore an instance of the CONDUIT metaphor. These diverse motivations allow *hon* with all these senses to fit the ecology of the Japanese classifier system.

Letters and telephone calls are intermediate steps in a chain. Radio and TV programs are also classified with *hon*. They are forms of communication at a distance, like letter-writing and and telephone communication. They, too, are motivated by the CONDUIT metaphor for communication. Given that letters and telephone calls are classified by *hon*, radio and TV programs constitute a well-motivated extension. Movies are also classified by *hon*. They are also instances of communication at a distance; in addition, one of the principal conventional images associated with movies is the movie reel, which looks like a spool of tape, which is classified with *hon*.

The phenomenon of category-chaining shows very clearly that the classical account of categorization is inadequate. Sticks and TV programs are both in the *hon* category, but they share no relevant common properties. They are categorized in the same way by virtue of the chain structure of the *hon* category.

Finally, let us turn our attention to judo matches and contests between Zen masters and students. Judo matches are in the same domain of experience as martial arts contests with staffs or swords. A win in a judo match can also be classified as a *hon*. Similarly, Zen contests are, in Japanese culture, in the same experiential domain as martial arts contests, and a win there also can be classified as a *hon*.

Incidentally, the noncentral cases of the *hon* category vary in some cases from speaker to speaker. Thus some speakers do not include baseball pitches and some do not include wins in Zen contests. But to my knowledge, every speaker of Japanese includes the central members—the candles, staffs, baseball bats, etc. Moreover, many of the extensions have become conventionalized for speakers in general: letters, telephone conversations, home runs, spools of thread. The variation just displayed involves chaining that has not yet stabilized but which shows the same principles at work as in the stable conventionalized extensions.

Categories of Mind or Mere Words

A possible objection to the kind of analyses we have been discussing is that classifiers are mere linguistic devices and do not reflect conceptual structure. That is, one might object that, say, the things categorized by *hon* in Japanese do not form a single conceptual category. Thus, one might suggest that the analysis of *hon* given above may show something about principles of linguistic organization, but that it shows nothing about our conceptual system.

Let us, for the sake of argument, consider such a suggestion. Whatever their precise cognitive status is, principles of linguistic organization are some part or other of our cognitive apparatus. Just what would such "principles of linguistic organization" involve? In particular, they would involve all the things we discussed above in the analysis of *hon*:

- central and peripheral members
- basic-level objects at the center
- conventional mental images
- knowledge about conventional mental images
- Image-schema transformations
- Metonymy applied to mental imagery
- Metonymy applied to domains of experience
- Metaphors (which map domains into other domains)

These mechanisms are needed, no matter whether one calls them linguistic or not. Moreover, they appear to be the kinds of things that one would tend to call conceptual—mental images and image transformations do not appear to be merely linguistic. Moreover, linguistic categories can be used in nonlinguistic tasks, as Kay and Kempton (1984) have demonstrated (see chap. 18 below for a discussion). But whether they are used in nonlinguistic tasks or not, linguistic categories *are* categories—and they are part of our overall cognitive apparatus. Whether one wants to dignify them with the term "conceptual" or not, linguistic categories are categories within our cognitive system and a study of *all* categories within our cognitive system will have to include them.

Cognitive Categories or Mere Historical Relics

Another objection occasionally raised to the kind of analysis proposed above is that the noncentral cases are "mere historical relics" not parts of a live cognitive system. Dixon has already rebutted this persuasively for the Dyirbal cases in his observation that speakers do not learn the system one case at a time but use general principles. Moreover, Schmidt's study of the decay of the Dyirbal system provides dramatic evidence that Dixon's analysis was basically correct and psychologically real. Schmidt has shown that parts of the *system*, and not just individual cases, are being lost. This is a fact that cannot be explained by the claim that classifiers are mere historical relics, learned one by one, with no cognitively real system.

In addition, the "mere historical relics" argument cannot be used to argue that cognitive mechanisms of the sort we have postulated do not exist. There is nothing "mere" even about historical relics. When categories get extended in the course of history, there has to be some sort of cognitive basis for the extension. And for them to be adopted into the system, that is, "conventionalized," they must make sense to the speakers who are making these innovations part of their linguistic system, which is, after all, a cognitive system. Chances are, the kinds of cognitive operations used to extend categories are pretty much the ones we have discussed. At the time the extension of the category occurs, such mechanisms are quite real. And any theory of historical semantic change must include an account of such mechanisms. At the time of an extension, the extension is *not a relic*! Since *hon* is in a period of extension right now, the mechanisms of extension are now operative and the extended senses cannot be considered relics.

In the two cases we have discussed, we have excellent reason to believe that the radial analyses we have given represent something alive in the minds of speakers. To see why, let us consider a possible retort to such radial analyses:

- Showing that there are real principles of extension that work over the course of history does not show that there are radial categories. Everything you have said is consistent with the following view: There are no radial categories. All such cases reflect the following historical development: At stage 1 there is a classical category *A*. At stage 2 a new classical category *B*, based on the old *A*, emerges. The principles of change may be exactly the principles of extension that you describe. But at both stages, there are only classical categories, but no radial categories in the minds of speakers. But the new classical category *B* will happen to look to a linguistic analyst like a radial category.

This position has an important consequence:

- At stage 2, there would be no radial structure, that is, no distinction between central and peripheral members. Future changes therefore could not be based on a central-peripheral distinction. The mechanisms of change should apply equally well to what we have called "central" and "peripheral" members.

It is this consequence that is demonstrably false for Dyirbal and Japanese. The evidence in Dyirbal has to do with language learning and language death. Dixon observed in his early fieldwork that children learned the category system according to the principles he described, principles that correlate with a radial structure. Schmidt has shown that the decay of the system reflects the same radial structure. The evidence in Japanese has to do with ongoing contemporary change. The use of *hon* varies in the peripheral cases; the central cases of *hon* show no variation. Here the evidence from change supports the radial analysis for *synchronic* description.

However, such evidence is not always available. Other cases which can be analyzed radially may reflect the presence of a contemporary live system or a system which was once alive. It is an empirical question whether such systems are now present in the minds of speakers, or whether they used to be and are no longer. And, of course, there is also the possibility that the system present now does not directly reflect history, but may be a product of restructuring. Additional cases that reflect a live system are discussed in case study 2, where we raise the issue of the status of folk etymologies.

Experiential, Imaginative, and Ecological Aspects of Mind

We are now in a position to see how classifier systems reflect the experiential, imaginative, and ecological aspects of mind. Let us begin with the experiential aspects.

As Denny (1976) observes, "the semantic function of noun classifiers is to place objects within a set of classes different from and additional to those given by the nouns. These classes are concerned with objects as they enter into human interactions." Denny notes that, cross-linguistically, classifiers fall into three basic semantic types, all having to do with human interaction: "*physical interaction* such as handling, *functional interaction* such as using an object as a vehicle, and *social interaction* such as interacting appropriately with a human compared to an animal, or a high status person compared to a low status one." Denny argues persuasively that the range of physical interaction classifiers correlates with the kinds of significant physical activities performed in the given culture.

Denny's observations fit nicely with observations by Berlin, Rosch, and their co-workers on basic-level categorization. What they found was that basic-level categorization depended on the nature of everyday human interaction both in a physical environment and in a culture (see Berlin, Breedlove, and Raven 1974 and Rosch 1977.) Factors involved in basic-level categorization include gestalt perception, motor interaction, mental images, and cultural importance.

Taken together, these observations support the view that our conceptual system is dependent on, and intimately linked to, our physical and cultural experience. It disconfirms the classical view that concepts are abstract and separate from human experiences.

The use of *hon* in Japanese and the Dyirbal classifier system display many of the imaginative aspects of mind, especially the use of mental images, image-schema transformations, conceptual metonymies, and conceptual metaphors.

Finally, the fact that extensions from the center of categories are neither predictable nor arbitrary, but instead are motivated, demonstrates the ecological character of the human mind. I am using the term "ecological" in the sense of a system with an overall structure, where effects cannot be localized—that is, where something in one part of the system affects things elsewhere in the system. Motivation depends on overall characteristics of the conceptual system, not just local characteristics of the category at hand. In addition, the existence of the Dyirbal miscellaneous category indicates that categorization is not local, but at the very least depends upon contrasting alternatives.

Summary

Language is among the most characteristic of human cognitive activities. To understand how human beings categorize in general, one must at least understand human categorization in the special case of natural language. The two cases we have just discussed are quite typical of the way human categorization functions in natural language. What is it about the human mind that allows it to categorize in this way? Is there some general cognitive apparatus used by the mind that gives rise to categorizations of this sort? The theory of cognitive models is an attempt to answer these questions.

The analyses given above suggest that such categories can be characterized using cognitive models of four types:

Propositional models specify elements, their properties, and the relations holding among them. Much of our knowledge structure is in the form of propositional models. Thus, a model of a domain (like fighting in Dyirbal) would include elements that occur in that domain (like fighting spears). A propositional model characterizing our knowledge about fire would include the fact that fire is dangerous. A taxonomic model, like the base model for Dyirbal given above, would include four elements corresponding to each of the categories, and a condition stating that anything not a member of the first three categories is in the fourth.

Image-schematic models specify schematic images, such as trajectories or long, thin shapes or containers. Our knowledge about baseball pitches includes a trajectory schema. Our knowledge about candles includes a long, thin object schema.

Metaphoric models are mappings from a propositional or image-schematic model in one domain to a corresponding structure in another domain. The CONDUIT metaphor for communication maps our knowledge about conveying objects in containers onto an understanding of communication as conveying ideas in words.

Metonymic models are models of one or more of the above types, together with a function from one element of the model to another. Thus, in a model that represents a part-whole structure, there may be a function from a part to the whole that enables the part to stand for the whole. In Dyirbal knowledge about the hairy mary grub, that is, knowledge of its sunburnlike sting, may stand for the grub itself in determining that it is a member of the same category as the sun.

Such models can characterize the overall category structure, indicate what the central members are, and characterize the links in the internal chains.

CHAPTER 7

Features, Stereotypes, and Defaults

Feature Bundles

At this point it is possible to show why certain early attempts to account for prototype effects failed. Both of these are versions of what we have called propositional models. One popular approach was the theory of *feature bundles*. A *feature* is a symbol representing a property. A *feature bundle* is an unstructured set of such features, representing a set of properties. A *weighted feature bundle* assigns weights to the features in a bundle; the weights indicate the relative importance of the features. *Weighted feature bundles* are used to account for prototype effects in the following way: the weighted feature bundle is taken as a representation of the prototypical category member. Approximations to the prototype are defined in terms of shared features. Deviation from the prototype in highly weighted features places a member further away from the prototype than deviation in a less highly weighted feature.

The Coleman-Kay (1981) analysis of *lie* is a representative use of *weighted feature bundles*. The Coleman-Kay weightings for *lie* were: first, lack of belief; second, attempt to deceive; third, being false. Thus, a statement that has the first and second properties, but not the third, is a pretty good example of a *lie*. But a statement that has the second and third properties but not the first is a less good example of a *lie*.

As Sweetser (1981) showed, weighted feature bundles simply do not provide enough structure to account for all the facts about *lie*, while a theory based on independently needed cognitive models of knowledge and communication can do the job. And in general, weighted feature bundle theories cannot account for most of the prototype effects discussed above. Since they don't differentiate background from foreground, they cannot account for the Fillmore (1982*a*) *bachelor* examples. Since they have no account of metonymy, they cannot account for the effects that result from metonymic models. And they cannot account for radial structures for a number of reasons. First, feature bundles cannot provide descriptions of the *types* of links—metaphoric, metonymic, and image-schematic. Second, feature bundles cannot describe *motivated, conventional* extensions that have to be learned one by one, but are motivated by general linking principles. Weighted feature bundles simply don't come close to being able to account for the full range of prototype effects.

Defaults and Stereotypes

In this chapter, we have attempted to show how superficial prototype effects can be accounted for by highly structured cognitive models. But the scholars cited above are not the only ones who have suggested such an approach. Outside of linguistics, the best-known advocates for something akin to a cognitive models account of prototype effects have been Marvin Minsky (see Minsky 1975) and Hilary Putnam (see Putnam 1975).

Minsky's *frames*, like Schank and Abelson's *scripts* (1977), and Rumelhart's *schemas* (1975), are akin to Fillmore's *frames* and to what we have called *propositional models*. They are all network structures with labeled branches that can code propositional information. In fact, Rumelhart's schemas, which are widely used in computational approaches to cognitive psychology, were developed from Fillmore's earlier work on case frames (Fillmore 1968). Frames, scripts, and schemas are all attempts to provide a format for representing human knowledge in computational models of the mind. They attempt to do so by providing conventional propositional structures in terms of which situations can be understood. The structures contain empty slots, which can be filled by the individuals occurring in a given situation that is to be structured.

Minsky's frames are equipped with *default values*. These are values for a slot that are used if no specific contextual information is supplied. For example, a default value for tigers will indicate that they are striped. A default value for gold will indicate that it is yellow. Default values define normal cases. But they can be overridden in nonnormal situations. Thus, Minsky's frames can accommodate stripeless tigers and white gold.

Hilary Putnam has used the term *stereotype* for roughly what Minsky has described as a frame with default values. A *stereotype* for Putnam is an idealized mental representation of a normal case, which may not be accurate. What we have called social stereotypes are, in a sense, special cases of Putnam's concept. In Putnam's stereotypes, tigers have stripes and gold is yellow, despite the real-world occurrence of stripeless tigers and white gold.

The Minsky-Putnam proposals appear to be capable in principle of accounting for the same range of prototype effects as propositional ICMs. They could probably be elaborated to duplicate Fillmore's *bachelor* analysis. They would thus be able to account for simple prototype effects. They do not, however, appear to be capable of accounting for most of the prototype effects we have discussed. They seem, at least on the face of it, to be inadequate to the task of describing the full range of effects that arise from metonymic models. And they are incapable of describing radially structured categories.

The Minsky-Putnam approaches are thus deficient in two respects. First, they have only propositional models; they do not include any of the "imaginative" models—metonymic, metaphoric, and image schematic. Second, they have a single representation for each category; this makes it impossible for them to account for complex radial structures like those in Dyirbal. Despite these deficiencies, Putnam and Minsky deserve a great deal of credit for seeing early on that superficial prototype effects should be accounted for in terms of deviations from idealized cognitive models.

What was right about the Putnam-Minsky approaches was that they used cognitive models. Their problem was that their concept of a cognitive model was too restricted in that it was limited to propositional models. I believe that a general notion of cognitive model of the sort characterized in this book will be able to account for categorization phenomena in general. But before we can proceed with that argument, there are certain properties of cognitive models that have to be discussed.

CHAPTER 8

More about Cognitive Models

We use cognitive models in trying to understand the world. In particular, we use them in theorizing about the world, in the construction of scientific theories as well as in theories of the sort we all make up. It is common for such theories not to be consistent with one another. The cognitive status of such models permits this. As we shall see, it also permits us to make sense of phenomena such as analyticity and presupposition, which don't make sense in accounts of meaning where cognition is not considered. Let us begin with theories.

Folk Models and Scientific Models

Ordinary people without any technical expertise have theories, either implicit or explicit, about every important aspect of their lives. Cognitive anthropologists refer to such theories as *folk theories* or *folk models.* As we have seen, we even have a folk model of what categories themselves are, and this folk model has evolved into the classical theory of categorization. Part of the problem that prototype theory now has, and will face in the future, is that it goes beyond our folk understanding of categorization. And much of what has given the classical theory its appeal over the centuries is that it meshes with our folk theory and seems like simple common sense. It is extremely important that we be made aware of what our folk theories are, especially in such fundamental areas as categorization, reference, meaning, etc., on which all technical understanding is founded.

Biology

There is a common idea, at least in the West, and I would suspect in other cultures, that there is a single correct taxonomy of natural things—plants, animals, minerals, etc. A taxonomy is a cognitive model of a particular kind. Taxonomic models are common in cognition, and they are built into languages throughout the world. They are among the most common means that human beings have used to make sense of their experience.

People have many ways of making sense of things—and taxonomies of all sorts abound. Yet the idea that there is a single right taxonomy of natural things is remarkably persistent. Perhaps it arises from the relative stability of basic-level concepts. But whatever the source, the idea is widespread. Taxonomies, after all, divide things into kinds, and it is commonly taken for granted that there is only one correct division of the natural world into natural kinds. Since scientific theories develop out of folk theories, it is not at all surprising to find that folk criteria for the application of taxonomic models find their way into science. A particularly interesting example of this is discussed by Gould (1983) in his classic "What, If Anything, Is a Zebra?"

Gould describes the heated disputes between two groups of biologists, the cladists and the pheneticists. Each of these applies different criteria for determining the one "correct" taxonomy of living beings. The pheneticists look at overall similarity in form, function, and biological role, while the cladists are primarily concerned with branching order in the course of evolution and look at *shared derived characters*, that is, features present only in members of an immediate lineage and not in distant primitive ancestors. Ideally, overall similarity ought to converge with evolutionary branching order and yield the same taxonomy. Traditional evolutionary taxonomists use both kinds of information. But in a considerable number of cases there is a divergence between the cladistic and phenetic taxonomic models. The zebra is a case in point. There are three species of zebra: Burchell's zebra, the mountain zebra, and Grevey's zebra. Burchell's zebra and Grevey's zebra form an evolutionary group, but the mountain zebra appears to form a genealogical unit with the true horse rather than with the other two species of zebra. Judging by the cladists' criteria, there is no true biological category that consists of all and only the zebras.

Gould's discussion is particularly interesting:

> Some of our most common and comforting groups no longer exist if classifications must be based on cladograms [evolutionary branching diagrams]. . . . I regret to report that there is surely no such thing as a fish. About 20,000 species of vertebrates have scales and fins and live in water, but they do not form a coherent cladistic group. Some—the lungfish and the coelacanth in particular—are genealogically close to the creatures that crawled out on land to become amphibians, reptiles, birds, and mammals. In a cladistic ordering of trout, lungfish, and any bird or mammal, the lungfish must form a sister group with the sparrow or elephant, leaving the trout in

its stream. The characters that form our vernacular concept of "fish" are all shared primitives and do not therefore specify cladistic groups.

At this point, many biologists rebel, and rightly I think. The cladogram of trout, lungfish, and elephant is undoubtedly true as an expression of branching order in time. But must classifications be based only on cladistic information? A coelacanth looks like a fish, tastes like a fish, acts like a fish, and therefore—in some legitimate sense beyond hidebound tradition—*is* a fish. Unfortunately, these two types of information—branching order and overall similarity—do not always yield congruent results. The cladist rejects overall similarity as a snare and delusion and works with branching order alone. The pheneticist attempts to work with overall similarity alone and tries to measure it in the vain pursuit of objectivity. The traditional systematist tries to balance both kinds of information but often falls into hopeless confusion because they really do conflict. Coelacanths are like mammals by branching order and like trout by biological role. Thus cladists buy potential objectivity at the price of ignoring biologically important information. And traditionalists curry confusion and subjectivity by trying to balance two legitimate, and often disparate, sources of information. What is to be done?

. . . In an ideal world, there would be no conflict among the three schools—cladistics, phenetics, and traditional—and all would produce the same classification for a given set of organisms. In this pipe-dream world, we would find a perfect correlation between phenetic similarity and recency of common ancestry (branching order). . . . But let the reverie halt. The world is much more interesting than ideal. Phenetic similarity often correlates very poorly with recency of common ancestry. Our ideal world requires a constancy of evolutionary rate in all lineages. But rates are enormously variable. . . . By branching order, the modern coelacanth may be closer to a rhino than a tuna. But while rhinos, on a rapidly evolving line, are now markedly distant from that distant common ancestor, coelacanths still look and act like fish—and we might as well say so. Cladists will put them with rhinos, pheneticists with tunas; traditionalists will hone their rhetoric to defend a necessarily subjective decision. . . . I do not believe that nature frustrates us by design, but I rejoice in her intransigence nonetheless. (Gould 1983, pp. 363–64)

There are several things here worth noticing. First, both the cladists and pheneticists are seeking categories based on shared characteristics. They differ on which shared characteristics are to be considered. Second, the cladists, the pheneticists, and traditionalists like Gould, who try to balance both kinds of criteria, all follow the folk theory that there is only one correct taxonomy. Even though Gould recognizes the scientific validity of the cladists' views, he cannot simply say that there are two, or even three, different taxonomies, equally correct for different reasons. As a traditional taxonomist, he feels forced to make a choice. Third, his choice is based on what he calls "subjective" criteria—what a coelacanth looks like and tastes like to a human being. Of course, there is a long tradition of using such human-based criteria in taxonomic biology.

The general point should be clear. There are at least two kinds of taxonomic models available to traditional biologists: the cladistic and the phenetic. Ideally, they are supposed to converge, and they do in a great many cases, but by no means in all. One may admit, as Gould does, that both have scientific validity. Still the force of the folk theory of taxonomic models is so strong that a choice must be made—if not one or the other exclusively, then a third choice combining elements of both. Above all, there must be one correct taxonomy.

Why? Why does the view that there is only one correct taxonomy have that kind of force? There is nothing wrong with saying that there are just two different taxonomic models of life forms, which are concerned with different and equally valid issues. Yet it doesn't seem like a possible alternative for many biologists.

My guess is that we have a folk theory of categorization itself. It says that things come in well-defined kinds, that the kinds are characterized by shared properties, and that there is one right taxonomy of the kinds.

It is easier to show what is wrong with a scientific theory than with a folk theory. A folk theory defines common sense itself. When the folk theory and the technical theory converge, it gets even tougher to see where that theory gets in the way—or even that it is a theory at all. Biology has conflicting taxonomic models that reflect different aspects of reality. The folk theory that there can be only one correct taxonomy of living things seems to be at least partly behind the conflict between the pheneticists, the cladists, and the evolutionary taxonomists.

Language

We not only have folk models of categorization, we even have folk models of reference. Ordinary English comes with not only one folk model of reference, but with two. And the two are not consistent. This, in itself, should not be surprising. There are many areas of human experience in which we have conflicting modes of understanding. We have both folk and expert theories of medicine, politics, economics, etc. Each theory, whether folk or expert, involves some idealized cognitive model, with a corresponding vocabulary. A given person may hold one or more folk theories and one or more expert theories in areas like medicine or economics or physics. It is commonplace for such idealized cognitive models to be inconsistent with one another.

In fact, recent studies of adults' understanding of physics shows that most of us do not have a single coherent understanding of how the physical world works. Instead, we have a number of cognitive models that are inconsistent. For example, many of us have two ways of understanding electricity—as a continuous fluid that flows like water and as a bunch of electrons that move like people in a crowd. Gentner and Gentner (1982), in a remarkable study of how people actually learn about and understand science, showed that it is common for people to have both of these folk models of electricity and to apply one in solving some problems and the other in solving other problems. As they observed, these are conflicting models, in that they give different results in a certain range of problems. One has to learn which model to apply in which range of problems.

Similarly, Paul Kay (1979, 1983*b*) has shown that ordinary speakers of English have two conflicting theories of how we use words to refer to things in the world. Kay demonstrates this through a careful reanalysis of the hedges *loosely speaking, strictly speaking, regular*, and *technically*, which were first analyzed (inadequately) by Lakoff (1972). Kay shows that these expressions are understood in terms of certain idealized cognitive models of the relationship between language and the world. In other words, we are all folk philosophers of language in that we have folk theories of reference.

Kay takes a principle like (1) to be a folk-theoretical counterpart of semantic theories in the tradition of the philosopher Gottlob Frege:

1. WORDS CAN FIT THE WORLD BY VIRTUE OF THEIR INHERENT MEANING.

Kay argues convincingly that *loosely speaking* and *strictly speaking* are defined with respect to an ICM embodying 1. Kay puts it this way:

> One of the implicit cognitive schemata by which we structure, remember, and image acts of speaking assumes that there is a world independent of our talk and that our linguistic expressions can be more or less faithful to the non-linguistic facts they represent. Thus we can lie, innocently misrepresent, speak loosely, speak strictly, and so on. (Kay 1979, p. 37)

In short, if words can fit the world, they can fit it either strictly or loosely, and the hedges *strictly speaking* and *loosely speaking* indicate how narrowly or broadly one should construe the fit. For instance, take Kay's example:

Loosely speaking, the first human beings lived in Kenya.

In a strict sense, there were no such things as "the first human beings"—at least assuming continuous evolution. But loosely speaking, this expression can be taken to refer to primates with important human characteristics. And Kenya, if you want to be picky, didn't exist then. But loosely speaking, we can take "in Kenya" to be in the general part of Africa where Kenya now exists (Kay 1979).

Kay thus identifies "loosely speaking" and "strictly speaking" as pragmatic hedges, which take for granted the ICM in 1 above. That is, they assume words can fit the world by virtue of their inherent meanings, either strictly or loosely. With respect to this sentence "the first human beings" and "in Kenya" property fit things they wouldn't fit under a strict construal, given the inherent meanings of the words.

But "technically" is defined relative to a different folk theory of how words refer. "Technically" assumes the following folk conception of the relation between words and the world—a folk version of the theory put forth by philosophers Hilary Putnam (1975*a*) and Saul Kripke (1972):

2. THERE IS SOME BODY OF PEOPLE IN SOCIETY WHO HAVE THE RIGHT TO STIPULATE WHAT WORDS SHOULD DESIGNATE, RELATIVE TO SOME DOMAIN OF EXPERTISE.

Sometimes these people are taken to be experts who know better than the common man what the world is like, as in the example:

Technically, a dolphin is a mammal.

Here professional biologists have the relevant expertise. In other cases, *technically* may refer in context to some immediately relevant body of experts:

Technically, a TV set is a piece of furniture.

This may be true with respect to the moving industry and false with respect to the insurance industry. Kay suggests that *technically* should be glossed as something like "as stipulated by those in whom society has vested the right to so stipulate" (Kay 1983*b*, p. 134). Let us call such people "experts." Now when the relevant area of expertise of these experts happens to be the nature of the world, then their stipulation as to how a term should be used dovetails with our assumptions about how the world really is. In this case, *technically* has a "semantic" effect, and it produces truth conditions that converge with those of *strictly speaking.*

Technically, a dolphin is a mammal.
Strictly speaking, a dolphin is a mammal.

Both sentences have the same truth conditions, but for different reasons. Since "mammal" is a term from scientific biology, the relevant body of expertise for *technically* is biology, which is about how the world is. *Strictly speaking* assumes that words, via inherent meanings, fit the world as it is.

Of course, the sentences have very different linguistic meanings and conditions of use, since the two hedges evoke different ICMs.

Now when the relevant body of experts are people like Quaker church officials and Internal Revenue agents, the truth conditions for *technically* and *strictly speaking* diverge, as we would expect, since their expertise is not about the way the world really is. Thus, given that Richard Nixon happens to be a member of the Quaker church, but does not share strict Quaker pacifist values, the following sentences have different truth values.

Technically, Richard Nixon is a Quaker.
Strictly speaking, Richard Nixon is a Quaker.

The first is true and the second is false. Similarly, Ronald Reagan owns a ranch that provides him a tax shelter, but is not primarily a professional cattle rancher.

Technically, Ronald Reagan is a rancher.
Strictly speaking, Ronald Reagan is a rancher.

The first sentence is true and the second is false.

The folk-theoretical principles given in ICMs 1 and 2 will happen to produce the same truth conditions for *strictly speaking* and *technically* if the domain of expertise in 2 happens to be the nature of the world. But in general they produce different truth conditions. Since 1 and 2 make very different assumptions about the mechanisms by which words designate things, they are not consistent with each other. Yet there are English expressions that make use of each of them. There are even expressions in English that make use of both theories of reference simultaneously. Consider the expression *so-called* in a sentence like

The general is president of a so-called democracy.

Here the speaker is assuming that the country in question has been dubbed a "democracy" (according to the folk version of the Kripke-Putnam theory), but that the word "democracy" does not really fit the country (according to the folk version of the Fregean theory). Both folk theories are needed if one is to characterize the meaning and actual use of such hedges. In communicating, we make use of both principles in appropriate situations. Despite their inconsistency, 1 and 2 both play roles in characterizing the reality of language use.

As we mentioned above, these two conflicting folk theories of reference actually correspond to two conflicting and competing technical theories within the philosophy of language. There are debates over which theory is "correct," that is, objectively true. Here two folk theories have been made into technical theories. But rather than being viewed as idealized cognitive models, each of which is suitable to some purpose, they are each taken by their various advocates to be objectively correct and to have a universal correct applicability. It is apparently intolerable to philosophers of language to have two conflicting models of reference, with different ranges of applicability. Yet both are present in the conceptual system on which ordinary English is based. The grammar of English is such that each can be used precisely, correctly, and effectively in the appropriate situations.

Seeing

The apparatus used by philosophical logicians does not allow for the sorts of things that cognitive models are needed for and can do. Here are two of the areas where ICMs have an advantage:

- the ability to distinguish prototypical from nonprototypical situations in which a given concept is used
- the ability to account for concepts that are inherently nonobjective, for example, concepts involving human perception

Perhaps the clearest way to see these advantages is by comparing the theory of ICMs to situation semantics, as developed by Barwise and Perry (1984). One of the principal claims made for situation semantics is that it can adequately account for the logic of human perception, particularly the logic of seeing. Since human perception is an area that appears to be nonobjective, Barwise and Perry's claim is of special interest, since situation semantics is a version of objectivist semantics—a semantics where meaning is defined in terms of the capacity of symbols to fit the objective world directly, without the intervention of any human understanding that either goes beyond or does not accord with what is really "out there." Can an objectivist semantics really deal adequately with a nonobjective conceptual domain?

There is one superficial similarity between situation semantics and theory of ICMs, which is set within Fauconnier's (1985) theory of mental spaces. Both use partial models. But in the theory of ICMs, they are both cognitive and idealized. This means that (*a*) they are characterized relative to experiential aspects of human psychology and (*b*) they do not necessarily fit the external world "correctly." Neither of these is true of situation semantics.

A situation for Barwise and Perry is a partial model, which contains some entities and some specification of their properties and the relationships between them—what Barwise and Perry refer to as "the actual 'common sense' world that language reflects [sic!], the one that consists of objects having properties and standing in relation to one another." The specifications are left incomplete, just as our knowledge of the world is necessarily incomplete. As Barwise (1980) puts it, "If we represent the way the world is as some sort of set-theoretical structure *M*, then types of situations in *M* will be some sort of partial substructures." A Barwise and Perry situation can thus be understood as a subpart of the world as observed from a particular viewpoint. Barwise and Perry's situations thus contrast with possible worlds in intensional semantics, in that possible worlds are *complete* specifications of all entities in a world and all their properties and interrelationships.

Within situation semantics, truth is defined with respect to situations and so is the concept of entailment. Situation semantics is an "objectivist" semantics: what's there in the situation is really there in the world; it's just not all that's there. As we mentioned above, an idealized cognitive model is very different. First of all, it's idealized. It provides a conventionalized way of comprehending experience in an oversimplified manner. It may fit real experience well or it may not. The ways in which ICMs are inconsistent with an objectivist semantics will become clearer as we go through some examples.

Let us begin with Barwise's attempt to provide a logic of perception (Barwise 1980). Barwise discusses naked infinitive (NI) constructions such as *Harry saw Max eat a bagel*, where *eat* is in naked infinitive form. He proposes several principles governing the logic of such sentences, including the following:

> The Principle of Veridicality: If *a* sees *P*, then *P*.

For example, if Harry saw Max eat a bagel, then Max ate a bagel.

> The principle of Substitution: If *a* sees $F(t_1)$ and $t_1 = t_2$, then *a* sees $F(t_2)$.

Barwise's example is:

> Russell saw G. E. Moore get shaved in Cambridge. G. E. Moore was (already) the author of *Principia Ethica*. Therefore, Russell saw the author of *Principia Ethica* get shaved in Cambridge.

I find both of these principles problematic if taken as objectively true and absolute—which is how they are intended. The basic problem is this: SEEING TYPICALLY INVOLVES CATEGORIZING. For example, seeing a tree involves categorizing an aspect of your visual experience as a *tree*. Such categorization in the visual realm generally depends on conventional mental images: You categorize some aspect of your visual experience as a tree because you know what a tree looks like. In the cases where such categorizations are unproblematical, we would say that you really saw a tree.

It is well known in the psychology of perception that seeing involves seeing-as. (For a discussion, see Gilchrist and Rock 1981.) To take a simple well-known example, two lights, A and B, flashed in quick succession will appear to subjects as a single light moving from the location of A to the location of B. In other words, what subjects *see* is a single light move across the screen; they do not see two lights flash in quick succession (see Johansson 1950). Thus if Harry is a subject in such an experiment, it will be true that

– Harry saw a single light move across the screen.

and false that

– Harry saw two lights flash on the screen.

What one sees is not necessarily what happens externally. And sentences of the form "NP sees NP VP," that is, sentences of the form given above, depend for their truth on what an individual perceives, not on what external occurrences happen to give rise to that perception. Thus, it would be incorrect to say in the above example that Harry really saw two lights flash on the screen, but he didn't know it and thought he saw a single light move across the screen. (For a discussion, see Goodman 1978, chap. 5.)

Moreover, an important body of twentieth-century art rests on the fact that ordinarily seeing is seeing-as, that is, categorizing what is perceived. A good example is discussed in Lawrence Weschler's *Seeing Is Forgetting the Name of the Thing One Sees*, a biography of artist Robert Irwin (Weschler 1982). A substantial part of Irwin's career was devoted to creating art pieces that could not be seen as something else, that were exercises in pure seeing without categorization. Irwin's discs provide the best examples I have come across of such experiences. The point is that seeing experiences of this sort—seeing without seeing-as, seeing without categorization—are rare. They require extraordinary works of art or very special training, often in a meditative tradition. The existence of such extraordinary seeing experiences highlights what is typical of seeing: SEEING TYPICALLY INVOLVES CATEGORIZING.

For an objectivist, seeing-as is a matter of human psychology and should never enter into questions of meaning, which are objective. But seeing-as, in the form of visual categorization, typically enters into seeing. This fact creates all sorts of problems for any logic of perception set up on objectivist principles. Among the places where the problems show up are in the principles of veridicality and substitution. Given the principle of veridicality, it should follow from the truth of

– Harry saw a single light move across the screen.

that

– A single light moved across the screen.

even though this need not be the case, since there could have been two lights flashing in quick succession. Thus the principal of veridicality does not always work.

Nor does the principle of substitution. Take for example the following case:

(*a*) The princess saw the frog jump into bed with her.
(*b*) The frog was really the prince.
(*c*) The princess saw the prince jump into bed with her.

Is (*c*) a valid conclusion to draw from (*a*) and (*b*)? Well, yes and no. The case is problematic. The frog doesn't look at all like the prince, and assuming that the princess has no idea the prince has been turned into a frog, she certainly did not perceive the prince as having jumped into bed with her. She would presumably agree with (*a*), but not with (*c*). One can always claim that she did not know what she saw. But it's harder to claim that she didn't see what she saw, and she saw a frog but not a prince.

The problem is very much the same as the classic problem with *want.*

(*a*) Oedipus wanted to marry Jocasta.
(*b*) Jocasta was Oedipus' mother.
(*c*) Therefore, Oedipus wanted to marry his mother.

Logicians generally agree that the principle of substitutability does not apply with *want*, since (*c*) does not unproblematically follow from (*a*) and (*b*). The cases with *want* and *see* are parallel. Yet Barwise's analysis requires that the principle of substitution work for *see* but not for *want*.

Though Barwise's principles of veridicality and substitution do not hold unproblematically in the way they were intended, they are not altogether wrong. They seem to follow from our commonsense folk theory of seeing, which might be represented as an idealized cognitive model of seeing.

THE ICM OF SEEING

1. You see things as they are.
2. You are aware of what you see.
3. You see what's in front of your eyes.

These aspects of our idealized cognitive model of seeing have various consequences, among them the folk-theoretical forms of Barwise's principles.

Consequences of 1:

If you see an event, then it really happened. (Veridicality)

You see what you see, regardless of how it's described. (Substitution)

If you see something, then there is something real that you've seen. (Exportation)

Consequence of 1 and 2:

To see something is to notice it and know it.

Consequences of 3:

If something is in front of your eyes, you see it. (The causal theory of perception)

Anyone looking at a certain situation from the same viewpoint at a given place and time will see the same things. You can't see what's not in front of your eyes. You can't see everything.

This idealized cognitive model of seeing does not always accurately fit our experience of seeing. Categorization does enter into our experience of seeing, and not all of us categorize the same things in the same way. Different people, looking upon a situation, will notice different things. Our experience of seeing may depend very much on what we know about what we are looking at. And what we see is not necessarily what's there, as the experiment with the two flashing lights shows. Moreover, everyone knows that there are optical illusions, that we sometimes don't see what's right in front of our eyes, that we make mistakes in perception, and that our eyes can deceive us, as in magic shows. Yet we still use the ICM OF SEEING, because it works most, if not absolutely *all*, of the time. It defines what we take to be the representative cases of seeing. The problem with the Barwise principles is that they are logical principles stated in an objectivist semantics, which means that they must *always* hold, even in that small percentage of cases where the ICM OF SEEING doesn't work. Because the Barwise principles are absolute principles of objectivist logic, all cases where the ICM OF SEEING doesn't work are counterexamples.

If Barwise's principles of veridicality and substitution were taken as special cases of the ICM OF SEEING, rather than as logical principles, then the problematic cases we noted above could be accounted for straightforwardly as cases where the situation is not normal and where the idealized cognitive model does not fit the situation in certain respects. For instance, the flashing lights situation and frog-prince situation are not representative situations. This is exactly what is predicted by the ICM OF SEEING. Whenever what one sees is not what there is, cases like those with the flashing lights and the frog-prince can arise. Such cases are not representative and will be judged so. Here the theory of ICMs works where the Barwise principles as interpreted within situation semantics fail. Within situation semantics, the Barwise principles are absolute logical principles and cannot recognize unrepresentative cases as being unrepresentative. The theory of ICMs allows one to recognize unrepresentative cases and to say precisely what is unrepresentative about them. It also permits the statement of general principles like Barwise's, but accords them a different status, cognitive rather than logical.

The point is this: Situation semantics cannot account for the semantics of perception. The reason is that it is an objectivist semantics—that is, it only takes account of the world external to the perceiver. But perception has to do with the interaction between the perceiver and the world external to him. The appropriate domain for the logic of seeing is cognitive, not objectivist. ICMs are idealized models used by perceivers, and they seem to be appropriate as domains for the logic of human concepts like seeing. Though Barwise's principles do not hold in general, they do seem to hold for a semantics that uses ICMs that structure mental spaces (see Book II below). This suggests to me that the general study of human concepts should proceed using a cognitive semantics of this sort.

Analyticity

As we have seen, the theory of idealized cognitive models makes very different claims about meaning than objectivist theories do. The differences become even more striking when we consider the issue of analyticity. In objectivist theories, if *A* is defined as *B*, then *A* and *B* must have the same meaning. Moreover, sentences of the form "All *A*'s are *B*'s" and "All *B*'s are *A*'s" are true by virtue of the meanings of the words "analytically true."

But this is not the case in the theory of ICMs. Suppose *A* is *bachelor* and *B* is *unmarried man.* In the theory of ICMs, a *bachelor* could be defined as an unmarried man, but only with respect to the BACHELORHOOD ICM—an ICM in which all the background assumptions about bachelorhood hold. But *unmarried man* is not defined with respect to the BACHELORHOOD ICM. It is for this reason that the pope is clearly an unmarried man, but not so clearly a bachelor. Since *bachelor* and *unmarried man* do not evoke the same ICMs, they do not have the same meaning. And "All unmarried men are bachelors" is not analytically true *in general.*

What allows this to happen is that definitions are made relative to cognitive models that are *idealized*, models that may or may not fit the world well and need not be consistent with one another.

Presuppositions

Presupposition is one of the most interesting of linguistic and conceptual phenomena. The empirical study of presupposition blossomed in linguistics in the late 1960s, but was pretty much killed off by the mid-1970s, a victim of objectivist semantics and psychology. It was a case where an interesting empirical study became disreputable because it did not make sense in terms of the reigning theoretical assumptions of the times.

Let us consider a simple example of a presupposition.

(*a*) I regret that Harry left.
(*b*) I don't regret that Harry left.
(*c*) Harry left.

Normally, the speaker who says (*a*) or its negation, (*b*), is taking (*c*) for granted. In the 1960s there were two alternatives available for trying to account for this phenomenon.

LOGICAL PRESUPPOSITION: Both (*a*) and its negation, (*b*), logically entail (*c*).

Logical entailment is defined in terms of truth in the world. Thus, whenever (*a*) or (*b*) is true in the world, (*c*) must be true in the world. This leads to problems for sentences like

(*d*) I don't *regret* that Harry left—in fact, he didn't leave at all.

If the theory of logical presupposition were correct, then (*d*) should be a logical contradiction, since the first half entails the truth of (*c*) and the second half denies (*c*). But since (*d*) is not a logical contradiction, the theory of logical presupposition cannot hold for such cases.

The only other method of comprehending presupposition available at that time was pragmatic (or psychological) presupposition, which was a matter of the speaker's assumptions rather than any logical entailment.

PRAGMATIC PRESUPPOSITION: P is a presupposition of sentence S if, whenever a speaker says S, he is committed to assuming P.

This doesn't help very much with (*d*). One might claim that the speaker was assuming (*c*) in the first half of the sentence and then changed his mind. But that doesn't seem to be what's going on at all. Let us take a case like the following, taken from Fillmore (1982*b*, 1984).

(*e*) John is thrifty.
(*f*) John isn't thrifty.
(*g*) Spending as little money as possible is good.

(*h*) John is stingy.
(*i*) John isn't stingy.
(*j*) Spending as little money as possible is not good.

Here (*g*) is taken for granted in both (*e*) and (*f*), and (*j*) is taken for granted in both (*h*) and (*i*). Now consider (*k*).

(*k*) John isn't stingy, he's thrifty.

According to the theory of pragmatic presupposition, the speaker should be assuming a contradiction—(*g*) and (*j*), since the first half of (*k*) presupposes (*g*) while the second half presupposes (*j*). For such cases, neither logical nor pragmatic presupposition will work. For a superb discussion of many such cases, see Horn 1985; Horn refers to the phenomenon as "metalinguistic negation."

Fillmore (1984) has observed that a theory of presupposition based on the theory of ICMs can account for examples like (*k*). The reason is that ICMs are cognitive models that are idealized. They do not have to fit the world and they can be used by speakers to suggest how to, or not to, understand a given situation. Fillmore suggests that *thrifty* is defined relative to an ICM in which (*g*) holds, and that *stingy* is defined relative an ICM in which (*j*) holds. Negation, Fillmore suggests, can either "accept" an ICM (that is, take that ICM for granted) or "reject" that ICM (that is, it can negate the applicability of the ICM evoked by the negated word). In (*k*), the negation is operating to reject the ICM associated with *stingy*. That is, the speaker is suggesting that the ICM evoked by *stingy* isn't the right way to look at the situation, while the ICM evoked by *thrifty* is.

This solution will also work for (*d*) above. Assume that *regret* is defined with respect to an ICM in which the object complement of *regret* holds; in this case it would be (*c*) above. Recall that (*c*) holds in the ICM, not in the world. In sentence (*d*) above, the negation is functioning not merely to negate *regret*, but to indicate the inapplicability of the ICM evoked by *regret.*

There are many examples similar to these. Consider

– You didn't *spare* me a trip to New York; you *deprived* me of one.

Here the ICM evoked by *spare* has as a background condition that what is spared someone is bad for that person, while the ICM for *deprive* has as a background condition that what someone is deprived of is good for that person. The sentence asserts that a given action should be looked upon as an act of depriving, not of sparing. That is, the *spare*-ICM is being rejected and the *deprive*-ICM substituted for it. The negative is negating the applicability of the *spare*-ICM. A similar case is

– Sam is more stupid than malign.

This suggests that the ICM associated with *stupid* is more appropriate for understanding Sam's behavior than the ICM associated with *malign*. The comparative *more than* is comparing the relative appropriateness of the ICMs. The best survey of such cases is given by Wilson (1975).

ICMs permit the distinction between what is backgrounded and what is foregrounded—what gestalt psychologists called the figure-ground distinction. They thus fit with Fauconnier's account of presuppositions in terms of mental spaces. Taken together, ICMs and mental spaces go a long way toward solving the classical problem of accounting for the presuppositions of complex sentences. Solutions such as the one given above are not available either in possible world semantics or in situation semantics, where there are no idealized cognitive models. In particular, the solution for example (*k*) would be impossible in ordinary logical and model-theoretical frameworks, since it would require having cognitive models that not only don't have to fit the world, but which provide contradictory ways of understanding situations. Contradictory cognitive models are not the stuff of logic as it is usually understood.

The interaction between negation and cognitive models is particularly "unlogical." There are three kinds of relationship possible between a negative and a cognitive model:

1. The negative is "outside" the cognitive model and functions to reject the ICM as being an inappropriate way to understand the situation.
2. The negative is "outside" the cognitive model, accepts the ICM as an appropriate way to understand the situation, and denies the truth of the foregrounded conditions of the ICM.
3. The negative is "inside" the ICM.

A case like *Sam didn't spare me a trip to New York, he deprived me of one* has a use of the negative in 1. Here the *spare*-ICM is rejected by the negative, and it is asserted that the *deprive*-ICM is more appropriate. A case like *Sam didn't spare me a trip to New York, he forced me to go* has the use of the negative in 2. Here the *spare*-ICM, which characterizes the trip to New York as being bad for me, is accepted as a way of characterizing the situation.

Cases where the negative is inside the cognitive model are often marked linguistically with prefixes like *dis-*, *un-*, and *in-*. For example, *dissuade* assumes a cognitive model which has a background in which someone has been intending to do something and a foreground in which he is persuaded *not* to do it. The *not* is internal to the model associated with *dissuade.* A case that is not marked by a negative prefix is *lack. Lack* is defined with respect to an ICM with a background condition indicating that some person or thing *should have* something and a foreground condition indicating that that person or thing does *not* have it. Since the negative is internal to the ICM, *lack* and *not have* are not synonymous, as the following examples show.

- My bike doesn't have a carburetor.
- My bike lacks a carburetor.

- The pope doesn't have a wife.
- The pope lacks a wife.

In each pair, the second example is inappropriate since the background conditions for *lack* are not met: a bike should no more have a carburetor than the pope should have a wife. The difference is especially pronounced in cases where there is a numerical quantifier in object position.

- I don't have four hands.
- I lack four hands.

- I don't have two wives.
- I lack two wives.

But *lack* and *not have* do have the same meaning when we would normally make the assumption that is the background condition of the *lack*-ICM:

- India doesn't have enough food for its people.
- India lacks enough food for its people.

In the theory of ICMs, it is expected that these three relationships between negatives and ICMs should exist.

Summary

ICMs have a cognitive status. They are used for understanding the world and for creating theories about the world. Consequently, they are often in conflict with one another or with some piece of knowledge that we have. This is important for the theory of meaning in the following ways.

First, the cognitive status of ICMs permits us to make sense of what presuppositions are. Presuppositions are background assumptions of ICMs. As such, they are not subject to the criticisms that have been made of the logical and pragmatic notions of presupposition.

Second, they allow us to understand more clearly what went wrong with the notion of *analytic truth.* Before the advent of the theory of cognitive models, certain philosophers defined analytic truth as an important semantic concept. An analytic truth was taken to be a sentence that was true solely by virtue of the meanings of its words. Word meaning was assumed to be defined in terms of conditions on the world, not in terms of idealized cognitive models. Sentences like the following were supposed to have characterized analytic truths:

- Someone is a bachelor if and only if he is an unmarried man.
- Someone lacks something if and only if he doesn't have it.

Such analytic truths containing if-and-only-if conditions were supposed to characterize definitions of words, and hence to play a major role in semantics.

We can now see that *bachelor* and *lack* are defined relative to ICMs that are not involved in the definitions of *un-, married*, and *man* in the first case and *not* and *have* in the second. As a result there turned out to be relatively few analytic truths, and some philosophers have claimed that there are none. Since lexical items tend to differ greatly in the ICMs that they are defined relative to, analytic truths would be expected to be hard, if not impossible, to come by. Even if some analytic truths do exist, they would not play any significant role in semantic theory.

Cognitive models allow us to make sense of a wide variety of semantic phenomena. The cognitive models approach to prototype phenomena is one of the most important of these. Its value can perhaps best be appreciated by seeing where other approaches are inadequate.

CHAPTER 9

Defenders of the Classical View

The experimental results that have led to prototype theory have been replicated often and, so far as I know, have not been challenged. Unfortunately, they are still being interpreted incorrectly—in accord with Rosch's interpretation of her results at Phase II of her research. Rosch maintained this interpretation for only a few years and discovered in a short time that it did not make very much sense. But, because this incorrect interpretation is the most direct and obvious one, given the assumptions of information-processing psychology, it has come to be identified with prototype theory by a great many cognitive psychologists. As a result, a number of prominent cognitive psychologists became disenchanted with what they mistakenly took prototype theory to be. And some, assuming the classical theory to be the only alternative, have sought a return to the classical theory.

To recall what the incorrect interpretations are and why they are incorrect, let us consider Rosch's basic findings. Rosch and her co-workers demonstrated the existence of *prototype effects*: scalar goodness-of-example judgments for categories. For example, in the case of a category like *bird*, subjects will consistently rate some birds as better examples than others. The best examples are referred to as *prototypes*. Such effects are superficial. They show nothing *direct* about the nature of categorization. As we saw above, Rosch (1978) made this clear: "to speak of a *prototype* at all is simply a convenient grammatical fiction; what is really referred to are judgments of degree of prototypicality. . . . Prototypes do not constitute a theory of representation for categories."

Despite Rosch's admonitions to the contrary in the late 1970s, prototype effects have been interpreted most often as showing something *direct* about the nature of human categorization. This is the mistake. It shows up in two incorrect interpretations of prototype effects:

THE EFFECTS = STRUCTURE INTERPRETATION: Goodness-of-example ratings are a direct reflection of degree of category membership.

According to this interpretation, scalar goodness-of-example ratings occur if and only if category membership is not all or none, but a matter of degree. It thus makes a claim that Rosch has since explicitly denied—that category membership is scalar whenever goodness-of-example ratings are scalar.

THE PROTOTYPE = REPRESENTATION INTERPRETATION: Categories are represented in the mind in terms of prototypes (that is, best examples). Degrees of category membership for other entities are determined by their degree of similarity to the prototype.

There are at least two variations on this interpretation: one in which the prototype is an abstraction, say a schema or a feature bundle, and another in which the prototype is an exemplar, that is, a particular example.

Despite the fact that Rosch has disavowed both of these interpretations and despite the fact that they are incompatible with much of what is known about prototype effects, they have remained popular. In fact, a whole school of research has developed within cognitive psychology which takes these interpretations as defining prototype theory. Smith and Medin's *Categories and Concepts* (1981) is a survey of research based on these interpretations.

It is no accident that these interpretations have been widely accepted by cognitive psychologists. A great many cognitive psychologists accept some version of the information-processing model of the mind. That model makes two central assumptions:

- Concepts are internal representations of external reality.
- Many, if not all, cognitive processes are algorithmic in nature.

Both interpretations fit these assumptions. The PROTOTYPE = REPRESENTATION INTERPRETATION sees the prototype as a representation of the structure of the entire category, and sees similarity as a way of computing category membership for other entities given the properties of the prototype. The EFFECTS = STRUCTURE INTERPRETATION reflects a working hypothesis of many cognitive psychologists: make the interpretation of the data as direct as possible.

If one compares these two interpretations with the examples cited above and the case studies presented below, it will become clear that these interpretations are not consistent with any of the examples in this book. It is not surprising then that problems with these interpretations should have been noticed. What is unfortunate is that many researchers have taken these overly restrictive interpretations of Rosch's experiments as defining prototype theory. The result has been a reaction against prototype theory—as it is defined by these interpretations. Since the classical theory has been seen as the only alternative, the researchers involved have seen themselves as upholding a version of the classical theory. As it turns out, their arguments against the EFFECT = STRUCTURE and PROTOTYPE = REPRESENTATION INTERPRETATIONS are reasonable. But their criticisms do not not extend to the cognitive models interpretation of prototype effects presented above. And they do not support a return to the classical theory. The remainder of this chapter will be an account of those arguments.

But before we begin, a bit of history is in order. In my 1972 paper, "Hedges," I began by taking for granted the EFFECTS = STRUCTURE INTERPRETATION, and I observed that Zadeh's fuzzy set theory could represent degrees of category membership. Later in the paper, I observed that the EFFECTS = STRUCTURE INTERPRETATION was inadequate to account for hedges like *strictly speaking, loosely speaking, technically*, and *regular*. To account for the use of *regular* one must distinguish *definitional* properties from *characteristic but incidental* properties. This corresponds to the semantics-pragmatics distinction in the objectivist paradigm, the distinction between what the word "really means" and encyclopedic knowledge that you happen to have about the things the word refers to.

However, my observation that the distinction was necessary was not in the service of supporting the semantics-pragmatics distinction; my purpose was to provide a counterexample. Here is the relevant passage:

> But hedges do not merely reveal distinctions of degree of category membership. They can also reveal a great deal more about meaning. Consider (6).
>
> (6) *a*. Esther Williams is a fish.
> *b*. Esther Williams is a regular fish.
>
> (6*a*) is false, since Esther Williams is a human being, not a fish. (6*b*), on the other hand, would seem to be true, since it says that Esther Williams swims well and is at home in water. Note that (6*b*) does not assert that Esther Williams has gills, scales, fins, a tail, etc. In fact, (6*b*) presupposes that Esther Williams is not literally a fish and asserts that she has certain other characteristic properties of a fish. Bolinger (1972) has suggested that *regular* picks out certain "metaphorical" properties. We can see what this means in an example like (7).
>
> (7) *a*. John is a bachelor.
> *b*. John is a regular bachelor.
>
> (7*b*) would not be said of a bachelor. It might be said of a married man who acts like a bachelor—dates a lot, feels unbounded by marital responsibilities, etc. In short, *regular* seems to assert the connotations of "bachelor", while presupposing the negation of the literal meaning. (Lakoff 1972, pp. 197–98)

Edward Smith (personal communication) has remarked that this passage started him on a line of research that he has pursued ever since. What interested him was the distinction between definitional and incidental properties. The passage had provided counterevidence to the objectivist view of this distinction, which *absolutely requires* that "semantics" be kept independent of "pragmatics"; that is, definitional properties are completely independent of incidental properties. The use of the hedge *regular* violates this condition, since it makes use of incidental properties in *semantics.* Kay (1979) has argued that the definitional-incidental distinction is not objectively correct, but rather part of our folk theory of language. The hedge *regular* makes use of this folk theory. If Kay's argument is correct, then the semantics-pragmatics and definitional-incidental distinctions are invalidated in an even deeper way than I first suggested.

Smith seems not to have been aware that this example was in conflict with the theory of semantics in which the classical theory of categorization is embedded. He drew from the distinction a way to keep the classical theory of categories, while still accounting for prototype effects. His idea was that the definitional properties fit the classical theory and that the incidental properties gave rise to prototype effects. This idea is developed in more detail in a classic paper by Osherson and Smith (1981). It may seem ironic that a passage providing counterevidence to the classical view should provide the impetus for a defense of that view.

Osherson and Smith

Osherson and Smith begin their paper with the following definition of prototype theory:

> Prototype theory construes membership in a concept's extension as graded, determined by similarity to the concept's "best" exemplar (or by some other measure of central tendency).

Here Osherson and Smith are assuming both the EFFECTS = STRUCTURE INTERPRETATION and the PROTOTYPE = REPRESENTATION INTERPRETATION. Their paper is an argument against these interpretations. Osherson and Smith also make additional assumptions:

- They assume that fuzzy set theory in the earliest of its many versions (Zadeh 1965) is the appropriate way of modelling the EFFECTS = STRUCTURE INTERPRETATION.
- They assume *atomism*, that is, that the meaning of the whole is a regular compositional function of the meaning of its parts. As a consequence, gestalt effects in semantics are eliminated as a possibility.

- They assume *objectivist semantics*, that is, that meaning is based on truth.
- They assume that all noun modifiers are to be treated via conjunction. This is commonly done in objectivist semantics, though as we will see it is grossly inadequate.

In the light of the previous chapters, we can see that these assumptions are not well founded. As we show in chapter 13, almost all prototype and basic-level effects are inconsistent with objectivist semantics. However, the EFFECTS = STRUCTURE INTERPRETATION is not inconsistent with objectivist semantics. The reason is that it treats all categories as graded categories, and as we will see in chapter 13, graded categorization is consistent with most of the objectivist assumptions.

If we grant all of Osherson and Smith's assumptions, their argument follows. The examples they give are well worth considering. Like classical set theory, classical fuzzy set theory has only three ways of forming complex categories: intersection, union, and complementation. Osherson and Smith take each of these and show that they lead to incorrect results. Their first counterexample involves three drawings:

a. a line drawing of a normal-shaped apple with stripes superimposed on the apple
b. a line drawing of a normal-shaped apple
c. a line drawing of misshapen apple with only a few stripes

They now consider three concepts: *apple, striped*, and *striped apple.* They correctly observe that within classical fuzzy set theory there is only one way to derive the complex category *striped apple* from the categories *apple* and *striped*, namely, by intersection of fuzzy sets—which is defined by taking the minimum of the membership values in the two component fuzzy sets.

They assume the following:

The apple in drawing *a* is a good example of a striped apple.
The apple in drawing *a* is not a good example of an apple, since apples generally aren't striped.
The apple in drawing *a* is not a good example of a striped thing, since apples are not among the things that are typically striped.

It follows that:

The apple in drawing *a* will have a high value in the category *striped apple.*
The apple in drawing *a* will have a low value in the category *apple.*
The apple in drawing *a* will have a low value in the category *striped.*

But since the minimum of two low values is a low value, it should follow from fuzzy set theory that *a* has a low value in the category *striped apple.* Thus fuzzy set theory makes an incorrect prediction. It predicts that an excellent example of a striped apple will have a low value in that category, since it has low values in the component categories *apple* and *striped.*

There is a general moral here: GOOD EXAMPLES OF COMPLEX CATEGORIES ARE OFTEN BAD EXAMPLES OF COMPONENT CATEGORIES.

Osherson and Smith cite a similar example: *pet fish.* A guppy might be a good example of a pet fish, but a bad example of a pet and a bad example of a fish. Set intersection in classical fuzzy set theory will give incorrect results in such cases.

Osherson and Smith also use some of what might be called "logicians' examples":

P AND NOT P: an apple that is not an apple
P OR NOT P: a fruit that either is, or is not, an apple

They assume the correctness of the usual logician's intuitions about such cases: There is no apple that isn't an apple and so the first category should have no members to any degree; and all fruits either are or are not apples, so the second category should contain all fruits as full-fledged members. Such intuitions have been disputed: a carved wooden apple might be considered an apple that is not an apple. And a cross between a pear and an apple might be considered a bad example of a fruit that clearly either is, or is not, an apple. Osherson and Smith do not consider such possibilities. They correctly argue that classical fuzzy set theory cannot account for the usual logician's intuitions in such cases.

The argument goes like this. Take an apple that is not a representative example of an apple, say a crabapple. According to classical fuzzy set theory, this would have a value in the category *apple* somewhere in between zero and 1. Call the value *c*. Its value in the category *not an apple* would then be $1 - c$, according to the definition of set complementation in fuzzy set theory. If *c* is in between 0 and 1, $1 - c$ will also be between 0 and 1. And both the maximum and the minimum of *c* and $1 - c$ will be in between 0 and 1. Thus, according to fuzzy set theory, a nonrepresentative apple, like a crabapple, would have a value greater than zero in the category *an apple that is not an apple*, and it would have a value less than one in the category *a fruit that either is, or is not, an apple.* This is inconsistent with the intuitions assumed to be correct by Osherson and Smith. If we accept their intuitions, their argument against fuzzy set theory is correct.

Osherson and Smith's last major argument depends on their assumption of the PROTOTYPE = REPRESENTATION INTERPRETATION, namely, that in prototype theory, degree of membership is determined by degree of similarity to a prototypical member. They correctly produce a counterexample to this interpretation. It is based on the following use of the PROTOTYPE = REPRESENTATION INTERPRETATION. Consider grizzly bears and squirrels. Since one can find some (possibly small) similarities between grizzly bears and squirrels, it follows on the PROTOTYPE = REPRESENTATION INTERPRETATION that squirrels are members of the category *grizzly bear* to some degree greater than zero. Now consider the statement:

– All grizzly bears are inhabitants of North America.

Suppose someone were to find a squirrel on Mars. Since that squirrel is a member of the category *grizzly bear* to some extent, and since Mars is far from North America, the discovery of a squirrel on Mars would serve as disconfirmation of the claim that all grizzly bears are inhabitants of North America. But this is ridiculous. The existence of squirrels on Mars should have nothing to do with the truth or falsity of that statement. Given Osherson and Smith's assumptions, this is indeed a counterexample to the PROTOTYPE = REPRESENTATION INTERPRETATION of prototype effects. (For detailed discussion of problems with fuzzy logic, see McCawley 1981, chap. 12.)

What Osherson and Smith have correctly shown is that, given all their assumptions, the EFFECTS = STRUCTURE and PROTOTYPE = REPRESENTATION INTERPRETATIONS are not correct. Of course, each one of their assumptions is questionable. One need not use the classical version of fuzzy set theory to mathematicize these interpretations. The assumption that noun modifiers work by conjunction is grossly incorrect. And objectivist semantics and atomism are, as we shall see in chapter 13, inadequate to handle the kinds of prototype phenomena that we have discussed. But, most important, the EFFECTS = STRUCTURE and PROTOTYPE = REPRESENTATION INTERPRETATIONS are wildly inaccurate ways of understanding prototype and basic-level effects. To show that they are wrong is to show virtually nothing about any reasonable version of prototype theory. And their argument shows nothing whatever about the cognitive models interpretation that we offered in the chapters above. But Osherson and Smith seem unaware of all this, and conclude (p. 54) that they have provided arguments against *all* versions of prototype theory.

Osherson and Smith then endorse a proposal reminiscent of that suggested by Miller and Johnson-Laird (1976) for saving the classical theory while accounting for the experimental results of prototype theory. What they adopt is a hybrid theory: each concept has a *core* and an *identification procedure*. The core works according to the traditional theory; the identification procedure accounts for the prototype effects that show up in experiments. As they put it:

> The core is concerned with those aspects of a concept that explicate its relation to other concepts, and to thoughts, while the identification procedure specifies the kind of information used to make rapid decisions about membership. . . . We can illustrate this with the concept *woman*. Its core might contain information about the presence of a reproductive system, while its identification procedures might contain information about body shape, hair length, and voice pitch.

The core, in other words, would be where the real work of the mind—thought—is done. The identification procedure would link the mind to the senses, but not do any real conceptual work. As they say,

> Given this distinction it is possible that some traditional theory of concepts correctly characterizes the core, whereas prototype theory characterizes an important identification procedure. This would explain why prototype theory does well in explicating the real-time process of determining category membership (a job for identification procedures), but fares badly in explicating conceptual combination and the truth conditions of thoughts (a job for concept cores).

This hybrid theory assumes that traditional theories actually work for complex concepts. The fact is that this is one of the most notorious weaknesses of traditional theories. The only traditional theories in existence are based on classical set theory. Such theories permit set-theoretical intersection, union, and complement operations, and occasionally a small number of additional operations. But on the whole they do very badly at accounting for complex categorization. We can see the problems best by looking first at the classical theory, without any additional operations. The traditional set-theoretical treatment of adjective-noun phrases is via set intersection. That is the only option the traditional theory makes available. So, in the classical theory, the complex concept *striped apple* would denote the intersection of the set of striped things and the set of apples.

The literature on linguistic semantics is replete with examples where simple set intersection will not work. Perhaps we should start with some that Osherson and Smith themselves mention (p. 43 n. 8 and p. 50 n. 12).

small galaxy—not the intersection of the set of small things and the set of galaxies

good thief—not the intersection of the set of good things and the set of thieves

imitation brass—not the intersection of the set of imitations and the set of brass things

Other classic examples abound:

electrical engineer—not the intersection of the set of electrical things and the set of engineers
mere child—not the intersection of the set of mere things and the set of children
red hair—since the color is not focal red, it is not merely the intersection of the set of red things and the set of hairs.
happy coincidence—not the intersection of the set of happy things and the set of coincidences
topless bar—not the intersection of the set of topless things and the set of bars
heavy price—not the intersection of the set of heavy things and the set of prices
past president—not the intersection of the set of past things and the set of presidents

Such examples can be multiplied indefinitely. There is nothing new about them, and no serious student of linguistic semantics would claim that such cases could be handled by intersection in traditional set theory. At present there is no adequate account of most kinds of complex concepts within a traditional framework, though a small number of isolated analyses using nonstandard set-theoretical apparatus has been attempted. For example, various logicians have attempted a treatment of the "small galaxy" cases using Montague semantics, and there have been occasional attempts to account for the "good thief" cases, and a couple of the others. But the vast number have not even been seriously studied within traditional approaches, and there is no reason whatever to think that they could be ultimately accounted for by traditional set theory, or any simple extension of it.

Let us turn now from the adequacy of the traditional set-theoretical core of the Osherson and Smith hybrid theory to the identification procedures. They do not give an indication of what such identification procedures might be like. But what is more important is that Osherson and Smith do not consider the question of what the identification procedures for complex concepts would be like and how they would be related to the identification procedures for component concepts. Take, for example, Osherson and Smith's case of *pet fish*. As Osherson and Smith correctly observe, "A guppy is more prototypical of *pet fish* than it is of either *pet* or *fish*." In the hybrid theory, the identification procedure for *pet* would not pick out a guppy as prototypical, nor would the identification procedure for *fish*. How does the hybrid theory come up with an identification procedure for the complex concept *pet fish* that will pick out a guppy as prototypical? In short, the hybrid theory has not solved the problem of how to account for the prototypes of complex concepts. It has just given the problem a new name.

Perhaps the most inaccurate part of the hybrid theory is that it views prototype phenomena as involving no more than "identification." But metonymic cases of prototypes function to a large extent in the service of reasoning; in general, what Rosch calls *reference-point reasoning* has to do with drawing conclusions and not mere identification.

Arithmetic submodels are used for doing computations and making approximations.
Social stereotypes are used to make rapid judgments about people.
Familiar examples are used to make probability judgments.
Paragons are used to make comparisons.
Ideals are used to make plans.
Generative prototypes are not used just for identification; they are necessary to define their categories.
Radial structures characterize relationships among subcategories and permit category extension, which is an extremely important rational function.

Most actual cases of prototype phenomena simply are not used in "identification." They are used instead in thought—making inferences, doing calculations, making approximations, planning, comparing, making judgments—as well as in defining categories, extending them, and characterizing relations among subcategories. Prototypes do a great deal of the real work of the mind and have a wide use in rational processes.

In short, Osherson and Smith have said nothing whatever that bears on the version of prototype theory that we have given. Nor have they provided any reason to believe that their proposal for saving the classical theory will work. Indeed, the fact that prototypes are used widely in rational processes of many kinds indicates that the classical theory will not account for all those aspects of rational thought.

Complex Categorization

The EFFECTS = STRUCTURE INTERPRETATION, as Osherson and Smith correctly observed, cannot handle problems of complex categorization. But it would be a mistake to think that the EFFECTS = STRUCTURE INTERPRETATION alone was responsible for that failure. The real source of the difficulties, they correctly note, is their acceptance of the objectivist characterization of the problem of complex categorization.

Suppose one makes the assumption of objectivist semantics:

- There are atomic concepts.
- Meaning is truth conditional.
- The meaning of the whole is a truth-conditional function of the meanings of the parts.

Then and only then does the classical problem of complex categorization arise:

- Exactly what are the atomic predicates?
- Exactly how do you get the meanings of the wholes from the meanings of the parts?

But Rosch's basic-level results contradict the assumptions of the classical theory. They suggest that:

- There are basic-level concepts, but these are not atomic concepts.
- Meaning is based on human perception, interaction, and understanding, and is therefore not truth conditional.

Within the theory of natural categorization, the problem of complex categorization in its classical form does not arise at all. But the classical problem was based on a correct empirical observation:

- People create new sentences all the time and are able to understand new sentences they've never heard before.

Take, for example, the sentence *People whose grandmothers were strippers are likely to be repressed.* This has the novel noun phrase *people whose grandmothers were strippers*, which denotes a novel category, but one which is immediately comprehensible. The question naturally arises: How is this possible? People do learn a finite stock of linguistic expressions and they do put them together to form new ones that they can understand. Exactly how?

Within prototype theory, this problem is very different from the classical problem of complex categorization. The problem is set within a cognitive theory that is neither atomistic nor objectivist. The things available to such a theory are mental images (not just visual images, but sound images, force images, etc.), perceptual and other cognitive processes, patterns of motor activity, intentions, cognitive models, and an extremely rich background of knowledge and experience.

In the classical theory, you have two choices for characterizing set membership: you can predict the members (by precise necessary and sufficient conditions, or by rule) or you can arbitrarily list them, if there is a finite list. The only choices are predictability (using rules or necessary and sufficient conditions) and arbitrariness (giving a list). But in a theory of natural categorization, the concept of *motivation* is available. Cases that are fully motivated are predictable and those that are totally unmotivated are arbitrary. But most cases fall in between—they are partly motivated.

Differences like these make possible suggested solutions to Osherson and Smith's examples of *striped apple* and *pet fish*. Consider, for example, Kay's Parsimony Principle (Kay 1983*a*), which was originally introduced for an entirely different reason—to handle discourse-based inferences. Adapted to the theory of ICMs, it says (informally and somewhat oversimplified): *When a number of ICMs are evoked, make them overlap as much as possible, consistent with your background knowledge.* In this case, the relevant aspects of the evoked ICMs in the *striped apple* example are our idealized image of stripes and our idealized image of an apple. The Parsimony Principle yields a simple image overlap—an apple with stripes—for our new complex ICM. This is Osherson and Smith's prototypical striped apple, and it works just as it should. The clause "consistent with your background knowledge" is a version of Wilensky's Law (Wilensky 1983, pp. 25, 145):

> More specific knowledge takes precedence over more general knowledge.

In other words, if you don't know about specific cases, use whatever general principles you have. But if you know something about a specific case, use what you know. This accounts for cases like *pet fish*. We happen to know about the kind of fish many people (at least in the United States) keep in their houses in fishbowls and fish tanks and that guppies are typical of such fish. That knowledge overrides the general Parsimony Principle. An incidental consequence is that the expression *pet fish* as used to describe guppies is not completely motivated by the meanings of *pet* and *fish*, but it is partly motivated. This accounts for the feelings on the part of most of the people I've asked that the expression *pet fish* is not an ideal description of the guppylike creature in the fish tank, but in the absence of anything better it will do.

Many of the examples we cited above, *topless bar, electrical engineer*, etc., are what linguists call "compounds." It is often the case that the meanings of compounds are not compositional; that is, the meaning of the whole cannot be predicted from the meanings of the parts and the way they are put together. The parts do play a role in the meaning of the whole expression—they *motivate* that meaning—but more is required: a relevant ICM where each part of the compound fits some element of the ICM. In most cases, we need to learn what the relevant ICM is for each compound.

In some cases the compounds can form chains, for example, *topless dress, topless waitress, topless dancer, topless bar, topless district.* These are based on related ICMs. *Topless dress* requires knowing what the top of a dress is meant to cover. *Topless waitresses and dancers* wear *topless dresses* while working. *Topless bars* employ *topless waitresses and/or dancers.* A *topless district* is a district with a concentration of *topless bars.* Thus compounds can be motivated not only by their parts, but by related compounds.

When an appropriate ICM is provided by context, a compound can be made up spontaneously. Pamela Downing (1977) provides the classic example of *apple juice seat*, an expression actually used by a hostess to an overnight guest coming down to breakfast. There were four place settings at the table, three with glasses of orange juice and one with a glass of apple juice. She said *Please sit in the apple juice seat*, and the new compound made perfect sense given what was understood about the setting.

What all this adds up to is this: The objectivist paradigm assumes that the meaning of the whole is a computable function of the meanings of the parts plus the syntactic relationship between the parts. This is simply wrong. There are a variety of reasons, but the one that I think should be stressed most is that the objectivist theories lack a concept of motivation. The meaning of the whole is often motivated by the meanings of the parts, but not predictable from them. What is required is a theory of motivation. Such a theory will be a cognitive theory and will go beyond any possible objectivist theory.

Armstrong, Gleitman, and Gleitman

The hybrid theory, despite all the arguments against it, is not likely to disappear. The classical theory that it incorporates as its "core" has two thousand years of tradition behind it. Within the past hundred years, theories of the form *core plus everything else* have appeared repeatedly as attempts to preserve the classical theory of categories. A particularly interesting recent attempt to argue for some form of the Osherson and Smith "core + identification procedure" theory has been made by Armstrong, Gleitman, and Gleitman (1983). Armstrong, Gleitman, and Gleitman argue that the very ubiquity of prototype phenomena provides support for a classical theory over a prototype theory.

Like Osherson and Smith, Armstrong, Gleitman, and Gleitman equate prototype theory with the EFFECTS = STRUCTURE INTERPRETATION. That is, they assume that every version of prototype theory would have to claim that all categories are graded and that goodness-of-example ratings correspond to degrees of membership. The form of their argument is roughly as follows:

(*a*) *Basic assumption:* Prototype theory assumes that whenever there are prototype effects for a category that category is graded. Goodness-of-example ratings correspond to degrees of membership. Conversely, it is assumed that prototype theory claims that ungraded categories would not yield prototype effects, since it is assumed that prototype effects only reflect degrees of membership.

(*b*) *Secondary assumption:* Concepts from formal mathematics are defined in terms of the classical theory, that is, by necessary and sufficient conditions, and therefore are not graded. By assumption (*a*), they should not show prototype effects. "Odd number" is an example.

(*c*) Armstrong, Gleitman, and Gleitman perform Rosch's experiments using the concept "odd number." They show that Rosch's prototype results appear and that subjects give graded responses when asked if some numbers are better examples of the category "odd number" than other numbers.

(*d*) From (*a*), they reason that prototype theory must interpret these results as indicating that the category "odd number" is graded. But (*b*) shows that it is not graded.

(*e*) Since we know that (*b*) is true, prototype effects cannot show that a category is graded. Therefore, (*a*) must be false, and so prototype theory does not show anything about the real structure of categories.

(*f*) But Rosch's results must show something. The core + identification procedure theory gives a plausible answer. Rosch's reproducible experiments reflect the identification procedure, but not the core, that is, the real cognitive structure of a category.

Like Osherson and Smith, Armstrong, Gleitman, and Gleitman assume the EFFECTS = STRUCTURE INTERPRETATION, and it is this interpretation that they, very reasonably, find wanting. They do not even consider the possibility of anything like the Cognitive Models Interpretation. But in the Cognitive Models Interpretation, their results make perfect sense.

To see why, let us first distinguish natural numbers as they are defined technically in formal arithmetic from natural numbers as ordinary people understand them. In formal arithmetic, the natural numbers are defined recursively. "Zero" is taken as a generator and "successor" as an operator. "One" is a name given to the successor of 0, "2" is a name given to the successor of the successor of 0, and so on. In mathematics, it is important to distinguish numbers from their names. We have a naming system for numbers that takes 10 as a base; that is, we have ten single-digit number names (0, 1, . . . , 9) and form multiple-digit number names thereafter. There is an indefinitely large number of possible naming systems. The best-known one after the base-10 system is the binary system, which takes 2 as a base and has only two single-digit number names, 0 and 1.

Most nonmathematicians do not distinguish numbers from their names. We comprehend numbers in terms of our base-10 naming system. The single-digit numbers are all generators. Multiple-digit numbers are understood as sequences of single-digit numbers. In order to compute with numbers, we must learn the generators 0 through 9 plus the addition and multiplication tables, plus algorithms for adding, multiplying, dividing, etc. Computation with large numbers is understood in terms of computation with smaller numbers—ultimately single-digit numbers. Without understanding large numbers in terms of single-digit numbers, we could not do arithmetic computations.

Thus, single-digit numbers have a privileged place among the numbers. Double-digit numbers, especially those in the multiplication and addition tables, are somewhat less privileged. Larger numbers in general are less privileged still. A model for understanding all natural numbers in terms of single-digit numbers is, by our definition, a metonymic model. We would, therefore, expect that, all other things being equal, single-digit numbers should be judged as better examples than double-digit numbers, which should be judged as better examples than larger numbers.

However, our understanding of numbers is more complicated than that. To aid in computation and in judging the relative size of numbers, we have learned to comprehend numbers using various submodels. The most common submodel consists of powers of ten (ten, a hundred, a thousand, etc.). Another common subsystem consists of multiples of five; the American monetary system is based on this submodel and it is helpful in doing monetary calculations. Other common submodels are multiples of two, powers of two, etc. As we pointed out above, each submodel produces prototype effects. Taking all such submodels together, we would expect prototype effects of complex sorts.

On the cognitive models interpretation, such prototype effects for numbers would not correspond to degrees of membership. All numbers are equal with respect to membership in the category *number*. But with respect to the various models we use to comprehend numbers, certain numbers have privileged status.

Another submodel we use with numbers is one in which numbers are divided into odd numbers and even numbers; the even numbers are those divisible by two, while the odd numbers are those of the form $2n+1$. The odd-even submodel has no gradations; all numbers are either odd or even.

Let us now consider all the models together: the model used to generate the numbers, the powers-of-ten model, the multiples-of-five model, the powers-of-two model, the prime number model, the odd-even model, and any others that we happen to have. Each model, by itself, produces prototype effects, except for the odd-even and prime number models. Suppose we take the integers together with all those prototype effects and superimpose the all-or-none odd-even model. Given that those prototype effects are there for other reasons, one would not expect the superimposition of an all-or-none odd-even model to make them disappear. Instead we would expect to get prototype effects within the odd numbers and other prototype effects within the even numbers. We would expect these effects to be complex, since they would be the product of all the models together.

If we then asked subjects if the odd-even distinction was all-or-none or graded, we would expect them to say it was all-or-none. If we then asked them to give goodness-of-example ratings for odd numbers and for even numbers, we would expect them to be able to perform the task readily, and to give rather complex ratings. This is exactly what Armstrong, Gleitman, and Gleitman did, and those were the results they got. It is exactly what prototype theory would predict—under the cognitive models interpretation.

Unfortunately, Armstrong, Gleitman, and Gleitman were using the EFFECTS = STRUCTURE INTERPRETATION of prototype theory, and the results they got were, not surprisingly, inconsistent with that interpretation. They assumed that since the odd-even distinction was all-or-none, there should be no prototype effects, since there was no degree-of-membership gradation. When they found prototype effects in a nongraded category, they concluded that prototype effects occurred in all categories regardless of structure and therefore reflected nothing about the structure of the category. Thus, the same experiment that confirms prototype theory under the Cognitive Models Interpretation disconfirms it under the EFFECTS = STRUCTURE INTERPRETATION.

Conclusion

Osherson and Smith, together with Armstrong, Gleitman, and Gleitman, have provided even more evidence that the incorrect EFFECTS = STRUCTURE and PROTOTYPE = REPRESENTATION INTERPRETATIONS of prototype theory are indeed incorrect. They have not shown that the core plus identification procedure theory *is* correct. In fact, the considerations we discussed above indicate that such a view is not viable for a number of reasons.

First, the classical theory of categories is hopelessly inadequate for complex concepts.

Second, there is a correspondence between prototype effects and metonymically based reasoning. Such prototype effects can be accounted for by metonymic models, which are needed independently to account for what Rosch has called "reference point reasoning." Thus, prototype effects are not independent of reasoning.

Third, there do exist direct correlations between conceptual structure and prototype effects. They are of two types: cognitive models containing scales that define gradations of category membership and radial categories.

The best way to account for prototype effects in general seems to be through a theory of cognitive models.

CHAPTER 10

Review

Up to this point, we have surveyed a number of empirical phenomena that concern categorization: family resemblance, centrality, gradience, metonymic reasoning, generativity as a prototype phenomenon, the embodiment of concepts, basic-level categorization and primacy, and the use of cognitive categories in language. We have surveyed some of the research demonstrating the reality of prototype effects, and we have made a number of suggestions as to what the sources of those effects might be. Those suggestions all involve the use of cognitive models of various sorts: propositional, metaphoric, metonymic, and image-schematic. Our description of cognitive models thus far has been superficial. A much more detailed account will be given in the case studies below.

The overall view we have presented so far has the following characteristics:

- The structure of thought is characterized by cognitive models.
- Categories of mind correspond to elements in those models.
- Some cognitive models are scalar. They yield categories with degrees of membership. These are the source of some prototype effects.
- Some cognitive models are classical; that is, they have rigid boundaries and are defined by necessary and sufficient conditions. They can be the source of prototype effects when their background conditions are partly consistent with our knowledge about certain given entities.
- Some cognitive models are metonymic, in that they allow a part of a category (a member or subcategory) to stand for the category as a whole for some purpose, usually reasoning. They too can be sources of prototype effects.
- The most radical prototype phenomena are radial categories. They cannot be represented by single model plus general principles. They involve many models organized around a center, with links to the center. The links are characterized by other cognitive models in the

conceptual system or by a similarity relation. The noncentral models are not predictable from the central model, but they are *motivated* by the central models and other models that characterize the links to the center.

- In the conceptual system, there are four types of cognitive models: propositional, image-schematic, metaphoric, and metonymic. Propositional and image-schematic models characterize structure; metaphoric and metonymic models characterize mappings that make use of structural models.
- Language is characterized by symbolic models, that is, models that pair linguistic information with models in the conceptual system. (See case study 3 for details.)
- Cognitive models are embodied, either directly or indirectly by way of systematic links to embodied concepts. A concept is embodied when its content or other properties are motivated by bodily or social experience. This does not necessarily mean that the concept is predictable from the experience, but rather that it makes sense that it has the content (or other properties) that it has, given the nature of the corresponding experience. Embodiment thus provides a *nonarbitrary* link between cognition and experience.

We are now in a position to address the questions with which we began.

- Are concepts and reason "transcendental," that is, independent of the nature and bodies of the reasoning beings?
- Is reason just the mechanical manipulation of abstract symbols that are meaningless in themselves, but get their meaning through conventional correspondences to things in the world—and only in that way?
- Do concepts provide "internal representations of external reality"?
- Is the mind a "mirror of nature"? Does correct reason merely mirror the logic of the external world?

Though we will be answering *no* to all these questions, we will begin by describing what we will call the *objectivist paradigm* in philosophy and cognitive science, in which the answer to all these questions is *yes*.

PART II

Philosophical Implications

CHAPTER 11

The Objectivist Paradigm

Philosophy matters. It matters more than most people realize, because philosophical ideas that have developed over the centuries enter our culture in the form of a world view and affect us in thousands of ways. Philosophy matters in the academic world because the conceptual frameworks upon which entire academic disciplines rest usually have roots in philosophy—roots so deep and invisible that they are usually not even noticed. This is certainly true in my own field, linguistics, where the classical theory of categories and certain attendant philosophical assumptions have been taken so much for granted that alternative assumptions seem unthinkable. One of my purposes is to show that the classical theory of categories is inadequate for the study of natural language as well as other aspects of the mind and that new philosophical assumptions are required in order to make sense of linguistic phenomena and other aspects of cognition.

The classical theory of categories has not evolved in a vacuum. It has developed side by side with some of the most widespread philosophical views in the West. And although it is possible to hold the classical theory of categories without being committed to those philosophical views, the reverse does not seem to be true. The philosophical views we will be discussing seem to require the classical theory of categories. If the classical theory of categories falls, those philosophical views fall with it.

The objectivist paradigm, as I will describe it, is an idealization. Each of the doctrines described here is widely held, though perhaps not all are held by any one person. Moreover, the versions I've given of the doctrines are fairly general; many philosophers hold more sophisticated versions, some of which are discussed below. It would take a volume much longer than this one to try to sort out exactly which philosophers, linguists, and psychologists hold which versions of which doctrines. Moreover, it would be beside the point, since it is the issues, not the personalities, that matter. These doctrines have evolved over two millennia; no single individual is responsible for them. Nor can one blame any individual for holding views that he or she was brought up to hold without question, not as opinions, but as part of the background relative to which one could have meaningful opinions.

It is our job here to bring our intellectual background into the foreground, to show that what have been taken as self-evident truths are really questionable opinions. We will argue that *all* of the objectivist doctrines concerning human thought and language are problematic if not downright wrong. These arguments, if correct, present problems for anyone who holds *any* of these doctrines.

We will be primarily concerned with objectivist epistemology—especially the objectivist view of thought and language. But there is also an objectivist metaphysics—an objectivist view of the nature of reality. We will be arguing against that view *in part,* but not in toto. Specifically, we will be arguing that the objectivist view of the nature of life forms is incorrect. But before we begin, it is important to point out that there is a certain common ground shared by objectivism and experientialism: we will refer to that common ground as *basic realism.*

Basic Realism

Basic realism involves at least the following:

- a commitment to the existence of a real world, both external to human beings and including the reality of human experience
- a link of some sort between human conceptual systems and other aspects of reality
- a conception of truth that is not merely based on internal coherence
- a commitment to the existence of stable knowledge of the external world
- a rejection of the view that "anything goes"—that any conceptual system is as good as any other.

Objectivism, as I will describe it, is one version of basic realism. Experientialism is another. Objectivism is a version that *requires* the classical theory of categories and is therefore inconsistent with the categorization results cited above. But basic realism, in the general form in which I have characterized it, is consistent with all of the empirical data on human categorization. When we present arguments against objectivist metaphysics, semantics, and cognition in the next two chapters, we will be arguing against objectivism, but not against basic realism.

The Two Aspects of Objectivism

The objectivist paradigm can be broken down into two parts:

1. Metaphysics, or the nature of the world, independent of any human understanding
2. Epistemology, or the nature of human cognition, language, and knowledge

In brief, objectivism holds that reality is structured in a way that can be modeled by set-theoretical models; that is, the world consists of

entities
the properties of those entities
the relations holding among those entities

A set-theoretical model consists of

entities
sets of entities (defined by the common properties of the members)
sets of *n*-tuples (corresponding to relations among entities)

The classical theory of categories provides a link between objectivist metaphysics and set-theoretical models: given any property (or collection of properties), there exists a category in the world consisting of the entities that have that property. Similarly, given an *n*-place relation, there is a category of *n*-tuples of entities standing in that relation. Since categories are understood as sets, it follows that the world (which is taken to consist of entities, properties, and relations) can be accurately modeled by set-theoretical models.

In this way, objectivist metaphysics goes beyond the metaphysics of basic realism. Basic realism merely assumes that there is a reality of some sort. Objectivist metaphysics is much more specific. It additionally assumes that reality is *correctly* and *completely* structured in a way that can be modeled by set-theoretical models—that is, in terms of entities, properties, and relations. On the objectivist view, reality comes with a unique, correct, complete structure in terms of entities, properties, and relations. This structure exists, independent of any human understanding.

Such structuring is necessary in order to get the objectivist view on cognition and language off the ground. If, as objectivists hold, thought is the manipulation of abstract symbols, then such symbols must be made meaningful somehow. The objectivist answer is that symbols (that is, words and mental representations) are made meaningful *in one and only one way:* via a correspondence to entities and categories in either the existing world or in possible worlds.

We will be arguing below that the data we have discussed concerning human categorization will turn out to be inconsistent with objectivist views on thought and language. Since that data concerns human cognition, that is, how human beings categorize, it will not have any bearing on objectivist metaphysics. However, there is independent evidence from biology that indicates that objectivist metaphysics is not adequate to account for the nature of life forms. We will discuss that evidence in the next chapter.

To avoid any possible misunderstanding before it occurs, I should make it clear that I will not be claiming that classical categories are never relevant to cognition. Quite the opposite! The classical theory of categorization is a product of the human mind. As I will argue below, many (though by no means all) cognitive models use classical categories. As such, they are part of our folk models of most domains of our experience. We use those folk models to understand what we experience. Thus, classical categories, *because of the role they play in the structure of many of our cognitive models,* do play a significant role in what we understand.

To say that classical categories are an invention (an *important* invention) of the human mind is not to say that no classical categories really exist. Certainly it is possible to create artificial categories of things to fit our cognitive models. It may even be the case that some classical categories do exist in nature. The point is that not all categories—either of mind or of nature—are classical, and therefore we cannot assume, a priori, as objectivist metaphysics does, that all of nature is structured by classical categories.

Let us now turn to the details of objectivism, beginning with objectivist metaphysics.

The Objectivist World

To appreciate the philosophical importance of the classical theory of categorization, we must first consider the worldview in which it is embedded—a metaphysical view of reality that is taken as being so obviously true as to be beyond question.

> OBJECTIVIST METAPHYSICS: All of reality consists of entities, which have fixed properties and relations holding among them at any instant.

Objectivist metaphysics is often found in the company of another metaphysical assumption, essentialism.

> ESSENTIALISM: Among the properties that things have, some are essential; that is, they are those properties that make the thing what it is, and without which it would not be that *kind* of thing. Other properties are accidental—that is, they are properties that things happen to have, not properties that capture the essence of the thing.

The classical theory of categories relates properties of entities to categories containing those entities.

> CLASSICAL CATEGORIZATION: All the entities that have a given property or collection of properties in common form a category. Such properties are necessary and sufficient to *define* the category. All categories are of this kind.

In the standard view, every entity either does or does not have a given property. As a result, categories have well-defined rather than fuzzy boundaries. However, one could extend the standard objectivist position to allow a category to have a property to some degree. We will discuss such an extended version of objectivism later in this chapter.

Given that properties have objective existence, and that properties define categories, it can make sense to speak of categories as having objective existence.

> THE DOCTRINE OF OBJECTIVE CATEGORIES: The entities in the world form objectively existing categories based on their shared objective properties.

If one adds essentialism, one can distinguish a special kind of objective category—one based on shared essential properties, as opposed to shared incidental properties.

> THE DOCTRINE OF NATURAL KINDS: There are natural kinds of entities in the world, each *kind* being a category based on shared essential properties, that is, properties that things have by virtue of their very nature.

Thus, what characterizes a natural kind is

> some 'essential nature' which the thing shares with other members of the natural kind. What the essential nature is is not a matter of language analysis but of scientific theory construction. (Putnam 1975*a*, p. 104)

The examples usually given are things that occur in nature—animals, plants, and minerals—but man-made artifacts can be viewed as having essential properties as well and so can also be viewed as falling into man-made *kinds*.

Since the entities of the world fall into objective categories, there are logical relations among those categories—logical relations that are purely objective and independent of any minds, human or otherwise.

OBJECTIVIST LOGIC: Logical relations exist objectively among the categories of the world.

Some categories, for example, may be completely included in other categories. Suppose category *G* is included in category *F*. Thus, everything that is a *G* is an *F*. That is, everything with the properties that characterize *G* also has the properties that characterize *F*. Or suppose *F* and *G* are mutually exclusive. Then nothing that is an *F* is a *G*, and nothing that is a *G* is an *F*. Thus, the existence of classical categories in an objectivist world guarantees the existence of logical relations within that world.

Some properties may be made up of logical combinations of other properties; these are complex. Those properties which have no internal logical structure are simple, or *atomic*.

REAL-WORLD ATOMISM: All properties either are atomic or consist of logical combinations of atomic properties.

The world, as objectivist doctrine envisions it, is extremely well-behaved. It is made up of discrete entities with discrete logical combinations of atomic properties and relations holding among those entities. Some properties are essential; others are accidental. Properties define categories, and categories defined by essential properties correspond to the *kinds* of things that there are. And the existence of classical categories provides logical relations that hold objectively in the world.

Objectivist Cognition and Language

Objectivism is very largely concerned with certain problems. How is it possible for someone to know something? What is *correct* human reason? What is truth? What is meaning? How can we characterize such meaning relationships as logical consequence and sameness of meaning?

The general approach an objectivist takes toward answering these questions is by assuming that the mind can function as a mirror of nature. That is, it is possible for the symbols used in language and thought to correspond to entities and categories in the world. Given objectivist metaphysics, the world can be assumed to have the kind of structure that makes such symbol-to-world correspondences possible. Symbols get their meaning via a conventional correspondence with things in the world. Thus, a system of symbols, linked to the world in this way, can be said to be a *representation* of reality—a mirror of nature. And human reason is correct when it accurately mirrors the logical relations in the objective world.

Thus, the objectivist answers his questions by assuming that the mind and language can reflect, or match up with, the world as he conceives of it. Here are the basic doctrines in somewhat more detail:

> OBJECTIVIST COGNITION: Thought is the manipulation of abstract symbols. Symbols get their meaning via correspondences to entities and categories in the world. In this way, the mind can represent external reality and be said to "mirror nature."
>
> OBJECTIVIST CONCEPTS: Concepts are symbols that (*a*) stand in a relation to other concepts in a conceptual system and (*b*) stand in correspondence to entities and categories in the real world (or possible worlds).

This account of cognition is objectivist in that it is independent of the nature of the beings doing the cognizing.

In objectivist cognition, the mind can achieve real knowledge of the external world only if it can represent (that is, *re-present*, make present again) what is really in the world; true knowledge must not be in any way an artifact of the nature of the thinking beings. Hence, the concern in the objectivist tradition with cognitive *representation* of external reality. The position is not that mental representations must resemble the external world. It is only that they must be able to correspond directly to them in a systematic way. Mental representations must thus be "semantically evaluable"—capable of being true or false, of referring correctly or failing to refer correctly.

> OBJECTIVIST RATIONALITY: Human reason is accurate when it matches objectivist logic, that is, when the symbols used in thought correctly correspond to entities and categories in the world and when the mind reproduces the logical relations that exist objectively among the entities and categories of entities in the world.

From an objectivist point of view, there is a transcendent rationality to the universe, a rationality that goes beyond all beings or minds. That rationality is defined by the logical relations holding among the entities and categories in the world. The successful functioning of human beings in the world is taken to be largely attributable to an ability to meet the standards of objectivist rationality. Human error is typically attributed to a failure to meet that standard.

> OBJECTIVIST KNOWLEDGE: Knowledge consists in correctly conceptualizing and categorizing things in the world and grasping the objective connections among those things and those categories.

To know something is to correctly isolate one or more entities (the things you know something about) and to *correctly* categorize them as to their properties and the relationships holding among them. Objectivism assumes that correctness is independent of the state of people's minds.

THE INDEPENDENCE ASSUMPTION: Existence and fact are independent of belief, knowledge, perception, modes of understanding, and every other aspect of human cognitive capacities. No true fact can depend upon people's believing it, on their knowledge of it, on their conceptualization of it, or on any other aspect of cognition. Existence cannot depend in any way on human cognition.

The world is the way it is, regardless of what people believe or perceive and regardless of any way in which human beings understand the world. Consequently, there is a correct categorization of things in the world independent of human perception or cognition—what we might call a God's eye view. A prerequisite for knowledge is that the symbolic system used in thought be capable of correctly corresponding to objectively existing entities and categories in the world.

Objectivist cognition comes in two common varieties, which differ on the question of how we come to get our concepts. Are we born with them, or do we acquire them through sense perception? The nativist position may have either a religious or evolutionary version. Either God made us so that the symbolic systems of our minds could correspond to the entities and categories in the world, or evolution operated so that creatures whose innate symbolic systems could mirror the world had the best chance of survival.

NATIVIST OBJECTIVIST COGNITION: Our conceptual systems, that is, the symbol systems that we use in thought, are innate and are made meaningful via their capacity to correspond correctly to entities and categories in the world. In other words, our inborn mental representations are "semantically evaluable," that is, capable of being true or false and of referring correctly to entities and categories in the world.

EMPIRICIST OBJECTIVIST COGNITION: We acquire our concepts, that is, the symbol systems that we use in thought, through accurate sense perceptions in such a way that they correspond systematically to entities and categories in the world.

It should be pointed out, incidentally, that *not all nativists are also objectivists.* One can be a nativist and hold a variety of nonobjectivist positions. Thus, for example, there are nativists who believe that some or all of our concepts are inborn but that they do not get their meaning only via their capacity to correspond to things in the world. Nativists who are not objectivists require some other account of the meaningfulness of concepts. As we will discuss in more detail below, it is also possible to be a nativist and an experientialist: one can hold the position that at least some concepts are inborn and that those concepts mean what they do because we are the kinds of beings that we are, rather than because they correspond to some external reality. In fact, we will defend such a position in chapter 17 below.

Objectivist cognition strongly constrains what the categories of mind can be like. Since they must be capable of corresponding to the categories of the world in cases where we can be said to have real knowledge, they must do so via the properties objects have and the relations objects bear to one another. This is done by imposing limitations on what can and cannot constitute a *concept.* Concepts in objectivist cognition are mental representations of categories and objects in the world. In objectivist cognition, concepts by definition exclude all nonobjective influences. If concepts are to be used for representing true knowledge of the external world, they must exclude anything that is outside of correspondences between symbols and things in the real world (or possible worlds.) For example, the properties of basic-level concepts that make them basic-level concepts—dependence on gestalt perception, motor movement, image-formation, and the organization of most knowledge at that level—cannot be true properties of concepts in an objectivist theory. They must be excluded because they are not objective, since they depend on the nature of the beings doing the thinking. Similarly, products of the imagination such as metaphor, metonymy, and mental imagery, which may not be (and usually are not) capable of corresponding to entities in an objectivist world, are banned from the realm of true concepts. Fictional and mythological entities (e.g., Superman and Santa Claus) are another matter. Objectivists usually accommodate them to the objectivist world by making minor modifications, such as permitting possible worlds in which fictional characters reside.

The objectivist's rationale for excluding such imaginative aspects of human psychology as metaphor, metonymy, and mental imagery from the realm of concepts is that these human factors may introduce nonobjective considerations. If these were to enter into our concepts which we use to represent knowledge, then we could not ever be sure of having accurate representations of knowledge. In order to guarantee the possibility of accurate representations of knowledge, our conceptual system, which must be capable of correctly mirroring the world, must by definition be free of metaphor, metonymy, and other such aspects of human cognition. The way knowledge happens to be understood or organized in the human mind, as well as such things as memory or real-time processing, are excluded because they do not mirror the external world. Knowledge is knowledge, regardless of how it is organized, processed, or remembered. Objectivist cognition does not deny the reality of memory or other aspects of cognitive processing, nor does it exclude them from study. It simply requires that our system of concepts be defined independent of cognitive processing. Aspects of cognition can have nothing whatever to do with truth or meaning or correct reason or real knowledge.

Given the goals of objectivist epistemology, we can see how the classical theory of categorization can be seen as working not only for categories of the world but also for conceptual categories.

> A CONCEPTUAL CATEGORY is a symbolic representation of a category in the real world (or some possible world). Members of a conceptual category are those symbolic entities that correspond to entities in the corresponding real-world category (or possible-world category).

The basic properties of conceptual categories follow immediately:

> A conceptual category is defined in terms of necessary and sufficient conditions shared by all members. Such conditions include properties of entities and relations holding among entities.

This allows for complex categories to be logical combinations of less complex categories. And it provides a concept of a conceptual category that excludes experiential aspects of human psychology.

Those categories that are not logical combinations of other categories are taken to be "primitive" building blocks out of which complex categories are constructed.

> CONCEPTUAL ATOMISM: All categories are either primitives or logical combinations of primitives.

The classical theory comes with two general principles of organization for categories: hierarchical categorization and cross-categorization.

> HIERARCHICAL CATEGORIZATION: A partition of a category into subcategories such that all members are in one, and only one, subcategory.

Biological taxonomies are common examples. For instance, we view animals as being elephants, raccoons, tigers, or the like. These group together into larger categories (mammals, etc.) and can be split up into smaller categories (e.g., various kinds of elephants).

> CROSS-CATEGORIZATION: A number of hierarchical categorizations at the same level.

For example, people can be categorized according to an adult-child distinction and a male-female distinction. Each of these is part of a hierarchical categorization: thus, human is hierarchically subcategorized simultaneously as human adult and human child, as well as male human and female human. Terms like *boy, girl, man,* and *woman* are typically used to cross-categorize people in this way. Thus, *boy* is both male and child, *woman* is both female and adult, etc. In the classical theory, hierarchical categorization and cross-categorization are the only organizations of categories that exist.

It is a commonly held assumption that sister categories in a hierarchy can always be minimally distinguished from one another by a single property, called a *distinctive feature.* This assumption has led to the common normative principle that "good" definitions must minimally distinguish sister categories. We will refer to this as the MINIMAL DISTINCTION PRINCIPLE. This principle contrasts with the idea that distinctions among sister categories can be due to clusters of properties, no one of which alone distinguishes the categories. For example, it is this principle that has led scholars to try to find *one* essential characteristic of man that distinguishes him from the other animals. That characteristic is usually taken to be rationality. Of course, there are a great many other ways in which human beings are different from other animals. But it is the view that there must be *one* minimal distinction that leads to such silly debates as whether one should classify man as a rational animal or a featherless biped.

There are also objectivist theories of language and meaning. They are attempts to show how language functions in the service of objectivist rationality, that is, how we can reason correctly about the world using language. Such theories are motivated by a certain narrow conception of meaningfulness. Statements are meaningful only if they can be true or false. Sentences used to express speech acts, like promising or requesting, are meaningful only if there can be a fit between the words of the sentences and objectively existing aspects of the world. Meaning is therefore to be based on truth or, to be more precise, on the capacity to correspond to the objective world. For example, a request is an attempt to make the world conform to the words (see Searle 1979).

Given that objectivist semantics is an attempt to show how language functions in correct human reason, it requires the following fundamental assumption:

> OBJECTIVIST SEMANTICS: Linguistic expressions get their meaning only via their capacity to correspond, or failure to correspond, to the real world or some possible world; that is, they are capable of referring correctly (say, in the case of noun phrases) or of being true or false (in the case of sentences).

Objectivist semantics comes in two common varieties, cognitivist and noncognitivist.

COGNITIVIST OBJECTIVIST SEMANTICS: Linguistic expressions (e.g., words) get their meaning indirectly via a correspondence with concepts which are taken to be symbols used in thought. Those symbols, in turn, get their meaning via their capacity to correspond to entities and categories in the world.

NONCOGNITIVIST OBJECTIVIST SEMANTICS: Linguistic expressions can correspond to objects and categories of objects in the world directly, without reference to any system of concepts used by human beings.

In both versions, expressions in a natural language are seen as being capable of corresponding to the world in basically the same way. Referring expressions (like proper names and definite noun phrases) designate entities, like *the Eiffel Tower*. Predicates (like verbs and adjectives) designate properties, like *tall,* and relations, like *taller than.* And sentences are true when the entities designated have the properties predicated of them (*The Eiffel Tower is tall*) or stand in the relations predicated of them (*The Eiffel Tower is taller than the Lincoln Memorial*).

Meaning is then based on truth. The meaning of a sentence is taken to be its truth conditions—the conditions under which the sentence would be true. Basic meaning-relations are defined as follows:

ENTAILMENT: *A* entails *B* if and only if *B* is true in every situation in which *A* is true.

SAMENESS OF MEANING: *A* and *B* have the same meaning if and only if *A* and *B* are true in exactly the same situations and false in exactly the same situations.

Another bifurcation, one that we mentioned above, occurs within objectivist semantics.

THE REFERENCE-VIA-MEANING DOCTRINE (Frege): Words have inherent meanings (called *intensions*) and designate objects by virtue of those meanings. Competent speakers of a language know and make use of those meanings.

THE DIRECT-REFERENCE DOCTRINE (Putnam 1975*b*): The meaning of a word has three parts: (1) an indication of what *kind* of thing in the world the word correctly refers to; (2) an extension, that is, a direct specification of exactly which things in the world the word correctly refers to; and (3) a *stereotype,* that is, a conventional idea associated with a word, which might well be inaccurate. Competent users of the language must know the stereotype. But the stereotype may be wrong, and so even a competent user may not be able to apply the word correctly. In the case of words denoting natural kinds, the correct application of the word is to be determined by a community of experts.

The reference-via-meaning doctrine is usually attributed to Gottlob Frege (1966), while the direct-reference doctrine originated with Hilary Putnam's essay "The Meaning of Meaning" (1975*b*) and, in a somewhat different form, with Saul Kripke's "Naming and Necessity" (1972). Putnam justifies his view with the example of a tiger. The tiger stereotype would contain the information that tigers have stripes, even though the existence of entirely white tigers has been authenticated. Stripes may not be correctly ascribed to every tiger, but they are part of the conventional idea of what a tiger is.

Putnam's 1975 account of meaning is objectivist in most, but not quite all, ways. His account of direct reference and of natural kinds assumes the correctness of objectivist metaphysics. Since his account of direct reference (the inclusion of extensions as part of meaning) tells how words can fit the world directly, Putnam's theory is a variety of objectivist semantics. His account also takes for granted the independence of metaphysics from epistemology, since his stereotypes (which are purely epistemological) may not determine correct reference or truth.

Putnam does, however, take one important step away from objectivism, in that he does not assume objectivist cognition: his account of stereotypes does not require that the concepts we think in terms of correspond to entities and categories in the world. For this reason his account of stereotypes is sometimes linked to prototype theory, even though his technical term *stereotype* is not exactly either a prototype or a social stereotype. Putnam's stereotypes come closest to what we have called ICMs, though they are specified much more vaguely, and, as we saw in chapter 7 above, differ from ICMs in crucial ways.

Reference and Natural Kinds

Before we go on, we should make clear the crucial role that the concept of *natural kind* plays in the objectivist accounts of reference. Take a sentence like

– All zebras eat grass.

In order to determine whether such a sentence is true, on an objectivist account, one must be able to pick out all the members of the category *zebra*. This means there must *be* a category *zebra* objectively existing in the world. It is the doctrine of natural kinds that makes this appear unproblematical. On the reference-via-meaning doctrine, the meaning (more precisely, the intension) of the word *zebra* denotes the natural kind *zebra,* and the sentence is true if and only if all the members of that natural kind category eat grass. On the direct-reference doctrine, there must be an objectively existing natural kind *zebra* for the word to "correctly" refer to, before one can determine whether all its members eat grass. Putnam (1975*b*) assumes that the correct application of the word *zebra*—that is, the natural kind that the word correctly refers to—would be determined by a community of experts, in this case, biologists. Both accounts of reference rely on the objective existence of natural kinds in order for statements about classes of objects to be meaningful.

Brute Facts and Institutional Facts

All objectivists recognize brute facts, those that are true regardless of any human institution. Thus, someone's height is a brute fact, as is the atomic weight of gold. Many objectivists also recognize institutional facts—those that are true by virtue of some human institution. Someone's social standing and the dollar value of gold are institutional facts.

Institutional facts have not been studied in any great depth within objectivist philosophy, linguistics, and cognitive psychology. And as we shall see below, they present problems for certain objectivist positions, especially the Independence Assumption. The problem arises in the following way:

> Since institutions are products of human cognition, institutional facts must depend on human cognition, which violates the Independence Assumption, which states that *no* facts can be dependent on human cognition.

To my knowledge, this is an unresolved problem within objectivist philosophy. Also unresolved is the question of whether a clear division exists between brute facts and institutional facts. This question arises in its most controversial form in the case of scientific institutions (e.g., scientific theories, criteria for measurement, etc.). Scientific institutions are devised by communities of scientists and they are concerned with what are taken to be brute facts. The problem is that those so-called brute facts are dependent in many ways on those institutions—on agreements about measuring instruments, theories of measurement, acceptable uses of statistics, and broad scientific theories—all of which are in significant part the products of the minds of scientists. This problem has not been adequately resolved within the objectivist tradition, and it appears unresolvable.

Within objectivist philosophy of language, the only important use that has been made of the idea of institutional facts has been to try to make natural languages fit the objectivist paradigm by viewing them as human institutions that can be accounted for in an objectivist framework. With a language considered as a human institution, linguistic expressions and their meanings are then taken to be objectively real entities that have an existence independent of their use by any particular person on any given occasion. Thus, the distinction is drawn between sentence meaning—the meaning of a sentence, which is fixed regardless of how anyone uses it—and speaker meaning, which might, for example, in the case of irony be the opposite of sentence meaning. Within objectivist semantics, it is sentence meaning—which is fixed and defined in terms of its capacity to fit a real or possible world—that is of central importance. "Semantics" then is taken to be a technical term having to do with sentence meaning and truth conditions. The study of how sentences are used and what speakers mean by what they say is segregated off as "pragmatics." Semantics is by definition independent of pragmatics, since semantic meaning is defined in terms of fixed truth conditions independent of the use of a sentence by any speaker.

The semantics-pragmatics distinction introduces an all-important set of values into the study of meaning. Semantics is given a central role, because it specifies connections between language and the objective world. Pragmatics is taken to be peripheral, and of secondary interest, since it is not concerned with anything having to do with objective reality, but "merely" with human communication. The assumption that pragmatics is based on semantics is used to justify these values: semantics must be understood first, before pragmatics can be approached. Semantics is also taken to be much more philosophically important than pragmatics, since it deals with matters of ontology and truth, rather than merely with matters of human psychology.

The Doctrine of Correct Definition

Recall that entities are assumed to have two *kinds* of properties, essential and accidental. The accidental properties are those that the object just happens to have, while the essential properties characterize the kind of object it is. The assumption is that accidental properties might have been different, but essential properties could not have been, given that the entity is the kind of thing it is. Thus, elephants might have evolved in

North America rather than Africa and Asia, and they would still have been elephants. But if no mammals with trunks, large ears, large bodies, and thick legs had evolved, then there wouldn't have been any elephants.

The metaphysical distinction between essential and contingent properties induces an epistemological distinction between two kinds of knowledge—definitional knowledge and encyclopedic knowledge. Definitional knowledge is knowledge of the essential properties of words, and encyclopedic knowledge is knowledge of the contingent properties of words. On this view, the words of a language have an objective institutional status. Since words are objectively existing entities, they have essential and contingent properties. For this reason, objectivists hold that words have *correct definitions*—definitions that are objectively correct as a matter of institutional fact.

The correspondence between words, on the one hand, and entities and categories in the world, on the other, induces a correspondence between the essential properties of words and the essential properties of those entities and categories:

- Our *definitional* knowledge of words corresponds to the *essential* properties of the entities and categories that the words designate.
- Our *encyclopedic* knowledge of words corresponds to the *contingent* properties of the entities and properties that the words designate.

Objectivist linguists refer to this distinction between definitional and other knowledge as the *dictionary-encyclopedia* distinction. It is a technical distinction, induced by the rest of the objectivist paradigm. It is a consequence of the objectivist paradigm extended to include language as a matter of objective institutional fact.

The objectivist paradigm also induces what is known as the *literal-figurative* distinction. A literal meaning is one that is capable of fitting reality, that is, of being objectively true or false. Figurative expressions are defined as those that do not have meanings that can directly fit the world in this way. If metaphors and metonymies have any meaning at all, they must have some other, related literal meaning. Thus, metaphor and metonymy are not subjects for objectivist semantics at all. The only viable alternative is to view them as part of pragmatics—the study of a speaker's meaning. Moreover, it follows from the objectivist definition of *definition* itself that metaphor and metonymy cannot be part of definitions. They cannot even be part of concepts, since concepts must involve a *direct* correspondence to entities and categories in the real world (or a possible world). These are not empirical results. They are simply further consequences of the objectivist paradigm.

An interesting discussion within this tradition is Rey 1983. Writing from a direct-reference perspective, Rey hails the Putnam-Kripke view as properly distinguishing metaphysics from epistemology and "denying definitions any essential epistemological role." Thus, he maintains, Putnam and Kripke save the classical view of categorization from "often capricious epistemological possibilities" and "purported psychological evidence." "The correct definition of a concept," Rey claims, "need not be known by the concept's competent users." The reason is that *correct definition* has nothing to do with anything in any speaker's mind. It has to do with the *correct* relationship between words and the objective world. "The appeal to experts for the correct definition simply becomes a piece of the appeal to experts on behalf of *any* knowledge."

In summary, the objectivist paradigm bases cognition on a metaphysical account of reality—all reality is made up of objectively existing entities with properties and relations among them. Some properties are essential and others are not. Classical categorization links categories to properties. Objectivist cognition assumes that people reason in terms of abstract symbols and that those symbols get their meaning via a correspondence between those symbols on the one hand and entities and categories in the world on the other. Concepts are symbols used in thought that stand in correspondence to entities and categories in the world—the actual world or some possible state of the world. Objectivist semantics assumes that linguistic meaning is based on a correspondence between words and the world, in some versions via concepts and in some versions not. The objectivist concept of *definition* is itself *defined* using all these assumptions. But since the assumptions are taken for granted and barely noticed, the objectivist concept of definition is assumed to be natural—the only one possible. Other views of definition, for example, Fillmore's view that definition is relative to ICMs, cannot not be considered since ICMs are not part of the objectivist world view.

The Relationship between Concepts and the Body

The objectivist account of cognition, meaning, and rationality makes no mention of the nature of who or what is doing the thinking. The nature of the human organism and the way it functions is irrelevant to the objectivist account of meaningful thought and reason. Thought is characterized as symbol-manipulation. Concepts are characterized as symbols in a system bearing a fixed correspondence to things and categories in the world. Those symbols are made meaningful *only* via symbol-to-word correspondences. Correct reason is viewed as symbol-manipulation that accurately mirrors the rational structure of the world. Meaning and rationality are *transcendental*—they transcend the limitations of any particular kind of being. Rational beings merely partake of transcendental rationality. Thus, in the characterization of what concepts and meaning and rationality are, there can be no mention of the nature of the human organism.

This is as it should be if "real knowledge" on the objectivist account is to be possible. Real knowledge must be expressed in concepts that must be about things as they really are—objectively, from a God's eye view. If human beings are to have real knowledge, then the idiosyncrasies of human organisms had better not get in the way. But this does not mean that bodies can play no role at all in objectivist cognition. Far from it.

Take perception, for example. The perceptual mechanisms of the body, on the objectivist view, are means of gathering information and checking on it. It is assumed that, on the whole, perception is veridical—what you see (and hear and touch, etc.) is by and large an accurate guide to what there is. Perception is viewed as the means by which we establish correct correspondences between external reality and the symbol system in terms of which we think. Of course, perception isn't perfect by any means. Perception is limited. It sometimes fools us. And many kinds of knowledge are beyond what we can perceive directly. The body thus aids in the acquisition of conceptual information, and it may limit our ability to conceptualize.

What the human body does not do, on the objectivist account, is add anything essential to concepts that does not correspond to what is objectively present in the structure of the world. The body does not play an essential role in giving concepts meaning. That would introduce a nonobjective aspect to meaning. And the body plays no role in characterizing the nature of reason.

The Intuitions behind Objectivism

What we have here is a collection of fairly abstract claims about the world, the mind, reason, and language. The concept of a category sits in the center of this collection of metaphysical and cognitive claims and holds them together. It is the *classical* concept of a category, the concept that contemporary research on prototype theory claims is untenable as a fully general approach. If that concept changes in an essential way, then most, if not all, of objectivist metaphysics and epistemology goes. What is at stake is a world view, especially a view of thought, rationality, and language. As we have stated these positions, they sound fairly obscure—the sort of thing only a philosopher could care about, much less believe. But putting aside what from our view are minor variations (nativism versus empiricism, mentalism versus nonmentalism, direct-reference versus reference-via-meaning), this metaphysics is at the center of much of our ordinary commonsense understanding of the world.

There is a certain range of everyday experiences with physical objects that make such metaphysical assumptions seem natural and inescapable. There is a table next to me. It has a top and is brown. I am an entity and so is the table. Having a top is a property of the table, as is being brown. "Next to" is a relation between me and the table. All this fits objectivist metaphysics. If the table had no top at all, it wouldn't be a table; it would be a different kind of object. But if I painted it red, it would still be table—in fact, it would be the same table. This fits essentialist metaphysics. Having a top seems to be an essential property of a table, while being brown is an incidental property.

And much of commonsense psychology is a version of objectivist cognition. I have a concept of what a table is. That concept corresponds to tables, not to tigers, clouds, or baseball gloves. And if something is a table, I can conclude by correct human reason that it has a top and that it isn't a kangaroo. And many of our commonsense conceptions of language fit objectivist semantics. The word "table" in English designates tables; it doesn't designate elephants or roses or automobiles. And if I use the word "table" consistently to refer to roses, then I am misusing the word.

Such observations are often used to justify objectivist metaphysics as being simply a matter of ordinary common sense. And there is at least a grain of truth in it. Such metaphysical assumptions certainly won't get us into trouble when we are dealing with tables and other familiar physical objects. But such commonsense assumptions about physical objects do not necessarily extend to other domains. When we use them to deal with political movements, inflation, friendships, marriage, our emotions, and our foreign policy, the results are not always happy ones. In such cases, the entities and properties are by no means so clear, nor is the distinction between what is essential and what is accidental. And rationality in such matters is not merely a matter of computing objectively existing logical relations among objectively existing categories of objectively existing entities. It is a much more creative enterprise.

Providing an alternative to the classical theory of categorization will require going beyond the discussion of categorization alone. What will be ultimately involved is providing a viable alternative to the objectivist world view—an alternative that works at least as well for the commonsense cases, yet one that fits the kind of phenomena that go beyond the classical theory.

Scientific Objectivism

Objectivism as we have been describing it is a general view of the nature of language, meaningful thought, and rationality. As such, it makes claims about all of natural language and all human concepts. There is, however, a much more restricted version of objectivism that makes no claim about human concepts and human language in general. Instead, it limits the claims of objectivism to the domain of science. We will refer to this as *scientific objectivism.*

Scientific objectivism grew out of the now-discredited view that science works strictly by the hypothetico-deductive method. According to that view, scientists frame hypotheses, deduce logical consequences from those hypotheses, and test those consequences to see if they accord with the facts. If scientific knowledge was to be true, objective knowledge, hypotheses would have to be stated in a precisely formulated symbolic language, free of vagueness and ambiguity. Deductions would have to be performed using a precisely formulated calculus. And systematic connections would have to be made between the symbols in the language and the appropriate things in the physical world. The physical world, of course, was taken to be structured according to objectivist metaphysics.

The assumption made was that natural languages and everyday human concepts were too vague or ambiguous or otherwise unsuitable to the needs of science. Objectivist views might not hold for the sloppy or fanciful concepts of everyday language and thought, but they could be made to hold for the "hard" sciences—physics, chemistry, and biology at least, with physics taken as a model of what a science should be. If objectivist constraints could be placed on the language and concepts of the hard sciences, then true, objective knowledge would be possible in science on the assumption that objectivist metaphysics is correct for the subject matter of the physical sciences.

Scientific objectivism, therefore, does not claim to be a general approach to the study of language, meaningful thought, and human reason. It does not have, and does not claim to have, an account of how people ordinarily think, or of what makes our ordinary concepts meaningful, or of what constitutes human reason. So far as most ordinary language and thought are concerned, it has nothing whatever to say. It makes claims only for the "hard"sciences.

It is important to distinguish scientific objectivism from scientific realism in general. Scientific realism is a form of basic realism. Scientific realism assumes that there is a real physical world and that scientific knowledge of it is possible within appropriate standards set by communities of scientists. Scientific realism is thus compatible both with scientific objectivism and with experientialism as we will discuss it in chapter 17. Both are forms of scientific realism.

What scientific objectivism adds to scientific realism is the entire objectivist paradigm, especially objectivist metaphysics, with its commitment to classical categorization, and objectivist semantics, with its view that symbols are given meaning independent of the nature of the human organism. Such assumptions are by no means necessary to scientific realism, nor to responsible science. In fact, as we shall see in chapter 12, scientific objectivism can get in the way of responsible science.

Incidentally, scientific objectivism says nothing whatever about ordinary human concepts and language. It has no account at all of most meaningful human thought. It is, at least in principle, willing to grant that objectivist philosophy may not be applicable at all outside of the physical sciences and that a general account of language and thought will not be objectivist in nature.

The Mathematization of Objectivist Semantics

The great achievements in mathematical logic and the foundations of mathematics, stemming from the work of Gottlob Frege, have led to the use of mathematical techniques to formalize objectivist metaphysics and semantics precisely. There is a good reason for this. Classical mathematics can very naturally be viewed as an objectivist universe, consisting of entities (numbers, points, lines, planes, etc.) with fixed properties (prime, even) and relations among them (greater than, square of). With this in mind, it is not surprising that the techniques that provided the foundations for classical mathematics should have been applied to the formalization of objectivist metaphysics and semantics.

Such techniques have the very great merit of making objectivist approaches sufficiently precise so that they can be evaluated. But before we argue that the techniques that work so well in the foundations of mathematics are deficient for human cognition and human language, we need to have some idea of what those techniques are.

Let us start with objectivist metaphysics, in which the world consists of entities, with properties and with relations holding among them. The goal is to construct mathematical models that can correspond one to one with any given objectivist universe. That is, we need to construct one-to-one correspondences for objects, their properties, and the relations among them.

OBJECTS: Let objects be represented by abstract entities of any kind.

PROPERTIES OF OBJECTS: In a given state of affairs, every property will be in one-to-one correspondence with the set of objects having that property. Let that set of objects correspond to the property.

RELATIONS AMONG OBJECTS: For any n-place relation, there will be a set of n-tuples (e.g., pairs, triples) of objects standing in that relation. Let the set of n-tuples correspond to that relation.

Since *n*-tuples can be defined entirely in terms of sets, the model uses nothing but entities and sets. This gives us a set-theoretical model of an objectivist universe at a single instant. This is called a "state description." To add a time dimension, we take another set of abstract entities. Let each of them correspond to an instant of time, and add a relation ordering them linearly so that they form a model of a time line. A model of an objectivist universe that extends through time is a set of pairings of entities on the time line with state descriptions of the universe at each instant.

Using set-theoretical apparatus in this way, it is possible to construct variations on such models. "Situation semantics," for example, uses only partial state descriptions, that is, models of "local" situations, in which only parts of objectivist universes are modeled. "Possible world semantics" adds a set of abstract entities called "worlds" and constructs pairings of such world entities and state descriptions. Abstract entities specifying times, worlds, and various situational factors are called "points of reference."

Before proceeding, I should point out that people who do model theory of this kind don't really construct set-theoretical models of the universe, picking out abstract entities for each entity in the universe. This is obviously an impossible and pointless task. What is done instead is to give precise representations that will characterize (or "generate") the class of such models.

Given such representations of models of objectivist universes (including possible ones), one can construct the notion of a "concept" in objectivist cognition. They are sometimes also called "intensional concepts," or just "intensions." "Intensions" are contrasted with "extensions." Extensions are just things in an individual state description, that is, entities, sets of entities, sets of pairs of entities, etc. Consider the concept of United States senator. At present, its extension is just the set containing the present one hundred U.S. senators. But the people who happen to be U.S. senators at present don't characterize the general concept of what a U.S. senator is. What we need is a set-theoretical construction that will be in one-to-one correspondence with the concept of U.S. senator. The following is such a construction:

- An *intension* is a function from points of reference to extensions.

That is, an intension is a set of pairs of the form "(*P*,*E*)", where "*P*" is point of reference (say a time, possible situation, etc.) and "*E*" is an extension—namely, an element in a model of an objectivist universe (say an entity, a set of entities, etc.). Thus, for example, one pair in the intension might be

(1984, {Ted Kennedy, Gary Hart, ... })

and another pair in the intension might be

(1960, {John Kennedy, Hubert Humphrey, ... }).

Each pair would consist of a time paired with the set of senators at that time. Given a time, the function would pick out the set of U.S. senators at that time. Intensions are often taken as characterizing meanings of linguistic expressions. As a consequence, two expressions with the same meaning are assumed to have the same intensions. For example, the same intension would have to be assigned to "U.S. senator" as to the synonymous expression "member of the upper house of the U.S. Congress." This is in principle possible in such a theory and is often cited as a justification for using intensions as representations for categories of mind. Such details are, however, seldom worked out.

Incidentally, there are concepts where the extension is the same in all points of reference—at all times and in all possible situations. Mathematical concepts are taken to be the clearest such examples. For example, the extension of "prime number" is assumed not to vary with time or circumstance. This is also true of concepts that are based on essential properties. Since essential properties supposedly don't change from context to context, the intension of such a concept will correspond one to one with the extension, namely, the set of things with the given essential properties.

In summary, intensions are commonly taken as models of objectivist concepts. Technically, intensions are functions from points of reference (abstract entities) to extensions. Since a function is definable in terms of sets of pairs, and pairs are definable in terms of sets, and extensions are definable in terms of abstract entities and sets, an intension is a purely set-theoretical construction. A major issue that we will be discussing below is whether such set-theoretical models of concepts are adequate to account for the facts of human categorization. As should be obvious, such models of concepts make no use of any experiential aspects of human cognition. That is, intensions have nothing in them corresponding to human perceptual abilities, imaging capacities, motor abilities, etc. In this respect, they fit the requirements of objectivist cognition. If objectivist cognition is wrong, if gestalt perception, mental images and motor abilities do play a role in our conceptual system—then intensions are not the right kinds of mathematical tools for modeling human concepts. Studies of natural categorization seem to lead to this conclusion.

Classical Categorization within Linguistics

In the past, linguists have generally shied away from the question of what categories are like and have either accepted the classical theory without question, or have left the matter to the philosophers, psychologists, and anthropologists. But most of the discussion of categorization within the philosophical, psychological, and anthropological literature is focused on concrete objects—plants, animals, artifacts, people. It is important that the focus be enlarged to include categories in nonphysical domains. The nonphysical domains—emotions, language, social institutions, etc.—are perhaps the most important ones for the study of mind. Since the conceptual structure of such domains cannot be viewed as merely a mirror of nature, the study of such domains may thus provide a clearer guide to the workings of the mind. Here is where linguists may be of help. Human language provides an immensely rich source of examples of categorization that is not only abstract, but also automatic and almost entirely unconscious.

Each human language is structured in terms of an enormously complex system of categories of various kinds: phonetic, phonological, morphological, lexical, syntactic, semantic, and pragmatic. Linguistic categories are among the kinds of abstract categories that any adequate theory of the human conceptual system must be able to account for. Human language is therefore an important source of evidence for the nature of cognitive categories. Conversely, general results concerning the nature of cognitive categorization should affect the theory of categorization used in theorizing about language. If languages make use of the kinds of categories used by the mind in general, then the theory of language is very much bound up with general issues in cognition.

On the whole, linguists have simply taken for granted the classical theory of categorization, which has been with us since the time of Aristotle and which has been given a contemporary mathematical treatment in terms of set-theoretical models of the sort discussed above. Contemporary formal semantics is almost entirely based on such models, which consist of nothing but abstract entities and sets, and sets of sets, and sets of sets of sets, etc. Sets are at the heart of all modern versions of the classical theory of categorization and formal semantics as well.

This is also true of every aspect of generative linguistics, whether phonology, syntax, or semantics. In generative phonology, distinctive features correspond to sets. Segments marked $+F$ are in the set, and those marked $-F$ are in the complement of the set. In generative phonological notation, square brackets indicate set intersection and curly brackets indicate set union. The same is true of syntactic features, and since they define syntactic categories, syntactic categories are defined within generative linguistics in terms of classical sets. A language, within generative linguistics, is defined as a set of sentences, and a grammar as a set of rules that characterizes the set of sentences. The sentences are sequences (ordered sets) of phonological feature matrices (set intersections). The semantics is Fregean. In virtually every respect, generative linguistics rests on the classical theory of categorization as it has been interpreted in the Fregean tradition—the assumption that the humanly relevant notion of a category can be adequately represented via a set-theoretical version of an objectivist theory of categories.

Should the classical theory of categorization turn out to be inadequate, as we will be claiming, then the foundations of contemporary linguistic theory are called into question.

Some of the basic results discussed here are not new. Wittgenstein's discussion of family resemblances and Rosch's early results are, at least in their bare outlines, well-known. Yet they have not been taken seriously enough. Within linguistics, on the contrary, great pains have been taken to insulate generative linguistics from such results. Generative linguistics has set up two major lines of defense against any such empirical findings.

First, there is the performance-competence distinction, which is sufficiently manipulable so that almost any experimental result from psychology can, at least initially, be claimed to be in the realm of mere performance and thus can be ignored. Such an interpretation of Rosch's experimental results has been attempted by Osherson and Smith (1981) and by Armstrong, Gleitman, and Gleitman (1983). In both cases, it is claimed that Rosch's results are due to the vagaries of perception and not to cognitive structure. Counterarguments were provided in chapter 9 above.

Second, generative grammar is *defined* so as to be independent of general cognitive capabilities. Consequently, any demonstration that classical categorization is inadequate for general cognition will be irrelevant to generative linguistics. Since this is not a widely known property of generative linguistics, it is worth a brief discussion.

Generative linguistics (in the Chomskyan tradition) takes for granted that there is an autonomous language faculty that makes no use at all of *general* cognitive capacities. This is not an idle assumption on the part of generative linguistics. It is an assumption that is necessary in order to maintain the basic metaphor on which generative linguistics is based, namely, A GRAMMAR IS A FORMAL SYSTEM. A *formal system* is a collection of rewriting rules that can mimic an algorithmic computation. The theory of generative linguistics is mathematically characterized in terms of such algorithmic systems, which manipulate symbols without regard to their meaning. By definition, an algorithmic system is one in which no algorithm can be sensitive to the way a symbol is semantically interpreted. If a generative grammar is such a system, then it is by definition required that no interpretation of the symbols—no meaning, no understanding of them—can be made use of in any rule of grammar. To do so would be to abandon the theory of generative linguistics—to give up on the basic metaphor that a grammar is a formal system in the technical sense.

All mathematical results having to do with the generative capacity of such systems require that no interpretations of the symbols can be used in the rules. Similarly, any use of a general cognitive capacity would require a step outside of the formal system metaphor and thus would constitute an abandonment of the mathematical concept of generative capacity as it is defined for such systems. The paradigm in which generative linguistics is defined absolutely requires a strong assumption of the autonomy of syntax from semantics and of the language faculty from any external cognitive influence.

Generative linguistics seeks to find a class of such systems that is both rich enough and restricted enough to account for the formal properties of natural languages. Generative linguistics claims that some collection of algorithmic devices—devices that manipulate symbols without recourse to their meaning or to any general cognitive capacity—will *constitute* the human language capacity. The entire framework requires that categorization be set-theoretical in nature. And any discussion of general cognitive capacities is simply beside the point, as is any discussion of empirical disconfirmation by reference to any general properties of cognition. Phenomena that do not fit must be, *by definition*, due to influences outside the linguistic system.

It seems extremely unlikely that human beings do not make use of general cognitive capacities in language. It is bizarre to assume that language ignores general cognitive apparatus, especially when it comes to something as basic as categorization. Considering that categorization enters fundamentally into every aspect of language, it would be very strange to assume that the mind in general used one kind of categorization and that language used an entirely different one. But strange as such an assumption is, it is a standard assumption behind mainstream contemporary linguistics. We will be challenging that assumption below, by arguing that the classical theory of categorization is as wrong for language as it is for the rest of the mind.

The Empirical Status of the Objectivist Paradigm

The objectivist doctrines on what semantics is, what concepts are, and what definitions are, as well as objectivist distinctions such as the semantics-pragmatics distinction and the dictionary-encyclopedia distinction are widely accepted in Anglo-American philosophy, linguistics, and cognitive psychology. Given the wide acceptance of these doctrines and the distinctions based on them, one might think that the objectivist paradigm rested upon a broad range of in-depth empirical studies of languages and conceptual systems. But that is not true at all. There have been relatively few detailed studies and the analyses that have been given either don't work very well or don't extend very far. At present the use of the objectivist paradigm in empirical semantic studies is simply an article of faith. As we shall see in the case studies given below, the objectivist paradigm does not even come close to working.

The Objectivist Legacy

According to the objectivist paradigm, true knowledge of the external world can only be achieved if the system of symbols we use in thinking can accurately represent the external world. The objectivist conception of mind must therefore rule out anything that can get in the way of that: perception, which can fool us; the body, which has its frailties; society, which has its pressures and special interests; memories, which can fade; mental images, which can differ from person to person; and imagination—especially metaphor and metonymy—which cannot fit the objectively given external world.

It is our objectivist legacy that we view rationality as being purely mental, unemotional, detached—independent of imagination, of social functioning, and of the limitations of our bodies and our memories. It is our objectivist legacy that leads us to view reasoning as mechanical and to glorify those kinds of reasoning that in fact *are* mechanical. It is our objectivist legacy that leads us to view machines that are capable of algorithmic computation as being capable of human reason. And it is our objectivist legacy that we view it as progress when we are able to structure aspects of our physical and social environment to make it more like an objectivist universe.

The advent of the digital computer has accelerated our attempts to make our environment and our society fit objectivist metaphysics. This has nothing to do with the computer itself, which is a marvelous tool capable of all sorts of uses—humane and inhumane. But the development of computer science is bound up with the development of the foundations of mathematics. As a result, the most common kind of data base now in use happens to fit an objectivist metaphysics: It stores representations of entities, their properties, and the relations holding among them. In your bank's computer, you might be represented by your bank account number, together with your bank balance on various dates, your credit rating on various dates, etc. The data base of your bank's computer is an objectivist universe. In it you *are* your account number and your properties are your bank balance and your credit rating. People have been treated as numbers and collections of records for a long time, and they will be treated much more so in the future.

Such treatment serves an important function in our society. There is a major folk theory in our society according to which being objective is being fair, and human judgment is subject to error or likely to be biased. Consequently decisions concerning people should be made on "objective" grounds as often as possible. It is the major way that people who make decisions avoid blame. If there are "objective" criteria on which to base a decision, then one cannot be blamed for being biased, and consequently one cannot be criticized, demoted, fired, or sued.

Another reason for the attempt to construct our institutions according to objectivist metaphysics is that it is supposed to be efficient. In some cases it may be, in others it may not be. But an awful lot of time and effort goes into trying to make matters of human judgment fit what are supposed to be objective pigeonholes. If the classical theory of categorization is not correct, then the wholesale importation of objectivist metaphysics into our institutions may be not only inhumane, but it may in the long run be an inefficient way for human beings to function. At the very least we should be aware that our institutions are being structured in terms of a particular metaphysics and a psychological theory of categorization which, as we shall see, is highly questionable.

One of the reasons why the classical theory of categorization is becoming more, rather than less, popular, is that it is built into the foundations of mathematics and into much of our current computer software. Since mathematical and computer models are being used more and more as intellectual tools in the cognitive sciences, it is not surprising that there is considerable pressure to keep the traditional theory of classification at all costs. It fits the available intellectual tools, and abandoning it would require the development of new intellectual tools. And retooling is no more popular in the academy than in industry.

CHAPTER 12

What's Wrong with Objectivist Metaphysics

Evidence from fields such as linguistics and cognitive psychology can only have a bearing on objectivist semantics and cognition—it can have no bearing on the correctness of objectivist metaphysics. The only kind of evidence that has a bearing on the question of what exists external to human beings is scientific evidence from fields that study appropriate phenomena. Biology is one such area. The objectivist claim that classical categories exist objectively in the external world is usually taken to be supported by biological evidence. Objectivist philosophers typically point to biological categories like *tiger, crow, fish, zebra,* etc., which they take as paradigm cases of *natural kinds*—classical categories that occur in nature and that are defined by essential necessary and sufficient conditions. This view of natural kinds is taken as being supported by scientific biology.

But, as we have seen, the situation in biology is more complex than that. There are three competing views of biological taxonomy: the cladistic, the phenetic, and the evolutionist position. The latter makes use of both phenetic and historical criteria. We will begin by considering what the dispute between the cladists and pheneticists means for objectivist metaphysics, and then we turn to a close look at why evolutionary biology disconfirms objectivist metaphysics.

Zebras and Fish

Let us begin with Gould's cases of *zebra* and *fish* (see chap. 8 above). In these cases, there are at least two different categorizations of living things, based on conflicting scientific criteria. By phenetic criteria (overall similarity), there are taxonomic catetories *zebra* and *fish*. But by cladistic criteria (shared derived characters), no such "natural kinds" exist, because there are no such categories in a cladist's taxonomy. If each kind of criterion reflects an aspect of reality, what is an objectivist to say? For an objectivist, natural kinds must either exist or not—independent of any criteria judged relevant by human beings. Objectivists must make a choice—just as Gould felt he had to. The common sense alternative—that if you ask different questions, you get different answers—is not available.

Take the example

- There are two zebras in my yard.

Suppose there are two animals in my yard, and one is a Grevey's zebra and the other is a mountain zebra. By phenetic criteria, there is a natural kind *zebra* that both animals belong to. But by cladistic criteria, there is no natural kind that both animals belong to. Both kinds of criteria have some real status, but they address different concerns—history versus current similarity. Is only one of these objectively true? Does there exist a natural kind that both animals belong to or doesn't there? This question must have a single, determinate answer in order to provide truth conditions for the above sentence; the sentence is true just in case there are two entities in my yard that are members of an objectively existing natural kind denoted by the word *zebra*. In objectivist semantics, the truth conditions of the sentence depend on a preexisting metaphysical reality of the right kind.

The same problem arises for a sentence like

- Harry caught a fish.

Suppose he caught a coelacanth. By phenetic criteria, this sentence would be true, but by cladistic criteria it would be false. Objectivism requires that there be an absolutely correct answer. But there is no objectivist rationale for choosing one set of scientific criteria over another, and there isn't even any reason to believe that there is one and only one objectively correct answer. The objectivist criterion for being in the same category is having common properties. But there is no objectivist criterion for *which properties* are to count. The cladists and pheneticists have different criteria for which properties to take into consideration, and there is no standard, independent of human interests and concerns, that can choose between them and provide a unique answer. But objectivist metaphysics requires just such an objective standard. Either there is an objectively existing natural kind *zebra* or not—there is no third choice.

So which is it? Is *fish* a natural kind or not? What about *zebra?* What kinds of properties are *really,* that is objectively, essential—the cladists' (shared derived characters) or the pheneticists' (those that characterize overall similarity). If each answer has *some* scientific validity, then any *one* answer misses a truth. If both kinds of criteria have some claim on reality, then the philosophical concept of a natural kind does not accord with our scientific understanding of the natural world. Rather, *natural kind* seems to be part of our folk conception of the world, not part of any scientific conceptual system that there will ultimately be general agreement on. As we saw, the concept *natural kind* plays an absolutely crucial role in objectivist metaphysics. Yet any objectivist notion of natural kind will miss some scientific criterion for categorization.

There is an obvious escape route here than an objectivist might reasonably attempt—saying that one scientific view is right and the other wrong. Let us look closely at exactly what that would entail. The most remarkable consequence is that the objectivist metaphysician who wants to keep the familiar natural kinds in biology must give up the theory of evolution! But that is perhaps the best supported scientific theory of our time.

The Species

According to evolutionary biology, species are not natural kinds in the technical objectivist sense, namely, classical categories defined by common essential properties. In fact, species in evolutionary biology are not classical categories at all.

Perhaps the best place to start is with the discussion of various concepts of the species by Ernst Mayr (1963, 1984*a*). As Mayr observes, the preevolutionary Linnaean view of a biological category did fit the objectivist picture.

> The typological species concept, going back to the philosophies of Plato and Aristotle (and thus sometimes called the essentialist concept), was the species concept of Linnaeus and his followers (Cain 1958). According to this concept, the observed diversity of the universe reflects the existence of a limited number of underlying "universals" or types (*eidos* of Plato). . . . The presence of the same underlying essence is inferred from similarity, and morphological similarity is, therefore, the species criterion for the essentialist. (Mayr 1984a, p. 532)

Preevolutionary Linnaean taxonomy is an instance of the classical theory of categories. It turned out not to be consistent with the theory of evolution. One major problem is variation. A species does not have a uniform internal structure, with all members sharing a given set of defining properties uniformly. Instead, there are subdivisions within a species defined by statistical correlations among a collection of properties. As David Hull puts it,

> After evolutionary theory was accepted, variation was acknowledged as the rule not the exception. Instead of ignoring it, taxonomists had to take varia-

tion into account by describing it statistically. No one specimen could be typical in any but a statistical sense. Species could no longer be viewed as homogeneous groups of individuals, but as polytypic groups, often with significant subdivisions. Polythetic definitions, in terms of statistically covarying properties, replaced essentialist definitions. (Hull 1984, p. 587)

In this century, attempts have been made to define the concept of a species in such a way that it could play an appropriate role in evolutionary theory. Dobzhansky and, especially, Mayr developed what came to be called the *biological species concept.* It not only considers morphological similarities, but also takes into account the parameters of evolutionary theory—reproduction, adaptation to ecological niches, gene pools, etc.

According to this concept, then, the members of a species constitute (1) a reproductive community. The individuals of a species of animals respond to one another as potential mates and seek one another for the purpose of reproduction. . . . The species is also (2) *an ecological unit* that, regardless of the individuals composing it, interacts as a unit with other species with which it shares the environment. The species, finally, is (3) *a genetic unit* consisting of a large intercommunicating gene pool, whereas an individual is merely a temporary vessel holding a small portion of the contents of the gene pool for a short period of time. The species definition that results from this theoretical species concept is: *Species are groups of actually or potentially interbreeding populations, which are reproductively isolated from other such groups.* (Mayr 1984*a*, p. 533)

Mayr correctly saw that such a concept of the species put evolutionary biology in conflict with a venerable and powerful philosophical tradition.

The development of the biological concept of the species is one of the earliest manifestations of the emancipation of biology from an inappropriate philosophy based on the phenomena of inanimate nature. (Mayr 1984*a*, p. 533)

The species, characterized in this way, is not a natural kind in the classical sense; in fact, it is not even a classical category. There are seven ways in which it fails to qualify as a natural kind of a classical sort:

First, as we saw above, species do not have a homogeneous structure with all members sharing defining properties. Only statistical correlations among properties can be given.

Second, a biological species is defined not with respect to intrinsic properties, but only with relation to other groups. In a classical natural kind, the relevant properties are defined intrinsically with respect to each member, not relationally with respect to other groups.

A population is a species with respect to all other populations with which it exhibits the relationship of reproductive isolation—noninterbreeding. If only a single population existed in the entire world, it would be meaningless to call it a species. (Mayr 1984*a*, p. 535).

Third, a species is not defined in terms of properties of its *individual* members. For example, it is defined in terms of its gene pool, though no individual has anything more than a small portion of the genes in the pool. Classical categories, on the other hand, are always defined in terms of properties that *each* of the individual members has.

Perhaps the most interesting ways in which species diverge from natural kinds as they were classically defined can be seen in Mayr's characterization of the kinds of situations that provide difficulties for fitting the biological species concept into traditional taxonomies. Such difficulties exist because the biological concept of the species is also defined relative to time and space. Time is involved because new species develop over time. Place is involved because adaptation to a particular geographical environment is crucial in evolutionary theory. Natural kinds, on the other hand, are defined only by properties of individual members and thus are constant across time and geographical areas. Factors involving time and space lead to further ways in which the biological concept of the species differs from classical natural kinds.

Fourth, if one considers populations distributed over broad areas, there is not always a distinct point at which one can distinguish one species from two. Instead, there is often a gradation.

Because the development of species is a gradual process and involves many factors, there are inevitably intermediate stages at which a binary same-or-different species distinction is impossible or meaningless. Mayr speaks of such cases as presenting "difficulties" for taxonomies.

> More interesting to the evolutionist are the difficulties that are introduced when the dimensions of time and space are added. Most species of taxa do not consist merely of a single local population, but are an aggregate of numerous local populations that exchange genes with each other to a greater or lesser degree. The more distant two populations are from each other, the more likely they are to differ in a number of characteristics. I show elsewhere (Mayr 1963, ch. 10 and 11) that some of these populations are incipient species, having acquired some but not all characteristics of species. One or another of the three most characteristic properties of species taxa—reproductive isolation, ecological difference, and morphological distinguishability—is in such cases only incompletely developed. The application of the species concept to such incompletely speciated populations raises considerable difficulties. (Mayr 1984*a*, p. 536)

In other words, biological species show prototype effects. Populations that are best examples of the biological species concept have all three of these characteristics. But the biological world is sufficiently complex that a clear same-or-different species judgment cannot be given in a great many cases. Mayr suggests that the best way to think about biological species in such difficult cases is not in terms of collections of individuals, but in terms of gene pools. "A species," as he puts it, "is a protected gene pool." The mechanisms of protection are relative to a habitat and to stages of evolutionary development. The following cases make sense in these terms, but provide further counterevidence to classical views of natural kinds.

Fifth, the concept "belongs to the same species as" is not transitive.

On the classical theory of natural kinds, the relation "belongs to the same natural kind as" is transitive. If *A* and *B* are of the same kind, and *B* and *C* are of the same kind, then *A* and *C* are of the same kind. Mayr cites a class of cases well-known in the biological community where transitivity fails. As he puts it,

> Widespread species may have terminal populations that behave toward each other as distinct species even though they are connected by a chain of interbreeding populations. (Mayr 1984*a*, p. 536)

To put it another way, consider the following situation: There is a sequence of adjacent geographical areas and a population of organisms in each area. Let us call these populations *A, B, C, D,* and *E. A* can interbreed with *B, B* with *C, C* with *D,* and *D* with *E.* But *A* cannot interbreed with *E.* Are *A* and *E* (the terminal populations of the chain) instances of the same species or not?

In a chain of this sort each adjacent pair of populations act like they are instances of the same species, but the relation is not transitive, since the terminal members *A* and *E* meet the conditions for being different species. Moreover, such chains can form rings, where *A* and *E* coexist in the same habitat. For a discussion of such "racial rings," see Stansfield 1977, pp. 438–39, and Dobzhansky 1955, pp. 184–85.

Looking globally at the entire situation, one cannot call these populations either the same species or different species. However, if one looks at the situation locally, one can speak of protected gene pools in each environment. The classical notion of natural kind, with its transitivity condition, is defined globally. It must be defined globally, since *essential* conditions cannot change from time to time and place to place. Such real populations of plants and animals in the world thus do not behave as classical natural kinds with respect to the biological concept of the species.

Sixth, the biological species concept cannot be interpreted as having any absolutely necessary conditions.

The biological species concept includes a cluster of two conditions that go together in typical cases: a morphological condition and an interbreeding condition. Two populations represent different species if they are morphologically distinguished and do not interbreed, and they represent the same species if they do interbreed and are morphologically similar to an appropriate degree. However, these two conditions do not always go together. Mayr cites the following situations (Mayr 1984*a*, p. 537):

- Reproductive isolation without corresponding morphological change; that is, their physical characteristics are the same, but they can no longer breed.
- Morphological differentiation without reproductive isolation; that is, they can breed despite having very different physical characteristics.
- Uniparental reproduction, e.g., self-fertilization, parthenogenesis, pseudogamy, vegetative reproduction, etc.; here the issue of interbreeding cannot arise.

These cases are important in two ways. First, they show that there can be no necessary degree of correlation between morphological similarity and interbreeding capabilities. That is, one cannot predict interbreeding capacity from similarity of physical properties, and hence one cannot base an account of the role of species in evolution on a definition of species purely in terms of physical properties. Second, the cases, taken together, show that the very *concept* of a biological species is not a classical concept. Both morphological similarity and interbreeding capability are parts of the definition of a biological species, but neither is a necessary part. Thus, none of the defining characteristics of the biological concept *species* is necessary, and so the concept is not definable by necessary and sufficient conditions.

Seventh, status as a separate species may depend on geographic location.

A natural kind in the objectivist tradition is defined by *inherent* necessary and sufficient conditions. Classical natural kinds are not defined relative to location. In terms of the classical definition of natural kinds, the following statements are nonsense:

- Populations *A* and *B* are the same kinds at one place and different kinds at another place.
- Populations *A* and *B* live in a given habitat. They used to be different kinds and they have not changed. But the habitat has changed and now they are the same kind.

Yet, with respect to the biological concept of the species both cases actually occur. Here is Mayr's description of such situations:

Attainment of different levels of speciation in different local populations. The perfecting of isolating mechanisms may proceed in different populations of a polytypic species (one having several subspecies) at different rates. Two widely overlapping species may, as a consequence, be completely distinct at certain localities but may freely hybridize at others.

Reproductive isolation dependent on habitat isolation. Numerous cases have been described in the literature in which natural populations acted toward each other like good species (in areas of contact) as long as their habitats were undisturbed. Yet the reproductive isolation broke down as soon as the characteristics of these habitats changed, usually by the interference of man. (Mayr 1984*a*, p. 537)

In short, the characterization of biological species from evolutionary perspective shows that the biological world is not divided up into clearly distinguished natural kinds as objectivist metaphysics requires. Yet, as Mayr points out, such phenomena are "consequences of the gradual nature of the ordinary process of speciation." In short, evolution, which works gradually in local habitats to create new species, is inconsistent with objectivist metaphysics. Because of evolutionary theory, there has had to be, in Mayr's terms, "an emancipation of biology from an inappropriate philosophy."

To summarize, the biological species concept fails to be a classical natural kind in the following ways:

- It does not have a homogeneous internal structure.
- It is defined relative to other groups.
- It is not defined solely with respect to properties of individuals.
- It does not have clear boundaries.
- It is not transitive.
- It does not have necessary conditions.
- It is dependent on geography.

These are all consequences of characterizing a species within evolutionary theory.

Mayr's biological concept of the species is by no means accepted throughout biology. It represents a middle ground between the pheneticists and the cladists since it uses both kinds of criteria. As such, it is not accepted by either pheneticists or cladists. But this does not mean that other biological theories, either purely phenetic or purely cladistic, provide comfort to those who accept objectivist metaphysics. Let us start with pheneticists.

Sokal and Crovello (1984) provide a critique of the biological species concept. They accept Mayr's observation that the role of a population in evolution (its capacity to interbreed with other populations) cannot be predicted on the basis of overall similarity (that is, by phenetic criteria). Their solution is to disengage the concept of the species from evolutionary theory. They argue that the concept of a species is indeed phenetic (based on overall similarity) and that the concept of a species has nothing whatever to do with evolution.

If we examine the evolutionary situation within some ecosystem, we can generate the same theory based on localized biological populations without grouping sets of interbreeding populations into more abstract biological species. Parenthetically, we may point out that what are probably the most important and progressive books on evolutionary theory that have been published within the last year or so essentially do not refer to the biological species at all. . . . We conclude that the phenetic species as normally described and whose definition may be improved by numerical taxonomy is the appropriate concept to be associated with the taxonomic category "species," while the local population may be the most useful unit for evolutionary study. (Sokal and Crovello 1984, pp. 562–63)

But their alternative is not a classical one:

Insistence on a phenetic species concept leads inevitably to a conceptualization of species as dense regions within a hyperdimensional environmental space. (P. 564)

The phenetic species concept is statistical, not discrete. The "dense regions" represent high statistical correlations of attributes. Thus, this species concept does not have clear boundaries and is not defined by necessary and sufficient conditions. It is very much like Wittgenstein's view of categories as defined by family resemblances.

It should be pointed out that, even among pheneticists, there is considerable disagreement on these matters. First, there are different kinds of statistical methods, which yield different results. Second, there do exist attempts to characterize a phenetic species concept that plays a role in evolution. (See Sober 1984)

Cladistic categorization looks like a form of classical categorization, but it provides little comfort to the classical view of natural kinds. On the cladistic view, all categorization is historical, and based only on the history of derived characters. This view results in categories that seem like anything but natural kinds. As Gould has observed, cladistic categorization produces a taxonomy in which lungfish are closer to rhinos than to tuna. As Mayr points out (Mayr 1984*b*, pp. 654–55), cladistic categorization yields one category that includes only birds and crocodiles, but not other reptiles. This example is worth some discussion, since it gives one a sense of what cladistic categorization is all about.

Birds descended from a branch of the reptiles, the Archosauria. So did pterodactyls, dinosaurs, and crocodilians. After the Archosauria branched off from other reptiles, it acquired certain characteristics which distinguished it from other reptiles. These characteristics, called "synapomorphies," are shared by birds and crocodiles today. After birds and crocodiles branched off from Archosauria, they each acquired new characteristics all their own, called "autapomorphies." The crocodiles didn't acquire very many of them; they remained pretty much the same. But birds, which had to adapt to living in the air, acquired a great many autapomorphic characters, that is, characteristics that birds have but crocodiles don't.

In setting up taxonomies, cladists only count synapomorphies and not autapomorphies. Hence, the surviving descendants of Archosauria, birds and crocodiles are grouped together by cladists; crocodiles are not grouped with other reptiles, even though they are much more like other reptiles today than they are like birds. Thus, the cladists pretty much ignore the ecological component of evolution in ignoring the autapomorphies in birds, those characteristics that birds developed in adapting to an aerial environment. Such cases are not rare; there are hundreds of them. Cladistic categorization tries to be true to history, at least to one aspect of it.

But a history-only view of categorization is not what classical theorists had in mind. Objective similarities on this view means objective similarities of derived (that is, synapomorphic) characters. Thus, when a given property got there in the history of the species is all that matters when a cladist decides whether that property is to count for establishing categories on classical grounds. Even current biological function does not matter. Nor do major aspects of evolutionary theory matter—selection pressures, shifts of adaptive zones, evolutionary rates, etc. On the cladistic view, a great many important aspects of biology play no role in determining biological categories. Objectivist metaphysics requires that there be only one correct categorization scheme. If that is a cladistic scheme, then many of our most familiar categories, like *zebras* and *fish*, will be seen as nonexistent. And a number of evolutionary processes that play an important role in determining the development of species will be left out of the picture.

The cladistic view, with a little charitable stretching in the time dimension, may be seen as fitting objectivist metaphysics. It, of course, does not fit objectivist semantics and cognition, since the categories it yields do not fit the categories of language and mind, like *zebra* and *fish*. Thus, the only version of contemporary biology that seems consistent with objectivist metaphysics is still inconsistent with other aspects of objectivist philosophy. It is also inconsistent with the *spirit* of the view of classification built into objectivist metaphysics. It may be construed as being consistent with the letter of objectivist metaphysics, in which case crocodiles are objectively categorized only with birds and not with other reptiles. Of all the current biological theories, only cladism might be interpreted as being consistent with objectivist metaphysics on the issue of categorization—and then only by ignoring vital aspects of evolutionary biology.

Objectivist philosophy likes to view itself as having science on its side. In the case of biological categories, science is not on its side. Classical categories and natural kinds are remnants of pre-Darwinian philosophy. They fit the biology of the ancient Greeks very well, and even the biology of local naturalists such as Linnaeus. But they do not accord with phenomena that are central to evolution—variation within species, adaptation to the environment, gradual change, gene pools, etc. Whatever one's choices are in the styles of contemporary biology, objectivist semantics and cognition and, to a large extent, even objectivist metaphysics are in conflict with post-Darwinian biology. I'd put my money on biology.

CHAPTER 13

What's Wrong with Objectivist Cognition

The objectivist paradigm is not just about the world. It is very largely about the mind and language. And it has had an overwhelming impact. Most contemporary theories of the mind and language take for granted at least some objectivist doctrines. To the extent that these doctrines rest upon the classical theory of categories, they are at least potentially in conflict with the results of prototype theory as I have reported them. It is of the greatest importance to determine whether such objectivist foundations for cognitive science can be maintained in the face of empirical studies of natural human categories. I would like to suggest that *none* of the objectivist doctrines concerning language and the mind can stand up to such scrutiny. But before getting into such a discussion, it is worth pointing out that there is one source of prototype effects that leaves objectivist cognition pretty much intact.

Fuzzified Objectivism

In objectivism as we have characterized it, entities either do or do not have a given property, and so they either are or are not in the category defined by that property. However, one can, within the spirit of objectivism, allow for the possibility that objects have a property to a certain degree, and thus are a member of the corresponding category to that degree. Zadeh's fuzzy set theory is a way of extending classical categorization to fit such a fuzzified version of objectivism.

A fuzzified objectivism would be somewhat different in that it would permit degrees of truth and a somewhat different logic. (For details, see Goguen 1969 and Lakoff 1972.) But on the whole, the change would not be all that dramatic. The objectivist account of cognition and language would not change at all, so far as I can tell. If there are fuzzy categories of the world, allowing fuzzy categories of the mind that fit them would not alter the basic premise of objectivist psychology: the categories of the mind would still fit the categories of the world. Objectivist rationality would also remain intact: if a fuzzy logic captures regularities about properties of objects in the world, then the same fuzzy logic would define human rationality on the objectivist account. Similarly, the objectivist accounts of epistemology and semantics would remain unaltered. Fuzziness and category gradience, though real phenomena, do not have much to do with the main themes of this book.

The Inadequacies

Although objectivist cognition can be adjusted to accommodate graded categories, it does not fare so well with other categories, especially those that show prototype effects of other kinds. There is only one argument given that objectivist metaphysics is incorrect; it has to do with the biological concept of the species. All the other arguments concern the inadequacy of objectivist semantics and cognition. On the whole, these arguments are of the following form: Suppose we assume, for the sake of discussion, that objectivist *metaphysics* is correct; that is, that the world *does* consist of objects with properties and relations holding among them and that the natural world *does* contain classical categories. The data that we have discussed nonetheless show that objectivist *cognition* and *semantics* are incorrect. The reason is that there are a great many categories of mind and language that are not reflections of alleged categories of the world. Each such case creates problems of the following sort for objectivist cognition and semantics.

The Problem for Objectivist Cognition: Concepts are not internal representations of external reality, since there is no corresponding external reality—there are no *categories* of the right kind of objectively "out there" for the concepts to mirror.

The Problem for Objectivist Semantics: Symbols (e.g., words) do not match up with *categories* in the world, since there are no categories of the right kind in the world for them to match up with.

Recall that the only objectively existing categories in the world as objectivists conceive of it are classical categories. All the examples we have given of nonclassical categories of mind are thus counterexamples to objectivist cognition and semantics, because there is nothing in objectivist metaphysics for them to correspond to. Here are the cases we will be discussing: color, folk-biological categories, conflicting models, and categories showing prototype effects that come from the following sources: idealizations, cluster models, metonymic models, and radial categories. Let us begin with perhaps the most obvious case, color.

Color

Wavelengths of light exist in a world external to human beings; color categories do not. The fact that we categorize different wavelengths as being in the same color category partly depends on human physiology—on the cones in the retina and the neural pathways between the eye and the brain. Colors arise from our interaction with the world; they do not exist outside of us. Color categorization is also partly a matter of cultural convention since different cultures have different boundaries for basic color categories. Color categorization also involves cognitive mechanisms, which are needed to account for the existence of focal nonprimary colors, like orange. Thus colors are categories of mind that do not exist objectively in the world exclusive of seeing beings.

A possible objectivist response to this might go as follows: Why not simply make use of the fact that human beings are part of the world and say that colors are two-place relations between objects and human beings? Fine, but that would not make up for the discrepancy between categories of mind and categories of the world. *Red*, as a category of the mind, is not a two-place predicate. People understand objects as having color in and of themselves. Thus, color as a category of mind (represented by a one-place predicate) would not fit color as a category of the world (represented by a two-place predicate). The doctrine of objectivist cognition would still be violated.

Red is an interactional property, and this argument works in general for interactional properties. The existence of interactional properties contradicts the doctrine of objectivist cognition, which says that the categories of mind fit the categories of the world. In order for this to be true, the number of argument-places must be the same for each category of mind and its corresponding category of the world. One might objectively represent the interactional quality of a given property by adding an argument-place, but only at the cost of violating the doctrine of objectivist cognition.

Color also provides problems for the doctrine of objectivist logic. Consider the issue of conjunction. Many colors are mixtures of basic colors; turquoise, for example, partakes of both blue and green. It is understood as being *both* blue and green. But that is not possible for red and green. It is possible for objects in the world to reflect both the wavelengths perceived as red and those perceived as green from the same spot at the same time and with the same intensity. But such an object is not perceived as a color in between red and green that simultaneously partakes of both. It is not understood as being both red and green. Rather it would be perceived as a murky brown. The reason is that red and green arise from opposing responses of the same neurons, while green and blue arise from responses of different neurons. Thus, there is a general fact about the logic of color categories that cannot be expressed within objectivist logic:

No object (or part of an object) is simultaneously red and green.

This is a true logical relationship between conceptual categories that does not fit an objectivist framework. On an objectivist account of color—according to which colors in the world correspond to the wavelengths that give rise to those colors—this would be false since an object can simultaneously reflect the wavelengths that give rise to both red and green. Thus, the objectivist account of logical relationships among categories simply does not work. The doctrine of objectivist logic is false for color categories.

Basic-Level Categories

One would expect, on an objectivist account, that cognition would reflect the logical organization of categories: that is, one would expect that the psychologically most basic categories would correspond to conceptual primitives and that those categories that were more complex from the point of view of conceptual primitives would be cognitively more complex. But this is not the case. The categories that are easiest to process—in a number of ways—do not correspond to conceptual primitives, that is, concepts with no internal structure. Basic-level concepts are in the middle of taxonomic hierarchies and have a great deal of internal structure. But they have the kind of structure that human beings find easy to process—that is, easy to learn, remember, and use. In short, what should be cognitively complex from an objectivist point of view is actually cognitively simple.

If Berlin (Berlin, Breedlove, and Raven 1974) and Hunn (1977) are correct, basic-level categories very closely fit discontinuities in nature as described at the level of the genus in Linnaean classification. However, categories above and below the basic level do *not* closely fit discontinuities in nature as described by biologists. As we saw above, discontinuities in nature are clearest in local environments. It is in such environments that most of the world's folk-biological taxonomies are made up. Yet even there, where the problems of evolutionary biology do not manifest themselves, Berlin et al. and Hunn have found that people are much less accurate in dealing with discontinuities above and below the level of the genus than at the level of the genus. The accuracy of fit between folk-biological categories in a local environment and the categories of scientific biology in that environment is a measure of how well objectivist semantics and cognition really work. They work pretty well in local environments at the basic level. But they are supposed to work equally well at *all* levels. The Berlin-Hunn research disconfirms the objectivist view at levels other than the basic level.

If the objectivist account of conceptual categories were correct, we would expect there to be an objectivist account of the organization of such categories into levels: basic, superordinate, subordinate, and the like. But the factors that actually determine basic-level structure do not correspond to anything in objectivist cognition. The factors include: gestalt perception of part-whole organization, imaging capacity, motor organization, and knowledge organization. On the objectivist account, conceptual structure *represents external reality,* that is, the only factors involved in structuring the categories of mind are those that can match up to something in the external world. If we look at the factors that determine basic-level structure one-by-one, we can see that none of them are part of an objectivist account of category organization:

- What is perceived by human beings as gestalts (that is, overall shapes that characterize basic-level categories) do not necessarily correspond to categories of the external world.
- The mental images formed by human beings do not necessarily correspond to objectively existing categories of the external world.
- The way one moves one's body while interacting with an object is partly determined by the nature of the object, but just as much by the nature of one's body. It is not completely determined by the nature of the object.
- On the objectivist account, real knowledge is supposed to fit the facts of the world; but the *organization* of that knowledge, particularly the organization at the basic level, is not objectively part of the external world. Thus the fact that knowledge about objects is clustered at the basic level is not something that can be accounted for within the objectivist tradition.

Each of these determinants of category structure is outside of the objectivist account of conceptual structure.

Incidently, basic-level structure is reflected in the structure of language. As Zubin and Köpcke (1986) observe, the German gender system is governed by a number of semantic principles. One important principle is based on the distinction between superordinate and basic-level categorization. In general superordinates are neuter, while basic-level concepts are typically either masculine or feminine (as determined by other principles). For example,

Superordinate: *das Instrument* musical 'instrument'
Basic-level: *die Guitarre* 'guitar', *die Trompete* 'trumpet', *die Trommel* 'drum'

Superordinate: *das Fahrzeug* 'vehicle'
Basic-level: *der Wagen* 'car', *der Bus* 'bus', *der Laster* 'truck'

Superordinate: *das Gemüse* 'vegetable'
Basic-level: *der Spinat* 'spinach', *die Erbse* 'pea', *der Kohl* 'cabbage'

If Zubin and Köpcke are correct, basic-level structure is one of the semantic determinants of German gender. But, as we have seen, "semantics" as defined in the objectivist paradigm is not capable of distinguishing semantic structure of this kind.

Alternative Models

Objectivist semantics assumes that in any domain there is only one correct way to understand what is going on. It is one thing to make such a claim for theories in the physical sciences. It is quite a different matter to make such a claim for social or abstract domains, where alternative models may be equally valid.

Sweetser's (1981, 1984) analysis of the Coleman-Kay (1981) data on *lie* is a good example. Take the case of a social lie, for example, saying *I had a wonderful time* when I was bored stiff. Part of the judgment as to whether this was a lie and if so, how good an example it was, depends on how the situation is understood. Framing it as a "social situation," where being nice is more important than telling the truth, affects one's judgment. But the choice of framing a situation one way or another is outside of objectivist semantics. In objectivist semantics, the world simply is the way it is, and truth cannot be affected by the way one understands a situation.

Similarly, sentences like *Harry's not stingy, he's thrifty* and *You didn't spare me a trip to New York, you deprived me of one* are about alternative framings. The *not* does not deny any fact; instead, it denies the appropriateness of using the cognitive model in terms of which *stingy* and *spare* are defined. The sentence is about which of two alternative cognitive models should be used to understand a situation where the facts are clear. Since objectivist semantics is based on truth, it has no way of talking about the appropriateness of using one cognitive model and the inappropriateness of using another, in a situation where both will fit the facts.

Kay's analysis of the hedges *strictly speaking, loosely speaking,* and *technically* are perhaps even more problematic for objectivist semantics. On the assumption that language itself is part of the world, objectivist semanticists assume that there is one correct account of reference, that is, of how linguistic expressions come to denote nonlinguistic entities. At present, there are two conflicting views—the reference-via-meaning doctrine and the doctrine of direct reference.

What Kay (1979, 1983*b*) showed was that English makes use of both models. *Strictly speaking* and *loosely speaking* make use of an ICM that incorporates a version of reference-via-meaning, which *technically* makes use of a version of direct reference. The two contradictory models are both in use.

None of these cases would be difficult for a cognitive semantics in which meaning and truth are based on understanding. In a cognitive semantics, the existence of contradictory modes of understanding a situation is no problem. But in an objectivist semantics, where meaning is based on truth, serious problems arise. Two contradictory models cannot both be true for an objectivist.

The Sources of Prototype Effects

Most of the sources of prototype effects are incompatible with objectivist views on cognition and language. As we saw above, graded category membership is consistent with objectivist cognition, and it is just about the only source of prototype effects that is. Let us consider the cases discussed above one by one.

Idealizations That Contradict Reality

Fillmore (1982*a*), in his analysis of *bachelor*, argued that the concept was based on the classical theory of categorization and that prototype effects were due to the concept being defined in terms of an idealization—a cognitive model whose background conditions are inconsistent with the existence of priests, Moslems with only three wives, divorced people, and Tarzan. The prototype effects, according to Fillmore, arise because those background conditions can be partially compatible with what is known about various situations. The prototype effects arise not from the model itself, but from the degree to which the background conditions fit a given situation.

Such an explanation does not jibe with a strict construal of objectivist principles. Since the background conditions contradict what is true, and known to be true, of the world, the ICM should simply not fit at all. To permit Fillmore's explanation, one would need to allow background conditions to fit partially and to allow partial contradictions. Allowing contradictions is not in the spirit of objectivism, but perhaps a revised objectivism could tolerate them in certain circumstances.

ICM Clusterings

In the analysis of *mother* given above, I argued that the concept is defined by a cluster of cognitive models. The cluster has the fundamental property of a gestalt, namely, that the entire cluster is easier to comprehend than its individual parts or any collection of them. Thus, *mother* is an easier concept to comprehend than other concepts defined in terms of just some of the models in the cluster: *birth mother, genetic mother, legal mother,* etc. In such cases, the modifiers (*birth, genetic, legal*) serve to isolate a single model in the cluster. Thus *birth mother*, based on a single model in the cluster, is more complex than *mother*, which is based on the entire cluster.

Such an analysis is outside the scope of objectivist semantics. It contradicts the doctrine of atomism, according to which concepts are either complex or primitive; primitives have no internal structure and are cognitively simpler that complex concepts. On the objectivist account, greater complexity of internal structure always results in greater cognitive complexity. In other words, objectivism has no place for gestalts in conceptual structure. The gestalt properties of the cluster than defines *mother* is inconsistent with the doctrine of conceptual atomism (sometimes known as *feature semantics*).

The doctrine of conceptual atomism, incidentally, is not something that the objectivist paradigm could easily jettison. It is a consequence of real-world atomism and the assumption that meaning is based on truth. These views are in turn tied to the objectivist concept of rationality: on the assumption of real-world atomism, there are logical relations holding among the categories in the world, and correct human reason mirrors those logical relations. Conceptual atomism is therefore tied to objectivist rationality, and abandoning conceptual atomism would lead to a change in the concept of rationality. For this reason, the existence of concepts with gestalt properties has very serious consequences.

Metonymic Models

These are the cases that come to mind most often when prototype effects are considered. They are all cases where some subcategory or individual member of a category is used to comprehend the category as a whole—typically for some limited purpose. They all involve metonymic understanding—understanding the whole in terms of some part or parts.

If we are correct in claiming that metonymic models of various sorts are the sources of a wide variety of prototype effects, then the existence of such effects is in conflict with objectivist psychology. According to objectivist cognition, the only true concepts are those that represent external reality, that is, those that mirror nature. Metonymic models do not mirror nature. If metonymic models are real—if they are used to make judgments and draw inferences, and if they lead to prototype effects—then they constitute counterevidence to objectivist cognition. They constitute a kind of conceptual resource that is not objectivist. It is important at this point to note that objectivist cognition does not merely claim that *some* concepts are objectivist; it claims that *all* of them are. The very existence of metonymic models is in contradition to the objectivist view of cognition.

All of the cases that Rosch (1981) refers to as instances of reference-point reasoning are well-substantiated empirically. They are the cases we cited above in our discussion of sources of prototype effects. If our analysis of reference-point reasoning in terms of metonymic models is correct, then it provides further evidence against the objectivist paradigm. Metonymic sources of prototype effects are at odds with an objectivist world view.

Incidentally, the same is true for metaphoric models. Johnson and I argued at length in *Metaphors We Live By* that metaphoric models exist and that they are inconsistent with objectivist semantics. The case studies we will present below provide additional evidence for the existence of metaphoric cognitive models and, hence, against objectivist cognition.

Radial Structures

The radial structuring of categories involves the following:

- A conventional choice of center.
- Extension principles. These characterize the class of possible "links" between more central and less central subcategories. They include metaphoric models, metonymic models, image-schema relations, etc.
- Specific conventional extensions. Though each extension is an instance of the extension principles, the extensions are *not* predictable from the center plus the principles. Each extension is a matter of convention and must be learned. The fact that specific extensions are instances of general principles makes them easier to learn.

Every aspect of radial structuring is inexpressible in a view of objectivist cognition. Let us begin with the extension principles. As we have seen, metaphoric and metonymic models do not fit into the objectivist framework, since they are matters of understanding and do not correspond to anything in an objectivist universe. The same is true of relations among image schemas. Human beings understand trajectories as being systematically related to long, thin objects— but such a relationship does not exist objectively in the external world. Thus there is nothing in objectivist psychology that corresponds to the principles of extension for radial categories.

Similarly, the choice of category center and the choices of particular extensions do not have any correlates in objective reality. There is nothing in objective reality corresponding to either the structure of the *hon* category in Japanese or the structure of the *balan* category in Dyirbal. This is also true of the English radial category that includes extensions of *mother*. The objective world does not contain a radial category corresponding to English *mother* with the cluster described above at the center of the category and *adoptive mother, birth mother, genetic mother, legal mother, unwed mother, stepmother,* and *surrogate mother* all extensions.

Objectivist cognition requires that every aspect of category structure be expressible in objectivist terms. In radial categories, no aspect of category structure is expressible in objectivist terms.

Beyond Markerese and Model Theory

There is a standard objectivist critique of cognitive approaches to semantics that needs to be answered. The best known example is David Lewis's (1972) reply to Katz and Postal's (1964) use of "semantic markers" to represent meaning.

> Semantic markers are *symbols:* items in the vocabulary of an artificial language we may call *Semantic Markerese.* Semantic interpretation by means of them amounts merely to a translation algorithm from the object language to the auxiliary language Markerese. But we can know the Markerese translation of an English sentence without knowing the first thing about the meaning of the English sentence: namely, the conditions under which it would be true. Semantics with no treatment of truth conditions is not semantics. Translation into Markerese is at best a substitute for real semantics, relying either on our tacit competence (at some future date) as speakers of Markerese or on our ability to do real semantics for at least the one language Markerese. (Lewis 1972, p. 169)

Lewis's critique is aimed not just at the theory of semantic markers, but at any nonobjectivist account of meaning, that is, any account on which meaning is not based on truth. It applies, for example, to schema theories of the sort used in cognitive psychology and artificial intelligence. Those theories use network representations of meaning, which are also composed of just "*symbols:* items in the vocabulary of an artificial language." Lewis is right about the inadequacy of doing semantics by translating one set of symbols into another.

Objectivism is one answer to going beyond mere symbols. Experientialism is another. What keeps the Lewis critique from being applicable to cognitive models is *embodiment*. Cognitive models that are embodied are not made up merely of items in an artificial language. In experientialist semantics, meaning is understood via real experiences in a very real world with very real bodies. In objectivist accounts, such experiences are simply absent. It is as though human beings did not exist, and their language and its (not *their*) meanings existed without any beings at all. What research on categorization shows clearly is that human categories are very much tied to human experiences and that any attempt to account for them free of such experience is doomed to failure.

Model-theoretic semantics applied to natural language attempts to account for human reason without taking human beings into account at all. The assumption that the mind is a mirror of nature allows model-theoretic semanticists to bypass the mind altogether. Where model theory appears to make sense, it does so by incorporating into models aspects of commonsense folk theories about the world, as in the case of the Barwise-Perry (1984) account of seeing discussed above. Our commonsense folk theory of colors has red as a property of objects, and so it seems intuitively correct when model-theoretic semantics treats red as a one-place predicate holding of objects in the world. But this is not a correct description of the world. It is a correct description of a human folk theory.

It is important for cognitive science to describe human folk theories and to explicate commonsense reasoning. To the extent that model theory does that, it is useful. But in doing so, model theory is not doing what it claims to do: describe the objectively existing world in the models. The human conceptual system is a product of human experience, and that experience comes through the body. There is no direct connection between human language and the world as it exists outside of human experience. Human language is based on human concepts, which are in turn motivated by human experience.

Experientialism thus goes along with Putnam's dictum, in his classic essay "The Meaning of Meaning" (Putnam 1975), that "Meaning is not in the mind." In experientialism, it is the embodiment of concepts via direct and indirect experience that takes experientialist semantics beyond mere symbol-manipulation. We agree with Putnam about what he called the "linguistic division of labor." Putnam observed that meaning is partly socially determined—determined by communities of experts to whom we give the authority to say what things are like in technical matters that go beyond most people's direct experience. For example, I have only the vaguest idea of what molybdenum is. I know that it's a metal, and an element, and that it's used in alloys, including steel. That's all. And what I do know comes not through any direct experience, but indirectly from some community of people whom we take to be "experts." Though I personally have not had any first-hand experience with molybdenum, I assume that such experts have had such experience, and I am willing to take their word for it. Ultimately, meaning is based on experience—in this case, their experience and not mine. My understanding is based on what has been indirectly communicated to me of their experience. And that is very little. Much of our knowledge and understanding is of this sort, where meaningfulness to us is very indirectly based on the experience of others.

Metaphysics and Epistemology

One of the cornerstones of the objectivist paradigm is the independence of metaphysics from epistemology. The world is as it is, independent of any concept, belief, or knowledge that people have. Minds, in other words, cannot create reality. I would like to suggest that this is false and that it is contradicted by just about everthing known in cultural anthropology. Take the examples cited above in our discussion of Lounsbury's research on kinship. Is there a real category *nehcihsähA* that includes not just maternal uncles but all the relatives characterized by the rules formulated by Lounsbury? Fox culture is real. And such a category is real in Fox culture. But it would be very strange to say that such a category existed independent of human minds and human conceptual systems. In such cases, human minds have produced such realities. This is the case for institutional facts of all kinds. Institutions are created by people. They are culture-specific. They are products of the human mind. And they are real.

In general, extending objectivism to include institutional facts gets one into trouble with the assumption that metaphysics is independent of epistemology. The reason is that institutions are products of culture and hence products of the human mind. They exist only by virtue of human minds. Let's take an example closer to the majority culture of the United States. Consider the category *mother*. This category includes women who have given birth to children (whether the genetic material originated with them or not), women whose eggs have developed into children (whether inside them or not), women who raise children, women who are given the legal right to raise children (whether they actually do any raising or not), and women who are married to a prototypical father. *Mother* is a real category in American culture. It is a radial category whose members cannot be defined by common properties. It would be ridiculous to claim that the category *mother* does not really exist. But it would be equally ridiculous to claim that the category *mother,* as it exists in American culture at the present time, is an objective category independent of any human minds. Only human beings could create such a reality.

Cultural Categories and the Creation of Reality

Cultural categories are real and they are made real by human action. Governments are real. They exist. But they exist only because human beings conceived of them and have acted according to that conceptualization. In short, the imaginative products of the human mind play an enormous role in the creation of reality. Trees and rocks may exist independently of the human mind. Governments do not. Physical objects are, no doubt, the best examples of things that exist, but they are by no means the only examples. An enormous number of the products of the human mind exist, though not in the way that trees and rocks exist. In the case of social and cultural reality, epistemology precedes metaphysics, since human beings have the power to create social institutions and make them real by virtue of their actions.

To Be Is Not To Be the Value of a Variable

One of the most important properties of objectivist semantics is elegantly expressed in Quine's famous slogan, "To be is to be the value of a variable." Quine saw clearly that objectivism requires that languages and conceptual schemes carry implicit ontological commitments. Categories of language and mind, in an objectivist theory, not only mirror the world but also project onto it. For an objectivist to accept as true *There are two zebras in the yard* is not merely to accept the existence of two individuals in the yard, but also to accept the existence in the world of the objectively existing classical category (or natural kind) *zebra.*

Taking into account this characteristic of objectivist semantics, Quine argued that the general concept of a *set* should be banned from formal languages used in responsible philosophical discussion. Thus, my brother, my teapot, and my desk may all exist, but it does not follow from the fact that the *set* containing exactly those three entities exists as an entity in the world. But this is what classical set theory—*on an objectivist interpretation*—claims. Quine has become a latter-day Occam, crusading against philosophical "irresponsibility," against claims for the existence of entities that don't really exist in the world as entities. Sets of arbitrarily thrown-together entities are prime examples.

Quine considers natural kinds to be sets, but he is happy about admitting these sets into his ontology.

> Kinds can be seen as sets, determined by their members. It is just that not all sets are kinds. (Quine 1969, p. 118)

Quine is, in fact, quite optimistic about the possibility that science will help us find out what the true kinds are.

> Since learning about the evolution of species, we are in a position to define comparative similarity suitably for this science by consideration of family trees. . . . When kind is construed in terms of any such similarity concept, fishes in the corrected whale-free sense of the word qualify as a kind while fishes in the more inclusive sense do not. (Quine 1969, p. 137)

Interestingly, Quine sounds like a cladist when he speaks of "family trees" and like a pheneticist when he speaks of a "similarity concept." He implicitly assumes that such cladistic and phenetic criteria are compatible. But as we have seen above, the conflict between phenetic and cladistic criteria for establishing kinds makes such optimism seem unwarranted. In any "true" objectivist ontology, it appears that kinds will have to go the way of other sets.

Quine's crusade against the undue multiplication of entities comes out of a deep understanding of, and commitment to, certain tenets (by no means all) of objectivist semantics. But even if one does not believe in objectivist semantics, as I do not, Quine's point is worth taking seriously. Our every day folk theory of the world is an objectivist folk theory. We create cognitive models of the world, and we have a natural tendency to attribute real existence to the categories in those cognitive models. This is especially true of conventional metaphorical models. Take, for example, our cognitive model in which time is understood metaphorically as a moneylike resource. Thus, time can be *saved, lost, spent, budgeted, used profitably, wasted,* etc. (See Lakoff and Johnson 1980, chap. 2.) This is not a universal way of conceptualizing time, but it is very pervasive in American culture, so much so that many people lose sight of its metaphorical character and take it as part of an objective characterization of what time "really is." Consider, for example, the following excerpt from an article in the Business Section of the *San Francisco Chronicle* (14 November, 1984):

> The Great Employee Time Robbery
>
> Employees across the nation this year will steal $150 billion worth of time from their jobs in what is termed by an employment specialist as the "deliberate and persistent abuse" of paid working hours.
>
> The study, released by Robert Half International, Inc., reported that the theft of working time is America's No. 1 crime against business, surpassing employee pilferage, insurance fraud, and embezzlement combined.
>
> Robert Half, president of the firm bearing his name, said that time is the

most valuable resource to business because it "cannot be replaced, recovered, or replenished."

He defined time theft as leaving work early or arriving late, extended lunch hours, excessive personal phone calls, conducting personal business during company hours, unwarranted sick days and non-stop chitchat at the proverbial water cooler.

The study showed that the average weekly time theft figure per employee amounted to four hours and 22 minutes.

This report was seriously and favorably commented on on the editorial page of the *San Francisco Examiner* (18 November, 1984):

News that American employees steal from their bosses an average of four hours and 22 minutes of time every week will come as no surprise to even a casual observer of the business office scene.

Here is a conscious attempt to project onto our understanding of reality a further branch of the TIME IS MONEY metaphor. It is an attempt to take a cognitive model of time, much of which is already taken to be objectively real, and extend it further. Though I doubt that this one will succeed, it is important to understand just what makes such attempts possible. Strangely enough, it is our objectivist folk theory: If categories of mind fit the categories of the world, and if TIME IS MONEY (since it can be saved, lost, wasted, budgeted, etc.), then time can be stolen. There is no reason to believe that those who commissioned and carried out the time-theft study were not sincere. From their point of view, they were presumably not just trying to extend a well-entrenched conventional metaphor; they were pointing out a *truth.* From their point of view, *time is really being stolen.* That is, for them, there is a real, objectively existing category of the world: *stolen time.*

Objectivism, as Quine realized, is a double-edged sword. The attempt to stick to what is real and characterize real knowledge leads to the imposition of categories upon the world. One reason is that objectivism leaves no room for metaphorically defined concepts and treats conventional metaphorical concepts that we use in everyday reasoning as if they were part of an objectivist conceptual system. One of the reasons that Johnson and I undertook our study of metaphorical concepts was to point out how many were being projected onto the world—in the name of objectivism! Experientialism is actually a lot pickier than objectivism about what categories are accorded "real existence." The reason is that experientialism focuses on the way we use our imaginative capacities to comprehend what we experience. It is important to distinguish those concepts that are understood indirectly via metaphorical models from those that are understood directly.

The World-As-Understood Defense

One apparent way to save objectivist semantics from such criticisms might be by redefining it to apply not to the would as it is, but to the world as it is understood to be. Although this goes against the realist spirit in objectivist philosophy, it does permit one to sidestep many of our criticisms of standard objectivist semantics. Under this revision, many of our criticisms become irrelevant. For example, it no longer matters whether there really are natural kinds in the animal kingdom or whether colors really exist externally to human beings. It no longer matters whether perception is veridical, that is, whether what we see is what there is. As long as we understand perception as veridical, we can characterize a logic of seeing that way in a semantics that has the *structure* if not the content of an objectivist semantics.

But the world is not always the way it is understood to be. One cannot claim that one has a semantics based on truth that deals with objective reality and simultaneously with reality as it is understood to be. Take, for example, the semantics suggested in Barwise and Perry's (1984) *Situations and Attitudes.*

Barwise and Perry are very clear about their objectivist metaphysics. It is about reality—objective reality—not merely reality as understood.

> Reality consists of situations, individuals having properties and standing in relations at various spatio-temporal locations.
> . . . The Theory of Situations is an abstract theory for talking about situations. We begin by pulling out of real situations the basic building blocks of the theory: individuals, properties and relations, and locations. These are conceived of as invariants or, as we shall call them, *uniformities* across real situations; the same individuals and properties appear again and again in different locations. We then put these pieces back together, using the tools of set theory, as *abstract situations.* Some of these abstract situations, the *actual situations,* correspond to the real ones; other do not. . . . Abstract situations are built up from locations and *situation types*. . . . [A situation type is] a partial function from n-ary relations and n individuals to the values 0 ("false") and 1 ("true"). . . . All these entities are set-theoretic objects, built up from individuals, properties, relations, and locations abstracted from real situations.
> . . . Situation types are partial. They don't say everything there is to say about everyone, or even everything there is to say about everyone appearing in the situation type. (Barwise and Perry 1984, chap. 1)

Among the examples of properties given by Barwise and Perry is the color red. But neither red nor any other color exists objectively in the world external to human beings, and no one knowledgeable in the neurophysiological and anthropological studies of color would make such a claim. What we see as red is determined partly by the reflective properties of the objects, partly by neurophysiology and partly by culturally imposed boundaries of regions in the color spectrum. Redness is not an objectively existing property of any object. In our folk understanding of the world we conceive of redness as a property, and any adequate account of that folk understanding would say as much. But Barwise and Perry are not claiming to give an account of folk understandings; they are claiming to give an account of reality itself, and they treat colors as objectively existing properties of objects. What they are doing instead is taking our objectivist folk theory of color and claiming that reality is what our folk theory says it is.

As we saw above, Barwise and Perry do the same thing in their account of seeing. They correctly describe the normal *folk theory* of seeing and then attribute it to *reality*. But, as we saw in our discussion of the flashing-lights example, the Barwise-Perry account of seeing fails in cases when what one sees is not what is there. Thus, when two lights are flashed in quick succession, people really see one light moving. The situation-type that characterizes what is seen does not match up with the situation-type that characterizes what really happened. In fact, there aren't even the same number of individuals; one light was perceived when two lights flashed.

Barwise and Perry cannot have it both ways. If they are proposing a semantics based on objective, mind-free reality, then they are simply wrong on factual grounds. But perhaps it would still be possible to preserve the *mechanisms* if not the substance of objectivist semantics by adopting a world-as-understood defense. Suppose one were to suggest that the real subject matter of objectivist semantics was the world as understood, not the world as it is. Suppose, further, that one were to propose that one could simply keep all the mechanisms of objectivist semantics and just give it this new interpretation. What would be wrong with that?

Plenty. The mechanisms of objectivist semantics would still not be able to account for human categorization. All that is available in set-theoretical models is structures made up of entities and sets. But human categories have richer structures, as we have seen—radial structures, metaphorical structures, metonymic structures, and other kinds of structures that yield prototype effects. At the very least, much richer structures would have to be introduced. But this is not a trivial step. Objectivist semantics is supposed to be merely a matter of entities and sets. But now it would become much more: the models would need all kinds of structures that a general theory of cognitive models would have.

Nor do the problems end there. Objectivist semantics also makes assumptions about the nature of reference. It assumes that there is a unique and objectively correct way of assigning reference to entities in a formal language, that there is a mathematical function from symbols in the formal language to entities and sets in the models. But Paul Kay's (1979) study of hedges shows that this, too, is empirically incorrect. As Kay observed, the hedges *technically* on the one hand, and *strictly speaking* on the other, employ two different and contradictory folk theories of reference. That is, we have at least two different and inconsistent ways of determining what our words refer to! This is beyond the scope of the mechanisms in objectivist semantics for linking symbols to elements of models.

There are even further referential problems—what we might call "split reference." Consider the flashing lights example once more. The world-as-understood view does not avoid this problem. The reason is that the world is understood differently by different people—say, the subject in the flashing-light experiment and the person running the experiment. One would have to have at least *two* real worlds-as-understood with one light in one world and more than one light in the other. This would be required in order to account for the use of pronouns in sentences like the following:

- Harry saw *one light* move, but there were really many of *them* flashing. He saw *it* move in a circle, but *they* were just arranged in a circle and were flashing rapidly in sequence.

What is needed is a referential correspondence between a single entity in one world-as-understood and multiple entities in another. This is also required by sentences like the following:

- If Ted Turner had been born twins, *they* would have had competing sports networks, but as things are *he* has no competition.

Technically, this is beyond classical systems of objectivist semantics. Such systems do not permit an entity in one world to correspond referentially to multiple entities in other worlds. There is, however, a nonobjectivist semantics where such problems are handled naturally and routinely—Fauconnier's (1985) theory of mental spaces.

Fauconnier's theory bears certain similarities to situation semantics. Both of them are successors to Kripke's possible world semantics, in that they can do certain kinds of things that possible world semantics was set up to do, e.g., provide the basis for an account of referential opacity and propositional attitudes. Both differ from possible world semantics in that they provide for partial representations, whereas possible worlds had to specify the totality of information about a world. Both are constructed to be used in an account of discourse. And both permit objectivist representations—representations of entities, their properties, and relations among them. In short, Fauconnier's approach has many of the same advantages over possible world semantics that the Barwise-Perry approach has.

But Fauconnier's theory does not have the disadvantage of being limited by objectivist philosophy. Fauconnier's approach therefore permits a straightforward account of the flashing lights example, in which there is a mental space corresponding to what is seen and a reality space. In the vision space, there is one light moving; in the reality space, there are two lights flashing; and there are connectors relating the single light of the vision space with the multiple lights of the reality space. Such one-many relations cannot be dealt with in situation semantics or in classical possible world semantics.

Each of these problems requires a remedy that goes beyond the *mechanisms* of objectivist semantics. That is, one cannot simply give up the realist philosophy and keep the formal mechanisms by going to a world-as-understood interpretation. But there is still one more major and, I think, irremediable problem with the formal mechanisms of objectivist semantics. The world-as-understood interpretation does not separate the world from the way it is understood. That is, the model structure that defines a possible world (or situation) *is* that world (or situation). A model structure for a world (or situation) consists of an entity-and-set structure; the sets not only structure the world (or situation), they *are* part of the world (or situation). There is no separation between the world and the structured understanding.

But such a separation is necessary. The reason is that it is possible for individuals to understand the world—the one real world—in more than one way, in fact, in two inconsistent ways. Take color, for example. A specialist in the physiology of color vision has at least two conflicting understandings of color: the normal folk-theoretical one, according to which colors are in the external world, and a scientific one, according to which they are not. In doing research on color and in talking to colleagues, such a researcher may simultaneously use both understandings in the same sentence to discuss a single real world. We can see this in a sentence like this:

- We weren't able to use red objects in the experiment because there is no single wavelength that can be perceived as focal red.

Here the phrase *red objects* makes use of the normal folk theory that color is a property of objects in the world, while *there is no single wave-*

length that is perceived as focal red makes use of the scientific theory that color does not exist as such in the world but is a product of the world plus human perception and cognition. The use of such a sentence would normally involve the simultaneous use of two different and inconsistent understandings of one real-world situation! Such a sentence cannot be satisfied by a model that is structured according to only one single consistent understanding of what color is. But that is the only kind of model that is possible given the mechanisms of objectivist semantics. The reason is that, technically, in such a theory each situation (or world) has only one structure—either *red* is in it as a property (technically a set), or it isn't. There can be only one consistent set-theoretical structure per situation. For this reason, the mechanisms of objectivist semantics fail here too.

Such cases are common not only in scientific discourse, but also in everyday commonsense discourse. Quinn (1987) has found, in studying conversations about marriage in minute detail, that each spouse in a marriage has multiple, and often contradictory, understandings of what marriage is. But it is common in a discussion of marriage for a spouse to shift in mid-sentence to a different understanding which is inconsistent with the one the sentence started out with.

What all this shows is that objectivist semantics is empirically incorrect in *two* ways: first, in its philosophical claims, and second, in its use of the mechanisms of mathematical logic.

Gibson and the Interactionist Defense

One version of the world-as-understood defense of objectivist semantics invokes the ecological psychology of J. J. Gibson (see Gibson 1979). Gibson stressed the importance of the constant interaction of human beings with, and as an inseparable part of, their environments. Our views concerning interactional properties and embodiment mesh with Gibson's on this issue. Gibson's insight here is of the greatest importance.

But Gibson's work was on perception, not on cognition. And there is an aspect of Gibson's psychology of perception that appears not to extend to cognition. Gibson distinguished between physical reality and the environment. Physical reality is independent of all animate beings. The environment is defined relative to how beings can interact with it. Thus, trees, for example, are *climb-up-able.* Gibson speaks of such opportunities for interaction provided by the environment as *affordances.* Gibson's *environment* is, thus, close in some respects to what we have called the world-as-experienced.

There is, however, a major difference. Gibson defines affordances as being invariants of the environment. As Gibson says (p. 137), affordances are "properties of things *taken with reference to an observer* but not properties of the *experience of the observer*. . . . The observer may or may not perceive or attend to the affordance, according to his needs, but the affordance, being invariant, is always there to be perceived." The Gibsonian environment sounds in important respects like an objectivist universe, but with physical reality replaced by a single unified world-as-experienced.

In fact, Barwise and Perry (1984) reach just this conclusion. Citing Gibson, they say, "a new realism has emerged, Ecological Realism, a view that finds meaning located in the interaction of living things and their environment." They don't go into the matter in any depth, but it would appear that the version of objectivism that Barwise and Perry are appealing to is not one based on purely objective *physical reality,* but on the Gibsonian environment, which is defined by interactions (or the possibility of them).

The problems with such an approach are just those cited above. The Gibsonian environment is not the kind of world-as-experienced that is needed in order to account for the facts of categorization. Suppose Gibson is right for perception. His account only deals with *individual* phenomena, not *categories* of phenomena. And it does not—and could not—deal with *abstract* categories. Another problem is that the Gibsonian environment is monolithic and self-consistent and the same for all people. Human categories of the sort we have discussed do not exist as invariants of a Gibsonian environment. They vary from culture to culture and are not consistent with each other. They are also mostly abstract and are not the kinds of things that could exist as part of a Gibsonian environment. Ecological realism cannot make sense of experiential or cultural categories. The category of *anger,* for example, cannot be accounted for in those terms. Nor can the category *mother* in English (which includes birth mothers, adoptive mothers, step mothers, etc.), nor the *nehcihsähA* category of Fox, and certainly not the *balan* category of Dyirbal. Even color categories, which one might expect to find in a Gibsonian environment, are not invariant; they vary from culture to culture. And categories that are metaphorically defined would certainly not be among the affordances of the environment. Nor would linguistic categories, or categories of senses of the sort discussed in case study 2 below. And ICMs are certainly not part of a Gibsonian environment.

Part of Gibson's ecological approach is absolutely essential to the experientialist approach that Johnson and I have proposed: his stress upon the constant interaction of people with their environment. His view of the environment and its affordances may or may not work for perception. But in the realm of cognition, ecological realism cannot account for most of the examples in this book.

Natural Logic

In 1970, I proposed for linguistics a program of study that I referred to as "natural logic"—the study of the human conceptual system, human reason, and their relationship to natural language (see Lakoff 1970, 1972). At that time, I believed that the approach to human reason taken in the formal logic of the time—using possible world semantics and model theory—would provide the right set of conceptual tools for studying natural logic. Prominent among the objectivist semanticists I have been criticizing is me—or me as I was in the late 1960s and early 1970s. In 1968, I proposed the introduction of model theory into linguistics (Lakoff 1968). Jim McCawley was immediately enthusiastic. And at about the same time, Edward Keenan and Barbara Partee had decided for independent, but very similar reasons on the same course. What was then a highly controversial proposal put forth by a handful of us has since developed into an extremely active branch of linguistics. A number of real insights about the nature of language and thought—not very many of them, but certainly very important ones—have come from that tradition. Predicate-argument structure, scope differences, coreference, variable binding, operators, referential opacity, propositional functions, etc. represent real insights into the structure of language. Any adequate theory of language and thought will have to preserve those insights in some form or other.

During the early 1970s I became acquainted with certain of the phenomena discussed above concerning categorization. They shook my faith in objectivist semantics, and I set out on the course of work described in this book. I still believe that natural logic is a reasonable project, but not within the framework of objectivist philosophy and not using exactly the mechanisms of classical model theory. Instead, new mechanisms will have to be proposed, as well as a new view of philosophy to frame them in. Logic is too important a field to be limited by an unfortunate marriage to objectivist philosophy. I propose a divorce, or at least polygamy. A redirection of creative energies is needed.

My purposes in discussing the inadequacies of objectivist semantics is constructive, rather than destructive. In chapter 17 below, I will suggest how the real insights of classical model theory can be preserved and expanded on in a *cognitive model theory*—and how different philosophical framework can make sense of this endeavor. In the case studies below, I will present some examples of what conceptual, lexical, and syntactic research would be like from such a viewpoint. In the midst of all this discussion of what is wrong with objectivist semantics, it should be borne in mind that my primary goal is to preserve and to build on what is right with objectivist semantics.

CHAPTER 14

The Formalist Enterprise

Mathematical logic—one of the great marvels of twentieth-century intellectual life—has been used to justify an objectivist approach to cognitive science in general, and to linguistics and the philosophy of language in particular. As we have seen, the study of categorization phenomena suggests that it has been applied inappropriately. It's not that there is anything wrong with the tools of mathematical logic. It's just that they are inadequate to deal with the empirical facts that have been discovered about human categorization. Mathematical logic has been asked to do a job that it was not designed to do, and it is not surprising that it has failed.

The mathematical tools that have been used are formal syntax and model theory. It is sometimes assumed that the way they have been applied to the study of natural language syntax and semantics is simply natural and obviously correct—that natural language syntax and semantics is just a special case of formal syntax and semantics. This is not true.

The formalist enterprise in linguistics and in cognition generally is an attempt to impose formal syntax and formal semantics on the study of language and human reason *in a particular way,* which, as we have seen, is empirically inadequate. It is important to know *that* it is inadequate; but it is equally important to be aware of exactly *where* it goes wrong. That is the question we will take up in this chapter and the one to follow. But before we can approach that, we should provide some background for those readers who are not acquainted with the reasons—the good reasons—for the development of the formalist approach in mathematics and mathematical logic.

Formalist Mathematics

Formalism is an approach to the study of the foundations of mathematics. It arose as an attempt to make sense of the discovery of noneuclidean geometries. That discovery showed that the axiomatic method, taken since Euclid as being at the heart of mathematics, was itself not properly understood.

The program of euclidean geometry was to demonstrate how *all* the truths of geometry could be shown to follow, by reason alone, from a small number of clear and intuitively obvious definitions, together with a small number of clearly understandable and obviously true propositions. Geometric knowledge was to be codified by showing which truths followed from which other truths.

For Euclid, the meaning of the terms he used was taken for granted. When he defined a "point" as that which has no parts, or no magnitude, a "line" as that which has length without breadth, and "surface" as that which has only length and breadth, it was assumed that everyone would know what these terms meant. Similarly, it was assumed that everyone would know what the basic truths meant: *A straight line may be drawn from one point to any other point. A circle may be described from any center, at any distance from that center. All right angles are equal.* In short, geometry was assumed to have an intuitively clear subject matter. The definitions, axioms, and postulates were taken as providing a *clear understanding* of the fundamental truths, from which all of the other truths could be deduced by reason alone. That clear understanding was part of the point of doing euclidean geometry.

Noneuclidean geometry was a consequence of the attempt to demonstrate that Euclid's postulates were independent of one another—that none could be deduced logically from the others, and that they really were an irreducible minimum. The postulate at issue was the parallel postulate:

> Suppose a straight line, A, intersects two other straight lines, B and C, so that the two interior angles on the same side of A have a sum of less than two right angles; then lines B and C will meet on the side of A on which the interior angles are less than two right angles.

It was eventually shown that a consistent geometry could be produced in which this postulate was false and all the others were true. In such a geometry, the following basic truth of euclidean geometry would be false:

> Through a point outside of a straight line, L, there can be drawn exactly one straight line parallel to L.

But what could it *mean* for such a truth of geometry to be false? What could it mean for there to be no straight line parallel to L? Or more than one? The answer provided was that noneuclidean geometries were about different subject matters. In addition to the geometry of a flat plane surface, there is the geometry of the surface of a sphere. Suppose we take "straight line" to mean a great circle on a sphere. Then, given a straight line, *L, no* straight lines parallel to *L* can be drawn through a point outside of *L*. And if we take the subject matter to be about a saddle-shaped surface and we take a "straight line" to be a geodesic on that surface, then the parallel postulate will be false: *B* and *C* need never meet.

Noneuclidean geometry represented a great advance in mathematics, but it caused a crisis in the understanding of the axiomatic method, and hence in the understanding of what mathematics itself was about. The crisis was this: Spherical and hyperbolic geometry "shared" other postulates with euclidean geometry, and differed in the parallel postulate. But the concepts used in those shared postulates were concepts taken from euclidean geometry—concepts like point, line, and plane. However, in euclidean geometry, "line" did not mean "great circle" and "plane" did not mean "the surface of a sphere." What could it mean for postulates of different geometries to be "shared" when the concepts used in those postulates were not the same? How could a postulate about lines and planes be the *same* as a postulate about great circles and surfaces of spheres?

It is possible to give an answer like the following: Euclid was too specific; his postulates should have mentioned concepts one level higher. Thus, instead of *planes* he should have said *two-dimensional surfaces*, instead of *lines* he should have said *geodesics*, etc. Such an answer would change the concepts used in the postulates to more general concepts. But substituting these new interpretations of the concepts used in the axioms was not a general solution. There might be still other geometries with still different concepts than geodesics and surfaces. There was no guarantee that any fixed concepts would be general enough to avoid such problems in the future.

David Hilbert (see Kleene 1967, chap. 4) came up with a solution that was completely general—his program of *formalism.* Hilbert viewed mathematical proofs as merely matters of form, with questions of meaning put aside to be discussed outside mathematics proper in "metamathematics." Mathematics, Hilbert suggested, is the study of meaningless symbols, and mathematical proofs are sequences of strings of uninterpreted symbols, with the lines of a proof related to one another by regular rules. In a formal axiomatic system, as Hilbert defined it, axioms are strings of uninterpreted symbols, and theorems are other strings of uninterpreted symbols derived from the axioms by rules. In what Hilbert called "metamathematics," the symbols in the axioms could be interpreted. In formal axiomatic geometry, the axioms consist only of uninterpreted symbols like *PT, L*, and *PN*. One might interpret these in plane geometry as meaning "point," "line," and "plane," respectively, but from the point of view of axiomatic geometry they are nothing but symbols. Proofs are deduced mechanically from the axioms. The axioms, strictly speaking, contain no concepts at all. Only in metamathematics are the symbols in the axioms given an interpretation. Thus, in euclidean geometry, symbols *L* and *PN* in an axiom might be interpreted by "line" and "plane," while in spherical geometry the same symbols would be interpreted by "great circle" and "surface of a sphere." But any interpretations of the symbols play no role at all in deducing theorems. In this way, the shared axioms of the various geometries would be the same not because they contained the same concepts, but because they consisted of the same strings of symbols.

In mathematical logic, Hilbert's version of the axiomatic method is applied to logic itself. A deductive logical system consists of a collection of uninterpreted symbols, formation rules that combine these into well-formed formulas, and transformation rules that permit certain strings of symbols to be substituted for other strings of symbols. A finite number of well-formed formulas are taken as axioms. Theorems are derived from axioms by transformation rules. A proof is just a sequence of strings of symbols. The symbols in such a deductive system are, technically, completely meaningless. Such a system of formation rules and rules of transformation is called a formal "syntax."

"Semantics" is a technical way to "give meaning" to the uninterpreted symbols of the "syntax." A model-theoretical semantics consists of a model structure and rules for mapping the symbols of the deductive system into elements of that model structure. The most typical kind of model structure consists of a set of entities, and various other set-theoretical constructions—sets of entities, sets of *n*-tuples of entities, etc. Strictly speaking, the models are also meaningless. They are just structures with entities and sets. The only structure they have is set-theoretical structure.

Mathematical logic provides mathematics with a completely precise and mechanical definition of a "proof" in a completely formal "language" where the question of what the symbols mean does not arise. It also provides mathematics with a completely precise definition of a mathematical structure, namely, a model with entities and sets. Here too the question of how the model is to be understood does not arise. Formal semantics is a way of pairing, *in a completely precise way,* strings of symbols that have structure but no meaning with models that also have structure but no meaning. The models are understood as "giving meaning" to the sentences. All that means is that the sentences are associated with a model. Everything—the sentences, the models, and the pairings—is completely precise. No problems of human understanding get in the way.

What makes this *mathematics,* rather than just the study of how structured symbol-sequences can match up with structures made up of entities and sets? The answer is that human mathematicians can *understand* both the sentences and the models in terms of mathematics that they have an intuitive familiarity with. If the subject matter were euclidean plane geometry, the entities in the models would be *understood* intuitively as being points, lines, and planes, and symbols like *PT, L,* and *PN* in the axioms would be *understood* as referring to points, lines, and planes. If the subject matter were spherical geometry, there would be a model with a different structure, and the entities in the model would be *understood* intuitively as being points, great circles, and surfaces of spheres, while symbols like *PT, L,* and *PN* would be *understood* as referring to points, great circles, and spheres. Technically, such understandings are irrelevant to the mathematics. Understandings of this sort do no more than make all this intuitively comprehensible to a human mathematician. It becomes mathematics for us because we can *understand* the models as being about geometric figures, numbers, etc.

Similarly, mathematical logic is technically no more than the study of sequences of symbol strings (proof theory) and the way symbol strings can be paired with structures containing entities and sets (model theory). What makes it the study of reason? The answer is: objectivist philosophy plus a way of understanding the models. The subject matter is taken to be the world. Objectivist metaphysics says the world consists of objects with properties and relations. We now add a way of understanding models. Understand the abstract entities in the models as objects, sets of entities as properties, and sets of ordered pairs of entities as relations. So much for the understanding of the models; now for the understanding of the symbol strings. Understand a set of symbol strings as a "language" in which we reason. Understand a sequence of these symbol strings as a chain of reasoning. Understand some of the symbols as referring expressions, expressions that refer to objects. Understand other symbols as predicates, that is, expressions that refer to properties and relations. If we view the formal language as a "language of thought," then the relationship between the symbols and the models can be understood as constituting a way in which the things we think in terms of (the symbols) can correspond to the world (the model consisting of entities and sets). Similarly, if we understand the formal language as a natural language, we can understand the words (symbols) as corresponding to things in the world (the entities and sets). It is only by assuming the correctness of objectivist philosophy and by imposing such an understanding that mathematical logic can be viewed as the study of reason in general. Such an understanding has been imposed by objectivist philosophers. There is nothing inherent to mathematical logic that makes it the study of reason.

There is a big difference between the application of mathematical logic in mathematics and its use as a tool to characterize human reason in general. The difference is this: Its use in mathematics has been justified by a magnificent tradition of mathematical research. What Bolzano, Dedekind, Cauchy, Peano, Hilbert, Frege, Russell, and others did was to demonstrate in minute detail exactly *why* it was reasonable to understand familiar branches of mathematics—arithmetic, geometry, algebra, topology, calculus, etc.—in terms of models made up of entities and sets. They also demonstrated why it was reasonable to understand the kinds of proofs that human mathematicians constructed as sequences of symbol strings constructed by mechanical means. In addition, they showed why it was reasonable to understand the formal rules of deduction used in mathematical logic as *the limited form of reasoning used by mathematicians to construct mathematical proofs*.

Hilbert was wrong about mathematics being nothing more than the study of meaningless symbols and their relationship to meaningless structures. Two things make formal mathematics mathematics: (*a*) the way those symbols and structures are *understood* as being about familiar mathematical domains and (*b*) the detailed *justifications* for adopting such an understanding. Here is the difference between the use of mathematical logic in mathematics and its use in the cognitive sciences. In the cognitive sciences, its use has not been adequately justified. The assumptions of objectivist philosophy have been assumed to be sufficient justification. But that is no justification at all. What is needed is *empirical* justification. In particular, three kinds of empirical justification would be needed:

- Justification for the use of models made up of abstract entities and sets to characterize the world.
- Justification for the use of strings of uninterpreted symbols to characterize human reason.
- Justification for the "objectively correct" interpretive links between the symbols in the mind and the entities and sets in the world.

But empirical studies of human categorization, on the one hand, and the world, on the other, suggest that no adequate justification will ever be forthcoming. Here are some reasons:

- Let's start with the world: Studies in evolutionary biology suggest that living things do not fall neatly into natural kinds as defined by simplistic set-theoretical taxonomic definitions. Biology is simply more complicated than that. Moreover, colors do not exist as neat set-theoretical divisions of the physical world external to beings with visual systems—in fact, they do not exist at all external to beings with visual systems.

- As for the mind, human conceptual categories have a structure that does not appear to be adequately characterized by primitive symbols or complex strings of them.
- And there does not appear to be any sort of direct relationship between the mind and the world of the sort hypothesized in model theory. Color categories exist in the mind, but simply do not correspond to anything like set-theoretical entities in the world. Radial categories, like *mother* in English, *balan* in Dyirbal, and *nehcihsähA* in Fox, do not correspond to sets in the world characterized by shared properties. Metaphorically defined categories do not seem to correspond to anything that exists independent of human conceptual systems. And perception, which is often taken as characterizing the links between the mind and world, is not veridical; it does not even preserve the number of entities, since people can see one light moving when there are two lights flashing.

In short, the empirical studies discussed in this book suggest that, on all three grounds, there can be no justification for extending mathematical logic from the domain of mathematical reasoning to the domain of human reason in general.

Autonomous Syntax

The idea that natural language syntax is independent of semantics derives from the attempt to impose the structure of mathematical logic on the study of human language and human thought in general. In mathematical logic, there are an independently existing "syntax," independently existing model structures, and principles for mapping the syntax into the model structures. The "semantics" consists of the model structure plus the mapping principles. It is a consequence of the *definition* of this kind of system that the syntax exists independent of the semantics, but not vice versa. The syntax could thus be viewed as a "module" independent of the semantics, and the semantics as a "module" that takes the syntax as input.

It is important at this point to recall that we are discussing man-made systems constructed for the purpose of making sense of mathematics. Euclid's axiomatic method was a way of comprehending and systematizing knowledge about a subject matter: geometry. Euclid's conception had the following two characteristics:

1. The definitions and the axioms were meaningful. To Euclid, "line" meant line, not great circle.

2. The axioms were precisely characterized in such a way that consequences would follow by reason alone.

Geometry for Euclid was something to be done in natural language—with terms that are meaningful and understandable. Part of the point was to use definitions, axioms, and postulates that had a fixed, understandable meaning.

The advent of noneuclidean geometry showed that these two characteristics were in conflict. Hilbert "saved" the axiomatic method by splitting off half of it—the half having to do with meaningfulness—and consigning it to metamathematics. It was a technical solution and a brilliant one, which led to an incredibly interesting new form of mathematics and to insights about the nature of mathematical proof, as well as the nature of mathematical truth.

But from its very birth, formalist mathematics, with its idea of an uninterpreted formal "language," was at odds with natural language. Natural language comes with meaning, and when we normally reason using natural language, we reason *about things in terms that are meaningful;* we don't just reason, and then find out what we were reasoning about and what our concepts meant. How did it come about that philosophers, linguists, and even many cognitive psychologists have come to view natural human languages in terms of formal syntax and formal semantics?

The principal reason was the rise of mathematical logic, the enormous prestige that it acquired, and the fact that it was taught in European and American universities by objectivist philosophers, who viewed it as the study of reason. When logic was turned into a form of mathematics by Frege, Russell, Hilbert, and others, the axiomatic method was adopted into logic itself. It was assumed that there were a finite number of fundamental truths of logic from which all others followed. These were adopted as axioms and used as the basis on which to make logical deductions. This was crucial to making mathematical logic "mathematical."

The formalist program of separating syntax from semantics accompanied the mathematicization of logic and the unification of logic with mathematics. The separation was needed in order to make sense of axiom systems. Through the influence of Bertrand Russell, British and American philosophers eventually adopted the objectivist equation of reason with mathematical logic. Along with that development came the idea that natural languages also had a division between syntax and semantics, with syntax being a matter of uninterpreted symbols and semantics providing a separate interpretation. To objectivist philosophers trained in mathematical logic, the division came to seem natural.

This division has, in recent years, been attributed to natural language and human reason by the professionals whose job it is to study such things: linguists, philosophers, artificial intelligence researchers, and cognitive psychologists. It has seemed natural to them precisely *because* they have been trained in mathematical logic. By now, it has largely been forgotten just why the division into formal syntax and formal semantics was made in the first place—and what an alien division it is relative to human language and thought.

Formalist mathematics changed Euclid's understanding of the axiomatic method in *two* fundamental ways: first, by making the axioms and postulates of geometry independent of the meanings of the terms in them and, second, by taking "reason" to be mathematical logic. It is important to remember that, although mathematical logic contributes a great deal to the study of the foundations of mathematics, it is *not* a general approach to the study of natural language and human reason. Formalist "syntax" and "semantics" in the tradition of mathematical logic are artificial constructions invented to serve certain mathematical purposes. They are not about natural language syntax and human reason.

The Formal System Metaphor for Grammar

The theory of formal deductive systems was generalized by Emil Post, who viewed them as special cases of systems of "production rules" which replace strings of uninterpreted symbols by other strings of uninterpreted symbols. Generative linguistics *defines* a language as a set of strings of uninterpreted symbols, generated by some appropriately restricted version of production rules (see Chomsky 1957). Rules of syntax within generative linguistics are thus, by definition, independent of semantics. Semantics is, by definition, interpretive; that is, it gives meaning to the uninterpreted symbols of the syntax. There are two general approaches to semantics within generative grammar. One is the sort used in mathematical logic, where the symbols in the syntax are mapped onto models. This approach has been taken in generative semantics, Montague grammar, and other theories. The other approach uses what Lewis called the "Markerese" strategy of algorithmically translating symbols of the syntax into symbols of another formal system which is taken to be a "language of thought," sometimes referred to as "mentalese." This approach is taken by Katz, Fodor, Chomsky, and others and is also characteristic of researchers in artificial intelligence.

As we have seen, such a "definition" of grammar as a kind of system of production rules and a language as a set of strings of symbols generated by that system is not a consequence of mathematical logic. It is not merely a value-free application of mathematics to natural language. It is the imposition of a metaphor—a metaphor based on objectivist philosophy. It characterizes a commitment to try to understand natural language in terms of such systems. The autonomy of syntax—the independence of syntax from semantics—is a consequence of that metaphor. If you accept the metaphor, then it is true by definition (metaphorical definition!) that natural language syntax is independent of semantics, but not conversely.

Within generative linguistics, the syntax is independent of everything else. This is not an empirical result; it is a consequence of a metaphorical definition, which characterizes a commitment to study language according to that metaphor.

The question of whether there is an independent syntax for natural language comes down to the question of whether the metaphorical definition that defines the enterprise of generative grammar is a reasonable way to comprehend natural language. Intuitively the idea that a natural language is made up of uninterpreted symbols is rather strange. The primary purposes of language are to frame and express thoughts and to communicate, not to produce sequences of uninterpreted sounds. If thought is independent of language (as it seems, at least in part, to be), and if language is a way of framing and expressing thought so that it can be communicated, then one would expect that many (not necessarily all) aspects of natural language syntax would be dependent in at least some way on the thoughts expressed. Indeed, evidence for this is presented in case study 3 below.

The formalist program in mathematics was a way to make the axiomatic method comprehensible and it has led to extraordinarily interesting mathematics. But the attempt to apply it to language and cognition in accordance with objectivist principles will not work for the empirical reasons given above. In fact, there is even reason to believe that formalist methods are *logically* inconsistent with the requirements for an objectivist theory of meaning.

CHAPTER 15

Putnam's Theorem

The Inconsistency of Model-Theoretic Semantics

The argument we gave in chapter 13 against objectivist epistemology and objectivist semantics was an empirical argument. It was based on evidence about how people categorize. But Hilary Putnam, in *Reason, Truth, and History* (1981), has gone one step further. He has provided a devastating logical critique of the view of meaning and reference in what he calls *metaphysical realism,* which is a generalized version of what we have called objectivist semantics. He has given a proof that, with a little work, will enable us to show that objectivist semantics, as it is characterized mathematically using model theory, is internally inconsistent. In particular, the following two claims are inconsistent:

- Semantics characterizes the way that symbols are related to entities in the world.
- Semantics characterizes meaning.

In short, the relationship between symbols and the world does not characterize meaning. This is a remarkable result. It has been arrived at by taking model theory as a general characterization of the relationship between symbols and entities in the world and by imposing on it standard requirements for an objectivist theory of meaning. The result is all the more remarkable since both statements are definitions. They have also been taken by a great many researchers in semantics as both being true—and obviously true. It is news that they are inconsistent—and important news! The inconsistency can be demonstrated by taking model theory and adding to it two things:

1. The standard model-theoretic definition of meaning.
2. A necessary requirement that any theory of meaning must fulfill.

The standard model-theoretic definition of meaning is:

1. The meaning of a sentence is a function which assigns a *truth value* to that sentence in each possible situation (or possible world).

Similarly, meanings are defined for parts of sentences, for example, for terms and for *n*-place predicates.

- The meaning of a term (a noun or noun phrase) is a function which assigns a *referent* (an individual or kind) to that term in each possible situation (or possible world).
- The meaning of an *n*-place predicate is a function which assigns a *referent* (a set of *n*-tuples of entities) to that predicate in each possible situation (or possible world).

Thus meaning is defined in terms of truth for whole sentences and in terms of reference for parts of sentences.

Any theory of meaning at all, model-theoretic or not, must obey the following constraint:

2. The meanings of the parts cannot be changed without changing the meaning of the whole.

It is the nature of meaning that the meanings of the parts of a sentence contribute to the meaning of the whole in a nontrivial way. Requirement 2 is a way of stating that. It is such an obvious requirement, that it is usually taken for granted in empirical semantic theories and not stated explicitly. Yet any putative theory of "meaning" that violates requirement 2 is not really a theory of *meaning*.

For example, the correct meanings of *cat* and *mat* should be required in order to get the correct meaning of *The cat is on the mat.* In other words, it should be impossible to get the correct meaning of *The cat is on the mat* without the correct meanings of *cat* and *mat* making their appropriate contributions. Any purported theory of meaning in which one can radically change the meanings of *cat* and *mat* without changing the meaning of *The cat is on the mat* would fail requirement 2 and hence fail as a theory of meaning.

Putnam argues the model-theoretic semantics fails as a theory of meaning in just this way. The reason is that the mathematical properties of model theory are inconsistent with requirement 2 taken together with the definition of meaning in 1. Without a definition of meaning (like 1), and without constraints on what constitutes meaning (like 2), model theory is just model theory—not a theory of meaning. The definition in 1 is the standard definition of meaning used in model-theoretic semantics. The constraint in 2 is simply a requirement on any theory of meaning. There is nothing wrong with model theory in itself. The problem lies in the use of model theory in the service of a theory of meaning. In short, if Putnam is right, model theory cannot be made into a theory of meaning at all. Model theory is, of course, the natural mathematization of objectivist semantics. What Putnam is suggesting is that there can be no such possible mathematicization. That is, objectivist semantics cannot be made precise without contradiction.

Rampant and Moderate Indeterminacy

Before we go on, it should be pointed out that, as it applies to objectivist semantics, requirement 2 must hold for all sentences of all languages. If a given theory cannot guarantee that requirement 2 will hold for *every* sentence, then it fails as a theory of meaning. This is an extremely strong condition: for any such theory, one counterexample can blow the whole works. In other words, the meaning of the whole sentence cannot be kept the same when the meanings of the parts change significantly—for any sentence!

This is an important point. Any purported theory of meaning that *necessarily* allows the meaning of, say, *The cat is on the mat* to be kept the same when the meanings of *cat* and *mat* change radically is not a theory of meaning. The word "necessarily" is crucial here. We are not talking about minor things that might be patched up. The problem has to be essential to the theory. We are also not talking about idioms or cases whose analysis is up for grabs. We are talking only about cases where it is clear that the meaning of the parts *should* play a role in the meaning of the whole.

Of course, if a theory fails in that way for one straightforward case, it will probably fail for an infinity of other cases. But, to prove inconsistency, it is not necessary to demonstrate failure for an infinity of cases. One *unavoidable* failure would show that requirements 1 and 2 are inconsistent with model theory. The point is that such a *necessary,* rather than incidental, failure provides a real counterexample, since it would fail an *essential requirement* of a theory of meaning. What needs to be shown is that such failures are necessary for at least one case and that they cannot be avoided by minor adjustments.

As we shall see, Putnam makes an infinitely stronger claim, that in model-theoretic semantics condition 2 can be violated for *every* sentence of a language. Let us refer to this as *rampant indeterminacy* of reference. Rampant indeterminacy occurs where reference can be changed throughout the language while the truth-conditional meaning is preserved. But this stronger claim is not necessary to show that objectivist semantics is internally inconsistent, that is, that conditions 1 and 2 cannot be added to model theory without inconsistency. Any such indeterminacy, however moderate, will do. The reason I mention this is that replies to Putnam, as we shall see below, suggest ways to avoid rampant indeterminacy of reference, but not moderate indeterminacy. But any number of violations of requirement 2 will be sufficient to show inconsistency. To make his point, Putnam only needs to demonstrate the inevitability of moderate indeterminacy of reference.

"Truth" in Model Theory

In what follows we will be speaking a good deal about "truth" as it is characterized in model theory. It should be pointed out that in model theory "truth" is a technical term that does not mean what we ordinarily mean by the English word *truth*. When we normally speak of a sentence being *true* or *false,* it is assumed that we understand the sentence prior to any determination of its truth or falsity in a given situation. We do not usually speak of the *truth* or *falsity* of sequences of nonsense words.

But that *is* what is done in model theory. "Truth" in model theory is a relation between a sequence of meaningless symbols and a structure consisting of abstract entities and sets. If a relation of a specified kind holds between the sequence of symbols and the model structure, then the model is said to "satisfy" the symbol sequence, which is referred to as a "sentence." That "sentence" is then called "true" in that model. It is "truth" in this technical sense that we will be discussing throughout this chapter. And it is this concept of "truth" that is used in requirement 1, where "meaning" is defined in terms of "truth."

This use of the term "truth" has come to us from formalist mathematics. There it is a very reasonable extension of the ordinary word "truth." The reason is that both the symbol sequences and the model structures are taken as *understood* in terms of familiar mathematical concepts. When both the symbol sequences and the models are meaningful beforehand, then it makes sense to use the ordinary English word "true" to speak of satisfaction in a model. And when that understanding is justified by mathematical research, the use of the word "true" is further justified.

But, as we observed in the previous chapter, such a prior understanding cannot be taken for granted in the case of ordinary natural language sentences. In the absence of any prior understanding of the sentences and the models that is justified in terms of research on cognition, it is more than a bit strange to use the word "true" to speak of sequences of meaningless symbols that are "satisfied" by a set-theoretical structure containing abstract entities and sets. Nonetheless, we will use "true" in this technical sense throughout this chapter, since it is the term used in objectivist semantics. When we speak below of "truth" being preserved when reference is changed, it is this technical sense of "truth" that we shall be talking about.

The Inconsistency

To approach Putnam's result, let us begin with a well-known result from the theory of models, the Löwenheim-Skolem theorem:

> If a countable collection of sentences in a first-order formalized language has a model, it has a denumerable model.

This was a rather surprising result in its day, and it still surprises a great many people. To see what is surprising about it, suppose that the collection of sentences is intended to be true of the real numbers, which are not countable—that is, there are too many of them to be put in a one-to-one correspondence with the positive integers. A mathematician might, for example, set up an axiom system for the real numbers. Such an axiom system would be intended to characterize the real numbers and only the real numbers. One thing an axiom systsem would have to do would be to *distinguish* the real numbers from the integers, that is, to state truths about the real numbers that would not be true of the integers. Before the Löwenheim-Skolem theorem, it was assumed that this would be possible in a first-order language with a countable number of terms. What the Löwenheim-Skolem theorem says is that this is not possible—no matter what axioms you set up. No matter what collection of sentences it is, if it is true of the real numbers, it can also be satisfied by the positive integers, structured in some way or other. Within the theory of models, you cannot come up with a set of sentences that will be true of the real numbers alone and not true of some structure or other (usually quite exotic) whose underlying set is the positive integers. If you intend that the collection of sentences have model A (the real numbers), then it will also have model B (the positive integers). In short, within the theory of models you can't construct a collection of sentences that will always refer exactly to what you want them to refer to.

Before we go on, it is important to see exactly *why* the Löwenheim-Skolem theorem is true. It has to do with the nature of formal syntax and formal semantics.

- A formal language is a set of strings of meaningless symbols. If the number of terms in the language is countable, and if each sentence is of finite length, then the number of "sentences," that is, strings of meaningless symbols in the formal language is countable: they can be put into one-to-one correspondence with the integers.
- A set of axioms is a finitely specifiable collection of strings of symbols that are meaningless in themselves and must be given an interpreta-

tion to be made meaningful. The theorems that follow from those axioms are countable—since they must be subset of the sentences of the language.

- Since the axioms are meaningless, they are, at least conceivably, open to interpretations that are unintended. The models, after all, exist independent of the formal language. Some model you hadn't thought about may just happen to satisfy the axioms you've set up.
- What is sometimes forgotten is that *the models are also meaningless in themselves without some interpretation being imposed on them.* Technically, each model is just a set of abstract entities with a structure. The structure is defined only by sets. The *interpretation of the model* as being about, say, mathematics or the physical world is not part of the model itself. It is an interpretation imposed by people.
- The models, which are supposed to supply *meaning* to the axioms, have no meaning themselves without some understanding being imposed on them. They are just a set of entities structured further into other sets, and sets of sets, etc.
- Given that you have a countable number of meaningless strings of symbols (your theorems), it should not be surprising that a model with a countable number of entities should satisfy them. In other words, if you have only countably many meaningless things to say, it only takes a countable number of objects to satisfy those statements.

The result shouldn't have been surprising, but it was. Even mathematicians using such systems forgot that both the language and the models were meaningless. Each of them has structure and no more. It was (and still is) common for mathematicians to project intended meanings onto their axioms and their models. But unintended interpretations are nonetheless unavoidable when you are matching meaningless strings of symbols to meaningless structures. Our purpose in discussing the Löwenheim-Skolem theorem has been to cite a well-known case that demonstrates this fact about formal systems. It is this fact that Putnam uses in demonstrating that the pairing of *meaningless* strings of symbols with *meaningless* structures cannot provide a theory of *meaning*.

To understand Putnam's result, it is important to bear in mind that the models in model theory are as meaningless in themselves as the symbols in the formal languages. All they have is structure. What objectivist semantics tries to do is use meaningless but structured models to give *meaning* to a meaningless but structured formal language. It attempts to do this by adding to model theory definition above. What Putnam argues is that this addition is inconsistent, given the constraint in 2 above. To show this, he uses the fact that formal languages can have unintended models.

Recall what it means for a collection of sentences to have two models, A and B. It means that model A makes all the sentences true and model B also makes all sentences true. Thus, in switching from model A to model B, one can keep all the sentences true while changing what the sentences are talking about. In short, preserving "truth" (in the technical model-theoretical sense of the word) does not mean preserving reference. It is this fact about model theory that Putnam makes use of to get his result.

Before we go on, we should make it clear that Putnam's result is *not* an application of the Löwenheim-Skolem theorem itself, but only an application of what the techniques for proving that theorem reveal about the nature of formal systems in general. The distinction is important, because the Löwenheim-Skolem theorem is about first-order systems, and does not apply to second-order systems. In first-order systems one cannot quantify over properties and predicates (as in *Herb has all of Sammy's good qualities*), while in second-order systems such quantification is possible. Since natural language permits such quantification, the Löwenheim-Skolem theorem does not apply to it. But the property of model-theoretic interpretation discussed above, namely, that truth in a model can be preserved while reference is changed, holds in general, not just in first-order systems. It is this property of such systems that Putnam is using. I mention this because the point has been misunderstood by Hacking (1983, pp. 102–9), who mistakenly describes Putnam's argument as an application of the Löwenheim-Skolem theorem and takes Putnam to task incorrectly for not distinguishing between first-order and second-order languages.

The crucial fact that Putnam uses is that model-theoretic semantics tries to use truth (that is, satisfaction in a model) and reference to define meaning. In model-theoretic semantics, the meaning of a sentence (the whole) is identified with its truth conditions in every possible situation. And the meaning of the terms (the parts) is identified with their referents in every possible situation (requirement 1 above). But truth underdetermines reference in model theory. Preserving the truth of sentences across models does not mean that the reference of the parts will be preserved. One can change the reference of the parts, while still preserving truth for the whole in every interpretation. But if sentence meaning is defined in terms of truth, and if the meaning of terms is defined in terms of reference, then one can change the "meaning" of the parts while preserving the "meaning" of the whole sentence.

What Putnam does is show exactly how this can be done and how that possibility violates requirement 2 above. For example, he shows how in model theory it is possible to keep the so-called meaning of *A cat is on a mat* constant while changing the reference of "cat" from cats to cherries and changing the reference of "mat" from mats to trees. This violates the condition that the meanings of the parts must contribute to the meaning of the whole.

To get an idea of the way Putnam's theorem accomplishes this, let us consider first his construction for the *cat-mat* case. Putnam begins with the sentence

(*A*) A cat is on a mat.

where "cat" refers to cats and "mat" refers to mats. He then shows how to give (*A*) a new interpretation:

(*B*) A cat* is on a mat*.

The definitions of cat* and mat* make use of three cases:

(*a*) Some cat is on some mat and some cherry is on some tree.
(*b*) Some cat is on some mat and no cherry is on any tree.
(*c*) Neither (*a*) nor (*b*) holds.

Here are Putnam's definitions:

DEFINITION OF CAT*
x is a cat* if and only if case (*a*) holds and *x* is a cherry; or case (*b*) holds and *x* is a cat; or case (*c*) holds and *x* is a cherry.

DEFINITION OF MAT*
x is a mat* if and only if case (*a*) holds and *x* is a tree; or case (*b*) holds and *x* is a mat; or case (*c*) holds and *x* is a quark.

These are obviously absurd, unnatural, gerrymandered definitions—and that is exactly Putnam's point. Given these definitions, it turns out that *A cat* is on a mat** is true in exactly those possible worlds in which *A cat is on a mat* is true, and thus according to the truth-conditional definition of meaning, these sentences will have the same meaning. To see why, consider the three cases, (*a*), (*b*), and (*c*):

In possible worlds where cases (*a*) holds, *A cat is on a mat* is true and *A cat* is on a mat** is also true—because a cherry is on a tree, and all cherries are cats* and all trees are mats*.
In possible worlds where case (*b*) holds, both sentences are true, because "cat" and "cat*" are coextensive terms, as are "mat" and "mat*."
In possible worlds where case (*c*) holds, *A cat is on a mat* is false, and *A cat* is on a mat** is also false—because a cherry can't be on a quark!

Since the sentences are true (or false) in exactly the same possible worlds, they have the same "meaning," given the definition of "meaning" in objectivist semantics. Thus it is possible to reinterpret "cat" to have the intension of "cat*" and to simultaneously reinterpret "mat" to have the intension of "mat*." This would leave *A cat is on a mat* with exactly the same meaning, while the meanings of "cat" and "mat" were changed drastically. But this violates requirement 2 above. But the very fact that Putnam's cat-mat construction is possible shows that requirements 1 and 2 are inconsistent with a fundamental property of model theory, namely, the property that truth can be maintained while reference is changed. On pages 217–18 of *Reason, Truth, and History,* Putnam gives a general proof that such meaning-preserving changes of reference are always possible. Putnam's Theorem is stated as follows:

Theorem Let L be a language with predicates $F_1, F_2, \ldots, F_k$ (not necessarily monadic). Let I be an interpretation, in the sense of an assignment of an intension to every predicate of L. Then if I is nontrivial in the sense that at least one predicate has an extension which is neither empty nor universal in at least one possible world, there exists a second interpretation J which disagrees with I, but which makes the same sentences true in every possible world as I does.

Unless such truth-preserving changes of reference are ruled out, the program of objectivist semantics—using model theory as a theory of meaning—is internally inconsistent. The reason is that conditions 1 and 2 cannot be added to model theory without a contradiction.

At this point, we have seen where the inconsistency lies in attempts to use model theory as a theory of meaning. But to get a better feel for what Putnam has accomplished, we should go through a range of attempts to avoid the consequences of Putnam's proof.

Why Fixing Reference Does Not Help

One might think that the solution to this problem would lie with providing a better account of reference—one that would eliminate the possibility that *cat* might refer to anything but cats. This has some initial plausibility. Language, after all, is fixed by convention—and that includes the meanings of words. Words do have correct meanings. What the words of a given language mean, at any point in history, is a matter of fact. The word *cat* in English at present does not mean cherry. Let us consider what would be required to use this fact about language *within model theory* as a way out of the dilemma.

Within model theory, meanings are defined in terms of reference. For words to have correct meanings in model theory, the references (which are used to define meaning) must be correct—objectively correct—in each model. What is required is an objectively correct reference assignment for each model. If such an objectively correct account of reference could be found, it would rule out the incorrect assignment of *cat* to cherries, and presumably all examples like Putnam's cat-mat example.

But even that would not solve the problem. Even finding an objectively correct reference assignment function would not eliminate the force of Putnam's example. The reason is that requirement 2 is a *necessary* condition for any theory of meaning. It entails that, if the meanings of parts are assigned *incorrectly,* then the meaning of the whole must be *incorrect.* An incorrect assignment of meaning is, after all, a change away from the correct assignment of meaning. Requirement 2 says that such a change in the meaning of the parts must result in a corresponding change in the meaning of the whole. Thus, *A cat is on a mat* should not be able to have its correct meaning if *cat* and *mat* do not have their correct meanings. However, Putnam's critique shows that truth-conditional meaning can be preserved even when *incorrect* reference is assigned. This violates requirement 2.

It is simply not enough to have an objectively correct reference assignment function. The reason is that requirement 2 entails a condition on *incorrect* as well as correct reference assignments: *Meaning cannot be preserved under incorrect assignments.* Any theory in which incorrect reference assignments have no effect on meaning is not an adequate theory of meaning. If there is a way out for model-theoretic semantics, it does not lie with finding an objectively correct account of reference.

Why There Can Be No Objectivist Account of Reference

As we have just seen, model-theoretic semantics cannot provide an adequate account of meaning, even if there could be an objectively correct account of reference. But Putnam's critique extends even further. It shows that *no objectively correct account of reference is even possible!*

On the objectivist view, a language, with its interpretation, is taken as an institutional fact. The references, and hence the meanings, of terms are fixed by convention. Once fixed, they become facts, on a par with other objective facts. Frege believed that "senses," or "intensions," of terms determined their reference. This is what we have called the reference-via-meaning view. It amounts to the idea that a description of the properties of either a single entity or a category will be sufficient to correctly "pick out" that entity or category. But Putnam (in earlier work) and Kripke have observed that no descriptions of properties will be sufficient to determine reference within model theory—just as truth-conditional "meanings" of sentences do not determine reference. They suggested instead that reference is "direct"—fixed not "indirectly" by a description of properties, but directly by acts of naming. But for the purpose of the present discussion, the difference between these two views doesn't matter. On both views, reference-via-meaning and direct-reference, once the interpretation of a language is chosen, reference is an objective fact.

In such cases, the model of the actual world must contain a model of the reference relation itself. In a model, the reference relation is given by a set of ordered pairs, with each pair consisting of (1) an element of the formal language being interpreted and (2) an entity or set in that model. Let us call this set of pairs defining the reference relation *S*. But now a problem arises. What does the expression "refer" refer to? One possible suggestion is that the referent is the set *S* itself. But this leads to vicious circularity, a characterization of *S* in terms of itself.

$S = \{. . . , (\text{"refer,"}\ S), . . .\}$.

The circularity can be avoided by attempting to provide a *theory* of reference, that is, a characterization of "refer" in terms of some other relation, *R*. Thus, it would have to be objectively true that:

x refers to y if and only if *x bears R to y*.

There have been various attempts to provide such a theory, for example, Kripke's causal theory (Kripke 1972). But what would such a theory be like? It would have to be some collection of sentences about the relation *R*. And it would have to characterize a unique, objectively correct relation *R*. That is, there would have to be a unique, objectively correct model of any such theory about *R*. But, as Putnam's theorem shows, that is impossible within model theory. Any collection of sentences about *R* could be satisfied by an indefinitely large number of models. There is an infinity of relations holding between words or mental representations on the one hand and objects or sets of objects on the other, and an infinity of models that will make any theory of reference true. Thus, there is no way to determine reference uniquely by providing a *theory* of reference. The reason is that a theory, on the objectivist view of semantics, is itself a set of meaningless sentences requiring an interpretation. Any objectivist theory of reference would, like all other objectivist theories, be subject to indeterminacy of reference!

Given that objectivist *theories* don't help, one might try to avoid the pitfalls of Putnam's theorem by fiat. One might argue that people just *do* refer correctly, so we might as well just give a name, say R^*, to the reference relation defined by people's acts of referring. But, if this is done within model-theoretic semantics the same old problem arises. To designate R^* as the name of the objectively real relation of reference is to make the claim that the sentence,

R^* is the *real* relation of reference.

is true. But Putnam's theorem would apply to this sentence too. There are an infinite number of referents for R^* that would make this sentence true. Without additional apparatus, there is simply no way to fix reference to avoid the consequences of Putnam's theorem.

Thus, not only is the theory of meaning compromised, but the theory of reference—whether reference-via-meaning or direct-reference—is compromised as well. Neither the objectivist theory of meaning nor the objectivist theory of reference will work.

Possible Defenses for Objectivist Semantics

Putnam has not shown that no model-theoretic approach to objectivist semantics of any kind will ever be possible. What he has demonstrated is that no existing approaches are consistent. It is, of course, conceivable that a way can be found to avoid the inconsistency. So far, several defenses of model-theoretic semantics have been offered. They are, in brief:

The Naturalist Defense: Putnam's critique makes use of unnatural categories. Suppose we assume the *world* does not contain unnatural categories of the kind Putnam uses.

The Cognitive Constraint Defense: Suppose we assume that the *mind* does not have such unnatural categories.

The Gradualist Defense: Putnam's theorem assumes that meaning is fixed all at once. Suppose we assume that it is fixed gradually—one or two terms at a time.

The Small-Models Defense: Putnam's theorem holds for very large models. Suppose models are kept to a small size.

The Character Defense: Putnam's critique assumes that meaning is defined *only* in terms of truth conditions. Suppose we let meaning be defined in terms of truth conditions plus *something else* (called "character").

The Situations Defense: Putnam's critique assumes that meaning is defined in terms of truth values. Suppose we grant that truth values are inadequate and suggest instead that meaning be defined in terms of factuality—facts of the matter holding in real-world situations.

These are all reasonable and interesting suggestions. It is all the more interesting that none of them works. Putnam's critique, as we shall see, holds up under *all* the defenses. This does not mean that no defense is possible. But the failure of such a variety of reasonable proposals suggests that there may be no adequate defense of model theory against Putnam's critique. Let us now turn to these defenses and see exactly why they fail.

The Naturalist Defense

Lewis has correctly perceived the devastating nature of Putnam's observations.

> Hilary Putnam has devised a bomb that threatens to devastate the realist philosophy we know and love. He explains that he has learned to stop worrying and love the bomb. He welcomes the new order that it would bring. But we who still live in the target area do not agree. The bomb must be banned. (Lewis 1984, p. 221)

Lewis is a dyed-in-the-wool objectivist, one of the world's finest philosophical logicians, and a principal developer of model-theoretic semantics. If there is a way out, he will look for it.

> Putnam's thesis is incredible. . . . It is out of the question to follow the argument where it leads. We know in advance that there is something wrong, and the challenge is to find out where. (Lewis 1984, p. 221)

Lewis starts by attacking the kind of device Putnam makes use of in the cat-mat example.

As we observed, Putnam's definitions of *cat** and *mat** are extremely unnatural. They do, of course, accord with the classical theory of categorization, in that they provide clear necessary and sufficient conditions for category membership. In part, they were constructed to be unnatural in order to show what crazy results are possible when model theory is used as a theory of meaning. But Lewis claims that Putnam's rampant reference-switching effects can *only* be achieved by the use of such unnatural properties. Such overall reference shifts can be achieved, Lewis claims, only by substituting less natural properties for more natural properties. To block such reference shifts, he adopts a version of a strategy suggested by Merrill (1980).

According to Lewis, the rampant indeterminacy demonstrated by Putnam's theorem can be avoided by blocking massive reference shifts in what he takes to be an intuitively correct way. Lewis claims that certain properties of objects in the world are objectively natural and that others are objectively less natural. His "saving constraint" makes use of this.

> This constraint looks not to the speech and thought of those who refer, and not to their causal connections to the world, but rather to the referents themselves. Among all the countless things and classes that there are, most are miscellaneous, gerrymandered, ill-demarcated. Only an elite minority are carved at the joints, so that their boundaries are established by objective sameness and difference in nature. Only these elite things and classes are eligible to serve as referents. The world—any world—has the makings of many interpretations that satisfy many theories; but most of the interpretations are disqualified because they employ ineligible referents. When we limit ourselves to the eligible interpretations, the ones that respect the objective joints in nature, there is no longer any guarantee that (almost) any world can satisfy (almost) any theory. It becomes once again a worthy goal to discover a theory that will come true on an eligible interpretation, and it becomes a daring and risky hope that we are well on the way to accomplishing this.
>
> Merrill makes eligibility an all-or-nothing matter; I would prefer to make it a matter of degree. The mereological sum of the coffee in my cup, the ink in this sentence, a nearby sparrow and my left shoe is a miscellaneous mess of an object, yet its boundaries are by no means unrelated to the joints in nature. It is an eligible referent, but less eligible than some others. . . . Likewise, metal things are less of an elite, eligible class than the silver things, and the green things are worse, and the grue things are worse still—but all these classes belong to the elite compared to the countless utterly miscellaneous classes of things that there are. *Ceteris paribus,* an eligible interpretation is one that maximises the eligibility of referents overall. Yet it may assign some fairly poor referents if there is a good reason to. After all, 'grue' is a word of our language! *Ceteris* aren't *paribus*, of course; overall eligibility of referents is a matter of degree, making total theory come true is a matter of degree, the two desiderata trade off. . . . The terms of the trade are vague; that will make for moderate indeterminacy of reference; but the sensible realist won't demand perfect determinacy. . . . To a physicalist like myself, the most plausible inequalitarianism seems to be the one that gives a special elite status to the "fundamental physical properties': mass, charge, quark colour and flavour, . . . It is up to physics to discover these properties and name them. (Lewis 1984, pp. 227–28)

In short, Lewis's "saving constraint" is this:

- associate a degree of naturalness with each property in each model, and
- constrain reference so that it maximizes naturalness.

Given such an extension of model theory, Lewis claims, Putnam's rampant reference-switching can be avoided, since there won't be all that many natural properties.

If the natural properties are sparse, there is no reason to expect any over-abundance of intended interpretations. There may even be none. . . . Because satisfaction is not guaranteed, we manage to achieve it by making a good fit between theory and the world. (Lewis 1983, p. 372)

What's Wrong with the Naturalist Defense

The naturalist defense is intended to rule out rampant indeterminacy of reference. By Lewis's own admission, it will still permit moderate indeterminacy of reference. The reason is that for each degree of naturalness, reference-switching can occur among properties at that degree. All that is ruled out is reference-switching across degrees of naturalness. But as we pointed out above, even moderate indeterminacy is enough to guarantee inconsistency with requirement 2. The reason is that moderate indeterminacy will permit a "moderate" number of violations of requirement 2; there will still be a moderate number of cases where the truth-conditional "meaning" of the whole will be preserved, while the "meanings" of the parts are changed to something completely irrelevant. The resulting theory, whatever it is a theory of, will not be a theory of *meaning* that satisfies the objectivists' own requirements. A "moderate" number, incidentally, would seem to be in the hundreds of thousands or more. But even one such example would leave objectivist semantics with an inconsistency.

Though this is sufficient to counter the naturalist defense, some further problems with it ought to be noticed.

First, it seems rather farfetched that nature would conveniently provide such a neat, objectively correct sorting-out of properties along a linear naturalness scale. That is an extreme assumption for even the most rabid physicalists. Imagine trying to convince a working physicist that there ought to be a theory of physics that characterizes such a scale. If the physical universe includes such a scale, then physicists ought to be in the business of characterizing the entire scale theoretically. After all, if Lewis is right, the existence of such a naturalness scale would be one of the most remarkable properties of the physical universe. But frankly, I can't imagine Lewis finding any takers.

Second, Lewis's naturalness scale would leave out functional properties, as Putnam (personal communication) has observed. Functional properties have to do with human beings' purposes and the way people think about objects. Thus, tables, chairs, baseball gloves, pinwheels, lugnuts, stereos, sailboats, fire escapes, garlic presses, venetian blinds, carburetors, chopsticks, garter belts, and tambourines would be no more "natural" than other randomly-put-together physical objects. These do not qualify under Lewis's "traditional realism that recognises objective sameness and difference, joints in the world, discriminatory classifications not of our own making."

Third, it would leave out culturally constituted entities and events. You can carve nature at any joints you like and not carve out a government. Yet governments exist. So do strikeouts, adoptive mothers, and bar mitzvahs. But these involve discriminatory classifications that are of our own making.

Fourth, Lewis has not presented a *proof* that rampant indeterminacy would be ruled out by his proposal. Since indeterminacy would still be possible for each degree of naturalness, and since an indefinitely large amount of reference-switching could go on at each level of naturalness, it is by no means clear that rampant indeterminacy would really be ruled out. That is only an educated guess on Lewis's part, but it still requires proof.

Although the naturalist defense is not an adequate "saving constraint," Lewis does have a point. Definitions like those of *cat** and *mat** should be ruled out—but by an adequate theory of human cognition and human language, which is the only relevant theory where meaning is concerned. But this, I take it, was just Putnam's point.

The Cognitive Constraint Defense

At this point, the obvious suggestion to make—at least to a linguist or psychologist—would be to rule out "unnatural" categories not by objectivist criteria but by cognitive criteria. Thus, one might propose to keep classical model-theoretic semantics, but add cognitive criteria to rule out gerrymandered categories like CAT* and MAT*.

There are three problems with such a suggestion.

First, it is not clear what such criteria should be. It is doubtful that any formal criteria—that is, constraints on the form rather than the content of concepts—would rule out all the gerrymandered concepts without ruling out any real ones. The suggestion is nothing more than a vague research program in the absence of a thorough study of the nature of real human concepts around the world, and suggestions as to what such cognitive constraints might be like.

Second, no constraints that merely *rule out* possible concepts would help in the case of radial and metonymic categories, which are not classical categories at all. Nor would it help with basic-level category structure, which does not exist in classical category structure. In such cases, something must be added, not just ruled out.

Third, the input to such cognitive constraints would still be an objectivist semantics—and that would require an objectively correct reference relation prior to the application of any constraints. But *that*—the input to the constraints—is what Putnam has shown is impossible.

The last objection is fatal. In order to have an objectivist semantics plus cognitive constraints, one must have an objectivist semantics to begin with. Without one, the project can't even get started.

The Gradualist Defense

Putnam's theorem, strictly speaking, concerns the assignment of reference all at once. Lewis observes, correctly, that people don't operate that way. They learn what refers to what a bit at a time. Though he is vague on the subject, Lewis seems to be suggesting something like adding a temporal dimension to model theory, and some small upper limit on how many references can be fixed at any one time. Thus reference can be fixed gradually along the temporal dimension, and future reference can be fixed relative to past fixings of reference. Such a gradualist approach would prevent the assignment of reference all at once and would make future reference assignments dependent upon past ones. This, Lewis claims, would eliminate rampant indeterminacy.

This is a reasonable suggestion. Lewis hasn't presented a proof that it will wipe out rampant indeterminacy, but I would not be surprised if it did. But even a gradual fixing of reference would not wipe out moderate indeterminacy. Lewis acknowledges this.

> There might be two candidates that both fit perfectly; more likely, there might be two imperfect candidates with little to choose between them and no stronger candidate to beat them both. If so, we end up with indeterminate reference . . . the new term refers equally to both candidates. . . . Note well that this is moderate indeterminacy, in which the rival interpretations have much in common; it is not the radical indeterminacy that leads to Putnam's paradox. I take it that the existence of moderate indeterminacy is not to be denied. (Lewis 1984, p. 223)

But, as we saw above, moderate indeterminacy still leads to inconsistency. Any theory in which the meaning of *A cat in on a mat* remains unchanged when "cat" is made to refer to something other than cats and "mat" is made to refer to something other than mats is just not an adequate objectivist theory of meaning. Even that modest an indeterminacy will be inconsistent with requirement 2.

The Small-Models Defense

The gradualist approach is very much like what might be called the *small-models approach*, typical of theories like that of Barwise and Perry's (1984) "situation semantics." In situation semantics, each model is partial and may be quite small. Thus, the fixing of reference is done a little bit at a time. This will certainly eliminate rampant indeterminacy, but not *all* indeterminacy, as Lewis points out. Thus, allowing models to be small will still not provide a "saving constraint." Some indeterminacy is simply inherent in the use of model theory, no matter how small the models.

If anything, the problem is even more pernicious in small, partial models. The reason is this: To ban indeterminacy in small models, one would have to rule out models with isomorphic substructures. For example, take a model with two individuals, *a* and *b*. Suppose it contained only two sets, each with one two-place relation: {(*a*, *b*)} and {(*b*, *a*)}. These sets have isomorphic structure and therefore would be subject to indeterminacy. Such a model would be necessary to satisfy a sentence like *Someone loves someone who hates him.* The indeterminacy arises when one asks which set is the "objectively correct" referent of *loves:* {(*a,b*)} or {(*b,a*)}. Consider the following possible reference relations:

1: { (*love*, {(*a,b*)}), (*hate*, {(*b,a*)}) }
2: { (*love*, {(*b,a*)}), (*hate*, {(*a,b*)}) }

Any interpretation would have to include one of these reference relations, or something essentially equivalent. This would be tantamount to the claim that the reference relation included is "objectively correct," while the other is not. But since they are isomorphic, the truth conditions will come out the same no matter which one is picked.

But on the objectivist assumption that there is one and only one right choice, and that that choice is the one that determines what the sentence "really means," it would be possible to make the "wrong" choice and get the "right" truth conditions. That is, one could let "love" mean hate and "hate" mean love on that interpretation and have no effect on truth-conditional meaning. The meanings of the parts would change, but the meaning of the whole would not. This would violate requirement 2, just as the *cat-mat* case did.

This example shows just why model theory will not do as a theory of meaning. The models just contain sets. The sets are not *understood* in any way within a model. If all you've got is sets in your models, then interchanging them while preserving the structure of the model won't affect truth conditions. But if meaning is based on truth alone, and if reference is taken to be objectively correct, then Putnam's critique will always apply whenever a model contains isomorphic substructures.

So why not let the "saving constraint" be this: *No model can have isomorphic substructures.* That won't work simply because such models are needed—in a variety of cases. For example, they are needed when two different predicates are symmetric. Moreover, they will be needed if small models are used to characterize belief. Suppose that someone had just one belief, that *someone loves someone who hates him*. If belief is to be characterized model-theoretically using partial models, then one will need a small model like the one we just discussed. But it has isomorphic substructures!

In short, small partial models are no help at all—except to make the nature of the problem more apparent. What makes Lewis's discussion of the gradualist defense sound reasonable is that *people* do tolerate moderate indeterminacy. But that has to do with a humanly relevant semantics, not with an objectivist semantics, as characterized by requirements 1 and 2. But this again is just what Putnam is pointing out. People may tolerate some indeterminacy, but the God's eye view does not—it requires that reference be objectively correct and that truth be absolute. Objectivist semantics, which takes a God's eye point of view with respect to reference, truth, and meaning, is in essential conflict with humanly relevant semantics. The problem is how to eliminate the God's eye point of view and make semantics humanly relevant, while preserving what *is* humanly relevant about logic and not giving in to total relativism. As I understand it, this is what Putnam's *internal realism* is about, and it is certainly what Johnson's and my *experientialism* is about.

The Character Defense

So far, the arguments against the use of model theory as a theory of meaning have rested upon the standard attempt to define meaning in terms of truth conditions alone. A number of philosophical logicians have realized that truth conditions alone will not suffice to characterize meaning. They have suggested that meaning be characterized in terms of truth conditions plus something else. There are at present no theories of what that something else is. It is usually defined as whatever is needed to bridge the discrepancy between truth conditions and meaning: Meaning minus truth conditions equals *X*. A common term for the *X* in this equation is "character" (the term is David Kaplan's). The character defense against the Putnam critique would go like this:

> The Putnam critique requires that it be possible to hold the meaning of a whole sentence constant while changing the meanings of the parts. If meaning is defined *only* in terms of truth conditions then Putnam's critique will hold. But if meaning is defined as truth conditions plus character (whatever that is), then Putnam's critique can be avoided under the following condition: If changing the meaning of the parts always results in a change of character, then it will always result in a change of meaning. We may not know what "character" is, but if we place that condition on it, then we can keep model theory as a theory of meaning and we can keep the truth-conditional component of meaning.
>
> The crucial part of this rebuttal is the following:
>
> - "Character" must be defined in such a way that the character of the sentence always changes whenever there is a change in the meaning of the parts of the sentence.
> - To stay within model-theoretical semantics, the "character" of a sentence must be assigned by a mathematical function on the basis of the meaning of the parts.

To see just what is involved in this, let us take a case where a model has two submodels that are isomorphic, that is, that have the same structure. As we have seen, the existence of such submodels cannot be ruled out. Let us call the isomorphic submodels *A* and *B*. Let us refer to the sentence in question as *S* and the part of the sentence in question *P*. Thus, the character of *S* must change when the meaning of *P* is changed from *A* to *B*.

But this is impossible if the character of *S* is assigned by a function. The reason is this: If *A* and *B* are isomorphic, then no function could tell the difference between *A* and *B*. By the definition of a function, a function can only "look at" the *structure* of its input. It cannot differentiate between inputs with the same structure.

What this means is that "character," whatever it is, cannot be characterized model-theoretically. To differentiate between two isomorphic submodels, one must be able to step outside of the model-theoretical apparatus. And if character cannot be defined model-theoretically, then adding "character" to the definition of meaning cannot save a model-theoretical approach to meaning.

One might be tempted to interpret this result in the following way: there are two aspects of meaning, one of which is model-theoretical (truth-conditional meaning) and the other of which is not model-theoretical (character). But even this is not really possible. The reason is that the truth-conditional aspects of meaning-so-defined don't look like they have anything at all to do with meaning, since those aspects of sentence meaning can remain constant when the meanings of the parts change. In other words, they are not even *aspects* of meaning. Thus, the only remaining aspect of meaning is "character," which is completely undefined—except for the fact that, whatever it is, it cannot be model-theoretical. In short, meaning is just not model-theoretic in nature.

The Situations Defense

One possible response to Putnam's critique of model-theoretic semantics might be to try to save a model-theoretic approach while giving up the idea that meaning is based on truth. In each model, there are only two truth values that a proposition can have—true and false. Two values do not distinguish among the structures of the indefinitely large number of propositions that might be assigned truth values on any given interpretation. So it should be no surprise that one can hold the truth values constant model by model and change the denotations of the parts of the sentence.

One might think that the solution to the problem lies in changing the model-theoretic definition of meaning—replacing truth values with something that has enough structure to guarantee that if the meaning of the whole is held constant, then the meaning of the parts cannot be changed. One way to do this would be to try to define the meaning of the whole in such a way that the meanings of the parts are contained in it. Suppose, for example, that meaning were to be based not just on truth values, but on the "facts" that make a sentence true. Since the "facts" of a given situation, as represented in the model, would contain the parts of the proposition, one would think that one could not hold the facts constant while changing the meanings of the parts. One would think that such a move would avoid the effects of Putnam's theorem.

Thus, one might make a counterproposal of the following sort: Instead of relying on truth values to provide a basis for the definition of meaning, let us instead base the definition of meaning on something with the appropriate kind of structure: the "facts" that make a proposition true. Thus, in the spirit of Barwise and Perry (1984), we might define a "fact" as a quadruple of the form: (L, S, R, T), where L is a location in space-time, S is a sequence of length n of entities, R is an n-place relation, and T is a truth value. For example, the fact that some cat is on some mat at location k, might be represented in a model by the following collection of facts, called a *situation*:

⟨*k*, (*a*,*b*), ON, 1⟩ '*a* is on *b*'
⟨*k*, *a*, CAT, 1⟩ '*a* is a cat'
⟨*k*, *b*, MAT, 1⟩ '*b* is a mat'

Reference relation:

{ (*cat*, CAT), (*mat*, MAT), (*on*, ON) }

Here, *a* and *b* are entities and CAT, MAT and ON are relations, while *cat, mat*, and *on* are words. The expression ⟨*k*, (*a*, *b*), ON, 1⟩, describes the fact that at space-time location *k*, it is true that entity *a* is on entity *b*. If 0 were to replace 1 in this expression, yielding ⟨*k*, (*a*,*b*), ON, 0⟩, it would describe the opposite fact, namely, that entity *a* is not on entity *b* at space-time location *k*. The reference relation simply specifies what words are matched up with what entities and sets. Thus, the ordered pair (*cat*, CAT) says that the word *cat* is matched up with the set which we have accorded the name CAT. And ⟨*k*, *a*, CAT, 1⟩ states the fact that entity *a* is a member of the set CAT.

Let us call such a collection of "facts" a *situation*. A sentence is true in a situation just in case the facts of the situation make it true. The facts in the above situation make the sentence *Some cat is on some mat* true at *k*. We can now define meaning in terms, not of truth, but of situations. Let the meaning of a sentence be defined as the collection of situations whose facts make a statement of the sentence true. As in classical model-theoretic semantics, the meaning depends on looking at all interpretations, but now one looks not just at truth values, but at situations and all the relevant "facts" in them. Two sentences will have the same meaning if and only if they are true in the same situations—that is, if they are made true by the same collections of facts.

The crucial part of such a model-theoretic redefinition of meaning is to attempt to take account of the meanings of the parts in forming the meaning of the whole, interpretation by interpretation. In the case described above, the denotations of the words *cat* and *mat* play a direct role in characterizing the facts that make the sentence true. By such a redefinition of "meaning" within model theory, one might seek to avoid the effects the Putnam's critique, since it would appear that one could not keep the meaning of the whole constant while changing the meanings of the parts.

But Putnam's critique extends even to such a redefined concept of meaning in model-theoretic terms. The reason is this: the models still do no more than characterize structure; they are still meaningless. Replacing such models by different models with an isomorphic structure will yield the same "meanings." Suppose, for example, we replace CAT and MAT by CAT* and MAT* in the above interpretation. The situations that now make *Some cat is on some mat* true at *k* will include the following "facts":

⟨*k*, (*a*,*b*), ON, 1⟩
⟨*k*, *a*, CAT*, 1⟩
⟨*k*, *b*, MAT*, 1⟩

Reference relation:

{ (*on*, ON), (cat, CAT*), (*mat*, MAT*) }

This interpretation is isomorphic to the one given above. The only difference is that it has CAT* and MAT* in place of CAT and MAT. Thus, the meanings of the words *cat* and *mat* are different in such interpretations, and may even denote cherries and trees, respectively. However, the facts that make *Some cat is on some mat* true will be the same, given the gerrymandered definitions of CAT* and MAT*, cited above. Because of those definitions, *Some cat* is on some mat** will be made true by the fact that some cat is on some mat, even though *cat** and *mat** do not refer to cats and mats. Similarly, it won't matter whether *cat* and *mat* refer to CAT and MAT or CAT* and MAT*. The facts that make the sentence true will be the same.

The reason for this is that the definitions of CAT* and MAT* constrain the factual content of possible situations in the following way:

> All and only the situations whose facts make *Some cat is on some mat* true under the CAT*-MAT* interpretation will happen to contain the fact that some cat is on some mat.

This will be true despite the fact that the word *cat* may refer to cherries and the word *mat* to trees in some of those situations. Putnam's gerrymandered definitions, cited above, yield this effect automatically via the constraint they place on the factual content of situations.

Thus, the "meaning" (defined in terms of factuality and situations) of *Some cat is on some mat* will be the same whether the CAT-MAT interpretation or the CAT*-MAT* interpretation is used. Even under the situational account of meaning, it is possible to change the meaning of the parts without changing the meaning of the whole. This will be true not only of the CAT*-MAT* cases; it is true in general. The move from truth to situations in the attempt to define meaning using model theory does not avoid the effects of Putnam's critique.

In short, defining meaning in terms of situations makes no difference, as long as situations are defined in terms of model theory, that is, in terms of models consisting only of entities and sets. The reason is that such models are themselves meaningless and yield the same results if replaced by isomorphic models. Thus, Putnam's critique applies not merely to model-theoretic accounts where meaning is based on truth; it also applies to model-theoretic accounts of meaning which are based on situations as characterized above. The problem is not that truth conditions do not have enough structure. The problem is that structure is not enough to confer meaning.

Why No Defense Seems Possible

We seem to have the following situation:

- Model theory cannot eliminate moderate indeterminacy of reference. (Lewis seems to admit that there can be no such "saving constraint.")
- Even moderate indeterminacy of reference leads to a violation of requirement 2.
- Therefore, model theory cannot be a theory of *meaning*, if meaning is defined in terms of truth (or situations).
- Furthermore, nothing (e.g., "character") can be added to the truth-conditional definition of meaning to avoid this result.

Model-theoretic semanticists had better change something if they want a consistent theory of meaning. Some version of requirement 2 must be kept: no theory of meaning can allow the meaning of the whole to be preserved when the meaning of its parts is changed and still be a theory of meaning. Anyway you look at it, requirement 1 must go: meaning is not definable in terms of truth in a model, or in terms of situations. The reason is clear: *Meaningless structures cannot give meaning to meaningless symbols.*

But this would leave model-theoretic semantics without an account of meaning at all! And that is one of Putnam's major points. It is impossible to keep model theory and still have an objectivist theory of meaning. Giving up on model-theoretic semantics need not, of course, result in chaos. Alternatives like Putnam's internal realism and our experiential realism are available. And they need not be vague, mushy alternatives. Cognitive model theory, as we will describe it below, can provide a detailed and precise account of meaning. But it is not an account of meaning independent of the nature of thinking beings. It is a theory of meaning based on what is meaningful to a person—a humanly relevant theory of meaning.

Putnam's bomb is still ticking. But all it threatens to blow up is a theory of meaning that is not humanly relevant.

The General Character of Putnam's Critique

Putnam's critique is not merely a critique of a particular mathematicization of objectivist semantics. It is a very general result:

– Meaning cannot be characterized by the way symbols are associated with things in the world.

Let us call the view that meaning concerns the association of symbols with things in the world the *symbolic* theory of meaning. The symbolic theory is objectivist in nature, since it does not depend in any way on the nature or experience of any thinking being. All that is relevant is the pairing of symbols with things. In order to qualify as a theory of meaning, the symbolic theory must sanction the pairing of symbols not only with individual things, but also with *categories* of things. But what is an objectively existing category? Symbolic theories all take for granted that classical categories are the only kind of objectively existing category. This is based on the assumption that things in the world have objectively existing properties and that categories of things sharing those properties are also things in the world with which symbols can be associated.

A symbolic theory of meaning must also assign a meaning to whole sentences, or other symbolic structures, as well as to parts of those sentences or structures. If a symbolic theory is to be a theory of meaning, the meanings of the wholes cannot be kept the same when the meanings of the parts change. Since a symbolic theory of meaning concerns only the association between symbols and things, any characteristics of any beings using the symbols must be irrelevant to the relationship between the meaning of the parts and the meanings of the wholes. In short, there must be an objective relation between the meanings of parts and the meanings of wholes, in which the meaning of the whole is dependent on the meanings of the parts.

This characterization of a symbolic theory of meaning is beginning to sound like model theory, and there is a good reason for it. Model theory is exactly what it takes to make a symbolic theory of meaning precise with a minimum of added assumptions. Since model-theoretic semantics is just the symbolic theory of meaning made precise, it follows that the symbolic theory of meaning cannot be made precise in a consistent manner. In other words, meaning is not merely a matter of the association of symbols with things.

Is There a Consistent Version of Objectivist Semantics?

There is no way to fix up models or model theory to make model-theoretic semantics an internally consistent theory of meaning as long as requirements 1 and 2 are kept. Model-theoretic semanticists are not likely to give up on model theory, when they have spent so long developing it. They will most likely tinker with models and with requirement 1 to try to arrive at a theory that is at least provably consistent. Perhaps those requirements can be changed to eliminate the inconsistency and still stay within the objectivist spirit. The answer is not clear, and it probably never will be. The reason is that what constitutes the "objectivist spirit" is anything but a clear-cut matter. Any new conditions to replace 1 and 2 will be subject to endless philosophical debate as to whether they are really realist.

Such debates do not lend themselves to easy clarification or straightforward resolution. They are debates of the sort that have kept philosophers arguing for centuries, and it would not surprise me if this one goes on for a long time without anything like a clear resolution. But in this case, what the debate is about is internal consistency: What can *reasonably* be added or changed so that model theory can be put together with a somewhat revised version of conditions 1 and 2 without inconsistency? In this case, inconsistency would invalidate the entire endeavor, since the case for objectivist semantics rests on the claim of mathematical rigor. For this reason, mathematical rigor cannot be taken for granted, since it depends on what constitutes a "reasonable" way to avoid the inconsistency and still be objectivist enough according to some still to be determined philosophical standard—and that is likely to be a matter of unclear, interminable, and perhaps ultimately unresolvable debate. There is no reason for defenders of mathematical rigor to feel comfortable with model-theoretic semantics. Model-theoretic semanticists are starting from a position of internal inconsistency. If they want to remain objectivists (metaphysical realists), then they must replace condition 1 to get a consistent theory of meaning. But it is the *philosophical* not the *mathematical* considerations that will determine whether any such resulting theory is "really realist," that is, whether it is "objectivist enough." Mathematical rigor will necessarily be at the mercy of philosophical speculation. It ought to be enough to make a mathematical logician who is interested in investigating meaning and human reason insist on a divorce from objectivist philosophy.

Where Model Theory Goes Wrong

Putnam's results were presented in his presidential address to the Association for Symbolic Logic in 1977, which was published in the *Journal of Symbolic Logic* in 1980. In that paper, Putnam explains very eloquently just why this problem occurs. It has to do with viewing a language as separate from its interpretation, as is done in standard formalist mathematics. And natural languages (or any "language of thought" consisting of mental representations) are viewed as being like formal "languages" as they are characterized in formalist mathematics.

A formal "language" is made up of uninterpreted symbols. The use of this formal language is characterized in terms of symbol manipulation procedures, for example, procedures for proving theorems. "Understanding" a formal "language" is characterized in terms of knowing what it is, knowing how to use it, i.e., knowing how to perform symbolic manipulations such as deductions, and knowing what sentences follow from what other sentences via manipulations such as proof procedures. On this account, one can know a language and understand how to use it, and even know what sentences entail what other sentences—without the language meaning anything at all! "Meaning" is the study of how one can provide interpretations for a "language" in this technical sense. Putnam's insight is that this very separation of the "language" from its interpretation—that is, making syntax independent of semantics—makes it in principle impossible to characterize meaning adequately.

> The predicament only is a predicament because we did two things: first, we gave an account of understanding the language in terms of programs and procedures for *using* the language (what else?); then, secondly, we asked what the possible "models" for the language were, thinking of the models as existing "out there" *independent of any description*. At this point, something really weird had already happened, had we stopped to notice. On any view, the understanding of the language must determine the reference of the terms, or must determine the reference given the context of use. If the use, even in a fixed context, does not determine reference, then use is not understanding. The language, on the perspective we talked ourselves into, has a full program of use; but it still lacks an *interpretation*.
>
> This is the fatal step. To adopt a theory of meaning according to which a language whose whole use is specified still lacks something—viz. its "interpretation"—is to accept a problem which *can* only have crazy solutions. To speak as if this were the problem, "I know how to use my language, but, now, how can I single out an interpretation?" is to speak nonsense. Either the use *already* fixes the "interpretation" or *nothing* can. . . . Models are not lost noumenal waifs looking for someone to name them; they are constructions within our theory itself, and they have names from birth. (Putnam 1980, pp. 481–82)

Set-theoretical models are products of the human mind, not objective things just "out there" that the world happens to conform to. Models of reality are *our* models and we might as well own up to it and make the best of it. People do not just manipulate meaningless symbols; they use symbols *because* they already mean something, and reasoning with those symbols takes account of that meaning.

Some Consequences

Putnam's result is of the greatest immediate importance to the study of semantics. Model-theoretic semantics can no longer be bolstered by the claim that it uses an appropriate mathematics. Quite the reverse. The mathematics it has been using is inconsistent with the requirements for a theory of meaning. No clearly and unequivocally "reasonable" method has been demonstrated so far that avoids the inconsistency. At present, the mathematical considerations argue against model-theoretic semantics, not for it. The burden of proof is on model-theoretic semanticists to demonstrate once and for all that they can avoid the effects of Putnam's theorem.

The problem lies not with the use of model theory per se. It lies with objectivist philosophy and the attempt to base a theory of meaning on truth (or on other structurally defined notions such as "situation"). Putnam's critique does not rule out the possibility that one might be able to use model theory, or at least some of its apparatus, in an adequate theory of semantics. What it appears to rule out is the idea that meaning is based on truth or "situations," and that there is a unique correct God's eye view of reference, that is, of the link between mental representations or language and the world. At least it rules it out until some demonstration that model-theoretic semantics has been revised to avoid the effects of Putnam's theorem. That will certainly not be a trivial matter. And it is not clear that it is even possible.

Putnam's argument has immediate consequences for the study of both natural language semantics and syntax. Many of the consequences of objectivist semantics have simply been taken over wholesale into linguistics. For example, model-theoretic semantics presupposes that syntax is independent of semantics, and that semantics is independent of pragmatics (i.e., speech acts, implicatures, etc.). Those assumptions can no longer be made with impunity; and as we shall see in case study 3, there is good reason to believe that they are false. We will suggest in case study 3 that what have been called semantics and pragmatics are both structured using cognitive models, and we will argue that cognitive models have structure of the appropriate kind to provide a base for a theory of syntax.

If Putnam is right about the source of the difficulty, then no autonomous syntax (of the sort required by generative grammar) could in principle be supplied with an adequate theory of meaning. A theory of grammar that takes syntax as the study of uninterpreted formal symbols will forever be meaningless. What is required is something like what is suggested in case study 3, a theory of syntax in which syntactic categories are semantically motivated and grammatical constructions come with meaning.

Putnam's argument also matters for the empirical study of natural language semantics. For more than a decade, detailed empirical study of the wide range of semantic phenomena in natural language has been seriously curtailed because of the influence of model-theoretic semantics. The research strategy in model-theoretic semantics has been to start with traditional logical operators and slowly work outward to subject matter that philosophical logicians happen to have thought about to some extent—tenses, modalities, some adverbs, comparatives, belief, etc. The idea was to keep everything mathematically rigorous at each step. Putnam's theorem shows that the mathematical rigor was an illusion. The systems have been inconsistent with the most fundamental of requirements for a theory of meaning. No unimpeachable method now exists to remove the inconsistency.

The empirically enlightening results coming out of model-theoretic semantics during the past decade and a half have been underwhelming. Most of the work has gone into taking well-known results and formalizing them. But, if Putnam is right, all this formalizing has been for naught. What, after all, could be more pointless than trying to "formalize" something in an inconsistent theory! Meanwhile, the empirical study of all the semantic phenomena in the world's languages has been languishing, a victim of objectivist philosophy.

Objectivist baggage has been sinking the empirical study of meaning for too long. It is about time it was cast off. For the past decade, linguists doing empirical semantics had to justify not doing model-theoretic semantics. Putnam's theorem (pardon the expression) puts the theoretical shoe on the other foot. Now a justification is required for doing model-theoretic semantics. Model-theoretic semantics must come up with suitable constraints either on model theory or on the theory of meaning that will avoid Putnam's results. Until then, there can be no justification for using an inconsistent approach to semantics in the name of mathematical rigor.

Not that rigor should, or needs to, be abandoned. At the end of chapter 17 below, we will outline a much-revised version of model theory—a cognitive model theory—which is not subject to Putnam's critique. It will be a model theory embedded in a nonobjectivist view of philosophy.

Finally, it should be borne in mind that Putnam's theorem is about categories—so-called objective reference to categories. Just as we have found empirical reasons why the phenomenon of categorization invalidates objectivist semantics, so Putnam has found technical logical reasons. What is remarkable is the way in which our empirical results dovetail with Putnam's logical results. To me, as a cognitive scientist, the empirical reasons are the most important ones. Perhaps it will be possible for logicians who like objectivist philosophy to revise objectivist semantics to make it internally consistent. What cannot be avoided are the *empirical* phenomena that are inconsistent with objectivist semantics, those discussed in chapter 13 above.

The Mentalist Alternative

Objectivist assumptions are important to many philosophers. They are not so important to most linguists and psychologists. A number of linguists and psychologists who like model-theoretic semantics have responded to Putnam's critique by saying, "Okay. Suppose the models aren't models of the world. Suppose they are just mental models, models of what you believe the world to be. Why not keep model theory and just reinterpret it in this way?"

The most obvious, and perhaps the most forceful, objection is that it would leave one without a theory of meaning. The entities and sets in a model are still meaningless in themselves; viewing them as mental entities does not tell how to make them meaningful. As Lewis observed in his critique of Markerese, translating one collection of meaningless symbols into another collection of meaningless symbols does not create meaning.

This point cannot be stated strongly enough. When linguists use models, they use them *with an imposed understanding.* It is this understanding of what the elements in the model are supposed to be that makes model theory seem plausible. But the understanding is not in the model itself! All that is in the model is meaningless structure.

A second objection is that one could not just take over model theory wholesale from the objectivist tradition and rechristen it as mentalistic. Consider, for example, the standard intended model for the expression "all the real numbers." That model is uncountably infinite. In the objectivist tradition, it is assumed that there is an objectively existing Platonic realm of numbers, and there is no problem with models that have an uncountably infinite number of elements. However, if such models are to be considered cognitively real, and if the same concept of a model is to be used, then one would be claiming that mental models could contain an uncountable infinity of mental elements. But this contradicts the usual assumption that the mind is finite.

One way out might be to say that mental models of such things as the real numbers only include samples, or some typical cases, or finite mechanisms for generating the full set. But, sensible as that would be, it would make a radical change in the character of model theory. The definition of satisfaction in a model would be changed utterly.

That brings up an interesting point. Model theory, as it has developed, is constrained by objectivist philosophy. If objectivist philosophy is to be abandoned,

- Why keep those constraints on model theory that came out of objectivist philosophy?
- Why continue to base meaning on truth or situations?
- Why keep classical categories when we know that, cognitively, most categories are nonclassical?
- Why try to limit models to literal meanings when we know that much of everyday conventional language and thought is metaphorical?
- Why not include mental images in mental models?
- Why keep the classical semantics-pragmatics distinction?

In short, it makes no sense to abandon the objectivist understanding of model theory but to keep all the constraints that were imposed by objectivist philosophy. Abandoning objectivist epistemology requires questioning all the constraints imposed by the epistemology.

In our proposal for cognitive model theory below in chapter 17, we will be suggesting ways to incorporate what seems empirically correct about model theory into a cognitive model theory, while changing other aspects of models when such changes better accord with the empirical facts. We will also propose ways to make such models meaningful without running afoul of Putnam's criticisms. In addition, we will try to show how to keep the sensible aspects of realism, and to avoid the pitfalls of idealism, subjectivism, and total relativism. The key, as we shall see, is Putnam's philosophy of internal realism.

In summary, Putnam has shown that existing formal versions of objectivist *epistemology* are inconsistent: there can be no objectively correct *description* of reality from a God's eye point of view. This does not, of course, mean that there is no objective reality—only that we have no *privileged access* to it from an external viewpoint.

CHAPTER 16

A New Realism

What we have referred to as *objectivism* is a special case of what Putnam calls *metaphysical realism.* As we saw above, Putnam has argued that metaphysical realism is internally incoherent. Its incoherence lies in its epistemology—its view of meaning, reference, knowledge, and understanding. The source of the incoherence is what Putnam calls its *externalist* perspective, that one can stand outside reality and find a unique correct way to understand reality.

Such an understanding, on the view of metaphysical realism, would involve a symbol system standing external to the rest of reality and a reference relation pairing symbols and aspects of reality. The reference relation is assumed to "give meaning" to the symbols. First, Putnam shows that this is logically impossible, without violating what we mean by "meaning." Second, Putnam points out that in order for such an understanding to be unique and correct, the reference relation itself must be part of reality. He then observes that this too is logically impossible.

Putnam's result is a result about symbol systems and their interpretations. The epistemology of metaphysical realism (and objectivism, in the special case) is formulated in terms of symbol systems and their interpretations. The metaphysical realist views of meaning, reference, knowledge, and understanding all make presuppositions about symbol systems and their interpretations that are logically incoherent.

Thus, Putnam concludes, there cannot be such a thing as "exactly one true and complete description of 'the way the world is ' "—that is, there can be no God's eye view of reality. The crucial words here are "description" and "view." They presuppose an external perspective: a symbol system external to reality, related to reality by a reference relation that gives meaning to the symbols. Putnam is not saying that there is no reality. And he is not saying that there is no "way the world is." He is not denying basic realism. He is only denying a certain epistemology. He is not saying that we cannot have correct knowledge. What he is saying is that we cannot have a privileged correct description *from an externalist perspective.*

The problem is the external perspective—the God's eye view. We are not outside of reality. We are part of it, *in* it. What is needed is not an externalist perspective, but an internalist perspective. It is a perspective that acknowledges that we are organisms functioning as part of reality and that it is impossible for us to ever stand outside it and take the stance of an observer with perfect knowledge, an observer with a God's eye point of view. But that does not mean that knowledge is impossible. We can know reality from the inside, on the basis of our being part of it. It is not the absolute perfect knowledge of the God's eye variety, but that kind of knowledge is logically impossible anyway. What *is* possible is knowledge of another kind: knowledge from a particular point of view, knowledge which includes the awareness that it is from a particular point of view, and knowledge which grants that other points of view can be legitimate.

Internal Realism

In the place of metaphysical realism, Putnam proposes another form of realism—internal realism—a realism from a human point of view that accords real status to the world and to the way we function in it. Putnam expresses the contrast between metaphysical and internal realism as follows:

> One of these perspectives is the perspective of metaphysical realism. On this perspective, the world consists of some fixed totality of mind-independent objects. There is exactly one true and complete description of 'the way the world is'. Truth involves some sort of correspondence relation between words or thought-signs and external things and sets of things. I shall call this perspective the *externalist* perspective, because its favorite point of view is a God's Eye point of view.
>
> The perspective I shall defend has no unambiguous name. It is a late arrival in the history of philosophy, and even today it keeps being confused with other points of view of a quite different sort. I shall refer to it as the *internalist* perspective, because it is characteristic of this view to hold that *what objects does the world consist of?* is a question that it only makes sense to ask *within* a theory or description. Many 'internalist' philosophers, though not all, hold further that there is more than one 'true' theory or description of the world. 'Truth', in an internalist view, is some sort of (idealized) rational acceptability—some sort of ideal coherence of our beliefs with each other and with our experiences *as those experiences are themselves represented in our belief system*—and not correspondence with mind-independent 'states of

affairs'. There is no God's Eye point of view that we can know or usefully imagine; there are only various points of view of actual persons reflecting various interests and purposes that their descriptions and theories subserve. (Putnam 1981, pp. 49–50)

By taking an internalist perspective, Putnam avoids the problems with reference that plague the objectivist. Our way of understanding the world in terms of objects, properties, and relations is an imposition of our conceptual schemes upon external reality; reality as we understand it is structured by our conceptual schemes. Because objects and categories of objects are characterized internal to conceptual schemes, not external to them, the problem of the indeterminacy of reference disappears.

In an internalist view also, signs do not intrinsically correspond to objects, independently of how those signs are employed and by whom. But a sign that is actually employed in a particular way by a particular community of users can correspond to particular objects *within the conceptual scheme of those users.* 'Objects' do not exist independently of conceptual schemes. We cut up the world into objects when we introduce one or another scheme of description. Since objects *and* the signs are alike *internal* to the scheme of description, it is possible to say what matches what. (Putnam 1981, p. 52)

It is important not to read Putnam out of context here, especially when he talks about objects. An "object" is a single bounded entity. According to metaphysical realism, there is a correct and unique division of reality into objects, with properties and relations holding among them. Each "object" is a single bounded entity, and that is *the only correct description* of that object. It cannot also be correctly described as a plurality of objects or a mass of waves. That is what metaphysical realism says: there is only one correct way in which reality is divided up into objects.

Putnam, being a realist, does not deny that objects exist. Take, for example, the chair I am sitting on. It exists. If it didn't, I would have fallen on the floor. But that chair can be viewed *correctly* in many ways. From the molecular point of view, it is an enormous collection of molecules and not a single undifferentiated bounded entity. From the point of view of wave equations in physics, there is no chair, but only wave forms. From a human point of view, it is a single object. Thus, whether the chair is a particular object—a single bounded entity—or a bunch of molecules or a wave form is not a question that has a unique correct answer. All the answers can be correct, but correct within different conceptual schemes. The chair is real in all those schemes, but it has a status as a single particular object in only one of them. Thus, when Putnam says that "'Objects' do not exist independently of conceptual schemes," he is not denying the reality of objects; rather, he is leaving open the possibility that what is characterized as a particular object of a particular sort in one conceptual scheme could be described otherwise in another, equally legitimate conceptual scheme. The issue is not whether reality exists, but whether there is only one right way to describe it in all cases.

Internal realism is a form of realism. What makes it a form of realism is:

- a commitment to the existence of a real world external to human beings
- a link between conceptual schemes and the world via real human experience; experience is not purely internal, but is constrained at every instant by the real world of which we are an inextricable part
- a concept of truth that is based not only on internal coherence and "rational acceptability," but, most important, on coherence with our constant real experience
- a commitment to the possibility of real human knowledge of the world

What makes it "internal" is that it does not take an external perspective that stands outside of reality. Rather, it focuses on the way that we make sense of reality by functioning within it. The internalist perspective acknowledges the contribution of our conceptual schemes to our understanding of our real experiences in a real world.

> Internalism does not deny that there are experiential *inputs* to knowledge; knowledge is not a story with no constraints except internal coherence; but it does deny that there are any inputs *which are not themselves to some extent shaped by our concepts*. . . . Even our description of our own sensations, so dear as a starting point for knowledge to generations of epistemologists, is heavily affected (as are the sensations themselves for that matter) by a host of conceptual choices. The very inputs upon which our knowledge is based are conceptually contaminated. (Putnam 1981, p. 54)

In recognizing the way that our conceptual schemes shape our comprehension of our experience, and even our experience itself, internal realism abandons the traditional distinction betweeen fact and value; but because it is still a form of realism, it retains a notion of objectivity without descriptions from a God's eye point of view.

> [Our conceptions] depend upon our biology and our culture; they are by no means 'value-free'. But they *are* our conceptions and they are conceptions of something real. They define a kind of objectivity, *objectivity for us*, even if it is not the metaphysical objectivity of the God's Eye view. Objectivity and rationality humanly speaking are what we have; they are better than nothing. (P. 55)

Objectivity cannot be a matter of conforming to a God's eye point of view, since the very existence of such a point of view is impossible on logical grounds. But that does not mean that there is no objectivity. Objectivity involves rising above prejudices, and that begins by being aware that we have those prejudices. The primal prejudice is our own conceptual system. To be objective, we must be aware that we have a particular conceptual system, we must know what it is like, and we must be able to entertain alternatives. Practical standards of objectivity are possible in a great many domains of human endeavor. Acknowledging alternative conceptual schemes does not abandon objectivity; on the contrary, it makes objectivity possible.

Although internal realism is a form of realism, its internal character permits the existence of alternative, incompatible conceptual schemes. It is not a total relativism because of the limits placed on it by experience of the real world. It is not the case that "anything goes" in internal realism.

> Why should there not sometimes be equally coherent but incompatible conceptual schemes which fit our experiential beliefs equally well? If truth is not (unique) correspondence then the possibility of a certain pluralism is opened up. But the motive of the metaphysical realist is to save the notion of the God's Eye Point of View, i.e., the One True Theory. (Putnam 1981, pp. 73–74)

Putnam is all too aware of the departure he is making from most traditional philosophical views, as well as from traditional everyday views of the world.

> What we have is the demise of a theory that lasted for over two thousand years. That it persisted so long and in so many forms in spite of the internal contradictions and obscurities which were present from the beginning testifies to the naturalness and strength of the desire for a God's Eye View. . . . The continued presence of this natural but unfulfillable impulse is, perhaps, a deep cause of false monisms and false dualisms which proliferate in our culture; be this as it may, we are left without the God's Eye View. (Putnam 1981, p. 74)

But isn't it irresponsible to claim to be a realist and not believe in the existence of a unique correct description of reality? On the contrary. Given that metaphysical realism (objectivism) has been empirically disconfirmed and given that objectivist semantics is now inconsistent pending the unlikely discovery of some "saving constraint," the only responsible kind of realist to be is an *internal* realist.

Doesn't the abandoning of the idea of a unique correct description of reality make science impossible? Isn't it giving up on scientific realism?

Not at all. It only gives up on scientific objectivism. The difference is all important.

Scientific objectivism claims that there is only one fully correct way in which reality can be correctly divided up into objects, properties, and relations. Accordingly, the correct choice of objects is not a matter of a choice of conceptual schemes: there is only one correct way to understand reality in terms of objects and categories of objects. Scientific realism, on the other hand, assumes that "the world is the way it is," while acknowledging that there can be more than one scientifically correct way of understanding reality in terms of conceptual schemes with different objects and categories of objects. The scientific community can have standards of objectivity and correctness (or "rightness" in the sense of Goodman 1978), according to which it is possible for theories with very different divisions into objects and categories of objects can be correct relative to community standards. Since no God's eye view standard is possible, that is the best we can do—and it's pretty good. Good enough to provide us with reasonable standards for stable scientific knowledge.

Experiential Realism

Objectivist philosophy is inconsistent both with the facts of human categorization and with the most basic of requirements for a theory of meaning. Those inconsistencies are deep ones; they cannot be patched up easily, and probably cannot be patched up at all. The result is a crisis. We need new theories of meaning, truth, reason, knowledge, understanding, objectivity, etc. Such theories must be capable of coping with the facts of categorization, while avoiding the pitfalls pointed out by Putnam. We need to keep what was right about the old accounts of logical relations and logical structure, while replacing both the descriptive apparatus of classical model theory and its philosophical underpinnings.

Internal realism looks like a viable alternative. It preserves basic realism, and avoids Putnam's critique. But it needs to be further developed. So far it hasn't offered new theories of meaning, reason, categorization, etc. Experiential realism, or experientialism, as Johnson and I (1980) called it, is a version of internal realism that attempts to provide at least some of what is needed:

- alternative accounts of meaning, truth, knowledge, understanding, objectivity, and reason
- a theory of cognitive models capable of dealing with the facts of categorization and natural language semantics

- an account of relativism that avoids the problems of total relativism and makes sense of what stability there is in scientific knowledge

All of this must be done while maintaining basic realism, that is, while acknowledging (*a*) the reality of a world existing independent of human beings, (*b*) constraints on our conceptual systems due to the nature of that reality, (*c*) a conception of truth that goes beyond mere internal coherence, (*d*) a commitment to objectivity, and (*e*) an account of how scientific knowledge can be stable.

The Experientialist Strategy

Mark Johnson and I have developed a strategy for expanding internal realism to deal with these issues. We have taken meaning to be the central issue. The central question, as we see it, is how linguistic expressions and the concepts they express can be meaningful. Our basic strategy is to isolate what we take to be the central problem in the objectivist approach and to take a very different and, we believe, more promising approach.

The objectivist approach to the problem of meaning was this:

- Linguistic expressions and the concepts they express are symbolic structures, meaningless in themselves, that get their meaning via direct, unmediated correlation with things and categories in the actual world (or possible worlds).

This account of meaning nowhere mentions human beings. It does not depend in any way on the nature of the thinking and communicating organisms, or on the nature of their experience. We take this to be the central problem with the objectivist approach.

The experientialist approach is very different: to attempt to characterize meaning in terms of *the nature and experience of the organisms doing the thinking.* Not just the nature and experience of individuals, but the nature and experience of the species and of communities. "Experience" is thus not taken in the narrow sense of the things that have "happened to happen" to a single individual. Experience is instead construed in the broad sense: the totality of human experience and everything that plays a role in it—the nature of our bodies, our genetically inherited capacities, our modes of physical functioning in the world, our social organization, etc. In short, it takes as essential much of what is seen as irrelevant in the objectivist account.

The experientialist approach to meaning, in its most general outlines, thus contrasts with the objectivist approach. Where objectivism defines meaning independently of the nature and experience of thinking beings, experiential realism characterizes meaning in terms of *embodiment,* that is, in terms of our collective biological capacities and our physical and social experiences as beings functioning in our environment. At this point, we divide the problem into two parts: (1) structure and (2) the embodiment of that structure.

Let us begin with structure. Our concepts are structured, both internally and relative to one another. That structuring permits us to reason, to comprehend, to acquire knowledge, and to communicate. The theory of cognitive models, as we will be describing it, is concerned with conceptual structure. But structure alone does not make for meaningfulness. We additionally need an account of what makes that structure meaningful. Experientialism claims that conceptual structure is meaningful because it is *embodied,* that is, it arises from, and is tied to, our preconceptual bodily experiences. In short, conceptual structure exists and is understood because preconceptual structures exist and are understood. Conceptual structure takes its form in part from the nature of preconceptual structures.

But there are two immediate problems that arise:

First, it must be assumed that our bodily experience itself has structure, that it is not an unstructured mush. Structure, after all, cannot arise from something that has no structure whatever. If conceptual structure arises from preconceptual experience, that preconceptual experience must itself be structured. The first problem is: What kind of preconceptual structure is there to our experience that could give rise to conceptual structure?

Second, it is obvious that not all of our concepts are physical concepts. Many of them are abstract. Reason is abstract. The second problem is: How can abstract concepts and abstract reason be based on bodily experience?

Johnson and I have proposed the following solutions to these problems:

1. There are at least two kinds of structure in our preconceptual experiences:
   A. Basic-level structure: Basic-level categories are defined by the convergence of our gestalt perception, our capacity for bodily movement, and our ability to form rich mental images.
   B. Kinesthetic image-schematic structure: Image schemas are relatively simple structures that constantly recur in our everyday bodily experience: CONTAINERS, PATHS, LINKS, FORCES, BALANCE, and in various orientations and relations: UP-DOWN, FRONT-BACK, PART-WHOLE, CENTER-PERIPHERY, etc.

These structures are directly meaningful, first, because they are directly and repeatedly experienced because of the nature of the body and its mode of functioning in our environment. (For a detailed discussion, see Johnson, 1987.)

2. There are two ways in which abstract conceptual structure arises from basic-level and image-schematic structure:
   A. By metaphorical projection from the domain of the physical to abstract domains.
   B. By the projection from basic-level categories to superordinate and subordinate categories.

Abstract conceptual structures are indirectly meaningful; they are understood because of their systematic relationship to directly meaningful structures.

Given such an approach to meaningfulness, we will go on to characterize understanding in terms of meaningfulness, truth in terms of understanding, entailment in terms of truth, knowledge in terms of truth and understanding, and objectivity in terms of understanding how we understand. The entire structure will stand on our account of meaningfulness, which in turn has dual preconceptual foundations in bodily experience: basic-level structures and kinesthetic image schemas.

This solution has the following basic characteristics:

- It is not subject to Putnam's critique because the concepts that are directly meaningful (the basic-level and image-schematic concepts) are directly tied to structural aspects of experience. This makes the account of meaningfulness *internal* to human beings.
- Since bodily experience is constant experience of the real world that mostly involves successful functioning, stringent real-world constraints are placed on conceptual structure. This avoids subjectivism.
- Since image schemas are common to all human beings, as are the principles that determine basic-level concepts, total relativism is ruled out, though limited relativism is permitted.

Experiential realism thus meets the criteria for being a form of internal realism. It is at present the only form of realism that makes sense of the phenomena discussed in this book.

CHAPTER 17

Cognitive Semantics

A philosophy of experiential realism requires a cognitive semantics. Our goal in this chapter is to provide a general outline of what such a semantic theory would be like. This will require a discussion of three general issues:

- Foundations: What makes concepts meaningful.
- Cognitive model theory: What is known about the nature of cognitive models.
- Philosophical issues: General approaches to meaning, understanding, truth, reason, knowledge, and objectivity.

In chapter 18, we will take up the issue of relativism and alternative conceptual systems.

Dual Foundations

Empirical studies by such prototype theorists as Berlin, Rosch, Hunn, Mervis, B. Tversky, and others have isolated a significant level of human interaction with the external environment (the basic level), characterized by gestalt perception, mental imagery, and motor movements. At this level, people function most efficiently and successfully in dealing with discontinuities in the natural environment. It is at this level of physical experience that we accurately distinguish tigers from elephants, chairs from tables, roses from daffodils, asparagus from broccoli, copper from lead, etc. One level down, things are much more difficult. It is much harder to distinguish one species of giraffe from another than to distinguish a giraffe from an elephant. Our capacity for basic-level gestalt perception is not tuned to make easy, clear-cut distinctions at such lower levels.

The studies of basic-level categorization suggest that our experience is preconceptually structured at that level. We have general capacities for dealing with part-whole structure in real world objects via gestalt perception, motor movement, and the formation of rich mental images. These impose a preconceptual structure on our experience. Our basic-level *concepts* correspond to that preconceptual structure and are understood directly in terms of it. Basic-level concepts are much more richly structured than kinesthetic image schemas, which have only the grossest outlines of structure. Gestalts for general overall shapes (e.g., the shape of an elephant or a giraffe or a rose) are relatively rich in structure. Still, they occur preconceptually as gestalts, and although one can identify internal structure in them, the wholes seem to be psychologically more basic than the parts. In short, the idea that all internal structure is of a building-block sort, with primitives and principles of combination, does not seem to work at the basic level of human experience. At this level, "basic" does not mean "primitive"; that is, basic-level concepts are not atomic building blocks without internal structure. The basic level is an intermediate level; it is neither the highest nor the lowest level of conceptual organization. Because of their gestalt nature and their intermediate status, basic-level concepts cannot be considered elementary atomic building blocks within a building-block approach to conceptual structure.

At the basic level of physical experience, many of the principles of objectivism appear to work well. Our intuitions that objectivism is "just common sense" seem to come from the preconceptual structure of our physical experience at the basic level. It is no accident that most of the examples used to justify objectivism come from this level of physical experience.

Those real discontinuities in nature that are easy for people to perceive—say the differences between elephants and giraffes—correspond to the *natural kinds* that objectivists cite in justifying their views. The common philosophical examples of natural kinds—tigers, cows, water, gold, etc.—are all basic-level categories in the physical domain. Similarly, the kinds of examples that philosophers of language like to cite as justifying objectivist semantics, sentences like

The cat is on the mat.
The boy hit the ball.
Brutus killed Caesar.

all involve basic-level categories of physical objects, actions, and relations. Moreover, most basic human artifacts are constructed so that our bodies can interact optimally with them. Chairs, tables, houses, books, lamps, coats, cars, etc. are constructed with our basic-level interactional abilities and purposes in mind.

We have basic-level concepts not only for objects but for actions and properties as well. Actions like *running, walking, eating, drinking,* etc. are basic-level, whereas *moving* and *ingesting* are superordinate, while kinds of walking and drinking, say, *ambling* and *slurping,* are subordinate. Similarly, *tall, short, hard, soft, heavy, light, hot, cold,* etc. are basic-level properties, as are the basic neurophysiologically determined colors: black, white, red, green, blue, and yellow.

It is basic-level physical experience that has made objectivism seem plausible. And it is basic-level physical experience that I believe will ultimately provide much of the basis for an experientialist view of epistemology that supersedes objectivism without giving up on realism.

Kinesthetic Image Schemas

One of Mark Johnson's basic insights is that experience is structured in a significant way prior to, and independent of, any concepts. Existing concepts may impose further structuring on what we experience, but basic experiential structures are present regardless of any such imposition of concepts. This may sound mysterious, but it is actually very simple and obvious, so much so that it is not usually considered worthy of notice.

The Body in the Mind: The Bodily Basis of Meaning, Imagination, and Reason (Johnson, 1987) makes an overwhelming case for the embodiment of certain kinesthetic image schemas. Take, for example, a CONTAINER schema—a schema consisting of a *boundary* distinguishing an *interior* from an *exterior.* The CONTAINER schema defines the most basic distinction between IN and OUT. We understand our own bodies as containers—perhaps the most basic things we do are ingest and excrete, take air into our lungs and breathe it out. But our understanding of our own bodies as containers seems small compared with all the daily experiences we understand in CONTAINER terms:

> Consider just a small fraction of the orientational feats you perform constantly in your daily activities—consider, for example, only a few of the many *in-out* orientations that might occur in the first few minutes of an ordinary day. You wake *out* of a deep sleep and peer *out* from beneath the covers *into* your room. You gradually emerge *out* of your stupor, pull yourself *out* from under the covers, climb *into* your robe, stretch *out* your limbs, and walk *in* a daze *out* of your bedroom and *into* the bathroom. You look *in* the mirror and see your face staring *out* at you. You reach *into* the medicine cabinet, take *out* the toothpaste, squeeze *out* some toothpaste, put the toothbrush *into* your mouth, brush your teeth, and rinse *out* your mouth. At breakfast you perform a host of further *in-out* moves—pouring *out* the coffee, setting *out* the dishes, putting the toast *in* the toaster, spreading *out* the jam on the toast, and on and on. (Johnson, 1987)

Johnson is not merely playing on the words *in* and *out*. There is a reason that those words are natural and appropriate, namely, the fact that we conceptualize an enormous number of activities in CONTAINER terms. Lindner (1981) describes in detail what is involved in this for 600 verbs containing the particle *out,* not just physical uses like *stretch out* and *spread out,* but in metaphorical uses like *figure out, work out,* etc. As Lindner observes, there are a great many metaphors based on the CONTAINER schema and they extend our body-based understanding of things in terms of CONTAINER schemas to a large range of abstract concepts. For example, emerging *out* of a stupor is a metaphorical, not a literal emergence from a container.

Let us consider some of the properties of this schema.

The CONTAINER Schema

Bodily experience: As Johnson points out, we experience our bodies both as containers and as things in containers (e.g., rooms) constantly.

Structural elements: INTERIOR, BOUNDARY, EXTERIOR.

Basic logic: Like most image schemas, its internal structure is arranged so as to yield a basic "logic." Everything is either inside a container or out of it—*P* or not *P*. If container *A* is in container *B* and *X* is in *A,* then *X* is in *B*—which is the basis for modus ponens: If all *A*'s are *B*'s and *X* is an *A,* then *X* is a *B*. As we shall see in case study 2, the CONTAINER schema is the basis of the Boolean logic of classes.

Sample metaphors: The visual field is understood as a container, e.g., things *come into* and *go out of sight.* Personal relationships are also understood in terms of containers: one can be *trapped in a marriage* and *get out of it.*

The "basic logic" of image schemas is due to their configurations as gestalts—as structured wholes which are more than mere collections of parts. Their basic logic is a consequence of their configurations. This way of understanding image schemas is irreducibly cognitive. It is rather different from the way of understanding logical structure that those of us raised with formal logic have grown to know and love. In formal logic there are no such gestalt configurations. What I have called the "basic logic" of a schema would be represented in formal logic by meaning postulates. This might be done as follows: Let CONTAINER and IN be uninterpreted predicate symbols, and let *A, B,* and *X* be variables over argument places. The logic of the predicates CONTAINER and IN would be characterized by meaning postulates such as:

For all A, X, either IN(X,A) or not IN(X,A).
For all A, B, X, if CONTAINER(A) and CONTAINER(B) and IN(A,B) and IN(X,A), then IN(X,B).

Such meaning postulates would be strings of meaningless symbols, but would be "given meaning" by the set-theoretical models they could be satisfied in.

On our account, the CONTAINER schema is inherently meaningful to people by virtue of their bodily experience. The schema has a meaningful configuration, from which the basic logic follows. In fact, on our account, the very concept of a set, as used in set-theoretical models, is understood in terms of CONTAINER schemas (see case study 2 for details). Thus, schemas are not understood in terms of meaning postulates and their interpretations. Rather, meaning postulates themselves only make sense given schemas that are inherently meaningful because they structure our direct experience. The logician's meaning postulates are nonetheless useful—if they are construed as precise statements of certain aspects of the logic inherent in schema configurations.

Let us consider a few more examples of image schemas.

The PART-WHOLE Schema

Bodily experience: We are whole beings with parts that we can manipulate. Our entire lives are spent with an awareness of both our wholeness and our parts. We experience our bodies as WHOLES with PARTS. In order to get around in the world, we have to be aware of the PART-WHOLE structure of other objects. In fact, we have evolved so that our basic-level perception can distinguish the fundamental PART-WHOLE structure that we need in order to function in our physical environment.

Structural elements: A WHOLE, PARTS, and a CONFIGURATION.

Basic logic: The schema is asymmetric: If A is a part of B, then B is not a part of A. It is irreflexive: A is not a part of A. Moreover, it cannot be the case that the WHOLE exists, while no PARTS of it exist. However, all the PARTS can exist, but still not constitute a WHOLE. If the PARTS exist in the CONFIGURATION, then and only then does the WHOLE exist. It follows that, if the PARTS are destroyed, then the WHOLE is destroyed. If the WHOLE is located at a place P, then the PARTS are located at P. A typical, but not necessary property: The PARTS are contiguous to one another.

Sample metaphors: Families (and other social organizations) are understood as wholes with parts. For example, marriage is understood as the creation of a family (a whole) with the spouses as parts. Divorce is thus viewed as *splitting up*. In India, society is conceived of as a body (the whole) with castes as parts—the highest caste being the head and the lowest caste being the feet. The caste structure is understood as being structured metaphorically according to the configuration of the body. Thus, it is believed (by those who believe the metaphor) that the maintenance of the caste structure (the configuration) is necessary to the preservation of society (the whole). The general concept of structure itself is a metaphorical projection of the CONFIGURATION aspect of PART-WHOLE structure. When we understand two things as being *isomorphic,* we mean that their parts stand in the same configuration to the whole.

The LINK Schema

Bodily experience: Our first link is the umbilical cord. Throughout infancy and early childhood, we hold onto our parents and other things, either to secure our location or theirs. To secure the location of two things relative to one another, we use such things as string, rope, or other means of connection.

Structural elements: Two entities, *A* and *B,* and LINK connecting them.

Basic logic: If *A* is linked to *B,* then *A* is constrained by, and dependent upon, *B*. Symmetry: If *A* is linked to *B,* then *B* is linked to *A*.

Metaphors: Social and interpersonal relationships are often understood in terms of links. Thus, we *make connections* and *break social ties*. Slavery is understood as bondage, and freedom as the absence of anything tying us down.

The CENTER-PERIPHERY Schema

Bodily experience: We experience our bodies as having centers (the trunk and internal organs) and peripheries (fingers, toes, hair). Similarly, trees and other plants have a central trunk and peripheral branches and leaves. The centers are viewed as more important than the peripheries in two ways: Injuries to the central parts are more serious (i.e., not mendable and often life threatening) than injuries to the peripheral parts. Similarly, the center defines the identity of the individual in a way that the peripheral parts do not. A tree that loses its leaves is the same tree. A person whose hair is cut off or who loses a finger is the same person. Thus, the periphery is viewed as depending on the center, but not conversely: bad circulation may affect the health of your hair, but losing your hair doesn't affect your circulatory system.

Structural elements: An ENTITY, a CENTER, and a PERIPHERY.

Basic logic: The periphery depends on the center, but not vice versa.

Sample metaphors: Theories have central and peripheral principles. What is important is understood as being central.

The SOURCE-PATH-GOAL Schema

Bodily experience: Every time we move anywhere there is a place we start from, a place we wind up at, a sequence of contiguous locations connecting the starting and ending points, and a direction. We will use the term "destination" as opposed to "goal" when we are referring to a specifically *spatial* ending point.

Structural elements: A SOURCE (starting point), a DESTINATION (end point), a PATH (a sequence of contiguous locations connecting the source and the destination), and a DIRECTION (toward the destination).

Basic logic: If you go from a source to a destination along a path, then you must pass through each intermediate point on the path; moreover, the further along the path you are, the more time has passed since starting.

Metaphors: Purposes are understood in terms of destinations, and achieving a purpose is understood as passing along a path from a starting point to an endpoint. Thus, one may *go a long way toward* achieving one's purposes, or one may get *sidetracked,* or find something getting *in one's way*. Complex events in general are also understood in terms of a source-path-goal schema; complex events have initial states (source), a sequence of intermediate stages (path), and a final state (destination).

Other image schemas include an UP-DOWN schema, a FRONT-BACK schema, a LINEAR ORDER schema, etc. At present, the range of existing schemas and their properties is still being studied. Image schemas provide particularly important evidence for the claim that abstract reason is a matter of two things: (*a*) reason based on bodily experience, and (*b*) metaphorical projections from concrete to abstract domains. Detailed evidence is provided by Johnson (1987). Johnson's argument has four parts:

- Image schemas structure our experience preconceptually.
- Corresponding image-schematic concepts exist.
- There are metaphors mapping image schemas into abstract domains, preserving their basic logic.
- The metaphors are not arbitrary but are themselves motivated by structures inhering in everyday bodily experience.

We have briefly discussed the first three parts of the argument, and will discuss them further in case study 2. Let us turn to the fourth part.

Experiential Bases of Metaphors

Each metaphor has a source domain, a target domain, and a source-to-target mapping. To show that the metaphor is *natural* in that it is *motivated by the structure of our experience,* we need to answer three questions:

1. What determines the choice of a possible well-structured source domain?
2. What determines the pairing of the source domain with the target domain?
3. What determines the details of the source-to-target mapping?

Let us take an example.

MORE IS UP; LESS IS DOWN

The crime rate keeps *rising*. The number of books published each year keeps going *up*. That stock has *fallen* again. Our sales *dropped* last year. You'll get a *higher* interest rate with them. Our financial reserves couldn't be any *lower.*

The source domain is VERTICALITY; the target domain is QUANTITY. The questions to be answered are:

1. What makes VERTICALITY appropriate as a source domain?
2. Why is VERTICALITY rather than some other domain (such as containment, front-back, or any other) used to understand QUANTITY?
3. Why is MORE mapped onto UP, rather than onto DOWN?

In short, why does this particular mapping occur, when so many others are possible? Is it just an arbitrary fact, or is there a reason?

The answer to question 1 is straightforward:

1. To function as a source domain for a metaphor, a domain must be understood independent of the metaphor. VERTICALITY is directly understood, since the UP-DOWN schema structures all of our functioning relative to gravity.

The answers to questions 2 and 3 come from the existence of a *structural correlation* in our daily experience that motivates every detail in this particular metaphorical mapping. Whenever we add *more* of a substance—say, water to a glass—the level goes *up.* When we add *more* objects to a pile, the level *rises.* Remove objects from the pile or water from the glass, and the level goes down. The correlation is overwhelming:

MORE correlates with UP.
LESS correlates with DOWN.

This correlation provides an answer to questions 2 and 3:

2. VERTICALITY serves as an appropriate source domain for understanding QUANTITY because of the regular correlation in our experience between VERTICALITY and QUANTITY.
3. The details of the mapping are motivated by the details of structural correlation cited above. Every detail of the metaphor is motivated by our physical functioning.

Let us take another example, the PURPOSES ARE DESTINATIONS metaphor that we discussed above. The three questions that need to be answered are:

1. What makes MOVEMENT appropriate as a source domain for PURPOSE?
2. Why is MOVEMENT used to understand purpose, rather than some other domain, such as CONTAINMENT, FRONT-BACK, VERTICALITY, or any other?
3. Why is DESIRED STATE mapped onto the DESTINATION, rather than onto the SOURCE, or some other point?

Again, the answer is that this metaphor is motivated by a structural correlation in everyday experience. Consider the common purpose of getting to a particular location. From the time we can first crawl, we regularly have as an intention getting to some particular place, whether for its own sake, or—even more commonly—as a subpurpose which must be fulfilled before some main purpose can be achieved. In such cases, we have a *purpose*—being in that *location*—that is satisfied by moving our bodies from a starting point *A*, through an intermediate sequence of locations, to the end point *B*—and that satisfies the purpose.

In this particular case, there is an identity between the domain of purpose and the physical domain. In the domain of purpose, there is an initial state, where the purpose is not satisfied, a sequence of actions necessary to achieve the final state, and a final state where the purpose is satisfied. Thus, there is a correlation in our experience, between a structure in the purpose domain and a structure in the domain of movement:

Initial State = Location *A* (starting point)
Final (Desired) State = Location *B* (end point)
Action Sequence = Movement from *A* to *B* (motion along path)

This pairing in our experience is not metaphorical; it is a special case of achieving a purpose, where that involves movement. It is, of course, an extremely important special case, since it is used over and over, every day, and is absolutely vital to our everyday functioning in the physical environment.

If we compare this structural correlation in a common experience with the details of the PURPOSES ARE DESTINATIONS metaphor, we find that there is an isomorphism between the structural correlation and the metaphorical mapping. In the metaphor,

A. The state where the desire is unfulfilled and no action toward fulfilling it has been taken is the starting point.
B. The desired state is the end point.
C. The sequence of actions that allow one to achieve the purpose is the movement.

Thus, our three questions get answered in the following way:

1. The SOURCE-PATH-GOAL schema is one of the most common structures that emerges from our constant bodily functioning. This schema has all the qualifications a schema should have to serve as the source domain of a metaphor. It is (*a*) pervasive in experience, (*b*) well-understood because it is pervasive, (*c*) well-structured, (*d*) simply structured, and (*e*) emergent and well-demarcated for these reasons. In fact, characteristics *a–d* provide some criteria for what it means for a structure to "emerge" naturally as a consequence of our experience.
2. There is an experiential correlation between the source domain (movement along a path to a physical location) and the target domain (achievement of a purpose). This correlation makes the mapping from the source to the target domain natural.
3. The cross-domain correlations in the experiential pairing (for example, desired state with final location) determine the details of the metaphorical mapping (for example, desired state maps onto final location).

There are many structural correlations in our experience. Not all of them motivate metaphors, but many do. When there is such a motivation, the metaphor seems *natural.* The reason it seems natural is that the pairing of the source and target domains is motivated by experience, as are the details of the mapping.

The point is this: Schemas that structure our bodily experience *preconceptually* have a basic logic. *Preconceptual* structural correlations in experience motivate metaphors that map that logic onto abstract domains. Thus, what has been called abstract reason has a bodily basis in our everyday physical functioning. It is this that allows us to base a theory of meaning and rationality on aspects of bodily functioning.

The Issue of Primitives

We have argued that our conceptual system has dual foundations—that both basic-level and image-schematic concepts are directly meaningful. This gives us a system that is grounded at two points. It also provides us with a situation that is odd from the point of view of objectivist semantic systems: strictly speaking, this system has foundations, but no primitives.

In objectivist semantic systems, the following principles of conceptual structure hold by definition:

A. Every concept is either primitive or built up out of primitives by fully productive principles of semantic composition.
B. All internal conceptual structure is the result of the application of fully productive principles of semantic composition.
C. The concepts with no internal structure are directly meaningful, and only those are.

But in the human conceptual system, as opposed to artificially constructed semantic systems, none of these principles holds.

- Basic-level and image-schematic concepts are the only directly meaningful concepts, but both have internal structure. This violates C.
- The internal structure of both basic-level and image-schematic concepts is not the result of the application of fully productive principles of composition. This violates A and B.

In objectivist semantic systems, the following criteria converge to characterize what a conceptual primitive is. When we say that a conceptual system has primitives, we usually mean that all of the following conditions hold:

1. There are fully productive principles of semantic composition, building up more complex concepts from less complex ones. Those concepts not put together by fully productive principles of semantic composition are primitive.
2. Every concept either has internal structure or it does not. The ones with internal structure are complex. The concepts with no internal structure are primitive.
3. Some concepts get their meaning directly. Those are the primitive concepts. Other concepts—the complex concepts—get their meaning indirectly via the principles of composition that relate them to primitive concepts.

By criterion 3, the directly meaningful concepts are primitive. This means that basic-level and image-schematic concepts would have to be primitive. Neither of them is put together by productive principles of semantic composition, so criterion 1 would hold. But since both have internal structure, they both violate criterion 2. Thus, the three criteria do not converge.

Both basic-level and image-schematic concepts meet two of the three criteria for conceptual primitives. Perhaps we should redefine "primitive" so as to rule out criterion 2. This would do violence to the notion of a primitive, since it allows primitives to have internal structure.

It would also create the bizarre situation in which one primitive concept could contain other primitive concepts. Consider the concept of a MAN. It comes with a rich mental image, characterizing overall shape. But that mental image also comes with a schematic structure. The image of the man is structured as having an UP-DOWN organization; it is structured as a container having an INSIDE and an OUTSIDE; it is also structured as WHOLE with PARTS; and so on. In general, rich mental images are structured by image-schemas, but they are not *exhaustively* structured by them. The mental image is more than just the sum of the schemas. Since the mental image is part of what makes MAN a basic-level concept, the basic-level concept must contain image schemas. If both basic-level concepts and image schemas are primitives, then we have the situation where one primitive contains other primitives.

Moreover, one could not just get out of this problem by saying that just the image schemas are primitives. Basic-level concepts would then neither be primitive nor constructed out of primitives—another bizarre result. The only sensible recourse is to give up on the traditional concept of a primitive.

But this does not require us to give up on semantic compositionality altogether. Within a theory that contains basic-level concepts and image schemas, it is still possible to have rules of semantic composition that form more complex concepts from less complex ones. (For example, see Langacker 1986.) This is a rather interesting point. All that semantic compositionality requires is a starting point—something for the compositional principles to work on. That starting point has to be something that is directly understood; in this case, basic-level and image-schematic concepts will do. Conceptual primitives, in the sense characterized above, are not required for compositionality.

The Conceptualizing Capacity

What gives human beings the power of abstract reason? Our answer is that human beings have what we will call a *conceptualizing capacity*. That capacity consists in:

- The ability to form symbolic structures that correlate with *preconceptual* structures in our everyday experience. Such symbolic structures are basic-level and image-schematic concepts.
- The ability to project metaphorically from structures in the physical domain to structures in abstract domains, constrained by other structural correlations between the physical and abstract domains. This accounts for our capacity to reason about abstract domains such as quantity and purpose.
- The ability to form complex concepts and general categories using image schemas as structuring devices. This allows us to construct complex event structures and taxonomies with superordinate and subordinate categories.

We have only touched on this last ability—the general capacity to form idealized cognitive models. It is the nature of such ICMs and the capacity to form them to which we now turn.

Cognitive Models

Mental Spaces

Following Fauconnier (1985), we take cognitive model theory as involving (*a*) mental spaces, and (*b*) cognitive models that structure those spaces. A mental space is a medium for conceptualization and thought. Thus any fixed or ongoing state of affairs as we conceptualize it is represented by a mental space. Examples include:

- our immediate reality, as understood
- fictional situations, situations in paintings, movies, etc.
- past or future situations, as understood
- hypothetical situations
- abstract domains, e.g., conceptual domains (e.g., subject matters such as economics, politics, physics), mathematical domains, etc.

Mental spaces have the following basic properties:

- Spaces may contain mental entities.
- Spaces may be structured by cognitive models.
- Spaces may be related to other spaces by what Fauconnier calls "connectors."
- An entity in one space may be related to entities in other spaces by connectors.
- Spaces are extendable, in that additional entities and ICMs may be added to them in the course of cognitive processing.

- ICMs may introduce spaces. For example, a storytelling ICM introduces the mental space of the story.

Fauconnier hypothesizes that the following strategies are used in cognitive processing involving mental spaces:

- Avoid contradictions within a space.
- Maximize common background assumptions across adjacent spaces.
- Foregrounded elements introduced into a space become backgrounded in future spaces.

Mental spaces are what cognitive model theory uses in place of possible worlds and situations. They are like possible worlds in that they can be taken as representing our understanding of hypothetical and fictional situations. Connectors between spaces play the role of "alternativeness relations" in possible world semantics, though they differ from alternativeness relations in certain respects. Spaces are like situations in situation semantics in that they are partial; they do not require that everything in the world be represented.

The major difference is that mental spaces are conceptual in nature. They have no ontological status outside of the mind, and hence have no role in an objectivist semantics. A mental space, unlike a situation or a possible world, is not the kind of thing that the real world, or some aspect of it, could be an instance of. It is therefore not the kind of thing that could function within a theory of meaning based on the relationship between symbols and things in the world. Because their status is purely cognitive, mental spaces are free to function within a semantics based on internal or experiential realism. Yet they allow for a semantics with all the explicitness of a model-theoretic semantics. (For details, see Fauconnier 1985.)

Let us now turn to the nature of the cognitive models that provide structure to mental spaces.

The Structure of Cognitive Models

We have argued that basic-level and image-schematic concepts are directly understood in terms of physical experience. We will now argue that these provide sufficient foundations for a theory of general conceptual structure. The basic idea is this:

- Given basic-level and image-schematic concepts, it is possible to build up complex cognitive models.
- Image schemas provide the structures used in those models.

Recall for a moment some of the kinds of image-schemas that we have discussed: schemas for CONTAINER, SOURCE-PATH-GOAL, LINK, PART-

WHOLE, CENTER-PERIPHERY, UP-DOWN, FRONT-BACK. These schemas structure our experience of space. What I will be claiming is that the same schemas structure concepts themselves. In fact, I maintain that image schemas define most of what we commonly mean by the term "structure" when we talk about abstract domains. When we understand something as having an abstract structure, we understand that structure in terms of image schemas.

The Spatialization of Form Hypothesis

In particular, I maintain that:

- Categories (in general) are understood in terms of CONTAINER schemas.
- Hierarchical structure is understood in terms of PART-WHOLE schemas and UP-DOWN schemas.
- Relational structure is understood in terms of LINK schemas.
- Radial structure in categories is understood in terms of CENTER-PERIPHERY schemas.
- Foreground-background structure is understood in terms of FRONT-BACK schemas.
- Linear quantity scales are understood in terms of UP-DOWN schemas and LINEAR ORDER schemas.

I will refer to this general view as The Spatialization of Form hypothesis.

Strictly speaking, the Spatialization of Form hypothesis requires a metaphorical mapping from physical space into a "conceptual space." Under this mapping, spatial structure is mapped into conceptual structure. More specifically, image schemas (which structure space) are mapped into the corresponding abstract configurations (which structure concepts). The Spatialization of Form hypothesis thus maintains that conceptual structure is understood in terms of image schemas plus a metaphorical mapping.

Additionally, metaphorical mappings themselves can also be understood in terms of image schemas:

- Conceptual domains (in particular, the source and target domains) are understood as being set off from one another within CONTAINER schemas.
- Mappings from entities in one domain to entities in another domain are understood in terms of SOURCE-PATH-GOAL schemas, though the PATH is unspecified in these cases.

Image schemas thus play two roles: They are concepts that have directly-understood structures of their own, and they are used metaphorically to structure other complex concepts.

The Structure of ICMs

Each cognitive model (or ICM) is a structure consisting of symbols. There are two kinds of complex symbolic structures: building-block structures and gestalt structures.

- A complex symbolic structure has a *building-block structure* if its structural elements all exist independently, and if the meaning of the whole is a function of the meanings of the parts.
- Otherwise, it has a gestalt structure, that is, a structure (*a*) whose elements do not all exist independent of the whole or (*b*) whose overall meaning is not predictable from the meanings of its parts and the way those parts are put together.

Directly-meaningful symbols all have gestalt structures. For example, the CONTAINER schema has an INTERIOR, EXTERIOR, and BOUNDARY; those parts do not all exist independent of the schema. The concept INTERIOR, for example, does not make sense independently of the CONTAINER gestalt. Similarly, all the other image-schemas are gestalts with structures of the sort described above. Basic-level concepts also have a gestalt structure, defined by in part by images and motor movements.

It should be noted that the term "symbol" is not used in the same way as in most other symbolic systems. In most symbolic systems, symbols are either entities (with no significant internal structure) or complexes with a building-block structure. The symbolic system we are describing differs in that it has gestalt structures as well.

ICMs are typically quite complex structures, defined by image schemas of all the sorts just discussed. Some symbols in an ICM may be directly meaningful: the basic-level and image-schematic concepts. Other symbols are understood indirectly via their relationship to directly understood concepts. Such relationships are defined by the image schemas that structure the ICMs.

We previously described ICMs as falling into five basic types: (*a*) image-schematic; (*b*) propositional; (*c*) metaphoric; (*d*) metonymic; (*e*) symbolic. We have already described image schemas. Let us now turn to the propositional ICM. I will describe several common types: (*a*) the proposition; (*b*) the scenario (sometimes called a "script"); (*c*) the feature bundle; (*d*) the taxonomy; (*e*) the radial category. The examples are intended to be suggestive, rather than authoritative or exhaustive. That is, I will be illustrating the idea of a cognitive model, rather making any serious claims about what our cognitive models are like in detail.

Propositional ICMs

By a *propositional* ICM, I mean one that does not use *imaginative devices*, i.e., metaphor, metonymy, or mental imagery. Each ICM has an *ontology* and a *structure*. The ontology is the set of elements used in the ICM. The structure consists of the properties of the elements and the relations obtaining among the elements. The elements in the ontology may be either basic-level concepts—entities, actions, states, properties, etc.—or they may be concepts characterized by cognitive models of other types.

Propositional models have an objectivist flavor to them, since they contain entities, with their properties and the relations holding among them. It must be recalled, however, that they are *cognitive* models, not slices of reality. The "entities" are mental entities, not real things. I believe that the common tendency to view the world in objectivist terms comes from the fact that many of our cognitive models are objectivist in this limited respect. It seems to me that when we understand our experience by projecting propositional models onto it, we are imposing an objectivist structure on the world.

The Simple Proposition

The simple proposition itself is an example of what we are calling "propositional ICMs." A simple proposition consists of an ontology of elements (the "arguments") and a basic predicate that holds of those arguments. The overall structure of the proposition is thus characterized by a part-whole schema, where the proposition = the whole, the predicate = a part, and the arguments = the other parts. In addition, certain semantic relations may hold among the arguments: there may be an agent, a patient, an experiencer, an instrument, a location, etc. Semantic relations are represented structurally by link schemas, and the kinds of schemas are represented by assignments of links to categories of relations (e.g., the agent category).

Complex propositions may be formed from simple ones by such well-known devices as modification, quantification, complementation, conjunction, negation, etc.

The Scenario

A scenario consists fundamentally of the following ontology: an initial state, a sequence of events, and a final state. In other words, the scenario is structured by a SOURCE-PATH-GOAL schema in the time domain, where

- the initial state = the source
- the final state = the destination
- the events = locations on the path

and the path stretches through time. The scenario is a WHOLE and each of these elements is a PART.

The scenario ontology also consists typically of people, things, properties, relations, and propositions. In addition, there are typically relations of certain kinds holding among the elements of the ontology: causal relations, identity relations, etc. These are represented structurally by link schemas, each of which is categorized as to the kind of relation it represents. Scenarios also have a purpose structure, which specifies the purposes of people in the scenario. Such structures are represented metaphorically via SOURCE-PATH-GOAL schemas, as discussed above.

The Relation between Concepts and Categories

In general, concepts are elements of cognitive models. Many concepts, for example, are characterized in terms of scenario ICMs. The concept WAITER is characterized relative to a restaurant scenario. The concept BUYER is characterized relative to a commercial exchange scenario. The concept SECOND BASEMAN is characterized relative to a baseball game scenario.

For every such concept, there can be a corresponding category: those entities in a given domain of discourse that the concept (as characterized by the cognitive model) fits. If the concept is characterized in the model purely by necessary and sufficient conditions, the category will be classically defined. It can give rise to simple prototype effects if it is possible for entities in the domain of discourse to meet some background conditions of the model. It will give rise to metonymic prototype effects if the ICM contains a metonymic mapping from part of the category to the whole category. And if the concept is defined not by necessary and sufficient conditions but by a graded scale, then the resulting category will be a graded category.

Feature-Bundle Structures

A feature bundle is a collection of properties. The elements in the ontology are properties. Structurally, the bundle is characterized by a CONTAINER schema, where the properties are inside the container. Classical categories can be represented by feature bundles.

Classical Taxonomic Structures

Classical categories and classical taxonomies are not built into nature or part of some transcendental rationality that goes beyond thinking beings. They are inventions of the human mind. Each classical taxonomy is an idealized cognitive model—a hierarchical structure of classical categories. The elements in the ontology of the taxonomic model are all categories. Each category is represented structurally by a CONTAINER schema. The hierarchy is represented structurally by PART-WHOLE and UP-DOWN schemas. Each higher-order category is a whole, with the immediately lower categories being its parts. Each higher-level category contains all of its lower-level categories. At each level, the categories are nonoverlapping.

Classical taxonomies have fundamental semantic constraints. Each category is classical—defined by feature bundles. Each member of each category has each of the properties contained in the feature bundles for that category. The feature bundles defining lower-level categories include all the features of the bundles defining higher-level categories.

A classical taxonomy is intended to be exhaustive—to categorize all the entities in some domain in terms of their properties. The highest category in the taxonomy encompasses the entire domain.

Taxonomic ICMs are one of the most important structuring devices we have for making sense of what we experience. But it is important to recall that the taxonomic models are imposed by us, for our purposes. If we are fortunate, they will serve those purposes.

Radial Category Structure

Like other categories, a radial category is represented structurally as a container, and its subcategories are containers inside it. What distinguishes it is that it is structured by the CENTER-PERIPHERY schema. One subcategory is the center; the other subcategories are linked to the center by various types of links. Noncentral categories may be "subcenters," that is, they may have further center-periphery structures imposed on them.

Graded Categories

Simple classical categories are represented as containers, with an interior (containing the members), an exterior (containing the nonmembers), and a boundary. In classical categories, the boundary is sharp and does not have any interior structure. But in graded categories, the boundary is fuzzy; it is given a "width," defined by a linear scale of values between 0 and 1, with 1 at the interior and 0 at the exterior. Elements are not merely in the interior or exterior, but may be located in the fuzzy boundary area, at some point along the scale between 0 and 1. That point defines the degree of membership of the given element.

It is, of course, possible for two graded categories to be adjacent to one another (e.g., blue and green, chair and stool) and for their fuzzy boundaries to overlap in such a way that a given element may be in the fuzzy boundaries of both at once, and therefore to be a member of each to some degree between 0 and 1.

Graded Propositions

ICMs characterizing propositions may, of course, contain linear scales. These may define the degree to which a given property holds of an individual (e.g., the degree to which someone is tall or rich). That property can be taken as defining a graded category, where the degree of membership equals the degree to which each member has the given property. This is a common way in which graded categories arise.

Metaphoric and Metonymic Models

A metaphoric mapping involves a source domain and a target domain. The source domain is assumed to be structured by a propositional or image-schematic model. The mapping is typically partial; it maps the structure of the ICM in the source domain onto a corresponding structure in the target domain. As we mentioned above, the source and target domains are represented structurally by CONTAINER schemas, and the mapping is represented by a SOURCE-PATH-GOAL schema.

A metonymic mapping occurs within a single conceptual domain, which is structured by an ICM. Given two elements, *A* and *B,* in the ICM, *A* may "stand for" *B*. The "stands-for" relation is represented structurally by a SOURCE-PATH-GOAL schema. If *B* is a category and *A* is a member, or subcategory, of *B,* the result is a metonymic category structure, in which *A* is a metonymic prototype.

Prototypes

Given the various possible category structures, prototype effects can arise in a number of ways:

- Metonymy: Given category *B,* where *A* is either a member or subcategory of *B,* suppose that *A* metonymically "stands for" *B*. That is,

it is either a social stereotype, or a typical case, or an ideal, or a submodel, etc. Then, *A* will be a *best example* of *B*.
- Radial Category: Given category *B* with a radial structure and *A* at its center, then *A* is the *best example* of *B*.
- Generative Category: Suppose *B* is a category generated by rule from a subcategory or member, *A*. Then *A* is a *best example* of *B*.
- Graded Category: Given a graded category *B* with *A* being a member of degree 1, then *A* is a *best example* of *B*.
- Classical Category: Consider a cognitive model containing a feature bundle that characterizes a classical category *B*. If *A* has all the properties in the feature bundle, it is a *best example* of *B*. An element *C*, having some of the properties in the feature bundle, may be judged a less-good example of *B*. Strictly speaking, *C* will be outside *B*; but people, in such cases, may consider *B* a graded category, such that elements bearing a degree of similarity to members of *B* will be viewed as being members of *B* to a degree.

These, of course, are "pure" cases. Mixed cases also exist. Categories of numbers, for example, may have both generators and submodels. In such cases, there is no theory of which kinds of best examples take precedence. No serious study of such phenomena exists at present.

Symbolic Models and Cognitive Grammar

Thus far, we have not discussed language at all. All the ICMs we have discussed so far have been purely conceptual; they have contained no elements of particular languages in them. The distinction is important. Purely conceptual ICMs can be characterized independently of the words and morphemes of particular languages. When linguistic elements are associated with conceptual elements in ICMs, the result is what we shall call a *symbolic* ICM. Let us now turn to the question of how natural languages can be described within this framework. We will begin with lexical items, grammatical categories, and grammatical constructions.

As Fillmore has established in his papers on frame semantics (Fillmore 1975, 1976, 1978, 1982*a*, 1982*b*, and 1985), the meanings of lexical items—words and morphemes—are characterized in terms of cognitive models. The meaning of each lexical item is represented as an element in an ICM. The ICM as a whole is taken as the background against which the word is defined.

The traditional definition of the grammatical category noun as the name of a person, place, or thing is not that far off. The best examples of nouns are words for basic-level physical objects. *Noun* is a radial category. Its central subcategory consists of names for physical entities—people, places, things. Those are the prototypical nouns. There are, of course, noncentral nouns: abstract nouns (like *strength*), and strange nouns that occur only in idioms (like *umbrage* in *take umbrage at*). *Verb* is also a radial category, with basic-level physical actions as central members (e.g., *run, hit, give,* etc.). Thus, although grammatical categories as a whole cannot be given strict classical definitions in semantic terms, their central subcategories can be defined in just that way. The remaining members of the each grammatical category can then be *motivated* by their relationships to the central members.

Prototype theory thus permits us to state the general principles that provide the semantic basis of syntactic categories. In a classical theory of categories, one would be forced to say that there is no semantic basis at all. The reason is that classical categories have a homogeneous structure—there are no prototypes—and everything that is not completely predictable must be arbitrary. Since syntactic categorization is not completely predictable from semantic categorization, a classical theory of categories would be forced to claim, incorrectly, that it is completely arbitrary. Take the case of adjectives, for example. As Dixon has shown in his classic *Where Have All The Adjectives Gone?* (Dixon 1982), languages may have no adjectives at all, or they may have a very small number: Igbo has eight, Hausa twelve, etc. These are not arbitrary. When a language has a very small number of adjectives, one can pretty well predict what they will be: central adjectival meanings like BIG-SMALL, GOOD-BAD, WHITE-BLACK, OLD-YOUNG, HARD-SOFT, etc. Thus, it is clear that general principles relating semantic to syntactic categories do exist.

The theory of ICMs is especially useful in characterizing grammatical constructions. Let us begin with the matter of linguistic structure in general. As we observed above, image schemas characterize conceptual structure. They also characterize syntactic structure.

- Hierarchical syntactic structure (i.e., constituent structure) is characterized by PART-WHOLE schemas: The mother node is the whole and the daughters are the parts.
- Head-and-modifier structures are characterized by CENTER-PERIPHERY schemas.
- Grammatical relations and coreference relations are represented structurally by LINK schemas.
- Syntactic "distance" is characterized by LINEAR SCALE schemas.
- Syntactic categories, like other categories, are characterized structurally by CONTAINER schemas.

Empirical evidence for this way of conceiving of syntactic structure is provided in chapter 20 of Lakoff and Johnson 1980.

Given such a view of the nature of syntactic structure, we can represent grammatical constructions as ICMs. We can also characterize the meanings of grammatical constructions by directly pairing the syntactic aspect of the construction with the ICM representing the meaning of the construction. Once this is done, it is possible to state many generalizations governing the relationship between syntax and semantics. As we shall see in case study 3, many, if not most, of the details of syntactic constructions are consequences of the meanings of the constructions. (See Langacker 1986.) This allows for a great simplification of the description of grammatical constructions.

The concept of a radial category also permits us to show regularities in the structure of the grammar and the lexicon. Most words and morphemes have multiple meanings—meanings that are related to one another. These meanings can be seen as forming a radial category, in which there is a central meaning and a structure of related meanings which are motivated by the central meaning. (See Brugman 1983.) This view of the lexicon allows us to state general principles relating meanings of words. An extremely detailed example is worked out in case study 2.

The idea of a radial category also allows us to state otherwise unstateable syntactic generalizations governing the relation of grammatical constructions to one another. (See Van Oosten 1984.) This is done by making use of the concept of *ecological location,* the location of a construction within a grammatical system. Constructions form radial categories, with a central construction and a number of peripheral constructions linked to the center. Certain generalizations about the details of grammatical constructions can be stated only in terms of where a construction is located in such a radial structure. For details, see case study 3.

In summary, linguistic expressions get their meanings via (*a*) being associated directly with ICMs and (*b*) having the elements of the ICMs either be directly understood in terms of preconceptual structures in experience, or indirectly understood in terms of directly understood concepts plus structural relations.

Language is thus based on cognition. The structure of language uses the same devices used to structure cognitive models—image schemas, which are understood in terms of bodily functioning. Language is made meaningful because it is directly tied to meaningful thought and depends upon the nature of thought. Thought is made meaningful via two direct connections to preconceptual bodily functioning, which is in turn highly constrained, but by no means totally constrained, by the nature of the world that we function within.

In experiential realism, there is no unbridgeable gulf between language and thought on one hand and the world on the other. Language and thought are meaningful because they are motivated by our functioning as part of reality.

Philosophical Issues

We are now in a position to characterize a general approach to a variety of philosophical issues: meaning, understanding, truth, knowledge, and objectivity. Basic-level and image-schematic concepts are the foundations of the approach. They are directly meaningful, since they put us in touch with preconceptual structures in our bodily experience of functioning in the world. It is because *the body is in the mind,* as Johnson puts it, that our basic-level and image-schematic concepts are meaningful.

Meaning

Meaning is not a thing; it involves what is meaningful to us. Nothing is meaningful in itself. Meaningfulness derives from the experience of functioning as a being of a certain sort in an environment of a certain sort. Basic-level concepts are meaningful to us because they are characterized by the way we perceive the overall shape of things in terms of part-whole structure and by the way we interact with things with our bodies. Image schemas are meaningful to us because they too structure our perceptions and bodily movements, though in a much less detailed way. Natural metaphorical concepts are meaningful because they are based on (*a*) directly meaningful concepts and (*b*) correlations in our experience. And superordinate and subordinate concepts are meaningful because they are grounded in basic-level concepts and extended on the basis of such things as function and purpose.

Understanding

Let us begin with *direct* understanding. This requires characterizations of directly understood sentences and directly understood situations:

- A *sentence* is *directly understood* if the concepts associated with it are directly meaningful.
- *Aspects of a particular situation* are *directly experienced* if they play a causal role in the experience. For example, I am not directly experi-

encing everything in the room I am sitting in. My chair, for example, is held together by glue. I directly experience the chair, but not the glue. The chair is playing a causal role in my experience. The glue's causal role involves the chair, but not my experience of the chair.

- *An aspect of a directly experienced situation* is *directly understood* if it is preconceptually structured.

Thus we have characterizations of directly understood sentences and directly understood situations. *Truth relative to direct understanding* can then be characterized as a correspondence between the understanding of the sentence and the understanding of the situation.

Let us take the usual example. Start with a directly understood sentence. It is possible to have a direct understanding of the proverbial *The cat is on the mat,* since CAT and MAT are basic-level concepts (presumably with associated mental images) and ON is composed of three kinesthic image schemas: ABOVE, CONTACT, and SUPPORT. CAT, MAT, and ON are all directly understood concepts.

Now let us consider a directly understood situation. Say, you are looking at (and thereby directly experiencing) a cat on a mat. Since both *cat* and *mat* are basic-level concepts, you will have a perception of the overall shape of both, as well as a perception of the relationship between them. Your perceptions of overall shape for the cat and the mat are preconceptually structured experiences of the cat and the mat. Your perception of the relationship between the cat and the mat is a preconceptually structured experience of the kinesthic relations ABOVE, CONTACT, and SUPPORT. This makes the situation one that is directly understood.

The fit of the direct understanding of the sentence to the direct understanding of the situation works like this:

- The mental image associated with your basic-level concept of CAT can accord with your perception of the overall shape of a cat.
- The mental image associated with your basic-level concept of MAT can accord with your perception of a mat.
- The image schemas that constitute your understanding of ON can accord with your perception of the relationship between the cat and the mat.

If the direct understanding of the sentence is in overall accord with the direct understanding of the situation, then we can characterize truth relative to a direct understanding. This is, of course, not unproblematical, since one must also take the understanding of the background of the situation into account, as Searle (1979, chap. 5) has observed. And, most important, we need a precise account of "accord with."

Sentences and situations are by no means all understood directly. The bulk of our understanding may well be indirect. An account of indirect understanding of both sentences and situations will therefore be needed. Sentences are not a problem: a sentence is indirectly understood if the concepts associated with it by the grammar are indirectly meaningful. But providing for the indirect understanding of situations is more difficult. Lakoff and Johnson (1980, chap. 24) provide an account of indirect metaphorical understanding. But at present there is no fully general account of how we understand situations indirectly.

Part of such an account of situational understanding will be a criterion of relative accuracy and good sense. Such a criterion would maximize directness of understanding. It would prefer understandings that are more direct to those that are less so. This would be analogous to Lewis's naturalness condition. Thus, although one might (metaphorically) try to understand a cherry in terms of the concept CAT, that understanding would be very indirect and therefore not nearly as accurate or as sensible as using the concept CHERRY.

Experientialism is committed to a general account of understanding along these lines. This is necessary for an account of truth. Such an account of truth would make the following claim: If a sentence is true, it is true by virtue of what it means and how it is understood. Truth depends on meaningfulness.

Truth

We understand a statement as being *true* in a given situation if our understanding of the statement fits our understanding of the situation closely enough for our purposes.

That is the basis of an experientialist account of truth. It is not absolute, God's eye view truth. But it is what we ordinarily take truth to be. One might well object, in response, that we ordinarily understand truth as being absolute truth, objective truth, and not truth relative to any understanding. Fair enough. But the discrepancy is readily explainable.

Truth is relative to understanding. But we commonly take understanding to be an absolute. That is, we have a folk theory to the effect that:

– There is one and only one correct way to understand reality.

If truth is relative to understanding, and if understanding, according to our folk theory, is fixed, then (in that folk theory) there is one and only one truth—absolute truth. This is our normal folk theory of truth. As with most folk theories, we can abandon it when forced to. When people are placed in a situation where they can see that there are two or more equally plausible understandings of a situation, then it is generally possible for them to see that truth can be relative to those understandings.

To conclude: The folk view that truth is absolute is a result of two things—a characterization of truth as relative to an understanding *plus* a folk theory that there is one and only one correct way to understand reality. When there is only one conceivable understanding of a situation, then truth appears to be absolute. But when it is clear that more than one understanding is possible, then it becomes clear that truth is relative to understanding. (For *empirical* evidence supporting this, see Sweetser, in press.) Such an account of truth also explains how metaphors can be true, since metaphors provide understandings of experiences. (For details, see Lakoff and Johnson 1980, chap. 23.)

Objectivist philosophers happen to take as paradigm cases situations that can be understood in only one plausible way. That is why they like to talk about cases like *The cat is on the mat.* On the assumption that it is clear what a cat is and what a mat is (they are, after all, basic level objects) and that we have a normal situation—that we're not in outer space or something weird like that—then *The cat is on the mat* is either true or not, absolutely, objectively true or not. But take a trickier case like the story about "time theft" discussed above in chapter 13. The researcher, Robert Half, and the editors of the *Oakland Tribune* take it as *true* that employees *steal time* from their employers. But in order to have such a belief, they must understand time metaphorically as the sort of entity that can be stolen. Relative to such an understanding, the sentence *Employees steal time from their employers* can be true. The question is whether that way of understanding time should be accepted. Ways of understanding situations change in the course of history. The metaphorical understanding of time as something that can be "wasted" is only a recent innovation in the history of man, and it is certainly not a universally shared way of understanding time. But because it is accepted in present-day Western culture, there is no problem evaluating the truth of sentences like *I wasted an hour this morning.* They have achieved cat-on-the-mat status, because our understanding of time as something that can be wasted has become conventional.

Created Realities

One of the major inadequacies of objectivist metaphysics is that it has no room for such humanly created realities as "wasted time." If we view time as a resource that can be wasted, and act upon that view, and even set up institutions that take such a view for granted, then, by our actions, we can create "wasted time." If I live in a society that is constructed on the TIME IS

A RESOURCE metaphor, and if I accept and function in terms of that metaphor, then it can be *true* that *someone wasted an hour of my time this morning*. This makes sense on an experientialist account of truth; it makes very little sense on an objectivist account of truth. Many of our most important truths are not physical truths, but truths that come about as a result of human beings acting in accord with a conceptual system that cannot in any sense be said to fit a reality completely outside of human experience. Human experience is, after all, real too—every bit as real as rocks and trees and cats and mats. Since we act in accord with our conceptual systems and since our actions are real, our conceptual systems have a major role in creating reality. Where human action is concerned, metaphysics, that is, our view of what exists and is real, is not independent of epistemology in the broad sense of human understanding and knowledge.

Truth as a Radial Concept

We saw above that categories of mind are often radially structured, with a central subcategory and extensions. I would like to suggest that the category of truths is similarly structured. Because, as we have seen, truth cannot be characterized simply as correspondence to a physical reality, we must recognize truth as a human concept, subject to the laws of human thought. It should come as no surprise that it is structured the way other human concepts are structured.

Put briefly, the suggestion is this: there are central and noncentral truths. The central truths are characterized in terms of directly understood concepts, concepts that fit the preconceptual structure of experience. Such concepts are (*a*) basic-level concepts in the physical domain and (*b*) general schemas emerging from experience (what I have called "kinesthetic image-schematic concepts"). Here are some examples of such central truths:

> I am writing this. There are three pens and a telephone on my desk. I am sitting on a green chair. There is a table to my left. There is a lamp to my right and it is on. Through my window, I can see houses, trees, the bay, some mountains, and a bridge.

There is nothing exciting or controversial here, just simple truths. Note the basic-level physical objects: pens, a telephone, a chair, a table, a desk, a lamp, a window, houses, trees, the bay, a bridge. These sentences (like many of the example sentences in the philosophical literature) have a decidedly Dick-and-Jane quality about them. They are very different from the other sentences in this book, most of which I hope you will find true, but few of which are simple central truths, concerning only basic-level physical objects. Central truths are true by virtue of the directness of the fit between the preconceptual structure of experience and the conceptual structure in terms of which the sentence is understood. But most of the sentences we speak and hear and read and write are not capable of expressing central truths; they are sentences that contain concepts that are very general or very specific or abstract or metaphorical or metonymic or display other kinds of "indirectness" relative to the direct structuring of experience. Not that they need be any less true, but they aren't central examples.

Truth is very much a bootstrapping operation, grounded in direct links to preconceptually and distinctly structured experience and the concepts that accord with such experience. But most cases of truth involve indirectness. That is, they make use of indirect understanding: higher-level categories, metaphoric and metonymic understanding, abstractions, etc. To me, this is the most interesting kind of truth—noncentral truth. Such truths are the ones least compatible with objectivist views of truth.

Knowledge

What does it mean to know something and how is knowledge possible? When an objectivist asks this question, certain parts of the answer are taken to be obvious: If you know something, then what you know is true—objectively true. Knowledge is possible at least partly because the categories of mind can fit the categories of the world—the objectively given external world, which comes complete with objective categories. We have scientific knowledge when our scientific theories fit the objective facts of the world.

When objectivism is abandoned, our understanding of what knowledge is must change. What takes its place? If truth, as we suggested, is a radial concept, then so is knowledge. The best examples of knowledge are things that we know about basic-level objects, actions, and relations in the physical domain—what might be called our cat-on-the-mat knowledge, our knowledge about chairs and tables and trees and rocks and our own bodies and other basic-level objects in our immediate environment. The best examples of truths are best examples of objects of knowledge.

We get our basic knowledge of our immediate physical environments from our basic-level interactions with the environment, through perceiving, touching, and manipulating. We may get our other knowledge either directly (as in the case of emotional and social knowledge) or indirectly (as in the cast of knowledge acquired by others and transmitted, say, by newspapers, textbooks, etc.). But the things we feel we know best are those that can be most closely related to basic-level experience.

Much of our technology is aimed in the direction of expanding basic-level experience. Telescopes, microscopes, photography, and television all extend basic-level perception in the visual domain. How do we *know* that Saturn has rings? We can see them through a telescope—or at least see pictures taken through somebody else's telescope. How do we know that there are bacteria? We can see them through a microscope—or at least see photographs of them. It doesn't really matter if one doesn't know why a microscope works or that one has to learn to see through microscopes. (See Hacking 1983, chap. 11 for a discussion.) Microscopes turn things that previously couldn't be seen into basic-level percepts, and they do so in a consistent manner—which is good enough for most practicing scientists. Knowledge that we are confident of can grow because we see science as having the potential to extend our basic-level perception and manipulation very much further, perhaps indefinitely further. For an extension of basic-level perception and manipulation to be acceptable, standards of consistency, reliability, and (to a lesser extent) rational explanation must be met. The microscope is consistent and reliable, so the fact that we may not really know why it works is not so important—as long as we think there *is* someone who knows or that someone will someday know. But rationality helps in getting such extensions of basic-level perception and manipulation accepted by the scientific community; understanding why something works is preferable.

It is the technological extension of basic-level perception and manipulation that makes us confident that science provides us with real knowledge. And if photographs aren't possible, graphs and diagrams are the next best thing. And photographs that show patterns and shapes that are good gestalts for us are more convincing than photographs that show patterns and that don't fit our gestalt perception.

Take, for example, an NMR spectrometer (NMR = nuclear magnetic resonance). A chemist can insert a substance and get an NMR spectrogram, which is in the form of a curve (a continuous function in 2-dimensional space). The shape of this curve is taken by chemists to be a *property* of the substance—as much a property as its crystal configuration and an even more fundamental and revealing property than its color. The NMR spectrometer is thus taken as providing a basic-level understanding of some aspect of electrochemical structure. It does this *very* indirectly, in a way that is dependent on theoretical considerations of many sorts: the theory of nuclear magnetic resonance, Fourier analysis, methods for computing Fourier transforms, methods for displaying Fourier transforms, etc. The result of all this is a *curve* that makes sense in terms of basic-level perception. Because the *curve* is comprehensible, it can be used to *understand* something about substances. And chemists intuitively understand such curves as *being* properties of the substances—so much so that they refer to the spectrograms as "NMR spectra," as if the graph were the thing itself. The intervening theoretical assumptions on which NMR spectroscopy is based are taken as givens relative to the everyday functioning of the practicing chemist. NMR curves are used to understand substances and are taken as primary data for the purpose of theorizing. A substance's NMR structure is taken as something that is *known* about the substance, just as its color is. Within the knowledge structure of science, extended basic-level perceptions (such as curves on NMR spectrograms) are taken as *primary* data. And this is legitimized by their consistency and their regular relationship to other data within general physical and chemical theories.

The experientialist account of knowledge that we have given depends on our account of truth, which in turn depends on, among other things, the structure of our basic-level experience. Scientific "knowledge," and scientific understanding, to a large degree, depend on the technological extension of basic-level perception. Chemists take the NMR spectra of substances as known and understood via the curves on the NMR spectrograms.

This view of what we understand knowledge to be is very much in accord with the view of truth given above. Knowledge, like truth, depends on understanding, most centrally on our basic-level understanding of experience. For the most part, we take our basic-level perception to be unshakable (unless there is very good reason to believe otherwise). What we perceive at the basic level is taken as real and known, pending very good reasons to the contrary. The same is true for scientific theories. They must be coherent with our basic-level perceptions and accepted by the relevant scientific communities in order to be generally accepted as true. Once they are, they become part of our knowledge—again pending good reasons to believe otherwise—because they provide the only socially acceptable understanding available. In this respect, scientific knowledge is like *ordinary* "knowledge."

Can knowledge ever be secure? Of course it can. Take our knowledge of the existence of cells. As we technologically extend our basic-level abilities to perceive and to manipulate, our understanding of organisms as being made up of cells remains unchallenged. It is stable and remains so because of the large number of observations of cell structure made through microscopes and the large number of manipulations of cell structure brought about through various technological extensions of our basic-level capacities. Our knowledge of the existence of cells seems secure, as secure as any knowledge is likely to be. Nonetheless, it is human knowledge based on human understanding, not on any neutral, or

God's-eye-view, understanding. There is no such thing as a neutral way to understand things. But as long as our human understanding remains stable, it is possible for our knowledge to be secure.

Knowledge, like truth, is relative to understanding. Our folk view of knowledge as being absolute comes from the same source as our folk view that truth is absolute, which is the folk theory that there is only one way to understand a situation. When that folk theory fails, and we have multiple ways of understanding, or "framing," a situation, then knowledge, like truth, becomes relative to that understanding. Likewise, when our understanding is stable and secure, knowledge based on that understanding is stable and secure.

Is such knowledge "real knowledge"? Well, it's as real as our knowledge ever gets—real enough for all but the most seasoned skeptics.

Common Sense

Objectivism is often justified by the claim that it accounts for common sense observations. For example, suppose there is an apple on the table next to me. I pick up the apple and take a bite out of it. Common sense tells us that there really was an apple there and I really did take a bite out of it. This is what experientialism says, too. The apple and the table are basic-level objects. By our best understanding of basic-level experience, they are real—pending some revelation that I have been duped. *On* is a basic-level spatial relation in our conceptual system, which is a gestalt consisting of a cluster of three kinesthetic image schemas—one for *above* on a vertical axis, one for *contact*, and one for *support.* Given our best (and only) understanding of the situation, it is true that the apple is on the table. And it is not merely true, it is a *central truth*—a truth for which we are not likely to find a better understanding.

This story sounds a little like an objectivist story, and there is a good reason for it: our common sense folk theories are very largely objectivist folk theories. Our basic-level gestalt perception tells us that there are *objects* in the world. By looking more closely, we can distinguish aspects of the objects, which we understand as *properties.* Our kinesthetic image schemas characterize *relations* between objects. And we naturally understand groups of objects in terms of our container-schemas: trees are *in* forests. Thus, our common sense folk theory of categories is that they are containers of some sort. And we use this folk theory of categories to consciously construct taxonomies as an aid to comprehending various domains of experience.

The term "folk theory" should not be thought of as having negative connotations. Our folk theories are imaginative products of the human mind that we absolutely could not do without. They allow us to function in everyday life, to go about our everyday business. In many vital domains—basic-level physical experience, communication, vision, etc.—they work most of the time. But our folk theories, as invaluable as they are, are neither indefinitely extendable nor applicable to every domain of experience. Their applicability is limited, and it is important to know what those limitations are. To a significant degree, they coincide with the limits of expert objectivist theories.

Objectivity

Within the objectivist tradition, objectivity meant eliminating any aspects of the subjective so as to better see things from an objective, God's eye point of view. But the fact that a God's eye view is not possible does not mean that objectivity is impossible or any less a virtue. Objectivity consists in two things:

First, putting aside one's own point of view and looking at a situation from other points of view—as many others as possible.
Second, being able to distinguish what is directly meaningful—basic-level and image-schematic concepts—from concepts that are indirectly meaningful.

Being objective therefore requires:

- knowing that one has a point of view, not merely a set of beliefs but a specific conceptual system in which beliefs are framed
- knowing what one's point of view is, including what one's conceptual system is like
- knowing other relevant points of view and being able to use the conceptual systems in which they are framed
- being able to assess a situation from other points of view, using other conceptual systems
- being able to distinguish concepts that are relatively stable and well-defined, given the general nature of the human organism and our environment (e.g., basic-level and image-schematic concepts), from those concepts that vary with human purposes and modes of indirect understanding

Indeed, the belief that there is a God's eye point of view and that one has access to it (that is, being a hard-and-fast objectivist) virtually precludes objectivity, since it involves a commitment to the belief that there are no alternative ways of conceptualizing that are worth considering. Interestingly enough, to be objective requires one to be a relativist of an appropriate sort. The range of possibilities for relativism are discussed in the following chapter.

The existence of directly meaningful concepts—basic-level concepts and image schemas—provides certain fixed points in the objective evaluation of situations. The image-schematic structuring of bodily experience is, we hypothesize, the same for all human beings. Moreover, the principles determining basic-level structure are also universally valid, though the particular concepts arrived at may differ somewhat. Thus, certain things will remain constant in assessing situations. Hunger and pain are basic-level, directly meaningful concepts. Water, wood, stone, and dirt are basic-level concepts, as are people, horses, cats, chairs, tables, and houses. And technology has provided ways of extending basic-level categorization, by extending the means for gestalt perception and for the manipulation of objects.

Thus, it is not the case that anything goes in assessing a situation objectively. Basic-level and image-schematic understanding in the physical domain must be preserved. Directly meaningful concepts must be preserved if we are to assess any situation objectively. If our capacity for categorization and reason is based on our basic bodily functioning and on our purposes, then it follows that the preservation of our bodily functioning and the maximal freedom to pursue our purposes are basic human values. Relativism, as we shall see, does not mean giving up on either basic concepts or basic values. Instead, it means considering additional alternative possibilities for assessing situations using concepts that are *not* directly meaningful, for example, concepts that are understood via metaphor or concepts that are more abstract than basic-level concepts.

Above all, objectivity requires a proper understanding of human categorization, since one always assesses situations in terms of human categories. And human categorization, as we have seen, is based, in part, on the nature of human bodies.

Summary

It is embodiment of the sort discussed above that makes the theory of cognitive models more than a mere mentalistic theory. Meaningfulness involves not merely mental structures, but the *structuring* of experience itself. Some kinds of experiences are structured preconceptually because of the way the world is and the way we are. We have suggested that at least two forms of preconceptual structure exist: basic-level structure and image-schematic structure. What is known about basic-level categorization suggests the existence of basic-level preconceptual structure, which arises as a result of our capacities for gestalt perception, mental imagery, and motor movement. The consideration of certain gross patterns in our experience—our vertical orientation, the nature of our bodies as containers and as wholes with parts, our ability to sense hot and cold, our experience of being empty (hungry) as opposed to filled (satiated), etc.—suggests that our experience is structured kinesthetically in at least a gross way in a variety of experiential domains.

Cognitive models derive their fundamental meaningfulness directly from their ability to match up with preconceptual structure. Such direct matchings provide a basis for an account of truth and knowledge. Because such matching is "internal" to a person, the irreconcilable problems pointed out by Putnam in the case of objectivist theories do not arise in experientialist theories.

In domains where there is no clearly discernible preconceptual structure to our experience, we import such structure via metaphor. Metaphor provides us with a means for comprehending domains of experience that do not have a preconceptual structure of their own. A great many of our domains of experience are like this. Comprehending experience via metaphor is one of the great imaginative triumphs of the human mind. Much of rational thought involves the use of metaphoric models. Any adequate account of rationality must account for the use of imagination and much of imagination consists of metaphorical reasoning. Such an account is outside the realm of objectivist theories. (See Lakoff and Johnson 1980, chap. 27.)

The idea of a conceptualizing capacity is central to the experientialist enterprise. Such a capacity would take preconceptual structures of experience as input and use them to motivate concepts that accord with those preconceptual structures. Such a capacity would explain (*a*) how we acquire our concepts, (*b*) how concepts are linked to preconceptual structures, (*c*) why concepts have the peculiar properties they have, and (*d*) how we can understand our present concepts and how we can come to understand even very different conceptual systems.

CHAPTER 18

Whorf and Relativism

For the past few decades, most "responsible" scholars have steered clear of relativism. It has become a bête noire, identified with scholarly irresponsibility, fuzzy thinking, lack of rigor, and even immorality. Disavowals and disproofs are de rigueur—even I felt obliged to cite the standard disproof of "total relativism" in the previous chapter. In many circles, even the smell of relativism is tainted.

At the same time, relativism has been championed by those who see "responsible scholarship" as wearing blinders and being oblivious to realities—realities that are not irresponsible, but liberating. The issue is an emotional one—and for good reason. Most of us like and feel comfortable with our world views. Many who view themselves as committed to science assume that scientific thinking requires an objectivist world view—a commitment to there being only one "correct" conceptual system. Even proposing that there may be many conceptual systems as reasonable as our own around the world is all too often taken as spitting in the eye of science.

Before we can enter into a reasonable discussion of conceptual relativism, it is important to defuse some of the emotionalism surrounding the issue. I will first observe that alternative ways of conceptualizing things are normal in the everyday lives of most people, including scientists. Second, I will try to sort out as many as possible of the issues that come up in discussions of relativism. The point is to show that there is not one concept of relativism but literally hundreds and that much of the emotion that has been spent in discussion of the issue has resulted from confusions about what is meant by "relativism." Third, I will discuss the views of the most celebrated relativist of this century, Benjamin Lee Whorf. Fourth, I will review the results of the remarkable Kay-Kempton experiment. And last, I will discuss my own views on relativism and the reasons why I hold them.

Alternative Conceptualizations in Everyday Life

Human beings do not function with internally consistent, monolithic conceptual systems. Each of us has many ways of making sense of experience, especially of those domains of experience that do not come with a clearly delineated preconceptual structure of their own, such as the domains of emotion and thought. As we pointed out above, Kay (1979) has demonstrated that speakers of English have two inconsistent folk theories of the way words refer to things in the world. Lakoff and Johnson (1980, chaps. 16–17) show that our very concept of a logical argument is structured in terms of three mutually inconsistent metaphors. Case study 1 below shows that we have several metaphorical models for comprehending anger.

Many functioning scientists, in their everyday work, depend on the ability to shift from one conceptualization to another. In fact, *learning* to become a scientist requires learning alternative conceptualizations for scientific concepts. Take electricity for example. What intuitive understanding of electricity is required to be able to solve problems with circuit diagrams correctly? As Gentner and Gentner (1982) observe, there are two prevalent ways of metaphorically understanding electricity: as a fluid and as a crowd made up of individual electrons. Both conceptualizations are needed. Those who understand electricity only as a fluid tend to make systematic errors in certain kinds of problems—those where the crowd metaphor works better. Students who understand electricity only as a crowd of electrons tend to make mistakes on a different set of problems—those where the fluid metaphor works better. Understanding electricity, at a certain level of sophistication, requires metaphors—more than one. Knowing how to solve problems in electrical circuitry involves knowing which metaphor to use in which situation.

A similar point has been made by Kuhn (1970, appendix) for physics. The equation $f = ma$ (force equals mass times acceleration) cannot be applied using a single monolithic interpretation of mass and acceleration. The equation is not applied in the same way to billiard balls, to pendulums, and to black-box radiation. Learning how to apply this equation correctly to pendulums and to black-box radiation involves learning a certain way of looking at pendulums and black-box radiation that is very different from the way we look at billiard balls. In the case of pendulums, one must learn to conceptualize $f = ma$ in terms of point masses and angular momentum. Force becomes a summation of the changes in angular momentum at each point. In black-box radiation, $f = ma$ becomes a complex set of differential equations. To get the right set of equations, one must learn the right way to conceptualize the problem. Each such conceptualization is a way of comprehending the domain. A physicist has to have many ways of conceptualizing force, and he has to know which one to use in which physical domain. There is no single correct way to conceptualize force that will work for all physical domains.

We all have alternative methods of conceptualization at our disposal, whether we are trying to understand our emotions or trying to comprehend the nature of the physical universe. In well-understood areas of physics, there are conceptualizations that are accepted as correct. But in dealing with our emotions, as in much of the rest of our daily lives, there are no clear and unequivocal externally "correct" standards, though there are many constraints. In trying to find ways of comprehending love, anger, friendship, morality, illness, death, misfortune, and other such normal phenomena, we make use of many alternative means of conceptualization, not just novel ones made up on the spot but conventional alternatives used throughout our culture. In American culture, love is conventionally understood in terms of physical force (there is *attraction, electricity, magnetism,* etc.), in terms of health (is the relationship *healthy, sick, on the mend, dying, on its last legs?*), and many more (see Lakoff and Johnson 1980, chap. 10).

Alternative conceptualizations are extremely common and we all make use of them. There is nothing exotic or mystical about the ones we use every day. But when we talk about how people living in unfamiliar cultures and speaking unfamiliar languages think, the stakes rise.

Conceptions of Relativism

There is a wide variety of reaction to the idea that other human beings comprehend their experience in ways that are different from ours and equally valid. Some people are scared by the idea: *How can we ever communicate with people who think differently?* Others are repelled by the idea: *There should be a universal language so that we can minimize misunderstanding and conflict.* Others are attracted by the idea: *Maybe I could learn to think differently too. Maybe it would make my life richer and more interesting.* Still others think the very idea is ridiculous: *People are pretty much the same all around the world. There may be differences here and there, but they don't amount to very much.* All of these reactions are fairly widespread.

There are also very different views of what relativism is. Here are a number of questions, the answers to which define a number of parameters along which views of relativism can vary:

- How much variation is there across conceptual systems?
- How deep is the variation?
- What is the nature of the variation?
- What is the difference between a conceptual system and the capacity used to understand that system?
- Do conceptual systems that are organized differently count as different systems?
- Are conceptual systems monolithic, or are there alternatives even within a single system?
- Are differences "located" in language or elsewhere in the mind?
- Do systems that are used differently count as different systems?
- What ways are there to define the "commensurability" of different systems?
- Are alternative conceptual systems good or bad things?
- Do you behave differently if you have a different conceptual system?
- Do you have control over which concepts you use?
- What is the difference, if any, between conceptual and moral relativism?

As we will see, the answers to these questions define hundreds of different varieties of "relativism."

The Degree of Variation Issue

How different is different? How different do two conceptual systems have to be before one is willing to say that they are different. As one might imagine, opinions differ wildly.

- Total difference: No concepts are shared.
- Radical difference: Most concepts are different, though there may be some overlap.
- Small difference: Most concepts are the same, but there are some differences.
- Any difference: Even one will do.

For some people, relativism means total difference, whereas for others it means radical difference. Others will claim to have demonstrated relativism by showing small differences, or even one difference.

The Depth of Variation Issue

Many scholars believe that some parts of a conceptual system are more fundamental than others. Concepts like space and time are usually taken as the most fundamental. Concepts like *chutzpah* in Yiddish or *agape* in Ancient Greek are taken as more superficial. Discussions of conceptual relativity, therefore, tend to be about fundamental concepts like space and time, rather than about less fundamental concepts like *chutzpah*. It is for this reason that Whorf focused on Hopi time and why Brugman and Casad have focused on space in Mixtec and Cora.

There are two intuitions behind such a conception of what is fundamental and what is superficial. The first is that concepts that are fundamental, like space and time, are used in many other concepts throughout the system, while concepts like *chutzpah* and *agape* are localized to isolated domains of experience, and therefore don't affect much else. The second intuition is that fundamental concepts tend to be grammaticized, that is, to be part of the grammar of the language. As such, they are used unconsciously, automatically, and constantly. In general, grammaticized concepts are viewed as more fundamental than the concepts expressed by vocabulary items. For example, classifiers such as Dyirbal *balan* and Japanese *hon* are part of the grammars of those languages and, on this view, would be much more fundamental than concepts associated with lexical items like *chutzpah* or *sushi*.

The depth issue is therefore tied to the degree issue, since it is assumed that if fundamental concepts vary, then other concepts dependent on them will vary as well. That is, the more fundamental the variation, the greater the degree of variation.

The Nature of Variation Issue

Possibly the most boring thing a linguistics professor has to suffer at the hands of eager undergraduates is the interminable discussion of the 22 (or however many) words for snow in Eskimo. This shows almost nothing about a conceptual system. Snow is not fundamental to a conceptual system; it is isolated and doesn't affect much else. And it is not part of the grammar. There are no great conceptual consequences of having a lot of words for snow. English-speaking skiers have reported to me that there are at least a dozen words for snow (e.g., *powder*) in their vocabularies, and yet their conceptual systems are largely the same as mine. Anyone with an expert knowledge of some domain of experience is bound to have a large vocabulary about things in that domain—sailors, carpenters, seamstresses, even linguists. When an entire culture is expert in a domain (as Eskimos must be in functioning with snow), they have a suitably large vocabulary. It's no surprise, and it's no big deal. It is no more surprising than the fact that people who sail have a lot of sailing terms, like *lee, port, jib,* or that Americans have lots of names for cars.

All that such observations indicate is the following: different people may have different domains of experience that are highly structured. Given a general conceptualizing capacity and a language capacity, they can conceptualize and name structured aspects of that domain of experience.

The 22-words-for-snow phenomenon does, however, raise an issue: What kind of conceptual differences count for showing significant differences in conceptual systems? This issue is important because many people who have written about it, especially philosophers, have assumed that there is only one kind of difference: how a conceptual system (or a language) "carves up nature." (See Quine 1939, 1951, 1983.) This view arises from objectivist philosophy, a philosophy that assumes that the job of concepts is to fit objective physical reality and no more. On this view, a conceptual system can succeed for fail to fit well, that is, to "carve nature at the joints." It can choose different joints to carve at, that is, it can conceptualize different aspects of reality. In addition, conceptual systems can vary in their "fineness of grain," that is, they can carve nature into big chunks or small artful slices: as Whorf puts it, with a "blunt instrument" or a "rapier." But a conceptual system cannot create new joints, because objectivism assumes that all the joints are given ahead of time, objectively, once and for all. A conceptual system is accurate if it always finds joints in nature (though it certainly won't find all of them) and inaccurate if it misses the joints and hits a bone or nothing at all.

The discerning reader will not have failed to notice the oddness of the objectivist metaphor: Conceptual systems are butchers and reality is a carcass. Cultures differ only in the way they have their meat cut up. On such a view, relativism may be real, but it doesn't matter all that much. It's just a matter of carving here rather than there, in bigger or smaller chunks.

But such a view leaves out virtually every phenomenon discussed in this book, concepts which are not to be found objectively in nature, but which are a result of the human imaginative capacity: cognitive models involving metaphor and metonymy, radial categories, and nonuniversal socially constructed concepts. And, as we have repeatedly observed, such concepts can be made real by human action. These characterize important ways in which conceptual systems may differ across cultures. They are particularly interesting because they involve different uses of our imaginative capacities to create social reality.

Thus, we must ask more about a conceptual system than where it fits the joints and what is the fineness of grain. We must also ask how imaginative capacities have been differentially employed and how those imaginative concepts have been made real through action.

The System Versus Capacity Issue

As we pointed out above, there is a distinction between conceptual systems and conceptualizing capacities. The same capacities can give rise to different systems in the following ways:

First, highly structured preconceptual experiences may be different. For example, for the Cora, who live in the mountains of Mexico, basic hill shape (top, slope, bottom) is a highly structured and fundamental aspect of their constant experience. It is not only conceptualized, but it has been conventionalized and has become part of the grammar of Cora (Casad 1982). Cora speakers may have the came conceptualizing *capacity* as we do, but they have a different *system,* which appears to arise from a different kind of fundamental *experience* with space.

Second, since experience does not *determine* conceptual systems, but only *motivates* them, the same experiences may provide equally good motivation for two somewhat different conceptual systems. For example, the concept *front* has its basic characterization in the body and then is extended metaphorically to other objects. In English, it is extended to objects like bushes as follows: If you are looking at a bush, the "front" of the bush is the side facing you. In Hausa, the reverse is true: the "front" of the bush would be the side facing *away* from you, that is, in the same direction in which you are facing. Both choices are equally reasonable—equally consonant with our experience. In such situations, the same conceptualizing capacity and experiences can give rise to different systems.

Third, the same basic experiences and the same conceptualizing capacity may still result in a situation where one system lacks a significant concept that another system has. An extreme example of such "hypocognition" has been reported by Levy (1973). Tahitians, Levy found, not only do not have a word for sadness, they seem to have no *concept* of it and, correspondingly, no ritualized behavior for dealing with depression or bereavement. They appear to experience sadness and depression, but have no way to cope with it. They categorize sadness with sickness, fatigue, or the attack of an evil spirit.

It should be borne in mind that the system-capacity distinction cannot, in many cases, be clearly drawn. Take, for example, Rosch's study of color categories among the Dani people of New Guinea (Rosch 1973). Dani has only two basic color terms: *mili* (dark-cool) and *mola* (light-warm), which cover the entire spectrum. Rosch showed that Dani speakers were readily able to learn and remember arbitrary names for what Berlin and Kay (1969) called "focal colors," that is, focal red, blue, green, etc. But Dani speakers showed difficulty learning and remembering names for nonfocal colors. Did this show that they already had concepts for focal colors and just lacked labels for them? Or did it show that their experience of focal colors is just as well delineated as ours and that given the same conceptualizing and language capacities as we have, they readily conceptualize and name well-structured aspects of their experience? Both interpretations are possible.

Translation and Understanding

The capacity-system distinction is nonetheless important to make. The reason is this: A theory that does not recognize a conceptualizing capacity makes very different claims about translation and understanding. The issues of translation and understanding arise constantly in discussions of relativism. Here's how:

First, it is claimed that if two languages have radically different conceptual systems, then translation from one language to the other is impossible.

Second, it is often claimed that if translation is impossible, then speakers of one language cannot understand the other language.

Third, it is often claimed that if the languages have different conceptual systems, then someone who speaks one language will be unable to learn the other language because he lacks the right conceptual system.

Fourth, to confuse matters further, it is sometimes claimed that since people *can* learn radically different languages, those languages couldn't have different conceptual systems.

Such claims may seem to make sense if one recognizes only conceptual systems and not conceptualizing capacities. But the picture is different if one assumes that people share a general conceptualizing capacity regardless of what differences they may have in conceptual systems. Differences in conceptual systems do create difficulties for translation. Let us temporarily assume that such differences make translation impossible, pending a more realistic discussion below. What follows? It does *not* follow from the impossibility of *translation* that *understanding* is impossible.

Consider the following situation: Speakers of both languages share the same basic experiences and conceptualize the same domains of experiences to roughly the same degree. Nevertheless, their conceptual systems are different and translation is impossible. In such a situation, it would still be possible for a speaker of one language to learn the other. The reason: He has the same conceptualizing capacity and the same basic experiences. His conceptualizing ability would enable him to construct the other conceptual system as he goes along and to understand it via the shared preconceptual experiential structure. He may be able to *understand* the other language even if he cannot *translate* it into his own. Accurate *translation* requires close correspondences across conceptual systems; *understanding* only requires correspondences in well-structured experiences and a common conceptualizing capacity.

In short, differences in conceptual systems do not necessarily entail that understanding and learning are impossible. And the fact that one can learn a radically different language does not mean that it does not have a different conceptual system.

The difference between translation and understanding is this: translation requires a mapping from one language to another language. Understanding is something that is internal to a person. It has to do with his ability to conceptualize and to match those concepts to his experiences, on the one hand, and to the expressions of the new language on the other. Translation can occur without understanding, and understanding can occur without the possibility of translation.

Of course, ideal situations like the one described above do not always occur. Speakers of radically different languages may not share all the same basic experiences. Some of these experiences may be acquired by living in the culture where the language is spoken, though living in such a culture as a outsider may well not provide the right kind of experience to understand *all* of the concepts of those who have grown up in the culture. There are, however, many basic experiences that one can pretty reasonably take as being universal. Among them are the basic-level perception of physical objects and what we have called "kinesthetic image schemas": structured experiences of vertical and horizontal dimensions, balance, inside and outside, and many others. When an experienced field linguist goes about learning another language, this is where he begins: with concepts for well-structured experiences that his years in the field have led him to believe are universal. For concepts like these, translation is often possible and understanding is relatively easy, if not immediate. When one goes outside of these, the difficulties begin: culturally defined frames (in Fillmore's sense) that are not shared (e.g., American baseball and the Balinese calendar), metaphorically defined concepts (e.g., the Western TIME IS MONEY or the traditional Japanese idea that THE BELLY [*hara*] IS THE LOCUS OF THOUGHT AND FEELING), the categories like those in Dyirbal, and the metonymic understanding of answers to questions as in Ojibwa ("How did you get here? I stepped into a canoe"). Each language comes with an enormously wide range of such concepts and their corresponding expressions.

The Conceptual Organization Issue

Conceptual systems come with an organization, and people differ on the question of whether that organization matters in deciding whether two languages have different conceptual systems. This issue could equally well have been called any of the following:

- The Truth-Conditional Semantics Issue
- The Sentence-by-Sentence Translation Issue
- The Polysemy Issue

Let us take an example. In Chalcatongo Mixtec, an Otomanguean language of Western Mexico, spatial locations are understood via the metaphorical projection of body-part terms onto objects. For example, if you want to say, *The stone is under the table*, you say,

yuù wã́ híyaà čìì-mesá

which word-by-word comes out *stone the be-located belly-table*, where "belly-table" is a possessive construction equivalent to "the table's belly." This way of expressing relative location using body-part projections is systematic throughout the language; the language has no system like the Indo-European prepositions and cases. As Brugman (1983, 1984) demonstrates, it is not just a matter of using those words for our concepts, but rather a matter of systematically understanding spatial locations via conceptual relations among body parts.

Let us consider a few illustrative examples, cases where English speakers would use a preposition, say , *on*. In English, the basic spatial use of *on* make use of three image schemas—CONTACT, SUPPORT, and ABOVE—which form a single conceptual unit. In Mixtec, there is no such conceptual unit with that structure. Instead, a variety of body-part concepts are used. Suppose you want to say *He is on top of the mountain*. The Mixtec equivalent is *He is located the mountain's head*.

híyaà-ðe šini-yúku
be + located-3sg.m. head-hill
'He is on top of the hill.'

Incidentially, *head* is not just used for *on top of*, but also for the space above.

ndasa híyaà yóò šini-yúnu wã
how be + located moon head-tree det.
'How is it that the moon is over the tree?'

Returning to translation equivalents of *on*, suppose one wanted to say *I was on the roof*. Since roofs are horizontal and do not have an upper tip in that part of the world, *head* will not do. Instead, the term for the back of an animal is used, since animal backs are horizontal.

ni-kaa-rí sɨkɨ-ßeˀe
perfv.-be-1sg. back-house
'I was on the roof of the house.'

If you want to say *I am sitting on the branch of the tree*, you say the equivalent of *I am sitting the tree's arm.*

ndukoo-rí ndaˀa-yúnu
sit-1sg. arm-tree
'I'm sitting on the branch of the tree.'

To say *My son is lying on the mat*, you say the equivalent of *My son is lying the mat's face.*

seˀe-ri hitu nũũ-yuu
son-I lie face-mat
'My son is lying on the mat.'

In short, Mixtec speakers have conventional ways of projecting body parts metaphorically onto objects in order to conceptualize spatial location. We can understand the Mixtec system because we too have the capacity for metaphorical projection of this sort, even though our conceptual system is not conventionally organized in this way. Systems like this are neither rare nor obscure. Such systems for expressing spatial location via body-part concepts are common among the indigenous languages of Mesoamerica and Africa, though there are considerable differences in detail in each case.

The Mixtec system is much more complex than this example suggests. Brugman (1983, 1984) has described those complexities and, in the process, has provided overwhelming evidence that speakers of Mixtec have a different *conceptual organization* of spatial location from the one speakers of Indo-European languages have. She argues in much greater detail than we can provide here that this organization is metaphorical in nature. Let us consider some further examples that indicate the presence of metaphorical mappings in the Mixtec conceptual system.

Consider some further uses of *nũũ*, the word for 'face'. One of the most important uses of *nũũ* is in the characterization of spatial relationships understood in terms of face-to-face interaction. For example, *nũũ-maria* means 'Maria's face'. It can also mean 'in front of Maria'.

hindi-ri   nũũ-maría
stand-1sg. face-Maria
'I am standing in front of (facing) Maria.'

That is, the speaker is located as being in the area of the space associated with Maria's face, that is, in front of her. Now consider the expression *nũũ-mesa*, literally, 'the table's face'.

hindi-ri   nũũ̀-mesá
stand-1sg. face-table

This can have a meaning parallel to the example given above. It can mean 'I am standing in front of the table', where the table is understood as having a front—an orientation *facing* the speaker, as if the table were in face-to-face relationship with the speaker. But the sentence has another meaning as well. If the table has the right shape, this sentence can also mean 'I am standing *on* the table'. The reason for this is that 'the table's face' can also refer to the top of the table—the portion of the table which has a flat surface (roughly like a face, as in the English 'sur*face*') and the part of the table that a person mainly interacts with. These two senses involve two different metaphorical projections: one of the face onto the tabletop and one in which the whole table is understood as facing the speaker.

The face-to-face interaction evoked by *nṹũ̀* is used with prototypical face-to-face actions such as giving. In the following sentence, *nṹũ̀-seʔ*e -ro literally means 'your son's face'.

ni-haʔa-rí   ʔn kɨtɨ   nṹũ̀-seʔe-ro
perfv.-pass-1sg. one horse face-son-2sg.
'I gave a horse to your son.'

This can also occur with more abstract cases such as 'teach'.

ni-s-naʔa-rí   nũũ-séʔé-rí ha   sátĩ́ũ
perfv.-cause-know-1sg. face-son-1sg. compl. work
'I taught my son to work.'

In short, Mixtec has complex and conventionalized metaphors for understanding both spatial relations and more abstract relations in terms of body-part concepts.

Does this mean that Mixtec has an alternative conceptual system for understanding spatial location? Well, it depends on where you stand on the conceptual organization issue and other issues. Take, for example, the sentence-by-sentence translation issue. Consider the following claim:

If language *A* can be translated sentence-by-sentence accurately into language *B*, then *A* and *B* have the same conceptual systems.

With respect to spatial location, it appears that Mixtec can be translated accurately into English sentence-by-sentence. What that misses is the fact that Mixtec has a different *way of conceptualizing* and a different *conceptual organization* than English does. But if the *means* of conceptualizing matters and if conceptual organization matters, then Mixtec has a very different conceptual system than English does so far as spatial location is concerned.

The criterion of getting the *truth conditions* right in sentence-by-sentence translation ignores what is in the mind. It ignores how sentences are *understood*. And it ignores how concepts are organized, both internally and relative to one another.

The issue of conceptual organization is intimately linked to the issue of polysemy. Polysemy occurs when a single word has more than one meaning—and when those meanings are systematically related. Systematic relationship is crucial here. The two meanings of *bank*—place where you put your money and the edge of a river—are not systematically related. Such cases are called *homonyms*. Cases of polysemy are cases like *warm*, which refers both to the temperature and to clothing that makes you feel warm. Another example would be *newspaper*, which can name either what you read at the breakfast table or the company that produces it.

A case of polysemy in Mixtec would be *čii,* which can mean 'belly' or 'under'. In Mixtec, these meanings are systematically related by a general conventional system of projecting body-part concepts onto objects. Thus, it is no accident that *sɨkɨ* means both 'animal back' and 'on top of' for objects of the appropriate shape and orientation to be viewed as having a surface which is horizontal and off the ground, like the back of an animal. Polysemy is not just a matter of listing meanings disjunctively, as dictionaries do; a disjunctive entry would be a list like: *čii*, 'belly', 'under'. Such a listing does not tell us *why* the word for 'belly' is the same as the word for 'under'. And it does not explain *why* the word for 'animal back' is the same as the word for 'on top of'—for horizontal surfaces off of the ground. And so on for other body-part terms. To understand the reasons, one has to understand the conceptual system. An *explanation* for such polysemy in Mixtec would be a conventional, general mapping *within the conceptual system* (as opposed to the grammar or lexicon) from body-part concepts to spatial locations.

Do the conceptual systems of Mixtec and English differ with respect to spatial relations? Well, it depends on how one stands on the polysemy issue. If one insists upon an explanation for systematic polysemy in a language, then the answer is yes. English has a system of prepositional relationships that Mixtec lacks, and Mixtec has a very rich mapping from body-part concepts onto spatial locations that English has only a hint of (e.g., 'in *back* of').

On the other hand, if one's criterion is sentence-by-sentence translation that preserves truth conditions, then the answer appears to be no. The question is whether one is interested in explanations for polysemy rather than mere lists of meanings, and whether one is interested in *understanding* rather than mere truth conditions.

The Monolithic System Issue

It is often assumed that conceptual systems are monolithic, that is, that they provide a single, consistent world view. In particular, it is assumed that for each domain of experience, a conceptual system contains only one way of comprehending that domain. This is such a pervasive view that I thought it prudent to begin this chapter by reviewing a small amount of the evidence that calls it into question.

The monolithic system issue arises in discussions of relativism in the following way. It is commonly taken for granted that if speakers of another language have a different way of conceptualizing a given domain, then we cannot possibly ever understand them and they cannot possibly ever understand us. But once it is realized that people can have many ways *within a single conceptual system and a single language* of conceptualizing a domain, then the idea that other people have other ways of conceptualizing experience does not seem so drastic or so much of a threat to eventual communication.

The Locus of Variation Issue

People who agree that different languages have different means of conceptualizing experience may disagree about where to locate the difference. Some place it in the "language," the actual words, morphemes, and grammatical constructions. Others locate the difference in the realm of thought as opposed to language.

Such differences of opinion may hide deeper theoretical assumptions. Some people do not believe that there is something such as thought independent of language; others take the opposite view, that language is just a matter of providing arbitrary labels for thought. There are also mixed views that recognize the independence of a system of thought from its expression in words and syntax, but also hold that words themselves constitute a form of conceptual categorization. Some of the evidence for the mixed view will be given below, when we discuss the Kay-Kempton experiment.

The Functional Embodiment Issue

Are concepts disembodied abstractions? Or do they exist only by virtue of being embodied in a being who uses them in thinking?

Are conceptual systems just *collections* of concepts? Or are they *functioning organizations* of concepts, so that a conceptual system is different when it *uses* a concept differently?

These questions characterize the functional embodiment issue in its most basic form. They define three positions:

1. Concepts are disembodied abstractions. They exist independent of any beings who use them. The way in which concepts happen to be used is irrelevant to the characterization of a conceptual system.
2. Concepts only exist by virtue of being embodied in a being. Conceptual systems are collections of concepts (perhaps organized, perhaps not). But the way they are used is irrelevant to the characterization of a conceptual system.
3. Concepts only exist by virtue of being embodied in a being. A conceptual system is a functioning organization of concepts. The way concepts are used is part of what defines the system.

Position 3 has the following consequence: *If two conceptual systems contain the same concept but use it in different ways, then the systems are different.* For example, consider two systems *A* and *B*:

- *A* actively uses concept *C* automatically, unconsciously, and effortlessly as part of the process of thinking and trying to comprehend experience.
- *B* contains *C* as an *object* of thought—something to ponder, perhaps to be understood in some other terms, and once understood, perhaps to be *consciously and effortfully* used to understand still other things.

Position 3 says *A* and *B* are different conceptual systems with respect to *C*. Positions 1 and 2 say that concept *C* is as much part of one system as the other, since the difference between being an *object* of thought and being *used in thinking* doesn't matter.

Let us take as an example the *balan* category from Dyirbal, as discussed above. Recall from our discussion above that *balan* is not merely a category of language, as opposed to thought. It does not just serve to classify an unstructured list of nouns. The reason is that, with only a few exceptions, the category is organized on *conceptual* principles, e.g., same domain of experience.

Speakers of traditional Dyirbal use *balan* automatically and effortlessly in thinking and in speaking to distinguish the categories of things under discussion. Speakers of English, however, do not use the *balan* category in any normal everyday activity at all. They may learn about it by reading the works of R. M. W. Dixon and they may ponder it, try to comprehend it in terms of their normal categories of thought, and even try with effort (probably great effort!) to categorize the things in their everyday environment using it.

On positions 1 and 2, learning what a concept is is enough to incorporate it into your conceptual system. Positions 1 and 2 implicitly claim that speakers of English who learn what the *balan* category is have that cateagory in their conceptual systems just as speakers of traditional Dyirbal do. Positions 1 and 2 define "conceptual system" in such a way that the conceptual systems of English speakers who *learn about* the *balan* category do not differ from the conceptual systems of the Dyirbal speakers who *use* the *balan* category. On position 3, there is all the difference in the world between using *balan* as part of one's normal functioning system of categories and employing it as something to ponder, to understand in one's own terms, and perhaps occasionally to use in the act of deliberate, effortful categorization. Position 3 says that, with respect to *balan*, there is a fundamental difference between the conceptual systems of Dyirbal speakers and the conceptual systems of English speakers who have learned what the Dyirbal system is.

The embodiment-of-use issue is especially important to linguists. Linguists are concerned with the grammars of languages throughout the world. Grammars incorporate meaningful elements—parts of a conceptual system. In Dyirbal, for example, the classifier *balan* is part of the grammar, and the category it characterizes is part of the conceptual system of speakers of the language. Grammars of languages are used automatically, effortlessly, unconsciously, and almost continuously—as long as one is speaking, listening, or even dreaming in the language. The concepts that correspond to elements in the grammar are used the same way. In English, the word *in* is part of the grammar and used in this way. *In* has a very different status in our conceptual system than the word *relativism*, which we are now pondering, examining, clarifying, etc.—and which we will never use the way we use *in*.

This is the point that Benjamin Lee Whorf was making when he wrote in his classic essay, "The Punctual and Segmentative Aspects of Verbs in Hopi,"

> The Hopi aspect-contrast which we have observed, being obligatory upon their verb forms, practically forces the Hopi to notice and observe vibratory phenomena, and furthermore encourages them to find names for and to classify such phenomena. (Whorf 1956, p. 51)

Whorf was talking about verbal prefixes that make fine distinctions between types of motion: waving vs. swaying vs. flapping vs. 'a racking shake' vs. helical motion vs. turning vs. a quick spin. We English speakers make distinctions like this in our lexicon, that is, in our vocabulary as opposed to our grammar. Hopis make such distinctions in choosing a required verb prefix. They must make such distinctions instantaneously, automatically, unconsciously, and effortlessly. And they *must* choose—just as we choose singular vs. plural. There is no neutral choice. It's not that there is no way to describe such concepts in English. It's just that their *status* is different in Hopi. The difference is one between thinking *in* the language and translating *into* the language. It is a difference between using the *conceptual units* of the language and translating into other conceptual units that happen to have equivalent truth conditions. And it is also a matter of different modes of cognitive processing.

Types of Status

If one grants that functional embodiment matters in characterizing conceptual systems, then the question arises as to what *kinds* of status matter. Is it merely a matter of grammaticized vs. ungrammaticized, or are there more kinds of status that must be taken into account in characterizing a conceptual system? This is not an area that has been well thought out, but there are a number of candidates for distinctions that matter in characterizing a conceptual system.

Let us begin with distinctions that go into the grammaticized vs. ungrammaticized distinction. In the following list, the first property is characteristic of grammaticized concepts and the second is characteristic of ungrammaticized concepts:

used vs. pondered
automatic vs. controlled
unconscious vs. conscious
effortless vs. effortful
fixed vs. novel
conventional vs. personal

These "dimensions of grammaticization" are, of course, not independent of one another. Concepts that are automatic and unconscious are used in thinking and understanding; they are not merely pondered as objects of thought. Concepts that are used in this way are fixed in the mind, or "entrenched," as opposed to being novel, that is, newly made up. Conventional concepts, shared by members of a culture, are also fixed in the mind of each speaker. Concepts that we ponder are, of course, conscious. Though these implicational relationships exist, it is not the case that the first properties in the oppositions (e.g., used, automatic, etc.) always occur together, nor do the second members of the pairs always occur together. Thus, novel concepts may be either pondered as objects of thought or used in thinking consciously about something. A given person may have fixed concepts in his own conceptual system that are not shared with others in his community, that is, that are not conventional. We may ponder concepts that are either novel or fixed, conventional or not. And so on.

There are other dimensions of status that concepts may have that seem not to be involved in grammaticization:

conceptual scaffolding vs. conceptual substance
believed vs. not believed
lived by vs. merely used in understanding

These distinctions are especially important for distinguishing among types of metaphorically defined concepts. For example, the MORE IS UP metaphorical model constitutes conceptual scaffolding for, say, discussions about economics—price rises, depressions, downturns, etc. It is *not* believed. No one thinks MORE really is UP; it is just used in understanding. But there are people who really believe that TIME IS A RESOURCE, and who live by it: they budget their time, try not to waste their time, etc. As we saw above, there is a movement to conventionally extend the RESOURCE (or MONEY) metaphor for TIME, so that the concept of STOLEN TIME will become believed and lived by and not merely pondered, as it is now. Metaphorical concepts can also be lived by without being believed. For example, no one believes that SEEING really is a form of TOUCHING, in which there is a limblike gaze that goes out from the eyes and seeing occurs when the gaze touches something. There used to be a scientific theory of "eye-beams" that was of this sort and was widely believed, but not anymore. Yet we still use such a metaphor to comprehend vision, and that use is reflected in expressions like *I can't take my eyes off of her. Her eyes picked out every detail of the pattern. Their eyes met.* And so on. Moreover, the metaphor is lived by in certain respects; there are prohibitions in the culture against *eye contact* in many situations and against *undressing someone with your eyes*. Metaphors of this sort seem to be automatic, unconscious, fixed, conventional, effortless, and used—but they are not grammaticized.

The study of what kinds of status our concepts have has barely begun. But the idea that conceptual systems may differ in the kind of status a concept has is certainly worthy of further investigation.

The Commensurability Issue

Whorf, who was largely responsible for popularizing issues concerning relativism, claimed that the conceptual systems of languages could be so radically different that they could not "be calibrated," that there was no common measure, no common standard by which they could be compared. Since Whorf, the question of whether conceptual systems are *incommensurable* has surfaced repeatedly, especially in the philosophy of science, where Kuhn (1970) and Feyerabend (1975) have argued that scientific theories are incommensurable. Such claims have made relativism even more controversial, and a good deal of heat, if not light, has been generated on the incommensurability issue.

The problem with much of this discussion is that there are several *kinds* of commensurability, and commentators are by no means clear about which kind is being discussed. As we shall see, conceptual systems that are commensurable by one criterion may be incommensurable by another. Here are the basic kinds of commensurability criteria:

Translation seems to be the favored criterion of objectivist philosophers. Two conceptual systems are commensurable if each language can be translated into the other, sentence by sentence, preserving truth conditions.

Understanding is an experientialist criterion. Two conceptual systems are commensurable if they can both be understood by a person—presumably via the preconceptual structure of his experiences and his general conceptualizing capacity.

Use is one of Whorf's criteria. Two conceptual systems are commensurable if they use the same concepts in the same ways.

Framing derives from the work of Fillmore and Kuhn. Two conceptual systems are commensurable if they frame situations in the same way and if there is a one-one correspondence between concepts in the two systems, frame by frame.

Organization derives from the work of Brugman. Two conceptual systems are commensurable if they have the same concepts organized relative to one another in the same way.

All of these are criteria for *total* commensurability. They can be made into criteria for partial commensurability by characterizing "partial" either with respect to degree of commensurability, or with respect to corresponding parts of the total systems. For example, two systems may be commensurable in their concepts of space, but incommensurable in their concepts of time.

These criteria are obviously so different that no simple claims either for or against commensurability in general can be made. One must make comparisons criterion by criterion. To get an idea of how different the criteria are, let us consider some cases.

The Mixtec and English Spatial Location Systems (Brugman).—Mixtec and English sentences, or at least the parts dealing with spatial location, can be translated into one another, preserving truth conditions. But the systems definitely do not have the same conceptual organization and do not have the same concepts. Thus, they are commensurable on the translation criterion, but not on the organization criterion.

The Hopi Aspectual System (Whorf).—Whorf translates his Hopi examples into English, so the translation criterion is presumably met. But Whorf's point was that the use criterion was not met.

The Cora and English Locational Systems (Casad).—The organizational criterion is not met; Cora has an image-schema organizational structure that is totally alien to English. But the understanding criterion is met. It is possible to understand both systems, given the same experiences and the same ability to conceptualize.

The Russian Verbal Prefix System (Janda) and the English Verb-Particle System (Lindner).—The two systems appear to be roughly commensurable on the translatability, understanding, and use criteria, to come close on the framing criterion, but are strongly incommensurable on the organizational criterion.

The Dani and English Basic Color Term Systems (Rosch).—The color systems of Dani and English are incommensurable on the translatability, organization, framing, and use criteria, since Dani has too few basic color terms—only two. They are commensurable on the understanding criterion, since Dani speakers can readily understand and learn a system isomorphic to the basic English system, though not an arbitrary system.

These criteria are based on different assumptions about what a conceptual system is and, in some cases, even on different assumptions about what concepts are. The question of whether conceptual systems are commensurable cannot be answered in absolute terms; it can only be answered relative to the way the question is put. In a sense, the various criteria for commensurability are themselves incommensurable.

Commensurability is not a natural concept; it has arisen in the context of expert theories about language and thought. Yet what has emerged is very much like what we find in natural concepts like *mother*—a cluster of very different criteria based on very different kinds of considerations.

The issues discussed so far primarily have to do with characterizing the various things *relativism* can mean. But an important part of why people are interested in relativism has to do with the values associated with it. One point of the survey to follow is to show that there is no simple correlation between being a relativist on some of the above criteria and having some particular set of values about relativism.

The Fact-Value Issue

There is an old joke that goes:

Q: Do you believe in marriage?
A: Believe in it! Hell, I've *seen* it!

There is a big difference between believing that something *does* exist and believing that it *should* exist. One might decide on the basis of empirical observation that alternative conceptual systems do exist, while believing that they are a bad thing—that they lead to error, misunderstanding, conflict, etc. On the other hand, one might be under the impression that people do all think the same way, but wish they didn't. The fact-value issue is important for relativism, not just because you might be asked whether you believe in relativism, but also for historical reasons.

Whorf was certainly a relativist with respect to fact. He believed that languages, as a matter of fact, had different and incommensurable conceptual systems. But with respect to value, he was an objectivist. He believed that there was an objectivist reality, and he thought that some but not other conceptual systems built into language were capable of fitting it with reasonable preciseness. He believed that languages differed in their conceptual systems, but he believed that some languages were more accurate—and therefore better for doing science—than others. Part of what made Whorf special was that he was not an English chauvinist. He thought that Hopi was better equiped to fit external reality—physical reality—than English.

Whorf's objectivism came from two sources: he was a fundamentalist Christian, and he was trained as a chemical engineer at MIT in the 1910s. His interest in linguistics arose from the discrepancy between his two sources of objective truth: science and the Bible. He believed that the discrepancy was due to a misunderstanding of the original biblical text as a result of its having been translated into Indo-European languages. A new understanding of the semantics of the Bible, he thought, would remedy the discrepancy (Whorf 1956, p. 7). He came to view English and other

Indo-European languages as having a conceptual system that was misleading because it did not adequately fit the objective world. He correctly observed that English had an extensive metaphorical system, but he viewed this as a bad thing because it could lead one into error—like dropping a match into an "empty" gasoline drum (Whorf 1956, p. 135). Part of his romance with the Hopi language was that he thought it was superior because he saw it as making fine distinctions that English did not make—distinctions that enabled it to fit the objective world better. Hopi was for Whorf "a rapier" to the "blunt instrument" of English.

Whorf also claimed that Hopi had no metaphors, which he took as being another sign of its superiority. Whorf recognized that languages like English had rich metaphorical systems, but he thought that metaphors were false and misleading and not a good thing for a language to have. As Malotki has recently shown in his masterful *Hopi Time* (1983), Whorf was wrong about many aspects of Hopi. Hopi is replete with metaphor, especially in its temporal system. Whorf was also wrong about the Hopi concept of time. He had claimed that Hopi did not have anything like a Western concept of time. As Malotki documents in great detail, Hopi does have a concept of time—and a rich system of temporal metaphors.

Whorf did not view metaphor as having *no* positive value. He viewed metaphor as arising from synesthesia (which seems to be so in some cases) and since he viewed synesthesia as real, he took metaphor as an attempt to express the reality of synesthetic experience, despite its being a "confusion of thought" (Whorf 1956, p. 156).

Whorf was not an easy person to classify. To think of him just as a relativist is much too simplistic.

Other Issues

The importance of relativism comes out most clearly in the issue of its effect on action. Presumably, the way we think has a lot to do with the way we act. But exactly what is the connection? Not just any conceptual difference will necessarily affect actions. What kinds of conceptual differences will affect what kinds of actions? Are actions that we take to be natural and normal actually a product of the conceptual system we happened to grow up with? These are important questions. They go beyond mere curiosity about the human mind.

Can you choose your conceptual system, or is your conceptual system beyond your control? Are there parts you can choose, and parts where you are helpless to choose? Linguists tend to study those aspects of conceptual systems that are beyond any conscious control. Philosophers and sociologists tend to focus on those aspects where there seems to be a measure of conscious control, that is, where you have some say over what your conceptual system is. The issue is what control there is, how much, and how you should exercise whatever control you have.

For many people, relativism is primarily an ethical issue. If there is total relativism, it has been argued, then there can be no fixed ethical values. For those primarily interested in the ethics issue, the term "relativism" often stands for total relativism with respect to ethical values.

There are philosophers who believe that objectivism and relativism (total relativism) are the only possible choices. If you're not an objectivist, then you're a relativist. Some philosophers who find objectivism too confining opt for relativism. If concepts are not objectively fixed, then they must be relative. If the price of conceptual relativism is a lack of absolute ethical values, then so be it. Others retort that such a view is immoral in itself since it can be used to justify any barbarism. Given such assumptions, one can see why the issue of relativism can cause tempers to flare. One reason is that conceptual relativism is confused with moral relativism, and therefore any relativism at all is seen as the denial of the possibility of universal standards of ethical conduct.

As our discussion shows, the idea that there is only a binary choice, objectivism or total relativism, is ludicrous. There are hundreds of possible forms of conceptual relativism. But that does not mean that the ethics issue is silly. Far from it. The question of whether there is, or can be, a universal standard of ethical conduct is far from trivial.

The ethics issue, for conceptual relativism, can be recast as follows:

- Does any form of conceptual relativism that anyone actually holds and that has an empirical basis rule out the possibility of a universal standard of ethical behavior?
- Do empirically supported forms of relativism *impose* any standards of ethical behavior?

These are vital questions that need to be taken up in a serious way. What we have seen is that there are hundreds of views of conceptual relativism in which it is not the case that "anything goes." The central issues are these:

- Exactly what versions of conceptual relativism do entail total moral relativism and why?
- Given the apparent fact that relativism of some sort does exist, how can we find out what general moral constraints, if any, either follow from it or are consistent with it?

To a substantial extent, this involves *empirical* inquiry into the nature of existing conceptual systems and how they have changed over time.

Many objectivist philosophers would, of course, deny that empirical issues could have any bearing on ethical issues. Such philosophers assume that there is an objectively correct standard of human reason, that there are objectively correct concepts that mirror nature accurately—and they further assume that *their* conceptual system is adequate and that *they* are rational. This is, perhaps, the most immoral position of all. Given these assumptions, there is no point in studying how people around the world think. Objectivist philosophers assume that they have sufficient conceptual tools at their disposal to draw conclusions about *universally applicable* ethical standards. Moreover, from an objectivist point of view, relativism is wrong on a priori grounds, for reason we will now turn to.

The Objectivist Critique

From the objectivist point of view, there is a devastating critique of Whorf's arguments that there are alternative conceptual systems. Here it is, put in the form of a blunt retort to Whorf:

Well, Mr. Whorf, you have described to us the conceptual system of Hopi, which you claim is incommensurable with the conceptual system of English. But you have described it to us *in English* in terms that we can understand. Therefore, if you have described it correctly, you are wrong about its incommensurability. You have proven that Hopi and English are commensurable merely by correctly describing Hopi concepts in English.

From our discussion of the commensurability issue, we can see that the argument uses the *translatability* criterion, which is defined as the preservation of truth conditions in sentence-by-sentence translation. But this criterion is itself an objectivist criterion. All the critique shows is that if one assumes that objectivism is right, then it follows that relativism is wrong. No surprise.

There are, of course, four other criteria for commensurability. Whorf's arguments for relativism on the basis of Hopi verbal aspect fare as follows with respect to these criteria:

Understanding: Commensurable. A given person using his general conceptualizing capacities, *given the appropriate experiences,* can come to understand the Hopi aspectual system.

Use: Incommensurable. Hopi aspectual categories, being part of Hopi grammar, are used and not merely pondered. And they are used automatically, unconsciously, and effortlessly. They are both fixed in the minds of individual speakers and conventional in their culture. None of this is true of the Hopi categories as they are described in English.

Framing: Incommensurable. The Hopi aspectual system provides a way of framing events. Though such events can be *described* in other terms in English, that way of framing events is not part of the conceptual system on which English is based.

Organization: Incommensurable. The conceptual organization—especially the system for categorizing events—of the Hopi aspectual system is different from the organization of the conceptual system associated with English.

Whorf's Views

On the basis of arguments like those cited above, Whorf and relativism in general are widely assumed to have been discredited. But, as we have seen, there is no single relativism, but rather dozens, if not hundreds, of versions, depending on the stand one takes on various issues. All too often, arguments against Whorf are taken to be arguments against relativism in general. And arguments against Whorf, as we have just seen, may not be arguments against the position that Whorf advocated. Though Whorf's view of relativism is only one out of a great many, and though it has no privileged status from a scientific point of view, it does have a privileged *historical* status. For this reason, it would be useful to review where Whorf stood on the issues that we have discussed. Whorf was a complex thinker. It should be borne in mind throughout the following discussion that his stands on these issues by no means exhaust his views, nor convey their subtlety.

Degree of Variation: Whorf believed that conceptual systems could be radically different, but he did not believe that they could be totally different. That is, Whorf was not a total relativist. He did not believe that just anything at all could occur in a language. Quite the opposite. His manuscript "Language: Plan and Conception of Arrangement" (Whorf 1956, pp. 125–33) is a remarkably detailed account of the constraints on the structure of language, including both formal and conceptual categories. He was interested in discovering the full range of what can occur in languages, but was just as interested, if one can judge from this work, in discovering the limits.

Depth of Variation: Whorf was not particularly interested in superficial conceptual differences. He was not concerned with vocabulary, specialized terminology, words for obscure concepts, and the like. He was concerned with fundamental concepts that he saw as going to the heart of our conceptual systems: space, time, causation, event structure, aspect, evidentiality, fundamental classifications of objects, and so on. He observed that these concepts were so fundamental that they were incorporated into the very grammars of languages. As such, they are the concepts used the most—and used unconsciously and automatically.

Nature of Variation: Whorf was not merely interested in how languages "carve up nature"—though he was interested in fineness of distinctions. He also recognized metaphorical thinking, the existence of language-particular sound symbolism, and the existence of metaphoric gesture, and he was concerned with the conceptualization of the internal reality of kinesthetic experience as well as with external reality.

System Versus Capacity: So far as I can tell, Whorf did not say anything of significance about conceptualizing capacities.

Conceptual Organization: The idea that conceptual systems can differ because of their organizations is implicit in Whorf's work.

Monolithic System: So far as I can tell, Whorf seemed to think conceptual systems were monolithic. This may have been one source of his concern that we may be "prisoners" of our languages: it is as though there were no room for alternatives *within* a language and a conceptual system.

Locus of Variation: Whorf seemed to view the actual linguistic forms—morphemes, words, grammatical constructions—as the locus of variation in conceptual systems. He spoke of *language* determining thought and action, and he spoke of *linguistic* relativity.

Functional Embodiment: This was one of Whorf's big issues: the nature of use mattered. He recognized that grammaticized concepts were used unconsciously and automatically, and he viewed differences in such concepts as differences in modes of thought.

Commensurability: Another of Whorf's major issues. His principal criteria, in arguing for incommensurability, were use, framing, and organization.

Fact-Value: Whorf was a relativist so far as the facts were concerned, and an objectivist with respect to values.

Effect on Action: Whorf was primarily responsible for bringing this issue to our attention. He argued strongly that radical differences in linguistic structure led to radical differences in thinking, and hence to corresponding differences in behavior.

Control: Whorf did not seem to believe that one had control over the most important parts of one's conceptual system—the grammaticized parts.

Ethics: Though Whorf was deeply concerned with ethical behavior, he did not, to my knowledge, write about the kind of philosophical ethical issues that his work has evoked. He would have been horrified to see his "linguistic relativity" thesis lumped with a form of moral relativism that could be used to justify Nazism. Whorf was concerned with conceptual not moral relativism. He was not a total relativist and his actual views do not sanction total moral relativism. In fact, his work has the opposite force: it explicitly contradicts Nazi theories of Aryan superiority.

One all-important thing should be remembered about Whorf. He did most of his work at a time when Nazism was on the rise in Europe and jingoism was prevalent in America. At that time, white people were assumed, even in much of the U.S., to be more intelligent than people with skins of other colors. Western civilization was assumed to be the pinnacle of intellectual achievement; other civilizations were considered inferior. "Culture" meant European and American culture, not Hopi culture or Balinese culture. "Literature" meant European and American literature. "Logic" meant Western logic, not logic as it developed in China and India. "Scientific thought" was the last word in rationality, and it of course belonged to us. It was even thought that Western languages were "advanced" and that nonwestern languages were "primitive." The very idea that "uneducated" Indians, who were still considered savages by many, could reason as well as educated Americans and Europeans was extraordinary and radical. The notion that their conceptual system *better* fit scientific reality—that *we* could learn from *them*—bordered on the unthinkable.

Whorf was not only a pioneer in linguistics. He was a pioneer as a human being. That should not be forgotten.

The Kay-Kempton Experiment

To my mind, Whorf was the most interesting linguist of his day. One of the most important claims he made was that the structure of a language could influence nonlinguistic behavior. Another way to put the issue, as Kay and Kempton (1984) have done, is to ask whether there are cases where differences in nonlinguistic cognition correlate with, and depend on, differences in linguistic structure. Or, to put it still another way, is naming part of cognition? Do symbolic ICMs, which pair form and content, function as part of normal cognition, or do they stand apart from nonlinguistic cognition and just supply labels?

In case study 3 we provide grammatical evidence that symbolic cognitive models are part of cognition. In our study of *there*-constructions, we will show that grammatical constructions form radial categories of the same sort that occur in conceptual structure, for example, in the concept of anger (see case study 1). We have already seen some evidence for this in Fillmore's discussion of "frame-rejecting negation," that is, of sentences like *John isn't* stingy, *he's thrifty* and *John doesn't* regret *that he stole the money because he didn't steal it.* What is being negated in these cases is the applicability of the symbolic models that pair the words *stingy* and *regret* with the corresponding concepts. Here ICMs containing linguistic material are functioning with respect to negation like ICMs not containing any linguistic material. Another well-known case, brought to my attention by Haj Ross, is *John and Bill came into the room in that order*, where *that order* refers to the order of the words *John* and *Bill.* In most cases, deictic expressions like *that* refer to nonlinguistic entities in the world. But, since language is part of our experience, it too can be referred to by deictic expressions. In such cases, cognitive models containing linguistic expressions are acting like cognitive models not containing linguistic expressions.

What Kay and Kempton did was devise a very subtle and elegant experiment which demonstrates that differences in nonlinguistic cognition correlate with, and depend on, differences in linguistic structure. The experiment was done for the domain of color, and the languages used were English and Tarahumara (a Uto-Aztecan lanugage of Mexico). Tarahumara does not have separate words for blue and green. Instead, it has a single basic color name, *siyóname,* which covers both colors. In the Kay-McDaniel (1978) characterization, it would be represented as GREEN OR BLUE—the fuzzy union of the green and blue response curves. What is important for this experiment is that Tarahumara does not have names that differentiate green from blue.

The idea behind the experiment was to set up two nonlinguistic tasks that were minimally different in the following way: In task 1, having names for green and blue could help the English speakers, whereas in task 2, having the names could not help the English speakers. A "Whorfian" effect resulting from the English-Tarahumara difference in color names would be verified under the following conditions:

- If English speakers used names in performing task 1, while Tarahumara speakers could not use names, and if this led to a significant difference in performance of the task, then that would be prima facie evidence of a Whorfian effect.

– If that difference in performance disappears in task 2, which differs from task 1 only in that the naming difference cannot be utilized, then the Whorfian effect is confirmed.

Such an experiment would show that the naming difference, and that difference alone, could affect performance in a nonlinguistic cognitive task. Thus, linguistic differences would be shown to affect nonlinguistic behavior.

Kay and Kempton were, in fact, able to devise such minimally different tasks. In both tasks, subjects were presented with a linear array of three color chips in the blue-to-green range. In each case, the leftmost chip was greenest, the rightmost chip was bluest, and the middle chip was in between. In both tasks, subjects were asked to tell which of the three chips was most different from the other two. This was a judgment, in effect, on whether the middle chip was closer in color to the leftmost or rightmost chip. The chips were chosen so that there was a "right" answer (see Kay and Kempton 1984 for details).

The chips were chosen to be close enough in color to make the task difficult—sufficiently difficult so that speakers would use anything they could use to help them make the choice. It was hypothesized that English speakers would have a strategy available to help them that Tarahumara speakers would lack. Kay and Kempton referred to this as the "name strategy":

> We propose that faced with this situation the English-speaking subject reasons unconsciously as follows: "It's hard to decide here which one looks the most different. Are there any other kinds of clues I might use? Aha! A and B are both CALLED *green* while C is CALLED *blue*. That solves my problem; I'll pick C as the most different. (Kay and Kempton 1984, p. 72)

Moreover, the prediction is made that if the English speakers use the color names as part of the task, then the use of contrasting names should have the effect of accentuating the blue-green boundary; that is, colors near the boundary should be subjectively pushed apart by English speakers, but not by Tarahumara speakers. It is this distortion effect that the experiment tests for.

In task 1, subjects are shown all three chips and asked which is most different. As expected, English speakers showed systematic distortion at the blue-green boundary—"pushing" colors on the blue side more toward blue and colors on the green side more toward green. This systematic distortion occurred in 29 out of 30 cases. With Tarahumara speakers, the distortion was random—almost a perfect 50-50 split. Thus English speakers did seem to be using the naming strategy.

Task 2 was given only to English-speaking subjects. It differed from task 1 in the following way: In task 1, the chips were presented in an apparatus with a stationary window which permitted all three chips to be seen at once. In task 2, however, the apparatus had a sliding window that permitted only two chips to be seen at once. The effectiveness of the naming strategy is eliminated by the following method of presentation and instructions:

> Experimenter exposes pair (*A,B*). "You can see that this chip (points to *A*) is greener than this chip (points to *B*)." (All subjects readily agreed.) Experimenter slides cover so that *A* is covered and *C* is exposed along with *B*; that is, the pair (*B,C*) is now exposed. "You can see that this chip (points to *C*) is bluer than this chip (points to *B*)." (Again all subjects agreed without problems.) "Now," experimenter hands stimuli to subject, "you may slide the cover back and forth as often as you like. I'd like you to tell me which is bigger: the difference in greenness between the two chips on the left, or the difference in blueness between the two chips on the right." (Kay and Kempton 1984, p. 73)

Kay and Kempton reason as follows:

> The subject cannot reasonably ask himself (herself) whether chip *B* is called *green* or *blue* because he (she) has already in effect both called it *green* and called it *blue* in agreeing to compare *B* in *greenness* to *A* and in *blueness* to *C*. (Kay and Kempton 1984, p. 73)

And in fact, the Whorfian effect shown by English speakers in task 1 completely disappears! At least in this very restricted case, Whorf has been shown to be right. Choosing which of three colors is most different is a nonlinguistic task. Linguistic differences can—in the right circumstances—affect the performance of the task.

Beyond confirming one of Whorf's claims, the Kay-Kempton experiment has an additional important consequence. It counters an all-too-common view in cognitive psychology that language plays no cognitive role other than to provide labels for concepts—labels that stand outside of "real cognition." The Kay-Kempton experiment has shown experimentally, if only for one small case, that language is part of real cognition.

This is true not just for grammar, but for the lexicon as well. An important moral of Brugman's study of *over* (Brugman 1981) is that one cannot simply assume that, aside from accidental homonymy, there is a one-to-one labeling relationship between single words and single concepts. The lexicon involves much more than mere labeling concepts. In the case of *over,* as in other cases of polysemy, an individual word correlates with each member of a natural category of concepts—a prototype-based category. That is what polysemy is about. Polysemy involves cognitive organization in a lexicon. Even at the level of the individual word, language is an inseparable part of general cognition. Psychologists are no more justified in ignoring language as mere labeling than linguists are in ignoring general principles of cognition, such as principles of categorization.

My Own Views

Am I a relativist? Well, I hold views that characterize one of the hundreds of forms of relativism. My views derive from two sources: first, my concerns as a linguist and cognitive scientist; second, the empirical studies cited above. For the sake of clarity, I will state my positions on the issues discussed above, and why I hold them.

Organization: As a linguist, I am concerned with general principles governing linguistic phenomena. Polysemy is one such phenomenon. Among the most thorough research on polysemy is that done by Lakoff and Johnson (1980), Lindner (1981), Brugman (1981, 1984), Casad (1982), Janda (1984), and Sweetser (1984). All of these studies lead to the same conclusion: The generalizations governing polysemy can only be described and explained in terms of conceptual organization. Thus, the study of linguistic phenomena leads to hypotheses concerning conceptual organization.

The two studies that I have found sufficiently detailed to be convincing to me are the studies of the general principles governing the use of spatial location terms in Cora (by Casad) and Mixtec (by Brugman). Talmy's study of Atsugewi (Talmy, 1972) is also sobering in this regard. Such detailed empirical studies have convinced me in a way that Whorf's cursory studies did not, that these languages differ from English and from each other in the way they conceptualize spatial location. These differences are largely differences in conceptual organization. Because I take linguistic regularities, including polysemy, seriously as phenomena to be both described and explained and because that seems to require an understanding of how conceptual systems are organized, I must take the question of how a conceptual system is organized very seriously. It is for this reason that I view the organization of a conceptual system as part of what characterizes the system. For me, conceptual systems with different organizations are different systems.

Functional Embodiment: As a linguist, I am interested in the grammars of languages, especially in what concepts are grammaticized in the languages of the world and what concepts are not. I am also interested in what it means for a concept to be grammaticized, and it is here that the use issue arises. Whorf was right in observing that concepts that have been made part of the grammar of a language are used *in* thought, not just *as objects of* thought, and that they are used spontaneously, automatically, unconsciously, and effortlessly. As a cognitive scientist, I am interested not only in what our concepts are but also in how they are used. I am convinced by Whorf's arguments that the way we use concepts affects the way we understand experience; concepts that are spontaneous, automatic, and unconscious are simply going to have a greater (though less obvious) impact on how we understand everyday life than concepts that we merely ponder. To me, conceptual systems are different if they lead consistently to different understandings of experience. Therefore, conceptual systems whose concepts are used differently are, to me, different systems.

Monolithic Systems: As a cognitive scientist, I am concerned with how we understand our experience. It is simply a fact that it is possible for an individual to understand the same domain of experience in different and inconsistent ways. This has been demonstrated in studies by Gentner and Gentner (1982) for electricity, by Kay (1979) for reference, and by Lakoff and Johnson (1980) for a variety of concepts. The fact that systems are not monolithic indicates that one does not have to look *across* conceptual systems to find evidence of relativism.

System versus Capacity: As a cognitive scientist, I am interested in the following questions: Why do human beings have the conceptual systems they have? How is it possible for a child to acquire a conceptual system? What is the range of possible human conceptual systems? How is it possible for an adult to learn a new way to conceptualize something? The idea that people are born with a conceptualizing capacity seems to be the only plausible way to begin to provide answers for all these questions.

The alternative seems to be to assume that all children are born with all concepts that now exist in all cultures, as well as all concepts that have ever existed or will ever exist. On this view, learning a new concept is just the activation of an already existing concept (Fodor, 1975). I find such an idea too bizarre to take seriously. Moreover, it does not explain why human beings have the concepts they have and why the range of possible human conceptual systems is what it is.

Locus of Variation: The Kay-Kempton results show that words can impose categorizations that can be made use of in nonlinguistic tasks. But, for me, the most interesting variation does not have to do with *isolated* conceptual differences corresponding to individual lexical items, but rather with *systematic* differences in conceptualization.

Nature and Depth of Variation: What kinds of concepts is one most likely to find as one surveys conceptual systems? First, kinesthetic image schemas: concepts like UP-DOWN, IN-OUT, PART-WHOLE, etc. Second, basic-level concepts for things, states, activities in one's immediate experience: body parts, plants and animals, basic-level artifacts, basic colors, basic emotions, etc. Third, metaphorical concepts based on universal experiences: thus it would not be surprising to find MORE being UP, or ANGER being understood in terms of HEAT or PRESSURE. There are a fair number of such things that one would not expect to vary much. All of these are tied very closely to well-structured experience. I would not expect radical variation in these three areas. I *would* expect a fair amount of variation in organization and use.

Commensurability: I accept four of the five criteria: understanding, use, framing, and organization. If one is interested in cognition, these criteria ought to play a role in characterizing and comparing conceptual systems. But I do not take the criterion of translatability preserving truth conditions at all seriously as showing anything interesting about human conceptual systems that the other four criteria do not show. Given the understanding criterion, talk of truth conditions introduces irrelevant considerations: truth (from some *external* point of view) may be preserved when understanding varies. But truth, from a pont of view *external* to the conceptual systems being compared, is irrelevant. It tells us nothing about the systems being compared and can lead to judgments of commensurability on purely external grounds.

Degree of Variation: Given four criteria for commensurability, it should not be surprising that I estimate that variation should be substantial. However, such variations would not be all that radical, considering the nature of what is preserved.

Fact-Value: As far as facts are concerned, I am a relativist in the sense characterized by my stands on the above issues. Alternative conceptual systems exist, whether one likes it or not. They are not likely to go away, since they arise from a fundamental human capacity to conceptualize experience. Communication might be easier if everyone had the same conceptual system. But better communication would not eliminate conflicts of interest, which are the major sources of human conflict.

I view relativism of the sort that exists as a good thing. Just as the gene pool of a species needs to be kept diverse if the species is to survive under a wide variety of conditions, so I believe that diverse ways of comprehending experience are necessary to our survival as a species. I believe that vanishing cultures and languages need to be protected just as vanishing species do. And, like Whorf, I think we have a lot to learn from other ways of conceptualizing experience that have evolved around the world.

Effect on Action: Like Whorf, I believe that differences in conceptual systems affect behavior in a significant way. It is vitally important to understand just how our behavior is dependent on how we think. In areas like human relationships, where failure rates tend to be higher than we would like them to be, an understanding of differences in conceptual systems, and how behavior depends on them, might well be helpful. Quinn's study of how Americans understand marriage is classic in this regard. Quinn (in press) demonstrates how different conceptualizations of marriage on the part of spouses in a marriage affect behavior and lead to misunderstanding and marital difficulties.

Control: Much of our conceptual system is used unconsciously and automatically, in ways that we don't even notice. To refuse to find out how our behavior depends on our conceptual systems is to abdicate responsibility for much of what we do. I have no idea whether understanding our own conceptual systems will give us more control over our behavior, but I doubt that it will give us less.

Ethics: Conceptual relativism of the sort that appears to exist does not rule out universal ethical standards of some sort—at least as far as I can determine. Nor does it seem to tell us very much about what such standards should be. However, a *refusal* to recognize conceptual relativism where it exists does have ethical consequences. It leads directly to conceptual elitism and imperialism—to the assumption that our behavior is rational and that of other people is not, and to attempts to impose our way of thinking on others. Whorf's ethical legacy was to make us aware of this.

CHAPTER 19

The Mind-As-Machine Paradigm

Because of the recent technological innovations in computer science, the mind-as-computer metaphor has taken hold, not only in the popular imagination, but among professional cognitive psychologists as well. The mind-as-machine view shares the traditional mind-body distinction, according to which the mind is disembodied, abstract, and independent of bodily functioning. According to this view, the mind is a computer with biological hardware and runs using programs essentially like those used in computers today. It may take input from the body and provide output to the body, but there is nonetheless a purely mental sphere of symbolic manipulation that can be characterized in terms of algorithms of the sort used in computer programs. I will refer to this as the *mind-as-machine* view. I will argue that certain of the results cited above contradict the mind-as-machine view.

But before I begin, I should point out that the studies discussed in this volume do not in any way contradict studies in artificial intelligence (usually called "AI") in general. Far from it. First, not all AI makes claims to be of empirical relevance to the study of the mind, for example, AI approaches to expert systems and robotics. We shall have nothing to say about such approaches. We shall discuss only computational approaches to the study of mind. Even there, our results by no means contradict all such approaches. For example, they do not contradict what have come to be called "connectionist" theories, in which the role of the body in cognition fits naturally. Our results only contradict what we will characterize below as the mind-as-machine view—a view considered silly and overly simplistic by many sophisticated researchers in AI and cognitive psychology.

There is no single computational approach to the study of mind. Our results do not in any way contradict the work of those who take the following approaches:

- those researchers who use computer models because they are convenient—easier than pencil and paper
- those who devise computer models purely for practical purposes
- those who use computer models as a heuristic, to suggest problems and solutions
- those who are engaged in *simulating* some *limited* domain of cognitive activity.

I have found much research of this sort interesting and useful. Nothing in this book contradicts any such general approaches. Indeed, our results fit very well with certain computational approaches—those that are sympathetic to empirical studies of language and thought of the sort we have cited. Such approaches are attempting to characterize notions like "cognitive model," "metaphorical mapping," "mental space," "prototype," "radial category," etc.

Our results also fit well with what we will call, following Mark Johnson (1987), the body-in-the-mind approach to information processing, according to which what have traditionally been called "purely mental" capacities overlap with information processing capacities having to do with bodily functioning. Empirical research on categorization should be seen as providing support for these computational approaches over research done in a mind-as-machine paradigm that preserves the independence and separateness of what has traditionally been called the mind.

The categorization studies cited above are, however, in conflict with a variety of mind-as-machine approaches. The conflicts are of two kinds.

First, they are in conflict with an approach to AI that views the mind as independent of the body and consisting purely of disembodied algorithms.

Second, they are in conflict with objectivist approaches to AI, approaches that assume objectivist philosophy.

I take the mind-as-machine paradigm as consisting of two positions that are logically independent, but which often occur together: computational realism and objectivist AI.

Computational Realism

There are two aspects to computational realism. They are:

The Algorithmic Mind Position: Every cognitive process is algorithmic in nature; that is, thought is purely a matter of symbol manipulation.

The Disembodied Mind Position: Human reason is completely abstract and not dependent in any way on human bodily experience.

Objectivist AI

There are also two aspects to objectivist AI.

The Objectivist Representations Position: Concepts are internal representations of external reality. In other words, the symbols being manipulated are given meaning only via their capacity to correspond to aspects of reality.

The Universal Conceptual Framework Position: There is a completely general and neutral conceptual framework in terms of which all human knowledge can be represented.

It should be clear from these formulations that the mind-as-machine paradigm has nothing to do with a physical computer. It is an abstract position having to do with the character of mind. Computer programs are algorithmic in nature, and it is the algorithmic character of mind that is the central claim of the mind-as-machine position. Since algorithms are abstract entities, whose properties have nothing to do with bodies, human or otherwise, the disembodied mind position is a consequence of the algorithmic mind position.

Algorithms concern the manipulation of meaningless disembodied symbols. Since thought is meaningful, and the symbols in an algorithm are meaningless, the disparity must be made up somehow. Since algorithms are characterized independent of bodies, they cannot be viewed as "embodied" in our sense of the term. Algorithmic "thought" is usually seen as being made meaningful via the association of symbols with things in the external world.

Since human minds are capable of understanding, and since the mind is viewed as being disembodied, understanding cannot be defined in terms of embodiment, as we characterized it in chapter 17. It is viewed instead in terms of the *translation* of one symbolic representation into another. This has an important consequence with respect to the issue of commensurability of alternative conceptual systems discussed in the previous chapter. It eliminates the understanding criterion and collapses it with the translation criterion. But as we saw, the translation criterion is the least interesting of the commensurability criteria, while the understanding criterion is perhaps the most central. People do seem to be capable of understanding alternative conceptual systems. Within the mind-as-machine paradigm, such a capacity for understanding alternative conceptual systems is possible only if there is a single symbolic system they can be translated into. Hence the universal conceptual framework position.

We will begin our discussion with the objectivist representations position, since that is crucial to the view that thought is merely symbol manipulation. The reason is that thought is meaningful, and it is usually assumed that symbol manipulation can be made meaningful if and only if the symbols can be given an interpretation in the external world. If the objectivist representations position is false, it creates problems for the disembodied mind position, and hence for the algorithmic mind position.

The Objectivist Representations Position

The term *representation* is used with abandon in the cognitive sciences, especially in AI. Most practicing cognitive scientists don't care about the philosophical status of what they are studying, that is, they don't care whether philosophers interpret the conceptual structures that they call *representations* as "internal representations of external reality." However, that, or something akin to it, is what is required to make thought meaningful—given the assumption of the disembodied mind.

Cognitive models, as we have been discussing them throughout this book, might be called "representations" by many practicing cognitive scientists. If one uses that terminology—and it is a common terminology—then this book can be seen as advocating the reality of such nonobjectivist "representations." But, as was made clear in chapter 17, cognitive models in our sense are not *internal representations of external reality*. They are not for two reasons: first, because they are understood in terms of embodiment, not in terms of direct connection to the external world; and second, because they include imaginative aspects of cognition such as metaphor and metonymy.

The algorithmic mind position and the disembodied mind position rule out any interpretation of cognitive models as being embodied in our sense. In the absence of an account like ours in which meaning is based on bodily understanding, all that is left seems to be the view that symbols can be made meaningful by being associated directly with objectively existing things and categories of things in the world. This is the objectivist representations position of objectivist AI.

Putnam's critique, discussed in chapter 15 above, applies to the objectivist representations position, since it applies to all views on which there are *internal representations* of the *external world*. Because the objectivist representations position involves the separation of a formal language (the "language" of the internal representations) from its interpretation (external entities), it therefore runs into the same problems as objectivist semantics.

> The same problem has even surfaced recently in the field of cognitive psychology. The standard model for the brain/mind in this field is the modern computing machine. This computing machine is thought of as having something analogous to a formalized language with which it computes. (This hypothetical brain language has even received a name—"mentalese.") What makes the model of cognitive psychology a *cognitive* model is that "mentalese" is thought to be a medium whereby the brain constructs an *internal representation* of the external world. This idea runs immediately into the following problem: if "mentalese" is to be a vehicle for describing the external world, then the various predicate letters must have extensions which are sets of external things (or sets of *n*-tuples of external things). (Putnam, 1980, p. 476)

In short, the problem arises from the disembodied mind position, which forces *an objectivist understanding of computational models.* For a computational model to provide a "representation" of the external world, there must be a *correct* link—from a God's eye point of view—between the representation and what it represents. Without such a link, it cannot be said to *really* be a *representation* of the external world. This is what makes the objectivist representations position into a form of objectivism.

> But if the way "mentalese" is "understood" by the deep structures in the brain that compute, record, etc. in this "language" is *via* what artificial intelligence people call "procedural semantics"—that is, if the brain's *program for using* "mentalese" comprises its entire "understanding" of "mentalese"—where the program for using "mentalese," like any program, refers only to what is *inside* then computer—then how do *extensions* ever come into the picture at all? (Putnam, 1980, p. 476)

For a collections of symbols to constitute a *representation* of something, there must, on an objectivist view, be a natural (god's eye view) link of the right sort between the symbols and what the symbols "represent." This is what an objectivist means, and must mean, by a "representation *of* something."

Here is what is required for a computational model of the mind to qualify as an "internal representation of the external world" from an objectivist perspective:

- There must be systematic links between the language used in the computational model ("mentalese") and the external world; in Putnam's terms, there must be "extensions."
- To *really* constitute a "representation of the external world," these

links must be accurate; they must "really represent" the world, according to an external, objective standard of what constitutes a representation.

As Putnam has demonstrated, an objectivist interpretation of the expression "internal representation of the external world" is impossible. Meaning cannot be characterized by a relationship between symbols and entities in the world. AI researchers cannot count on the objectivist representations position to save the day and give meaning to the symbols in computer languages. Objectivist AI has no consistent theory of meaning! And neither does the mind-as-machine paradigm, because it incorporates the disembodied mind position.

Most practitioners of artificial intelligence and cognitive psychology will most likely not care about this. On the whole, they could not care less whether the computational models they come up with really count as "representations of the external world" of a sort that would satisfy objectivist philosophy. I think this is a perfectly reasonable attitude for practical researchers to take. My own feeling is that something like the experientialist approach (outlined in chapter 17) to what AI researchers call "representations" and what I have called "cognitive models" will mesh better with empirically responsible AI research. But such a position is in conflict with the claims being made by other AI researchers—those who really believe in the mind-as-machine paradigm, in computational realism, in objectivist AI, and in the idea that the symbols in a computer language really can be "internal representations of external reality." They are simply wrong.

The Predicate Calculus Position

There is a version of objectivist AI according to which all human reasoning is done in some form of predicate calculus. Those advocating such a position attempt to use theorem-proving programs to characterize forms of human reason. Of course, the concept of a category used in such research is the classical category. To the extent that the evidence cited in this book disconfirms the classical view of categorization, it also disconfirms the predicate calculus position.

Experientialism

On the whole the experientialist program is at odds with the mind-as-machine view. As we saw, the universal conceptual framework and objectivist representations positions are both objectivist in nature, and so it is not surprising that they are in conflict with experientialism. Experientialism is also at odds with computational realism in a number of ways, especially on the issue of whether concepts are disembodied.

Let us start with the conceptualizing capacity hypothesis of chapter 17. Experientialism is concerned with *explaining* why the human conceptual system is as it is. It claims that aspects of the conceptual system are a consequence of the nature of human physical experience and the way that it is structured preconceptually by the fact that we have the bodies that we have and that we interact continuously as part of a physical and social environment. Basic-level concepts and kinesthetic image schemas are products of such experience plus a general capacity to construct concepts, especially concepts that fit those of our experiences that have a preconceptual structure.

The question of why our knowledge is structured as it is—primarily at the basic level—is also something that experientialism takes as something requiring an explanation. Such an explanation is possible under the assumption that there is a conceptualizing capacity that accounts for the acquisition of basic-level concepts in terms of the perception of overall part-whole structure (B. Tversky, 1986).

Experientialism is also concerned with understanding—both with how we understand our own concepts and how we can learn and comprehend another conceptual system. The hypothesis of a conceptualizing capacity is central to explaining both phenomena.

The mind-as-machine view does not seem to provide a basis for explaining any of these phenomena. Take the question of how we can learn another conceptual system. Under the mind-as-machine view, learning another system would require a *translation* into one's own language of thought. But as we have seen, there is more to understanding another conceptual system than translation. On the conceptualizing capacity hypothesis, it is possible to construct another system using one's capacity for understanding in terms of experience. The mind-as-machine view doesn't allow for this.

As a consequence there is an important aspect of mind that cannot be characterized in the mind-as-machine paradigm: different conceptual organizations in different conceptual systems. As we saw in chapter 18, the Mixtec and English spatial location systems have different conceptual organizations, even though they permit sentence-by-sentence translation. It is possible for a human being to understand both systems, while maintaining the two different conceptual organizations. But if understanding another conceptual system is viewed as translation into a single symbolic system, then the difference in the *organization* of the two conceptual systems will be lost in the translation, since any single symbolic system will have only one such organization. For this reason, the mind-as-machine paradigm fails in such cases.

In addition, the mind-as-machine view would appear to require that the "language of thought" be digital. But there is evidence for the existence of kinesthetic image schemas (see case study 2). They are largely analog, not digital. They can be simulated by digital means, but that would not do for computational realism. We will discuss the reason why below.

Experientialism also requires an account of meaning. It provides it via an account of the meaningfulness of experience. Again the conceptualizing capacity plays a large role here. The only account of meaning available to the mind-as-machine view appears to be some sort of objectivist account, using the notion of an internal representation of external reality. But this, as we have seen, cannot work.

The mind-as-machine view is hopeless if we wish to find an account of meaning and explanations for how we can understand our own concepts and those in other conceptual systems. It offers no help in explaining why we have the concepts we have, and what role human physical experience plays in this. And it is in conflict with what is known about image schemas. Overall, the mind-as-machine view seems inadequate both in coping with empirical phenomena and in providing *explanations* of central cognitive phenomena.

The Simulation Position

It is important to distinguish the computational realism position from the computational simulation position. Simulationism claims that some (perhaps many) significant cognitive processes can be simulated by a computer. I do not doubt that this is true for at least some cognitive processes. But computational realism says something very different: It says that the mind really is algorithmic in nature. The difference is easy to see. A computer can simulate aspects of the flow of water in a river. That does not mean that the river itself is directed by any algorithm. The difference is anything but trivial.

So far as I can tell, nothing in this book contradicts the simulation position. Such a position is entirely responsible. It does not claim that *all* mental processes can be simulated by a computer. It does not claim that all thought is disembodied and algorithmic. It does not claim that there is a universal conceptual framework. It does not claim that symbols in computer programs are internal representations of external reality. And it does not claim that people use predicate calculus to reason. What it claims is that one can learn something significant about the mind by doing computer simulations of certain cognitive activities. It is a responsible position that cannot in any way be faulted on the basis of evidence in this book. And it is a far cry from computational realism.

To discuss the issue substantively, let us turn to a phenomenon which is not characteristic of algorithms themselves, but which might be simulated by an algorithm. The phenomenon is *motivation*, as we have characterized it briefly in chapter 6 above and, at length, in case studies 2 and 3 below. Something in language or thought is *motivated* when it is neither arbitrary nor predictable. Motivated phenomena include category extensions (as with *mother*, the Dyirbal classifiers and *hon*), polysemy (see *over* in case study 2), related grammatical constructions (see case study 3), most idioms (see case study 2), etc. In natural language, motivation seems to be more the norm than the exception.

Motivation is not the kind of phenomenon that algorithms were designed to characterize. Algorithms permit one to state rules, or principles, that will compute an output given an input. One can interpret such computation metaphorically as "prediction." Algorithms are good for prediction (that is, the computation of outputs from given inputs). With respect to an algorithm, things are either predictable (that is, computable from an input) or they are arbitrary. But in human conceptual and linguistic systems, most things are neither. They are motivated, to some degree and in various respects. Motivation is a central phenomenon in cognition. The reason is this: *It is easier to learn something that is motivated than something that is arbitrary.* It is also easier to *remember* and *use* motivated knowledge than arbitrary knowledge.

The phenomenon of motivation creates the following problem for the algorithmic mind position, and hence for computational realism. Recall that knowledge that is motivated is motivated *by* something—other knowledge. To state it overly simplistically: Let *K* be something one knows. Let *M* be a piece of knowledge motivated by *K*. Assume that *M* cannot be computed by algorithm from *K* or anything else. Assume furthermore that *M* and *K* are related in one of the ways specified in the examples of motivation given above or in the case studies. Here is the phenomenon:

1. Given that one knows *K*, it is easier to learn, remember, and use *M* than if one did not know *K*.
2. *K* is one of the following:
   - the center of a radial category to which *M* is systematically related
   - a metaphoric model such that *M* is either an instance of a category in the target domain of the model (or of some novel extension of it)

– a metonymic model where *M* is in the domain of the metonymic function.

From a computational point of view, here is what makes this interesting: Having something *extra* in memory makes it easier to learn, remember, and use something which is not computable. In most algorithmic systems, having something extra in memory just uses up *more* not *fewer* computational resources—whether those resources be computational steps, storage space, etc. There are (I am told) computational organizations where it is easier to remember more than less. But these are abstract organizations that do not have the peculiar properties of human conceptual systems cited in condition 2.

Now, given a particular *K* and *M* in a particular system, it might well be possible to write a computer program that *simulates* the phenomenon. For example, one might construct a simulation of radial categories, metaphoric models, and metonymic models. And one might define some measure called *D* = *difficulty of processing*, and construct a program so that *D* gets a lower value for *M* when *K* is present in memory than when it is not. Such a simulation might even be revealing of something real about the phenomenon.

There are two problems here. First, what is a required is a *general* solution that will work for all the real cases. Second, the measure *D* would have to *really be* a measure of processing difficulty of the relevant sort. For example, if one were to hard-wire the simulation, that is, build a machine that naturally does what the simulation does, *D* would have to be a real measure of processing difficulty.

Of course, all this is pie in the sky right now. There are no such simulations. At present, motivation phenomena have just begun to be studied from a computational point of view. Given this situation, what can we conclude?

The most important point to bear in mind is this: simulations are not good enough to satisfy computational realism. On the computational realism position, the simulation *program* itself (the algorithm) would be real—that is, the mind would be *simulating* a machine that could account for the motivation phenomenon: but it would not *be* such a machine. For this reason, simulations do not satisfy the mind-as-machine hypothesis as a solution for the phenomenon of motivation.

At present, there is no existing computer model for representing knowledge that has the property that *adding* knowledge to memory under just the conditions stated above (in condition 2) makes it possible to learn, remember, and use certain kinds of information *more efficiently*. For all such models, including all those that presently exist, the computational realism position is false. I doubt that any algorithm will have such properties—properties that depend on detailed characteristics of human conceptual systems, such things as radial categories, metonymic models, and metaphoric models.

The Fundamental Problem

I believe that computational approaches to the study of mind incorporate an important insight into the mind. There is a flow of thought. It is not just a mushy flow, but rather a highly structured flow. The view of thought as algorithmic computation is presently our best model of a highly structured flow of thought. That does not mean that it is the only possible correct model. Most of the inadequacies that we have found with that model boil down to one inadequacy—the lack of what we have called "conceptual embodiment." The symbols used in the computation are meaningless. Thought is not meaningless, and a nonobjectivist account must be given of what makes it meaningful. That, I claim, is conceptual embodiment.

The need for meaningfulness has been lost on many AI researchers. The reason is that when those researchers construct those algorithms, they do so with their own understanding of what the symbols used in knowledge representation languages are supposed to mean. For this reason, the symbols don't seem meaningless to *them.* The input is meaningful to them and the output is meaningful to them—and the symbols used in the computation may be chosen with an intended interpretation. But their computational models do not incorporate an adequate nonobjectivist account of what makes the symbols meaningful *to the being whose thinking is being modeled*, not to the researcher doing the modeling. In typical AI research, either no account is given at all, or else it is assumed that the symbols are internal representations of external reality. But the phenomena we have been discussing require such a nonobjectivist account of the meaningfulness of the symbols used in the computations.

An adequate solution would involve more than just giving some interpretation to the symbols. The reason is that the understanding of the symbols is, strictly speaking, external to the algorithm, yet must enter into the computation. For example, in the case of motivation, the computation must proceed more efficiently if the symbols mean the right kinds of things, and not if they don't. For example, basic-level concepts are easier to learn, remember, and use. Simply giving the concept a name doesn't account for that. The reason it is easier is that its meaning bears a certain relationship to perception, motor abilities, and imaging capacities. An adequate account of mind requires an *explanation* for this. Such an explanation is unlikely to come from a purely algorithmic account of mind, since the efficiency of an algorithm cannot depend on the interpretation of the symbols used in the algorithm. We need a theory of mind that can account adequately for the difference in cognitive efficiency—that is, learning, memory, and use—between basic-level concepts and other concepts. A purely algorithmic view of mind is unlikely to provide it.

It is important to note that one cannot get out of the problem just by giving distinct names to the symbols that have meanings of a certain sort. Such names may tell the researcher what the symbols are supposed to mean, but they are still arbitrary names. They do not constitute a theory of why those symbols mean what they do to the person whose thought is being modelled. Setting up a model in which symbols with one kind of name are processed more efficiently than symbols with another kind of name is doing nothing more than giving a name to the problem. It is not a theory that explains why that happens. An adequate theory must take into account how the *content* of a concept is related to bodily experience. And that is outside the realm of the algorithmic mind.

It is equally important to realize that one cannot solve such problems simply by grafting an interpretation on the symbols in the algorithm. The reason is that there are external factors that make the mind work more efficiently in such cases. One would have to show how something *outside* of the algorithm can make that algorithm work more efficiently in just such cases.

What all this shows is that there are limits on the computer metaphor for the mind. The computer metaphor may be insightful in many other ways, but it fails here. With respect to categorization phenomena, those limits all concern the inability of the algorithmic mind position to allow for a theory of meaning of the sort needed to account for the empirical data.

Is There a Joint Body-Mind System?

AI researchers, confronted by such arguments, are quick to point out that the categorization data we have discussed do not provide any evidence against a general information-processing view. What these indicate is that the mind is not separate from and independent of the body. That is, the mind cannot just be considered an independent module, algorithmic in character, that takes input from the body and provides output to it. There is, however, a perfectly reasonable information-processing view that is consistent with such results, namely, that the information processing capacities needed for bodily functioning overlap significantly with what have previously been considered purely mental information-processing capacities.

The Body-Mind System Position

The information-processing system of the body is a joint body-mind system, not factorable into purely mental and purely bodily functions in a way that fits the classical theory of concepts and categories. Instead, information-processing capacities used in bodily functioning are also adapted to at least certain areas of what has traditionally been called purely mental functioning. It is conceivable that such a unified information-processing system could have the properties that categorization studies have uncovered.

Another way of thinking about this is in terms of the difference between *signal processing* and *symbol processing*. Both are forms of information processing. But individual symbols are assumed to have meaning, while individual signals are not. Information processing in the central nervous system involves signal processing, not symbol processing. Information processing in the mind is usually assumed to involve symbol processing, not signal processing. A joint body-mind system might involve both signal and symbol processing, without a single, clearly isolatable symbol-processing subsystem. I know of no evidence from the study of categorization that is in conflict with such a joint body-mind position.

Such a view should not be at all shocking to cognitive psychologists in the information-processing tradition or to AI researchers. However, it does contradict widely held views in philosophy and linguistics, views that even some cognitive psychologists have come to accept. The heart of what I have called the mind-as-machine position has to do with the *separateness* and *independence* of what has traditionally been considered to be purely mental. It is that separateness and independence that is challenged by the categorization results.

Conclusion

In summary, categorization phenomena are in conflict with a mind-as-machine paradigm that insists on a separate, independent, disembodied, and algorithmic character of mind. The conflicts are as follows:

- The disembodied mind position is in conflict with embodiment of content:
  (*a*) basic-level perception, motor movement, and imaging capacities that jointly characterize basic-level concepts (see chap. 2);

(*b*) general experiential structures that determine the character of kinesthetic image schemas (see chap. 17 and case study 2); and
(*c*) experiences that form the basis of metaphorical concepts (see case study 1).

Computer simulation may someday be able to *describe* such things, but only an understanding of the dependence of mind upon the body for the content of its concepts can *explain* such characteristics of human conceptual systems.

- The algorithmic mind position is in conflict with the phenomenon of motivation. Again, computational *simulation* of such phenomena may someday be possible, but algorithms *themselves* do not have the properties of motivated systems of the sort that have been empirically discovered (see chap. 6 and case studies 2 and 3).
- The objectivist representations position is in conflict with Putnam's critique (see chap. 15).
- The universal conceptual framework position is in conflict with two facts:
  (*a*) conceptual systems have different conceptual *organizations*, such differences being cognitively significant; and
  (*b*) the understanding of another conceptual system on the basis of experience can occur without full translatability into any single system (see chap. 18).

The problem here for the algorithmic mind position is that the only way it can make sense of the understanding of two different conceptual systems is via the *translation* of one into the other, or of both into a third system. But if the two different systems have different conceptual *organizations*, say, like the organizations of Mixtec and English (discussed in chap. 18), then translation into a single system—a universal conceptual framework—would eliminate that organizational difference. Understanding in terms of experience, on the other hand, does not eliminate such organizational differences. Thus, the mind-as-machine paradigm can only provide an account of understanding in which differences in conceptual organization are eliminated. In this way, it is inadequate as an account of real cognition, in which differences of conceptual organization are preserved in the understanding of alternative conceptual systems of the sort that actually occur in the languages of the world.

For all these reasons, I believe that the mind-as-machine paradigm, taken literally, is hopeless. It cannot even account for the phenomena discussed in this book. I know that many AI researchers share my skepticism and do not accept the mind-as-machine paradigm—neither computational realism nor objectivist AI. Those researchers feel, as do I, that the computational metaphor for the mind is important, interesting, and useful, but it has definite limitations, including those discussed above. Personally, I am strongly in favor of continued computational research outside the mind-as-machine paradigm on interesting empirical matters. I feel we have learned a great deal from such research in the past and that future prospects are excellent, even in the area of modelling human categorization. The phenomena discussed in this book should keep empirically minded AI researchers who are looking for interesting problems busy for quite a while. But ultimately we must look outside of the mind-as-machine paradigm for solutions to the kind of problems that we have discussed.

Going outside the mind-as-machine paradigm does not necessarily mean going outside of a more general information-processing paradigm. For example, within connectionist approaches, it may ultimately be possible to maintain a joint body-mind position that might make sense of categorization phenomena. It would require that the information-processing functions of the mind overlap with and significantly determine many of what have traditionally been called purely mental functions.

CHAPTER 20

Mathematics as a Cognitive Activity

Categorization is a form of reason. To say that classical categories exist external to any beings or any minds is to claim that there is a transcendent logic of the universe, a rationality that transcends any being or any mind. Classical categorization and classical logic are two sides of the same coin. Most of the subject matter of classical logic is categorization. A statement like *All* A*'s are* B*'s* says that the category *A* is a subcategory of the category *B*, which implies that any member of *A* is a member of *B*. *All* A*'s are not* B*'s* says that the category *A* and the category *B* do not overlap, which implies that any member of category *A* is not a member of category *B*. Classical modus ponens concerns category structure. To reason

All *A*'s are *B*'s
X is an *A*.
Therefore, *X* is a *B*.

is to stipulate something about category structure in the premises, namely, that

Category *A* is contained in category *B*.
X is contained in category *A*.

and to notice something about the stipulated category structure, namely,

X is contained in category *B*.

This aspect of category structure is, moreover, a consequence of the fact that we understand categories as metaphorical containers. The structure of the syllogism is an observation about container structure. To apply the syllogism to a given domain is to say that it is appropriate to understand that domain in terms of metaphorical containers. But objectivism says more than this. It says that that domain is objectively structured, independent of any understanding, in terms of containers. That is what it means to say that classical categories have an objective existence.

The experientialist alternative does not commit one to the existence of a transcendental rationality that goes beyond the understanding of any beings. It says instead that there is a logic to *our* rationality. Image schemas, as we saw in chapter 17, each have a basic logic. Those schemas structure our preconceptual experience as functioning beings. And they appear to have all the logical structure that is needed to characterize rationality—without positing a transcendental rationality. Container schemas, for example, arise out of our bodily experience, and they have the basic logic of the syllogism. The syllogism can be viewed as arising out of our bodily experience and our capacity for metaphorical projection, rather than having some transcendental existence.

It does not follow from the existence of logical reasoning that there is a transcendent rationality to the universe. All that follows is that many aspects of real experience can be consistently understood in terms of container metaphors—and metaphors based on other image schemas—in a way that is sufficient for our purposes. Logic, from this point of view, consists of the study of constraints on our modes of understanding. It is no less worthwhile an enterprise. It is simply not the same enterprise that objectivist philosophy has thought it to be.

What Is Mathematics?

Those who claim that there is a rationality to the universe that transcends all beings usually point to mathematics as an example. Mathematicians commonly view mathematics as a "Platonic ideal"—a unique body of absolute truths that hold of a timeless realm of mathematical objects, independent of the understandings of any beings. I would like to argue that mathematics need not be construed as transcendentally true, true independent of the understanding of any beings. Instead, it can be construed as growing out of the nature of human rationality.

Take, for example, the view that mathematics is the study of pure form. What is pure form? Under the spatialization hypothesis (see chap. 17), form is the metaphorical projection of image schemas and other ways of understanding space onto an abstract domain. To take the example of containers again, a container form might be called a "pure form." Under the spatialization hypothesis, it is a metaphorical projection of the container schema onto another domain. It not transcendental, because it is not beyond the experience or understanding of any beings. Rather it is a consequence of the experience and understanding of human beings. If "pure form" is not transcendental, and if mathematics is the study of pure form, then mathematics is not transcendental. Mathematics instead is the study of the structures that we use to understand and reason about our experience—structures that are inherent in our preconceptual bodily experience and that we make abstract via metaphor.

Is Mathematics Unique?

We thus have two possible views of the nature of mathematics. They correspond to two views of "pure form." On the one view, pure form is transcendental: it inheres in the nature of the universe. On the other view, what we understand as form arises from our bodily experience, especially our experience of functioning in space. Kinesthetic image schemas are structured in such a way that they have a basic logic, and it is that structure that is used in reasoning and that gives rise to mathematics.

The view that reason is transcendental goes along with the view that mathematics is transcendental. Mathematics is taken as an example—the prime example—of a transcendental rationality. Such a transcendental mathematics would, of course, be unique. The claim is not that there are many transcendental rationalities to the universe, but only one. I would like to suggest that *if mathematics is transcendentally true, then it is not unique.* This would undercut the view that mathematics is an instance of some unique transcendental rationality of the universe, and the existence of mathematics could no longer be seen as supporting the existence of a single transcendental rationality.

It may sound odd at first to think that, if mathematics is transcendentally true, then it is not unique. But the result, as we shall see, has to do with the fact that there is mathematics about mathematics. If the higher-level mathematics (the metamathematics) is true in the transcendental Platonic realm, then the mathematical objects that it is about exist in that realm. If those higher-level mathematical objects themselves characterize distinct forms of mathematics, then the Platonic realm—the realm of transcendental truths—contains more than one body of mathematical truths.

The relevant evidence upon which our argument will be based comes from mathematics itself. It will involve Putnam's theorem plus certain recent "independence proofs." But before we can see what those proofs imply, we must look a little more closely at the view of mathematics as not merely transcendental, but also unique. That view has a strong emotional appeal. Much of the appeal of mathematics for many practicing mathematicians is the satisfaction of being able to *prove* which mathematical propositions are absolutely and ultimately *true*. From this point of view, part of the glory of being a mathematician is to be able to transcend one's humanness, to plug in to the transcendent rationality of the universe and discover some of its ultimate truths.

Mathematics, on the transcendentalist view, is thus "Platonic" in the sense that it concerns a realm of abstract mathematical objects, standing outside of time and history and the experience of any beings, and a unique body of absolute truths that hold of those objects. In addition, it is commonly held that such a unique transcendental mathematics is *complete*, that is, that every mathematical conjecture is either true or false. This is not a necessary concomitant of the transcendentalist view. One could imagine an incomplete transcendentally true mathematics, in which some mathematical conjectures were neither true nor false in the Platonic realm.

It should be noted that the issue of transcendental completeness (whether all mathematical conjectures are either true or false in the Platonic realm) is separate from the issue of the "completeness" of a mathematical system (whether all true conjectures are provable in the system). Gödel's famous incompleteness proof was about the latter issue, provability. Gödel showed that, for any collection of axioms for arithmetic that could either be listed or specified by rule, there will be an infinity of truths of arithmetic that cannot be proved. This means that what many mathematicians had taken as the job of mathematics—providing proofs for absolute mathematical truths—can in principle never be completed. Gödel's result did not show that there could be no complete and unique, transcendentally true mathematics. Gödel, himself, was a Platonist, and assumed that there was such a mathematics. All his proof showed was that, if there is one, it contains an infinity of unprovable truths, truths inherently unestablishable by the techniques of mathematics. Since mere unprovability does not assault the idea of a transcendental mathematical rationality, we will set aside the issue of provability. When we refer to "completeness," we will be talking about transcendental completeness, the issue of whether all mathematical conjectures are either absolutely true or false in the transcendental Platonic realm or whether there are some that are neither.

Although Gödel himself believed in the existence of complete and unique transcendental mathematical truth, his work has led to results that allow us to understand mathematics in a rather different way. To approach this alternative view, let us begin with the most commonly held view of the foundations of mathematics:

- There is some collection of axioms that characterizes set theory.
- For each subdivision of mathematics, there is a collection of definitions that characterizes the concepts of that subdivision in terms of set theory.

Under this characterization of mathematics, the concept of a set assumes an enormous importance. To see why, take group theory as an example. A group is a set with an added structure, given by the definitions that characterize what a group is. Conjectures about group theory are of the form: *For all groups, . . .* or *There is some group. . . .* Whether a given conjecture is true or not will depend on what groups there are. And that in turn, depends on what sets there are.

Since it is the axioms for set theory that provide a precise understanding of what a set is, the precise understanding of the various branches of mathematics depends on the understanding of the axioms of set theory. The set-theoretical axioms that are usually taken for granted are the Zermelo-Fraenkel axioms plus the axiom of choice (called "ZFC"). The following question may be asked about ZFC:

Is ZFC sufficient to characterize the concept of a set in such a way that all natural, basic, and relatively simple conjectures in the various subdivisions of mathematics will be either absolutely true or absolutely false?

Another way of putting this is the following:

Does ZFC plus the definitions that characterize the various branches of mathematics fix a "Platonic" mathematics—a mathematics that is complete, unique, and transcendentally true, at least for all natural, basic, and relatively simple mathematical conjectures?

The answer is no! This has been shown by a number of what have been called "independence results." The proofs establishing these results are of the following form:

- Consider two collections of set-theoretic axioms, A and B, which are both consistent with ZFC and not consequences of ZFC.
- Consider a mathematical proposition P.
- Prove that P is true in a model of ZFC + A, and that P is false in a model of ZFC + B.

Proofs of this form show at least the following:

- The truth of P is *independent* of ZFC.

The most celebrated of the independence results is the Gödel-Cohen result proving the independence of the continuum hypothesis from ZFC. The continuum hypothesis is a conjecture of Cantor's. Cantor had shown that the cardinality (that is, the "size") of the set of rational numbers is the same as the cardinality of the integers. He had also shown that the cardinality of the real numbers is greater than the cardinality of the rational numbers. (The set of real numbers is called the "continuum" since it has the same cardinality as any continuous line segment.) The continuum hypothesis states that there is no set larger than the integers and smaller than the reals. ZFC does not constrain the concept of a set sufficiently so that the continuum hypothesis is either true or false when sets are characterized by ZFC alone.

In recent years, other mathematical propositions in other branches of mathematics have been proven independent of ZFC.

- Whitehead's conjecture, a well-known proposition in the theory of abelian groups, has been shown independent of ZFC for groups of cardinality aleph-one. See Eklof 1976 and Shelah 1974).
- Souslin's hypothesis has also been shown to be independent of ZFC. See Martin and Solovay 1970, Solovay and Tennenbaum 1971, Rudin 1969 and Schoenfield 1975.

In short, there are propositions in algebra and topology that are independent of ZFC.

These are the mathematical results that we will use below in arguing that, if mathematics is transcendental, it is not unique. But, before we begin, let us look at a more basic consequence of these results.

To say that the continuum hypothesis is independent of ZFC is simply to say that both the truth and the falsity of continuum hypothesis is consistent with the ZFC axioms for set theory. But a mathematics in which the continuum hypothesis is true is substantively different from a mathematics in which it is false. Thus, the ZFC axioms for set theory do not determine a complete, unique mathematics: ZFC determines either (*a*) a mathematics which is unique, but incomplete, or (*b*) more than one complete mathematics, for example, one mathematics in which the continuum hypothesis is true and another in which it is false.

Given the independence results for Whitehead's conjecture and Souslin's hypothesis, it follows that the concept of a set as characterized by the ZFC axioms cannot determine a unique and complete algebra or topology: either (*a*) algebra and topology are incomplete (containing conjectures that are neither true nor false—not merely unprovable), or (*b*) there is more than one complete algebra (where every algebraic conjecture is either true or false) and more than one complete topology (where every topological conjecture is either true or false). Given that ZFC defines the only generally accepted conception of a set, if follows that at present there is no generally accepted conception of a set that is sufficient to determine a mathematics that is *both* complete and unique.

We will argue presently that if mathematics is transcendental, it is not unique. In doing so, we will be claiming that the various substantively different algebras and topologies that arise as a result of assuming extensions of ZFC—ZFC + A and ZFC + B—must all have an existence in the "Platonic realm" of mathematical entities. Since these are substantively different varieties of mathematics, it will follow that mathematics, if transcendental, is not unique and therefore that the mere existence of mathematical truths does not provide prima facie evidence for a *unique* transcendental rationality.

Let us proceed:

- Suppose mathematics is transcendental, that is, there is a "Platonic realm" of abstract mathematical objects and a body of absolute mathematical truths concerning those objects.
- We assume that the independence results—those concerning the continuum hypothesis, Whitehead's conjecture, and Souslin's hypothesis—are among the mathematical truths.
- It follows that the entities that those results are *true of* are entities in the Platonic realm.
- Among those entities are two kinds of "setlike" things, namely, the "sets" defined by the ZFC + A axioms (where A is Gödel's axiom of constructibility) and the "sets" defined by ZFC + B (where B is, say, Martin's axiom, in the case of the Whitehead and Souslin conjectures).

We may not want to call these objects transcendentally correct "sets," but whatever we call them, they must exist as real mathematical objects under any Platonistic interpretation of the independence results. For the sake of discussion, let us call them "A-sets" and "B-sets."

- Given that A-sets and B-sets both exist in the Platonic realm of mathematical objects, it follows that the two varieties of mathematics characterized by A-sets and B-sets also exist in that Platonic realm. In other words, the bodies of truths about A-sets and B-sets are truths in the Platonic realm.

So, for example, Whitehead's conjecture is true in the mathematics defined by A-sets and false in the mathematics defined by B-sets. We may not want to dignify these bodies of truths by the name "mathematics," but they must nonetheless exist as bodies of truths about A-sets and B-sets in the Platonic realm of abstract entities. Let us give them the names "A-mathematics" and "B-mathematics." What makes them "mathematics-like" is that they include all of the traditional mathematical truths that are based on ZFC set theory, while also including others that are based on extensions of ZFC. They each include most of the truths most mathematicians care about, but they are not completely identical.

We now have the following situation: From the Platonic interpretation of the independence results, it follows that *A*-sets and *B*-sets both exist as entities of some sort in the Platonic realm, and as a consequence the bodies of truths that we have called *A*-mathematics and *B*-mathematics both exist in that realm, as bodies of truth of some sort or other.

Now a mathematical monotheist may still want to say that mathematics is unique; in particular, there is only one body of algebraic truths, topological truths, etc. He could maintain this by claiming that *A*-sets and *B*-sets are not both really *sets,* and that the body of truths of *A*-mathematics and *B*-mathematics are not both really bodies of truths of *mathematics.* In other words, the mathematical monotheist would be claiming that the word *mathematics* really designates one and only one body of truths with a mathematical subject matter. That is, the word *mathematics* would have to have one and only one objectively correct referent in the Platonic realm.

But Putnam's (1981) critique in *Reason, Truth, and History,* discussed in chapter 15 above, argues that there can be no objectively "correct" reference relation. Given alternative models of set theory, there are corresponding alternative candidates (which are very similar but not identical) for referents of the term *mathematics*. Without an objective reference relation, no single "correct" meaning of *mathematics* can be fixed. Since the alternative versions of algebra and topology are all true, and since there is no way to establish that one of them is *really* mathematics and that the others are not, it follows that there is no unique body of transcendental truths that we can call the one and only *mathematics*. Therefore, the mere existence of mathematical truths does not constitute prima facie evidence for a unique transcendental rationality.

Here we see the profundity of Putnam's results once more. The independence results demonstrate the existence of distinct alternative candidates for the referents of the terms "set" and "mathematics." The claim that the words "set" and "mathematics" have unique correct referents in some abstract Platonic realm requires that there be a unique, objectively correct reference relation to pick out the *real* referent of "set" and the *real* referent of "mathematics." But Putnam showed that no unique, objectively correct reference relation could exist. Taking Putnam's result and the independence results *together*, it follows that there can be no unique body of truths that we can correctly call "mathematics." That result is itself a truth of mathematics, *whatever* plausible referent that term has.

It may seem bizarre at first to think that there is no unique transcendental mathematics. But if what we understand mathematics to be is based on an understanding of what a set is, and if we have more than one way of understanding what a set is, then it should not be surprising that we have more than one form of mathematics.

We started out by contrasting objectivist and experientialist views of mathematics. On the objectivist view, mathematics is claimed to be part of a unique transcendental rationality. We have argued that that is false. It is merely one possible alternative. On that alternative view, mathematics arises out of human experience and is based on modes of human understanding. Interestingly enough, there is at least one very prominent mathematician who holds a view of this sort.

Mac Lane's Views

The most widely held view of the foundations of mathematics is that mathematics is based on set theory plus logic. But that is by no means the only view. One of the most interesting alternative conceptions I have found is in the recent writings of Saunders Mac Lane, one of America's most distinguished mathematicians. Mac Lane (1981, to appear) points out that set-theoretical foundations leave a crucial question unanswered:

Why does mathematics have the branches it has?

As Mac Lane puts it, the "grand set-theoretic foundation"

> does not adequately describe which are the relevant mathematical structures to be built up from the starting point of set theory. A priori from set theory there could be very many such structures, but in fact there are a few which are dominant. . . . Some mathematical structures (natural numbers, rational numbers, real numbers, Euclidean geometry) are intended to be unique but other structures are built to have many different models: group, ring, order and partial order, linear space and module, topological space, measure space. The "Grand Foundation" does not provide any way in which to explain the choice of these concepts. (Mac Lane, 1981, p. 468)

Mac Lane takes this question as central to any account of the foundations of mathematics. Set theory and logic cannot answer this question, nor were they intended to. But the question remains, and it is a nontrivial question. Mac Lane suggests that we look for the answer not merely in terms of mathematical form, but also in terms of the *function* of mathematics in human activity.

> The real nature of these structures does not lie in their often artificial construction from set theory, but in their relation to simple mathematical ideas or to basic human activities . . . mathematics is not the study of intangible Platonic worlds, but of tangible formal systems which have arisen from real human activities. (P. 470)

Mac Lane (1981, p. 463) provides the following list of "human activities, each one of which leads more or less directly to a corresponding portion of mathematics":

counting: to arithmetic and number theory
measuring: to real numbers, calculus, analysis
shaping: to geometry, topology
forming (as in architecture): to symmetry, group theory
estimating: to probability, measure theory, statistics
moving: to mechanics, calculus, dynamics
calculating: to algebra, numerical analysis
proving: to logic
puzzling: to combinatorics, number theory
grouping: to set theory, combinatorics

"These various human activities are by no means completely separate; indeed, they interact with each other in complex ways. . . . The two parts of this table should (and do) fit together by many crosslinks." Mathematical systems, Mac Lane observes, "codify deeper and nonobvious properties of the originating human activities," for example, properties of motion (rotation and translation), symmetry, algebraic manipulations, etc. "In this view, mathematics is formal, but not simply 'formalistic'—since the forms studied in mathematics are derived from human activities and are used to understand those activities" (p. 464).

Mac Lane claims that the branches of mathematics are as they are because they arise from human activities that each have a general schematic structure, made up of various substructures, or "basic ideas." These basic ideas both occur in the structure of the human activities that give rise to the various branches of mathematics. Mathematics describes them and their connections and interrelations in an absolutely rigorous way.

Mac Lane is suggesting that appropriate foundations for mathematics must come from outside mathematics, from the study of basic human activities and the ways we understand them. What he is, in effect, suggesting is that *cognitive* foundations are needed. It has occurred to me, in reading Mac Lane, that certain of these "basic ideas" that recur across the branches of mathematics are akin to what we have been calling "image schemas." The most obvious cases are sets and functions. Sets are akin to CONTAINERS, while functions are akin to nonbranching DIRECTED LINKS (a complex of a LINK and a DIRECTION). In fact, Mac Lane's own suggestion for an alternative foundation for mathematics begins with what he refers to as "arrows," that is, functions.

These are by no means the only basic ideas from mathematics that correspond to the kinesthetic image schemas that arise in the study of linguistic semantics. Here are some others, listed in no special order, with basic mathematical ideas on the left and image schemas (and other basic concepts) akin to them on the right:

entity — ENTITY
correspondence — LINK
continuity — PATH (OF MOTION)
order — DIRECTION
bounded — BOUNDARY (OF CONTAINER)
factor (or decomposition) — PART-WHOLE, SEPARATION
prime — PART (WITH NO OTHER PARTS)
finiteness — DISTINCTNESS, BEGINNING-MIDDLE-END
chain — ITERATION, LINK
equality (of amount) — BALANCE
identity — LINKING OF TWO ENTITIES TO ONE
unit (of measure) — MASS, DISTINCTNESS, BALANCE
cyclic — CIRCLE, DIRECTION
denseness — (LACK OF) SEPARATION
operator — AGENT
operation — CHANGE TO ANOTHER ENTITY
identity element ($1 \times a = a$) — AGENT CAUSING NO CHANGE
zero element ($0 \times a = 0$) — AGENT CAUSING CHANGE TO AGENT ITSELF

What this list is intended to show, probably to the surprise of no one, is that basic ideas in mathematics are understood in terms of basic concepts in cognition, as revealed by empirical studies in cognitive semantics. One may view this as speculation about the psychology of mathematical understanding, which is by no means an uninteresting subject. But, from Mac Lane's point of view, such basic cognitive concepts could be used to provide a foundation for mathematics that could begin to answer the questions he sees as needing answering.

If there were a correspondence between basic ideas of mathematics and kinesthetic image schemas (plus some other basic concepts like AGENT) that we use to comprehend experience, we could then answer not only the question

– How do we understand mathematics?

but also the question

– Why does mathematics "work" in the real world?

Mac Lane points out that the current set-theoretical foundations, which assume that mathematics is about nothing more than an ideal Platonistic realm, leave this a total mystery for such specific questions as the following (Mac Lane 1981, p. 466):

– How is it that the formal calculations by Newtonian mechanics of the motions of the bodies turn out to fit their actual motions?

- Why is it that the formal deduction of the possible groups of symmetry is matched by those groups as they occur in the world?
- How is it that the differential calculus seems to work both for physics and for the economists' problems of local maxima?

The question is not merely why mathematics works, but why it works *for the particular phenomena it works for.* The answer cannot merely be that the real world happens to conform to the Platonic ideal. That would not explain why the *same* branch of mathematics works for economics and physics, but not for the characterization of perceived symmetries. Platonism claims that ideals are realized in particulars. But the Platonic characterization of pure mathematics does not account for *which* ideals are realized in *which* particulars; it does not provide a pairing of applicable branches of mathematics and given phenomena.

Though Mac Lane provides no answer himself, the form of realism that we have been proposing—experientialism—may provide an answer that makes sense, one that makes no reference to Platonic ideals or pure essences. Suppose that mathematics is based on structures within the human conceptual system, structures that people use to comprehend ordinary experiences. Then groups of working scientists who closely observe real world phenomena may, over time, achieve a partial, but consistent understanding of those phenomena in terms of their ordinary, everyday concepts. To the extent that those concepts are also the basis for mathematics, the mystery disappears. If those phenomena can be consistently understood in terms of ordinary basic concepts, then the mathematical ideas corresponding to those concepts will be applicable. This does not tell us why there are regularities in the world. What it does tell us is that regularities that are consistently observed by human beings and understood in terms of certain basic human concepts will be characterizable using a corresponding mathematics.

There is nothing easy or automatic or magical about the success of mathematics in empirical domains. It arises from careful and insightful observation and the achievement by many people over long periods of time of a consistent understanding of the phenomena in ordinary, everyday terms, which are then translated into corresponding mathematical terms. It is the human capacity to understand experience in terms of basic cognitive concepts that is at the heart of the success of mathematics—that and hard work.

Finally, Mac Lane points out, as we have above, that there is no unique foundation for mathematics. He also argues that we shouldn't expect one. The reason, he claims, is that mathematics is about ways of understanding human experience, and there are many ways of understanding experience using different basic ideas of mathematics. To say that there is only one correct foundation for mathematics is to say that there is only one correct means for understanding the world.

> Our thesis as to the nature of mathematics might be formulated thus: Mathematics deals with the construction of a variety of formal models of aspects of the world and of human experience. On the other hand, this means that mathematics is not a direct theory of some underlying Platonic reality, but rather an indirect theory of formal aspects of the world (or of reality, if there is such). On the one hand, our thesis emphasizes that mathematics involves a considerable variety of models. The same experience can be modeled mathematically in more than one way. (Mac Lane 1981, p. 467)

Suppose for a moment that mathematics is the study of *cognitive* structures of the sort listed above—CONTAINERS, LINKS, etc. Mathematics would still be the study of form, but it would not be form that is *opposed to content*; form of that sort would *be conceptual content* in the following respect:

The forms are those that emerge from our bodily functioning in the world and which are used cognitively to comprehend experience.

This is form, but not pure disembodied Platonic form. It is form that emerges from our functioning—with our bodies in the world. Mac Lane's view of mathematics is thus very much like the view of human conceptual systems that has emerged in this book. Mathematics grows out of the structures of everyday experience and is used to understand other experiences. It allows for many modes of understanding. As he puts it, "Mathematics, we hold, deals with multiple models of the world. It is not subsumed in any one big model or by any one grand system of axioms" (Mac Lane 1981, p. 470).

A Richer View of Reason

To give up on a transcendental rationality—a God's eye view of reason—is not to give up on reason and rationality. To grant that reason and rationality are human and no more is to assume responsibility for finding out what human reason is like: Is it fixed or extendable? How much of it is common to all human beings? If there are differences, where do they lie? Where does human reason extend beyond the traditional concerns of logicians?

The concern with the God's eye view of reason has left us with a terribly impoverished view of human reason. The study of human categorization makes that clear. What is needed is a cognitive semantics—an empirically adequate account of what human reason is like. Research on cognitive semantics has barely begun, but there are already such significant results as Fauconnier's (1985) theory of mental spaces. Here are some ideas now being considered:

To the extent that systems like the predicate calculus correctly reflect some aspects of human reason, a corresponding cognitive semantics might be constructed using image schemas, metaphors, and metonymies as follows: Briefly, two basic metaphors are used: CLASSES ARE CONTAINERS and THE PROPER SUBCLASS RELATION IS THE PART-WHOLE RELATION. Putting together suggestions by Langacker (1986) and Fauconnier (1985), we can view the semantics of quantificational logic as involving (*a*) metaphorical mappings based on image schemas and (*b*) a metonymy:

> CONTAINER schemas metaphorically map onto classes.
>
> PART-WHOLE schemas metaphorically map onto subclass relations.
>
> LINEAR-SCALE schemas map onto scales defining relative degrees of quantification (e.g., *all* versus *most* versus *some* versus *none*).

The metonymy in which a TYPICAL CASE stands for the WHOLE CATEGORY characterizes the effects of variable binding. In this metonymy, a representative member of a category stands for the members of the category as a whole.

> IDENTIFICATION schemas metaphorically map into identity relations. In an IDENTIFICATION schema, two entities are directionally linked to a single entity. Directional links are characterized in terms of LINK schemas and DIRECTIONAL ORIENTATION schemas. The two entities metaphorically map onto what Fauconnier calls "roles" (logicians often use the term "descriptions"). The DIRECTIONAL LINKS metaphorically map onto denotation relations.
>
> ENTAILMENT is defined in terms of truth, as we characterized it in chapter 17. Sentence *A* entails sentence *B* if *B* is true in every situation in which *A* is true.

Each of these schemas is understood in terms of direct experience. Each of them has an internal structure, that is, there is a "logic" of each schema. Entailment is characterized in terms of truth, which is, in turn, characterized in terms of understanding. When made fully explicit, the result would be a cognitive semantics that covers the subject matter of predicate calculus. The resulting logic would apply to any subject matter that can be understood in terms of these schemas. Such a logic would cover pretty much the same subject matter as classical logic, but it would have an experientialist rather than an objectivist interpretation. This would avoid Putnam's critique of objectivist semantics. And it would provide an intuitively meaningful semantics.

But this is the least interesting aspect of cognitive semantics. What is more interesting about it is that there are other image schemas, metonymies, and metaphors and that these characterize real modes of human reason that go beyond predicate logic. Sweetser (1984) has argued that the logic of modal operators is to be characterized in terms of metaphors based on FORCE schemas. As we will see in case study 1, there is a logic of anger. There are also logics of other schemas. Carbonell (in press) has studied the logic of the BALANCE schema and has shown that it applies to many etaphorical domains: economics, politics, etc.

In our study of the sources of prototype effects, we discussed a number of metonymic models (stereotypes, ideals, submodels, etc.), all of which are used in reasoning, though not in logic as it is normally understood. These forms of metonymic, or "reference-point," reasoning are real and deserve further study. They include:

Social stereotypes: making quick judgments about people and situations
Typical cases: making inferences from typical to atypical cases, based on knowledge of the typical
Ideals: making judgments of quality and planning for the future
Paragons: making comparisons, using them as a model for behavior
Generators: defining concepts by principles of extension
Submodels: estimating size, doing calculations and making approximations
Salient examples: making judgments of probability

These are normal activities involving the use of human reason. They all involve imaginative projections based on understanding an entire category in terms of some subpart of that category. Because they are imaginative projections, they are outside of objectivist semantics, but within the domain of cognitive semantics.

What makes cognitive semantics interesting is that it opens up the study of human reason to areas that were previously closed off because reason was viewed as being limited to objectivist logic. In cognitive semantics, the study of the general forms of metaphoric, metonymic and image-schematic reason is no longer off-limits. This is human reason, not transcendental reason. It can in principle be characterized with appropriate precision. It can apply to any subject matter that we can understand using image schemas, metaphors, and metonymies. That is an extraordinarily wide range of subject matter. It includes the subject matter of classical logic as a small subpart.

By now, it should be clear what categories reveal about the mind. The study of categorization is a key to the study of reason. By looking at categorization phenomena, we have discovered that reason is embodied and imaginative. Reason is embodied in the sense that the very structures on which reason is based emerge from our bodily experiences. Reason is imaginative in the sense that it makes use of metonymies, metaphors, and a wide variety of image schemas.

Human beings are rational animals. But that does not mean that we have privileged access to a God's eye view of nature or to some transcendental rationality. Our forms of reason are our own—and they are remarkable. They are not independent of our animal nature; rather, they depend crucially on that animal nature. Imagination is not mere fancy, for it is imagination, especially metaphor and metonymy, that transforms the general schemas defined by our animal experience into forms of reason—forms even richer than the objectivists' transcendental reason has been taken to be.

Summary

On the objectivist view, there is an objectively true rationality to the universe that transcends all beings and all experience. According to this view, we reason correctly when our thoughts are in accord with that transcendental rationality. Mathematics is commonly assumed to be transcendentally true—true of pure mathematical entities in some abstract "Platonic" realm. The existence of mathematical truth is commonly taken as a demonstration that rationality is transcendental.

We have argued against this view on the following grounds: Any transcendental rationality must be unique; the objectivist view is that there is one rationality, not many. If mathematics is to be part of such a transcendental rationality, it too must be unique. But what we refer to as *mathematics* cannot be both transcendentally true and unique. The argument is complex. It has the following structure:

- Assume that the independence results are mathematical truths.
- Each independence result for a mathematical conjecture *P* is arrived at by constructing extensions of ZFC set theory. Call them "ZFC + *A*" and "ZFC + *B*."
- Each such extension characterizes a category of entities that must exist as mathematical objects of some sort in the Platonic realm. Call them "*A*-sets" and "*B*-sets."
- Each independence result shows that the mathematical conjecture *P* is true of *A*-sets and false of *B*-sets.

- There is only one body of truths that holds of *A*-sets and another that holds of *B*-sets. Call those bodies of truths "*A*-mathematics" and "*B*-mathematics." They are distinct, since *P* is true in one and false in the other.
- Both *A*-mathematics and *B*-mathematics are "mathematicslike," since both contain all the truths of ZFC-mathematics (the standard, generally accepted variety).
- Thus, the Platonic realm contains more than one plausible referent for the term *mathematics*.
- To say that what we call *mathematics* is both transcendentally true and unique is to say that there is one and only one body of truths in the Platonic realm that *mathematics* correctly refers to.
- For this to be the case, objectively correct reference must be possible.
- But Putnam has demonstrated that it is not possible (see chap. 15).
- Therefore, what we call *mathematics* is not both transcendentally true and unique.
- Consequently, the existence of mathematical truth does not support the claim for the existence of a unique transcendental rationality.

We suggested an alternative view of mathematics as being based on human rationality rather than being transcendental. We then discussed the views along these lines of Saunders Mac Lane. Finally, to make a case for the plausibility of the view that reason is not transcendental but grows out of bodily experience, we suggested tentatively how the mechanisms of cognitive semantics might be employed in characterizing reasoning of the sort discussed in traditional logic.

CHAPTER 21

Overview

We have now completed everything but the case studies. Let us review the territory we have covered. We set out to argue for an experientialist view of reason and against the objectivist view. Here were the first things that had to be shown:

- Meaningful thought is not merely the manipulation of abstract symbols that are meaningless in themselves and get their meaning only by virtue of correspondences to things in the world.
- Reason is not abstract and disembodied, a matter of instantiating some transcendental rationality.
- The mind is thus not simply a "mirror of nature," and concepts are not merely "internal representations of external reality."

The argument is based on the nature of categorization. Most of our concepts concern categories, not individuals (e.g., *dog* as opposed to *Fido*). If the objectivist view were correct, the following would have to be true of categories:

- Conceptual categories would have to be symbolic structures that get their meaning only by virtue of corresponding to objectively existing categories in the world (the world as it actually is or some possible state of the world).
- Categories in the world would have to be characterized objectively, in terms of objective properties of their members and not in any way taking into account the nature of the beings doing the categorization.
- Conceptual categories could only be mental representations of categories in the world.
- Conceptual categories, being mental representations of categories in the world, would have to mirror the structure of categories in the world, excluding anything that was not a reflection of the properties of the category members. Otherwise, they would not be true internal

representations of external reality and could not represent true knowledge of the external world.
- Conceptual categories must thus have the same structure as categories in the world: the structure of classical categories.

The classical theory of categories is thus central to the objectivist view of mind. It views categories as being defined solely by the objectively given properties shared by the members of the category.

Our goal was to show that the classical theory was wrong (1) for conceptual categories, (2) for categories in the world, and (3) for the hypothesized relationship between conceptual categories and categories in the world. Our strategy was to demonstrate three things:

1. Conceptual categories are not merely characterized in terms of objective properties of category members. They differ in two respects:

- Human conceptual categories have properties that are, at least in part, determined by the bodily nature of the people doing the categorizing rather than solely by the properties of the category members.
- Human conceptual categories have properties that are a result of imaginative processes (metaphor, metonymy, mental imagery) that do not mirror nature.

2. The real world cannot be properly understood in terms of the classical theory of categories.

3. The relationship between conceptual categories and real-world categories cannot be as the objectivist view claims.

Part I of the book was dedicated to reviewing the research needed to demonstrate the first item in the list:

- Basic-level category structure reflects the *bodily nature* of the people doing the categorizing, since it depends on gestalt perception and motor movements. Color categories also depend on the nature of the human body, since they are characterized in part by human neurophysiology.
- Basic-level structure is partly characterized by human *imaginative processes*: the capacity to form mental images, to store knowledge at a particular level of categorization, and to communicate. Prototype structure also testifies to imaginative processes of many kinds: metonymy (the capacity to let one thing stand for another for some purpose), the ability to construct and use idealized models, and the ability to extend categories from central to noncentral members using imaginative capacities such as metaphor, metonymy, mythological associations, and image relationships.

Thus, we were able to show that *conceptual* categories do not fit the objectivist view of meaningful thought and reason.

Chapter 12 demonstrated the second item. By showing that biological species do not fit the classical account of categorization, we were able to show that species, which are taken to be categories in the world, are not classical categories.

Chapter 15 demonstrated the third item, namely, that the purported relationship between categories in the world and their "mental representations" could not hold. In other words, mental representations for categories cannot be given meaning via their relationship to categories in the world. This is a consequence of Putnam's theorem together with a fundamental constraint on the nature of meaning.

Having argued against the objectivist view of meaningful thought and reason, we put forth an alternative in chapter 17. On the experientialist account, meaningful thought and reason make use of symbolic structures *which are meaningful to begin with.* Those that are directly meaningful are of two sorts: basic-level concepts and kinesthetic image schemas. Basic-level concepts are directly meaningful because they reflect the structure of our perceptual-motor experience and our capacity to form rich mental images. Kinesthetic image schemas are directly meaningful because they preconceptually structure our experience of functioning in space. They also have an internal basic logic that we believe is sufficient to characterize human reason. With such a dual basis for directly meaningful symbolic structures, indirectly meaningful symbolic structures are built up by imaginative capacities (especially metaphor and metonymy). But despite the fact that we rely centrally on our bodily natures and our imaginative capacities, experientialism has maintained a form of basic realism, since our conceptual structures are strongly (though by no means totally) constrained by reality and by the way we function as an inherent part of reality.

Finally, we defended the experientialist view of reason against objections having to do with three issues—relativism, artificial intelligence, and mathematics:

- Relativism is commonly and falsely identified with total relativism. Experiential realism permits a form of relativism, though one that is not at all like total relativism. Chapter 18 surveyed the forms of relativism and showed that there is not only nothing wrong with the relativism that we propose, and that there is positive evidence for it.
- Artificial intelligence is often given an objectivist interpretation, especially by philosophers. If accepted, that interpretation would place the field at odds with the experientialist view of reason. We ob-

served in chapter 19 that such an interpretation of the endeavor of artificial intelligence is not only unnecessary but in fact goes against the practice of many researchers in the field. The study of artificial intelligence does not in any way conflict with an experientialist view of reason. It is only an interpretation of artificial intelligence in terms of objectivist philosophy that is in conflict with our views.

- The very existence of mathematical truth is sometimes cited in support of the existence of a single transcendental rationality that we can have access to. We argued in chapter 20 that if mathematics is assumed to be transcendentally true, it cannot be unique. For example, there are versions of algebra and topology that differ substantively from one another because they are based on different models of set theory. They are all transcendentally true, not absolutely, but relative to what is taken to be a "set." Thus, the mere existence of mathematical truths cannot provide evidence of a unique transcendental rationality.It is at least as plausible that mathematics arises out of *human* rational structures.

We have argued that the objectivist views on meaningful thought and reason are incorrect on both empirical and logical grounds. No doubt, defenses of objectivism will be forthcoming. What is important is that objectivist views can no longer be taken for granted as being obviously true and beyond question. The questions have been asked and an alternative has been proposed. It is an alternative that opens up further inquiry into the nature of the human mind. The value of opening up such a path of inquiry can only be shown through detailed case studies of phenomena that reveal something about the nature of human reason.

BOOK II

Case Studies

Introduction

We have now completed our general overview. It is time to get down to the nitty-gritty. We have spoken about cognitive models in very general terms. It is time to give some idea of what they look like in detail: to show what propositional models, metaphoric models, image-schematic, and symbolic models look like up close. We have argued that an experientialist approach is needed so that phenomena involving metaphor, metonymy, image schemas, and radial categories can be adequately described. It is time to show what such an approach can do.

I will be presenting three case studies. Since I am a linguist, they will all involve language, but to show that the method of analysis is not limited to a single subject matter, these studies will cover three different domains—concepts, words, and grammatical constructions. Each of the case studies takes up a recalcitrant area of study, an area where classical techniques of analysis could not account adequately for the phenomena. The case studies are, therefore, intended not just as examples of how the cognitive models approach works. They are each of interest in their own right.

The first is the study of a concept—anger. It is taken from the domain of emotions for a number of reasons. Emotions are often viewed as feelings devoid of any conceptual content. But in addition to feeling what we feel, we also impose an understanding on what it is that we feel. When we act on our emotions, we act not only on the basis of feeling but also on the basis of that understanding. Emotional concepts are thus very clear examples of concepts that are abstract and yet have an obvious basis in bodily experience. Anger, as we shall see, is a particularly rich example: it has a very elaborate conceptual structure. Anger also has a very rich category structure, in that there are many kinds of anger, from righteous indignation, to wrath, to cold anger, and the like.

In the second study, we will consider a single word—*over*. *Over* is basically a preposition, but it can also function as an adverb, a prefix, a particle, and a predicate adjective. It has more than a hundred identifiable senses, which are linked to one another by family resemblances. Brugman (1981) has shown that the senses of *over* form a category with a radial structure, and we will be reviewing a portion of her analysis, as well as extending it to display the details of the relationships among the senses. Prepositions in English, as well as in other languages, have traditionally been difficult to describe, largely because of their proliferation of senses. It has only been through the advent of prototype theory that we have begun to make sense of the semantics of prepositions. Of course, prepositions are not the only kinds of words that have a multitude of related meanings. Most words are like that. Brugman's hypothesis ought to be extendable to cases of polysemy (multiple meaning) in general: polysemy appears to be a special case of prototype-based categorization, where the senses of the word are the members of a category. The application of prototype theory to the study of word meaning brings order into an area where before there was only chaos.

The third, and longest, case study concerns grammatical constructions. It demonstrates that grammatical constructions form categories with radial structures. Within contemporary linguistic theory, this is a very controversial claim. The case study will focus on an extremely complex and well-studied area of English syntax—*there*-constructions. A great deal is known about these constructions. Yet they have previously resisted all attempts at an adequate analysis. We will try to show that they can be analyzed adequately if we make three assumptions.

- Grammatical constructions are pairings of form and meaning.
- The structural aspect of meaning is describable using cognitive models.
- Grammatical constructions form radially structured categories.

The third case study is much longer than the other two. It has to be that way because of the current state of the theory of grammar. There are a great many theories of grammar now available, and almost all of them are based on the classical theory of categorization. Most of these theories are complex and have many kinds of descriptive devices available. Because of this, there appears to be only one way to present a thorough case for the necessity of cognitive models and prototype theory in grammar: One must take a phenomenon with a very large amount of recalcitrant data, show how to make sense of that data, state all the relevant generalizations, and show why those generalizations cannot be stated in other theories. It is a long and difficult enterprise, but it is the only way I know of to make the case in a responsible manner.

Each of these case studies demonstrates the reality of radially structured categories. As we have seen above, radial structure is not the only kind of category structure that yields prototype effects. But it is the kind of structure that departs most radically from classical theories:

First, there is no single representation for a radially structured category. One must provide a representation for the central subcategory and representations for each of the noncentral subcategories, since there are no general principles that can predict the noncentral cases from the central case.

Second, a theory of *motivation* is required, since the noncentral subcategories are neither arbitrary nor predictable from the central subcategory.

Third, a theory of the types of links between the central and noncentral subcategories is required.

Fourth, when the nature of these links is spelled out in detail, it turns out that an adequate account of these links requires an experientialist theory of meaningful thought and reason and all the kinds of cognitive models that we have mentioned above: propositional, metaphoric, metonymic, and image-schematic.

Since radially structured categories differ most radically from classical categories, it is important to have detailed case studies that document their existence.

Grand theories don't count for much, unless they are substantiated down to the minutest details. One of the most important things that cognitive linguistics has to offer to other branches of cognitive science is a methodology for studying linguistic and conceptual structure in very great detail—a level of detail much finer and richer than can be approached at present by other techniques. It is in that spirit that these case studies are presented.

CASE STUDY 1

Anger

The Conceptualization of Feeling

Emotions are often considered to be feelings alone, and as such they are viewed as being devoid of conceptual content. As a result, the study of emotions is usually not taken seriously by students of semantics and conceptual structure. A topic such as the logic of emotions would seem on this view to be a contradiction in terms, since emotions, being devoid of conceptual content, would give rise to no inferences at all, or at least none of any interest.

I would like to argue that the opposite is true, that emotions have an extremely complex conceptual structure, which gives rise to a wide variety of nontrivial inferences. The work I will be presenting is based on joint research by myself and Zoltán Kövecses. Kövecses had suggested that the conceptual structure of emotions could be studied in detail using techniques devised by Mark Johnson and myself (Lakoff and Johnson 1980) for the systematic investigation of expressions that are understood metaphorically. English has an extremely large range of such expressions. What we set out to do was to study them systematically to see if any coherent conceptual structure emerged.

At first glance, the conventional expressions used to talk about anger seem so diverse that finding any coherent system would seem impossible. For example, if we look up *anger* in, say, *Roget's University Thesaurus*, we find about three hundred entries, most of which have something or other to do with anger, but the thesaurus doesn't tell us exactly what. Many of these are idioms, and they seem too diverse to reflect any coherent cognitive model. Here are some sample sentences using such idioms:

- He *lost his cool.*
- She was *looking daggers* at me.
- I almost *burst a blood vessel.*

- He was *foaming at the mouth.*
- You're beginning to *get to* me.
- You make my *blood boil.*
- He's *wrestling* with his anger.
- Watch out! He's *on a short fuse.*
- He's just *letting off steam.*
- Don't *get a hernia!*
- Try to *keep a grip on yourself.*
- Don't *fly off the handle.*
- When I told him, he *blew up.*
- He *channeled* his anger into something constructive.
- He was *red with anger.*
- He was *blue in the face.*
- He *appeased* his anger.
- He was *doing a slow burn.*
- He *suppressed* his anger.
- She kept *bugging* me.
- When I told my mother, *she had a cow.*

What do these expressions have to do with anger, and what do they have to do with each other? We will be arguing that they are not random. When we look at inferences among these expressions, it becomes clear that there must be a systematic structure of some kind. We know, for example, that someone who is foaming at the mouth has lost his cool. We know that someone who is looking daggers at you is likely to be doing a slow burn or be on a short fuse. We know that someone whose blood is boiling has not had his anger appeased. We know that someone who has channeled his anger into something constructive has not had a cow. How do we know these things? Is it just that each idiom has a literal meaning and the inferences are based on the literal meanings? Or is there something more going on? What we will try to show is that there is a coherent conceptual organization underlying all these expressions and that much of it is metaphorical and metonymical in nature.

Metaphor and Metonymy

The analysis we are proposing begins with the common folk theory of the physiological effects of anger:

The physiological effects of anger are increased body heat, increased internal pressure (blood pressure, muscular pressure), agitation, and interference with accurate perception.

As anger increases, its physiological effects increase.

There is a limit beyond which the physiological effects of anger impair normal functioning.

We use this folk theory in large measure to tell when someone is angry on the basis of their appearance—as well as to signal anger or hide it. In doing this, we make use of a general metonymic principle:

The physiological effects of an emotion stand for the emotion.

Given this principle, the folk theory given above yields a system of metonymies for anger:

Body heat

- Don't get *hot under the collar.*
- Billy's a *hothead.*
- They were having a *heated argument.*
- When the cop gave her a ticket, she got all *hot and bothered* and started cursing.

Internal pressure

- Don't get a *hernia!*
- When I found out, I almost *burst a blood vessel.*
- He almost had a *hemorrhage.*

Increased body heat and/or blood pressure is assumed to cause redness in the face and neck area, and such redness can also metonymically indicate anger.

Redness in face and neck area

- She was *scarlet with rage.*
- He got *red with anger.*
- He was *flushed with anger.*

Agitation

- She was *shaking* with anger.
- I was *hopping mad.*
- He was *quivering with rage.*
- He's *all worked up.*
- There's no need to get so *excited* about it!
- She's *all wrought up.*
- You look *upset.*

Interference with accurate perception

- She was *blind with rage.*
- I was beginning to *see red.*
- I was so mad I *couldn't see straight.*

Each of these expressions indicate the presence of anger via its supposed physiological effects.

The folk theory of physiological effects, especially the part that emphasizes HEAT, forms the basis of the most general metaphor for anger: ANGER IS HEAT. There are two versions of this metaphor, one where the heat is applied to fluids, the other where it is applied to solids. When it is applied to fluids, we get: ANGER IS THE HEAT OF A FLUID IN A CONTAINER. The specific motivation for this consists of the HEAT, INTERNAL PRESSURE, and AGITATION parts of the folk theory. When ANGER IS HEAT is applied to solids, we get the version ANGER IS FIRE, which is motivated by the HEAT and REDNESS aspects of the folk theory of physiological effects.

As we will see shortly, the fluid version is much more highly elaborated. The reason for this, we surmise, is that in our overall conceptual system we have the general metaphor:

The body is a container for the emotions.

- He was *filled* with anger.
- She couldn't *contain* her joy.
- She was *brimming* with rage.
- Try to get your anger *out of your system.*

The ANGER IS HEAT metaphor, when applied to fluids, combines with the metaphor THE BODY IS A CONTAINER FOR THE EMOTIONS to yield the central metaphor of the system:

Anger is the heat of a fluid in a container.

- You make my *blood boil.*
- *Simmer* down!
- I had reached the *boiling point.*
- Let him *stew.*

A historically derived instance of this metaphor is:

- She was *seething with rage.*

Although most speakers do not now use *seethe* to indicate physical boiling, the boiling image is still there when *seethe* is used to indicate anger. Similarly, *pissed off* is used only to refer to anger, not to the hot liquid under pressure in the bladder. Still, the effectiveness of the expression seems to depend on such an image.

When there is no heat, the liquid is cool and calm. In the central metaphor, cool and calmness corresponds to lack of anger.

- Keep *cool.*
- Stay *calm.*

As we will see shortly, the central metaphor is an extremely productive one. There are two ways in which a conceptual metaphor can be productive. The first is lexical. The words and fixed expressions of a language can *code*, that is, be used to express aspects of, a given conceptual metaphor to a greater or lesser extent. The number of conventional linguistic expressions that code a given conceptual metaphor is one measure of the productivity of the metaphor. In addition, the words and fixed expressions of a language can *elaborate* the conceptual metaphor. For example, a stew is a special case in which there is a hot fluid in a container. It is something that continues at a given level of heat for a long time. This special case can be used to elaborate the central metaphor. "Stewing" indicates the continuance of anger over a long period. Another special case is "simmer," which indicates a low boil. This can be used to indicate a lowering of the intensity of anger. Although both of these are cooking terms, cooking per se plays no metaphorical role in these cases. It just happens to be a case where there is a hot fluid in a container. This is typical of lexical elaborations.

Let us refer to the HEAT OF FLUID IN A CONTAINER as the source domain of the central metaphor and to ANGER as the target domain. We usually have extensive knowledge about source domains. A second way in which a conceptual metaphor can be productive is that it can carry over details of that knowledge from the source domain to the target domain. We will refer to such carryovers as metaphorical entailments. Such entailments are part of our conceptual system. They constitute elaborations of conceptual metaphors. The central metaphor has a rich system of metaphorical entailments. For example, one thing we know about hot fluids is that, when they start to boil, the fluid goes upward. This gives rise to the entailment:

When the intensity of anger increases, the fluid rises.

- His pent-up anger *welled up* inside him.
- She could feel her *gorge rising.*
- We got a *rise* out of him.
- My anger kept *building up* inside me.
- Pretty soon I was in a *towering rage.*

We also know that intense heat produces steam and creates pressure on the container. This yields the metaphorical entailments:

Intense anger produces steam.

- – She got *all steamed up.*
- – Billy's just *blowing off steam.*
- – I was *fuming.*

Intense anger produces pressure on the container.

- – He was *bursting with anger.*
- – I could barely *contain* my rage.
- – I could barely *keep it in* anymore.

A variant of this involves keeping the pressure back:

- – I *suppressed* my anger.
- – He *turned his anger inward.*
- – He managed to keep his anger *bottled up* inside him.
- – He was *blue in the face.*

When the pressure on the container becomes too high, the container explodes. This yields the entailment:

When anger becomes too intense, the person explodes.

- – When I told him, he just *exploded.*
- – She *blew up* at me.
- – We won't tolerate any more of your *outbursts.*

This can be elaborated, using special cases:

Pistons: He *blew a gasket.*
Volcanos: She *erupted.*
Electricity: I *blew a fuse.*
Explosives: She's *on a short fuse.*
Bombs: That really *set me off.*

In an explosion, parts of the container go up in the air.

When a person explodes, parts of him go up in the air.

- – I *blew my stack.*
- – I *blew my top.*
- – She *flipped her lid.*
- – He *hit the ceiling.*
- – I *went through the roof.*

When something explodes, what was inside it comes out.

When a person explodes, what was inside him comes out.

– His anger finally *came out.*
– Smoke was *pouring out of his ears.*

This can be elaborated in terms of animals giving birth, where something that was inside causing pressure bursts out:

– She was *having kittens.*
– My mother will *have a cow* when I tell her.

Let us now turn to the question of what issues the central metaphor addresses and what kind of ontology of anger it reveals. The central metaphor focuses on the fact that anger can be intense, that it can lead to a loss of control, and that a loss of control can be dangerous. Let us begin with intensity. Anger is conceptualized as a mass, and takes the grammar of mass nouns, as opposed to count nouns:

Thus, you can say

How much anger has he got in him?

but not

*How many angers does he have in him?

Anger thus has the ontology of a mass entity, that is, it has a scale indicating its amount, it exists when the amount is greater than zero, and it goes out of existence when the amount falls to zero. In the central metaphor, the scale indicating the amount of anger is the heat scale. But, as the central metaphor indicates, the anger scale is not open-ended; it has a limit. Just as a hot fluid in a closed container can only take so much heat before it explodes, so we conceptualize the anger scale as having a limit point. We can only bear so much anger before we explode, that is, lose control. This has its correlates in our folk theory of physiological effects. As anger gets more intense the physiological effects increase and those increases interfere with our normal functioning. Body heat, blood pressure, agitation, and interference with perception cannot increase without limit before our ability to function normally becomes seriously impaired, and we lose control over our functioning. In the folk model of anger, loss of control is dangerous, both to the angry person and to those around him. In the central metaphor, the danger of loss of control is understood as the danger of explosion.

The structural aspect of a conceptual metaphor consists of a set of correspondences between a source domain and a target domain. These correspondences can be factored into two types: ontological and epistemic. Ontological correspondences are correspondences between the entities in the source domain and the corresponding entities in the target domain. For example, the container in the source domain corresponds to the body in the target domain. Epistemic correspondences are correspondences between knowledge about the source domain and corresponding knowledge about the target domain. We can schematize these correspondences between the FLUID domain and the ANGER domain as follows:

Source: HEAT OF FLUID IN CONTAINER   Target: ANGER

Ontological correspondences:

- The container is the body.
- The heat of fluid is the anger.
- The heat scale is the anger scale, with end points zero and limit.
- Container heat is body heat.
- Pressure in container is internal pressure in the body.
- Agitation of fluid and container is physical agitation.
- The limit of the container's capacity to withstand pressure caused by heat is the limit on the anger scale.
- Explosion is loss of control.
- Danger of explosion is danger of loss of control.
- Coolness in the fluid is lack of anger.
- Calmness of the fluid is lack of agitation.

Epistemic correspondences:

Source: The effect of intense fluid heat is container heat, internal pressure, and agitation.
Target: The effect of intense anger is body heat, internal pressure, and agitation.

Source: When the fluid is heated past a certain limit, pressure increases to the point at which the container explodes.
Target: When anger increases past a certain limit, pressure increases to the point at which the person loses control.

Source: An explosion is damaging to the container and dangerous to bystanders.
Target: A loss of control is damaging to an angry person and dangerous to other people.

Source: An explosion may be prevented by the application of sufficient force and energy to keep the fluid in.
Target: A loss of control may be prevented by the application of sufficient force and energy to keep the anger in.

Source: It is sometimes possible to control the release of heated fluid for either destructive or constructive purposes; this has the effect of lowering the level of heat and pressure.

Target: It is sometimes possible to control the release of anger for either destructive or constructive purposes; this has the effect of lowering the level of anger and internal pressure.

The latter case defines an elaboration of the entailment WHEN A PERSON EXPLODES, WHAT WAS INSIDE HIM COMES OUT:

Anger can be let out under control.

- He *let out* his anger.
- I *gave vent* to my anger.
- *Channel* your anger into something constructive.
- He *took out* his anger on me.

So far, we have seen that the folk theory of physiological reactions provides the basis for the central metaphor and that the central metaphor characterizes detailed correspondences between the source domain and the target domain—correspondences concerning both ontology and knowledge.

At this point, our analysis enables us to see why various relationships among idioms hold. We can see why someone who is in a towering rage has not kept his cool, why someone who is stewing may have contained his anger but has not got it out of his system, why someone who has suppressed his anger has not yet erupted, and why someone who has channeled his anger into something constructive has not had a cow.

Let us now turn to the case where the general ANGER IS HEAT metaphor is applied to solids:

Anger is fire.

- Those are *inflammatory* remarks.
- She was *doing a slow burn.*
- He was *breathing fire.*
- Your insincere apology just *added fuel to the fire.*
- After the argument, Dave was *smoldering* for days.
- That *kindled my ire.*
- Boy, am I *burned up!*
- He was *consumed* by his anger.

This metaphor highlights the cause of anger (kindle, inflame), the intensity and duration (smoldering, slow burn, burned up), the danger to others (breathing fire), and the damage to the angry person (consumed). The correspondences in ontology are as follows:

Source: FIRE Target: ANGER

- The fire is anger.
- The thing burning is the angry person.
- The cause of the fire is the cause of the anger.
- The intensity of the fire is the intensity of the anger.
- The physical damage to the thing burning is mental damage to the angry person.
- The capacity of the thing burning to serve its normal function is the capacity of the angry person to function normally.
- An object at the point of being consumed by fire corresponds to a person whose anger is at the limit.
- The danger of the fire to things nearby is danger of the anger to other people.

The correspondences in knowledge are:

Source: Things can burn at low intensity for a long time and then burst into flame.
Target: People can be angry at a low intensity for a long time and then suddenly become extremely angry.

Source: Fires are dangerous to things nearby.
Target: Angry people are dangerous to other people.

Source: Things consumed by fire cannot serve their normal function.
Target: At the limit of the anger scale, people cannot function normally.

Putting together what we've done so far, we can see why someone who is doing a slow burn hasn't hit the ceiling yet, why someone whose anger is bottled up is not breathing fire, why someone who is consumed by anger probably can't see straight, and why adding fuel to the fire might just cause the person you're talking to to have kittens.

The Other Principal Metaphors

As we have seen, the ANGER IS HEAT metaphor is based on the folk theory of the physiological effects of anger, according to which increased body heat is a major effect of anger. That folk theory also maintains that agitation is an important effect. Agitation is also an important part of our folk model of insanity. According to this view, people who are insane are unduly agitated—they go wild, start raving, flail their arms, foam at the mouth, etc. Correspondingly, these physiological effects can stand, metonymically, for insanity. One can indicate that someone is insane by describing him as foaming at the mouth, raving, going wild, etc.

The overlap between the folk theories of the effects of anger and the effects of insanity provides a basis for the metaphor:

Anger is insanity.

- I just touched him, and he *went crazy.*
- You're *driving me nuts!*
- When the umpire called him out on strikes, he *went bananas.*
- One more complaint and I'll *go berserk.*
- He got so angry, he *went out of his mind.*
- When he gets angry, he *goes bonkers.*
- She went into an *insane rage.*
- If anything else goes wrong, I'll *get hysterical.*

Perhaps the most common conventional expression for anger came into English historically as a result of this metaphor:

- I'm *mad!*

Because of this metaphorical link between insanity and anger, expressions that indicate insane behavior can also indicate angry behavior. Given the metonymy INSANE BEHAVIOR STANDS FOR INSANITY and the metaphor ANGER IS INSANITY, we get the metaphorical metonymy:

Insane behavior stands for anger.

- When my mother finds out, she'll *have a fit.*
- When the ump threw him out of the game, Billy started *foaming at the mouth.*
- He's *fit to be tied.*
- He's about to *throw a tantrum.*

Violent behavior indicative of frustration is viewed as a form of insane behavior. According to our folk model of anger, people who can neither control nor relieve the pressure of anger engage in violent frustrated behavior. This folk model is the basis for the metonymy:

Violent frustrated behavior stands for anger.

- He's *tearing his hair out!*
- If one more thing goes wrong, I'll start *banging my head against the wall.*
- The loud music next door has got him *climbing the walls!*
- She's been *slamming doors all morning.*

The ANGER IS INSANITY metaphor has the following correspondences:

Source: INSANITY Target: ANGER

- The cause of insanity is the cause of anger.
- Becoming insane is passing the limit point on the anger scale.
- Insane behavior is angry behavior.

Source: An insane person cannot function normally.
Target: A person who is angry beyond the limit point cannot function normally.

Source: An insane person is dangerous to others.
Target: A person who is angry beyond the limit point is dangerous to others.

At this point, we can see a generalization. Emotional effects are understood as physical effects. Anger is understood as a form of energy. According to our folk understanding of physics, when enough input energy is applied to a body, the body begins to produce output energy. Thus, the cause of anger is viewed as input energy that produces internal heat (output energy). Moreover, the internal heat can function as input energy, producing various forms of output energy: steam, pressure, externally radiating heat, and agitation. Such output energy (the angry behavior) is viewed as dangerous to others. In the insanity metaphor, insanity is understood as a highly energized state, with insane behavior as a form of energy output.

All in all, anger is understood in our folk model as a negative emotion. It produces undesirable physiological reactions, leads to an inability to function normally, and is dangerous to others. The angry person, recognizing this danger, views his anger as an opponent.

Anger is an opponent (in a struggle).

- I'm *struggling* with my anger.
- He was *battling* his anger.
- She *fought back* her anger.
- You need to *subdue* your anger.
- I've been *wrestling* with my anger all day.
- I was *seized* by anger.
- I'm finally *coming to grips with* my anger.
- He *lost control over* his anger.
- Anger *took control* of him.
- He *surrendered* to his anger.
- He *yielded* to his anger.
- I was *overcome* by anger.
- Her anger has been *appeased.*

The ANGER IS AN OPPONENT metaphor is constituted by the following correspondences:

Source: STRUGGLE Target: ANGER

- The opponent is anger.
- Winning is controlling anger.
- Losing is having anger control you.
- Surrender is allowing anger to take control of you.
- The pool of resources needed for winning is the energy needed to control anger.

One thing that is left out of this account so far is what constitutes "appeasement." To appease an opponent is to give in to his demands. This suggests that anger has demands. We will address the question of what these demands are below.

The OPPONENT metaphor focuses on the issue of control and the danger of loss of control to the angry person himself. There is another metaphor that focuses on the issue of control, but its main aspect is the danger to others. It is a very widespread metaphor in Western culture, namely, PASSIONS ARE BEASTS INSIDE A PERSON. According to this metaphor, there is a part of each person that is a wild animal. Civilized people are supposed to keep that part of them private, that is, they are supposed to keep the animal inside them. In the metaphor, loss of control is equivalent to the animal getting loose. And the behavior of a person who has lost control is the behavior of a wild animal. There are versions of this metaphor for the various passions—desire, anger, etc. In the case of anger, the beast presents a danger to other people.

Anger is a dangerous animal.

- He has a *ferocious* temper.
- He has a *fierce* temper.
- It's dangerous to *arouse* his anger.
- That *awakened* my ire.
- His anger *grew.*
- He has a *monstrous* temper.
- He *unleashed* his anger.
- Don't let your anger *get out of hand.*
- He *lost his grip* on his anger.
- His anger is *insatiable.*

An example that draws on both the FIRE and DANGEROUS ANIMAL metaphors is:

– He was *breathing fire.*

The image here is of a dragon, a dangerous animal that can devour you with fire.

The DANGEROUS ANIMAL metaphor portrays anger as a sleeping animal that it is dangerous to awaken, as something that can grow and thereby become dangerous, as something that has to be held back, and as something with a dangerous appetite. Here are the correspondences that constitute the metaphor.

Source: DANGEROUS ANIMAL Target: ANGER

- The dangerous animal is the anger.
- The animal's getting loose is loss of control of anger.
- The owner of the dangerous animal is the angry person.
- The sleeping animal is anger near the zero level.
- Being awake for the animal is anger near the limit.

Source: It is dangerous for a dangerous animal to be loose.
Target: It is dangerous for a person's anger to be out of control.

Source: A dangerous animal is safe when it is sleeping and dangerous when it is awake.
Target: Anger is safe near the zero level and dangerous near the limit.

Source: A dangerous animal is safe when it is very small and dangerous when it is grown.
Target: Anger is safe near the zero level and dangerous near the limit.

Source: It is the responsibility of a dangerous animal's owner to keep it under control.
Target: It is the responsibility of an angry person to keep his anger under control.

Source: It requires a lot of energy to control a dangerous animal.
Target: It requires a lot of energy to control one's anger.

There is another class of expressions that, as far as we can tell, are instances of the same metaphor. These are cases in which angry behavior is described in terms of aggressive animal behavior.

Angry behavior is aggressive animal behavior.

- He was *bristling* with anger.
- That *got my hackles up.*
- He began to *bare his teeth.*
- That *ruffled her feathers.*

- She was *bridling with anger.*
- Don't *snap* at me!
- I was *growling* with rage.
- He started *snarling.*
- Don't *bite my head off!*
- Why did you *jump down my throat*?

Perhaps the best way to account for these cases would be to extend the ontological correspondences of the ANGER IS A DANGEROUS ANIMAL metaphor to include:

- The aggressive behavior of the dangerous animal is angry behavior.

If we do this, we can account naturally for the fact that these expressions indicate anger. They would do so via a combination of metaphor and metonymy, in which the aggressive behavior metaphorically corresponds to angry behavior, which in turn metonymically stands for anger. For example, the snarling of the animal corresponds to the angry verbal behavior of the person, which in turn indicates the presence of anger.

Aggressive verbal behavior is a common form of angry behavior, as *snap, growl, snarl*, etc. indicate. We can see this in a number of cases outside of the animal domain:

Aggressive verbal behavior stands for anger.

- She gave him a *tongue-lashing.*
- I really *chewed* him *out* good!

Other forms of aggressive behavior can also stand metonymically for anger, especially aggressive visual behavior:

Aggressive visual behavior stands for anger.

- She was *looking daggers* at me.
- He *gave me a dirty look.*
- If *looks could kill*, . . .
- He was *glowering* at me.

All these metonymic expressions can be used to indicate anger.

As in the case of the OPPONENT metaphor, our analysis of the DANGEROUS ANIMAL metaphor leaves an expression unaccounted for—"insatiable." This expression indicates that the animal has an appetite. This "appetite" seems to correspond to the "demands" in the OPPONENT metaphor, as can be seen from the fact that the following sentences entail each other:

- Harry's anger is *insatiable.*
- Harry's anger cannot be *appeased.*

To see what it is that anger demands and has an appetite for, let us turn to expressions that indicate causes of anger. Perhaps the most common group of expressions that indicate anger consists of conventionalized forms of annoyance: minor pains, burdens placed on domestic animals, etc. Thus we have the metaphor:

The cause of anger is a physical annoyance.

- Don't be *a pain in the ass.*
- Get *off my back!*
- You don't have to *ride me so hard.*
- You're *getting under my skin.*
- He's *a pain in the neck.*
- Don't *be a pest!*

These forms of annoyance involve an offender and a victim. The offender is at fault. The victim, who is innocent, is the one who gets angry.

There is another set of conventionalized expressions used to speak of, or to, people who are in the process of making someone angry. These are expressions of territoriality, in which the cause of anger is viewed as a trespasser.

Causing anger is trespassing.

- You're beginning to *get to* me.
- Get *out of here*!
- Get *out of my sight*!
- *Leave me alone*!
- This is where I *draw the line*!
- Don't *step on my toes*!

Again, there is an offender (the cause of anger) and a victim (the person who is getting angry). The offense seems to constitute some sort of injustice. This is reflected in the conventional wisdom:

- Don't get *mad*, get *even*!

In order for this saying to make sense, there has to be some connection between anger and retribution. Getting even is equivalent to balancing the scales of justice. The saying assumes a model in which injustice leads to anger and retribution can alleviate or prevent anger. In short, what anger "demands" and has an "appetite" for is revenge. This is why warnings and threats can count as angry behavior:

- If I get mad, watch out!
- Don't get me angry, or you'll be sorry.

The angry behavior is, in itself, viewed as a form of retribution.

We are now in a position to make sense of another metaphor for anger:

Anger is a burden.

- Unburdening himself of his anger gave him a sense of *relief.*
- After I lost my temper, I felt *lighter.*
- He *carries* his anger around with him.
- He *has a chip on his shoulder.*
- You'll feel better if you *get it off your chest.*

In English, it is common for responsibilities to be metaphorized as burdens. There are two kinds of responsibilities involved in the folk model of anger that has emerged so far. The first is a responsibility to control one's anger. In cases of extreme anger, this may place a considerable burden on one's "inner resources." The second comes from the model of retributive justice that is built into our concept of anger; it is the responsibility to seek vengeance. What is particularly interesting is that these two responsibilities are in conflict in the case of angry retribution: If you take out your anger on someone, you are not meeting your responsibility to control your anger, and if you don't take out your anger on someone, you are not meeting your responsibility to provide retribution. The slogan "Don't get mad, get even!" offers one way out: retribution without anger. The human potential movement provides another way out by suggesting that letting your anger out is okay. But the fact is that neither of these solutions is the cultural norm. It should also be mentioned in passing that the human potential movement's way of dealing with anger by sanctioning its release is not all that revolutionary. It assumes almost all of our standard folk model and metaphorical understanding and makes one change: sanctioning the "release."

Some Minor Metaphors

There are a few very general metaphors that apply to anger as well as to many other things, and these are commonly used in comprehending and speaking about anger. The first we will discuss has to do with existence. Existence is commonly understood in terms of physical presence. You are typically aware of something's presence if it is nearby and you can see it. This is the basis for the metaphor:

Existence is presence.

- His anger *went away.*
- His anger eventually *came back.*
- My anger *lingered on* for days.
- She couldn't *get rid of* her anger.
- After a while, her anger just *vanished.*
- My anger slowly began to *dissipate.*
- When he saw her smile, his anger *disappeared.*

In the case of emotions, existence is often conceived of as location in a bounded space. Here the emotion is the bounded space and it exists when the person is in that space:

Emotions are bounded spaces.

- She flew *into* a rage.
- She was *in* an angry mood.
- He was *in* a state of anger.
- I am not easily roused *to* anger.

These cases are relatively independent of the rest of the anger system and are included here merely for completeness.

The Prototypical Scenario

The metaphors and metonymies that we have investigated so far converge on a certain prototypical cognitive model of anger. It is not the only model of anger we have; in fact, there are quite a few. But as we shall see, all of the others can be characterized as minimal variants of the model that the metaphors converge on. The model has a temporal dimension and can be conceived of as a scenario with a number of stages. We will call this the "prototypical scenario"; it is similar to what De Sousa (1980) calls the "paradigm scenario." We will be referring to the person who gets angry as *S*, short for the self.

Stage 1: Offending event

There is an offending event that displeases *S*. There is a wrongdoer who intentionally does something directly to *S*. The wrongdoer is at fault and *S* is innocent. The offending event constitutes an injustice and produces anger in *S*. The scales of justice can only be balanced by some act of retribution. That is, the intensity of retribution must be roughly equal to the intensity of offense. *S* has the responsibility to perform such an act of retribution.

Stage 2: Anger

Associated with the entity anger is a scale that measures its intensity. As the intensity of anger increases, *S* experiences physiological effects: increase in body heat, internal pressure, and physical agitation. As the anger gets very intense, it exerts a force upon *S* to perform an act of retribution. Because acts of retribution are dangerous and/or socially unacceptable, *S* has a responsibility to control his anger. Moreover, loss of control is damaging to *S*'s own well-being, which is another motivation for controlling anger.

Stage 3: Attempt at control

S attempts to control his anger.

Stage 4: Loss of control

Each person has a certain tolerance for controlling anger. That tolerance can be viewed as the limit point on the anger scale. When the intensity of anger goes beyond that limit, *S* can no longer control his anger. *S* exhibits angry behavior and his anger forces him to attempt an act of retribution. Since *S* is out of control and acting under coercion, he is not responsible for his actions.

Stage 5: Act of retribution

S performs the act of retribution. The wrongdoer is the target of the act. The intensity of retribution roughly equals the intensity of the offense and the scales are balanced again. The intensity of anger drops to zero.

At this point, we can see how the various conceptual metaphors we have discussed all map onto a part of the prototypical scenario and how they jointly converge on that scenario. This enables us to show exactly how the various metaphors are related to one another and how they function together to help characterize a single concept. This is something that Lakoff and Johnson (1980) were unable to do.

The course of anger depicted in the prototype scenario is by no means the only course anger can take. In claiming that the scenario is prototypical we are claiming that according to our cultural folk theory of anger, this is a normal course for anger to take. Deviations of many kinds are both recognized as existing and recognized as being noteworthy and not the norm. Let us take some examples:

- Someone who "turns the other cheek" does not get angry or seek retribution. In this culture, such a person is considered virtually saintly.
- Someone who has no difficulty controlling his anger is especially praiseworthy.
- A "hothead" is someone who considers more events offensive than most people, who has a lower threshold for anger than the norm, who cannot control his anger, and whose acts of retribution are considered out of proportion to the offense. Someone who is extremely hotheaded is considered emotionally "unbalanced."

On the other hand, someone who acts in the manner described in the prototypical scenario would not be considered abnormal at all.

Before turning to the nonprototypical cases, it will be useful for us to make a rough sketch of the ontology of anger: the entities, predicates, and events required. This will serve two purposes. First, it will allow us to show in detail how the nonprototypical cases are related to the prototypical model. Second, it will allow us to investigate the nature of this ontology. We will include only the detail required for our purposes.

It is part of our folk concept of a person that he can temporarily lose control of his body or his emotions. Implicit in this concept is a separation of the body and the emotions from the self. This separation is especially important in the ontology of anger. Anger, as a separable entity, can overcome someone, take control, and cause him to act in ways he would not normally act. In such cases, the self is no longer in control of the body. Thus, the ontology of anger must include a self, anger, and the body. A fuller treatment would probably also require viewing the mind as a separate entity, but that is beyond our present purposes.

Since anger has a quantitative aspect, the ontology must include a scale of anger, including an intensity, a zero point and a limit point. The basic anger scenario also includes an offending event and a retributive act. Each of these has a quantitative aspect and must also include an intensity, a zero point, and a limit. In the prototypical case, the offending event is an action on the part of a wrongdoer against a victim. The retribution takes the form of an act by an agent against some target.

The ontology of anger also includes a number of predicates: *displeasing, at fault, exert force on, cause, exist, control, dangerous, damaging, balance*, and *outweigh*. There are also some other kinds of events: the physiological effects; the angry behaviors; and the immediate cause of anger, in case it is not the same as the offending event.

Summary of the Ontology of Anger

Aspects of the person
- self
- body
- anger

Offense and retribution
- offending event
- retributive act

Scales of intensity
- intensity of anger
- intensity of offense
- intensity of retribution

End points
- zero
- limit

Predicates
- displease
- at fault
- cause
- exist
- exert force on
- control
- dangerous
- damaging
- balance
- outweigh

Other events
- physiological reactions
- angry behaviors
- immediate cause

Restatement of the Prototypical Scenario

Given the ontology and principles of the folk model, we can restate the prototypical anger scenario in terms that will facilitate showing the relationships among the wide variety of anger scenarios. We will first restate the prototypical scenario and then go on to the nonprototypical scenarios.

Prototypical anger scenario

Constraints

Victim = *S*
Agent of retribution = *S*
Target of anger = wrongdoer *(W)*
Immediate cause of anger = offending event
Angry behavior = retribution

Stage 1: Offending event

Wrongdoer offends *S*.
Wrongdoer is at fault.
The offending event displeases *S*.
The intensity of the offense outweighs the intensity of the retribution (which equals zero at this point), thus creating an imbalance.
The offense causes anger to come into existence.

Stage 2: Anger
Anger exists.
S experiences physiological effects (heat, pressure, agitation).
Anger exerts force on *S* to attempt an act of retribution.

Stage 3: Attempt to control anger
S exerts a counterforce in an attempt to control anger.

Stage 4: Loss of control
The intensity of anger goes above the limit.
Anger takes control of *S*.
S exhibits angry behavior (loss of judgment, aggressive actions).
There is damage to *S*.
There is a danger to the target of anger, in this case, the wrongdoer.

Stage 5: Retribution
S performs retributive act against *W* (this is usually angry behavior directed at *W*).
The intensity of retribution balances the intensity of offense.
The intensity of anger drops.

The Nonprototypical Cases

We are now in a position to show how a large range of instances of anger cluster around this prototype. The examples are in the following form: a nonprototypical anger scenario is followed by an informal description, with an account of the minimal difference between the given scenario and the prototype scenario, and finally, some example sentences.

Insatiable anger: You perform the act of retribution and the anger just doesn't go away.
In stage 5, the intensity of anger stays high.
Example: His anger lingered on.

Frustrated anger: You just can't get back at the wrongdoer and you get frustrated.
It is not possible to gain retribution for the offensive act. *S* engages in frustrated behavior. Option: *S* directs his anger at himself.
Examples: He was climbing the walls. She was tearing her hair out. He was banging his head against the wall. He's taking it out on himself.

Redirected anger: Instead of directing your anger at the person who made you angry, you direct it at someone or something else.

The target of anger is not the wrongdoer.

Examples: When I lose my temper, I kick the cat. When you get angry, punch a pillow until your anger goes away. When something bad happened at the office, he would take it out on his wife.

Exaggerated response: Your reaction is out of proportion to the offense.

The intensity of retribution outweighs the intensity of offense.

Examples: Why jump down my throat? You have a right to get angry, but not to go *that* far.

Controlled response: You get angry, but retain control and consciously direct your anger at the wrongdoer.

S remains in control. Everything else remains the same.

Example: He vented his anger on her.

Constructive use: Instead of attempting an act of retribution, you put your anger to a constructive use.

S remains in control and performs a constructive act instead of a retributive act. The scales remain unbalanced, but the anger disappears.

Example: Try to channel your anger into something constructive.

Terminating event: Before you have a chance to lose control, some unrelated event happens to make your anger disappear.

Anger doesn't take control of *S*. Some event causes the anger to go out of existence.

Example: When his daughter smiled at him, his anger disappeared.

Spontaneous cessation: Before you lose control, your anger just goes away.

Anger doesn't take control of *S* and the intensity of anger goes to zero.

Example: His anger just went away by itself.

Successful suppression: You successfully suppress your anger.

S keeps control and the intensity of anger is not near the limit.

Example: He suppressed his anger.

Controlled reduction: Before you lose control, you engage in angry behavior and the intensity of anger goes down.

S does not lose control; *S* engages in angry behavior and the intensity of anger goes down.

Example: He's just letting off steam.

Immediate explosion: You get angry and lose control all at once. No Stage 3. Stages 2 and 4 combine into a single event.

Example: I said "Hi, Roundeyes!" and he blew up.

Slow burn: Anger continues for a long time.
Stage 2 lasts a long time.
Example: He was doing a slow burn.

Nursing a grudge: *S* maintains his anger for a long period, waiting for a chance at a retributive act. Maintaining that level of anger takes special effort.
Stage 2 lasts a long time and requires effort. The retributive act does not equal angry behavior.

Don't get mad, get even: This is advice (rarely followed) about the pointlessness of getting angry. It suggests avoiding stages 2, 3, and 4, and instead going directly to stage 5. This advice is defined as an alternative to the prototypical scenario.

Indirect cause: It is some result of the wrongdoer's action, not the action itself, that causes anger.
The offense is not the immediate cause of anger, but rather is more indirect—the cause of the immediate cause.
Consider the following case: Your secretary forgets to fill out a form that results in your not getting a deserved promotion. Offending event = secretary forgets to fill out form. Immediate cause = you don't get promotion. You are angry *about* not getting the promotion. You are angry *at* the secretary *for* not filling out the form. In general, *about* marks the immediate cause, *at* marks the target, and *for* marks the offense.

Cool anger: There are no physiological effects and S remains in control.

Cold anger: S puts so much effort into suppressing the anger that temperature goes down, while internal pressure increases. There are neither signs of heat nor agitation, and there is no danger that *S* will lose control and display his anger. In the prototypical case, a display of anger constitutes retribution. But since there is no such display, and since there is internal pressure, release from that pressure can only come through retribution of some other kind, one that is more severe than the display of emotion. It is for this reason that cold anger is viewed as being much more dangerous than anger of the usual kind. Expressions like *Sally gave me an icy stare* are instances of cold anger. This expression implies that Sally is angry at me, is controlling her anger with effort, and is not about to lose control; it suggests the possibility that she may take retributive action against me of some sort other than losing her temper.

Anger with: To be angry with someone, *S* has to have a positive relationship with the wrongdoer, the wrongdoer must be answerable to *S*, the intensity is above the threshold but not near the limit. Perhaps the best example is a parent-child relationship, where the parent is angry with the child.

Righteous indignation: The offending event is a moral offense and the victim is not the *S*. The intensity of anger is not near the limit.

Wrath: The intensity of the offense is very great and many acts of retribution are required in order to create a balance. The intensity of the anger is well above the limit and the anger lasts a long time.

There appears to be a recognizable form of anger for which there are no conventional linguistic expressions, so far as we can tell. We will call this a manipulative use of anger. It is a case where a person cultivates his anger and does not attempt to control it, with the effect that he intimidates those around him into following his wishes in order to keep him from getting angry. This can work either by fear or by guilt. The people manipulated can either be afraid of his anger or may feel guilty about what anger does to him. This form of anger is fairly distant from the prototype and it is no surprise that we have no name for it.

Interestingly enough, there is a linguistic test that can be used to verify that what we have called the prototypical scenario is indeed prototypical. It involves the use of the word *but*. Consider the following examples (where the asterisk indicates a semantic aberration):

– Max got angry, but he didn't blow his top.
– *Max got angry, but he blew his top.

– Max blew up at his boss, but the anger didn't go away.
– *Max blew up at his boss, but the anger went away.

– Sam got me angry, but it wasn't him that I took my anger out on.
– *Sam got me angry, but it was him that I took my anger out on.

The word *but* marks a situation counter to expectation. In these examples, the prototypical scenario defines what is to be expected. The acceptable sentences with *but* run counter to the prototypical scenario, and thus fit the conditions for the use of *but*. The unacceptable sentences fit the prototypical scenario and define expected situations. This is incompatible with the use of *but*. Thus we have a linguistic test that accords with our intuitions about what is or isn't prototypical.

Each of the nonprototypical cases cited above is a case involving anger. There appear to be no necessary and sufficient conditions that will fit all these cases. However, they can all be seen as variants of the prototypical anger scenario. Prototypes often involve clusters of conditions and the prototypical anger scenario is no exception. The clustering can be seen explicitly in identity conditions such as: victim = self, target = wrongdoer, offending event = immediate cause, etc. When these identities do not hold, we get nonprototypical cases. For example, with righteous indignation, victim does not have to equal self. In the case of an indirect cause, offending event does not equal immediate cause. In the case of redirected anger, target does not equal wrongdoer. Usually the act of retribution and the disappearance of anger go together, but in the case of spontaneous cessation and insatiable anger, that is not the case. And in the "Don't get mad, get even" case, angry behavior is avoided and therefore is not identical to the act of retribution. Part of what makes the prototypical scenario prototypical is that it is sufficiently rich so that variations on it can account for nonprototypical cases, and it also has a conflation of conditions which are not conflated in nonprototypical cases.

The point is that there is no single unified cognitive model of anger. Instead there is a category of cognitive models with a prototypical model in the center. This suggests that it is a mistake to try to find a single cognitive model for all instances of a concept. Kinds of anger are not all instances of the same model; instead they are *variants* on a prototypical model. There is no core that all kinds of anger have in common. Instead, the kinds of anger bear family resemblances to one another.

Metaphorical Aspects of the Prototype Scenario

The analysis we have done so far is consistent with a certain traditional view of metaphor, namely:

- The concept of anger exists and is understood independently of any metaphors.
- The anger ontology and the category of scenarios represent the literal meaning of the concept of anger.
- Metaphors do no more than provide ways of talking about the ontology of anger.

This view entails the following:

- The elements of the anger ontology really, literally exist, independent of any metaphors.

A brief examination of the anger ontology reveals that this is simply not the case. In the ontology, anger exists as an independent entity, capable of exerting force and controlling a person. This is what Lakoff and Johnson (1980) refer to as an "ontological metaphor." In this case, it would be the ANGER IS AN ENTITY metaphor. A person's anger does not really, literally exist as an independent entity, though we do comprehend it metaphorically as such. In the ontology, there is an intensity scale for anger, which is understood as being oriented UP, by virtue of the MORE IS UP metaphor. The intensity scale has a limit associated with it—another ontological metaphor. Anger is understood as being capable of exerting force and taking control of a person. The FORCE and CONTROL here are also metaphorical, based on physical force and physical control. The anger ontology also borrows certain elements from the ontology of retributive justice: offense and retribution, with their scales of intensity and the concept of balance. These are also metaphorical, with metaphorical BALANCE based on physical balance. In short, the anger ontology is largely constituted by metaphor.

Let us now examine these constitutive metaphors. Their source domains—ENTITY, INTENSITY, LIMIT, FORCE, and CONTROL—all seem to be superordinate concepts, that is, concepts that are fairly abstract. By contrast, the principal metaphors that map onto the anger ontology—HOT FLUID, INSANITY, FIRE, BURDEN, STRUGGLE—appear to be basic-level concepts, that is, concepts that are linked more directly to experience, concepts that are information-rich and rich in conventional mental imagery. Let us call the metaphors based on such concepts "basic-level metaphors." We would like to suggest that most of our understanding of anger comes via these basic-level metaphors. The HOT FLUID and FIRE metaphors give us an understanding of what kind of entity anger is. And the STRUGGLE metaphor gives us a sense of what is involved in controlling it. Without these metaphors, our understanding of anger would be extremely impoverished, to say the least. One is tempted to ask which is more primary: the constitutive metaphors or the basic-level ones. We don't know if that is a meaningful question. All we know is that both exist and have their separate functions: The basic-level metaphors allow us to comprehend and draw inferences about anger, using our knowledge of familiar, well-structured domains. The constitutive metaphors provide the bulk of the anger ontology.

The Embodiment of Anger

We have seen that the concept of anger has a rich conceptual structure and that those who view it as just a feeling devoid of conceptual content are mistaken. But the opposite view also exists. Schachter and Singer (1962) have claimed that emotions are *purely cognitive* and that there are no physiological differences among the emotions. They claim that the feeling of an emotion is simply a state of generalized arousal and that *which* emotion one feels is simply a matter of what frame of mind one is in. The results of Ekman, Levenson, and Friesen (1983) contradict the Schachter-Singer claims with evidence showing that pulse rate and skin temperature do correlate with particular emotions.

Although the kind of analysis we have offered does not tell us anything direct about what the physiology of emotions might be, it does correlate positively with the Ekman group's results. As we saw, the conceptual metaphors and metonymies used in the comprehension of anger are based on a folk theory of the physiology of anger, the major part of which involves heat and internal pressure. The Ekman group's results (which are entirely independent of the analysis given here) suggest that our folk theory of the physiology of anger corresponds remarkably well with the actual physiology: when people experience anger their skin temperature and pulse rate rises.

Although the folk theory is only a folk theory, it has stood the test of time. It has made sense to hundreds of millions of English speakers over a period of roughly a thousand years. The Ekman group's results suggest that ordinary speakers of English by the millions have had a very subtle insight into their own physiology. Those results suggest that our concept of anger is embodied via the autonomic nervous system and that the conceptual metaphors and metonymies used in understanding anger are by no means arbitrary; instead they are motivated by our physiology.

From the Ekman group's results, together with our hypothesis concerning conceptual embodiment, we can make an interesting prediction, that if we look at metaphors and metonymies for anger in the languages of the world, we will not find any that contradict the physiological results that they found. In short, we should not find languages where the basic emotion of anger is understood in terms of both cold and freedom from pressure. The nonbasic case of *cold anger* discussed above is irrelevant, since it is a special form of anger and not an instance of the normal basic anger emotion and since it does involve internal pressure.

If Schachter and Singer are right and the Ekman group has made a mistake, then the English metaphors and metonymies for anger are arbitrary, that is, they are not embodied, not motivated by any physiological reality. The heat and internal pressure metaphors should thus be completely accidental. If there is no physiological basis for anger at all, as Schachter and Singer suggest, we would then expect metaphors for anger to be randomly distributed in the languages of the world. We would expect metaphors for cold and freedom from pressure to be just as common as metaphors for heat and pressure; in fact, on the Schachter-Singer account, we would expect that metaphors based on shape, darkness, trees, water—anything at all—would be just as common as metaphors based on heat and pressure. The research has not been done, but my guess is that the facts will match the predictions of the Ekman group. Cursory studies of non-Indo-European languages as diverse as Chinese and Hungarian indicate the presence of heat and pressure metaphors. If our predictions hold up, it will show that the match between the Ekman group's results and ours is no fluke, and it will give even more substance to our claim that concepts are embodied.

Review

We have shown that the expressions that indicate anger in American English are not a random collection but rather are structured in terms of an elaborate cognitive model that is implicit in the semantics of the language. This indicates that anger is not just an amorphous feeling, but rather that it has an elaborate cognitive structure. However, very significant problems and questions remain.

First, there are aspects of our understanding of anger that our methodology cannot shed any light on. Take, for example, the range of offenses that cause anger and the corresponding range of appropriate responses. Our methodology reveals nothing in this area.

Second, study of the language as a whole gives us no guide to individual variation. We have no idea how close any individual comes to the model we have uncovered, and we have no idea how people differ from one another.

Third, our methodology does not enable us to say much about the exact psychological status of the model we have uncovered. How much of it do people really use in comprehending anger? Do people base their actions on this model? Are people aware of the model? How much of it, if any, do people consciously believe? And most intriguingly, does the model have any effect on what people feel?

Certain things, however, do seem to be clear. Most speakers of American English seem to use the expressions we have described consistently and make inferences that appear, so far as we can tell, to be consistent with our model. We make this claim on the basis of our own intuitive observations, though to really establish it, one would have to do thorough empirical studies. If we are right, our model has considerable psychological reality, but how much and what kind remains to be determined. The fact that our analysis meshes so closely with the physiological study done by the Ekman group suggests that emotional concepts are embodied, that is, that the actual content of the concepts are correlated with bodily experience.

This is especially interesting in the case of metaphorical concepts, since the correlation is between the metaphors and the physiology, rather than directly between the literal sense and the physiology. It provides confirmation of the claim made by Lakoff and Johnson (1980) that conceptual metaphors are not mere flights of fancy, but can even have a basis in bodily experience.

Finally, we have shown that the anger category—the category consisting of basic anger and its conventionalized variations—is a radial category with a center and extensions. This provides confirmation of prototype theory in the domain of conceptual structure.

Anger, Lust, and Rape

We have shown that an emotion, anger, has a conceptual structure, and we have investigated various aspects of it. A deeper question now arises: How do such conceptual structures affect how we live our lives? To get some idea of how the emotional concepts function in our culture, let us consider an issue that has enormous social importance, but which most people would rather not think about: rape.

Not all cultures have a high incidence of rape. In some cultures, rape is virtually unknown. The high incidence of rape in America undoubtedly has many complex causes. I would like to suggest that the way we conceptualize lust and anger, together with our various folk theories of sexuality, may be a contributing factor.

Let us begin with an examination of our concept of lust. It is commonly thought that lust, as a sexual urge, is devoid of cognitive content and that there is not much to say about how lust, or sexual desire, is understood. On the contrary, lust is a complex concept which is understood via a system of conceptual metaphors. Here are some examples that Zoltán Kövecses and I have discovered:

LUST IS HUNGER; THE OBJECT OF LUST IS FOOD.

- He is *sex-starved.*
- You have a remarkable *sexual appetite.*
- She's quite a *dish.*
- Hey, *honey*, let's see some *cheesecake.*
- Look at those *buns!*
- What a piece of *meat!*
- She had him *drooling.*
- You look *luscious.*
- Hi, *sugar!*
- I *hunger* for your touch.

A LUSTFUL PERSON IS AN ANIMAL.

– Don't touch me, you *animal!*
– Get away from me, you *brute!*
– He's a *wolf.*
– He looks like he's ready to *pounce.*
– Stop *pawing* me!
– Wanna *nuzzle* up close?
– He *preys* upon unsuspecting women.
– He's a real *stud*—the Italian *Stallion!*
– Hello, my little *chickadee.*
– She's a *tigress* in bed.
– She looks like a *bitch in heat.*
– You bring out the *beast* in me.

LUST IS HEAT.

– I've got the *hots* for her.
– She's an old *flame.*
– Hey, baby, *light my fire.*
– She's *frigid.*
– Don't be *cold* to me.
– She's *hot stuff.*
– He's still carrying a *torch* for her.
– She's a *red hot mama.*
– I'm *warm* for your form.
– She's got *hot pants* for you.
– I'm *burning* with desire.
– She's *in heat.*
– He was *consumed* by desire.

LUST IS INSANITY.

– I'm *crazy* about her.
– I'm *madly* in love with him.
– I'm *wild* over her.
– You're driving me *insane.*
– She's *sex-crazed.*
– He's a real *sex maniac.*
– She's got me *delirious.*
– I'm a *sex addict.*

A LUSTFUL PERSON IS A FUNCTIONING MACHINE (ESPECIALLY A CAR).

– You *turn me on.*

- I got my *motor runnin'*, baby.
- Don't leave me *idling.*
- I think I'm *running out of gas.*
- *Turn my crank*, baby.

To return to examples of longer standing:

LUST IS A GAME.

- I think I'm going to *score* tonight.
- You won't be able to *get to first base* with her.
- He's a *loser.*
- I *struck out* last night.
- She wouldn't *play ball.*
- *Touchdown!*

LUST IS WAR.

- He's known for his *conquests.*
- That's quite a *weapon* you've got there.
- Better put on my *war paint.*
- He *fled from her advances.*
- He has to *fend off* all the women who want him.
- She *surrendered* to him.

SEXUALITY IS A PHYSICAL FORCE; LUST IS A REACTION TO THAT FORCE.

- She's *devastating.*
- When she grows up, she'll be a *knockout.*
- I was *knocked off my feet.*
- She *bowled me over.*
- What a *bombshell!*
- She's *dressed to kill.*
- I could feel the *electricity* between us.
- She *sparked* my interest.
- He has a lot of *animal magnetism.*
- We were *drawn* to each other.
- The *attraction* was very strong.

A particularly important fact about the collection of metaphors used to understand lust in our culture is that their source domains overlap considerably with the source domains of metaphors for anger. As we saw above, anger in America is understood in terms of HEAT, FIRE, WILD ANIMALS and INSANITY as well as a reaction to an external force. Just as one can have *smoldering sexuality*, one can have *smoldering anger.* One can be *consumed with desire* and *consumed with anger.* One can be *insane with lust* and *insane with anger*. Your lust, as well as your anger, can get *out of hand*. I believe that the connection between our conception of lust and our conception of anger is by no means accidental and has important social consequences.

One might suggest that these conceptual metaphors provide ways of passively understanding and talking about lust, but no more than that. What I would like to show is that, at the very least, it is possible for them to enter into reasoning. For this purpose, I will look in detail at the reasoning in a passage from Timothy Beneke's collection of interviews, *Men on Rape* (1982). The analysis of the passage was done jointly with Mark Johnson.

Before we get to the details of the analysis, we should bear in mind that it raises an important social issue. Many experts have argued that rape has nothing to do with sex or even lust, but is simply violence against women with no sexual aspect. But, as we have seen, sexual desire is partly understood in America in terms of physical force and war metaphors. This suggests that sex and violence are linked in the American mind via these metaphors. Since sex and violence are conceptually anything but mutually exclusive, it is quite conceivable that rape is not a matter of violence alone and that it may have a lot to do with lust and the fact that the metaphorical understanding of lust shares a considerable amount with the metaphorical understanding of anger.

The passage I'll be looking at is taken from Beneke's interview with a mild-mannered librarian in the financial district of San Francisco. It is a passage in which he gives a coherent argument providing what he would consider a justification for rape.

> Let's say I see a woman and she looks really pretty, and really clean and sexy, and she's giving off very feminine, sexy vibes. I think, "Wow, I would love to make love to her," but I know she's not really interested. It's a tease. A lot of times a woman knows that she's looking really good and she'll use that and flaunt it, and it makes me feel like she's laughing at me and I feel *degraded*.
>
> I also feel dehumanized, because when I'm being teased I just turn off, I cease to be human. Because if I go with my human emotions I'm going to want to put my arms around her and kiss her, and to do that would be unacceptable. I don't like the feeling that I'm supposed to stand there and take it, and not be able to hug her or kiss her; so I just turn off my emotions. It's a feeling of humiliation, because the woman has forced me to turn off my feelings and react in a way that I really don't want to.
>
> If I were actually desperate enough to rape somebody, it would be from wanting the person, but also it would be a very spiteful thing, just being able to say, "I have power over you and I can do anything I want with you"; because really I feel that *they* have power over *me* just by their presence. Just

> the fact that they can come up to me and just melt me and make me feel like a dummy makes me want revenge. They have power over me so I want power over them. (Beneke 1982, pp. 43–44)

Here is a clear and forceful statement in which a man is giving an account of his reality. On the face of it, there is nothing particularly difficult about this passage. It is fairly straightforward as explanations go. But when we make sense of a passage even as simple as this, there is a lot going on that we are not usually conscious of. What is most important in this passage are the conceptual metaphors and the folk theories of everyday experience that jointly make it cohere.

The logic of the passage is based on the SEXUALITY IS A PHYSICAL FORCE metaphor, which is reflected in the following expressions:

– She's *giving off very feminine, sexy vibes.*
– Just the fact that they can come up to me and just *melt me* . . .

In addition to the SEXUALITY IS A PHYSICAL FORCE metaphor, the passage draws upon a number of other metaphors and folk theories. Let us roughly trace the logic of the passage. The speaker assumes that A WOMAN IS RESPONSIBLE FOR HER PHYSICAL APPEARANCE and since PHYSICAL APPEARANCE IS A PHYSICAL FORCE, he assumes that, if she looks sexy ("giving off very feminine, sexy vibes"), she is using her sexy appearance as a force on him ("a woman knows that she's looking very good and she'll use that and flaunt it"). The speaker also assumes that SEXUAL EMOTIONS ARE PART OF HUMAN NATURE and that A PERSON WHO USES A FORCE IS RESPONSIBLE FOR THE EFFECT OF THAT FORCE. It follows that A WOMAN WITH A SEXY APPEARANCE IS RESPONSIBLE FOR AROUSING A MAN'S SEXUAL EMOTIONS. As he says, "they have power over me just by their presence." The speaker has an important additional folk theory about the relationship between sexual emotion and sexual action: SEXUAL EMOTION NATURALLY RESULTS IN SEXUAL ACTION ("because if I go with my human emotions I'm going to want to put my arms around her and kiss her."). This raises problems for him because "to do that would be unacceptable." This is based upon the folk theory that SEXUAL ACTION AGAINST SOMEONE'S WILL IS UNACCEPTABLE. It follows that TO ACT MORALLY, ONE MUST AVOID SEXUAL ACTION (in such a case as this one). Since sexual action is for him the natural result of sexual emotions, the only acceptable thing he can do is inhibit his emotions: AVOIDING SEXUAL ACTION REQUIRES INHIBITING SEXUAL EMOTIONS. As he says, "I don't like the feeling that I'm supposed to stand there and take it, and not be able to hug her or kiss her; so I just turn off my emotions." TO ACT MORALLY, ONE MUST INHIBIT SEXUAL EMOTIONS. So, as a consequence, a woman who looks sexy is responsible for his sexual emotions and for putting him in a position where he must inhibit them if he is to act morally. He explains, "It's a feeling of humiliation, because the woman has forced me to turn off my feelings and react in a way that I don't really want to."

The humiliation he feels is part of his sense that he has become less than human ("I feel degraded . . . I also feel dehumanized . . . I cease to be human"). The reason for this is, as we saw above, that he assumes that SEXUAL EMOTIONS ARE PART OF HUMAN NATURE and therefore that TO INHIBIT SEXUAL EMOTIONS IS TO BE LESS THAN HUMAN. Since she forces him to turn off his emotions, she makes him less than human. A WOMAN WITH A SEXY APPEARANCE MAKES A MAN WHO IS ACTING MORALLY LESS THAN HUMAN. The speaker feels (by a fairly natural folk theory) that TO BE MADE LESS THAN HUMAN IS TO BE INJURED. He also assumes the biblical eye-for-an-eye folk theory of retributive justice: THE ONLY WAY TO MAKE UP FOR BEING INJURED IS TO INFLICT AN INJURY OF THE SAME KIND.

Since the injury involves the use of sexual *power*, he sees rape as a possibility for appropriate redress: "If I were actually desperate enough to rape somebody, it would be from wanting the person, but also it would be a very spiteful thing, just being able to say, 'I have power over you and I can do anything I want with you'; because really I feel that *they* have power over *me* just by their presence. Just the fact that they can come up to me and just melt me and make me feel like a dummy makes me want revenge. They have power over me so I want power over them."

Here the overlap between lust and anger is even stronger. Our concept of anger carries with it the concept of revenge, as well as the idea of insane, heated, animal behavior. In this particular logic of rape, lust and anger go hand-in-hand.

In giving the overall logic of the passage, we have made explicit only *some* of the implicit metaphors and folk theories necessary to understand it. Little, if any, of this is explicit, and we are not claiming that we have presented anything like a conscious chain of deduction that the speaker has followed. Rather, we have tried to show the logic and structure that unconsciously lies behind the reality the speaker takes for granted.

There is an important, and somewhat frightening, sense in which his reality is ours as well. We may personally find his views despicable, but it is frightening how easy they are to make sense of. The reason that they seem to be so easily understood is that most, if not all, of them are deeply ingrained in American culture. All of the metaphors and folk theories we have discussed occur again and again in one form or another throughout Beneke's interviews. Moreover, it seems that these metaphors and folk theories are largely held by women as well as men. As Beneke's interviews indicate, women on juries in rape trials regularly view rape victims who were attractively dressed as "asking for it" or bringing it upon themselves and therefore deserving of their fate. Such women jurors are using the kind of reasoning we saw in the passage above.

Of course, not everyone's sense of reality is structured in terms of *all* the above metaphors and folk theories. And even if it were, not everyone would put them together in the way outlined above. Nor does it follow that someone with such a sense of reality would act on it, as the speaker supposedly has not. What the analysis of the passage does seem to show is that American culture contains within it a sufficient stock of fairly common metaphors and folk theories which, when put together in the way outlined above, can actually provide what could be viewed as a "rationale" for rape. Furthermore, if these metaphors and folk theories were not readily available to us for use in understanding—that is, if they were not ours in some sense—the passage would be simply incomprehensible to us.

The metaphorical expressions that we use to describe lust are not mere words. They are expressions of metaphorical concepts that we use to understand lust and to reason about it. What I find sad is that we appear to have no metaphors for a healthy mutual lust. The domains we use for comprehending lust are HUNGER, ANIMALS, HEAT, INSANITY, MACHINES, GAMES, WAR, and PHYSICAL FORCES.

CASE STUDY 2

Over

Polysemy: Categories of Senses

It is common for a single word to have more than one meaning. In some cases the meanings are unrelated, like the two meanings of *bank*—the place where you put your money and the land along the edge of a river. In such cases, there is not one word, but two. They are called instances of *homonymy,* where two words with two totally different meanings happen to be pronounced the same way. In other cases, the senses are related, often in such a close and systematic way that we don't notice at first that more than one sense exists at all. Take the word *window*, for example. It can refer either to an opening in a wall or to the glass-filled frame in that opening. Or take the word *open*. We open doors and open presents, and though the actions described by the words are very different, we would normally have to think twice to notice the difference. Or the word *run*. It is very different for Harry to run into the woods and for the road to run into the woods. Again, there is a single verb with two senses so intimately related that we have to think twice to notice the difference. Such cases are called instances of *polysemy*. They are cases where there is one lexical item with a family of related senses.

The classical theory of categories does not do very well on the treatment of polysemy. In order to have a single lexical item, the classical theory must treat all of the related senses as having some abstract meaning in common—usually so abstract that it cannot distinguish among the cases and so devoid of real meaning that it is not recognizable as what people think of as the meaning of a word. And where there are a large number of related senses that don't all share a property, then the classical theory is forced to treat such cases as homonymy, the same way it treats the case of the two words *bank*. Moreover, the classical theory has no adequate means of characterizing the situation where one or more senses are "central" or "most representative."

Fillmore (1982*a*) observes that the adjective *long* has two senses, one spatial and one temporal. The spatial sense is generally taken to be more central, or prototypical, and the temporal sense is related to it via metaphor. Another example would be the word *up*, which can mean happy, in "I'm feeling up today," or can have a spatial sense, in "The rocket went up." The spatial sense is generally taken as the more central sense.

These and other observations about prototypical uses of lexical items can be united with other data on natural categorization by viewing lexical items as constituting natural categories of senses. Thus some senses of a word may be more representative than other senses. The senses of a word are related to one another more or less closely by various means, one of which is conceptual metaphor. As Lakoff and Johnson (1980) observe, a metaphor can be viewed as an experientially based mapping from an ICM in one domain to an ICM in another domain. This mapping defines a relationship between the idealized cognitive models of the two domains. It is very common for a word that designates an element of the source domain's ICM to designate the corresponding element in the ICM of the target domain. The metaphorical mapping that relates the ICMs defines the relationship between the senses of the word. It is most common for the sense of the word in the source domain to be viewed as more basic. Thus, in the case of *up*, the source domain is spatial and the target domain is emotional, and the spatial sense is viewed as being more basic.

Polysemy Based on Correspondences within an ICM

In other cases, a single idealized cognitive model can be the basis on which a collection of senses forms a single natural category expressed by a single lexical item. *Window* is a good example. In our cognitive model of a window there is both an opening in the wall and a glass-filled frame fitting into it. This correspondence provides *motivation* for using the same word to refer to both. In isolation, an opening in the wall doesn't have much if anything *in common* with a glass-filled frame. Independent of any knowledge about the way windows happen to work, there would be no objective reason to place these two very different kinds of things in the same category. The fact that the opening in the wall and the glass-filled frame have been brought together to fit one another physically and to correspond to one another in the same cognitive model seems to make them members of the same cognitive category—so much so that in sentences like the following the word *window* doesn't seem to distinguish between them.

How many windows are there in your living room?

Here *window* seems to refer not to either the opening or the glass-filled frame, but to the combination. It takes sentences like the following to tease the senses of *window* apart.

- This room is too dark; we're going to have to cut a new window in that wall.
- They've just delivered our new windows.

Window can also refer to the frame alone or the glass alone:

- This window has rotted; we're going to have to replace it.
- The kids were playing ball and broke a window.

In the case of *window* the correspondences are physical: the glass fitting the frame, the frame fitting the opening in the wall. These correspondences within our model of what a window is motivate our use of the word *window* in these three senses, and in addition allow us to view these three senses (opening, frame, and glass) not as unrelated, but as forming a *natural category of senses*. The idea that lexical items are natural categories of senses has been studied extensively in the domain of English prepositions, and we will turn to those results next.

Chaining within Categories: The Case of *Over*

Most of the research on categorization within cognitive psychology has been in the domain of physical objects and physical perception. But perhaps the strongest evidence against traditional views of categorization and in favor of a prototype approach comes from the study of verb-particles and prepositions. The most detailed studies of prepositions by far are those done by Lindner (1981) and Brugman (1981). Lindner's study looked at more than 1800 verb-particle constructions using the two words *up* and *out* and surveyed the contributions to meaning made by the particles. Brugman's study is an extended survey of the highly complex network of senses of the English word *over*. It covers nearly one hundred kinds of uses. The two studies reach substantially the same conclusions, though Brugman's has a more thorough discussion of the consequences for the theory of categorization, and she is the first to explicitly propose the idea that lexical items are natural categories of senses. This case study presents part of that analysis and extends it in two ways: first, in showing the precise relations among the spatial senses and second, in describing metaphorical extensions of the spatial senses.

The Problem

To get some sense of the problem, let us consider a handful of the senses of *over*:

- The painting is *over* the mantle.
- The plane is flying *over* the hill.

- Sam is walking *over* the hill.
- Sam lives *over* the hill.
- The wall fell *over.*
- Sam turned the page *over.*
- Sam turned *over.*
- She spread the tablecloth *over* the table.
- The guards were posted all *over* the hill.
- The play is *over.*
- Do it *over*, but don't *over*do it.
- Look *over* my corrections, and don't *over*look any of them.
- You made *over* a hundred errors.

Even this small number of examples shows enormous complexity. Not all the complexity is semantic; the word *over* in these examples is in several grammatical categories, e.g., preposition, particle, adverb, prefix, etc. The problem Brugman undertook was how to describe all these senses and the relations among them. The analysis we will be presenting is a minor refinement of the semantic aspect of Brugman's analysis. Let us begin with what Brugman found to be the central sense.

The *Above-Across* Sense

The central sense of *over* combines elements of both *above* and *across.* In figure 1, the plane is understood as a trajector (TR) oriented relative to a landmark (LM). TR and LM are generalizations of the concepts figure

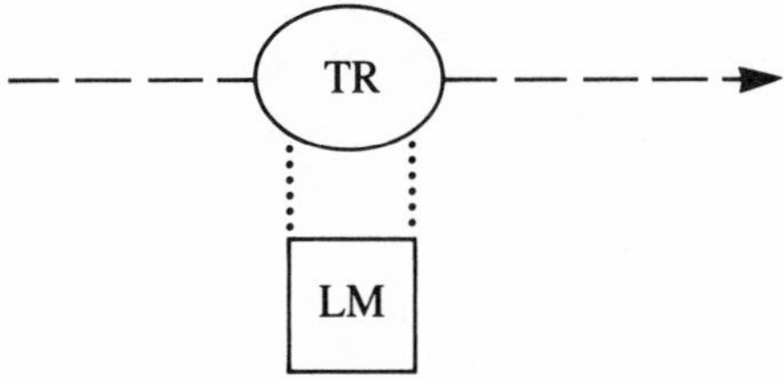

Fig. 1 The plane flew over.
Schema 1

and ground (Langacker 1986). In this case the landmark is unspecified. The arrow in the figure represents the PATH that the TR is moving along. The LM is what the plane is flying over. The PATH is *above* the LM. The dotted lines indicate the extreme boundaries of the landmark. The PATH goes all the way *across* the landmark from the boundary on one side to the boundary on the other. Although the drawing in figure 1 indicates noncontact between the TR and LM, this sense is actually neutral on the issue of contact. As we will see shortly, there are instances with contact and instances without contact. In this respect the schema cannot be drawn correctly. Any drawing would have to indicate contact or the lack of it. The image schema is neutral and that is part of what makes it schematic. What we have here is an abstract schema that cannot itself be imaged concretely, but which structures images. We will return below to the question of what it means for an image schema to structure an image.

Let us now turn to some special cases of the schema in figure 1. These are instances of the schema that are arrived at by adding information, in particular, by further specifying the nature of the landmark and by specifying whether or not there is contact. We will consider four kinds of landmark specifications: (1) LM is a point, that is, the landmark is an entity whose internal structure is irrelevant as far as the schema is concerned. (2) LM is extended, that is, the landmark extends over a distance or area. (3) LM is vertical, in that it extends upward (for example, a fence or a hill). (4) LM is both extended and vertical. For each such case, we will consider two further specifications: contact between TR and LM and noncontact. Each schema will be named using the following abbreviations: X, extended; V, vertical; C, contact; NC, no contact. Thus, the schema name 1.VX.C stands for the special case of schema 1 in which the landmark is both vertical and extended (VX) and there is contact (C) between the LM and the TR. The schemas in figures 2–7 can be related by a diagram of the sort shown in figure 8, where the links among schemas indicate similarity. Thus, all the contact schemas are linked, as are all the schemas that share noncontact. Moreover, each pair of schemas that share everything except contact are linked. In addition, they are all linked to schema 1, since they are all instances of that schema.

The schemas in figures 2–7 can be viewed in two ways. Take, for example, a sentence like *Sam walked over the hill* in figure 6. We can think of *over* in this sentence as being represented by the minimally specified schema 1 of figure 1, and we can think of the additional information as being added by the object and the verb. Thus, a hill is vertical and extended (VX) and walking requires contact (C) with the ground. Let us refer to this as the *minimal specification interpretation*. Equivalently, we can view the minimally specified *over* of figure 1 as generating all the fully specified schemas of figures 2–7. On this *full specification interpretation*, we can think of the *over* in *Sam walked over the hill* as having the full specification of schema 1.VX.C in figure 6. The verb *walk* would then match the contact (C) specification, and the direct object *hill* would match the vertical extended (VX) specification. The difference is whether the verb and direct object *add* the VX and C information or whether they *match* it.

These two interpretations make slightly different claims about the lexical representation of *over* in these sentences. On the minimal specifica-

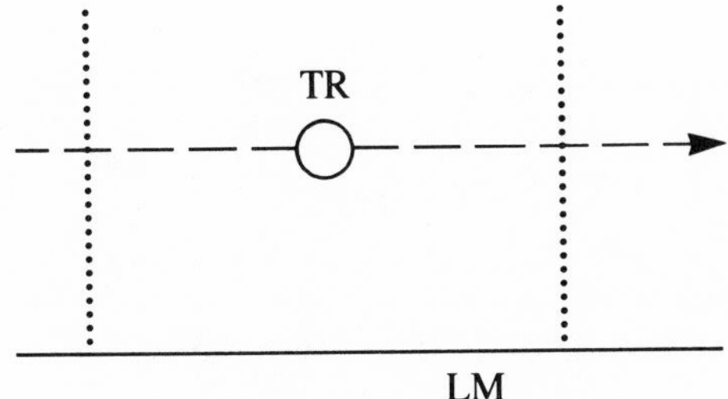

Fig. 2 The bird flew over the yard.
Schema 1.X.NC

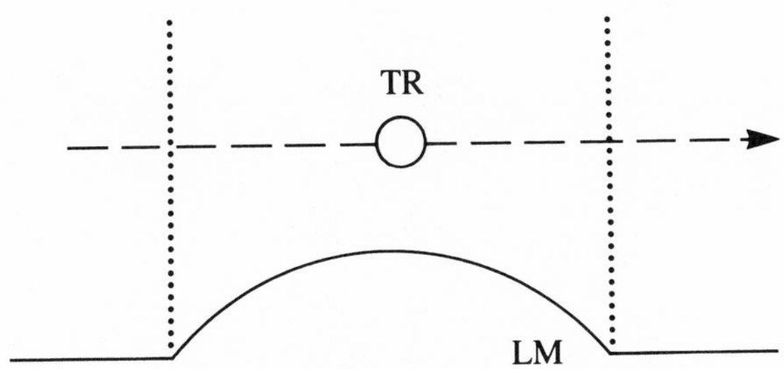

Fig. 3. The plane flew over the hill.
Schema 1.VX.NC

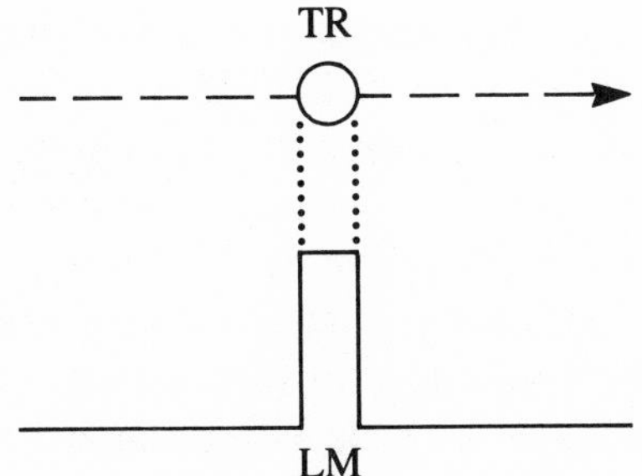

Fig. 4. The bird flew over the wall.
Schema 1.V.NC

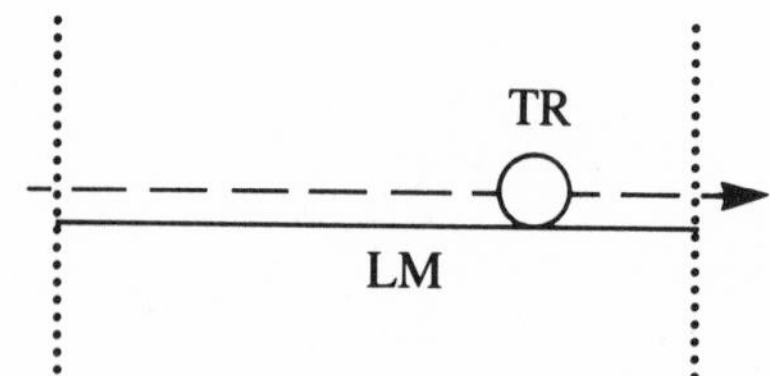

Fig. 5. Sam drove over the bridge.
Schema 1.X.C

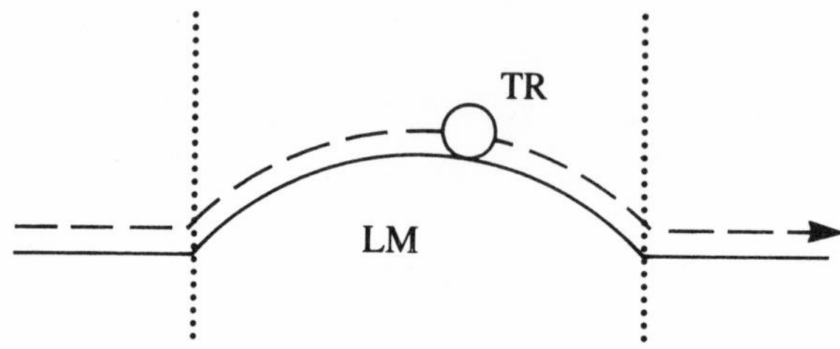

Fig. 6. Sam walked over the hill.
Schema 1.VX.C

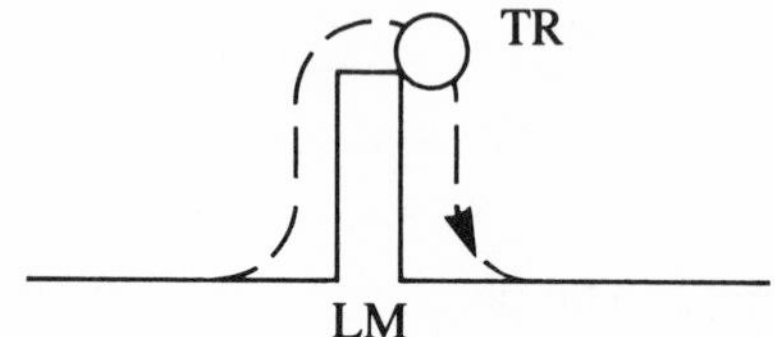

Fig. 7. Sam climbed over the wall.
Schema 1.V.C

tion interpretation, only schema 1 exists in the lexicon; the other schemas all result from information added by the verb and direct object. On the full specification interpretation, there is a lexical representation for all these schemas; the more specific schemas are generated by schema 1 plus the general parameters we have discussed: C-NC and X-VX-V.

On the basis of what we have said so far, these two interpretations are completely equivalent; there is no empirical difference between them and no a priori reason to choose between them. There is, however, additional evidence that favors the full specification interpretation, and we will be citing it throughout the remainder of this case study. We will be arguing that the senses of *over* form a chain with schema 1 at the center. On the full specification interpretation, the schemas in figures 2–7 are part of that chain. Some of those schemas form links to other senses. The existence of such links suggests that the full specification interpretation is correct.

Consider the following case, where there is a focus on the end point of the path. We will use the abbreviation E in naming schemas where there is end-point focus. In figure 10, there is an understood path that goes over the hill, and Sam lives at the end of that path. The end-point focus is not added by anything in the sentence, neither *hill*, nor *lives*, nor *Sam*. Here *over* has an additional sense which is one step away from schema 1.VX.C, a sense in which end-point focus (E) is added to yield schema 1.VX.C.E. As we shall see below, such end-point focus senses are the result of a general process that applies in many, but not all, English prepositions.

End-point focus cannot be freely added to just any of the schemas in figures 2–7. It can only be added to those with an extended landmark, as in

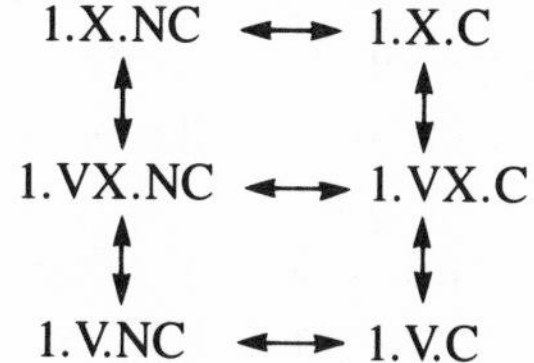

Fig. 8. Links among schemas

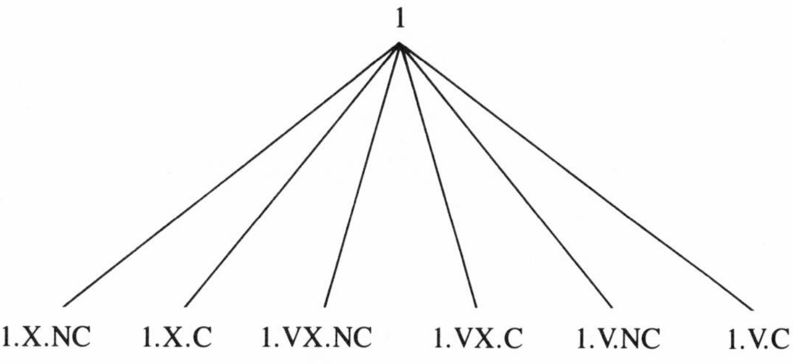

Fig. 9. Instances of schema 1

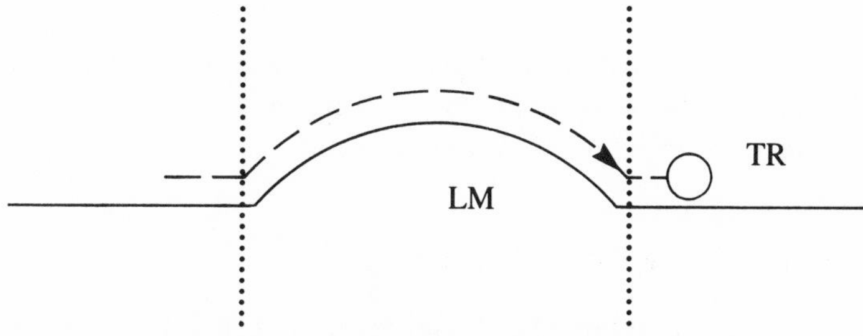

Fig. 10. Sam lives over the hill.
Schema 1.VX.C.E

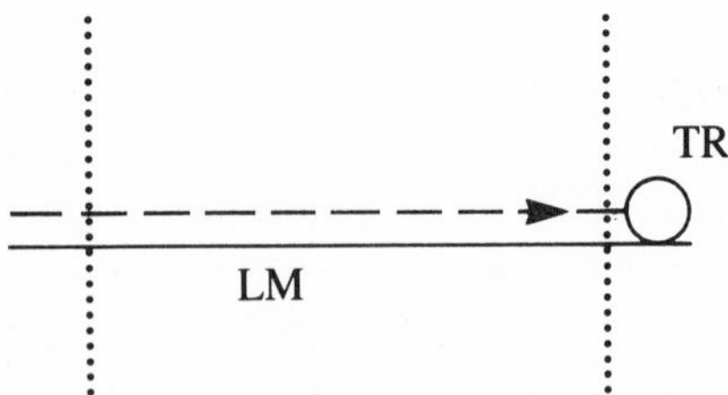

Fig. 11. Sausalito is over the bridge.
Schema 1.X.C.E

figure 11. In these cases, *over* has the sense of "on the other side of" as a result of end-point focus. However, *over* does not in general mean "on the other side of." For example, sentences like *Sam lives over the wall* and *Sam is standing over the door*, if they occur at all, cannot mean that he lives or is standing on the other side of the wall and the door. And a sentence like *Sam is sitting over the spot*, can only mean that he is sitting *on* it, not that he is sitting on the other side of it. Thus, there is no end-point focus schema corresponding to schema 1.V.C. of figure 7. Assuming the full specification interpretation, we can extend the chain in figure 8 to include the schemas in figures 10 and 11.

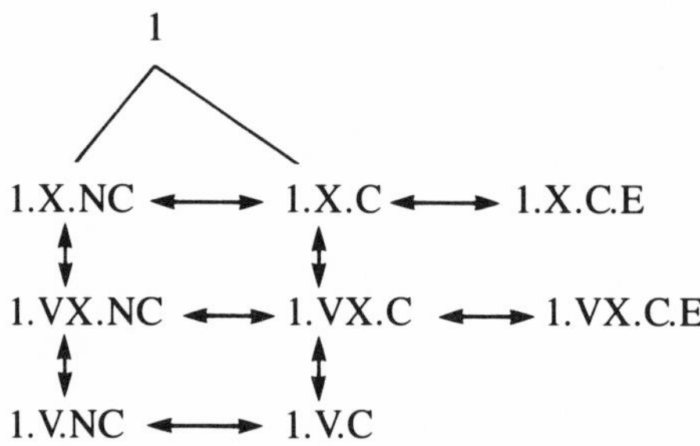

Fig. 12. Links among schemas

So far, we have considered two types of links among schemas: *instance links* and *similarity links*. Here are two examples, where → indicates an instance link and ↔ indicates a similarity link:

Instance link: 1.V.C. → 1

Similarity links: 1.VX.NC ↔ 1.VX.C

Thus, the link between schema 1 and schema 1.V.C is an instance link, with 1.V.C being an instance of 1. And the link between schema 1.VX.NC and schema 1.VX.C is a similarity link, where 1.VX is shared.

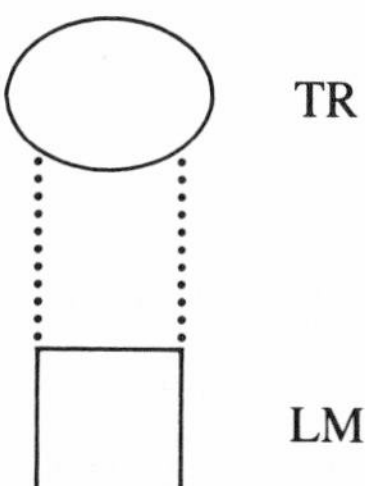

Fig. 13. Hang the painting over the fireplace.
Schema 2

So far, we have looked only at instances of the *above-across* sense. And we have only looked at the least interesting links between schemas. Let us now turn to other senses and more interesting kinds of links.

The *Above* Sense

Over has a stative sense, with no PATH. It is roughly equivalent in meaning to *above.* Schema 2 has no particular constraints on either the TR or LM. It is linked to schema 1 in that it has the TR above the LM. However, it differs from schema 1 in two respects: First, it has no PATH and no boundaries; in other words, the *across* sense is missing. Second, it does not permit contact between the TR and LM. The no-contact requirement can be seen in examples like *The helicopter is hovering over the hill.* If the helicopter lands, it is no longer *over* the hill, it is *on* the hill.

From time to time, linguists have suggested that schema 2 is the *core meaning* of the preposition *over*, that is, that schema 2 is present in all the uses of *over* as a preposition. It should be clear from what we have seen so far that this is false. Since schema 2 requires no contact, it cannot be present in those cases where contact occurs, for example, in schema 1.X.C exemplified by *Sam drove over the bridge.* Schema 2 also does not occur in the cases of end-point focus, such as schema 1.VX.C.E, which is exemplified by *Sam lives over the hill.* In this case, the TR is not above the LM.

One of the instances of schema 2 is the case where the TR is one-dimensional (which we will abbreviate as 1DTR). This schema is a minimal variant of schema 1.X.NC, exemplified by *The bird flew over the yard*, as shown in figure 2. The extended path in figure 2 corresponds to the one-dimensional solid trajector in figure 14. We will call this kind of link between schemas a *transformational link.* This particular link between an extended path (X.P) and a one-dimensional trajector (1DTR) will be represented as:

X.P $\leftrightarrow$ 1DTR

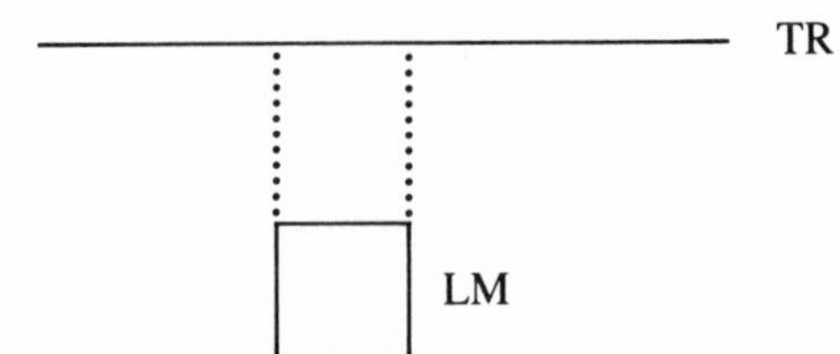

Fig. 14. The power line stretches over the yard.
Schema 2.1DTR

This relationship is not directly reflected in the naming system for schemas that we have adopted. However, we can state the relationship more systematically if we do a little renaming of a sort that reflects image-schema decompositions. Let us use ABV for the *above* subschema. And let us use PATH (P) for the *across* subschema. Schema 1 would be renamed ABV.P, and Schema 1.X.NC of figure 2 would be renamed ABV.NC.X.P. This name would reflect the fact that in this schema the TR is moving above (ABV) the LM, along a path (P), where the landmark is extended (X) and there is no contact between TR and LM (NC). Correspondingly, schema 2 would be renamed ABV.NC, and schema 2.1DTR in figure 14 would be renamed ABV.NC.1DTR.

Schema 1.X.NC = ABV.NC.X.P

Schema 2.1DTR = ABV.NC.1DTR

This decomposition displays the relationship between the schemas directly. The schemas are transforms of one another, given the transformational link X.P ↔ 1DTR.

It is important to bear in mind the difference between similarity links and transformational links. In the case of similarity links, the link is defined by shared subschemas. In the relationship described above, there are, indeed, shared subschemas: both schemas contain ABV.NC. But the transformational link is not a matter of *shared* subschemas, but of *related* subschemas.

The links among the schemas that we have described so far can be seen in figure 15.

The *Covering* Senses

There is a group of schemas for *over* that have to do with covering. This group is linked to the grid of figure 15 in two ways. The basic covering schema is a variant of schema 2, where the TR is at least two-dimensional and extends across the boundaries of the LM. There are two differences

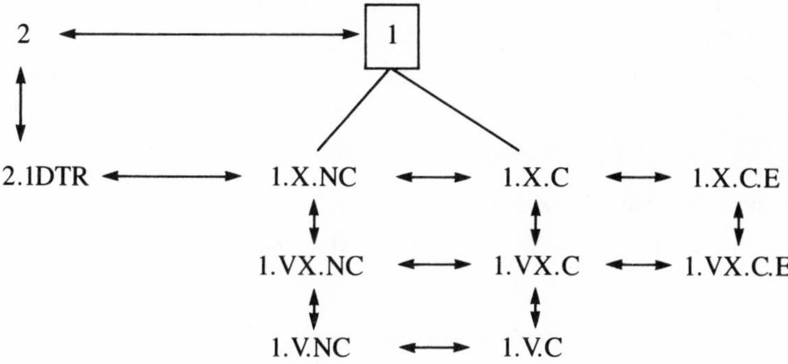

Fig. 15. Links among schemas

between schema 2 and schema 3. In schema 2 the dimensionality of the trajector is unspecified, while in schema 3 it must be at least two-dimensional. But whereas schema 2 requires noncontact, schema 3 is neutral with respect to contact, allowing either contact or lack of it.

There is a minimal variant of schema 3 in which the TR moves into the configuration of schema 3. This schema is composed of schema 3 plus a path (P) indicating motion to the final position. Schema 3.P.E is linked to schema 1. It shares motion of the TR above and across the LM. It also shares a lack of specification for contact. Schema 3.P.E differs from schema 1 in two ways. It is specified for the dimension of the trajector and it has end-point focus, which indicates that the final state is that of schema 3.

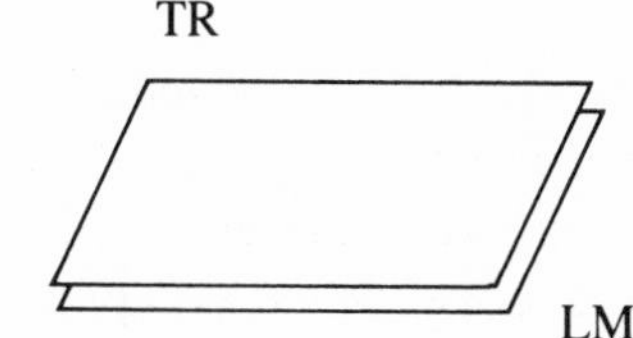

Fig. 16. The board is over the hole.
Schema 3

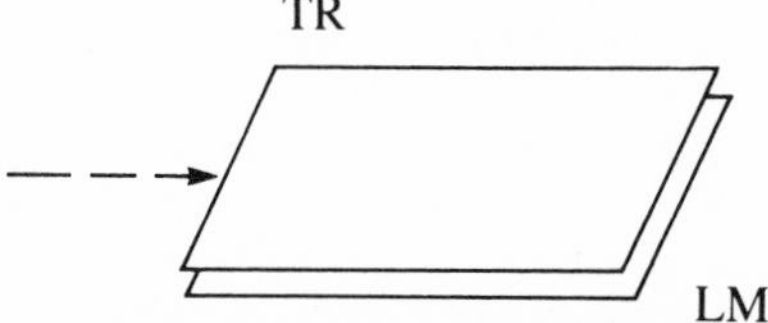

Fig. 17. The city clouded over.
Schema 3.P.E.

There are two covering schemas in which *over* is paired with a mass quantifier that quantifies regions of the landmark, e.g., *all, most, a lot of, entire*, etc. The quantifier *all* may combine with *over* in this sense to form the unit *all over.* The first of these two schemas has a multiplex (MX) trajector, that is, a trajector made up of many individuals.

- He has freckles *over most* of his body.
- There are specks of paint *all over* the rug.
- There is sagebrush *over* the *entire* valley floor.

In these cases, the individuals—the individual hairs, specks of paint, and bushes—don't completely cover the part of the landmark quantified by *over.* Rather, the landmark has small regions which jointly cover its surface (or most of it), and there is at least one trajector in each region. The relationship between schema 3 and schema 3.MX is the relationship between a continuous region (or mass) and a multiplex entity. Such relationships are very common in language. Compare *cows* (multiplex) and *cattle* (mass). Quantifiers like *all* and *most* can occur with either masses (*all gold, most wine*) or multiplex entities (*all ducks, most trees*). The relationship between multiplex entities and masses is a natural visual relationship. Imagine a large herd of cows up close—close enough to pick out the individual cows. Now imagine yourself moving back until you can no longer pick out the individual cows. What you perceive is a mass. There is a point at which you cease making out the individuals and start perceiving a mass. It is this perceptual experience upon which the relationship between multiplex entities and masses rests. The image transformation that relates multiplex entities and masses characterizes the link between schema 3 and schema 3.MX. We can characterize that transformational link as follows:

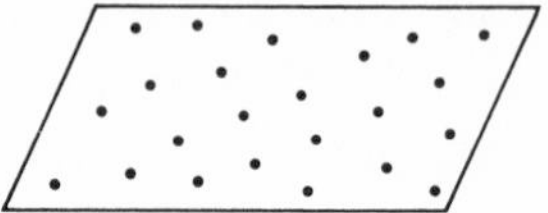

Fig. 18. The guards were posted all over the hill.
Schema 3.MX

MX ↔ MS

There is a second covering schema for *over* in which *over* is associated with a mass quantifier. It is a minimal variant on schema 3.MX in which the points representing the multiplex entity of 3.MX are joined to form a path (P) which "covers" the landmark. Examples are:

- I walked all over the hill.
- We've hiked over most of the Sierras.
- I've hitchhiked over the entire country.

We can represent this schema in figure 19. This schema is linked to schema 3.MX by an image transformation that forms a path through a collection of points. We will represent this transformational linkage as:

MX ↔ MX.P

Schema 3.MX.P is also minimally linked to schema 3.P. In schema 3.P, the landmark is gradually covered as the trajector moves along the path. This is also true in schema 3.MX.P.

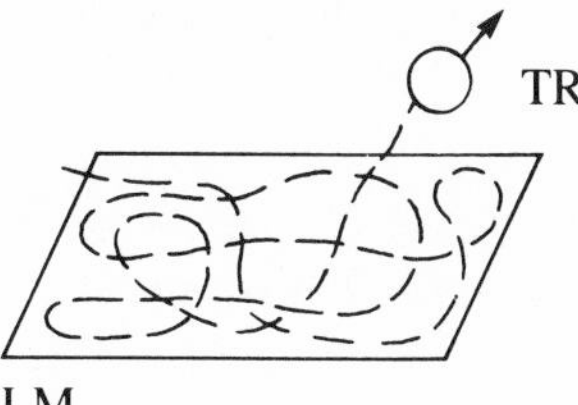

Fig. 19. I walked all over the hill.
Schema 3.MX.P

The covering schemas all have variants in which the TR need not be above (that is, higher than) the LM. In all cases, however, there must be an understood viewpoint from which the TR is blocking accessibility of vision to at least some part of the landmark.

- There was a veil *over* her face.
- As the rain came down, it froze and ice spread all *over* the windshield.
- There were flies all *over* the ceiling.
- The spider had crawled all *over* the ceiling.

We will refer to these as *rotated* (RO) schemas, though with no suggestion that there is actual mental rotation degree-by-degree involved. One might suggest that instead of rotation from the vertical, there is simply a lack of specification of orientation. If there were, we would expect that the contact restrictions would be the same in all orientations, but they are not. The rotated versions of the MX schemas (3.MX and 3.MX.P) require contact, while the unrotated versions do not. Here are some typical examples that illustrate the distinction:

- Superman flew all *over* downtown Metropolis. (TR above LM, non-contact)
- *Superman flew all *over* the canyon walls. (TR not above LM, non-contact)
- Harry climbed all *over* the canyon walls. (TR not above LM, contact)

Thus, Superman's flying *alongside* the canyon walls does not constitute flying *over* them.

We will add RO to the names of the unrotated covering schemas to yield names for the corresponding covering schemas. The rotated covering schemas have the following names: 3.RO, 3.P.RO, 3.MX.RO, and 3.MX.P.RO. Figure 20 is a diagram indicating the links among the covering schemas and the links to the other *over* schemas. And figure 21 indicates the overall linkage among the schemas discussed so far.

The Reflexive Schemas

Perhaps the most remarkable of the discoveries made by Lindner (1981, 1982) was the discovery of *reflexive trajectors.* The concept can be illustrated most simply using the example of *out.* The simplest use of *out* occurs in cases like *Harry ran out of the room.* In figure 22 the container (the room) is the landmark, and the trajector (Harry) moves from the interior to the exterior of the room. But this schema won't do for cases of *out* like:

- The syrup spread *out.*
- The posse spread *out.*

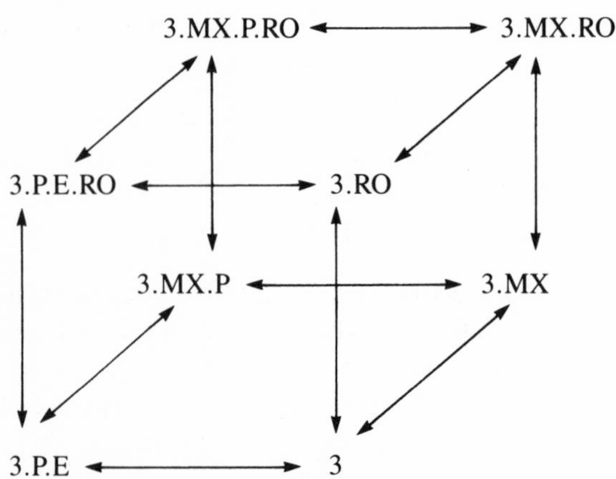

Fig. 20. Links among covering schemas

- They stretched *out* the taffy.
- We rolled *out* the carpet.

Here the relevant trajectors are the syrup, the posse, the taffy, and the carpet. But they are not moving *out* with respect to any other landmark. Take the case of the syrup. Pour some syrup on a table. It will have a certain outer boundary at first. But the boundary moves. Some of the syrup that was inside the initial boundary is now outside that initial boundary. The syrup, or at least part of it, is moving "out" relative to its own prior boundary. We can schematize this as in figure 23. In short, the syrup is its own landmark. TR = LM. Such a relation between a landmark and a trajector is called *reflexive.* Since there is only one entity under consideration, it is referred to as a *reflexive trajector.*

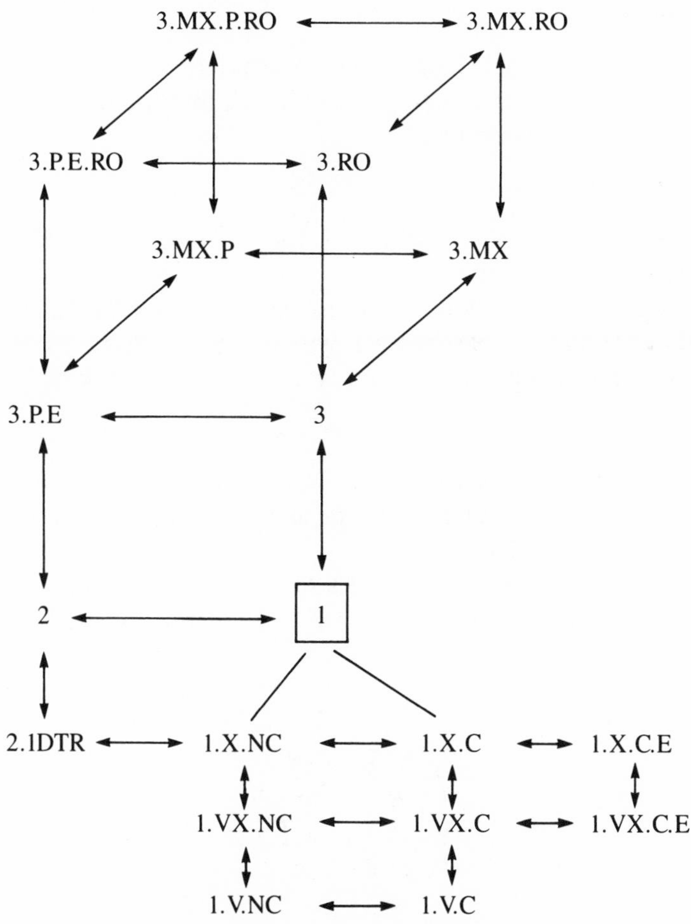

Fig. 21. Links among schemas 1–3

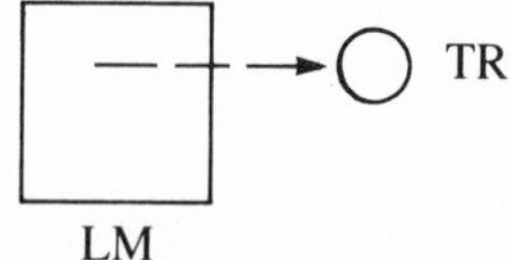

Fig. 22. Harry ran out of the room.

The equal sign in "TR = LM" is not strict identity; it is "identity" of *part of* a bounded mass relative to itself as it *used to be* bounded. As we will see below, there are several ways in which "TR = LM" can be realized. An important one is when parts of a single entity act as TR and other parts of the same entity act as LM. This kind of reflexive trajector occurs in the case of *over*. Consider examples like:

– Roll the log *over*.

Here a major part (roughly half) of the log is moving above and across the rest. That is, half the log is acting as landmark and the rest as trajector. The same is true in a case like

– Turn the paper *over*.

Both of these are variations on schema 1; they differ only in that LM = TR in the sense just described.

We can represent the schema for these cases in figure 24. Schema 4 can be viewed as a transform of schema 1, with schema 4 adding the condition TR = LM. We will represent such a transformational link as

NRF ↔ RF

where NRF means nonreflexive and RF means reflexive. If we had chosen to name schema 4 according to its status as a variant of schema 1, we would have called it 1.RF.

The path of *over* in schema 4 traces a semicircle above and across other parts of the thing being moved. We will refer to this as a *reflexive path.*

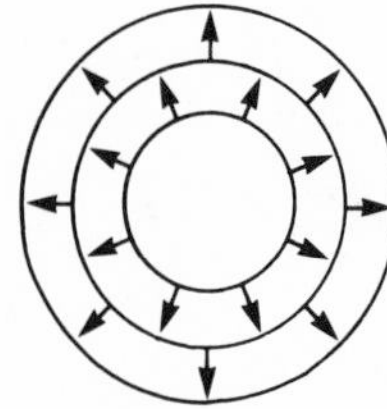

Fig. 23. The syrup spread out.

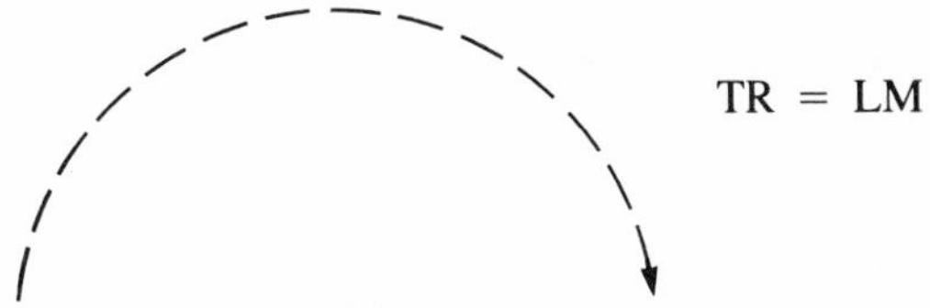

Fig. 24. Roll the log over.

There is a variant on schema 4 in which no part of the thing moving moves above or across any other part; instead, the entity as a whole traces the reflexive path:

- The fence fell *over.*
- Sam knocked *over* the lamp.

These are cases where the TR is initially vertical and moves so as to follow the last half of a reflexive path (RFP). The relationship between schemas 4 and 4.RFP (fig. 25) can be stated as follows: In schema 4, half of the TR follows the whole reflexive path; in schema 4.RPF, all of the TR follows the last half of the reflexive path.

This schema is not only a variant of schema 4. It is also a minimal variant of one of the most common instances of schema 1, the instance that characterizes *over* in *The dog jumped over the fence.* In this case, there is a vertical landmark and the path of the trajector both begins and ends on the ground (G). This results in a semicircular path, as in figure 26. If we take the reflexive transform of this schema, letting TR = LM, we get the schema of figure 25, schema 4.RFP. Thus, schema 4.RFP has close links to two other schemas.

The Excess Schema

When *over* is used as a prefix, it can indicate excess, as in:

- The bathtub *over*flowed.
- I *over*ate.
- Don't *over*extend yourself.

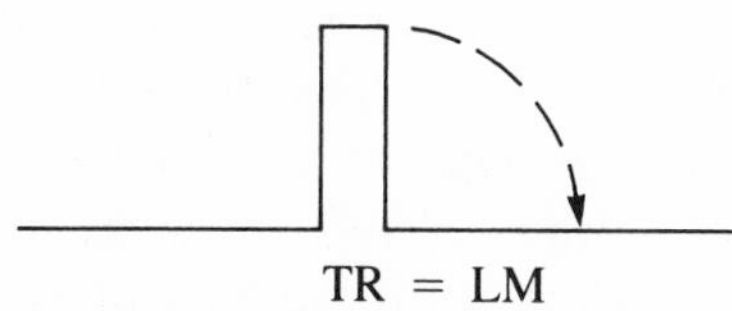

Fig. 25. The fence fell over.
Schema 4.RFP

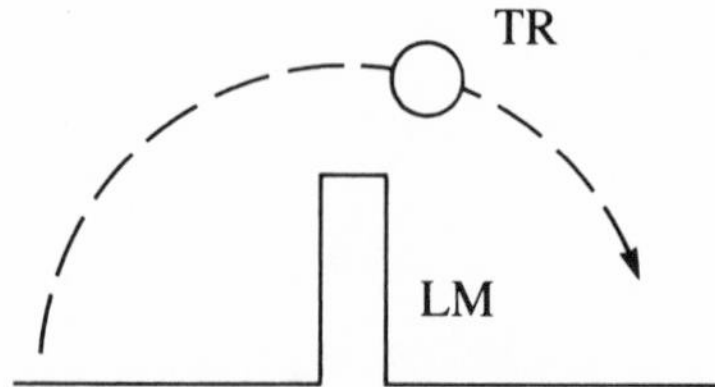

Fig. 26. The dog jumped over the fence.

Overflow provides a link between the excess schema in general and the schema of figure 26. For overflowing to take place, there must be a fluid in a container, which has vertical sides. The path of the overflowing fluid is upward and *over* the side of the container. This makes the *over* of *overflow* an instance of figure 26, where the LM = the side of the container, the PATH = the path of the flow, and the TR = the level of the fluid.

But overflowing is more than just flowing over the edge of a container. Semantically, it involves excess. Syntactically, the *over* becomes a prefix. Let us look at the semantics first. The concept of overflowing presupposes that there is a container with vertical sides and that the height of the sides characterizes the maximal normal amount of fluid, relative to some assumed norm. For example,

– The river *over*flowed.

Here the banks of the river are the vertical sides and define the maximal normal height of the river. Thus, we have in addition: the height of the LM *defines* the maximal normal amount of fluid. Thus, flowing over the LM constitutes exceeding the norm.

We regularly fill containers with fluids for some purpose, drinking, washing, etc. The container used defines a maximal normal amount of the fluid. *Overflowing* is a very common occurrence. When it occurs, the fluid put into the container is wasted and creates a mess. This regular correlation in experience is the basis of the metaphor on which the excess schema is based. The metaphor involved is not specialized to the excess schema; it is more general. In the metaphor, AN ACTIVITY IS A CONTAINER for the effort (or energy) *put into it.* The sides of the container define the maximal normal effort required to achieve the goal of the activity. *Overdoing* something involves putting more than the maximal normal amount of effort into an activity that is required to achieve the goal. This results in wasted effort, and sometimes in awkwardness (a social mess).

The excess schema is thus not merely an image schema, but an image schema (1.V.NC.G as in fig. 25) plus a metaphor. We will refer to it as schema 5.

The Repetition Schema

One of the most common uses of *over* is to indicate repetition, as in

– Do it *over.*

Here *over* is used as an adverb. As in the case of the *over* of excess, the *over* of repetition makes use of a complex schema built on an instance of schema 1, namely, schema 1.X.C. This schema has an extended landmark and indicates motion above and across it (cf. fig. 5). The repetition schema uses schema 1.X.C and adds two metaphors to it. Again, the path is metaphorically understood as the course of the activity. This is via the very general ACTIVITY IS A JOURNEY metaphor. There is, however, an important idiosyncrasy in this sense: the landmark is understood metaphorically as an earlier completed performance of the activity. This is a special-purpose constraint on the general metaphor, which is, to my knowledge, used only in this complex schema. This is the part of the repetition schema for *over* that is *not motivated by an occurrence elsewhere in the conceptual system.* For this reason, the repetition sense of *over* is less naturally tied into the category of senses than the other senses.

At this point, we are in a position to give a link diagram that shows a good deal of the complexity of *over.* In that diagram, we will refer to the repetition schema as schema 6. Figure 27 displays all the links we have discussed so far. A number of additional metaphorical links will be discussed below.

Figure 27 shows what is meant by a *radial* structure. Schema 1 occupies a central position; it and its instances are of primary importance in the system of links. The links correspond to what Wittgenstein called "family resemblances." The links are sometimes defined by shared properties, but frequently they are defined not by shared properties, but by transforms or by metaphors.

Some Metaphorical Senses

It is extremely common for metaphors to take image schemas as their input. A great many metaphorical models use a spatial domain as their source domain. Among the most common source domains for metaphorical models are containers, orientations, journeys (with paths and goals), vertical impediments, etc. In this section, we will give a number of cases where *over* has a metaphorical sense based on an image schema discussed above.

– She has a strange power *over* me.

This is an instance of a very common metaphor: CONTROL IS UP; LACK OF CONTROL IS DOWN (cf. Lakoff and Johnson 1980, p.15). *Over* in this sen-

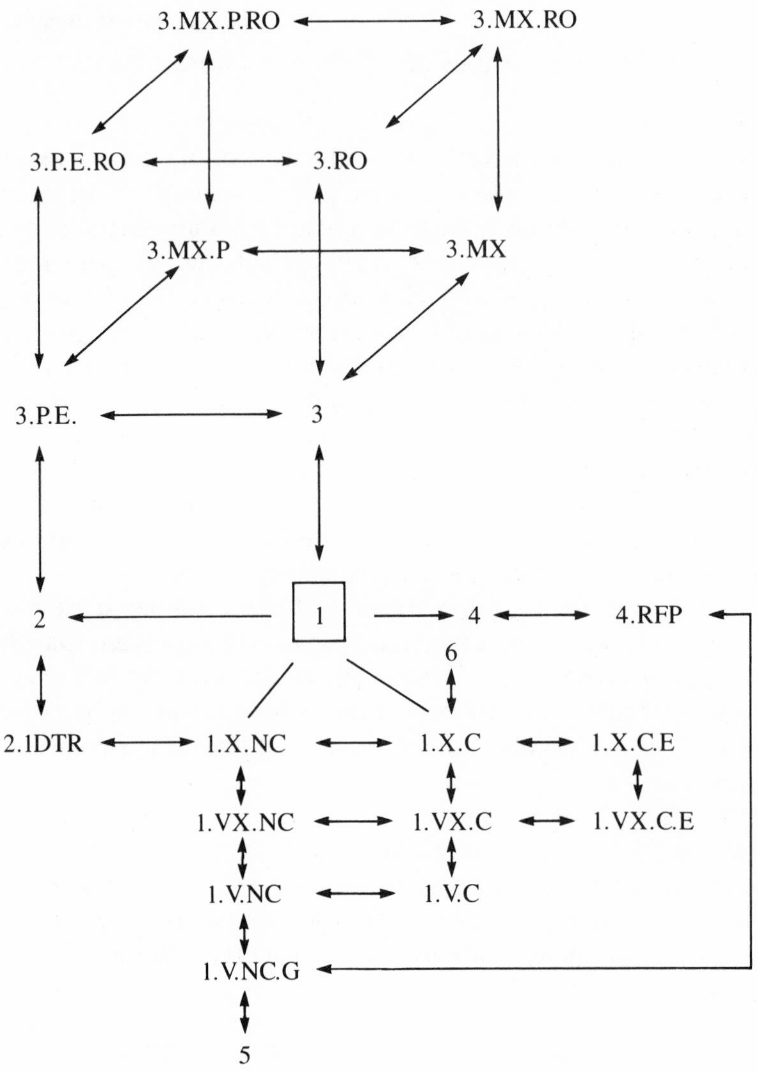

Fig. 27. Relations among the schemas

tence is an extension of schema 2 (fig. 14), where the trajector is simply above the landmark.

– Sam was passed *over* for promotion.

Here we have an instance of schema 1 (fig. 1). Two metaphorical mappings apply to it. The first is CONTROL IS UP; LACK OF CONTROL IS DOWN. This entails that the person who passed over Sam was in control of Sam's status. The second metaphor that applies to this schema is another common one: CHOOSING IS TOUCHING. This occurs in such sentences as *He was tapped for service* and *The boss handpicked his successor.* Since the schema indicates that there is no contact, it is entailed that Sam was not chosen.

We are now in a position to make sense of the difference between *overlook* and *oversee.*

- You've *over*looked his accomplishments.
- We need to find someone who can *over*see this operation.

The *over* in *overlook* is based on schema 2.1DTR (fig. 14). There are two metaphors involved. The first is a metaphor for understanding vision: SEEING IS TOUCHING. This occurs in examples like *I couldn't take my eyes off of her, Her eyes picked out every detail of the pattern, He undressed her with his eyes*, and *He fixed his gaze on the entrance.* According to this metaphor, one's gaze goes from one's eyes to what one sees. You see whatever your gaze touches. Under the metaphorical mapping, the path in schema 2.1DTR is the gaze. Since there is no contact in schema 2.1DTR, the metaphorical gaze doesn't touch the landmark; thus the subject of *overlook* is *not* looking at, and therefore does *not* see, the landmark. The second metaphor is the general MIND-AS-BODY metaphor (cf. Sweetser 1984). The relevant aspect of that metaphor is the part in which LOOKING AT SOMETHING IS TAKING IT INTO CONSIDERATION. Accordingly, *I'll take a look at it* normally entails *I'll consider it.* Therefore, to overlook someone's accomplishments is *not* to take them into consideration.

The *over* in *oversee* is based on schema 2 (fig. 13), in which the TR is above the LM. There are a metaphor and a metonymy that are relevant to this example. The metaphor is CONTROL IS UP. Thus, the one who does the overseeing has control over the persons overseen. The metonymy is SEEING SOMETHING DONE STANDS FOR MAKING SURE THAT IT IS DONE. This metonymy is based on an idealized model in which making sure of something typically involves seeing it. Because of this metonymic relation, *See that he gets his money* means *Make sure that he gets his money.* Thus, to *oversee* means to be in control and make sure that something is done.

We can now compare *overlook* to *look over.*

- Look *over* my corrections, but don't *over*look any of them.

The *over* in *look over* is based on schema 3.MX.P (fig. 19), and the SEEING IS TOUCHING metaphor. The resulting complex schema is one in which the subject's gaze traces a path that "covers" the direct object, *corrections.* In the resulting schema, the gaze does make contact with the landmark. The MIND-AS-BODY metaphor again yields a sense of *look* in which looking at something involves taking it into consideration. Thus, when one looks over X, one directs one's attention to a representative sampling that "covers" X, and one takes into consideration each subpart that one directs attention to.

Motivation

Before we go on, it is worth commenting on what is and what is not being explained in these analyses. We are not explaining why *oversee, overlook*, and *look over* mean what they mean. Their meanings cannot be predicted from the meanings of *over, look*, and *see.* But their meanings are not completely arbitrary. Given the range of spatial meanings of *over* and given the metaphors present in the conceptual system that English is based on, it *makes sense* for these words to have these meanings. We are explaining just why it makes sense and what kind of sense it makes.

In each of these cases, the metaphorical and metonymic models exist in the conceptual system independently of the given expression. For example, we understand seeing metaphorically in terms of a gaze that goes out of one's eyes and touches the object seen. This metaphorical understanding is present regardless of whether any of the expressions just discussed have those meanings. Similarly, the schemas for *over* exist for expressions in the spatial domain independent of the existence of *oversee, overlook*, and *look over.* What one learns when one learns these words is which of the independently existing components of their meaning are actually utilized. Each of these expressions is a specialized "assembly" of independently existing parts. The only arbitrariness involved is the knowledge that such an assembly exists.

The psychological claim being made here is that it is easier to learn, remember, and use such assemblies which use existing patterns than it is to learn, remember, and use words whose meaning is not consistent with existing patterns. What is being explained is not why those expressions mean what they mean, but why those are natural meanings for them to have. Thus, if one is going to have a word that means "to fail to take into consideration," it is more natural to use *overlook* than to use an existing unrelated word like *sew*, or a complex word whose components are in conflict with the meaning, such as *underplan*, or *taste at*, or *rekick*. It is common sense that such expressions would not be used with such a meaning, and we are characterizing the nature of that "common sense."

As we have mentioned before, such an explanation requires going beyond the predictable-arbitrary dichotomy. It requires introducing the concept of *motivation.* Thus, the meaning of *overlook*, though not predictable, is motivated—motivated by one of the spatial schemas for *over* and by two metaphors in the conceptual system. Similarly, all of the noncentral schemas for *over* in the chain given in figure 27 are motivated—motivated by other senses and by principles of linking.

More Metaphorical Senses

There are some additional common metaphorical senses of *over* that are worth discussing. Take *get over*, for example.

- Harry still hasn't gotten *over* his divorce.

This use of *over* is based on schema 1.VX.C (fig. 6) and two metaphors. In the first metaphor, obstacles are understood in terms of vertical landmarks—which may be extended or not. This metaphorical model is the basis for expressions such as *There is nothing standing in your way.* The second metaphorical model is one that understands LIFE as a JOURNEY. This occurs in sentences like *It's time to get on with your life.* In the above use, the divorce is an obstacle (metaphorically, a vertical extended landmark) on the path defined by life's journey.

- Pete Rose is *over* the hill.

Over the hill makes use of schema 1.VX.C.E (fig. 10) and a metaphor for understanding a career in terms of a journey over a vertical extended landmark like a hill. In this metaphorical model of a career, one *starts at the bottom*, may *go all the way to the top*, and then *goes downhill.* Thus, *over the hill* means that one has already reached and passed the peak, or "high point," of one's career and will never have that high a stature again.

- The rebels *overthrew* the government.

This is an instance of schema 4.RFP (fig. 25) which is the schema in *fall over*, and the CONTROL IS UP metaphor. Before the event takes place, the government is in control (metaphorically upright), and afterwards it is not in control (metaphorically, it has fallen over).

- He turned the question *over* in his mind.

This is an instance of schema 4 (fig. 24), plus an instance of the MIND-AS-BODY metaphor in which THINKING ABOUT SOMETHING IS EXAMINING IT. This metaphorical model occurs in such sentences as *Let us now examine the question of factory chickens.* In examining a physical object, one turns it over in order to get a look at all sides of it. Questions are metaphorically understood as having sides, and when one turns a question over in one's mind, one is examining all sides of it.

- The play is *over.*

Here we have an instance of schema 1.X.C.E (fig. 11). In general, activities with a prescribed structure are understood as extended landmarks, and performing such an activity is understood metaphorically as traveling along a prescribed path over that landmark. When one gets to the end, the activity is *over*. Thus, games, plays, and political campaigns can be characterized at their end as being *over.*

Image Schemas as Links between Perception and Reason

Two of our major sources of information are vision and language. We can gain information through either perceiving something directly or being told it. And we can reason about that information, no matter what its source. We can even reason using information from both sources simultaneously, which suggests that it is possible for us to encode information from both sources in a single format. I would like to suggest that image schemas provide such a format.

It is my guess that image schemas play a central role in both perception and reason. I believe that they structure our perceptions and that their structure is made use of in reason. The analysis of *over* that we have just given is rich enough for us to discuss such questions in some detail. Let us begin with the following question. Are the image-schema transformations we have discussed natural, and if so, what is the source of their "naturalness"?

The Nature of Image-Schema Transformations

There are certain very natural relationships among image-schemas, and these motivate polysemy, not just in one or two cases, but in case after case throughout the lexicon. Natural image-schema transformations play a central role in forming radial categories of senses. Take, for example, the end-point focus transformation. It is common for words that have an image schema with a path to also have the corresponding image-schema with a focus on the end point of the path, as Bennett (1975) observed. We saw this in *over* in cases like

- Sam walked *over* the hill. (path)
- Sam lives over the hill. (end of path)

Pairs such as this are common.

- Harry walked *through* that doorway. (path)
- The passport office is *through* that doorway. (end of path)

- Sam walked *around* the corner. (path)
- Sam lives *around* the corner. (end of path)

- Harriet walked *across* the street. (path)
- Harriet lives *across* the street. (end of path)

- Mary walked *down* the road. (path)
- Mary lives *down* the road. (end of path)

- Sam walked *past* the post office. (path)
- Sam lives *past* the post office. (end of path)

It should be noted that although such pairs are common, they are not fully productive.

- Sam walked *by* the post office. (path)
- Sam lives *by* the post office. (= *near*; ≠ end of path)

Here, *by* has a path schema, but no corresponding end-point schema.

- Sam ran *from* the house. (path)
- Sam stood three feet *from* the house. (end of path)

- Sam ran *to* the house. (path)
- *Sam stood (three feet) *to* the house. (not end of path)

From allows both path and end-of-path schemas, but *to* allows only a path schema.

Path schemas are so naturally related to end-point schemas that people sometimes have to think twice to notice the difference. The same is true of the schema transformation that links multiplex and mass schemas. It is natural for words that have a mass schema to have a multiplex schema as well.

- *All* men are mortal. (MX)
- *All* gold is yellow. (MS)
- She bought *a lot of* earrings. (MX)
- She bought *a lot of* jewelry. (MS)

This schema transformation, of course, doesn't hold for all quantifiers:

- She bought *two* earrings. (MX)
- *She bought *two* jewelry. (MS)

There are also verbs that have both schemas:

- He *poured* the juice through the sieve. (MS)
- The fans *poured* through the gates (MX)

This will also work for other verbs of liquid movement, such as *spill, flow*, etc.

- The wine *spilled* out over the table. (MS)
- The fans *spilled* out over the field. (MX)

There is a special case of the multiplex-mass transformation in which the multiplex entity is a sequence of points and the mass is a one-dimensional trajector. A variety of prepositions permit both schemas.

- There are guards posted *along* the road. (MX)
- There is a fence *along* the road. (1DTR)

- He coughed *throughout* the concert. (MX)
- He slept *throughout* the concert. (1DTR)

- There were stains *down* his tie. (MX)
- There were stripes *down* his tie. (1DTR)

There is a natural relationship not only between a one-dimensional trajector and a sequence of points, but also between a one-dimensional trajector and a zero-dimensional moving trajector that traces a path.

- Sam *went* to the top of the mountain. (0DMTR)
- The road *went* to the top of the mountain. (1DTR)

- Sam ran *through* the forest. (0DMTR)
- There is a road *through* the forest. (1DTR)

- Sam walked *across* the street. (0DMTR)
- There was a rope stretched *across* the street. (1DTR)

Finally, there is a natural relationship between nonreflexive and reflexive trajectors. Here are some examples:

- He stood *apart* from the crowd. (NRF)
- The book fell *apart.* (RF)

- She walked *up* to me. (NRF)
- Let's cuddle *up*. (RF)

- She poured the syrup *out* of the jar. (NRF)
- The syrup spread *out* over the pancakes. (RF)

Let us consider for a moment what is natural about these image-schema transformations.

Path focus ↔ end-point focus: It is a common experience to follow the path of a moving object until it comes to rest, and then to focus on where it is. This corresponds to the path focus and end-point focus transformation.

Multiplex ↔ mass: As one moves further away, a group of individuals at a certain point begins to be seen as a mass. Similarly, a sequence of points is seen as a continuous line when viewed from a distance.

0DMTR ↔ 1DTR: When we perceive a continuously moving object, we can mentally trace the path it is following. This capacity is reflected in the transformation linking zero-dimensional moving trajectors and a one-dimensional trajector.

NRF ↔ *RF:* Given a perceived relationship between a TR and a LM which are two separate entities, it is possible to perceive the same relationship between (*a*) different parts of the same entity or (*b*) earlier and later locations of the same entity, where one part or location is considered LM and the other TR.

In short, these schema transformations are anything but arbitrary. They are direct reflections of our experiences, which may be visual, or kinesthetic.

The fact that image schemas are a reflection of our sensory and general spatial experience is hardly surprising, yet it plays a very important role in the theory of image schemas. Perhaps we can see that significance most easily by contrasting the image-schema transformations we have described with the names we have given to them. Take the transformation name "MX ↔ MS." The names "MX" and "MS" are arbitrary relative to the character of what they name: a group of individual entities and a mass. The transformation is a natural relationship, but the name of the transformation is just a bunch of arbitrary symbols.

The distinction is important because of certain versions of the computational theory of mind. On one theory of image representation—the "propositional theory"—visual scenes are represented by arbitrary symbols which are linked together in network structures. Arbitrary symbols such as X and Y are taken as standing for some aspect of a scene, such as a point or an edge or a surface or an entire object. Other symbols are used to express relations among these symbols, for example, "ABV(X,Y)" and "C(X,Y)" might represent relations which are supposed to correspond to "X is above Y" and "X is in contact with Y," but which, so far as the computer is concerned, are just symbols. Such a symbolization describes how various parts—points, edges, surfaces, etc.—are related to one another. Objects in a scene are described using such symbolizations.

According to the computational view of mind as applied to visual information and mental imagery (Pylyshyn 1981), only such propositional representations are mentally real, while images are not real. This view stems from taking the computational model of the mind *very* seriously. Since digital computers work by the manipulation of such arbitrary symbols, the strong version of the computational theory of mind *requires* not only that visual perception and mental imagery be characterizable in such a "propositional" form, but also that such symbolic representations, and only those, are mentally real.

The names that we have given to image schemas, and to image-schema transformations, are very much in keeping with the kind of symbolization that might be used in studies of computer vision. But the names are not the things named. This is shown by the naturalness of image-schema transformations relative to visual experience, as opposed to the arbitrariness of the names for those transformations. It seems to me that image-schema transformations are cognitively real; the pervasiveness of the kinds of relationships between senses of lexical items that those transformations characterize is a strong indicator of their cognitive reality. And the naturalness of these transformations relative to our visual experience suggests that image-schema transformations and the schemas they relate are not propositional in character (in the sense of the term used in computer vision studies). Rather, they are truly imagistic in character.

Perceptions, Rich Images, and Schemas

The term *image* is not intended here to be limited to visual images. We also have auditory images, olfactory images, and images of how forces act upon us. But the only kind of nonvisual images that linguists have said anything of interest about are sound images (Rhodes and Lawler 1981, McCune 1983) and force images (Talmy 1985*b*). Sweetser (1982, 1984) has demonstrated that our image-schematic understanding of forces lies behind our understanding of modality, that is, the concepts represented by words such as *must, may, can*, etc. But, on the whole, research on image schemas has concentrated on visual images, and we will limit our discussion to those.

It is important at the outset to distinguish mental images from perceptions. A perception of a scene is rich in detail; every part of the visual field is filled. And one can focus on details that are very small and intricate. Moreover, since our eyes are constantly scanning different parts of the visual field, the details focused on are continually changing. We perceive in color, and we can perceive an incredible range of shades of color. Those of us with color vision cannot simply turn off the color. Moreover, we ordinarily perceive without noticeable effort, although paying attention and noticing is an effortful activity.

Mental images have a different character. They are not nearly as detailed as perceptions, and they do not allow anything like the full range of perceived colors. People who see in color can have mental images in black and white. Not all of the field of mental vision is filled. And although in daydreaming we form mental images without noticeable effort, constructing an image and keeping it in mind is an effortful activity. Moreover, we can form images of things we can't see. Imagine a basketball.

Imagine a trunk. Imagine the basketball inside the trunk. Our real eyes cannot see through the trunk to the basketball, but our mind's eye can.

Conscious Effortful Imagery

The study of mental images has recently come into its own in cognitive psychology, due primarily to the efforts of Roger Shepard, Stephen Kosslyn, and their co-workers (cf. Shepard and Cooper 1982, Kosslyn 1980, 1983). Shepard and his colleagues have studied rigid transformations of images, e.g., rotations, which unlike the schema transformations mentioned above, are structure-preserving. Kosslyn and his co-workers have studied such matters as what is involved in scanning images, putting parts of images together, and even how wide the field of "mental vision" is.

The kind of mental images studied by Shepard, Kosslyn, and others are what we will call *context-bound specific conscious effortful rich images.* Subjects are presented with pictures and are asked to form images of them. This makes the images context-bound. They are then asked to do such things as rotate them in their minds or scan them or make judgments about them. The images are *specific* in that the pictures presented are of specific objects or figures. They are *conscious* in that subjects form the images consciously and do conscious manipulations on them. The fact that it requires some mental effort for subjects to construct and manipulate the images makes them *effortful.* And the images are relatively *rich* in detail compared to the schemas that we have been discussing. They are the sort of images you would get if I showed you a detailed treasure map, asked you to memorize it as well as you could, and then took the map away and asked you to form an image of the map and scan various parts of it. This is a special kind of task that some people can do better than others, and the people who can do it well can do it very well. But people do vary greatly in their ability to function with such context-bound, specific, conscious, effortful, and rich imagery.

The Kinesthetic Nature of Mental Imagery

Mental imagery, as we pointed out above, is not merely visual. And image schemas are kinesthetic in nature, that is, they have to do with the sense of spatial locations, movement, shape, etc., independent of any particular sensory modality. Evidence for this comes from mental imagery experiments conducted with congenitally blind people. Experiments of the sort done by Shepard, Kosslyn, and their co-workers have been replicated with the congenitally blind. The principal experiments have been reported on in Marmor and Zaback (1976), Carpenter and

Eisenberg (1978), Zimler and Keenan (1983), and Kerr (1983). The basic result is this: When mental imagery experiments are run with the congenitally blind using touch instead of vision, the results are virtually the same as for sighted persons, except that people who can see perform the tasks faster.

Among the tasks used in these experiments were mental rotation and scanning tasks, both of which involve not just static images but continuous motion. It seems to me that the appropriate conclusion to draw from these experiments is that much of mental imagery is kinesthetic—that is, it is independent of sensory modality and concerns awareness of many aspects of functioning in space: orientation, motion, balance, shape judgments, etc. This includes image schemas, which are sufficiently general in character to be prime candidates for having a kinesthetic nature. If richer, more detailed images have been shown to be kinesthetic, then it would seem that schematic images could be kinesthetic as well.

Conventional Images

Imagery of this sort is real, and the studies done by Shepard, Kosslyn, and others have contributed a great deal to our understanding of images of this type. But they are by no means the only kind of mental images that people have. As a cognitive linguist, I am mainly interested in that aspect of cognition that is unconscious, automatic, and apparently effort-free and independent of skill. Language has this character, as does everyday commonsense reasoning. There also appear to be mental images that have these properties—what I will refer to as *conventional rich images.*

Being a member of a culture requires one to have a large stock of such conventional rich images. Americans, for example, tend to have images of Marilyn Monroe and Richard Nixon and Cadillac limousines and the Statue of Liberty. They also have images of horses and cats and roses and bicycles and engagement rings and baseball bats. As Rosch discovered, people often have images of prototypical members of categories—of typical cases, social stereotypes, paragons, and the like. And they tend to use such images in making goodness-of-example judgments. These images are conventional. They appear to be pretty much the same from person to person in the same culture. My image of a cup may be somewhat different from yours, but not all that different—unless you come from some part of the world where the things you eat and drink with are very different from those in America. Conventional images are not context-bound. You can form an image of a cup right now—without anyone presenting you with a particular cup or a picture of one. The image you form may or may not be of a specific cup. Most people are capable of forming nonspecific images. If I ask you to imagine an elephant and you do, it is unlikely to be any particular elephant. And it doesn't take any noticeable effort to imagine a cup or a car or an elephant, though it will probably take noticeable effort to imagine an elephant and turn your image 135 degrees. Moreover, conventional images seem to be unconscious. We seem capable of storing images of horses and sailboats and pizzas for very long periods without any effort and without even being aware that they are there. We also have conventional images of typical actions performed with these things. For example, we have conventional images of people eating pizza—most likely a wedge-shaped slice of a round pizza, with the point going in the mouth first, and probably not with a clean bite but rather with the cheese pulling away in its usual stringy fashion. Our conventional images may not all be exactly the same, but the degree of uniformity is remarkable.

Conventional images play an extremely important role in natural language. They are central to the formation of new idioms and to making sense of old ones. There is an extensive class of idioms that I will refer to as *imageable idioms.* These are idioms that have associated conventional images. Consider the idiom *to keep someone at arm's length.* I have asked hundreds of people if they have an image associated with this idiom. Almost everyone does, and it is almost always the same image.

Keeping Someone at Arm's Length

- The arm is oriented forward with respect to the body, perhaps a little to the side. It is never oriented backward, or upward, or downward, though these are all logical possibilities.
- The arm is chest high.
- The hand is usually open (though some have it making a fist).
- The open palm is facing away from the subject; it is never facing toward the subject.
- The angle of the hand relative to the forearm is roughly 90 to 135 degrees.
- The arm muscles are tense, not lax.
- The person being kept at arm's length is facing toward the subject.

The actual expression, *to keep someone at arm's length*, does not specify any of these details. In fact, it doesn't refer to a position of the arm at all, but only to a distance. The details just described are in the conventional image, not in the meanings of words. Interestingly, there are many things that are not specified in the image, things that are either simply absent or that vary indiscriminately from person to person. For example, is the arm clothed? Long sleeve or short sleeve? Answers to such questions are not consistent, or the image isn't clear. Thus, some parts of the image are relatively stable and clear, while other parts are unstable or vague.

In addition, speakers have knowledge about such images:

- The purpose of having one's arm in that position is defense.
- If the arm were let down, the other person could get close enough to inflict harm.

According to the classical theory of idioms, there is no reason at all why a conventional image with specific knowledge should be associated with an idiom. According to the classical theory, idioms have arbitrary meanings: any series of words could have any meaning at all. The idiom *to keep someone at arm's length* has a meaning which is not physical. It means *to keep someone from becoming intimate, so as to avoid social or psychological harm.* In the classical theory, all that there is to idioms is such a pairing of words with a meaning, and there is no reason whatever why speakers should have a conventional image accompanying the idiom. What is the image doing there? And how did people learn that association?

I would like to suggest that, in a very large number of cases, the meanings of idioms are not arbitrary. The reason that they have been thought to be arbitrary is that the meaning of the idiom is not predictable just from the meanings of the individual words that make it up. In traditional linguistic theory, anything that is not predictable is arbitrary. Hence, the meanings of idioms, given traditional theories, must be arbitrary. But, given the theory of cognitive models, there is a third alternative: motivation.

> The relationship between A and B is *motivated* just in case there is an independently existing link, L, such that A-L-B "fit together." L *makes sense* of the relationship between A and B.

The meaning of the idiom *to keep someone at arm's length* is motivated—in large part by the conventional image described above. That image, plus two metaphors that exist independently in our conceptual system, provide the link between the idiom and its meaning. The two metaphors are:

- INTIMACY IS PHYSICAL CLOSENESS.
- SOCIAL (or PSYCHOLOGICAL) HARM IS PHYSICAL HARM.

Given the image, and the knowledge that the image is associated with defense, we get a link to the meaning of the idiom. Keeping someone at arm's length physically is keeping him from getting physically close, and thereby protecting oneself from physical harm. The metaphors map this knowledge into the meaning of the idiom, which is *to keep someone from becoming intimate, so as to protect oneself from social or psychological harm.*

In detail, the explanation goes like this:

- The literal meaning of the idiom fits the conventional image (though it underdetermines it).
- The image has accompanying knowledge.
- The two metaphors map the literal meaning, the image, and its associated knowledge into the meaning of the idiom.
- Letting A be the idiom and B be its meaning, L is the conventional image plus its associated knowledge plus the two metaphors. L thus links A to B.

What it means for an idiom to "be natural" or to "make sense" is that there are independently existing elements of the conceptual system that link the idiom to its meaning.

Let us take another example, the idiom *spill the beans*. Whether or not a given speaker has a conscious vivid image associated with this idiom, most speakers that I have asked informally seem to be able to answer questions like the following about the associated image: Where are the beans before they are spilled? How big is the container? Are they cooked or uncooked? Is the spilling on purpose or accidental? Where are they afterwards? Are they in a nice, neat pile? Where are they supposed to be? After they are spilled, can they be easily retrieved? Was the spill messy or relatively neat? Even speakers who claim not to have a conscious image can answer such questions. This suggests that they have an unconscious image.

The images appear to have certain small variations. Speakers vary as to where the beans are before they are spilled: a pot, a crock, a bag, a jar. Most speakers have uncooked beans in their images; a small percentage have cooked beans. What is remarkable is that, despite such variations, the images are the same in the following respects: The container for the beans is almost always about the size of the human head; it is not barrel size, or silo size, or the size, say, of a small mustard jar. The beans were supposed to be kept in that container. The spilling is, or appears to be, accidental. The beans are never spilled into a neat pile; instead, they go all over the place. They are never easy to retrieve. The spill is always messy.

The uniformity of such answers is remarkable. On the usual theory that the meanings of idioms are arbitrary, there is no reason for any speaker to have any image at all, much less for most speakers to have images that are so much alike. But on the hypothesis that idioms are motivated, and that motivation may consist of a link of the form *image + knowledge + metaphors*, we can explain not only why there are such images, but also what forms they may and may not take. In this case, the relevant metaphor is the CONDUIT METAPHOR (cf. Reddy 1979, Lakoff and Johnson 1980). According to the conduit metaphor, THE MIND IS A CONTAINER, IDEAS ARE ENTITIES, and communication involves taking ideas out of the mind, putting them into words, and sending them to other people.

The CONDUIT METAPHOR applies to this image in the following way. The beans correspond to information. The container corresponds to the head. Therefore, the information is supposed to be kept in the head; that is, it is supposed to be kept secret. Spilling corresponds to letting the information out, either accidentally or apparently by accident. The information "goes all over the place," and the secret is out (the beans cannot all be retrieved). The result is messy. Thus, the image plus the knowledge about the image plus the CONDUIT METAPHOR provide a link between the idiom and its meaning, a link which makes the idiom motivated, not arbitrary.

Incidentally, it may be the case that the image is not stored, but generated when an investigator like myself asks someone. But this does not change the point. We can see this by asking how it would be possible for someone to generate such an image and why the images generated are relatively uniform rather than random. Under the traditional theory of idioms, the words are simply associated directly with their meanings, with no images or metaphors. There is no reason why speakers should be able to generate associated images or have knowledge about them. And if they generated them at all, one would, on the traditional theory, expect them to be random, not structured in this way.

If the images are newly generated, not stored, then the theory we have given makes a prediction: the generated images will be among the conventional images of the culture, they will make use of cultural knowledge, and there will be one or more metaphors already in the conceptual system that link the image and the knowledge to the meaning of the idiom. In short, the principles we have proposed to characterize the nature of motivation for imageable idioms constrain what such images can be like. If the images are newly generated, they are generated in accordance with these principles.

We should also make clear what is not being claimed. We are not claiming that either the meaning of idioms, or their form, is predictable. We are only claiming that the relation between them is not arbitrary. Instead, it is motivated, and the motivation makes the idiom "make sense." Thus, we cannot predict why there are beans in *spill the beans*. However, beans and spilling make sense since beans, when spilled, are hard to retrieve and make a mess, and spilling either is, or can be made to appear, accidental. Given the existence of the CONDUIT METAPHOR, there is a sensible link between our knowledge about spilling beans and the meaning of the idiom *spill the beans.*

Incidentally, there is an extremely important consequence of this kind of analysis: parts of idioms may have metaphorical referents. Thus, *the beans* in *spill the beans* refers to the information that is supposed to be kept secret. *Spill* refers to making that information public. This is important if we are ever to understand the grammar of idioms. For example, *spill the beans* can be passivized, as in *The beans have been spilled.* In this case, *the beans* is a noun phrase that has a referent both in the source domain (the beans in the image) and in the target domain of the CONDUIT METAPHOR (the information to be kept secret). It may be that being a noun phrase and having referents in both source and target domains will permit the idiom to be passivized.

It is important to bear in mind that we are, of course, not claiming that all speakers make complete sense of all idioms. Quite the contrary. There may be occasional idioms that are completely arbitrary for all speakers. There are certainly idioms that some speakers can't make any sense out of. Still most native speakers seem to make at least partial sense of most idioms, with much of the meaning being motivated and perhaps some being arbitrary. As one would expect, not all speakers make the same sense of all idioms. The best known case is *A rolling stone gathers no moss*, which not only varies in meaning from speaker to speaker, but has two primary meanings which are nearly opposites. On one reading, moss is taken to be a good thing, a symbol of the money and status to be accrued by staying in one place. The moral is that it's bad to move around a lot. On the other reading, the moral is the opposite. If you move around a lot, you don't get tied down. Moss is viewed as a bad thing, an encumberment that you get from staying in one place too long. It restricts your freedom.

Just as there are considerable speaker-to-speaker differences in the details of rules of grammar, and very great differences in vocabulary, so there are differences in the images associated with idioms. For most of the imageable idioms I have studied, there seem to be between one and three prevalent associated images, though in some cases there may be between a half-dozen and a dozen. This is by no means an unseemly amount of lexical variation. In fact, since associated images are hardly ever consciously taught or consciously learned, it is remarkable that there is any uniformity at all.

Motivating links for idioms—that is, cases where there is some link (L) of the form *conventional image + knowledge + metaphors* relating the idiom to its meaning—have traditionally been called *folk etymologies.* The term arose in historical linguistics, where the goal was to come as close as possible to the "real" etymology, the real history, of each word and idiom. Folk etymologies are, to historical linguists, things to avoid, things students are warned against. But since the real history of an idiom is hardly ever known, folk etymologies are just about all there is for a historical linguist to go on. Moreover, since hardly any ordinary person ever really knows for sure the real origin of an expression, the folk etymologies that people automatically—and unconsciously—come up with are real for them, not historically, but psychologically.

The fact that ordinary nonlinguists spontaneously and unconsciously make up folk etymologies is a truly remarkable psychological fact. Why should this happen? On the view that the meanings of idioms are always completely arbitrary, there is no reason at all. But if we recognize the need to find motivating links that make sense of idioms, that people function more efficiently with additional information that makes sense of otherwise random information, then it is clear why people would try to make sense of idioms by finding as many motivating links as possible.

The motivating links that people typically find to make sense of the relationship between an idiom and its meaning usually consist of conventional images and metaphors. In the case study of anger, we encountered a great number of idioms that worked this way: *simmer down, blow off steam, flip one's lid, keep one's anger bottled up, wrestle with one's anger*, and so on. There appear to be thousands of idioms that are at least partly motivated by associated conventional images. Such associated images have an important cognitive function. They make sense of the idioms, and therefore make them easier to understand, learn, remember, and use. This is important to bear in mind in considering the nature of lexical knowledge. Human lexicons are not just massive random lists of expressions and associated meanings. Motivating links are included that make sense of those associations. Any adequate psychological account of the learning of, and memory for, the human lexicon will have to take account of the phenomenon of folk etymology—that is, it will have to include an account of why expressions with motivating links are easier to learn and remember than random pairings.

Conventional images do not merely play a role in idiomatic expressions. They are also central to our use and understanding of even the simplest sentences. Rosch has observed that simple basic-level expressions are used to refer to a prototypical instance of a basic-level category, but that it is misleading to use such an expression to refer to a nonprototypical instance. For example, if a sparrow lands on the front porch, it is not misleading to report this by *There's a bird on the porch.* But it would be quite misleading to use such a sentence to report that an eagle had landed on the porch or that a penguin had waddled up the front steps.

Similarly, if John hit a baseball with a bat in the usual way by swinging the bat at the ball, we could straightforwardly report that *John hit a ball.* But if he hit a beachball with a pizza platter, or if he hit a ball by throwing a rock at it, it would be misleading to describe such an event to someone who didn't see it as *John hit a ball*, even though such a description, strictly speaking, would be true. *Hit a ball* has an associated conventional image that characterizes the normal case, and with no further modification we assume that the normal case holds. Thus, conventional images are used to understand even the simplest, most straightforward sentences with no idioms in them.

Image Schemas

Image schemas of the sort we have been discussing are more like conventional images than like the kind of images discussed by Shepard and Kosslyn. Like conventional images, they are neither context-bound, nor specific, nor conscious, nor effortful. They are unlike conventional images in two important respects: they are not rich (that is, fully detailed), and they do not have specific knowledge associated with them. They are relatively abstract schemas that organize what can be perceived and visualized, but they themselves cannot be directly visualized in the way a rich image can be. The drawings we gave above are not the schemas themselves, but only drawings that characterize some of the properties of the schemas and enable us to get some idea of what they are like. But any drawings will necessarily differ in many ways from the schemas themselves. Take, for example, a schema that involves motion and the tracing of a path that exists in time. We have drawn such schemas as static with a dotted line tracing the path. Drawings of schemas with vertical extended landmarks (such as fig. 6) must necessarily sketch the landmark in a particular shape, while the schemas are neutral with respect to the particular details of the shape of the landmark, as long as it is vertical and extended. Image schemas can be visualized or drawn only by making them overly specific. In this respect, they are much like Kant's "schema" for a triangle, which Kant conceived of as fitting equilateral, isosceles, acute, and obtuse triangles without being rich enough in detail to be visualizable as any particular one.

Let us turn now to the relationship between image schemas on the one hand and perceptions and rich mental images on the other. It is my hypothesis that image schemas structure both our perceptions and our rich images. This hypothesis appears to be necessary if we are to account for one of the most common of everyday phenomena, namely, the fact that sentences are judged as accurately describing visual scenes and mental images. Suppose you are either watching or imagining a plane flying and there is a hill on the terrain below. Take a simple sentence like

– The plane is flying over the hill.

You can now judge whether that sentence fits the scene you are watching or imagining. Part of that judgment will involve whether schema 1.VX.NC (fig. 3) fits what you are perceiving or imagining. If the plane, in your perception or imagination, is flying low to the ground around the base of the hill, you would presumably judge the sentence as not fitting the scene or image. A sentence like *A plane is flying around the hill* would no doubt be judged more appropriate in those circumstances. The only difference in these sentences is the choice of preposition: *over* versus *around. Over* is the appropriate choice just in case there is an *over* schema that fits the scene or image.

It is important to note that there are clear cases when a given schema fits a perception or image, clear cases when it does not fit, and intermediate cases when it fits to a degree. Suppose first that the path of the plane goes directly above (and not all that far above) the peak of the hill. Then schema 1.VX.NC fits and the use of *over* is sanctioned. Suppose now that the path of flight is not directly above the top of the hill but rather to one side. If the path of flight is reasonably near the top, the *over* is still appropriate. But the further the path of flight gets from being above the top, the less appropriate it is to use *over*. And when the path of flight is above the valley next to the hill and not even near the top of the hill, *over* is not appropriate at all. How well the schema fits the scene or image will also depend on the height of the flight path. Suppose that instead of being not far above the top of the hill, the flight path is 50,000 feet up. Then the path can be considered *over* the hill even though it is farther away from being directly above the top. Thus, *over* schema 1.VX.NC characterizes a fuzzy category of scenes and images. The central members of the category are those scenes and images that are clear cases of the schema. The less clear cases are less central members and those scenes and images that clearly do not fit are not members. The schema can thus be viewed as a generative prototype, with the schema as the generator and closeness of fit as the general principle defining degree of membership.

On Brugman's analysis, there are two levels of prototype structure for *over:* (1) the radial structure of the category of schemas, where each schema is a member of the category, and (2) the generative structure of the category of scenes and images, which is defined by each individual schema. The perceptions and images are correlated with words via a two-stage model; e.g., the perception of the plane flying over the hill is a member of the category of perceptions and rich images that fit schema

1.VX.NC. That schema is, in turn, a member of the *over* category, which consists of a group of radially structured schemas.

Let us now turn to the question of how it is possible for an image schema to fit a perception or an image. The hypothesis I am putting forth is that our perceptions and our mental images are structured by image schemas and that the schemas associated with lexical items are capable of fitting the schemas that structure our perceptions and images. On this hypothesis, we do not have pure unstructured perceptions and images. Perceptions and images are not merely pictorial. In perceiving and in forming images, we impose a great deal of image-schematic structure. It is this image-schematic structure that allows us to categorize what we perceive. And it is this image-schematic structure that allows us to fit language to our perceptions and rich images.

This hypothesis is anything but uncontroversial. For example, it appears to conflict with Kosslyn's cathode-ray-tube model of mental imagery.

> We can think of the computer's central processing unit (CPU) and memory locations as the means utilized by the program to get its job done. Similarly, the brain can be interpreted as the vehicle for performing the work of the mind.
>
> The analogy between brain and computer also allows us to see how visual imagery can be picturelike without being actual pictures. The cathode ray tube (CRT) that displays information stored in the computer works by translating data encoded as bits into a physical, visible screen. The computer is able to interpret certain stored information as spatial images (whether or not it actually projects an image onto a CRT) because its CPU treats these data as if they were organized in a matrix; that is, these data function as if they were stored in a matrix with some entries next to others, some diagonal from others, and so on. Thus, though the machine itself contains no actual screen, it can store and use material that is pictorial at the functional level. Our model suggests that the brain works this way too. (Kosslyn 1983, p. 205)

Thus, according to Kosslyn, images are stored in the mind in dot-matrix fashion, just as they would be in a computer. The computer-mind knows which cells of the matrix have black dots and which have white dots. Thus, it could compute, for example, whether the black dots happened to form a diagonal line against a field of white dots, without actually projecting any picture on a screen.

Kosslyn's theory is inconsistent with our hypothesis that perceptions and images are structured by image schemas. One of the reasons is that image schemas may not actually appear in the images. Take image schemas that indicate motion. The motion would not be represented in any individual dot-matrix image; it is a property of a sequence of such images, but doesn't occur in any of them. Moreover, in schemas with an end-point focus but no actual movement, such as 1.VX.C.E (fig. 10) "Sam lives over the hill," there is an understood path that goes over the hill. Such an understanding may be part of what is perceived or imagined, but it is not in a dot-matrix representation of the sort Kosslyn has in mind. Dot-matrix representations are simply too impoverished structurally to do the job—the job defined by the question: how can we represent the meanings of words to show how language can fit perceptions and rich images, while also showing how the senses of polysemous words are related to one another?

These, of course, are not questions that Kosslyn and his co-workers have taken seriously, in the way that linguists like Talmy, Langacker, Lindner, Janda, and Brugman have. Taking such questions seriously can yield answers very different from the ones Kosslyn and his associates came up with. The most important such question is the question raised by Rudolf Arnheim in *Visual Thinking* (Arnheim 1974): Do we reason imagistically? On the dot-matrix view of images, the answer would have to be no. There is not enough structure there to characterize reasoning, and what structure there is is not of the right kind. But on the image-schema view, the answer could be yes.

Are Image Schemas Used in Reasoning?

Image schemas appear to have the kind of structure that can be used in reasoning. Let us consider a very simple example. Edward Keenan and Aryeh Faltz (Keenan and Faltz, 1987) have argued that there are parts of English where the Boolean logic of classes is used in reasoning. This does not contradict the claim that real human categories go well beyond Boolean classes in the ways we have described. What the Keenan-Faltz claim says in our terms is that there exist cognitive models embodying the Boolean logic of classes; other kinds of models are not ruled out. This is in accord with the view expressed by Rosch (1981).

Keenan has observed (personal communication) that such Boolean reasoning can be understood as being based on the metaphorical understanding of classes as containers. In our terms, whatever Boolean classes we use are really metaphorical projections of a particular kind of image schema, the container schema, which is used as part of one of the *out*-schemas (fig. 28). It is a simple schema with an interior, a boundary, and an exterior. To flesh out Keenan's suggestion, we also need the part-whole schema, which relates parts to the whole (there is no drawing that captures this intuitively). Using container schemas, part-whole schemas, and a metaphorical mapping, we can construct complex schemas that match

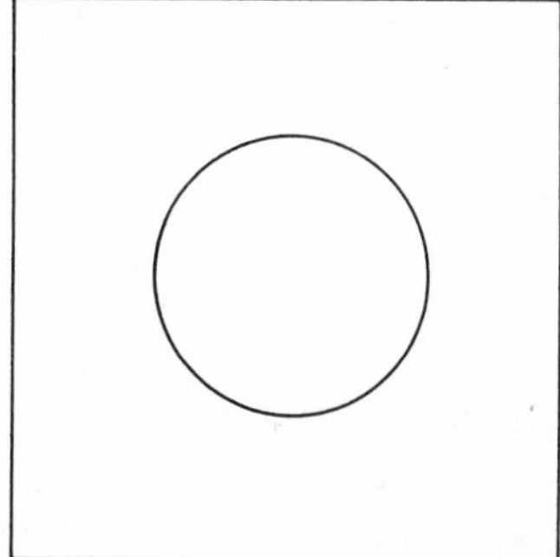

Fig. 28. The container schema

the structures needed to characterize the Boolean logic of classes. These structures will intuitively match Venn diagrams.

Here is an outline of how it can be done. Consider the following mapping from image schemas to classes:

- Container schemas are mapped into classes.
- Part-whole schemas, where both parts and wholes are container schemas, are mapped into subclass relations.
- Entities inside a container schema are mapped into members of the class corresponding to that schema.
- The exterior of the container schema is mapped into the complement of the corresponding class.

Thus, if A is a container schema, A' (the result of the mapping) is a class. And if A and B are container schemas, and B is a part of A, then B' is a proper subclass of A'. If E is the exterior of container schema A, then E' is the complement of A'. And if X is inside of container schema A, then X' is a member of class A'. Union and intersection are defined as follows:

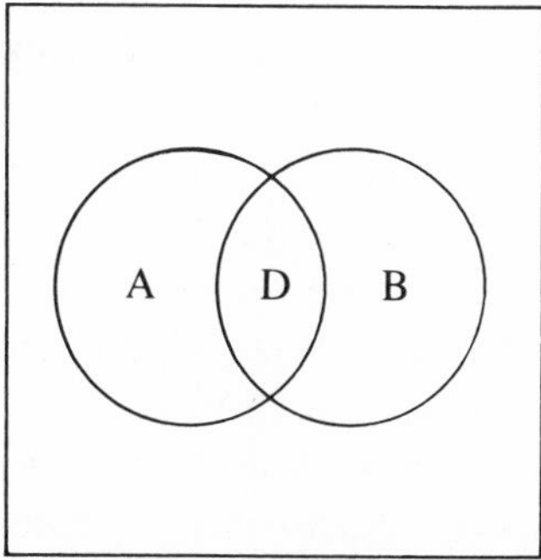

Fig. 29. Two overlapping container schemas

- Let container schemas B and C be the only parts of container schema A; A' is the union of B' and C'.
- Let container schema D be the largest container schema that is both a part of B and a part of C. D' is the intersection of B' and C'.

Given these definitions, the usual theorems of the Boolean logic of classes will be true.

Incidentally, this characterization of the logic of classes avoids the Russell paradox. The reason is that classes are defined metaphorically by a mapping from container schemas to classes. Given the nature of containers, no container schema can be inside of itself. Therefore, under the metaphorical mapping defined above, no class could possibly be a member of itself.

From the point of view of the theory of cognitive models, classes are understood metaphorically in terms of image schemas in just this way. Reasoning done with such structures can be viewed as image-schematic reasoning. For a further example of image-schematic reasoning, consider path schemas. If a trajector is at a given point on a path, it follows that it has been on all previous points on the path. Another example of image-schematic reasoning is scalar reasoning. Consider an extended landmark of the sort represented in figure 11. An extended landmark is a sequence of points. Each point can be understood metaphorically as a value of a scalar property P, and the landmark as a whole as the scale defining P. If X is at a given point on that scale, then X is more P than Y, if Y is lower on the scale, and less P than Y, if Y is higher on the scale. Langacker (1982) has even suggested how binding of variables and quantification might be done using complex image schemas. Variable binding can be viewed as a metonymic mapping in which a typical instance of a category stands for the category as a whole. The differences among *all, most, some*, and *no* can be represented by points on a scale, with *no* as the lowest point and *all* as the highest. Langacker (1986) has also described in detail how image schemas can be used to characterize the semantics of tense and aspect. Sweetser (1984) has suggested how reasoning with modalities can be done using metaphorical projections of force images. Given Fauconnier's (1985) treatment of such classical problems of semantics as referential opacity and presuppositions using mental spaces, it appears that a great deal of reasoning can be characterized using cognitive mechanisms that are not traditionally propositional in character.

At present, we do not know very much about the use of image schemas in reasoning. We have some glimmerings of how to do certain kinds of reasoning using classes, some quantifiers, tenses, aspects, modalities, scales, referential opacity, and presuppositions. But we do not understand these in anything like full detail as yet. We are not even close to knowing what kinds of image schemas are used in cognition and what kinds of reasoning can be done with them. And the fact that reasoning *can* be done with them does not prove that reasoning *is* done with them. Still, the very fact that it is possible to characterize modes of reasoning using image schemas is exciting. It may be the case that the same cognitive models that structure perceptions and images are also used in reason. If this is true, it would provide an account of how knowledge gained from perception and knowledge gained from language can function together in reasoning.

This is of special interest because it is usually taken for granted that only propositional structures are used in reason and that anything imagistic in character is not used in reasoning. Even so vociferous an advocate of mental imagery as Kosslyn is willing to grant that reason is purely propositional.

> Consider the most elementary logical operations, like negation, quantification, disjunction, and so on. How would one represent such things using only images? . . . what about classes of objects? . . . How do we distinguish quantification from addition and subtraction? Let alone *scope* of quantification? Disjunction is no easier. . . . What are we going to do about tenses? . . . I suspect that with enough sweat, tears, and worn-out erasers some kind of imagery logic could be concocted. But compared to the standard predicate calculus, an imagery calculus would be unwieldy and awkward in the extreme. (Kosslyn 1980, pp. 454–55)

Kosslyn, of course, is considering only rich images, not image schemas. As we saw above, his theory of imagery precludes the very possibility of image schemas. Kosslyn is also taking it for granted that predicate calculus is up to the task of accounting for all human reason. It simply isn't, and it doesn't even come close. But though Kosslyn is too sanguine about what classical logic can do, his challenges do have to be answered: Research into the logical properties of image schemas has barely begun, and we have no real idea of how much of human reason they can account for.

References and Conclusions

Detailed research on image schemas has mainly been done within linguistics. My own interest was kindled by Benjamin Lee Whorf's (1956) discussion of the role of image schemas in Shawnee stem composition. Over the past decade and a half, the most influential pioneer in this kind of research has been Leonard Talmy (1972, 1975, 1978*a*, 1981). Ronald Langacker's major foundational study (Langacker 1986) has provided an extremely important theoretical underpinning for all contemporary image-schema research. The most detailed description of image schemas in a non-Indo-European language is Eugene Casad's (1982) study of Cora, a short portion of which appears in Casad and Langacker (1985). The image-schematic structure of Cora is strikingly different from that of English, though the many of the elements and principles of image composition are similar. Keith McCune (1983) has demonstrated that Indonesian has a widespread system of language-particular sound symbolism that is structured around image schemas and metaphors. And within anthropology, Naomi Quinn (1987) has done a detailed study of the role of image schemas in reasoning about marriage.

Over is not the only linguistic expression that has been given an image-schematic analysis in considerable detail. Susan Lindner (1981, 1982) has provided at least as detailed an analysis of the English verb particles *up* and *out*. Laura Janda (1984) has done a similarly detailed study of the Russian verbal prefixes *za-*, *pere-*, *do-*, and *ot-*. And Brygida Rudzka-Ostyn (1983) has done a comparative study of Polish *vy* and Dutch *uit*. Bruce Hawkins (1984) has provided an overview of English prepositions, comparing the image-schematic approach to other approaches. And Claude Vandeloise (1984) has provided a detailed image-schematic analysis of certain French prepositions. All these scholars have reached essentially the same conclusions as Brugman:

- The expressions studied (*up, over, za-*, etc.) are all polysemous; they cannot be represented by a single core meaning that accounts for all and only the various senses.
- Image schemas and metaphorical models are required to represent the meanings of the expressions.
- The senses of each expression form a radially structured category, with a central member and links defined by image-schema transformations and metaphors.
- The noncentral senses cannot be predicted from the central senses, but are nonetheless not arbitrary. Rather, they are *motivated* by less central cases, image-schema transformations, and metaphorical models.

Brugman's study of *over*, like the studies by Lindner and Janda, shows that there is far less arbitrariness in the lexicon than has previously been thought. It may be arbitrary that the phonemic sequence /over/ has schema 1 as one of its meanings. But the fact that the same phonemic sequence denotes dozens of other schemas does not multiply the arbitrariness, because the other schemas are motivated. The pairing of /over/ with the central schema, schema 1, is an arbitrary form-meaning correspondence; the pairings of /over/ with the other schemas are motivated form-meaning correspondences. Thus, radial categories of senses within the lexicon serve the function of greatly reducing the arbitrariness of correspondences between form and meaning.

CASE STUDY 3

There-Constructions

Introduction

Before launching into this very lengthy case study, I feel I should say something about why I think a study this long and detailed is necessary. The short answer is this: I am proposing an alternative to standard theories of grammar. That is not something to be taken lightly. One of the principal merits claimed for the standard approaches is that they are rigorous and precise. For an alternative to be taken seriously, it must show that it is every bit as rigorous and precise. In addition, a new approach must show that it can succeed where previous approaches fail. That is why I have chosen *there*-constructions. They are classical cases that every theory of grammar must deal with, and where all previous approaches have been found wanting. Previous approaches have failed in two respects: First, they have not been able to account for the incredibly complex detail in these constructions. Second, they have not been able to account adequately for the relationship between the *there* of *There's Harry on the porch* and the *there* of *There's a man on the porch*. Standard theories simply throw up their hands and claim that there is no relationship. The principal purpose of this case study is to demonstrate how cognitively based grammar can be done with as much rigor as generative grammar, and why it succeeds in a complicated case where generative grammar fails.

There is, of course, not just one theory of generative grammar; there are dozens, if not hundreds, of actual theories, and the variations on them go into the millions, as McCawley's title *Thirty Million Theories of Grammar* suggests. We will be arguing that *all* generative approaches to grammar are inadequate. The argument will be an empirical one—based on a very large body of data. But before we get to the details, it should be pointed out that generative approaches to the study of language are inadequate not just for empirical reasons, but for theoretical reasons as well.

A generative grammar is technically a kind of formal syntax—a collection of principles for manipulating symbols without regard to their meaning. As such, generative grammars typically presuppose an objectivist approach to cognition. A semantics for a generative grammar is either model-theoretical or it consists of a translation into another system of symbols—a "mentalese" usually called a *logical form* or *semantic representation*—where the symbols are taken as being internal representations of external reality. In either case, generative grammar is subject to Putnam's critique (see chap. 15), which means that it cannot be provided with a consistent theory of meaning. We must simply look elsewhere for a theory of grammar. In particular, we must find a theory of grammar in which the syntax is not independent of the semantics.

We will be proposing a theory of cognitively based grammar that makes use of cognitive model theory as described in chapter 17. A grammar from this point of view will be a radial category of *grammatical constructions*, where each construction pairs a cognitive model (which characterizes meaning) with corresponding aspects of linguistic form. We will refer to this as a cognitive grammar.

Cognitive grammars avoid Putnam's critique for the following reason: Cognitive models are *internal* in Putnam's sense and are given meaning via their connection with experience, especially bodily experience (see chap. 17). The parameters of linguistic form in grammatical constructions are not independent of meaning; rather they are *motivated,* and in many cases even *predicted,* on the basis of meaning. On this view, many aspects of syntactic structure are motivated by, or are consequences of, the structure of cognitive models.

Cognitive Grammar

The present case study is intended to show that radial categories occur in grammar and that they have the same function as radial categories in the lexicon (see *over*), namely, motivating correspondences between form and meaning. We will be claiming that the category of clause structures in a language is radially structured, with a central subcategory and many noncentral subcategories. The central clause structures exhibit a direct and regular relationship between form and meaning, specified by general principles which we will refer to as *central principles.* Noncentral clause structures are systematically related to central clause structures, and their form-meaning correspondences derive in large part from those which are more central. Thus, the form-meaning correspondences of noncentral clause structures are highly motivated—by their relation to more central structures and by the form-meaning correspondences given by the central principles.

This general idea is not new. The idea of central and noncentral clause structures goes back to Zellig Harris's "kernel" sentences (Harris 1957) and has its roots in the tradition of descriptive grammars in which the "most basic" sentence types are described first, and the "less basic" types described later. The idea that form-meaning correspondences are direct and regular for central clause types goes back to Katz and Postal's *integrated theory* (Katz and Postal 1964) and to *generative semantics* (Lakoff 1963). The most popular version of this theory was Chomsky's *Aspects* theory (Chomsky 1965), in which "deep structures" played a role similar to that of central clause types. A recent incarnation of this view of central clause types is Gazdar, Klein, Pullum, and Sag's *Generalized Phrase-Structure Grammar* (1985), which makes a grammar-metagrammar distinction, which is roughly equivalent to the central-noncentral distinction. Other contemporary theories of grammar make a similar distinction.

None of these theories, or other contemporary theories, have been able to account adequately for the phenomena we will be discussing. There are a number of reasons for this.

First, the theory of meaning used in these theories has, on the whole, been a version of objectivist semantics. As we will see, a cognitive semantics is required instead—one that makes use of propositional, metaphoric, and metonymic models, as well as the theory of mental spaces.

Second, such theories do not have an adequate account—if they have any account at all—of *grammatical constructions,* direct pairings of parameters of form with parameters of meaning.

Third, such theories do not have an adequate concept of a category. As we will see, radial categories with prototypical centers are needed.

Fourth, other theories of grammar operate with the usual dichotomy between predictability and arbitrariness. Instead, a concept of *motivation* is needed.

Fifth, other theories relate central to noncentral cases by syntactic transformations, or roughly equivalent devices—metarules, redundancy rules, and the like. These usually provide only for syntactic relationships. We will argue that what is needed instead is a concept of an "ecological location" within a grammatical system as a whole. Ecological locations are defined by central subcategories plus links of noncentral to central categories. Such links are characterized by what we shall call "based on" relations. These differ from transformations and their equivalents in that they may specify semantic and pragmatic relationships, including some defined by metaphoric and metonymic models, and others defined by the addition (and sometimes the subtraction) of whole ICMs.

Sixth, most other theories (with the notable exception of generative semantics) assume that syntactic categories and grammatical relations are "autonomous," that is, entirely independent of meaning and use. We will see that, instead, syntactic categories and grammatical relations have radial structure, with a prototypical center that is predictable on semantic grounds; the noncentral members constitute extensions which are not predictable on a semantic basis, but which are typically semantically or pragmatically motivated.

Seventh, most other theories (again with the notable exception of generative semantics) assume that syntactic constraints on the occurrence of a construction cannot be predicted from the meaning of that construction. We will show that the opposite is the case, and that a great many syntactic constraints can be predicted on semantic grounds.

Eighth, other theories of grammar assume some form of atomism, namely, that the meaning of a grammatical construction is a computable function of the meanings of its parts. We will argue instead that grammatical constructions in general are holistic, that is, that the meaning of the whole construction is motivated by the meanings of the parts, but is not computable from them.

Ninth, just about all other theories assume that there is a clear division between the grammar and the lexicon, with the grammar providing structures and the lexicon providing meaningful words to plug into grammatical structures. We will see that such a clear division is problematic, and that there is more likely a continuum between the grammar and the lexicon (see Fillmore, Kay, and O'Connor, to appear; Sadock 1984).

Tenth, most other contemporary theories assume that grammar is independent of the rest of cognition. As we will show, grammar is dependent on many other aspects of cognition, which we will have represented via prototype theory, cognitive models, mental spaces, etc. In fact, we will argue that grammars are defined relative to nonuniversal conceptual systems.

The purpose of this case study is to show that, because of these differences, a cognitive grammar can provide both an adequate description and explanation of the complexities of *there*-constructions, while other theories cannot. Existential *there*-constructions, as in *There's a fly in my soup,* were originally viewed as a phenomenon that could be handled naturally and easily by generative theories. Over the years, however, they have proven to be extremely recalcitrant. It was also thought at first that the relationship between existential and deictic *there*-constructions, like *There goes a fly, into your soup,* could be easily accounted for by transformational grammar (cf. Fillmore 1968, Lyons 1968, Thorne 1973, Kuno 1971). Ultimately, this proved impossible for reasons that we will discuss below. The problem was not that there was no systematic relationship between the constructions; the problem, instead, lay with the theory of transformational grammar.

This case study thus brings to bear empirical evidence concerning the following ten issues:

1. Is objectivist semantics adequate, or is a cognitive semantics necessary?
2. Are grammatical constructions epiphenomena, or do they have a real cognitive status?
3. Are classical categories sufficient for grammar, or is prototype theory required?
4. Will a predictable-arbitrary dichotomy suffice for grammar, or is the concept of motivation necessary?
5. Can transformations (and their rough equivalents, metarules, redundancy rules, and the like) account for relationships among constructions, or do we need instead the concept of "ecologial location" defined in terms of radial structure and the "based on" relation?
6. Are syntactic categories and grammatical relations autonomous, or are they radially structured with a semantically defined center?
7. Must all syntactic constraints be accounted for only by rules of syntax that are oblivious to meaning, or can a great many syntactic constraints be accounted for on semantic grounds?
8. Is the meaning of every grammatical construction a computable function of the meaning of its parts, or are there constructions whose meaning is motivated by the meanings of its parts but is not computable from them by general rules?
9. Is there a strict dichotomy between grammar and lexicon, or is there a continuum between the two?
10. Is grammar a separate "module," independent of other aspects of cognition, or does it make use of other aspects of cognition such as prototype categorization, cognitive models, and mental spaces?

On the whole, generative approaches to grammar assume the first alternative in each case, while cognitive grammar maintains the second alternative. These are not the only differences between generative and cognitive grammar, but they are the ones that matter for an understanding of *there*-constructions. As we go along, we will try to show that the generative assumptions are inadequate, and that a cognitive approach is needed.

Grammatical Constructions

I am using the term *grammatical construction* in a somewhat enriched version of its traditional sense. Traditional grammarians took it for granted that the grammar of a language could be described in terms of a collection of constructions, where each construction was a configuration of syntactic elements (like *clause, noun, preposition, gerund,* etc.) paired with a meaning and/or use associated with that syntactic configuration. I will be speaking of grammatical constructions in just this sense. Each construction will be a form-meaning pair (F,M), where F is a set of conditions on syntactic and phonological form and M is a set of conditions on meaning and use. I have been working with my colleagues Charles Fillmore and Paul Kay on a general theory of such constructions (see Fillmore, Kay, and O'Connor, to appear).

I will try to be somewhat more precise than traditional grammarians were, and I will also be concerned with such contemporary issues as the relationships among constructions and the psychological reality of individual constructions and categories of constructions. It is my ultimate goal to place the theory of grammatical constructions within a general theory of *symbolic models.* Symbolic models are pairings of models of form with other cognitive models. A general theory of language would include an account of lexical items, motivated idioms, grammatical constructions, morphemes, etc. An even more general theory of symbolic models would account for the understanding of all sorts of form-meaning correspondences that have a cognitive reality. Such a general theory is far beyond the present study; for the present we will be concerned only with grammatical constructions.

It should be pointed out the concept *grammatical construction* is extremely controversial in contemporary linguistics. In most contemporary formal theories, grammatical constructions in our sense have no status whatever. They are considered epiphenomena—consequences of more general rules of a very different character. The types of general rules differ from theory to theory. What should be borne in mind throughout the following discussion is that grammatical constructions are left out of other contemporary formal theories not for any empirical reasons, but for reasons internal to those theories. Those theories are very much the poorer for it. Theories of grammar without grammatical constructions simply do not account for anything approaching the full range of grammatical facts of any language. In fact, they are limited to a relatively small range of phenomena. It is part of the objective of this case study to demonstrate the utility of grammatical constructions, as well as the utility of prototype theory. The point is to show that when prototype theory is taken together with grammatical constructions, it is possible to state regularities that cannot otherwise be stated. To my knowledge, there is no contemporary generative theory that accounts for anything approaching the range of phenomena discussed in this case study.

Some Basic Facts

Let us begin with certain basic and relatively well-known facts. There are two types of *there*-constructions, the deictics and the existentials:

Deictic: There's Harry with his red hat on.
Existential: There was a man shot last night.

The term *deictic* is used to refer to words like *this* and *that* that are used in pointing or are interpretable only relative to the context in which the sentence is uttered. In *There's Harry with his red hat on*, the word *there* is used to pick out a location relative to the speaker. It is a locative adverb in that it picks out a location, and it is deictic in that the location it picks out is relative to the speaker. In the *existential* case, it is not location but existence which is at issue, in this case the existence of an event. The *there* in *There was a man shot last night* does not pick out a location. Therefore, while the deictic *there* may take an accompanying pointing gesture the existential *there* cannot. In addition, the deictic *there* bears stress (not necessarily primary sentence stress), while existential *there* does not bear stress at all and its vowel may reduce.

Moreover, there are major syntactic differences between the constructions. The differences involve subjecthood, negatability, embeddability, and alternation with *here*.

Subjecthood: Existential *there* is grammatical subject; deictic *there* is not.

There are at least two clear tests that show this. Tag-questions require that a pronoun corresponding to the subject appear in the tag. This works fine for existentials, but not for deictics (asterisks indicate unacceptability):

- There was a man shot, wasn't there?
- *There's Harry with his red hat on, isn't there?

The existential works like the simple sentence,

- Debbie saw Harry last night, didn't she?

where *she* refers back to the subject, *Debbie.* Since deictic *there* is not a subject, it cannot occur in the tag. Similarly, only subjects can occur in what are called *raising*-constructions. Thus, in a central clause like *John is sick, John* is subject. It can therefore be subject of cases of *raising*-constructions like ______ *is believed to* ______ and ______ *is likely to* ______:

- John is sick.
- John is believed to be sick.
- John is likely to be sick.

This also works for existential *there*-constructions.

- There was a man shot.
- There was believed to have been a man shot.
- There is likely to be a man shot.

However, it does not work for deictic *there*-constructions.

- There is Harry with his red hat on.
- *There is believed to be Harry with his red hat on.
- *There is likely to be Harry with his red hat on.

In the above example, *Harry* is the subject, not *there*. This is clear from the fact that it goes into the nominative case when it is pronominalized.

- There *he* is with his red hat on.
- *There *him* is with his red hat on.

Note that inverted word order is forbidden with a pronoun subject:

- *There is he with his red hat on.

This restriction will be discussed below.

Negatability: Existential *there*-constructions can be negated; deictic *there*-constructions cannot be negated.

- There wasn't anyone in the room.
- *There isn't Harry with his red hat on.

Embeddability: Existential constructions can be freely embedded in subordinate clauses; deictic constructions can almost never be embedded (with exceptions to be discussed below).

- If there's anyone in the room with a red hat on, I'll be surprised.
- *If there's Harry in the room with his red hat on, I'll be surprised.

- I doubt that there's anyone in the kitchen.
- *I doubt that there's Harry in the kitchen.

Alternation with here: *Here* can occur in deictic constructions, but not in existential constructions.

- There's Harry with our pizza!
- Here's Harry with our pizza!

- There will be a man shot tomorrow.
- *Here will be a man shot tomorrow.

Yet, despite these very considerable differences, it is possible to find cases where the deictic and existential differ superficially only in stress. (Capitals indicate stress.) The following sentences minimally differ in form, and one has to think twice to differentiate them.

Deictic: THERE's an ape flirting with Harriet.

Existential: There's an APE flirting with Harriet.

Such similarities are by no means accidental. As Fillmore, Thorne, Kuno, and Lyons observed, it is no accident that the same word—*there*—occurs in both constructions. It is generally agreed that the deictic *there* is in some sense the more basic of the two and that the existential use is extended from the deictic use. The commonsense explanation seems to be that things that exist must exist in a location, or in slogan form: to be is to be located. I think this is essentially correct as far as it goes, but it is not an explanation, and needs to be made into one. However, the authors mentioned above attempted to relate the deictics and the existentials via a transformational rule. This attempt failed, and one of the principal reasons was that no transformational derivation could account for all the differences between the constructions. Thus, one of the central problems that we will have to deal with is:

How can we show the relationship between the existential and the deictic constructions while simultaneously accounting for the differences?

We will approach this question, among others, via a cognitively based grammar.

Some Pragmatic Distinctions

One of the things that grammatical constructions will enable us to represent is the pairing of pragmatic conditions (namely, conditions on the use of a construction) with syntactic conditions (e.g., conditions on word order, etc.). In fact, one of the major ways we have of identifying grammatical constructions is to find cases where pragmatic conditions are associated with syntactic conditions. In the case of deictic *there*-constructions, we can best reveal the pragmatic conditions on the construction by comparing instances of *there*-constructions to the corresponding simple sentences. This is especially important, since it is commonly believed that *there*-constructions have no special status as constructions at all, but rather are merely derived by regular transformational rules from the corresponding simple sentences. According to such a proposal, a transformation moving adverbs to the front of a sentence would apply, say, to *He comes here* to yield *Here he comes,* which would presumably be a mere stylistic variation of the simple sentence. Since transformations are, by definition, not paired with either pragmatic conditions or semantic conditions, the transformational analysis predicts that there should be no important semantic or pragmatic differences between *there*-constructions and simple sentences. To show that such differences do exist is to provide prima facie evidence for the existence of a construction, rather than a mere transformational variant. In other words, if we can show that *Here he comes* has different semantic and pragmatic properties from *He comes here*, then we can show that they are not merely related by a syntactic transformation and that *Here he comes* is really an instance of grammatical construction—a symbolic model that pairs syntactic conditions with semantic and pragmatic conditions.

Let us begin by considering the difference between sentences like:

- Here comes Harry.

and

- Harry comes here.

In *Here comes Harry*, there is a true present tense, that is, *comes* makes reference to the time the sentence is uttered and it is instantaneous. In *Harry comes here*, the present tense form has a generic meaning, that is, it picks out a general area of time around the present, and *comes* designates many instances of coming, not just one. This difference shows up in the way that these two constructions treat modifiers like *from time to time*, which is restricted to generic, not instantaneous, time reference.

- Harry comes here from time to time.
- *Here comes Harry from time to time.

The *here* also works differently in the two constructions. In *Harry comes here, here* designates the location of the speaker. In *Here comes Harry, come* places Harry on a trajectory aimed toward the speaker. *Here* has two functions. It both designates the end point of that trajectory (the location of the speaker) and designates Harry's location as being closer to the speaker than *there* (the contrasting term) would indicate. This difference shows up with locative adverbs that cannot refer to the location of the speaker, for example, *around the corner:*

- Here comes Harry around the corner.
- *Harry comes here around the corner.

In the first sentence, *here* designates Harry's location as he rounds the corner, and places him on trajectory aimed toward the speaker. But in the second sentence, the *here* is at the location of the speaker, which is inconsistent with *around the corner.*

A similar point can be made with a sentence where there is some variation among speakers. Roughly half the speakers of English I have asked find sentences like the following grammatical:

- %There comes Harry. (%indicates variation)

In this sentence, *there* indicates Harry's location, which is on the trajectory defined by *comes*, but is not the end point of that trajectory. But in the next sentence, *there* indicates the end point of the trajectory defined by *comes:*

- Harry comes there (regularly).

The two constructions also differ in their pragmatics, that is, in the conditions on their use. Thus, *Harry comes here* is a simple assertion like any other declarative sentence. But *Here comes Harry* is not only an assertion. In addition, the speaker is directing the attention of the hearer to the location specified by *here.*

Correlating with these differences in semantics and pragmatics are major syntactic differences. The simple sentences do not have any of the syntactic constraints that *there*-constructions have. Thus, they can take tag-questions.

- Harry comes here, doesn't he?

They can occur in raising constructions.

- Harry is likely to come here.

They can be negated.

- Harry doesn't come here anymore.

They can be embedded freely.

- If Harry comes here, let me know.
- I doubt that Harry comes here.

In short, deictic *there*-constructions have syntactic, semantic, and pragmatic properties that are markedly different from the corresponding simple sentences. This suggests that *there*-constructions really are constructions—pairings of form and meaning—rather than mere stylistic variants of simple sentences.

Pragmatics and Syntax

We have defined a grammatical construction in such a way as to include semantic and pragmatic constraints. As we have seen, ordinary simple sentences like *Harry comes here* differ considerably in such constraints from instances of deictic *there*-constructions like *Here comes Harry*. We are now in a position to see that defining constructions to include both semantic and pragmatic constraints allows us to predict much of their syntactic behavior.

We will begin by asking a very traditional question in syntax: what kinds of syntactic configurations can occur in what kinds of subordinate clauses? It is a syntactic question of the most basic kind, and it is usually assumed that a general answer to this question can be given in syntactic terms alone. We will try to show that this is not the case and that a general answer can be provided only within a theory that contains grammatical constructions that include semantic and pragmatic constraints.

We will approach the question by looking at what I will call *performative subordinate clauses*. The basic properties we will be concerned with can be seen in the sentences:

- I'm leaving, because here comes my bus.
- *I'm leaving, if here comes my bus.

If-clauses and *because*-clauses are both adverbial clauses. It is usually assumed that whatever can occur in one kind of adverbial clause can occur in another. These examples indicate that that simply isn't true. *Because*-clauses permit constructions that *if*-clauses forbid.

What is of particular interest in these examples is that the construction that differentiates them, as exemplified by *Here comes my bus*, is usually assumed to be a main-clause construction, that is, a construction that occurs only in main clauses. (See Emonds 1971, Hooper and Thompson 1973, and Green 1976.) What is a main-clause construction doing in a subordinate clause at all? And why does it occur in *because*-clauses but not in *if*-clauses? Do other main-clause constructions act in the same way? And if so, which ones do, and why?

A quick look at other constructions that are supposed to occur only in main clauses shows that *Here comes my bus* is not alone. Take, for example, a negative question like *Isn't it a beautiful day?!* It shows exactly the same behavior:

- We should go on a picnic, because isn't it a beautiful day!
- *We should go on a picnic, if isn't it a beautiful day!

This shows that whatever is going on, it is not restricted to individual constructions. It must involve some general property of a class of constructions that usually occur only in main clauses. Exactly what property is it?

Before going on to try to answer these questions, one more peculiarity of this phenomenon should be pointed out. Main-clause constructions occur in *because*-clauses only when they are in final position. Preposed *because*-clauses do not permit them:

- *Because isn't it a beautiful day, we should go on a picnic.
- *If isn't it a beautiful day, we should go on a picnic.
- *Because here comes the bus, I'm leaving.
- *If here comes the bus, I'm leaving.

Any adequate account of this phenomenon must explain why this is so.

Some Speech Act Constructions

I would like to suggest, as a first approximation, that what unites the constructions in question is that they are all speech act constructions, that is, constructions that are restricted in their use to expressing certain illocutionary forces that are specified as part of the grammar of English. Let us consider a number of such constructions, together with their illocutionary force constraints.

Deictic there-*constructions* direct the hearer's attention to something present.

- There goes Harry!

Negative questions convey positive hedged assertions.

- Didn't Harry leave?

Inverted exclamations express surprise (see N. McCawley 1973).

- Boy! Is he ever tall!

WH-exclamations express something that has just come to mind.

- What a fool he is!

Rhetorical questions convey corresponding negative statements.

- Who on earth can stop Bernard?

Reversal tags convey hedged assertions.

- He's coming, isn't he?

All of the above occur in final *because*-clauses:

- I'm gonna have breakfast now, because am I ever hungry!
- *I'm gonna have breakfast now, if am I ever hungry!
- We should have another party, because what a good time everyone had at the last one!
- *We should have another party, if what a good time everyone had at the last one!
- The Knicks are going to win, because who on earth can stop Bernard?
- *The Knicks are going to win, if who on earth can stop Bernard?
- I guess we should call off the picnic because it's raining, isn't it?
- *I guess we should call off the picnic if it's raining, isn't it?

However, not all speech act constructions occur in final *because*-clauses. Compare, for example, the differences between reversal tags and reduplicative tags.

- It's raining, isn't it? (reversal tag)
- It's raining, is it? (reduplicative tag)

Although reversal tags can occur in *because*-clauses, reduplicative tags cannot.

- *I guess we should call off the picnic because it's raining, is it?

The relevant difference between reversal and reduplicative tags seems to be that, whereas reversal tags convey assertions, reduplicative tags convey challenges to the assertions of others. We can see that this is the relevant distinction by looking at other speech act constructions that cannot occur in *because*-clauses, for example, true questions and imperatives.

- *I'm staying because go home!
- *I'm leaving because which girl pinched me?

Why should rhetorical questions like *Who can stop Bernard?* occur in *because*-clauses, while true questions like *Which girl pinched me?* cannot? The difference is that rhetorical questions convey statements (e.g., *No one can stop Bernard*) while true questions are requests for information. Such cases suggest the following hypothesis:

> Only speech act constructions that (directly or indirectly) convey statements can occur in performative subordinate clauses.

This hypothesis predicts that certain overt performatives but not others should be able to occur in *because*-clauses. The prediction is borne out, since only statements occur:

- I'm going to vote for Snurdley because I maintain that he's the only honest candidate.
- *I'm staying because I order you to leave.
- *I'm leaving because I ask you which girl pinched me.

The hypothesis also accounts for the range of speech act constructions that do occur. All of the cases cited above happen to convey corresponding statements:

- Here comes the bus!

conveys

- The bus is coming.

- Isn't it a beautiful day?

conveys

- It's a beautiful day.

- Am I ever hungry!

conveys

- I'm hungry.

- What a good time everyone had!

conveys

- Everyone had a good time.

- Who on earth can stop Bernard?

conveys

- No one can stop Bernard.

- It's raining, isn't it?

conveys

- It's raining.

Thus we can account in a straightforward way for the relationship between the speech act constructions and the semantics of the *because*-clauses:

When speech act constructions occur in *because*-clauses, the content of the statement conveyed by the speech act construction equals the content of the *because*-clause.

Thus, in a sentence like

– I'm gonna have breakfast now, because am I ever hungry!

the exclamation *Am I ever hungry!* conveys the statement *I'm hungry*. Thus, the reason given in this sentence is the same as the reason given in

– I'm gonna have breakfast, because I'm hungry.

Thus performative subordinate clauses perform two functions at once. They perform a speech act that conventionally conveys a statement, and they give the content of that statement as a reason for the first statement.

This general principle covers all the cases given above and excludes nonoccurring cases like pure questions and orders. It allows rhetorical questions that convey statements, and it predicts that if an imperative construction were to conventionally convey a statement, it could occur in these clauses. As it happens, there is such an imperative. Compare the pure imperative.

– Find out which girl pinched me.

with a sentence of the same syntactic form

– Consider which girl pinched me.

The first is simply an order. The second, however, assumes that the hearer already knows the answer. It directs the hearer to think about the answer and assumes that if the hearer does so, he will reach a specific conclusion that the speaker already has in mind. It is a roundabout, but nonetheless conventionalized, way of conveying a statement which is never overtly mentioned. As predicted, the difference between these two imperatives is reflected in their ability to occur in *because*-clauses. The second can occur, while the first cannot.

– *I'm staying because find out which girl pinched me.
– I'm staying because consider which girl pinched me.

Thus, we see that it is not the imperative construction per se that is ruled out. Most imperatives cannot occur in such clauses simply because they do not conventionally convey statements. Imperatives that do conventionally convey statements do occur in these *because*-clauses.

Initial Clauses

We are now in a position to explain why speech act constructions can occur in *because*-clauses in final position, but not in initial position. *Because*-clauses in sentence-initial position are presupposed, while those in sentence-final position are not. Consider the sentence:

- I'm going to vote for McSwain instead of Polanski because McSwain can win in November.

In this sentence the speaker is asserting that McSwain can win in November. However, in the following sentence, the speaker is taking it as a foregone conclusion that McSwain can win in November.

- Because McSwain can win in November, I'm going to vote for him instead of Polanski.

This can be seen even more clearly in the following examples.

- Do you think that John left early because he was tired?
- Do you think that, because he was tired, John left early?
- I doubt that John left early because he was tired.
- I doubt that, because he was tired, John left early.

In the first sentence of each pair, it is not necessarily taken for granted that John was tired, whereas in the second sentence of each pair it is.

Given the presuppositional character of initial *because*-clauses, we can explain why speech act constructions cannot occur in such clauses. In order for speech act constructions to occur in *because*-clauses at all, they must convey statements. However, it is impossible to both state and presuppose something simultaneously. It is for this reason that speech act constructions cannot occur inside initial *because*-clauses.

Further evidence for this explanation has been brought to my attention by James D. McCawley, who observes that in certain situations preposed *because*-clauses do not have to be presupposed. Thus, in sentences like

- My boss wants me to vote for Polanski, but because McSwain can win in November, I'm going to vote for him.

In this case, the speaker can be asserting, not presupposing, that McSwain can win in November. McCawley observes that in such cases speech act constructions *can* occur in preposed *because*-clauses.

- I want to stay, but because here comes my bus, I'd better leave.

This shows that the constraint on the occurrence of speech act constructions is pragmatic rather than syntactic. That is, it is not the preposed position of the *because*-clauses that rules out speech act constructions; rather, it is the presuppositional character of the position that rules out the speech act constructions. When that presuppositional character is removed, then speech act constructions can occur in preposed *because*-clauses.

The Range of Clauses

Let us now turn to the question of what kind of clauses speech act constructions can occur in. We have seen that they occur in *because*-clauses. They also occur in clauses that begin with *although, except, since* and *but.*

Although

- I'm not going to vote for Snurdley, although I maintain that he's the best candidate.
- I've decided to stay, although here comes Harry—and you know what I think of him!
- I'm going to stay on my diet, although could I ever go for a dim sum brunch!

Except

- I'd stay a little longer, except here comes my bus!
- We really shouldn't go on a picnic, except it is a nice day, isn't it?
- I'd go swimming with you, except am I ever tired!

Since

- I'd better leave, since here comes my bus!
- I'm going to cheat on my taxes, since who will ever find out?
- No one's going to be there, since it's going to be boring, isn't it?

(It should be noted, incidentally, that *since* is formal and many of these constructions are mainly used in informal speech. This can lead to register incompatibility, as in *?He must be a great player, since what a shot he hit!* This incompatibility is irrevelant to the present discussion.)

But

- I really should stay, but here comes my bus.
- I'm on a diet, but am I ever hungry!

In addition to *if*-clauses, all other adverbial subordinate clauses exclude these speech act constructions, e.g., *where, when, while, as,* etc.

- *There's Bill where isn't John sitting.

- *Harry left when did he ever get hungry!
- *John left as didn't Bill come in?
- *John was sitting in his favorite chair reading while was Harry ever sneaking up on him!

Speech act constructions occur in two classes of adverbials: reason adverbials (*because, since*) and concessives (*although, except, but*). Actually, these two classes form a single more general class for the following reason: In sentences of the form "A although B" and "A but B," B is a reason for *not* A. For example, in a sentence like *John stayed up although he was tired,* being tired would be a reason for *not* staying up. In short, concessive clauses give reasons for the opposite of the main clause. The generalization seems to be that speech act constructions occur in clauses expressing reasons of either sort.

What we have arrived at is a single general principle:

> Clauses expressing a reason allow speech act constructions that convey statements, and the content of the statement equals the reason expressed.

The observant reader will have noticed that not all of the examples given have been subordinate clauses. *But*-clauses are coordinate. Yet with respect to this phenomenon they work the same way as other clauses expressing reasons. In fact the general rule does not mention subordinate clauses at all. It only mentions "clauses expressing a reason." Such clauses may be subordinate and marked with subordinators like *because, although,* etc. They may be coordinate and marked with *but.* In addition, coordinate clauses marked with *and* and *or* may also take such constructions when one coordinate clause is expressing a reason for another.

- Here comes my bus and so I'd better leave.

Conclusions

The problem we began with was a conventional syntactic problem: What kinds of constructions can occur in what kinds of subordinate clauses? The solution to the problem requires constructions to be paired in the grammar with the illocutionary forces they express (both directly and indirectly). Once this is done, a general rule can be stated in purely semantic terms. In other words, a complex syntactic problem can be solved by a simple semantic principle—provided we have the means in the grammar to pair constructions with the meanings they convey. This phenomenon therefore provides support for a theory of grammatical constructions of the sort we will be using in the remainder of this case study—one in which semantic and pragmatic information is paired with syntactic information, which permits generalizations about syntax to be stated in semantic and pragmatic terms.

Of course, grammatical construction theory is not the only contemporary theory that permits the direct pairing of syntactic and semantic information. However, it is the only theory I am aware of that permits the pairing of complex syntactic configurations with the appropriate pragmatics—in this case, conveyed illocutionary force. Grammatical construction theory permits such pragmatic factors to enter directly into the composition of sentences. Generative theories with an autonomous syntax cannot do this. For example, they have no way of generating speech act constructions in exactly the right subordinate clauses while not generating them in the wrong subordinate clauses.

Pragmatics in the Grammar

Before we continue, an important but subtle distinction needs to be noted. The pragmatic constraints, that is, constraints on use, that we have been discussing are *in the grammar of English.* Constraints on use which are part of the grammar of a language are very different from knowledge about normal use which is not part of the grammar. Compare, for example, sentences like:

- There's Sadie.
- That's Sadie.

These two sentences are normally used in pretty much the same way: to direct the hearer's attention to something in the perceptual field of both speaker and hearer and to identify it with the expression given (in this case, *Sadie*). The semantic difference is minor: *there* directs attention to a location which has an entity located there, while *that* directs attention to the entity in that location.

But there is a major difference. In the case of *There's Sadie,* the speech act condition on the use of the sentence is absolutely required by the grammar of English. Deictic *there*-clauses can be used only when the speaker is directing the attention of the hearer. However, in the case of *That's Sadie*, the given condition is part of our knowledge of how the construction is normally used, but not part of the grammar of English. Just because a construction is normally used in a given way, it doesn't follow that it necessarily has to be used in that way. *That's Sadie* is, therefore, free to be used in ways that *There's Sadie* cannot be used. For example, it can be negated, questioned, and embedded freely.

- That isn't Sadie.
- Is that Sadie?
- I wonder if that's Sadie.
- I doubt that that's Sadie.
- I'm leaving if that's Sadie.

When we speak of pragmatic constraints on constructions, we will be speaking about those that are part of the grammar of English, not those that are part of our knowledge about how constructions happen to be normally used.

Grammatical constructions, as we will speak of them below, are complex cognitive models with two dimensions: one characterizing parameters of form and one characterizing parameters of meaning. We have seen that deictic *there*-constructions fit this characterization. At this point we are in a position to begin to discuss prototype theory. We will show that there is not just one deictic *there*-construction, but a whole category of them, and that the category is not a classical category, but a category centered around a prototype.

Deictic *There*-Constructions

We have seen nothing so far to indicate that there is more than one deictic *there*-construction. But as we will see shortly, there are many "subconstructions," and they form a prototype-based category—a category consisting of constructions. It is also a category that cannot be defined by necessary and sufficient conditions. That is, it is impossible to give conditions that all and only the constructions in this category share. What we can do is characterize the category by giving the properties of the central construction and then give the properties that minimally distinguish each of the subconstructions from the central construction. The result is a cognitive structure that is very much like the category structures that occur elsewhere in the conceptual system. The point is that structures like this are to be expected, given the way people normally construct categories. Prototype theory thus *explains* why such a grouping of constructions should exist in a language. According to traditional generative theories, such a clustering of constructions is simply an anomaly.

Here is a list of examples of the various subconstructions in the category of deictic *there*-constructions:

THE DEICTICS

Central: There's Harry with the red jacket on.

Perceptual: There goes the bell now!

Discourse: There's a nice point to bring up in class.

Existence: There goes our last hope.

Activity Start: There goes Harry, meditating again.

Delivery: Here's your pizza, piping hot!

Paragon: Now there was a real ballplayer!

Exasperation: There goes Harry again, making a fool of himself.

Narrative Focus: There I was in the middle of the jungle . . . .

New Enterprise: Here I go, off to Africa.

Presentational: There on that hill will be built by the alumni of this university a ping-pong facility second to none.

Some are distinct subconstructions, some are not. Their status, as we will see, is anything but obvious. As we go through them one by one, we will see what the differences are. But before we begin, it is important to see that such sentences present problems. Consider the following phenomena:

Only presentational constructions permit locative phrases after *there* and full auxiliaries; the others do not permit locatives and allow only simple tenses:

- There on that hill will be built a new library. (presentational)
- There goes Harry. (central)
- *There on that hill goes Harry. (central plus impermissible locative phrase)
- There goes Harry with the red sneakers on. (central)
- *There is going Harry with the red sneakers on. (central plus impermissible full auxiliary)

Only the narrative focus construction permits the past tense, and it does not permit *come.*

- Here I was, with a silly hat on. (narrative focus)
- Here he comes, with a silly hat on. (central)
- *Here I came, with a silly hat on. (narrative focus with *come*)

Only the delivery construction takes an elongated vowel, and it requires present tense:

- There was my pizza, ready to go. (narrative focus)
- The e e ere's your pizza, ready to go. (delivery)
- *The e e ere was your pizza, ready to go. (delivery with past tense)

A remarkable phenomenon occurs in the perceptual deictic. A percept (say, *the pain in my knee*) can be replaced by the thing perceived (in this case, *my knee*).

– There goes the pain in my knee.
– There goes my knee.

But this is not possible when the verb is *come*. Suppose you feel a twinge in your knee slightly before the pain appears. You can report this with the first sentence, but not the second.

– Here comes the pain in my knee.
– *Here comes my knee.

Similarly, suppose you have an alarm clock that clicks a few seconds before it is set to go off, and when it goes off it makes a beep. Upon hearing the warning click, one might say

– Here comes the beep.

but not

– *Here comes the alarm clock.

However, when the alarm clock goes off one can say either

– There goes the beep.

or

– There goes the alarm clock.

One last example: The discourse deictic construction, unlike the central construction, does not permit *go*. To see the contrast, suppose that you see a beautiful car go by. You can say either

– There's a beautiful car.

or

– There goes a beautiful car.

However, if you are listening to a lecture and you hear the lecturer make a beautiful point, you can say

– There's a beautiful point.

but not

– *There goes a beautiful point.

These are subtle distinctions, and previous accounts of these constructions have not been able to explain them. Within the theory of grammatical constructions, an explanation is possible. In attempting to provide both descriptions and explanations, I will adopt the following strategy: Describe the central construction in very great detail, enough to permit a description of all the variations on it. Enough detail must also be given to distinguish the deictic constructions from the existential constructions. After this is done, the noncentral constructions can be described very simply as variations of the central construction, and their peculiarities can be explained on this basis.

Notation

Because the phenomena we are discussing are extremely complex, it is necessary to use some sort of notation to keep track of everything involved in the analysis. The notation will be essentially the same as the notation used in case study 1 to characterize cognitive models. This notation has a number of virtues. First, it is the only notation I know of that is sufficiently precise to describe these phenomena. Second, it shows the unity between the theory of cognitive models and the theory of grammatical constructions, since cognitive models are used in grammatical constructions to represent meaning. Third, it has empirical consequences, since it is the only notational system now in use that can characterize *syntactic amalgams* (for details, see Lakoff 1974). An *amalgam* is a case where more than one proposition is represented in a single clause. This situation arises in deictic *there*-constructions. Consider the example

- %There comes Harry with his red hat on.

This is syntactically a single clause. But it corresponds to three semantic propositions:

- Harry is there.
- Harry is coming, that is, moving toward the speaker.
- Harry has his red hat on.

We will be using the following notation: a syntactic element, for instance the clause *There's Harry with his red hat on*, will be represented by an integer, say zero. The corresponding semantic elements, for instance the three propositions mentioned above, will each be represented by zero followed by one, two or three prime signs. When a syntactic element is represented by an integer, the corresponding semantic element will be represented by the same integer followed by one or more primes. The number of primes distinguishes among the different semantic elements corresponding to individual syntactic elements. Cases of this sort are common in natural language and the notation adopted is one way (by no means the only possible way) of describing such cases.

Cognitive Systems versus Formal Systems

The term *formal system* has been used in linguistics in two distinct senses:

Practical formal system: A system of principles of some sort expressed precisely, often in a notation which permits one to give precise names to concepts, to state hypotheses in appropriate detail, and to make detailed predictions.

Technical formal system: A special kind of mathematical system of production rules, in which arbitrary symbols are manipulated in an algorithmic fashion without regard to their meaning.

Generative linguistics makes use of technical formal systems, not merely practical formal systems. The difference is crucial, since technical formal systems have many properties that practical formal systems do not have. For example, the technical concept of "generative capacity" is defined only for technical formal systems, not for practical formal systems in general. Moreover, technical formal systems are defined in such a way that the meaning of the symbols does not enter into the rules of the system. Practical formal systems have no such limitations.

The basic metaphor of generative linguistics is that a grammar of a language is a technical formal system restricted to certain kinds of formal rules (e.g., phrase structure rules, transformations, etc.). However, many linguists have used the notational system of transformational grammar as a practical formal system, and a great deal of confusion has arisen as a result.

As a working linguist and cognitive scientist, I will not be using the technical formal system metaphor for grammars, since it is irrelevant to the concerns of cognitive science, and since it cannot be the basis for a theory of meaning. My concern, like that of other cognitive linguists, is to ask what we need to hypothesize about the nature of cognition in general in order to account for the phenomena of natural language. The notation I will be using is a practical formal system that has the merit of permitting appropriate precision. I view it as a practical notation for characterizing certain relevant aspects of cognitive models. It has no cosmic significance. It is simply one way of providing a precise description of certain things that need to be described precisely.

Our notation, incidentally, does not capture every relevant aspect of grammatical constructions. For example, grammatical constructions may constitute gestalts, where the whole is conceptually simpler than the sum of the parts. Our notation does not capture the gestalt characteristics of constructions. Another very important thing it cannot characterize adequately is the spatialization of form. As we argued above, syntactic form is characterized in image-schematic terms—using part-whole schemas, linear order, closeness, centrality, size, containers, etc. The notation we will be using *describes* such schemas but doesn't utilize them directly in the notation.

Throughout what follows it should be borne in mind that we are describing different kinds of entities than those described by any technical formal system of the sort used in generative linguistics. Here are some differences:

- Cognitive models and grammatical constructions use prototype theory to account for categorization. Technical formal systems do not use prototype theory.
- Cognitive models and grammatical constructions have gestalt properties. That is, the wholes may by psychologically simpler than the parts. Technical formal systems, on the other hand, are atomistic—that is, the wholes are just collections of the parts.
- In technical formal systems, syntactic elements are arbitrary symbols. In cognitive grammar, syntactic elements are not arbitrary but are *motivated* by corresponding semantic elements. The concept of *motivation* does not exist in technical formal systems. It will be discussed in some detail below.
- In technical formal systems, there is no notion of the *ecology* of the system and no concept of an ecological niche, a place where something fits into the system. Cognitive systems have such an ecology, and we will be discussing it below. The concept of a ecological niche will turn out to be an important part of the theory of grammatical constructions.
- Within classical formal linguistics, there is a concern with such mathematical notions as the generative power of formal systems and with ways of limiting generative power by constraining the forms of rules. These technical mathematical concerns are of no interest whatever in a cognitively based grammar. We are interested in the way general cognition places constraints on human languages and not in constraints having to do with cognitively irrelevant concepts like generative power. Any choice among alternative descriptions must be based on such cognitive criteria as the ability to account for language acquisition, the ability of a grammar to cohere with a conceptual system, the ease of cognitive processing, and the overall ecology of the grammar.

- In technical formal systems, syntax is independent of semantics and pragmatics. In cognitively based linguistics, syntax is to a very significant extent (though by no means entirely) dependent on semantics, pragmatics, and communicative function.

For these reasons, the system that we will be discussing is not just another technical formal system of the sort that a great many linguists have justifiably become disillusioned with. It is, instead, an attempt to provide a precise characterization of some central concepts in cognitive linguistics.

Before we go on, there is one further possible confusion that ought to be cleared up. It is sometimes maintained that the mind uses technical formal systems (e.g., phrase structure or transformational grammars). If this were true, some type of generative linguistics would be cognitively correct. One of the goals of this case study is to show that that is not the case, by actually working out cognitively based descriptions and explanations of subtle linguistic phenomena that technical formal systems seem not to be able to deal with.

Linguists trained within the generative tradition have sometimes claimed that only technical formal systems allow for the kind of precise formulation of principles that is necessary to adequately describe and explain linguistic phenomena. What is implicit in this claim is that cognitively based accounts of linguistic phenomena are necessarily imprecise and therefore incapable of providing adequate descriptions and explanations. Another goal of this case study is to take a problem area in English grammar and provide for it an account that is much more adequate, both descriptively and explanatorily, than any account in terms of mathematical formal systems can be. This is one reason why the present case study is as detailed as it is.

Finally, the present study is by no means antimathematical. It is quite conceivable that a mathematics appropriate to the kind of cognitive systems discussed here could be developed. In fact, I am rather hopeful about this. It is one of the reasons that I have taken the trouble to describe the phenomena as precisely as I have. I object only to the use of an inappropriate mathematics such as technical formal systems.

Some Notational Prerequisites

Each construction will be described in terms of the following parameters of form and meaning:

Parameters of Meaning

- Semantic elements (e.g., entities, locations, predicates, etc.)
- Overall semantics (e.g., any idealized cognitive model associated with the construction as a whole). The ICMs will often include background conditions, speech act conditions, and a specification of the function of the construction.

Parameters of Form

- Syntactic elements (e.g., clause, noun phrase, verb, etc.)
- Lexical elements (e.g., *here, there, come, go, be,* etc.)
- Syntactic conditions (e.g., linear order of elements, grammatical relations such as subject and object, optionality of elements, etc.)
- Phonological conditions (e.g., presence or absence of stress, vowel length, etc.)

Form-Meaning Pairings

Whenever there is a pairing between a syntactic element and a semantic element, we will express the pairing in the following way:

- The syntactic element will be represented by an integer, *i*.
- The semantic element with be represented by *i*′, the same integer followed by a prime.

No primacy of either syntax or semantics is indicated by this notation, though in general we will be trying to predict as much as possible of the syntax from the semantics. All that is indicated is a pairing of the form ⟨*i*,*i*′⟩. In some cases, one syntactic element will be paired with more than one semantic element. In such cases we will use more than one prime, i′′′, etc.

We are now in a position to begin the first of our major projects, motivating the syntax of deictic *there*-constructions on the basis of their parameters of meaning. We will begin with the idealized cognitive model (ICM) that represents the parameters of meaning of the central deictic construction. Once we do that, we can go on to account for various parameters of form of the central construction.

The Central ICM: An Experiential Gestalt

It is one of the principal findings of prototype theory that certain clusters of conditions are more basic to human experience than other clusters and also more basic than individual conditions in the cluster. Lakoff and Johnson (1980) refer to such a cluster as an *experiential gestalt.* Such a gestalt is often representable by an ICM. It should be borne in mind that in such cases the entire ICM is understood as being psychologically simpler than its parts—hence the term *gestalt.* Although a great many conditions may enter into the description of such a gestalt, it is important to realize that the complexity of the description is an artifact of our notational system. If we had a notational system that reflected psychological reality, the entire ICM would be representable by a simple description and its parts by a more complex one.

The reason it is important to bear this in mind is that it is normal to think of descriptions in the following way: the more complex the description, the more complex the concept. In the case of experiential gestalts, however, the reverse may hold: a complex description may correspond to a cognitively simple concept, while a relatively simple description of one of the parts of the concept may be cognitively more complex. This is so in the case of experiential gestalt we are about to describe.

One of the most basic things people do is point out things to other people. English-speaking children start to do this at the two-word stage with utterances like "Da shoe" (There's a/the shoe). When we pick out all the relevant parts of this very simple experiential gestalt, we find a fairly complex cluster of conditions:

> It is assumed as a background that some entity exists and is present at some location in the speaker's visual field, that the speaker is directing his attention at it, and that the hearer is interested in its whereabouts but does not have his attention focused on it and may not even know that it is present. The speaker then directs the hearer's attention to the location of the entity (perhaps accompanied by a pointing gesture) and brings it to the hearer's attention that the entity is at the specified location. Additionally (for older children and adults), if the entity is moving, the motion may be indicated. And the speaker may choose to describe the entity or its location.

Adopting the format given above for representing parameters of meaning, we can pick apart this experiential gestalt in even more detail and represent it as follows:

The Pointing-Out ICM

Semantic Elements

S: Speaker
H: Hearer

1′: a location
2′: a locational predicate
2″: a predicate of motion
3′: an entity
4′: a predicate

0′: a proposition of the form 2′(3′,1′) (the entity is at the location)
0″: a proposition of the form 2″(3′) (the entity is moving)
0‴: a proposition of the form 4′(3′) (the predicate holds of the entity)
(0″ and 0‴ are optional.)

Overall Semantics

Speech Act Background

B-1: 3′ exists
B-2: 0′ (3′ is located at 1′)
B-3: 3′ is in *S*'s visual field
B-4: *S* is focusing his attention on 3′
B-5: *S* assumes *H* is not focusing his attention on 3′

Speech Act

S directs *H*'s attention to 1′

Functional Condition

To focus *H*'s awareness on 3′

Gesture

S gestures in the direction of 1′, typically by pointing or turning the head. (optional)

In what follows, I will refer to all of the above simply as the pointing-out ICM.

Restricted Prediction and Cognitive Explanation

Part of the program of cognitive grammar is to show how aspects of form can follow from aspects of meaning. We will try to show, for example, that almost every syntactic property of the central deictic construction is a consequence of the fact that it is used to express the pointing-out ICM. There is a long tradition in linguistics of attempting to predict form from meaning. To date, none of these attempts has succeeded. Take some well-known and relatively simple-minded attempts:

- Actions are expressed by verbs.
- States are expressed by adjectives.
- Physical objects are expressed by nouns (or noun phrases).

If we take such principles as absolutes that hold for all cases, then there are abundant counterexamples. Thus, states like knowing can be expressed by verbs, as in *I know the answer*. Actions can be expressed by adjectives, as in *Be aggressive!* or *Be careful!* An expression denoting a physical object can be a verb, as in *He hammered in the nail.*

Yet, despite such counterexamples, the principles proposed above are by no means completely wrong. They are wrong only in having been proposed as absolutes. There are a number of reasons why I think attempts to do so have failed.

First, it was assumed that they should work for all cases in a language.

Second, it was assumed that they were all to be universal.

Third, it was assumed that they were to be absolute, rather than relative to other factors in a language.

Fourth, it was assumed that everything was either fully predictable or arbitrary. No other alternative was possible.

I would like to suggest an approach that avoids these pitfalls.

- Such principles may be limited to prototypical cases, in particular, to central subcategories of radial categories. We will refer to these as *central principles.*
- Such principles may be language-particular, rather than universal.
- Such principles may make use of the "ecological location" of a construction within a linguistic system.
- Specific cases may preempt general principles.

Central principles play a dual role. First, they characterize form-meaning regularities for central subcategories, e.g., prototypical clauses, nouns, verbs, adjectives, subjects, etc. Second, they characterize the way in which noncentral cases are like central cases. That is, they help characterize what it means for a noncentral case to be motivated by central cases.

A grammatical system is characterized as follows:

First, given a conceptual system, the central categories of the language are characterized by the *central principles* linking form and content.

Second, noncentral categories are "located" in the grammatical system via relations to central (or more central) categories. The relation which "locates," say, one constructional category relative to another is called the *based-on* relation.

Third, less central categories are characterized by those *minimal differences* that distinguish them from the categories they are *based on.*

Fourth, central principles are used to characterize redundancies in the following way: Any property of a noncentral category that can be predicted by *central principles* from a specification of *minimal differences* is *redundant.* Such prediction will be referred to as "restricted prediction," since it is prediction restricted to a given ecological location.

Fifth, relative motivation is characterized as follows: the more the properties of a given category are redundant, the more it is motivated by its ecological location, and the better it fits into the system as a whole.

Sixth, an optimal ecological structure for a language is a structure that maximizes motivation.

There is a tradition in linguistic analysis of identifying an optimal linguistic analysis (according to some criterion of optimality) with the cognitively correct analysis for some "ideal" speaker of the language (cf. Chomsky, 1965). I will follow that tradition, even though I am acutely aware of its pitfalls, which are legion. None of us, after all, is ideal. Our individual grammars may not be structured optimally. Moreover, there may be a point in development at which our grammars "freeze" and no further optimization of what we have learned up till then takes place. Perhaps the role of such an optimal grammar is that it represents the maximal motivations used in the speech community in general, though no individual may make full use of them. That is, a speaker may learn certain constructions by rote rather than fitting them into his grammar as a whole. But it is unlikely that any individual learns *all* constructions by rote, without understanding them as being motivated in any way by the rest of the grammar.

One thing we can be sure of is that a great deal of optimization of the sort we will be describing does occur. We know this from the fact that when new constructions are added to language, they are not random. Rather, they are motivated by existing structures, just as new senses of words are motivated by existing senses. New constructions and words that "fit well" into a language are easier to learn than those that don't. The theory we are proposing offers a characterization of just what it means to "fit well."

The kind of optimal analysis we will be giving—one which maximizes motivation—also allows us to characterize actual systems that may be nonoptimal. It will allow us to characterize individual variation and to ask whether speakers really use maximally motivated systems, and if not, just how their systems are motivated. It will also allow us to investigate the role that motivation plays in linguistic change and in language acquisition.

Before we embark on a spate of restricted predictions, it is important to point out what cognitive relevance such predictions are supposed to have. We are not claiming that speakers of natural languages go about making such predictions every time they produce an utterance. Quite the opposite. What speakers do is use a linguistic system that fits together well and is cognitively efficient for their purposes. What we are trying to do is characterize exactly what it means for a linguistic system to "fit together well" and be "cognitively efficient." We are attempting to characterize these concepts using the analytic notion "restricted prediction" as we have defined it. Another way of thinking of restricted prediction is that it characterizes the concept of "systemic redundancy," that is, the redundancy of the system as a whole given its overall ecological structure. We will discuss this concept in somewhat more detail after we have seen some examples.

We are trying to give cognitive explanations for linguistic phenomena. Part of our goal is to understand why languages are structured the way they are and what that can tell us about cognitive organization. Toward this end, we are trying to develop techniques of linguistic analysis that will allow us to get insight into cognitive organization. The hypothesis that we are offering is that restricted prediction (in the special sense in which we are defining it) is a measure of cognitive efficiency, given the linguistic and conceptual system as a whole. This in turn can allow us to *explain* why languages are structured the way they are.

If we can show, for example, that most of the syntax of the central deictic construction can be predicted, in our sense of the term, from the pointing-out ICM, then we will have shown that in English the central deictic construction is a cognitively efficient way to express the pointing-out ICM. Moreover, we will have shown in detail exactly *why* it is a cognitively efficient construction, given the rest of English. That is, we will have shown why it is easy to learn, remember, and use. And we will have explained, in cognitive terms, why it has the peculiar properties it has.

In the predictions to be made below, I am taking for granted certain central principles governing the correspondence of form and content in prototypical cases. Some appear to be universal, while others are English-specific. It is beyond the scope of this study to justify all of them or even to state all of them as precisely as necessary. That will have to be done in a fully worked out and fully explicit cognitive grammar. What we can do is give a few simple examples of the sort that we will be making use of below. Most of the central principles are relatively obvious, so obvious as to hardly be worth stating. We are bothering to state them only to provide some simple clear examples. We will state each principle both in simple English, and in the notation we will be using. Each of the examples given will be used in the discussion below.

Some Central Principles (CP)

CP1: Clauses correspond to propositions.

CLAUSE (X) iff PROPOSITION (X')

CP2: Noun phrases correspond to entities.

NP (X) iff ENTITY (X')

CP3: Motion predicates are expressed as verbs.

If MOTION PREDICATE (X'), then $V(X)$

CP4: Location predicates are expressed as verbs.

If LOCATION PREDICATE (X'), then $V(X)$

CP5: Locative adverbs correspond to locations.

LOCATIVE ADVERB (X) iff LOCATION (X')

CP6: Parts of a semantic structure correspond to parts of the corresponding syntactic structure.

PART(X',Y') iff PART(X,Y)

CP7: Semantically optional parts of ICMs correspond to syntactically optional elements.

If PART (X',Y') and OPTIONAL (X'), then OPTIONAL (X)

Some Detailed Predictions

The central deictic construction is based on the simple central clause and expresses the pointing-out ICM. Given this, we can make the following predictions:

Prediction 1: 0 is a CLAUSE.

A consequence of CP1. Since $0'$, $0''$, and $0'''$ are propositions which are expressed by 0, 0 is a clause.

Prediction 2: 0 has parts 1, 2, 3, and 4.

A consequence of CP6. Since $1'$, $2'$, $3'$, and $4'$ are parts of the propositions $0'$, $0''$, and $0'''$, it follows that 1, 2, 3, and 4 are parts of 0.

Prediction 3: 1 is a DEICTIC LOCATIVE ADVERB.

It is a consequence of CP5 that 1 is a LOCATIVE ADVERB. Moreover, an element located relative to the context of utterance is deictic. Since $1'$ is a location relative to the speaker, it is therefore relative to the context of utterance; thus, 1 is a deictic locative adverb.

Prediction 4: 3 is a NOUN PHRASE.

A consequence of CP2. Since $3'$ is an entity, 3 is a NOUN PHRASE.

Prediction 5: 3 is not a SENTENTIAL COMPLEMENT.

Since $3'$ is a physically present, visible entity, it cannot be a proposition or an event or a state. Since only propositions, events, or states are expressed by sentential complements, 3 cannot be a sentential complement.

Prediction 6: 2 is a verb.

A consequence of CP3 and CP4. Since 2′ is a locational predicate and 2″ is a predicate of motion, it follows that 2 is a verb.

Prediction 7: 2 is in the simple present tense.

In the pointing-out ICM, the predication of location or motion is simultaneous with the speech act. Therefore, it must be present tense, which expresses simultaneity with the speech act. Since the pointing-out event (the speech act) is instantaneous, and since the present tense marks simultaneity with that speech act, there is no progressive or perfect aspect, and hence no auxiliary verbs. Since the pointing-out ICM has no indication of modality, there are no modals. Consequently, 2 is in the simple present tense.

Prediction 8: 4 is optional.

A consequence of CP7. In the pointing-out ICM, the proposition describing 3′ is optional. The predicate 4′ occurs only in that proposition. Since 4′ is optional, the syntactic element expressing it, namely 4, is optional.

Prediction 9: 1 is first.

The speaker is directing immediate attention to location 1′. To direct immediate attention to something, you have to mention it immediately. Therefore, the syntactic element expressing 1′ must come first.

Prediction 10: 3 is subject of 0.

In central clauses, the subject of the clause must be a noun phrase expressing an argument of one of the propositions expressed by the clause. It must also be included among the semantic elements in the parameters of meaning of the construction. There are only two possible candidates, 3 and 1, since 3′ and 1′ are the only arguments listed among the parameters of meaning. But 1 is ruled out because, here, as in central clauses, an adverb cannot be the subject. That leaves 3.

Lexical Choices

In this construction there are three cases where lexical items are chosen: the deictic locative adverb (*here* or *there*), a locational predicate (*be, sit, stand,* or *lie*), and a predicate of motion (*go* or *come*). Most of these specific lexical items, but not all, are predictable from general principles. And the ones that are not predictable are nonetheless not arbitrary.

This construction contains lexical elements because it has semantic elements that are tightly restricted: a location relative to the speaker, a predicate of location, and a predicate of motion. These can only be expressed lexically; they cannot be expressed (at least not in English) by bound morphemes or word order or constituent structure. The general principle governing the choice of lexical elements can be called the lexical choice principle.

Suppose:
(*a*) there is a semantic element x' in a construction,
(*b*) there is a semantic constraint on x',
(*c*) x, the syntactic element corresponding to x', is a lexical category (e.g., noun, verb, adverb, etc.), and
(*d*) L is one of the most general individual lexical items available in the lexicon that is in the syntactic category of x and meets the semantic constraints on x'.

Then:
(*e*) L expresses x in the construction.

The lexical choice principle makes the following predictions:

Prediction 11: 1 is expressed by *here* or *there.*

Prediction 12: 2 can be expressed by *be, go,* or *come.*

Here and *there* are the most general individual lexical items that are deictic locative adverbs. *Be* is the most general single lexical item that expresses a predicate of location. And *go* and *come* are the most general verbs that express a predicate of motion.

What is not predicted by the lexical choice principle is that *sit, stand,* and *lie* can occur in the construction as element 2. But this particular collection of verbs is not an arbitrary collection. They happen to be the basic-level verbs of location. This construction allows verbs of location to be one level of generality lower than verbs of motion. The basic-level verbs of motion are *run, walk,* etc. These, of course, cannot occur. Their absence is to be expected from the lexical choice principle, but the fact that *sit, stand,* and *lie* do occur is not predicted. Instead it must be listed among the unpredictable parts of the construction that 2 may be expressed by basic-level locational verbs.

It may seem strange to have a condition mentioning basic-level verbs as part of a construction. However, the ability to refer to cognitive concepts like basic-level categorization may make sense of some otherwise inexplicable facts. Moreover, basic-level categorization must be appealed to in the description of grammatical facts in languages other than English. For example, in Swedish, one cannot say the equivalent of *The lamp is in the corner* or *The rug is on the floor.* One must say instead the Swedish equivalents of *The lamp stands in the corner* and *The rug lies on the floor.* Swedish appears to require basic-level verbs in simple locative clauses. The important thing in both the Swedish and English constructions is that one doesn't have to give a list of apparently unrelated items. What unites them is their level of categorization and that can be specified in a grammatical construction.

Before we leave the realm of the lexicon, we should make one more prediction that is related, at least tangentially, to lexical items.

Prediction 13: 1 bears stress.

Lexical items in major grammatical categories, including adverbs, normally bear some stress. Lack of stress occurs in a relatively small range of such cases—anaphoric pronouns and backgrounded elements that do not take part in any minimal contrast. As we will see below, the existential *there* is a backgrounded element that does not minimally contrast with anything else. It is unstressed for that reason. But the deictic *here* and *there* are not backgrounded and they do enter into a minimal contrast—with each other. Thus, there is no reason whatever for them to lack stress.

The Final Phrase

The final phrase—syntactic element 4—expresses semantic element 4′, which is a predicate. Predicates are typically expressed syntactically as verb phrases. For example, in a sentence like *Harry is carrying a huge herring,* the verb phrase *is carrying a huge herring* is predicated of *Harry.* The final phrase in the central deictic construction is, however, different from normal verb phrases in an important respect. Take the sentence

- There's Harry, carrying a huge herring.

The final phrase is only *carrying a huge herring*; there is no *is,* that is, no overt manifestation of the verb *be*, which is the head verb of the verb phrase *is carrying a huge herring*. This is typical of final phrases in this construction. They are phrases which, in simple sentences, normally occur in verb phrases where *be* is the main verb. We can see this in the following examples:

- There's Sally *in front of her house.*
- Here comes Max *with his new girlfriend.*
- There's Sammy *at work.*
- There goes the cop, *afraid of his shadow.*
- Here's the victim, *shot in the back.*
- There's Mary, *about to go into the bookstore.*

The final phrases in such examples seem very diverse. What all the expressions in italics have in common is that they are all remnants of verb phrases whose head verb would be *be* in a corresponding simple sentence.

This suggests the followng tentative hypothesis about final phrases:

> There is a construction in English that is arrived at in the following way: take a verb phrase whose head verb is *be*, and subtract the *be*. Let us call this: VP/*be*. The final phrase of the deictic *there*-constructions is VP/*be*.

Thus far we have hypothesized that final phrases are verb phrases with a missing *be*. Let us now consider a further bit of evidence supporting this position.

With Meaning "Have"

All of the cases we have mentioned happen to have corresponding simple sentences where the *be* is actually expressed:

- Sally is in front of her house.
- Max is with his new girlfriend.
- Sammy is at work.
- The cop is afraid of his shadow.
- The victim was shot in the back.
- Mary is about to go into the bookstore.

These are some of the many situations where *be* is required to be the head of the verb phrase in a simple sentence: with prepositional phrases in the first three examples, with adjective phrases (e.g., *afraid of his shadow*), with passive phrases (e.g., *shot in the back*), as part of the phrase *be about to*, and with progressive participial phrases (e.g., *carrying a huge herring*). Thus, where *be* occurs as the head of a verb phrase, the remainder of the verb phrase can occur as a final phrase in a central deictic *there*-construction.

We can find further support for this theory of final phrases in the behavior of a special class of *with*-phrases that have the meaning of *have* and appear to occur with an understood but unexpressed *be*. An example of such a phrase is *with her shoes off* in:

- There's Tammy with her shoes off.

At first, such expressions might appear anomalous because they cannot occur with an overtly expressed *be*.

- *Tammy is with her shoes off.

The corresponding full sentence has *have* instead of *be with*.

– Tammy has her shoes off.

If we look at a variety of contexts where there is an understood but unexpressed *be*, we find that this *with* can occur there. We will consider two such cases: reduced relative clauses and the complement of the verb *find*.

Full relative clauses that have a *be* following the relative pronoun, such as

– Anyone who is carrying a herring . . .

usually have variants without the relative pronoun and *be*:

– Anyone carrying a herring . . .

Here *carrying a herring* is a reduced relative clause, and the *be* that usually accompanies the progressive participle *carrying* is understood but not overtly expressed. Other constructions that usually occur with *be*, such as passives and *about to*, can occur here.

– Anyone shot in the back . . .
– Anyone about to leave . . .

Special *with* can occur in reduced relative clauses as well.

– Anyone with his shoes off . . .

Similarly, constructions that usually take *be* can occur in the complement of *find* without the *be*, as in:

– I found Harry carrying a herring.
– I found the victim shot in the back.
– I found Sally about to leave.

Special *with* can also occur here:

– I found Tammy with her shoes off.

The generalization governing the occurrence of special *with* seems to be that it expresses certain senses of *have* and that it occurs where one would expect to find a VP/*be*. Thus, the fact that special *with* can occur in the final phrases of central deictic *there*-constructions lends further support to our analysis of a final phrase as a VP/*be*.

There is, however, a slight wrinkle here. Not quite all verb phrases with *be* can occur as final phrases. There are two types that cannot: predicate nominals and adjectives that indicate what has been called an "inherent" property.

– Harry is a lawyer. (predicate nominal)
– Harry is tall. (inherent adjective)

- *There goes Harry a lawyer.
- *There goes Harry tall.

Noninherent adjectives, like *drunk*, specifying properties that vary with the occasion, can occur as final phrases:

- There goes Harry drunk!

This contrasts with

- *There goes Harry a drunk!

(Incidentally, we are discussing only sentences without comma intonation; the sentence *There goes Harry, a drunk* is, of course, well-formed but has a structure that is irrelevant here.) Noun phrases tend to express persisting properties. Thus *a drunk* indicates persistent drunkenness, while *drunk* does not. This explains why noun phrases tend to be ruled out as final phrases. However, some can occur, but only when they are clearly nonpersistent and noninherent.

- There goes Citation the winner by a nose!

This condition can be described in our format as follows:

Syntactic Elements
  4: a VP/*be*

Semantic Elements
  4′: a noninherent, nonpersistent predicate

The Last Word on Final Phrases

The description given above won't quite handle all final phrases. It misses cases where there is motion indicated and where the final phrase is directional, for example,

- There goes Harry into the bar.
- Here comes the bus into the terminal.

Since *into the bar* and *into the terminal* are directional phrases, they cannot occur with *be*, but rather require a verb of motion, like *go* or *come*. Since each of the sentences has an occurrence of a motion verb in it, it might seem reasonable to assume that the directional phrase modifies that motion verb—for example, that *into the bar* modifies *goes* and *into the terminal* modifies *comes* in the above sentences.

But this solution cannot be made to work in all cases. The reason is that the final phrases are part of a separate proposition from the rest of the construction. We can see this with the help of some added adverbs that have the function of separating out the component propositions. Let us begin with a nondirectional final phrase and then show the same for the directionals.

– There is Derek, running around the track.

Here *running around the track* is the final phrase. We can show that there are two propositions here by adding the adverbs *again* and *still.*

– There is Derek again, still running around the track.

Still presupposes that what it modifies has been going on continuously. *Again* presupposes that what it modifies has happened before, but that there has been some discontinuity. If they were modifying the same proposition, there would be a contradiction. What we have is two propositions equivalent to the separate sentences

– There is Derek again.
– Derek is still running around the track.

The same effect can be shown with directionals. Compare

– There goes Harry into the bar.

with

– There goes Harry again, into the bar this time.

Again indicates that Harry went by before, and *this time* indicates that he did not go into the bar before. There are two separate propositions, equivalent to the sentences:

– There goes Harry again.
– Harry is going into the bar this time.

The verb *goes* designates a number of occurrences of going, most of which did not include going into the bar. Thus, we cannot simply have *into the bar* modifying the *goes* of *There goes Harry again.*

We can describe such cases by making a minimal modification of the description of final phrases given in the preceding section. There we described the final phrase as a verb phrase missing a *be*. In this case the missing head verb would be either *go* or *come*, depending on which was chosen as syntactic element 2, the main verb of the whole construction. Since 2 = *be*, *go*, or *come*, the modified lexical condition in our descriptive format would now read as follows:

Syntactic Elements
    4: a VP/2

There is one further complication concerning final phrases: More than one of them can occur in a sentence. In fact, there can be an indefinitely large number.

- There's Sally at work on her new book, writing as quickly as she can, afraid that she might miss her deadline.

We can describe this in a straightforward way by indicating that syntactic element 4 can be iterated indefinitely. A standard way of notating iteration is to place an asterisk after the numeral marking the syntactic element, that is, changing "4" to "4*."

The last detail that needs to be mentioned is that the noun phrase of the construction—syntactic element 3—functions as the grammatical subject of the final phrase. This is predicted from the semantics. The final phrase is semantically a predicate, and it is predicated of 3′, the semantic entity corresponding to the syntactic noun phrase. Since 3′ is the only required argument of this predicate, it is the only possible candidate to be the grammatical subject of the final phrase. Thus, in a sentence like

- There's Derek again, still running around the track.

Derek is the grammatical subject of *(is) still running around the track.* In the notation given, 3 is grammatical subject of 4. It will thus govern such phenomena as reflexivization in final phrases, for example, *There's Derek again, still admiring himself.*

Technically, the grammatical subject relation is usually defined so that it holds between a noun phrase and a clause, not a verb phrase. To be technically correct, we need to pick out the clause that 3 is subject of. The entire construction constitutes a clause, represented by syntactic element 0. Let us define a subconstruction ⟨0; 3,4⟩, which consists of the clause, 0, together with the noun phrase, 3, and the verb phrase, 4. We will now say that 3 is the subject of ⟨0; 3,4⟩, or, in other words, that "Derek" in the above example is the subject of "Derek (is) still running around the track."

The Order of Verb and Noun Phrase

Thus far, we have not considered the relative order of syntactic elements 2 (the verb) and 3 (the noun phrase). The order is not fixed, and varies depending on whether or not the noun phrase is a pronoun. In general, the noun phrase precedes the verb if it is a pronoun and follows the verb if it is not.

- There he goes.
- *There goes he.
- There goes Harry.

These facts seem to be constant across all speakers. There is variation when the noun phrase is not a pronoun and precedes the verb. Some speakers find proper names well-formed in this position. (The "%" indicates variation.)

- %There Harry goes.

But in general, the longer the noun phrase, the worse this construction seems to be.

- *There the mayor goes.
- *There the tall man goes.
- *There the man with the purple hair goes.
- *There the man who I met yesterday goes.

This ordering of verb and noun phrase seems not to be confined to the central deictic construction. It also occurs with directional deictic adverbial constructions:

- Away ran Harry.
- Out jumped the cat.
- Up popped a mole.
- Into the room came a priest.

The same variation in the order of verb and noun phrase occurs with this construction:

- Away he ran.
- *Away ran he.
- Away ran Harry.
- %Away Harry ran.

Again, for those who find *Away Harry ran* grammatical, the sentences get worse as the noun phrases get longer:

- *Away the major ran.
- *Away the tall man ran.
- *Away the man with the purple hair ran.
- *Away the man who I met yesterday ran.

Incidentally, the pronoun constraint seems to work only for definite pronouns, like *he, she*, etc. The indefinite pronoun *one* works like other noun phrases:

- There goes one!
- %There one goes!

– I was waiting for a mole and up popped one!
– %I was waiting for a mole and up one popped!

This construction functions deictically for the following reason: it is used in what are sometimes called "vivid narratives," where a story that is supposed to be visualized is being told. Thus the construction functions as though the participants were in the presence of the speaker and hearer.

Consequently, there seems to be a word-order constraint that extends beyond the central deictic *there*-construction to spatial deictic adverbial constructions in general:

> In spatial deictic adverbial constructions, the noun phrase precedes the verb if it is a definite pronoun, and the verb precedes the noun phrase otherwise.

Given this constraint, the relative order of the verb and noun phrase in the central deictic *there*-construction is predicted.

One aspect of the central deictic construction that does not seem predictable is the choice of locational verbs in case there is no motion. In this construction, the basic-level locational verbs *sit, stand,* and *lie* may optionally appear as element 2.

– There sits Harry, chomping on a cigar.
– There he stands, ready to defend our country.
– Here lies a great American.

This extension from the superordinate locational verb *be* to the basic-level locationals seems to occur only in the central construction.

The Central Deictic Construction

We are finally in a position to represent the central deictic construction in maximally general terms. The following is a minimal representation, leaving out all predictable details.

The Central Deictic

Based on: The Central Clause

Parameters of Meaning
  The pointing-out ICM

Parameters of Form

Semantic Elements
    4: not inherent

Syntactic Elements

4*: a VP/2

Lexical Elements

If there is no 2″, 2 may be expressed by a basic-level locational verb. (These are *sit, stand, lie*.)

This is all that needs to be said about the construction. Everything else is predictable.

Although most of the syntax of the central construction is a consequence of its semantics, it is important to list all of the parameters of form, even the predictable ones, since many of them will be different in the noncentral deictic constructions. Here is the full representation, with the pointing-out ICM listed as a single unit.

The Central Deictic

Based on: The Central Clause

Parameters of Meaning

The pointing-out ICM

Parameters of Form

Syntactic Elements

0: CLAUSE, a whole with parts:

1: DEICTIC LOCATIVE ADVERB

2: VERB

3: NOUN PHRASE

4*: a VERB PHRASE minus 2

Lexical elements

1: *here* or *there*

2: either *be*, or a superordinate motion verb if there is a 2″, or a basic-level locational verb if there is no 2″

Syntactic Conditions

S-1: 1 is first

S-2: 2 is in the simple present tense

S-3: 2 precedes 3 unless 2 is a definite pronoun

S-4: 4 is optional

S-5: 4 is last

S-6: 3 is subject of 0

S-7: 3 is subject of ⟨0; 3,4⟩

S-8: 3 is not a sentential complement

Phonological Condition

P-1: 1 bears stress

One Construction or Many?

The bulk of this study will be concerned with the distinction between central and noncentral constructions. It is not an uncontroversial distinction, and since the validity of the entire study depends on the distinction, it is important to discuss the question of how one can tell whether one is dealing with one construction or many.

First, let us distinguish between a *special case* and a *minor variation*. Given a proposed analysis of a central construction, a subconstruction that meets all of the conditions of the analysis is a special case. A subconstruction that comes close to meeting all the conditions of the analysis, but doesn't quite make it, is a minor variation. The noncentral cases we will be discussing are all minor variations.

Incorrect Predictions

Given a proposed central construction and one class of minor variations, can one always revise the analysis of the central constructions to be more general, so that the minor variations can be considered special cases of the revised central construction? In other words, can one take what is in common between the old central and the old noncentral constructions and come up with a new, more general central construction that will work just as well?

The answer in general is no. Such a strategy can lead to incorrect predictions concerning form-meaning pairings. Such a reanalysis is possible only when the new, generalized central construction predicts no incorrect form-meaning pairings. In each of the cases we will be discussing below, we will argue that any attempt to generalize the central construction to include the noncentral construction will result in such incorrect predictions.

Increased Complexity Elsewhere

It may also be the case that even if such an analysis is possible, it may not be desirable. For example, consider an analysis with one central construction and ten noncentral constructions. Suppose that there is a possible reanalysis of the central construction that would eliminate the need for one noncentral construction, but that this would considerably increase the complexity of the analyses of the other nine noncentral constructions. In such a case, one might argue that such a generalization in the central construction is too costly. But to make such an argument one would have to be able to weigh generalizations in central constructions against generalizations in noncentral constructions. As yet, no such cases have been found, and so the question has not arisen for any real cases.

Lack of Full Predictability

Another important distinction that needs to be made is that between a *special case* and a *fully predictable variation*. In all of the noncentral constructions that we will discuss below, most of their properties are predictable from their relation to the central construction and from other more general principles of both universal grammar and the grammar of English. However, in no case that we will discuss can *every* aspect of the noncentral construction be predicted. That is, in each case there is at least some minimal part that we claim that a speaker of the language must learn.

It should be noted that we cannot *prove* that any given property is unpredictable. To do that, one would have to know all the correct general principles of both universal grammar and the grammar of English, and be able to show that each property listed is unpredictable. All that I can say is that at present I don't see any way of predicting them. But, although the analyses are not verifiable, they are falsifiable. To argue against any given analysis, all one has to do is show how *all* properties of a given subconstruction are predictable from other general principles.

But even if one could do this for all the cases given below, one would still not have succeeded in arguing against the applicability of prototype theory in grammar. If each of the constructions is a variation and not a special case, then all one would have succeeded in doing is arguing that the noncentral cases were predictable from the central cases. To argue against the applicability of prototype theory in general, one must provide an analysis according to which all of what we have called variations turn out to be special cases and which makes no incorrect predictions about form-meaning pairings.

In the following section, we will discuss a case that indicates that any such analysis is improbable, if not impossible.

The Noncentral Constructions

The noncentral constructions are variations on the central construction and will be described as such. To indicate the linkage, each noncentral construction will be marked "based on: the central deictic." This will be taken to mean that each noncentral construction will inherit from the central construction all parameters of form and meaning except for those that are explicitly contradicted by the parameters listed for the noncentral construction.

But this is too simple a concept of inheritance. Some of the subconstructions we will be discussing involve metaphoric and metonymic models—models that have a mapping function. For example, the next construction we will be looking at is the perceptual deictic, in which reference is made to sounds and other percepts in one's nonvisual perceptual field. The central deictic is adaptable for this purpose because we model perceptual space metaphorically on physical space. This allows us to pick out perceptual "locations," as in

– There's the buzzer!

What is "inherited" by such perceptual deictics is not the semantics of physical space used in the central construction, but a metaphorical mapping of physical space into perceptual space. One thing that we need to know about the perceptual deictic construction is that it makes use of this metaphorical mapping. Thus, one part of the representation of a subconstruction will be a listing of the names of any mapping models—metaphoric or metonymic—that it makes use of.

The Perceptual Deictic

It is commonly believed that the senses of lexical items are independent of the constructions that the lexical items appear in. Thus, it is assumed that if a word has a given sense when used in a special grammatical construction, it will also have that sense outside of that construction. This is true in many cases. For example, take the word *there*. In the central deictic construction, *there* designates a location in physical space.

– There's Harry.

Similarly, when used outside of this construction, say in a simple sentence, *there* also designates a location in physical space.

– Harry is there.

According to the usual belief, *there* has this meaning in the English lexicon, independent of any particular construction. When *there* happens to be used in a special construction, such as the central deictic, it has its normal lexical meaning. This view can be expressed as follows:

> *The Lexical Independence Hypothesis:* The meanings of words are independent of any grammatical constructions that the words occur in.

This hypothesis is assumed to be true by most contemporary theories of grammar. The fact that it is false is therefore by no means a trivial fact.

We can see that it is false by comparing the central deictic and perceptual deictic constructions. Corresponding to the central deictic

– There's Harry.

we have the simple sentence

– Harry is there.

But given the perceptual deictic

– There's the beep.

there is no corresponding simple sentence

– *The beep is there.

The perceptual sense of *there*, which refers to a perceptual rather than spatial location, only occurs in the perceptual deictic construction. If the lexical independence hypothesis were correct, the perceptual sense of *there* should occur in such simple sentences, since simple sentences do not have any constraints that would prohibit it from occurring there. The fact that the perceptual sense of *there* cannot occur in simple sentences must therefore be considered prima facie evidence against the independence hypothesis.

Incidentally, these facts can also be accounted for in an ad hoc way—by marking the appropriate sense of *there* in the lexicon to indicate that it can only occur in this construction. This solution misses the generalization that we stated. It also assumes that the lexical independence hypothesis is false.

One of the effects of the lexical independence hypothesis has been to confine the application of metaphor and metonymy to the lexicon and to keep the grammar independent of them. This phenomenon suggests, however, that this cannot be done. Instead, the perceptual deictic construction must, as a whole, make use of the relevant metaphors. This conclusion fits very harmoniously with grammatical construction theory as we have seen it at work so far. Grammatical constructions have complex parameters of meaning that are not just associated with individual lexical items. For instance, the central deictic has the entire pointing-out ICM as its semantics—and this goes well beyond the semantic contributions of the lexical items. The metaphors that relate spatial location to perceptual location must apply to the entire pointing-out ICM, not just to the meaning of *there*, in order to provide correct meanings for the perceptual deictic construction. To get the meaning right, metaphors must operate on entire constructional meanings, not just on the meanings of words. Let us turn to some examples that show why this is so.

In the perceptual deictic construction, *there* refers to a location in nonvisual perceptual space at a time that either is present or in the recent past, sufficiently recent so that the image (say the auditory image) still persists. *Here* refers to a location in nonvisual perceptual space at a time that is in the immediate future. Thus, one can say of a beep alarm that has just gone off, or may or may not have finished beeping:

– There's the beep.

If the beep is preceded by a clicking noise a few seconds before going off, one can say upon hearing the clicking noise:

– Here comes the beep.

Go and *come* are used in this construction not to indicate motion, but to indicate activation, for example, activation of a signaling device like an alarm or activation of a pain, as in:

– There goes the throbbing in my head again.

There appear to be three conceptual metaphors involved in these cases:

NONVISUAL PERCEPTUAL SPACE IS PHYSICAL SPACE; PERCEPTS ARE ENTITIES.

REALIZED IS DISTAL; SOON-TO-BE-REALIZED IS PROXIMAL.

ACTIVATION IS MOTION.

Once we know that these metaphors apply, they predict most of the uses of the construction. For example, in the description of the semantics these metaphors predict that:

1′ = a location in nonvisual perceptual space
2′ = a predicate of perceptual location
2″ = a predicate indicating activation
3′ = a percept
B-3: 3′ is in *S*'s nonvisual perceptual field

Incidentally, the gesture often accompanying this construction is pointing upwards with the index finger, as in

– There's the bell now! (speaker points upward and tilts ear upward)

This gesture can be used independently of the syntactic construction.

As I pointed out above, this construction interacts with metonymy in an interesting way. There seems to be a conceptual metonymy of the form

THE THING PERCEIVED STANDS FOR THE PERCEPT.

Among the percepts are sounds, smells, pains, etc., while the things perceived are entities that give rise to the percepts like alarm clocks, chemical factories, injured knees, etc. This metonymy shows up in the synonymy of sentences like

– There goes the beep.
– There goes the alarm clock.

when the alarm clock makes a beep. In the second sentence, the alarm clock isn't going anywhere; it is standing metonymically for the beep it makes when it goes off. Similarly, if you have an old knee injury that is acting up, you can say either of the following:

– There goes the pain in my knee.
– There goes my knee.

The second is, in fact, more idiomatic. Again the knee isn't going anywhere; it is becoming active in producing a perceived pain. The knee is standing metonymically for the pain.

But things are not so simple. The metonymy, at least as we have stated it so far, does not appear to work when the verb *come* is used. Thus, when one hears the click a few seconds before the beep of the alarm clock, one can say the first sentence, but not the second.

– Here comes the beep.
– *Here comes the alarm clock.

Similarly, when one senses that one's knee is about to act up, one can say the first sentence but not the second:

– Here comes the pain in my knee.
– *Here comes my knee.

There are two ways to account for this phenomenon. One can try a description that says that when the verb *come* appears in the construction, the metonymy cannot be used. One can state this in the following manner:

Lexical Condition

2 = *come*, only if it is not the case that 3′ stands for the percept of 3′.

Such a condition would claim that the phenomenon is not predictable, but must be listed as part of the nonpredictable part of English grammar.

However, such a condition can be made predictable by reanalyzing the metonymy. Instead of the formulation given above, one can revise the metonymy to read as follows:

THE THING PERCEIVED STANDS FOR THE PERCEPT WHILE THE PERCEPTION IS IN PROGRESS.

Adding the qualification "while the perception is in progress" permits the metonymy with *there goes*, but rules it out with *here comes*, since the perception has not yet started at the time it is appropriate to say *here comes*. This formulation of the metonymy accounts for the linguistic facts. It would predict the following change in the parameters of meaning:

3′: a percept or something perceived

But such a formulation of the metonymy does not merely account for the linguistic facts. It is also an account of what we normally *do* when we perceive—that is, we take our percepts as being actual things that give rise to our perceptions. Although it is possible for us to question our perceptions, by separating percepts from things perceived, it is not what we normally do—at least not in the case of vision. Distinguishing between percepts and the things that give rise to them is more common with the nonvisual modalities, where one is less likely to be certain what one hears, smells, feels, etc. Perhaps that is why the choice is grammaticized in the case of nonvisual modalities—so that one can indicate the distinction between the percept and the thing perceived, since that is a useful distinction to make.

Such a distinction does not show up everywhere in English. For example, words like *sight* and *sound* are not distinguished in cases like:

- I can't stand the sight of the bell.
- I can't stand the sound of the bell.

But such a grammaticized distinction between the modalities does show up in deictic *there*-constructions:

- There's the sound of the bell.
- *There's the sight of the bell.

The central deictic makes reference to entities, not to their visual percepts such as *the sight of the bell*. The noncentral deictic only makes reference to percepts and only to nonvisual percepts. This leaves visual percepts out in the cold, so far as *there*-constructions are concerned.

What a speaker of English has to learn about the perceptual deictic is that it is based on the central deictic and that the metaphoric and metonymic models concerning perception (which exist independently in the conceptual system) are used in the construction. Everything else is predictable. Therefore, all that needs to be mentioned in a minimal specification of the perceptual deictic is the name of the construction it is based on and the fact that the mapping models used are those that concern the domain of nonvisual perception. This will invoke the use of all of the metaphoric and metonymic models mentioned above, namely,

NONVISUAL PERCEPTUAL SPACE IS PHYSICAL SPACE; PERCEPTS ARE ENTITIES.

REALIZED IS DISTAL; SOON-TO-BE-REALIZED IS PROXIMAL.

ACTIVATION IS MOTION.

THINGS PERCEIVED STAND FOR THEIR PERCEPTS WHILE THEY ARE BEING PERCEIVED.

What the following minimal representation says is that there is a variant of the central deictic that is concerned with nonvisual perception.

The Perceptual Deictic
Based on: The Central Deictic
About: NONVISUAL PERCEPTION

This location in the grammatical system defines both a target domain (nonvisual perception) and a source domain (space), and thus the construction will automatically make use of the appropriate metaphorical mapping models in the conceptual system. Thus spatial *here* and *there* in the central deictic will be mapped onto the appropriate realized and soon-to-be-realized senses. Spatial *come* and *go* will also be mapped onto their activation senses. And this will occur only relative to their uses in this construction and will not apply to their use in the general lexicon. This will allow the appropriate sense of *there* in *There's the beep*, while blocking the occurrence of that sense in **The beep is there*.

Such a minimal representation, which mentions only the ecological niche of the construction, will generate a full grammatical construction with the same parameters of form as the central deictic has and the revised parameters of meaning cited above.

Learning

This description accounts automatically for how such a construction can be learned. Once a child has the appropriate conceptual system for comprehending perception—including the metaphoric and metonymic models mentioned above—all that the child has to learn is that there is such a construction based on the central deictic and about nonvisual perception. To learn that such a construction exists, all he has to do is hear instances of the construction used in appropriate contexts.

One Construction or Two?

This is a convenient point at which to discuss some of the problems that arise from trying to generalize the central deictic to account for the cases covered by the perceptual deictic. This is something I actually tried to do in a previous version of this analysis, and a description of my failure in this matter may be instructive.

My first instinct was to keep the number of senses of lexical items and the number of constructions from proliferating. Ideally, I preferred to have a single deictic sense of the word *there* in both central clauses and *there*-constructions, and I preferred to have a single construction to cover both the central and perceptual cases. Initially, I had placed two conditions on what I thought would be a reasonable analysis.

Condition 1: The Same Lexical Sense Condition

> The *there* in the simple sentence *Harry's there* is the same sense of the same lexical item as the *there* in *There's Harry*.

Condition 2: The Same Construction Condition

> *There's Harry* is an instance of the same construction as *There's the beep*.

The analysis of the central construction given above meets condition 1, but conditions 1 and 2 cannot be met simultaneously, while maintaining a maximally general account of the phenomena.

The first problem concerns the nonoccurrence of **The beep is there*. Suppose that the construction mentions the lexical items *here* and *there*. To meet condition 2, the same lexical item *there* with the same sense must occur in both *There's Harry* and *There's the beep*. Thus, there must be a single sense of *there* neutral between the spatial and perceptual senses. But now there is a problem with condition 1. This *there* that is neutral between the spatial and perceptual senses must occur in the simple sentence *Harry's there*, if the same lexical sense condition is to be met. But if the *there* in *Harry's there* is neutral between the spatial and perceptual senses, then there is no natural way to keep it from occurring in **The beep is there*.

There are, of course, some unnatural ways that could be tried. One might, by brute force, add a condition that says that this sense of *there* cannot occur in simple sentences whose subject refers to a nonvisual percept. This is a purely ad hoc constraint, and it would not only have to be placed on *there*, but also on *here*. Such ad hoc constraints are not in the spirit of conditions 1 and 2, which seek maximum generality.

Incidentally, the same problem arises even if we do not assume that the construction mentions the lexical items *here* and *there*. The construction might simply mention a deictic locative adverb, and the lexicon might include *there* and *here* with both spatial and perceptual senses. But this would give rise to the same problem. To block **The beep is there*, one would have to have the same ad hoc constraints keeping the perceptual sense from occurring in simple sentences with a subject referring to a nonvisual percept.

But it is not even clear that such a solution could be made to work at all. Having a construction neutral between the spatial and perceptual cases would require that the parameters of meaning be neutral between space and perception. But it does not appear that this is possible, when one looks in detail at what it would involve. The meaning of *there* would have to be neutral between DISTAL and REALIZED; the meaning of *here* would have to be neutral between PROXIMAL and SOON-TO-BE-REALIZED. And the meanings of *come* and *go* would have to be neutral between ACTIVATION and MOTION. While the members of each pair are obviously *related* in some way, there is no present account of semantics that permits such neutral meanings—and until such an account is forthcoming one cannot even consider the possibility of such a neutral semantics. Thus, there can be no general construction covering both the spatial and perceptual cases if it has any realistic semantics at all.

There is still one more possibility to be considered, namely, that the general construction covering both the spatial and perceptual cases does not mention any parameters of meaning at all. There are three things wrong with such a solution.

First, the construction would not account for the pairing of form and meaning. Since that job has to be done by maximally general principles somewhere in a grammar, the same problems raised above would arise elsewhere.

Second, the parameters of form would all have to be listed as arbitrary, instead of being mostly predictable from the parameters of meaning. Moreover, the syntactic constraints that are predictable from the pragmatics under the analysis given above would need to be accounted for in some other way.

Third, such a solution would be unable to account in any nonarbitrary way for the contrasts:

- There goes my knee.
- *Here comes my knee.

- There's the sound of the bell.
- *There's the sight of the bell.

- Harry is there.
- *The beep is there.

Arguments like these can be constructed for the noncentral constructions given below. I will not go into each case in as much detail but will present the data on which such arguments would be based.

We should take this opportunity to give a clear example of the distinction mentioned above between a *special case* of a construction and a *predictable variant* of a construction. As we saw above, the only thing about the perceptual deictic that we could not predict is that such a construction—a variant of the central deictic concerned with perception—exists. Suppose we could even predict that. What we would have would be a completely predictable variant of the central deictic. We would *not* have a special case of the central deictic. The reason is that no neutral semantics exists for the domains of space and perception. In order for the perceptual deictic cases to be special cases of the central deictic, the central deictic would have to have a semantics neutral between space and perception. Since that is impossible, the perceptual deictic construction cannot be a special case of the central deictic. It must be a variant—in this case, an almost but not quite predictable variant.

The Discourse Deictic

Here and *there* can be used to refer to something in a discourse. Let us first take up the case where the speaker is commenting on something that someone else has said. In that case, *there* is used to refer to something said in the immediate past. If the speaker thinks he can predict what is about to be said, he can refer to it with *here*.

- Now there's a good point. (past)
- Here comes the best part. (future)

The verb *go*, however, cannot be used in reference to a discourse.

- *There goes a nice point.

The most basic metaphor involved here is:

DISCOURSE SPACE IS PHYSICAL SPACE; DISCOURSE ELEMENTS ARE ENTITIES.

This metaphor is the basis of expressions like

- I'm lost.
- Where are we?
- Can we go back to your last point?

and many others. There also seems to be a metaphor such as:

IMMEDIATELY PAST DISCOURSE IS IN OUR PRESENCE AT A DISTANCE FROM US.

DISCOURSE IN THE IMMEDIATE FUTURE IS MOVING TOWARD US.

This would allow us to account for the fact that *there* in *There's a nice point* refers to discourse in the immediate past, and for the fact that *here comes* indicates something that has not yet been said but is anticipated. It would also account for the absence of the verb *go*, since past discourse is not conceptualized as moving. Here is what such a metaphorical account would predict:

1′ = a location in discourse space
2′ = a predicate of discourse location
2″ = a predicate of discourse motion toward the speaker
3′ = a discourse entity

B-3: 3′ is in or about to enter *S*'s perceptual field

2 ≠ *go*

If 1 = *there*, then discourse entity occurred in the immediate past.

If 1 = *here*, the discourse entity is anticipated in immediate future.

The minimal representation for the discourse deictic need only mention that it is based on the central deictic and that the mapping models used are the metaphors given above. The conditions given above will be consequences, and the full representation will be that of the central deictic with the above changes made.

The Discourse Deictic

Based on: The Central Deictic
About: DISCOURSE

The Existence Deictic

Things that exist exist in locations. To be is to be located. Moreover, we know that something exists if it is in our presence; otherwise, we cannot be sure. These common facts form the basis of a widespread metaphor:

EXISTENCE IS LOCATION HERE; NONEXISTENCE IS LOCATION AWAY.

This metaphor is the basis for many common expressions reporting birth and death:

- There's a baby on the way.
- The baby is here.
- The baby has arrived.
- The doctor delivered the baby.
- He's left us.
- He's gone.
- We've lost him.
- Let us pray for the dear departed.

The same general metaphor seems to be used for existence in general. Thus, something *comes* into existence and *goes* out of existence. The existential senses of *come, go, here,* and *there* are used in the deictic *there*-construction.

- There goes our last hope.
- There goes the possibility of a peaceful settlement.
- Here comes another outburst.
- Here comes the chance of a lifetime!

The metaphor would predict that elements of the central construction would take on the following values:

1′ = a location in a conceptual space, divided into two parts so that entities in locations near the speaker exist and those in locations far from the speaker do not exist.

B-1: 3′ is either coming into existence or going out of existence

B-3: 3′ is in *S*'s conceptual field

Again, the minimal representation only needs to mention that the construction is based on the central deictic and that the mapping model used is the metaphor given above.

The Existence Deictic

Based on: The Central Deictic
About: EXISTENCE

The Activity Start Deictic

Consider the sentence

- There he goes, meditating again.

There is no motion indicated—only an activity, which in this case involves a lack of action and motion. In general, one can point out the beginning of an activity by using a variant of the central deictic. The central deictic is made applicable by a metaphor in which activities are conceptualized in terms of motion along a path. The construction does, however, add one thing to the conceptual metaphor: the location designated by the deictic locative adverb is the beginning of the metaphorical activity path.

We can represent this as follows:

The Activity Start Deictic

Based on: The Central Deictic
About: ACTIVITY

Semantic Elements

1′: designates start of activity (starting point on activity path)

Outside of this construction, *there* does not have the meaning of designating the starting point of an activity, and this description of the construction accounts for that. In addition, it also predicts the absence of *come* in this sense. Thus, compare

- There goes Harry, thinking about linguistics again.
- Here comes Harry, thinking about linguistics again.

Both can be instances of the central deictic, in which *go* and *come* designate motion. But only the first sentence can indicate the beginning of an activity with no indication of motion.

Cases like *Here we go again!* will be discussed below when we get to exasperation constructions.

The Presentational Deictic

The presentational deictic differs from the central deictic in a number of ways. The most striking difference is in the syntax. Syntactic element 2, rather than being just a verb in the simple present tense, may be either a verb or a multiword verbal idiom (e.g., *laid to rest*), and it may be accompanied by a full auxiliary phrase. And syntactic elements 4*, rather than just occurring at the end of the construction, may occur in second position immediately following the deictic locative adverb, or in final position or both. Here are some examples with syntactic element 4 in second position and an auxiliary phrase.

- There in the alley had gathered a large crowd of roughnecks.
- There on the stage wearing an outrageous costume was standing one of our most distinguished public figures.
- Here honored by thousands of her fellow citizens will be laid to rest our beloved former mayor, Sally Stanford.
- There without a stitch on, staring at the ceiling, lay the beautiful KGB agent shot through the heart.
- Here isolated from all the noise of the city will be built large, comfortable estates to house our former presidents.

The auxiliary + verb combinations include *had gathered, was standing, will be laid to rest*, and *will be built*. The "final phrases" in second position include *in the alley, on the stage wearing an outrageous costume,* etc.

The permissible verbs are those that, directly or indirectly, specify a location. Indirect specifications of location include *will be laid to rest, will be built,* and even *can be seen*:

- There in the southern sky can be seen the largest comet ever to enter our solar system.

The presentational deictic has two uses. In a narrative, it can be used to indicate a discovery, thus introducing (or reintroducing) the referent of the noun phrase into the discourse:

- There in my favorite chair sat a fat man with a monocle.

It can also be used to point out something the speaker considers extremely significant. This makes it useful in pompous speeches, public relations pamphlets, public announcements, etc.

- If I am elected, I guarantee that here in this town will be built a multipurpose athletic facility second to none!

Moreover, the *there* can be omitted, provided the first non-null element of the construction still designates a location relative to the speaker.

- Behind the desk was sitting a bald-headed man.
- Strewn about the room were lying the victim's personal effects.
- Standing atop that mountain is the largest radiotelescope ever built.

However, if the initial phrase does not designate a location, syntactic element 1 cannot be null.

- There without a stitch of clothes on lay the victim.
- *Without a stitch of clothes on lay the victim.

- There, enjoying his solitude, can be found the country's most famous hermit.
- *Enjoying his solitude can be found the country's most famous hermit.

- There happy at last could be seen the smiling refugees.
- *Happy at last could be seen the smiling refugees.

The presentational deictic can be represented minimally as follows:

The Presentational Deictic

Based on: The Central Deictic
Discourse Conditions
Used in narratives or announcements when *S* considers 3′ significant
Lexical Conditions
2 = a VERB designating a location, directly or indirectly
Syntactic Conditions
2 may have a full auxiliary.
Instances of 4* may optionally occur before 2 and 3.

1 may be null if an initial instance of 4* designates a location, directly or indirectly.

Since the verb must pick out a location, rather than indicate motion, we can account for why *come* and *go* cannot occur with a full auxiliary:

- There goes the president.
- *There is going the president.
- *Here will come the president.

The Delivery Deictic

There is a deictic *there*-construction that is used to indicate delivery, as in:

- Here's your pizza, piping hot.
- Here's your hot and sour soup, with no MSG.
- There's your car, all washed and waxed.

One might think that this is just a special case of the central deictic construction, where the speaker happens to be delivering something to the hearer. For the most part this is correct. However, there is a phonological peculiarity that is linked to the delivery situation: the vowel in *here* and *there* can be elongated and the elongation only occurs with a "delivery" situation. The most famous case is Ed McMahon's introduction of Johnny Carson:

- H e e e e re's Johnny!

This occurs in delivery situations in general, for example:

- H e e e e re comes your soup!
- Th e e e e re's your car, all fixed and ready to go!

In delivery situations, the thing being delivered is either being brought to the hearer (as in the first sentence) or has been left in a temporary nearby location to be picked up (as in the second sentence). Consequently, the verb *go* cannot be used in the delivery deictic construction, as we can see from the incompatibility of *go* with the elongation of the vowel in *there*:

- *Th e e e e re goes your car, all washed and waxed!

Such a sentence might be used in a bizarre situation, say, on a TV comedy where the carwash attendant started to inform his customer that his car was ready and in the process noticed a thief driving off with it. But even then, it would be a joke rather than a normal thing to say.

As we observed above, deictic *there*-constructions can occur in the past tense in certain narrative situations:

– There I was in the middle of the jungle . . .
– There was my car with the key in the ignition . . .

Since the delivery deictic only occurs in the present tense, such sentences cannot have the elongated vowel that signifies delivery:

– *Th e e e e re I was in the middle of the jungle . . .
– *Th e e e e re was my car with the key in the ignition . . .

In addition, the *here* and *there* of the delivery deictic is unique among the deictics in that it need not bear stress and may take a reduced vowel.

Finally, this construction is unique in that it allows the second person pronoun, *you*, to replace syntactic element 3.

– H e e e e re you are.
– There you are—one pizza with sausage and mushrooms.

However, when this occurs the verb *go* is possible, but *come* is not.

– Here you go!
– There you go!
– *Here you come!
– *There you come!

The choice of *go* versus *come* with 3 = *you* is exactly the opposite of the choice when 3 ≠ *you*. We can see the reason for this difference of lexical choice if we compare the sentences:

– Here comes your pizza!
– Here you go!

Either could be used by a waiter delivering a pizza to a customer's table. But there are subtle differences. In the *come*-sentence, *come* refers to the movement of the pizza toward the hearer. It is typically uttered when the pizza hasn't quite yet reached the hearer. The *go*-sentence differs in both respects. It is usually uttered as the pizza (or whatever) reaches the hearer. And the *go* does not necessarily refer to any movement of any sort. Instead the *go* seems to refer to the hearer's embarking on some activity that could only begin with the delivery. Thus, the *come*-sentence focuses on the delivery, while the *go*-sentence focuses on what happens after the delivery.

Part of our understanding of what delivery is typically about is that the recipient is going to do something with what is delivered—if only to store it for later use. Given the ACTIVITY IS MOTION metaphor, it is natural for *go* to be used to refer to what the hearer is about to do with the delivered entity upon delivery. Thus, all of the following sentences pick out some aspect of the delivery scenario and express that aspect. Attention can be directed either to the delivered object and its location or to the hearer and his location on the activity path.

In the following examples, attention is directed to the location of the delivered object.

– Here it comes!

This focuses on the movement of the object toward the hearer.

– Here it is!

This focuses on the arrival of the object in the hearer's presence.

In the following examples, attention is directed to the location of the hearer on the activity path.

– Here you are!

This focuses on the presence of the hearer at the beginning of the activity path.

– Here you go!

This focuses on the start of the activity, that is, on the beginning of motion by the hearer along the activity path. It follows that only *come*, and not *go*, can refer to the motion of the delivered entity to the speaker and that only *go*, and not *come*, can refer to the "movement" of the hearer along the activity path.

Our knowledge about deliveries can be represented as a cognitive model. Here is a representation of such a model, restricted to the issues at hand.

The Delivery ICM

Metaphorical Mapping: ACTIVITY IS MOTION ALONG AN ACTIVITY PATH.

Semantic Elements

D: deliverer
R: receiver
E: entity
*L*1: location of *E*
*L*2: location of *R*
*M*1: predicate indicating motion through space
A: activity path
*M*2: predicate indicating motion along *A*

Scenario

Background

R is waiting for *D* to bring *E* to *L2*
R requires *E* in order to move along *A* (perform the activity)

Activity
D brings *E* to *L2*

Resultant State
E is at *L2*
R is at beginning of *A*

As in the case of the pointing-out ICM, the delivery ICM constitutes an experiential gestalt, which is psychologically simple, but whose analysis looks complex.

The delivery deictic can be used in situations that are structured by the delivery ICM. In such cases, the speaker is the deliverer ($S = D$). The construction is marked phonologically—either the deictic locative adverb is unstressed or its vowel is elongated.

We can represent this as follows:

The Delivery Deictic

Instance of: The Deictic Category
Overall Semantics
The Delivery ICM, with $S = D$.
Phonological Conditions
1 may be elongated with rising intonation and need not bear stress.

What is particularly interesting about the delivery deictic is that it can be an instance of more than one of the deictic constructions discussed above. Thus

– H e e e e re comes your pizza!

is an instance of the central deictic applied to the delivery situation, while

– H e e e re you go!

is an instance of the activity start deictic applied to the delivery situation. The reason this is possible is that the delivery ICM includes both motion of an object to a destination and the start of an activity.

We have represented this situation simply by indicating that the delivery ICM is an instance of the deictic category. This means that it can be an instance of any construction in the category that it can fit. It happens to be able to fit both the central deictic and the activity start constructions. It fits them in two different ways. That is, each construction takes a different perspective on the delivery situation. In the central deictic perspective, attention is focused on the entity being delivered, which is the thing being pointed out. Thus we have the following fit between the delivery ICM and the semantic elements of the central deictic:

The central deictic perspective on the delivery ICM:

$S = D$
$H = R$
$3' = E$
$1' = L1$
$2' = M1$

In the activity start perspective, the receiver (R) is both the hearer (H) and the entity being pointed out ($3'$).

The activity start perspective:

$H = R = 3'$
$S = D$
$1' = L2$
$2' = M2$

The delivery deictic is a case where there is a minor variation in phonological form which is used to signal the presence of a delivery situation. Minor variations in phonological form are often used to signal something about the nature of the situation. Such cases involve form-meaning pairings that can be represented by minimal constructions. We will now turn to such a case—one where an expression of awe is indicated phonologically and where this can intersect with deictic constructions.

Paragons

When one thinks that something is very good—among the best of its kind—it is common to direct attention to it and express awe at how good it is. (The capitals followed by three dots indicate extra-heavy stress, optionally accompanied by breathiness.)

- Now THAT's . . . a real cup of coffee!
- Now THIS . . . is chicken soup the way mama made it!
- THIS . . . soup is g o o o d!

This can also be done using a deictic *there*-construction.

- Now THERE . . . is a great centerfielder!
- Now HERE . . . is a great cup of coffee!

The semantics that is special to these cases can be represented by what I will refer to as the expression of awe ICM.

The Expression of Awe ICM

Semantic Elements

S: Speaker
H: Hearer
1′: an entity
2′: a predicate indicating the best of a type
0′: 2′(1′)

Speech Acts

S is expressing *S*'s awe at 0′

The paragon-intonation construction is quite simple and involves no syntactic or semantic parameters: it pairs the expression of awe ICM with the appropriate phonology—extra-heavy stress and breathiness on the appropriate element. It is independent of, and can be superimposed on, any construction with a consistent pragmatics.

The Paragon-Intonation Construction

Parameters of Meaning

The expression of awe ICM

Parameters of Form

1 is pronounced with extra-heavy stress and breathiness.

Such a pairing of form and meaning is so simple and obvious that it seems barely worth mentioning. Yet it produces some complex and not entirely obvious results. These complexities come from the fact that the paragon-intonation construction can form intersections with other constructions, among them simple sentences and deictic *there*-constructions.

Let us begin with simple cases of the sort discussed above. Suppose we take ordinary simple sentences like

- That's a cup of coffee.
- This is chicken soup.

Superimposing the paragon-intonation construction yields

- THAT's . . . a real cup of coffee!
- THIS . . . is chicken soup the way mama made it!

Here "real" and "the way mama made it" indicate that it is a paragon.

It is part of the semantics of the central deictic that there is an entity at the location referred to by *here* and *there*. There is a general metonymic mapping, according to which a place may stand for something located at that place. For example, *Toledo is late* may mean that our sales representative located in Toledo is late. When this metonymic mapping is employed, the location referred to by *here* or *there* stands for the entity at that location. This permits the paragon-intonation construction to be superimposed on the central deictic, and for *here* or *there* to refer to the entity to be described as a paragon.

– Now THERE . . . is a real cup of coffee!
– Now HERE . . . is chicken soup the way mama made it!

One source of complexity is the fact that the paragon-intonation construction brings along its own pragmatics. The speech act it conveys is expressive—in the same class of speech acts as exclamations. It can thus potentially intersect with other exclamation constructions. Consider the exclamation construction in

– Boy! Is HE ever tall!

This has the syntactic form of a question, but the phonological form and the illocutionary force of an exclamation. It requires that the heavily stressed element (HE, in this case) be a subject. Thus this construction can intersect with those instances of the paragon-intonation construction where the heavily stressed element is a subject.

– Boy! Was THAT ever a cup of coffee!

This construction cannot intersect with paragon *there*-sentences, since the stressed element in those cases is not a subject.

– *Boy! Was THERE ever a cup of coffee!

Since the paragon-intonation construction expresses awe at something positively being a paragon, it cannot take true negations.

– *Now THAT . . . wasn't a real cup of coffee!

Here the semantics of the negated construction, that the referent is not a paragon, contradicts the pragmatics, which expresses awe at its being a paragon.

However, it can occur with a negation that expresses a positive proposition.

– Now THAT . . . can't be beat!

Here *can't be beat* expresses a positive value, despite being syntactically negative. Another example is the construction that occurs in

– If JIM won't eat these ducks' feet, I don't know who will!

The effect of this construction is to suggest that Jim probably will eat the ducks' feet. Since this negation conveys a positive not a negative, it can occur with paragon-intonation constructions.

– If THAT . . . isn't a real cup of coffee, I don't know what is!

Not only can the paragon-intonation construction intersect with the central deictic, it can also intersect with other deictics, for example, the discourse deictic.

- Now THERE . . . was a nice point!

If one happens in the discourse to have been talking about old-time baseball players, one can say

Now THERE . . . was a great centerfielder!

If we are at a baseball game, we can point to a ballplayer and say, using the central deictic plus the paragon-intonation construction,

- THERE . . . goes a great centerfielder!

But if you are talking about old-time ballplayers, you cannot say

- *Now THERE . . . went a great centerfielder!

This would be an intersection of the paragon-intonation and the discourse deictic constructions. But the discourse deictic does not permit *go*, as we observed above.

- *There went a nice point!

The question raised by this analysis is whether the paragon deictic construction needs to be listed in the grammar of English at all. The traditional answer is, of course, no. If all of its properties can be predicted from the general paragon-intonation construction and other deictics, then there is no need to say anything more. However, one might argue, in response, that such complex constructions have some cognitive status as speech formulas—special things one says on certain occasions. We will discuss this issue in general below.

Exasperation

A deictic *there*-construction can be used to express exasperation over someone's behavior. Examples include:

- There goes Harry, sounding off again!
- There she is, making a fool of herself!

Go here does not refer to motion, but to actions on Harry's part. It appears that the ACTIVITY IS MOTION metaphor is at work here and that the *there* designates the beginning of an activity. Exasperation may be indicated by a sigh, a throat constriction, slight nasalization, or an intonation contour. But exasperation can be indicated by these means, not only with deictic *there*-constructions, but also with just about any sentence at all with the appropriate meaning.

– (sigh) He's insulting her again!

Let us, for the sake of discussion, represent such a pairing of form and meaning with a very simple construction, the exasperation construction.

Speech act

S expresses exasperation with 0′, a proposition.

Phonological Condition

The sentence is pronounced with a sigh, a throat constriction, slight nasalization, or the exasperation intonation.

Sentences like

– (sigh) There goes Harry, telling the same old jokes!

can now be seen as intersections of the activity start deictic and the exasperation construction. This explains why we don't have deictic exasperation expressions with *come*, except in the central, spatial sense. Thus,

– Here comes Harry, sounding off again!

suggests that Harry is actually moving toward the speaker, while the corresponding sentence with *there goes* does not require any motion at all. In the ACTIVITY IS MOTION metaphor, which is used in the activity start deictic, the metaphorical motion is never toward the speaker. This would explain why the *here comes* in the above example can only have a physical motion reading. The use of this metaphor in the activity start construction would also explain why such cases can have *here* without spatial motion, but only with a first-person subject.

– Here we go, making fools of ourselves again!
– *Here they go, making fools of themselves again!

According to the metaphor, the deictic locative adverb refers to the beginning of the activity path. If the speaker is at the beginning of the activity path, *here* may be used. This is not the case if someone other than the speaker is at the beginning of the activity path. The above distinction is, thus, a consequence of the ACTIVITY IS MOTION metaphor as used in the activity start deictic and the ordinary constraints on the use of *here*.

Narrative Focus

In the course of a vivid narrative, a speaker may want to focus on a participant in the narrative, perhaps himself. This can be accomplished with a deictic *there*-construction:

- There I was, alone on a desert island . . .
- There I am, alone on a desert island . . .
- Here I am, alone on a desert island . . .

In a vivid narrative, the hearer is expected to imagine the action—that is, to create a mental image of what is happening. *Here* and *there* function to focus on a location in the imagined scene. Both the past tense and the present may be used. The difference has to do with cognitive "distancing." The choice of *here* and the present tense bring the hearer "closer" to the imagined scene of the narrative. They do so in somewhat different ways. The present tense identifies the action of the narrative with the time of the telling. "Here" invites the hearer to imagine the action close to him and the speaker, rather than at a distance.

When the present tense is used and the imagined scene of the narrative is taken to occur simultaneously with the time of the narration, the narrative focus deictic merges with central deictic via the pretense that the elements of the narrative exist and are present. The full range of central deictic expressions can be used in such a situation, including verbs of motion:

- Here come the killer bees, blackening the sky . . .
- There go the jets, screaming overhead . . .

This seems to be a matter of general conventions of narration rather than anything peculiar to *there*-constructions.

Let us call these the vivid narrative conventions, and specify them as follows:

> The speaker assumes the hearer is forming a vivid mental image of the narrative. The things in the mental image are taken to be present. If the present tense is used, there is a pretense that the action is occurring at the time of the telling. If the past tense is used, the action is taken as happening prior to the telling.

When we apply the vivid narrative conventions to the use of the central deictic, we get the trivial consequence:

Semantic Elements
$1'$ = a location in the imagined scene of the narrative
$3'$ = an entity in the world of the narrative

The vivid narrative conventions may apply to many of the deictic constructions, to yield past tense forms that can be used in vivid narratives.

- There were the helicopters at last, coming to rescue us . . .
- There went Harry, out to buy some bread . . .

- There came the bus at last—and just as you might expect, it was full.
- There went the buzzer, and the children ran out the door!
- There went our last hope.

The fact that these conventions require one to imagine a scene vividly (presumably to form a mental image of it) explains the absence of certain forms. For example, things that have not yet happened are not part of a vivid mental image. Since *here comes* in certain constructions refers to the future, which has not yet happened, those cases are impossible as intersections with the narrative focus construction.

- *Here came the beep!
- *Here came another outburst!

Jeanne van Oosten has pointed out (personal communication) that some of the deictic constructions simply cannot occur at all as intersections with the vivid narrative conventions. Those ruled out are the delivery deictic and the exasperation deictic.

- *Here you went! (delivery plus past tense vivid narrative)
- *There came our pizza! (delivery plus past tense vivid narrative)
- *There he went again! (Exasperation plus past tense vivid narrative)

I do not know exactly why these intersections are impossible. My best guess is that there is some pragmatic constraint on the vivid narrative conventions that I have missed and that it is inconsistent with the pragmatics of these constructions. However, at present, these phenomena remain a mystery.

Enthusiastic Beginning

A continuous intonational rise with a fall at the very end can often be used to mark the enthusiastic beginning of some enterprise.

- Let's get going!
- Let's hit the road!
- Off we go!
- They're off!

Let us call this pairing of intonation with an expression of enthusiasm at the beginning of an enterprise the enthusiastic beginning construction. This can form an intersection with the activity start deictic:

- Here we go, off to Africa!

This seems to be nothing more than a predictable intersection of the two constructions.

A description of the idiom *Here goes nothin'* can be given as follows:

Intersection of: Activity Start Deictic and Enthusiastic Beginning
S = person making attempt
3 = *nothin'*
3′ = attempt with nothing to lose

The rest of the syntax, semantics, and phonology of the idiom is inherited from the enthusiastic beginning deictic. This idiom is therefore not completely arbitrary. The arbitrary parts are listed above in the minimal representation. The rest of the idiom is motivated by the constructions it is an instance of.

The Issue of Cognitive Status

The grammar of a language is a cognitive subsystem. Anything in the grammar that has to be learned by a native speaker must exist as part of that cognitive subsystem, and thus has some cognitive status. For example, anyone learning English must learn how to form passives (like *Harry was hit by someone*) and how to form questions (like *Did someone hit Harry?*). Presumably they must learn passive and question constructions. But having learned those, they can superimpose them to form passive questions (like *Was Harry hit by someone?*). They presumably do not have to learn a passive-question construction. They just intersect the passive construction and the question construction. The result, the passive-question construction, is made up anew each time and has no permanent cognitive status. That is, it does not exist as a unit in the conceptual subsystem we were calling a grammar.

According to the assumptions of traditional grammar, nothing that is predictable has any permanent cognitive status. The assumption was that if it can be predicted, then it is computed anew each time it is used. Though this seems plausible in the case of passive questions, it is not true in all cases. Perhaps the best-known example of this sort is the negative question. In terms of syntactic conditions, negative questions are just intersections of the question construction and the sentential negative construction. But negative questions have a special pragmatics—they are not questions of negatives, but rather hedged positive suggestions. For example, *Didn't Harry leave?* is a hedged suggestion that Harry did leave. Thus, negative questions must have a cognitive status of their own. The construction would be represented as an intersection of the negative and question constructions, with a special pragmatics indicated.

Some of the complex cases we have been discussing may be like this, though I do not at present have evidence to demonstrate it. Paragon deictics (like *THERE . . .is a cup of coffee!*) and exasperation deictics (like *There he goes again!* are intersections of other constructions, yet they seem to have the status of speech formulas—things that one learns to say on certain occasions. When one learns a language, one does not only learn those constructions from which you can form other, more complex, constructions. One also learns which constructions to use when. Even if such constructions are intersections of other constructions, they still have cognitive status because one must learn something about when to use them. For example, suppose one could specify conditions under which the exasperation deictic is used as a formula. All you would have to learn is that there is such a formula with such conditions, and the details would follow as a consequence.

What Do the Deictics Have in Common?

As we have just seen, the deictic *there*-constructions can be analyzed as forming a natural category with the central deictic as the prototype. It will be instructive to go back over the data we have considered to see exactly why the deictics cannot be analyzed as forming a classical category. If the deictics formed a classical category, then the properties they have in common would characterize all and only the members of the category. One way of seeing just how far away this is from being true is to survey what the various deictic *there*-constructions all share.

The Generalized Deictic

Parameters of Meaning

Semantic Elements

S: speaker
H: hearer

1′: an argument
2′: a predicate
3′: an argument
4′: a noninherent predicate

0′: a proposition, 2′(3′,1′)
0‴: a proposition, 4′(3′)

Speech Act
S is directing *H*'s attention to 1′

Parameters of Form

Syntactic Elements

1: a deictic locative adverb
2: a verb
3: a noun phrase
4*: VP/*be* or VP/2

Lexical Conditions
1 = *here, there*

Syntactic Conditions
1 is first
2 precedes 3 unless 3 is a pronoun
4 is last
4* is optional

These shared properties can be viewed as necessary conditions for a construction to be a deictic *there*-construction. But according to the classical theory, the shared properties should be both necessary and sufficient to characterize all the constructions. But these conditions are so vague that they are not sufficient to characterize any of the constructions. To get the individual constructions one would have to add to these necessary conditions various combinations of syntactic, semantic, pragmatic, lexical, and phonological properties. There is no way to preserve the classical theory and still get the correct pairings of form and meaning. Moreover, even if one left meaning out entirely, there would be no way to get sufficient conditions on the parameters of form. The presentationals take full auxiliaries, element 4 optionally in second position, and an optional deictic adverb. The others do not. Of the remaining constructions, two take the past tense. Lexically, one doesn't allow verbs of motion, another doesn't allow *come*, and one doesn't take *be*. The phonological conditions introduce even more complications. Any attempt to state shared sufficient conditions, even on parameters of form alone, simply will not work.

No matter what one does, one is going to wind up with a radially structured category of constructions. One possible analysis would be to have the abstract, generalized construction in the center and the actual constructions structured around the center and specifying it further. As I see it, there are two things wrong with such an analysis. First, it would fail to make correct predictions about prototype effects. Since none of the actual constructions are central on this analysis, the analysis fails to predict what appears to be a crucial fact, that the central deictic seems to be a better example of the category than the other cases. Intuitively,

– There's Harry.

seems to be a better example of a deictic construction than any of the following:

- THERE's . . . a real cup of coffee!
- There he was in the jungle . . .
- H e e e re's Johnny!
- There will stand the new stadium for the 1996 Olympics.

This is predicted on our analysis, but not on the analysis where the generalized deictic is central.

Second, such an analysis would preclude stating the generalizations that we pointed out above. The predictions that can be made on the basis of the central deictic cannot be made on the basis of the generalized deictic. If all of the actual constructions are based on the generalized deictic, then all one can do for each construction is give a big list of whatever needs to be added. This is an especially serious flaw in the area of semantics. Under our proposed analysis, it is possible to make use of metaphoric and metonymic models that exist independent of these constructions. By naming which metaphoric and metonymic models are used, we can predict most of the semantics of the noncentral constructions from the semantics of the central deictic. This is possible because the metaphoric models all take physical space as their source domains. However, if the generalized deictic is taken as the center of the natural category and if all the actual constructions are just extensions of it, then the metaphoric models that exist independently in the conceptual system cannot be used to predict semantic properties. One would be reduced instead to giving a list of the semantic properties in each case and would thereby miss the regularities that are possible with the analysis that makes use of the metaphoric models.

To summarize: Despite the fact that there are necessary conditions for membership in the category of deictic *there*-constructions, there are no sufficient conditions. This is why the classical theory will not work for such constructions. In addition, any attempt to analyze the generalized construction as central will fail for two reasons: First, it cannot predict prototype effects; in particular, it cannot predict that examples of the central deictic are better examples of the category than examples of, say, the presentational, paragon, or delivery subconstructions. Second, it does not permit the statement of generalizations, especially semantic generalizations.

Given that there are necessary conditions which can be stated in a generalized construction, one ought to ask whether such a generalized construction has any psychological reality or plays any role in the grammar of a language. At this point, there is no reason to believe that it plays any role whatever. It simply seems to be too general to be of any use, and in the absence of any reason to hypothesize it, I would tentatively suggest that it has no psychological reality whatever.

This is not a trivial matter. The generalized deictic represents the result of abstracting out the common properties of the various kinds of deictic *there*-constructions. To claim that it plays no cognitive role is to claim that seeking common properties—as linguists are trained to do—does not always lead to the best analysis, even when one can find such common properties.

Cognitive Organization and Cognitive Efficiency

The deictic *there*-constructions present a bewildering range of phenomena. We have found that we could make sense of these phenomena using the concept *grammatical construction*, together with prototype theory. Accordingly, if the deictic *there*-constructions are viewed as constituting a radially structured category of grammatical constructions, a wide range of phenomena can be seen to follow from general principles. The central deictic construction's parameters of form can be seen almost entirely to be consequences of the pragmatic function of the construction, namely, to express the pointing-out ICM. Given this, the noncentral constructions can be seen as minimal variants of the central construction. This account seems to explain a wider range of data than any other account available.

The key to this mode of explanation is the concept of *motivation.* We have characterized motivation in terms of (1) central principles of form-meaning correspondence; (2) ecological location within a grammatical system, defined by the based-on relation; (3) minimal differences; and (4) restricted prediction, using central principles, metaphors and metonymies already in the conceptual system, and minimal differences. If we assume that languages are structured to maximize motivation, we would *expect* radially structured categories to be prevalent, since such structures have the effect of maximizing motivation. Thus, radial structures in grammar have the same function that they do in the lexicon—that of reducing the arbitrariness of form-meaning correspondences.

Motivation is, therefore, concerned both with parameters of form *and* with parameters of meaning. In each language, parameters of meaning make use of concepts from a conceptual system which, in certain respects, is not universal. Since parameters of form depend on parameters of meaning, it follows that some grammars may be better-suited to certain cultures and conceptual systems than to others. For example, the English perceptual deictic construction, with expressions like *There goes my knee*, is very well suited to a conceptual system that has metaphoric and metonymic models like ACTIVATION IS MOTION, REALIZED IS DISTAL, and THE THING PERCEIVED STANDS FOR THE PERCEPT. Such a construction would not fit at all well into a language based on a conceptual system without a REALIZED IS DISTAL metaphor. Motivation is therefore a global property of both a conceptual system and a grammar that makes use of it.

Motivation may best be thought of as "systemic redundancy"—redundancy as defined by the overall structure of the grammar and conceptual system taken together. We have made a specific proposal for how to characterize such redundancy in terms of the analytic techniques at our disposal. In the theory we have outlined, it is possible for us to make certain "restricted predictions." It is our claim that there is a correspondence between each such "prediction" that can be made using this theory and some cognitively real redundancy within the grammatical system of a speaker.

We have *not* been claiming that speakers of a language go about making such predictions as part of everyday language use. Speakers do not algorithmically compute most of the properties of the constructions they use every time they speak. Quite the opposite. Speakers use constructions that are present in the grammatical system—present with a high degree of systemic redundancy.

We assume that constructions are used as wholes, as entire gestalts. But in order to make sense of viewing grammatical constructions as gestalts, one must have some account of gestalt formation for grammatical constructions, that is, an account of what it is that allows a construction to function as a gestalt rather than just as a random collection of properties. The account we are proposing is the following:

- The more a construction's properties are motivated, the better it functions as a gestalt.

There is a great deal that follows from this principle. Good gestalts are cognitively simple, easy to learn, easy to remember, and easy to use. They also have the following very important property:

- If *A* is a good gestalt, and *B* is a minimal variation of *A*, then *B* is almost as good a gestalt as *A*.

In other words, there is a very good reason why cognitive structure is organized in terms of good gestalts and minimal variations on them: it maximizes cognitive efficiency. Thus, we can see why there should be so many radially structured categories. If a cognitive model is a good gestalt, then minimal variations on it will be easy to learn, remember, and use. When there are many minimal variations on a cognitive model, the result is a radially structured category.

This provides a critical link between cognitive organization and cognitive efficiency. Radial category structure can make it easier for people to learn, remember, and use cognitive models, provided that the prototypical centers of the radial categories are good gestalts. But our proposed concept of a good gestalt is itself dependent on overall cognitive organization. The reason is that motivated properties are motivated not merely by the properties of an adjacent construction. They are also motivated by general principles governing the entire linguistic and conceptual system. The good-gestalt principles for geometric figures are local: they have to do with things like symmetry, continuity, etc. But the good-gestalt principles for grammatical constructions are global. They have to do with the overall ecology of the conceptual and linguistic systems. All sorts of factors outside the construction itself may enter in: cognitive models, including those metaphoric and metonymic models in the conceptual system, language-particular word-order constraints, lexical contrasts, rules governing stress and intonation, etc. To be a good gestalt, a construction must fit well into the linguistic and conceptual system as a whole. It is our claim that the more a construction is motivated, the better it will fit into the ecology of the system.

The concept of motivation therefore provides a cognitively based evaluation metric for grammars. Suppose we think of a language as a collection of form-meaning pairs, where the meanings are concepts in a given conceptual system. Incidentally, this is not an uncontroversial characterization of a language, since it takes a language as being defined relative to a conceptual system. We can then define the "expressive power" of a language as the collection of concepts in that conceptual system that the language can distinctively express. Incidentally, that collection is infinite, since it includes complex concepts. This is an intuitive way to define "expressive power" since it is based on what is expressed. For a language of a given expressive power, an optimal grammar is one that maximizes motivation. And there may be many equally optimal grammars since motivation may be maximized in many ways. An evaluation metric for grammars would rate grammars as to how well motivated they are (that is, how well they fit together overall) relative to the concepts expressed. The worst grammars would be those with no motivation at all, grammars where the form-meaning correlations are maximally arbitrary. Grammars of real natural languages (as opposed to hypothesized "possible" natural languages) always show a very high degree of motivation. People seem to learn and remember highly motivated expressions better than unmotivated expressions. We thus hypothesize that the degree of motivation of a grammatical system is a measure of the cognitive efficiency of that system relative to the concepts the system expresses.

Contemporary generative theories do not incorporate a concept of motivation at all, and they do not permit prototype-based categorization. The concept of expressive power used in generative theories has nothing whatever to do with what is expressed. Conceptual systems play no role. Expressive power there is concerned only with the set of strings of uninterpreted symbols that a formal grammar can generate. Generative theories are thus incapable of even approaching the kinds of issues raised in this case study, just as they are incapable of accounting for the kinds of regularities we found in the study of deictic *there*-constructions.

We will now turn to the relationship between the central deictic and central existential constructions. This has traditionally been a stumbling block for generative theories. Various attempts have been made to account for the relationship within transformational theories, and they have all been failures. One reason is that the relationship between these constructional categories is not a purely syntactic relationship. Another reason is that generative grammars cannot adequately characterize the overall ecology of grammatical systems. The relationship between the deictic and existential *there*-constructions in English is very much a matter of that overall ecology.

Comparison of Deictics and Existentials

The deictics and the existentials can look similar, as the following examples show (capitals indicate stress).

- THERE's a new Mercedes across the street. (deictic)
- There's a new MERCEDES across the street. (existential)

Despite the superficial similarities, the deictic and existential *there*'s differ in at least the following ways:

- Deictic *there* refers to a specific location; existential *there* does not.
- Deictic *there* contrasts with *here*; existential *there* does not.
- Deictic *there* occurs independently of the deictic *there*-constructions; existential *there* does not occur outside of existential *there*-constructions.
- Deictic *there* is a locative adverb; existential *there* is not.
- Deictic *there* is not a grammatical subject; existential *there* is a grammatical subject.
- Deictic *there* almost always bears stress; existential *there* almost never does.

The lone case I know of where deictic *there* does not bear stress is the delivery deictic (*Th e e e re's your pizza!*). The only case I know of where existential *there* does bear stress is when it occurs in WH-exclamations, which require a stressed subject:

- Were THERE ever a lot of problems!

Existential *there* is basically unstressed but appears to be able to acquire stress from a specialized construction. The only apparent counterexample I know to this generalization is the *What, ME worry?* construction, which requires a stressed subject, but disallows existential *there* as subject (Akmajian, 1984):

- *What, THERE a fire?

However, this construction excludes third person inanimate pronouns in general:

- *What, IT on fire?

This independently needed restriction also rules out sentences containing existential *there* and accounts automatically for the ill-formedness of **What, THERE a fire?* which eliminates such cases as counterexamples. The generalization, therefore, seems to stand:

- Existential *there* is unstressed in the existential *there*-constructions, but stress can be imposed by a construction imposing stress on a subject.

From the list of properties given above, it is clear that the spatial deictic *there* of the central deictic construction thus differs considerably from the existential *there*. Yet there are intermediate types of deictic *there* that are closer to the existential *there*. For example, the *there*'s of the perceptual and discourse subconstructions do not refer to a concrete location in space, but rather to abstract locations in perception and discourse. The *there* of the existence deictic construction, as in *There goes our last hope*, refers to a location in conceptual space that characterizes existence. Semantically, this comes very close to the existential *there*. And the *there* of the delivery deictic, when it does not bear stress, is phonologically indistinguishable from the existential *there*. Thus there is a continuum between the spatial deictic *there* and the existential *there*.

I would like to suggest that this continuum has a significance in the organizational structure of English grammar. I will argue that there is a category of existential constructions parallel to the deictic constructions, and that the central existential construction is based on the central deictic construction. I contend that there is only one fundamental difference between the constructions—the reference of existential *there*—and that all the other major differences are a consequence of that one distinction.

It is commonly assumed that existential *there* and the so-called ambient *it* of *It's raining* are semantically empty. Bolinger (1977) has provided evidence to show that ambient *it* is meaningful, and his claims have been corroborated by Gensler (1977). He also maintains that existential *there* is meaningful and that it functions to "bring something into awareness." Bolinger (1977, pp. 93–94) contrasts spatial locatives, which "bring something literally or figuratively before our presence," with existential *there*, which "presents something to our minds." Bolinger suggests that *there* designates the "awareness" of "bring into awareness" and that awareness is "abstract location." Bolinger observes, as we have, that deictic locatives are concerned with presence—presence in space, in our perception, in discourse, or in our vivid imaginations. "The less vividly on stage an action is," he notes, "the more necessary [existential] *there* becomes" (p. 96). Abstractions such as absence, probability, and generic activities are not "vividly on stage" and therefore require existential *there*. In demonstration, he cites contrasts like the following from Breivik (1975). Existential *there* is necessary when there is no concrete object "on stage."

- *In the house was no sign of life.
- In the house there was no sign of life.
- *On the table is probably a book.
- On the table there is probably a book.
- *At the party was dancing.
- At the party there was dancing.

Compare these with:

- On the table lay a book.
- On the table there lay a book.

"Abstractions," Bolinger concludes, "make poor actors in this drama."

The proposal we will be making is very much in the spirit of Bolinger's suggestion. We will substitute for the somewhat vague terms "awareness" and "consciousness" the concept of a *mental space*, proposed by Fauconnier (1985). A mental space is a medium in which thoughts occur and in which conceptual entities are located. Fauconnier's theory of mental spaces provides solutions to a great many previously recalcitrant problems in language and cognition, and I believe that it will help here too.

I propose that existential *there* designates a mental space in which a conceptual entity is to be located. A mental space is, however, not a location; it is a medium in which there are many locations. Entities are, of course, located in spaces—at some location or other. Following Fauconnier, I will assume that the function of the indefinite article is to set up a conceptual entity in a mental space. Let us take some examples:

- In my dream there was a rabbit.
- In his poem there is a rabbit.
- In the painting there is a rabbit.
- In the yard there is a rabbit.

The locative phrases indicate the nature of the space—a dream, a poem, a painting, and a portion of the physical world. The existential *there* designates the space, the indefinite article indicates that a new entity is being set up in the space, the noun *rabbit* tells what kind of entity it is, and the verb *be* is a locative relation indicating that the entity is located in the space.

Only in the last example, the one with *in the yard*, is there any concern with existence in the real world. The reason is that yards are part of the real world, and the mental space set up was designated as corresponding to the space of the yard. In the absence of modifiers like *in his poem* or others that specifically indicate that the mental space is not to correspond to the real world, it is assumed that mental spaces are meant to correspond to reality. In all such cases, the existential constructions are concerned with real-world existence. Since this includes the majority of uses, we can see why the constructions have come to be called "existential."

There is a very small but important difference between the *there* of the existence deictic, as in

- There goes our last hope.

and the existential *there* of

- There is still hope.

The existence deictic is based on the following metaphor: EXISTENCE IS UNDERSTOOD AS LOCATION IN A CONCEPTUAL SPACE. That part of the space in the speaker's presence is taken to represent existence. That part of the space not in the speaker's presence represents nonexistence. The deictic *there* of the first sentence designates a location in the speaker's presence. By contrast, the existential *there* designates a conceptual space itself, not a location in it. The existential is generally concerned with conceptual existence, which may or may not coincide with "real" physical existence.

Given the hypothesis that existential *there* designates a mental space, we can make a great many predictions. Let us suppose, in addition, that the central existential construction is based on the central deictic construction—that is, that it takes its properties from the central deictic construction, except for those that are incompatible with the assumption that *there* designates a mental space. Here are some predictions:

Prediction 1: Existential *there* is not a locative adverb.

The reason is that it does not designate a location. This makes *there* eligible to serve as grammatical subject, though we have not yet predicted why it does in fact serve that function.

Prediction 2: Existential *there* does not contrast with *here*.

Again the reason is that it does not designate a location and therefore cannot contrast with another location.

Prediction 3: Existential *there* does not exist as a "free" lexical item, independent of existential constructions.

Existential *there*, on our hypothesis, occurs in English only as a consequence of its appearance in this construction.

Prediction 4: Existential *there* does not bear stress.

Elements that are backgrounded, do not convey any new information, and are not involved in any contrast are unstressed. Nothing can be more backgrounded than the space itself. *There* is not involved in any contrast and conveys no new information. Because *there* is unstressed, the vowel in it is subject to vowel reduction.

Prediction 5: The existential *there* does not take a pointing gesture.

Since it doesn't designate a specific location, the pointing gesture that goes with the deictic *there* is inappropriate.

Prediction 6: The basic-level locational verbs *sit, stand*, and *lie* cannot occur in the central existential construction.

These verbs concern orientation in physical space and are not applicable to mental spaces.

Prediction 7: *There*-constructions cannot be used to point something out and therefore do not have the speech act condition of the central deictic.

Since existential *there* does not designate a location, it cannot serve the locating function that deictic *there* serves in the deictic constructions. The fact that existential *there* designates a mental space is incompatible with the speech act condition of the central deictic, which is to direct the hearer's attention to the specific location designated by *there* (or *here*).

Prediction 8: *There*-constructions can take negatives, questions, etc., and can be freely embedded.

This is a consequence of their not having the speech act condition associated with the deictic constructions.

Prediction 9: Existential *there*-constructions are not limited to simple present tense, but can take full auxiliaries.

This is also a consequence of their not having the central deictic's speech act condition.

Prediction 10: The central existential construction has the same functional condition as the central deictic, namely, to focus the hearer's awareness on the referent of the noun phrase.

Elimination of the speech act condition does not affect the functional condition. The reason is that the speech act condition made reference to element 1′, the location, whereas the functional condition made reference to element 3′, the entity located. Thus the existential construction, like the central deictic, functions to focus the hearer's awareness on the entity designated by the noun phrase.

Prediction 11: The noun phrase is not both definite and specific.

The function of the construction is to focus the hearer's awareness on the referent of the construction. If the construction is to serve this function, then either the hearer must not have been aware of the referent, or he must have forgotten about it. Let's put the case of forgetting aside for now, since we will discuss it in detail shortly. Reminding aside, it must be assumed that the hearer has not been aware of the entity referred to. If the noun phrase refers to a specific entity, then the definite article indicates that the hearer is already aware of it. This violates the functional condition on the construction. Hence, the noun phrase cannot be both specific and definite, unless it is serving a reminding function. We can factor out cases of reminding by introducing a negative into the sentence. This allows us to get clear cases where nonreminding existentials cannot have a specific definite noun phrase. Compare the following:

- There wasn't a man in the room.
- *There wasn't the man in the room.

- There isn't one in the house. (*one* is indefinite)
- *There isn't it in the house. (*it* is definite and specific)

Note, incidentally, that the definite article can be used freely with nonspecific noun phrases, for example:

- There was the usual argument in class today.
- There's the strangest smell coming from the refrigerator.
- There's this woman next door who plays the stereo too loud.

These uses of definite determiners *the* and *this* in these constructions do not function to pick out specific referents that the hearer is assumed to be already aware of. That is why they are permitted in the existential construction.

Let us return to our predictions.

Prediction 12: *There* is first; syntactic element 4, the "final phrase," is last.

These are inherited from the central deictic construction. But there is an additional reason why *there* is first. Backgrounded elements tend to occur earlier in a clause than foregrounded elements. Nothing can be more backgrounded than the space in which entities occur.

Prediction 13: The verb precedes the noun phrase.

The syntactic condition inherited from the central deictic is that the verb precedes the noun phrase, unless the noun phrase is a definite pronoun. Since definite pronouns are ruled out of the central existential construction altogether, the inherited condition has the verb always preceding the noun phrase.

Is *There* the Subject?

In the central deictic, syntactic element 3 (the noun phrase) is the grammatical subject. One might expect this condition to be carried over to the central existential. But it cannot be. The reason is that *there* occurs first. Like element 3, *there* is a noun phrase, not an adverb, and *there* is an argument of the main verb *be*. English is a subject-initial language, which means that when there are two nonadverbial noun phrase arguments of the main verb in a central clause, the subject *must* be first. Since *there* is first, only it can be subject. Otherwise one of the most basic constraints of English grammar would be violated. This constraint does not hold in special topicalization constructions, but *there* doesn't have the right kind of semantics to be a topicalized element—one doesn't topicalize the element referring to the background space.

Prediction 14: *There* is subject.

This prediction is borne out. There are three relevant tests for subjecthood. The first concerns tag formation. Tags like "will you?" and "didn't he?" can be appended to the end of declarative sentences. One of the conditions is that the pronoun in the tag agree with the subject, as in:

- John kicked the dog, didn't he?
- *John kicked the dog, didn't it?

In existential constructions, tags agree with *there*, indicating that *there* is subject:

- There was a dog in the yard, wasn't there?
- *There was a dog in the yard, wasn't it?

The second test has to do with a construction known as "raising." Consider a sentence like

- It is believed that Harry is sick.

In such situations, the subject of the *that*-clause, in this case, *Harry*, can be "raised" and can appear as the subject of the higher clause *is believed*:

- Harry is believed to be sick.

Now suppose there is an existential construction in the *that*-clause:

- It is believed that there is a dog in the yard.

Only subjects can be raised. To test for subjecthood of the existential construction, we ask whether *there* or *a dog* can be raised to become subject of *is believed*. The answer is *there*:

- There is believed to be a dog in the yard.
- *A dog is believed there to be in the yard.

The third test is subject-verb agreement. Here the results are not at all clear-cut. Sometimes *there* acts as subject and governs agreement, and sometimes the noun phrase does. There is also considerable variation from speaker to speaker. In my own speech, here is what happens: If the verb is contracted, it agrees with either *there* or the noun phrase. If the verb is not contracted, it agrees with the noun phrase.

- *There is problems with your proposal.
- There are problems with your proposal.
- There's problems with your proposal.
- There're problems with your proposal.

There are other speakers for whom only the noun phrase can govern agreement. For them, *there* does not act like a subject at all with respect to agreement, and the third sentence above (*There's problems with your proposal*) is ill-formed for such speakers. (For a general discussion of this phenomenon see Dixon 1977, Nathan 1981, and Sparks 1984.)

But even though the verb may agree with the noun phrase, that does not necessarily mean that the noun phrase is acting as subject. Cases where the verb agrees with the noun phrase can be handled in two ways: either straightforwardly, with the verb agreeing directly with the noun phrase, or indirectly, with *there* agreeing with the noun phrase and the verb agreeing with *there.* The second alternative—indirect agreement—may sound strange, but there seems to be strong evidence in its favor. The evidence comes from raising cases. Suppose the noun phrase is plural, like *problems* in the above example. Suppose further that the noun phrase is embedded in a *that*-clause:

- It is believed that there are problems with your proposal.

In the raising version, *there* is subject of *be believed* and *be* agrees with *there. Problems* remains in the *that*-clause and is not close enough to *be believed* to be available for direct agreement. Yet the *be* of *be believed* can be plural:

- There are believed to be problems with your proposal.

In fact, the same agreement paradigm occurs in my speech:

- *There is believed to be problems with your proposal.
- There are believed to be problems with your proposal.
- There's believed to be problems with your proposal.
- There're believed to be problems with your proposal.

These facts suggest that the indirect agreement proposal is correct, and that *there* must be represented as agreeing with the noun phrase, and all verb agreement occurs via *there.* This makes *there* undisputed grammatical subject of the construction. Yet even if such an analysis is adopted, there remains the question of why *there* should agree with the noun phrase, or to put it another way, why the subject of the construction should have the agreement properties of the noun phrase. The intuitive reason seems to be that the noun phrase, even if it is not the grammatical subject, has some right to the title, since it is subject in the base construction, that is, in the central deictic construction. The agreement properties might be construed as indicating that the noun phrase would have been subject if other considerations had not intervened. I believe that this should be included in any explanatorily adequate account of the agreement properties of this construction.

Why *There* and Not *Here?*

According to our hypothesis, semantic element 1′, which designated a location in physical space in the central deictic construction, will designate a mental space in the central existential construction. In the central deictic, the corresponding syntactic element, 1, was expressed by either of two contrasting lexical items—*here* and *there*. In the existential construction, the possibility for such a contrast has been eliminated and at most one of these modes of expressing semantic element 1′ can be inherited. The fact is that *there* is inherited and *here* is not. Is there a reason for this?

There seem to be at least two reasons why *there* is chosen, and no reasons at all for choosing *here*. The simplest and most straightforward rationale for the choice of *there* has to do with the fact that the referent is a mental space—the medium in which entities occur. A space is understood as the ultimate background relative to which the entities in the space are foregrounded and is therefore comprehended as being distant. This way of comprehending a space makes the choice of the distal *there* natural and the proximal *here* unnatural.

The second rationale concerns markedness. When a binary contrast is eliminated, it is most natural for the unmarked member of the pair to be chosen. *There* seems to be the unmarked member of the *here-there* pair. Deictic *there* appears earlier than *here* in children's speech. And it is much more frequent.

Prediction 15: 1 = *there.*

Final Phrases

Existential constructions, like deictic constructions, have final phrases. The exact nature of the final phrase in the central existential construction is a direct consequence of the nature of the final phrase in the existential construction. Here are some examples (with final phrases in italics).

- There is someone *in the yard.* (locative phrase)
- There's a boy *running away.* (progressive participial phrase)
- There wasn't any money *stolen.* (passive phrase)
- There isn't anyone *taller than Harry.* (adjective phrase)
- There was no one *with his shirt on.* (special *with*-phrase)
- There is a concert *at noon.* (temporal phrase)
- There is a man *about to leave.* (*about to*–phrase)

The range of final phrases permitted in the central existential construction is the same as that in the central deictic construction. Moreover, the same phrases are ruled out:

- *There is a man a doctor. (No predicate nominals)
- *There is a man tall. (No "inherent" adjectives)

As with the central deictic, the final phrases are optional and iterable. Here are some cases with no final phrase:

- There won't be any trouble.
- There's someone who wants to see you.
- There may be problems.

and a case of iteration:

- There's a man standing at the front door mad as hell about to call the cops.

Prediction 16: 4 is an optional VP/*be* and can be iterated.

Prediction 17: 3 is subject of 4.

From the central deictic construction, we also predict that syntactic element 3, the noun phrase, functions as grammatical subject of the final phrase, if it is present. This will allow us to account automatically for a great many common syntactic properties of final phrases, such as the occurrence of reflexive pronouns, equi constructions, floating quantifiers, etc. (For an idea of how such phenomena can be accounted for in a theory of constructions, see Lakoff 1977.)

No Verbs of Motion

Another prediction that can be made is that the central existential does not contain any verbs of motion—neither *go* nor *come*. As we shall see, some noncentral existentials do contain verbs of motion, but they function in special ways which we shall discuss below. The following are not possible existentials:

- *There will go a boy to the ballgame.
- *There can't come any muggers in here.

In the central deictic construction, the occurrence of *go* and *come* were consequences of the fact that one can point out things that are moving through physical space. But entities do not move *through* mental spaces (though they may come to be in them). Thus, the semantics of mental spaces rules out motion *through* a mental space, and hence predicts the absence of *go* and *come* in the central constructions.

Prediction 18: 2 = *be.*

To allay objections at this point, I should point out that perfectly fine existential sentences like

– There will come a time when you'll be sorry.

and

– There ran into the room three strange men dressed as walruses.

will be discussed below when we get to noncentral existential constructions.

Incidentally, we can now restate our description of 4 to read:

4 = VP/2

since 2 is *be*.

Constituent Structure

Prediction 19: 0 is a clause with parts 1, 2, 3, and 4.

In the central deictic construction, syntactic elements 3 and 4—the noun phrase and the final phrase—are sister constituents within the clause and not parts of a single larger noun phrase. For example, in

– There's Harry in the room.

Harry in the room is not a single unit—and in particular, not a single noun phrase. Our hypothesis predicts that this constituent structure is inherited by the existential construction. Thus, in the existential sentence

– There's a man in the room.

a man in the room has at least one analysis as a sequence of two disjoint constituents—a noun phrase followed by a final phrase. It is not just a single noun phrase.

We can prove this by making use of Ross constraints (see Ross 1967). Ross showed that WH-questions cannot leave gaps in either relative clauses or reduced relative clauses. The italicized portions of the following sentences are noun phrase units. The first contains a relative clause, while the second contains a reduced relative clause (with *who is* missing):

– John knows *a man who is in the room* extremely well.
– John knows *a man in the room* extremely well.

If we attempt to question *the room*, gaps will be left behind in the relative clause and the reduced relative clause.

– *Which room does John know *a man who is in* ____ extremely well?
– *Which room does John know *a man in* ____ extremely well?

Similarly, the italicized portion of the following sentence is a noun phrase unit containing a relative clause.

– There is *a man who is in the room.*

Thus we cannot get:

– *Which room is there *a man who is in* ____?

However, in the sentence

– There is *a man in the room.*

the italicized portion does not function like a single noun phrase unit with a reduced relative clause. Thus we have questions like:

– Which room is there *a man in* ____?

Thus, *a man in the room* functions not like a single noun phrase but like a sequence of two constituents, *a man* and *in the room*, just as predicted.

Minimal and Full Representations

Given all of the above predictions, we can represent the central existential *there*-construction in a remarkably minimal fashion:

The Central Existential

Based on: The Central Deictic
Semantic Element
1′: a mental space

This is all that needs to be said. The rest follows from the principle of inheritance, principles of language in general, and independently needed principles particular to English. One way of understanding this is that the central existential is just the central deictic applied to mental spaces instead of locations in physical space.

To see just how much is predicted, let us take a look at a full representation:

The Central Existential

Based on: The Central Deictic

Parameters of Meaning

Semantic Elements

1′: a mental space
2′: a predicate locating an entity in a mental space
3′: an entity
4′: a noninherent predicate
0′: a proposition, 2′(3′,1′)
0′: a proposition, 4′(3′)
S: Speaker
H: Hearer

Function

To focus *H*'s awareness on 3′

Parameters of Form

Syntactic Elements

0: a clause, with parts 1,2,3,4
1: noun phrase
2: verb
3: noun phrase
4*: VP/2

Lexical Conditions

1 = *there*
2 = *be*

Syntactic Conditions

S-1: 1 is first
S-3: 2 precedes 3
S-4: 4 is optional
S-5: 4 is last
S-6: 1 is subject of 0
S-7: 3 is subject of ⟨0; 3,4⟩
S-8: NUMBER (1) agrees with NUMBER (3); OPTIONAL if 1 governs contraction

Phonological Conditions

1 is unstressed

This should give some idea of the explanatory power of grammatical construction theory. All of the full representation is predictable from the ecological location and one semantic condition.

An Alternative

Suppose that, instead of analyzing the central existential as based on the central deictic, we had analyzed the central existential as being based on the central clause type. Something akin to this, though by no means exactly the same, is done in transformational grammar, where there is an attempt to derive existentials from central clauses.

Perhaps the best way to compare the analyses is to ask how much of the full representation of the central existential is predictable if we try to base the central existential on the central clause type. To find this out, what we have to do is construct a minimal representation in which the central existential *is* based on the central clause type, and then see how complex it is.

The syntactic elements of the central existential that correspond to simple sentences are elements 0, 2, 3, and 4—the clause, made up of the verb *be*, the noun phrase, and the final phrase. For example, corresponding to *There is a thief running away*, would be the central clause 0 = *A thief is running away*, where 2 = *is*, 3 = *a thief*, and 4 = *running away*. The semantic elements corresponding to such central clause types are proposition 0″, entity 3′, and predicate 4′, where 0″ = 4′(3′). In this case, 0″ is the meaning of *A thief is running away*. The noun phrase, 3, is the subject of the final phrase, 4—or as we have been writing it, ⟨0; 3,4⟩.

The parts of the central existential that are predictable are:

Semantic Elements
- 0″: a proposition, 4′(3′)
- 3′: an entity
- 4′: a predicate

Syntactic Elements
- 0: a clause, with parts 3, 4
- 3: a noun phrase

Syntactic Conditions
- S-7: 3 is subject of ⟨0; 3,4⟩

This is what is predictable simply from saying that the central existential is based on a central clause type. Most of the central existential construction is not predictable. Here is what a minimal representation would have to be like.

The Central Existential (Alternative Version)

Parameters of Meaning

Semantic Elements
- 1′: a mental space
- 2′: a predicate locating an entity in a mental space
- 4′*: noninherent
- 0′: a proposition, 2′(3′,1′)

S: Speaker
H: Hearer

Function

To focus *H*'s awareness on 3′

Parameters of Form

Syntactic Elements

0: a clause with parts 1, 2
1: a noun phrase
2: a verb

Lexical Conditions

1 = *there*
2 = *be*

Syntactic Conditions

S-1: 1 is first
S-3: 2 precedes 3
S-4: 4 is optional
S-5: 4 is last
S-6: 1 is subject of 0
S-8: NUMBER (1) agrees with NUMBER (3); optional if 1 governs contraction.

Phonological Conditions

1 is unstressed

Just about all of the central existential would be unpredictable if it were based on the simple sentence. In such an analysis, these properties would be arbitrary and unmotivated. The analysis given above can thus explain almost everything that this analysis would have to state as arbitrary.

Based on Versus *Derived from*

Those linguists who tried to relate existentials to deictics—Fillmore, Kuno, Lyons, and Thorne—had a correct intuition. Their problem was that they tried to use transformational grammar to show the relationship by transformationally deriving the existential from the deictic. Of the twenty predictions we were able to make using such an analysis in grammatical construction theory, a transformational analysis could make only two of the minor predictions—prediction 17 (that 3 is subject) and prediction 19 (the constituent structure).

Thus, the concept *based on* in grammatical construction theory is considerably different from the concept *derived from* in transformational grammar.

One Category or Two?

We have argued that the deictic constructions form a natural category with the central deictic as prototype. For the most part, the nonprototypical deictic constructions are based on the central deictic. But we have just argued that the central existential construction is also based on the central deictic. Does that make the central existential part of the deictic category?

The answer is no. The central existential, in its full representation, is so different from any of the deictics that it is in a category of its own. There are well over a dozen differences between the constructions, and many of them are major differences. The categories may be "adjacent," in that there are also many similarities as well as examples whose superficial form is differentiated only by stress. Yet the categories are distinct.

What is remarkable about this is that the difference between the central deictic and the minimal representation of the central existential is so small. Given just one difference, the difference between a location in physical space and a mental space, a great many major differences follow. This is an illustration of how a small difference, placed within a system of complex principles, can yield a very large difference. It is a dramatic illustration of the effects that the overall ecology of a grammatical system can have.

Some Consequences

We have claimed that the central existential construction is based on the central deictic and not, as many linguists have suggested, on the central clause. This allows us to explain a great deal more about this construction than we could explain by analyzing the construction as being based on a central clause. At the same time, it permits us to show how the central existential is related to the central clause. This is done via one of the propositions expressed, 0‴, which predicates 4′ of 3′, and which corresponds to the substructure ⟨0; 3,4⟩. Thus we can account for the fact that in a sentence like

– There's a man shaving himself.

the noun phrase *a man* (element 3) is understood as the subject of *shaving himself* (element 4). This allows us to relate existentials to central clauses corresponding to ⟨0; 3,4⟩ without basing the construction on those central clauses.

Explaining the relationship in this way avoids the problems that transformational grammarians have run into by trying to transformationally derive existentials from central clauses. Transformational treatments face problems like trying to derive the existential

- There's a man who wants to see you.

from the impossible central clause

- *A man who wants to see you is.

On our account there is no problem, since the existential construction is based not on the central clause type, but on the deictic construction.

Our analysis also allows us to account automatically for phenomena like the following.

- There's a Japanese executive in the waiting room.
- A Japanese executive is in the waiting room.

- There's a Japanese executive in our company.
- *A Japanese executive is in our company.

The difference is a consequence of a general principle of English grammar plus the difference between rooms and companies. Companies are institutions that are in part constituted by the people who are employed in them. Rooms are not like this. People in a room do not in part constitute the room, unless they are specifically placed there to be part of the makeup of the room—say, a receptionist.

- There's a receptionist in the waiting room.
- *A receptionist is in the waiting room.

The last sentence is not appropriate if the receptionist is there in her function as the receptionist in that room. It is however fine if someone who is a receptionist somewhere else happens to be in the waiting room.

A transformational analysis would have difficulties with these cases if it were to try to derive all existentials from corresponding simple sentences. The problem is that, in these cases, the corresponding simple sentences don't exist. Such a problem doesn't arise in the analysis we have proposed, since the existential sentences are not derived from simple sentences. All the existential sentences are straightforward cases of the central existential construction. The problem lies not with the occurrence of the existentials, but with the nonoccurrence of the simple sentences. The general principle involved, the part-whole predication constraint, seems to be something like the following:

> In a central clause with an indefinite subject and *be* as the main verb, the verb phrase cannot predicate that the subject is part of some whole with respect to some conceptual schema.

In the sentences given above, there is a company schema in which executives are understood as part of the company. Thus the principle rules out **A Japanese executive is in our company*. Similarly, there is a reception room schema in which the receptionist is part of the reception room. The principle will therefore rule out **A receptionist is in the reception room* if the receptionist is the one working in the reception room. Other examples abound:

- There is a flaw in the diamond.
- *A flaw is in the diamond.

- There is no lid to this jar.
- *No lid is to this jar.

- There are Szechuan peppercorns in this dish.
- *Szechuan peppercorns are in this dish.

Incidentally, English has a special construction to mark cases where there is a schema of the sort described above, where one entity is understood relative to that schema to be part of another entity. Here are some examples of that construction:

- The diamond has a flaw in it.
- The jar has no lid to it.
- This dish has Szechuan peppercorns in it.
- The reception room has a receptionist in it.
- *The reception room has a Japanese executive in it.

This accounts for the following phenomenon:

- There is a vase on the table.

This can be understood in two ways. Either a vase happened, incidentally, to be placed there, or the vase is part of the table setting. The existential is neutral between these two situations. However,

- A vase is on the table.

is restricted to the incidental-occurrence sense, while

- The table has a vase on it.

suggests that the vase is part of an overall image including both table and vase, as in the case of a table setting.

The part-whole predication constraint will also account for cases where the noun phrase designates a literal or metaphorical substance that inheres in some entity.

- There's not much to him.
- There's a great deal of merit in his theory.
- There's not much substance to his claims.

Here the final phrase is a prepositional phrase beginning with either *to* or *in*. The noun phrase which is the object of the preposition (e.g., *his theory*) designates the entity that the substance (e.g., *merit*) inheres in. Because substances are understood as part of the entities that they help to constitute, this construction fits a part-whole schema. As a consequence there are no corresponding simple sentences, but there are corresponding *have*-sentences:

- *Not much is to him.
- He doesn't have much to him.
- *A good deal of merit is in his theory.
- His theory has a good deal of merit in it.
- *Not much substance is to his claims.
- His claims don't have much substance to them.

Incidentally, the *to* in this construction has a bizarre and as yet unexplained quirk. Whereas *in* can occur in postnominal modifiers like *the merit in his theory*, *to* cannot occur in such cases:

- The merit in his theory is considerable.
- *The substance to his theory is considerable.

Though I cannot explain this quirk, the fact that it exists is of interest. It provides a test to distinguish final phrases from postnominal modifiers, and it shows that in

- There is not much substance to his claims.

to his claims is a final phrase, as suggested above, and not a postnominal modifier attached to *substance*.

Although the distribution of the prepositions in these examples is extremely peculiar, there is no reason to think that they are tied to the existential *there*-construction, and hence no reason to set up a special subconstruction to account for them.

The part-whole predication constraint does not cover a range of other cases where indefinite subjects cannot appear in simple sentences with *be* as the main verb.

- There's an hour before lunch.
- *An hour is before lunch.

– There's a concert at ten o'clock.
– *A concert is at ten o'clock.

These involve temporal, not part-whole, relationships, as the following examples show:

– *Lunch has an hour before it.
– *Ten o'clock has a concert at it.

Another principle will be required to rule out temporal predicates of indefinite subjects in central clauses.

To summarize: Cases like those above, where there is no central clause corresponding to an existential sentence, pose no problem for the analysis we have given of existentials. Principles to account for the ill-formedness of those central clauses are needed independently. Since the principles are restricted to central clauses, they have no effect on existentials.

Incidentally, one automatic consequence of our analysis of the central existential is that examples like the following are automatically predicted to be ill-formed:

– *There was being a man shot.

This is a clause of the form: NP–be–NP – . . . . Such a clause can take the progressive auxiliary on *be* (*is being*) only when the "be + noun phrase" can be understood as designating some action over which the subject is exercising control. For example,

– John is being a fool.
– Sally is being a nuisance.

are possible because one can actively be a fool or a nuisance, but

– *Harry is being the man she married.
– *Sam is being the worst hitter in the American League.

are impossible because the subject cannot exercise control over such things. Similarly, a mental space cannot exercise control over the entities in it. Thus, the *be* of the existential can never take the progressive auxiliary, and the ill-formedness of

– *There was being a man shot.

follows as a consequence. However,

– There was a man being shot.

is permitted in a straightforward fashion. *Being shot* is a final phrase, which is based on simple clauses. It is permitted because *A man was being shot* is permitted.

Reminders

The function of existential constructions is to focus the hearer's awareness on semantic element 3′, the referent of the noun phrase. This can happen in two situations: either the hearer has never been aware of 3′, or he has been aware of 3′ and forgotten about it. It is only in the latter case, where the speaker is reminding the hearer of 3′, that the noun phrase can be both definite and specific. Examples include:

- There's always Harry.
- But there's the dog!
- There's still the remains of Christmas dinner in the freezer.

Pronouns used deictically can also occur here.

- If you need a backup catcher, there's always *me*.
- If you need a good pinch-hitter, there's always *him*. (said pointing to someone)

It is predicted, however, that anaphoric pronouns cannot occur in this construction at all. Since their antecedents, if they are to function as antecedents, cannot have been forgotten, anaphoric pronouns cannot function as reminders.

On our analysis, all of these reminding uses are simply cases of the central existential. They just happen to be used in a reminding function. When the noun phrase is definite and specific, reminding is the only function compatible with the general constraints on the construction.

Lists

Examples of reminders are most commonly given in the form of lists:

- There's the cat to feed, the dog to walk, the horse to brush, . . .
- There'll be Max at the head of the table, Sally next to me, . . .

Lists of this sort are a general feature of English and are not peculiar to reminding uses of existentials. They apply to all sorts of other constructions:

- Joan is prettier than Sue, richer than Melanie, smarter than Eliza, . . .
- Bring the camera, the backpack, the canteen, . . .

– I want to give Tom a sweater, Jeff an espresso-maker, . . .
– Tom likes cats, Sally horses, Mike dogs, . . .

Existential lists are simply cases where the list construction has applied to an existential sentence. They are not part of the analysis of existentials at all.

A sentence with a definite NP like

– There's Harry.

can be either a central deictic (if *there* is stressed) or, under special circumstances, a central existential (if *there* is not stressed). The "special circumstances" are those that characterize reminders, namely, the hearer has been aware of the referent of the NP and has forgotten about it. The has-been-aware-of-it condition sanctions the definiteness, while the has-forgotten-about-it condition sanctions the existential *there*-construction, whose function is to introduce it to the hearer's awareness. If these "special circumstances" do not obtain, then it is pragmatically odd to take *There's Harry* as an existential construction.

This completes our study of the central existentials. We can now turn to the noncentral cases.

The Noncentral Existentials

Let us begin by considering examples of each of the constructions we will be discussing.

Central: There's a masked man outside.

Strange: There's a man been shot.

Ontological: There IS a Santa Claus.

Infinitival: There's making dinner to start thinking about.

Presentational: There walked into the room a tall blond man with one black shoe.

The Strange Existential

Guy Carden (1978) has observed that there is an existential construction that is a minimal variation of the central existential, but has some unusual properties. Compare the sentences:

– There's been a man shot. (central existential)
– There's a man been shot. (strange existential)

Although many speakers, on first inspection, don't notice that the strange existential is in any way different from the central existential, a little investigation reveals that it is unusual. It appears at first that the contracted verb is a contraction of *is*, but that is false. *Is* cannot appear in place of the contraction *'s* in these sentence types.

- *There is a man been shot.

Moreover, an inspection of possible tag questions shows that the verb is not *is*, but *has*!

- *There's a man been shot, isn't there?
- There's a man been shot, hasn't there?

Carden also observes that there is another construction that includes a pronominal copy of the subject and the main auxiliary.

- John's left, he has.

This also reveals that the contracted *'s* is *has*, not *is*.

- There's a man been shot, there has.
- *There's a man been shot, there is.

Yet *has* cannot appear uncontracted.

- *There has a man been shot.

Apparently, contracted *has* can appear in this construction because it looks like contracted *is*. Notice that the strange existential does not occur in the plural, since *'ve* (the contracted form of plural *have*) is not the same form as the contracted plural of *be*, namely *'re*.

- *There've many people been killed this week.

The corresponding central existential

- There've been many people killed this week.

is fine, as expected.

The strange existential not only occurs with passive final phrases, but also with just about any verb phrase minus *have* of the perfect.

- There's a strange dog been hanging around outside.
- There's an actor been president for almost six years now.
- There's a man robbed the drugstore down the street.
- There's someone fallen overboard.

We can represent this construction minimally as follows:

The Strange Existential

Based on: The Central Existential
Lexical Condition
  2 = *have* of the perfect
Phonological Condition
  2 = *'s*

Given that the central construction contains the condition that 4 = a verb phrase minus 2, the fact that 2 = the *have* the perfect will predict that 4, the final phrase, will be a verb phrase minus the *have* of the perfect.

Rational Properties

Although such an account of this construction is perhaps most perspicuous, it does miss something. It is no accident that the phonological form chosen is *'s*. This is the contracted form of *is*, which is the verb in the central construction. And the contracted form is, in fact, the most typical form used. That is, one usually finds *there's* rather than *there is* in casual conversation.

In short, there is a reason why the phonological form in the construction is *'s* and not some other random element. It is a rational thing to occur, not an arbitrary form. Yet it is not a motivated property of the construction, as we are using the term. To be "motivated" it would have to be predictable from the construction's ecological location (what it is based on) plus general principles of grammar. But it *is* predictable from one other piece of information—the fact that it is the same as the typical form of the corresponding element of the central construction.

We can represent this information in the following way. Let us refer to element 2 of the central existential construction as the "ancestor" of 2 in the strange existential construction. Let us abbreviate "the typical form of the ancestor of 2" as TFA(2). Were we to list "TFA(2)" as the phonological condition of the strange existential, it would follow that 2 = *'s*.

Given that 2 = *'s*, there are only two things that 2 could be—either *is* or *has* of the perfect auxiliary. Note that it is only the perfect *has* that contracts. Thus, *John has a book* does not contract to *John's a book*, while *John has been here* contracts to *John's been here*. Since there are only two possibilities, all we need to know about the lexical item chosen as 2 is that it is not *is*, that is, it is not the same as the lexical item chosen in the central construction, or equivalently that it is not the same as its ancestor. If we abbreviate "ancestor of 2" as A(2), then we can represent as:

Lexical Condition
2 = A(2).

With these two pieces of information about the relationship between element 2 in the strange construction and the corresponding elements in its ancestor construction, we can predict both of the above conditions that define the strange construction. The fact that this can be done shows that these are not arbitrary conditions. But they are not predictable in the way that motivated conditions are. That is, they lean somewhat more toward arbitrary properties than motivated properties do, but they are not by any means completely arbitrary. We will refer to such properties of constructions as *rational properties.*

I will use the term *rational property* for all nonarbitrary properties that are not *motivated*, in the technical sense in which we are using the term in this case study. Languages contain a great many rational properties, properties that are not arbitrary but make sense in terms of the rest of the system. I do not at present have anything approaching a general theory of rational properties. However, I think they are one of the most interesting aspects of natural languages, and they deserve serious study.

Like motivated properties, rational properties seem to be easier to learn, remember, and use than arbitrary properties. This suggests that they too have an important cognitive status.

The Ontological Existential

One of the existential constructions is actually concerned with ontology, that is, with whether an entity exists or not. In this construction, the verb *exist* can appear instead of *be,* and the verb bears stress. It is also common for the noun phrase to be an indefinite version of a proper name, since discussions of existence often center upon whether some entity for which there is a proper name exists.

- There is a Santa Claus.
- There is no God.
- If there exists a Valhalla, I want to go there.

Other examples include:

- There are five prime numbers below twelve.
- There weren't cars in 1876.
- How could there exist a God without a mother?
- There is work to be found.

We can represent this construction minimally in the following way:

The Ontological Existential

Semantic Elements

$2'' =$ a predicate of existence

$0'' = 2''(3')$

Lexical Condition

2 may be *exist*

Phonological Condition

2 bears stress

Incidentally, this is another construction that cannot have corresponding simple sentences:

- *A Santa Claus is.
- *No God is.

There are, however, corresponding simple sentences with the verb *exist:*

- Santa Claus exists.
- No God exists.

The above analysis accounts for the relationship between the existentials and such simple sentences via the proposition, $0''$, in the semantics, which expresses the proposition that the referent of the noun phrase exists. This is the proposition expressed by the corresponding simple sentences. In a sentence like *There exists a God,* the subpart corresponding to this proposition consists of syntactic elements 3 (*a God*) and 2 (*exists*) and bears a direct relationship to the corresponding simple sentence *A God exists.* Moreover, a sentence like

- There exists a Santa Claus living quietly at the North Pole.

is related to two simple sentences via the propositions $0''$ and $0'''$ in their semantics. $0''$ is of the form $2'(3')$, which corresponds to the syntactic subpart consisting of syntactic elements 3 (*A Santa Claus*) and 2 (*exists*). $0'''$ is of the form $4'(3')$, which corresponds to the syntactic subpart consisting of elements 3 (*A Santa Claus*) and 4 (*(is) living quietly at the North Pole*). The above existential sentence is thereby related systematically to the corresponding simple sentences:

- A Santa Claus exists.
- A Santa Claus is living quietly at the North Pole.

The difference between the way that *be* and *exist* function in these examples is the following: * *A Santa Claus is* ruled out as a simple clause because the copula *be* must take a following NP. *A Santa Claus exists* is allowed as a simple clause because *exist* is intransitive. Both *There is a Santa Claus* and *There exists a Santa Claus* are instances of the ontological existential construction. The *be* in this construction is permitted because the construction is based on the central existential, which in turn is based on the central deictic (which has a *be*). *Exist* can occur in this construction by the lexical choice principle, since the semantic conditions list a predicate of existence.

To my knowledge there is no transformational analysis of such existentials that adequately accounts for the way they are systematically related to *two* such simple sentences.

The analysis given above also accounts for the fact that definite specific noun phrases cannot occur with this construction.

- *There exists the negative square root of nine.

The reason is that one cannot both be predicating the existence of an entity and reminding someone about it. One can remind someone of something specific, but only if its existence is taken for granted.

The Infinitival Existential

In morphology, there is a distinction made between *bound* and *free* morphemes. Bound morphemes are those that cannot occur independently, but only occur as part of larger units. For example, the *-ing* of *working* and the *-s* of *cats* are bound morphemes. There is a similar distinction to be made in grammar between bound and free constructions. A bound construction is one that occurs only as part of other constructions.

There is an existential construction that contains a bound construction within it. I have in mind cases where the bound construction is an infinitival clause which contains a gap that is not in subject position. In the following examples, the gapped infinitival clause is in italics, and the noun phrase which is understood as fitting into that gap is in bold.

- There is **a bed** *for you to sleep in* _____.
- There's **food** *to eat* _____.
- There's still **getting himself into college** *for John to start thinking about* _____.
- There won't be **any producers** there *for Stephanie to be seen by* _____.

In these existential sentences, the gapped infinitival clause is the final phrase, and the noun phrase that is understood as fitting into the gap is syntactic element 3.

This construction can be given the following minimal representation:

The Infinitival Existential

Based on: The Central Existential
Syntactic Elements
4: a GAPPED INFINITIVAL CLAUSE

Incidentally, here are two other constructions that make use of the gapped infinitival clause—the bound construction used in the infinitival existential:

Object-to-Subject Raising

- **This bed** is easy *to fall asleep in* _____.
- **Getting myself to exercise regularly** is tough *for me to even consider* _____.

Nominal with an Infinitival Relative Clause

- Harry is **the man** *for you to see* _____.
- This is **a good bed** *to sleep in* _____.
- I just found **a good paper** *to assign* _____ in class.

The gapped infinitival clause construction can be characterized as follows:

The Gapped Infinitival Clause

Based on: The Central Clause Type

Parameters of Meaning

Semantic Elements

0′: a proposition, with 1′ as a part.
1′: an entity.
2′: an entity, not a part of 0′.

Semantic Conditions
1′ is coreferential to 2′

Parameters of Form

Syntactic Conditions
S-1: 0 is infinitival.
S-2: 1 is not subject of 0.
S-3: 1 is null.
S-4: 2 immediately commands 0.

Condition S-3 specifies that there is a gap. Since 1′ is an entity, 1 is an NP gap. The semantic element 2′ indicates that this is a bound construction.

The conditions on the pair (2′, 2) specify that this construction must fit an "external" entity, which is coreferential to 1′. Condition S-4 tells where this external entity must be relative this construction. Essentially, 2′ plays the same role that lambda-abstraction plays in theories such as generalized phrase-structure grammar and Montague grammar. That is, it links the equivalent of a variable inside the construction (1′) to a coreferential noun phrase entity (2′) in the next highest clause. The "immediate command" condition of S-4 specifies that there must be a noun phrase coreferential with the gap in the next highest clause. This condition must be consistent with whatever constraints there are on that next-highest clause. When the infinitival existential and the gapped infinitive clause constructions are superimposed, element 3′ of the infinitival existential will fit onto (that is, be identical to) element 2′ of the gapped infinitival clause. It is by such a mechanism that the theory of grammatical constructions in general achieves the same purpose as lambda-abstraction.

From this perspective, we can characterize the gapped infinitive clause in a minimal fashion, by first characterizing the bound clause construction.

The Bound Clause Construction

Based on: The Central Clause Type

Parameters of Meaning

Semantic Elements

- 0′: a proposition with 1′ as a part.
- 1′: an entity.
- 2′: an entity that is not a part of 0′.

Semantic Condition

- 1′ is coreferential to 2′.

Syntactic Conditions

- S-1: 1 is null.
- S-2: 2 immediately commands 0.

The bound clause construction is a general construction that has many instances—all clausal constructions containing noun phrase gaps. These include the equi-construction, the raising construction, the WH-question construction, the relative clause construction, etc. Among its instances is the gapped infinitival clause:

The Gapped Infinitival Construction

Based on: The bound clause Construction

Parameters of Form

Syntactic Conditions

S-1: 0 is infinitival.

S-2: 1 is not the subject of 0.

The Presentational Existential

Narratives create mental spaces of their own, and when an existential construction is used within a narrative, it is the mental space of the narrative that is designated by *there.* Moreover, it is the function of the *there*-construction to bring the entity designated by the noun phrase into the narrative. Thus when a sentence like *There was a loud noise!* occurs in a narrative, it functions to bring the noise into the mental space of the hearer, which is also the space of the narrative.

A good narrative is one that allows the hearer to vividly picture the events of the narrative as they are told. English has an existential construction that is specialized to narratives. It allows speakers to introduce a new narrative element, while simultaneously sketching a scene.

- From an asylum near Providence, R.I., there recently disappeared an exceedingly singular person.
- In the cubicle there was sitting alone a pretty young woman writing a term paper.
- Suddenly there burst into the room an SS officer holding a machine gun.
- There once lived in Translyvania an old woman with three sons.

This construction differs in certain important ways from other existentials. It permits an entire verb phrase, not just a verb alone, to appear as syntactic element 2. Thus, in the above examples, there are the verb phrases (including auxiliaries): *recently disappeared, was sitting alone,* and *burst into the room.* The verb phrase in such a sentence must be intransitive. Thus, we do not have sentences like:

- *Suddenly there hit Harry over the head a mugger brandishing a baseball bat.
- *Last year there sent me a Valentine's card an attractive older woman in my office.

These are ill-formed because the verb phrases *hit Harry over the head* and *sent me a Valentine's card* are transitive.

In my speech there is also a constraint on this construction having to do with the length (or possibly the information content) of the noun phrase and the verb phrase:

The verb phrase cannot be much longer (or have much more informational content) than the noun phrase.

Thus, I find the following sentences ill-formed:

- *In the cubicle there was sitting alone a girl.
- *Suddenly there burst into the room a man.
- *There once lived in Transylvania a woman.

The only difference between these sentences and the ones cited above is the length of the noun phrase. If we hold the verb phrase constant and vary the length of the noun phrase, we can see the sentences getting progressively better.

- *Suddenly there burst into the room a cop.
- *Suddenly there burst into the room a tall cop.
- ?*Suddenly there burst into the room a brawny cop.
- ?*Suddenly there burst into the room a mean-looking cop.
- Suddenly there burst into the room a tall, brawny, mean-looking cop.

Here ?* indicates pretty bad and ? indicates pretty good.

We can represent this constraint as a syntactic condition of the form:

Size (3) $\geq$ Size (2)

This seems at first like a strange constraint, until we consider the function it serves. The referent of the noun phrase is being set up as a new narrative element via the description give in the verb phrase and the noun phrase. The verb phrase must therefore set up an appropriate background against which the noun phrase will count as new information. The noun phrase must therefore convey more new content than the verb phrase. Given the fact that, for the most part, the longer a phrase is the more content it conveys, it follows that the size of the noun phrase must be greater that the size of the verb phrase. Thus, the syntactic condition is a consequence of the function of the construction—bringing a new element into a narrative via the descriptions given the verb phrase and the noun phrase.

We will refer to the predicate expressed by the verb phrase as semantic element 2″. This is predicated of the referent of the noun phrase, 3′. We will refer to the resulting proposition as 0″. We can now provide a minimal representation of this construction.

The Presentational Existential

Based on: The Central Existential

Semantic Elements

1′: a narrative space
2″: a predicate
0″: 2″ (3′)

Syntactic Elements

2: a verb phrase, with an intransitive head verb.

Given the narrative function of the construction, the syntactic constraint

Size (3) ≥ Size (2)

will follow.

The account we have given of the presentational existential has a number of important consequences. Note that the only constraint that we have placed on the head verb of the verb phrase is that it must be intransitive. This is an implicit claim that any intransitive verb should be able to work here providing that the verb phrase functions to set up an appropriate background for the noun phrase. This, of course, will depend on many factors—the nature of the verb, the nature of the auxiliary verbs, the time and locational adverbs present in the sentence, etc. Take, as an example, the intransitive verb *bleed.* By itself, this verb describes a process, but does not set up an appropriate background for the introduction of a narrative element. Thus we do not get sentences like:

- *There bled a hemophiliac.

But this does not mean that *bleed* cannot occur as the head verb of the verb phrase. With the right auxiliary verbs and adverbs modifying *bleed,* it too can function as the head verb of a presentational existential:

- For two hours there had been bleeding on the emergency room floor a poor hemophiliac who had fainted before he could sign his Blue Cross form.

So far, I have not found any intransitive verbs that cannot be made to fit this construction. It is just a matter of finding the right combination of auxiliaries and adverbs, a noun phase of the appropriate size, and a context that makes sense.

Of course, some intransitive verbs fit more easily than others. Verbs that have such meanings as "coming into existence," or "changing to a new state," or "moving to a new location," can occur in this construction most easily, usually without any help from auxiliaries or adverbs. Hence the oft-cited examples:

- There arose a commotion.
- There ensued a riot.
- There entered a policeman.

In a reminding use, the verb *remain* can be used, as one would expect.

- There remains one major problem.

These are just special cases of the presentational construction. The verb phrase happens to contain just a single verb. And since the verb phrase is short, the noun phrase can be relatively short. However, it cannot be too small; for example, the indefinite pronoun *one* is somewhat smaller than the above verbs, and so the following sentences are ill-formed:

- *There arose one.
- *There ensued one.
- *There entered one.

However, with the right context and a short enough verb, the indefinite pronoun is possible:

- Bill had said that he didn't expect any Christmas cards, so when there finally came one in the mail, he was surprised.

With the somewhat longer verbs *arrived* and *was delivered*, there is a corresponding decrease in acceptability.

- ?Bill had said that he didn't expect any Christmas cards, so when there finally arrived one in the mail, he was surprised.
- *Bill had said that he didn't expect any Christmas cards, so when there was finally delivered one in the mail, he was surprised.

Thus, the cases where the verb phrase is just a simple verb are just special cases of the presentational existential construction. No special construction is necessary to handle them.

The analysis given above makes a further prediction about the syntax of this construction, namely, that it cannot be negated. This is a consequence of our claim that the verb phrase functions either to predicate an entrance of the new element into the scene, as in

- There emerged from the cocoon a beautiful black and red butterfly.

or to set up a background against which a new element may be introduced, as in

- There were singing in the alley below a hearty group of carolers undaunted by the snow and the cold.

In either case, negation is inconsistent with the function of the construction. In the first case, it negates the entrance predicate, communicating the lack of an entrance:

- *There didn't emerge from the cocoon a beautiful black and red butterfly.

In the second case, it negates the predicate setting up the appropriate background, which results in the lack of such a background:

- *There weren't singing in the alley below a hearty group of carolers undaunted by the snow and the cold.

The analysis given also predicts that not all negatives will be excluded. It is possible for certain kinds of negatives to help set up a background, rather than negate one. *Never*, for example, sets up an extended counterfactual mental space which can serve as a background.

- While I was sheriff, there never occurred any demonstrations of significant proportions.

Even predicates like *end* can play a role in setting up a background for this construction.

- There recently ended the longest scoring streak in the history of professional hockey.

The pragmatic function of this construction also predicts where it can and cannot be embedded and what other constructions it can interact with. Let us begin with the sentence

- There jumped out of the hole a jackrabbit with enormous ears.

As Aissen (1975) points out, this sentence can form a relative clause modifying *the hole* under the right conditions.

- That's the hole out of which there jumped a jackrabbit with enormous ears.

However, it cannot be used as a relative clause modifying *jackrabbit.*

- *That's the jackrabbit that there jumped out of the hole.

In the construction, *jackrabbit* is constituent 3, the element being introduced into the narrative. If *hole* is relativized, it is still possible for *jackrabbit* to be introduced into the narrative via this construction. But if *jackrabbit* is relativized, then it has been introduced prior to the background given in the construction, which violates the pragmatic condition on the construction.

Let us now turn from the details of analysis to some theoretical issues.

What's in Common?

As in the case of the deictic constructions, it is possible to find a set of conditions shared by all the existential constructions.

The Generalized Existential

Parameters of Meaning

Same as the central existential

Parameters of Form

Syntactic Elements

0: clause, with parts 1, 2, 3, and 4

1: noun phrase

3: noun phrase

Lexical Conditions

1 = *there*

Syntactic Conditions

S-1: 1 is first

S-3: 2 precedes 3

S-6: 1 is subject of 0

S-8: NUMBER (1) agrees with NUMBER (3); OPTIONAL if 1 governs contraction

Phonological Conditions

1 is unstressed

This is a very strange set of conditions. There is no specification of the syntactic categories of elements 2 and 4. Since 2 is a verb phrase in the presentational construction, but a verb in all the other constructions, there is no syntactic category that can be uniformly assigned to 2 in all constructions. For the same reason, *be* cannot be assigned as the lexical representation of 2 in all constructions. Since 4 is a gapped infinitival clause in the infinitival construction, there can be no common value of 4 that is shared in all constructions. Similarly, the syntactic conditions that accompany 4 are not shared and so are not part of the generalized existential. What the existentials have in common is so skewed a set of conditions that it is difficult to imagine that it could have any linguistic significance whatever.

Since these are necessary but not sufficient conditions, no classical account of the category of existentials is possible. It would be technically possible to give a prototype-based account with the generalized existential as the prototypical construction, and all the other constructions as noncentral. As in the case of the similar proposal for the deictics, there are two objections. First, this would not account for the fact that central existentials are considered better examples of existentials than noncentral cases. Thus

- There is a boy in the room.

is a better example of the category than:

- There's a boy been hurt.
- There exists a God.
- Into the room there burst a policeman.

In addition, many of the generalizations that we stated above cannot be stated if the generalized existential is taken as the prototypical construction, with the other constructions based on it. Most notably, we could not use all the predictions that come from basing the central existential on the central deictic. That predicts *more* than is in the generalized existential, and there is no way to predict exactly what is in the generalized existential. The point here is that the concept "based on" allows us to predict exactly what is in the central existential, but there is no corresponding concept that would allow us to predict exactly what is in the generalized existential. This suggests that the shared properties of the existentials—those in the generalized existential—have no cognitive status at all.

Whereas we can predict all but one property of the central existential, we can predict nothing of the generalized existential. Were we to choose it as the central member, we would miss a great deal. We would also miss a great deal in the specification of each of the subconstructions. Instead of simply listing where the individual subconstructions diverge from the central existential, we would have to list considerably more for each subconstruction. The minimal representations would be much more complex. As in the case of the deictics, there seems to be no reason to accord any cognitive status whatever to the conditions that happen to be shared by the members of the category of *there*-constructions.

Distinguishing Versus Defining Properties

In the classical theory, shared properties, defining properties, and distinguishing properties are coextensive. The idea is that a category is *defined* by *shared* properties, and these *distinguish* the members of the given category from everything else. As we have seen, the collection of properties that incidentally happen to be shared by the constructions in the category seem to have no special cognitive status. If another subconstruction were added to the category, the shared properties might well change, but the category would otherwise remain intact.

We have also seen that there is no set of properties that exactly defines all and only the subconstructions in the category. The two constructional categories that we have studied are each defined by a central member and conventionalized variations on it.

Minimal distinguishing properties may, however, be found and may even be psychologically real. As their name suggests, distinguishing properties are those that minimally distinguish one category from another. They are a subset of the shared properties, but they do not define the category. In the case of deictic and existential *there*-constructions, it does seem possible for speakers to distinguish one category from the other directly, without using the prototype structure we have uncovered. My guess is that they use properties such as these:

Deictic: First element is either *here* or *there* and refers deictically to a real or abstract location.

Existential: First element is *there* and does not refer to any entity or location.

Such conditions will suffice to distinguish the deictics from the existentials. I have no evidence whatever that distinguishing properties play any role in the grammar of a language. It is possible that they play no role at all and that speakers, if asked, can come up with some minimal distinguishing characteristics that will enable them to make the distinction. But in ordinary language use, people don't have to engage in the task of distinguishing one category from another. Instead, they just have to pair form and meaning, and constructions of the sort we have discussed are sufficient for the task. This does not rule out the possibility that linguists will someday find that minimal distinguishing characteristics have some cognitive function in grammar. If so, something like the above may have to be added to what we have already described.

Let us suppose for the sake of discussion that there is some reason for the grammar of English to include minimal distinguishing features, like those cited above, to distinguish the deictics as a group from the existentials as a group. Such minimal distinguishing features would still not do very much of what has to be done to *define* the constructions—that is, to tell exactly what form-meaning pairings are, and are not, in the language. Such conditions would not exclude what needs to be excluded and would not get the constructional meanings and pragmatic conditions right. Nor would they account for the fine details of the syntax that differ from subconstruction to subconstruction. It might be the case that we need *both* the prototype-based analysis and minimal distinguishing features, but there is no way to do without the prototype-based characterization.

There Is Where

This case study would not be complete without a discussion of a class of sentences that look like they are deictic *there*-constructions but aren't. I have in mind sentences like

– There is where he put the money.

Such sentences may look superficially like

– There's Harry.

But they have different properties. They can be negated, questioned, embedded, and raised.

– There isn't where he put the money.
– *There isn't Harry.
– Is there where he put the money?
– *Is there Harry?
– There is believed to be where he put the money.
– *There is believed to be Harry.
– If there is where he put the money, our problems are over.
– *If there's Harry, our problems are over.

It is possible to get conjunctions of noun phrases of the form *Harry and where he put the money,* as in

– I keep thinking about Harry and where he put the money.

Such conjunctions, however, are impossible in deictic *there*-constructions. For example, if one discovered Harry getting the hidden money out of a secret cache, one could say either

– There's Harry.

or

– There's where he put the money.

but not

– *There's Harry and where he put the money.

Nothing needs to be said about *there*-constructions to account for these facts. They are automatic consequences of another phenomenon in English grammar.

English has a construction called the pseudo-cleft construction. Here are some examples:

- What Harry ate was a bagel.
- What bit me was a mosquito.
- Where he put the money was under the bed.

Under certain conditions, pseudo-clefts can be inverted:

- A bagel is what Harry ate.
- A mosquito is what bit me.
- Under the bed is where he put the money.

Inverted pseudo-clefts like these are remarkable in that they allow adverbs like *under the bed* to function as grammatical subjects. We can see that *under the bed* is a subject in the last sentence above from the fact that it can raise:

- Under the bed is believed to be where he put the money.

Inverted pseudo-clefts can also be negated, questioned, and embedded with relative freedom.

- Under the bed isn't where he put the money.
- Is under the bed where he put the money?
- I doubt that under the bed is where he put the money.
- I would be surprised if under the bed were where he put the money.

Since locative adverbs like *under the bed* can occur in pseudo-clefts and inverted pseudo-clefts, so can deictic locatives like *there.*

- Where he put the money was there (pointing).
- There is where he put the money.

Although *There is where he put the money* looks superficially like a deictic *there*-construction, it isn't one. It is simply an inverted pseudo-cleft, and functions exactly as one would expect.

A Short Recapitulation

We are now in a position to give a simple and elegant characterization of the *there*-constructions. We will make use of the following notation.

For: What the construction is used for.

About: What the construction is used to talk about.
On: What other construction it is based on.

The integers denote the following syntactic elements, which are consequences of their semantics:

1: *there* (or *here*)
2: V or VP
3: NP
4: Final Phrase

A slash indicates "minus." And lexical items are capitalized, as are rule names. In the "based-on" statements, the central deictic and existential constructions will be abbreviated by CD and CE.

The central deictic and existential constructions can be described simply as follows:

CENTRAL DEICTIC: *For:* Pointing out
2: If locational, then basic level.
4′: Not inherent.
4: VP/2. [That is, a VP minus a 2.]
CENTRAL EXISTENTIAL: *On:* CD
1′: Mental space.

This says that the central deictic construction is used for pointing out things (using the pointing-out ICM), and it gives the three properties of the construction that are not consequences of its use. The *on*-condition says that the central existential is based on the central deictic, and gives the single condition that differentiates the central existential from the central deictic. All the other differences are consequences.

There are nine minimal variants of the central deictic, and they can be characterized very simply. All of them are linked to the central deictic by the *on*-condition. First, there are five that are about various subject matters.

PERCEPTUAL DEICTIC: *On:* CD. *About:* Perception
DISCOURSE DEICTIC: *On:* CD. *About:* Discourse
EXISTENCE DEICTIC: *On:* CD. *About:* Existence
ACTIVITY START DEICTIC: *On:* CD. *About:* Activity
1′: Starting point.
DELIVERY DEICTIC: *On:* CD: *About:* Delivery
S: Deliverer
Option: 1: elongated, rising, unstressed

There are also three minimal variants that are simply intersections of the central deictic and another minimal construction that pairs a pragmatic condition with an intonation. All that needs to be said is that these constructions exist and are based on both the central deictic and an additional construction.

PARAGON DEICTIC: *On:* CD and PARAGON
EXASPERATION DEICTIC: *On:* CD and EXASPERATION
ENTHUSIASTIC BEGINNING DEICTIC: *On:* CD and ENTHUSIATIC BEGINNING

There are also two special purpose constructions, one of which is a minimal variant and one of which is more complex.

NARRATIVE FOCUS DEICTIC: *On:* CD. *For:* Vivid narrative
PRESENTATIONAL DEICTIC: *On:* CD. *For:* Announcements
  2: Verb of location
  Options: 2 has full auxiliary
    4 precedes 2 and 3
    If 4′ = location, then 1 is null.

The presentational deictic is the only complex variant, having one special condition and three options.

There are also three variants based on the central existential.

STRANGE EXISTENTIAL: *On:* CE
  2: Perfect HAVE & *'s*
ONTOLOGICAL EXISTENTIAL: *On:* CE. *About:* Existence
  2: stressed
  Option: 2 = EXIST
INFINITIVAL EXISTENTIAL: *On:* CE
  4: Gapped infinitival
PRESENTATIONAL EXISTENTIAL: *On:* CE
  1′: Narrative space
  2: Intransitive VP
  2′: No restriction

Given the enormous complexity of the data, it is hard to see how a more elegant account could be given that covers the same range of syntactic, semantic, and pragmatic phenomena, while also showing the relationships among the constructions.

Summary

This case study has had both a narrow and a broad purpose. The narrow purpose was to provide an adequate description of both deictic and existential *there*-constructions and to show how they are related. The broad purpose was to answer a number of deep and important questions about the nature of language. Here are the answers that have emerged from our study:

- Cognitive semantics is necessary for the description of the meanings of grammatical constructions. This includes mental spaces and cognitive models of many sorts, including metaphoric and metonymic models.
- Grammatical constructions have a real cognitive status. They are not mere epiphenomena arising from the operation of generative rules.
- Prototype-based categorization occurs in grammar. Radially structured categories exist there, and their function is to greatly reduce the arbitrariness of form-meaning correlations.
- The concept of motivation is needed in order to account for a great many of the regularities that occur in grammar.
- Syntactic categories are not autonomous, nor are they completely predictable from semantic considerations. Instead, their central subcategories are predictable from semantic considerations, and their noncentral subcategories are motivated extensions of central subcategories.
- A great many syntactic properties of grammatical constructions are consequences of their meanings.
- The meanings of whole grammatical constructions are not computable by general rules from the meanings of their parts. They are, however, motivated by the meanings of their parts.
- There is a continuum between the grammar and the lexicon.
- Grammars are not separate "modules" independent of the rest of cognition. The reason is that they make use of prototype categorization, which arises in other aspects of cognition, and they also make use of various aspects of conceptual systems, such as cognitive models (including metaphoric and metonymic models) and mental spaces.

Generative Semantics Updated

Cognitive grammar, as I have presented it, has developed gradually over a number of years, evolving from generative semantics and case grammar through the theory of linguistic gestalts to its present form. In recent years, I have been working on the theory of grammatical constructions with Berkeley colleagues Charles Fillmore and Paul Kay. I view cognitive grammar as an updated version of generative semantics.

Certain basic principles of cognitive grammar were also basic principles of generative semantics:

- Language is part of general cognition and makes use of general cognitive mechanisms.
- The primary function of language is to convey meaning. A grammar should therefore show as directly as possible how parameters of form are linked to parameters of meaning.
- Since meaning and communicative function are primary, grammars should attempt to explain as much as possible about parameters of form on the basis of parameters of meaning and communicative function.
- Pragmatics is taken to be the semantics of communication, and the same theoretical apparatus is used in the description of both domains.

The differences between generative semantics and cognitive grammar are a matter of implementation rather than a matter of basic assumptions. They have come about because our understanding of the basic mechanisms involved in cognition has increased considerably in recent years. Here are the principal areas of difference for semantics.

- Generative semantics assumed that model-theoretical approaches to logic could be adapted to account for semantics and pragmatics.
- Cognitive grammar recognizes that model theory will not account for most semantic and pragmatic phenomena. It hypothesizes that a theory of experientially grounded cognitive models can adequately account for semantic and pragmatic phenomena.

And here are the principal areas of difference for syntax:

- Generative semantics assumed that the classical arguments given for transformational grammar were essentially correct. It attempted to link form and meaning by taking logical forms as underlying syntactic structures. Global rules served the function of directly linking logical form and surface syntax and were viewed as preferable to transformations (which largely got in the way of direct form-meaning correspondences).
- Cognitive grammar recognizes recent results showing that transformational rules are not necessary. It also recognizes the empirical failure of generative theories of grammar to account for most grammatical phenomena. Grammatical construction theory proposes instead that symbolic models—direct form-meaning pairings—are basic

elements of grammar. Grammatical constructions are organized via prototype theory, using radially structured constructional categories.

Generative semantics succeeded in a great many ways:

- Generative semantics got linguists to pay attention to the role of logical form and model theory.
- Generative semantics showed how predicate-argument structure, logical operators, coreference, binding, propositonal functions, etc., played a role in such syntactic phenomena as negative polarity, anaphora, constraints on the occurrence of quantifiers, etc.
- Generative semantics showed how the internal structure of lexical items had syntactic consequences.
- Generative semantics got the linguistic community to pay attention to the relationship between syntax and pragmatics, especially phenomena involving performatives, presuppositions, implicatures, evidentials, etc.
- Generative semantics brought to the attention of the linguistic community an enormous number of syntactic and semantic phenomena.

Primarily as a result of the work of generative semanticists, such matters are now part of mainstream syntactic and semantic theories.
But generative semantics also failed as an empirical theory in many ways:

- Because it used transformational syntax, it could not deal adequately with syntactic amalgams (Lakoff 1974).
- Because it depended on a theory of classical syntactic categories, it could not deal adequately with prototype effects in syntax and with the semantic basis of syntactic categories.
- Because it used a generative grammar, it could not account for motivated grammatical constructions, which are not fully predictable by generative rules. (See Fillmore, Kay, and O'Connor, to appear.)
- Because the lexicon only had redundancy rules available to it, but not radial categories, it could not deal adequately with polysemy (Brugman 1981, Dixon 1968, Lindner 1981).
- Because it had no account of the spatialization of form, it could not deal with syntactic iconicity (Lakoff and Johnson 1980, chap. 20, Haiman 1980).
- Because it used an objectivist semantics, that is, a semantics containing logical forms and model theory, it could not deal adequately with:
  (*a*) basic-level categories and prototype effects in semantics
  (*b*) Fillmore's frame-semantic phenomena

(*c*) the Lakoff-Johnson metaphor phenomena
(*d*) the Borkin-Nunberg-Fauconnier metonymy phenomena (see Fauconnier 1985)
(*e*) the Lindner-Brugman-Janda image-schema phenomena
(*f*) alternative conceptual systems (Casad 1982, Brugman 1983)
(*g*) inconsistent cognitive models (Kay 1979, Gentner and Gentner 1982)
(*h*) such mental space phenomena as referential opacity and presupposition (Fauconnier 1985)
(*i*) the semantics of classifier systems (Dixon 1968, Downing 1984)
(*j*) metalinguistic negation (Fillmore 1984, Horn 1985)
(*k*) the inconsistency in the theory of meaning pointed out by Putnam (1981)

It should be pointed out that it was not only generative semantics that failed in these ways. Every theory that makes use of a generative syntax and either model-theoretic semantics or a semantics that involves only logical form has failed in the same ways. The appearance of failure has been avoided only by ignoring such phenomena. Luckily, a significant number of linguists have paid attention to them, and the result is cognitive linguistics.

Afterword

I began work on this book with the knowledge that objectivist views of the mind have a very wide currency in the academic world. Among my principal aims has been to characterize that view, name it, point out that it is an opinion, not a fundamental truth, and raise the question of its validity, so that it can be discussed in the open and no longer be presupposed automatically as part of an unquestioned background.

Many scholars do indeed take it for granted without question that conceptual categories are defined solely by the shared essential properties of their members, that thought is the disembodied manipulation of abstract symbols, and that those symbols get their meaning solely by virtue of correspondences to things in the world. The view of reason as abstract, disembodied, and literal is well-established.

It is well-established partly because there are certain aspects of it that are correct. Some conceptual categories do have the structure of a classical category. Certain aspects of classical logic do seem to be used in reason. But it does not follow from that that the whole objectivist paradigm must be accepted. Another of my goals has been to provide an alternative to objectivist views that preserves what is right about objectivism, while permitting research into the nature of reason that goes beyond the limits that objectivism had placed on that research.

What I could not have guessed when I began this book is just how many researchers have found evidence of one sort or another that contradicts objectivist views. One of the most gratifying aspects of this research has been the discovery that there is a large body of evidence from many fields that supports a view of mind that is centered in the bodily and imaginative capacities of human beings.

During the course of the writing, I had an opportunity to lecture on these topics not only at universities throughout the United States, but in many other countries, particularly in Europe, Asia, and South America. Everywhere I have gone, I have encountered researchers whose findings are, in one way or another, inconsistent with the objectivist view of mind, but who had no idea that so many others had reached similar conclusions. Such meetings have been important to me. They are like meetings between long-lost relatives, eager to share news of the family. As long as this book is, I have barely begun to follow up all the leads I have been given. My initial aim was to bring together whatever results I could find that supported an experientialist view of mind. I have come to the conclusion that it would take many lifetimes to do that. I am stopping here with the knowledge that there are many others involved in the enterprise.

The ideas I have put forth are, thus, by no means uniquely my own. Most of them are shared by a diverse group of scholars whose research has led them to question traditional views of reason, categorization, and language, but who have not yet formed themselves into a community. It is important to develop such a sense of community, and I hope that this book can contribute to it.

References

Adams, Karen, and Nancy Faires Conklin. 1973. Toward a Theory of Natural Classification. In *Proceedings of the Ninth Regional Meeting, Chicago Linguistic Society,* pp. 1–10. Chicago: Chicago Linguistic Society.

Aissen, Judith. 1975. Presentational There-Insertion: A Cyclic Root Transformation. In *Papers from the Eleventh Regional Meeting, Chicago Linguistic Society,* pp. 1–14. Chicago: Chicago Linguistic Society.

Akmajian, Adrian. 1984. Sentence Types and the Form-Function Fit. *Natural Language and Linguistic Theory* 2, no. 1, 1–24.

Armstrong, Sharon Lee, Lila Gleitman, and Henry Gleitman. 1983. What Some Concepts Might Not Be. *Cognition* 13:263–308.

Arnheim, Rudolf. 1974. *Visual Thinking.* Berkeley: University of California Press.

Austin, John L. 1961. *Philosophical Papers.* Oxford: Oxford University Press.

Barsalou, Lawrence W. 1983. Ad-hoc categories. *Memory and Cognition* 11:211–27.

———. 1984. Determinants of Graded Structure in Categories. Psychology Department, Emory University, Atlanta.

Barwise, Jon. 1980. Scenes and Other Situations. In Barwise and Sag, 1980.

Barwise, Jon, and John Perry. 1980. The Situation Underground. In Barwise and Sag, 1980.

———. 1984. *Situations and Attitudes.* Cambridge, Mass.: MIT Press.

Barwise, Jon, and Ivan Sag, eds. 1980. *Stanford Working Papers in Semantics,* vol. 1. Stanford University.

Bates, Elizabeth, and Brian MacWhinney. 1982. Functionalist Approaches to Grammar. In L. Gleitman and E. Wanner, eds., *Language Acquisition: The State of the Art,* pp. 173–218, Cambridge: Cambridge University Press.

Becker, Alton L. 1975. A Linguistic Image of Nature: The Burmese Numerative Classifier System. *Linguistics,* Whole 165, pp. 109–21.

Beneke, Timothy. 1982. *Men on Rape.* New York: St. Martin's Press.

Bennett, David. 1975. *Spatial and Temporal Uses of English Prepositions.* London: Longmans.

Berlin, Brent. 1968. *Tzeltal Numeral Classifiers.* The Hague: Mouton.

———. 1976. The Concept of Rank in Ethnobiological Classification: Some Evidence from Aguaruna Folk Botany. In Casson, 1981, pp. 92–113.

Berlin, Brent, Dennis E. Breedlove, and Peter H. Raven. 1974. *Principles of Tzeltal Plant Classification.* New York: Academic.

Berlin, Brent and Paul Kay. 1969. *Basic Color Terms: Their Universality and Evolution.* Berkeley: University of California Press.

Berlin, Brent, and A. Kimball Romney. 1964. Descriptive Semantics of Tzeltal Numeral Classifiers. In A. K. Romney and R. D'Andrade, eds., *Transcultural Studies in Cognition,* pp. 79–98. Special publication of *The American Anthropologist* 66, no. 3, part 2.

Bernstein, Richard. 1983. *Beyond Objectivism and Relativism.* Philadelphia: University of Pennsylvania Press.

Bolinger, Dwight. 1972. *Degree Words.* The Hague: Mouton.

———. 1976. Language and Memory. *Language Sciences.*

———. 1977. *Meaning and Form.* New York: Longmans.

———. 1982. Intonation and Gesture. In *Papers from the Parasession on Nondeclaratives,* pp. 1–22. Chicago: Chicago Linguistic Society.

Borges, J. L. 1966. *Other Inquisitions.* New York: Washington Square Press.

Breivik, Leif Egil. 1975. The Use and Non-use of Existential *There* in Present-Day English. *Forum Linguisticum* 7:57–103.

Brown, Roger. 1958. How Shall a Thing Be Called? *Psychological Review* 65:14–21.

———. 1965. *Social Psychology.* New York: Free Press.

Brugman, Claudia. 1981. Story of *Over.* M. A. thesis, University of California, Berkeley. Available from the Indiana University Linguistics Club.

———. 1983. The Use of Body-Part Terms as Locatives in Chalcatongo Mixtec. In Report No. 4 of the Survey of California and Other Indian Languages, pp. 235–90. University of California, Berkeley.

———. 1984. Metaphor in the Elaboration of Grammatical Categories in Mixtec. Linguistics Department, University of California, Berkeley.

Burgess, Don, Willett Kempton, and Robert MacLaury. 1983. Tarahumara Color Modifiers: Category Structure Presaging Evolutionary Change. *American Ethnologist,* no. 1, 133–49.

Bybee, Joan, and Carol Moder. 1983. Morphological Classes as Natural Categories. *Language* 59, no. 2, 251–70.

Cain, A. J. 1958. Logic and Memory in Linnaeus's System of Taxonomy. *Proceedings of the Linnaean Society of London* 169:144–63.

Carbonell, Jaime. In press. Towards a Computational Model of Metaphor in Commonsense Reasoning. In Holland and Quinn, in press.

Carden, Guy. 1978. *There*-insertion Makes a Mistake: A Global Rule and the Validation of Introspective Judgments. Linguistics Department, University of British Columbia, Vancouver.

Carpenter, P. A., and P. Eisenberg. 1978. Mental Rotation and the Frame of Reference in Blind and Sighted Individuals. *Perception and Psychophysics* 23:117–24.

Casad, Eugene. 1982. Cora Locationals and Structured Imagery. Ph.D. diss., University of California, San Diego.

Casad, Eugene, and Ronald Langacker. 1985. "Inside" and "Outside" in Cora Grammar. *International Journal of American Linguistics* 51.3:247–81.

Casson, Ronald, ed. 1981. *Language, Culture, and Cognition: Anthropological Perspectives.* New York: Macmillan.

Chomsky, Noam. 1957. *Syntactic Structures.* The Hague: Mouton.

———. 1965. *Aspects of the Theory of Syntax.* Cambridge, Mass.: MIT Press.

———. 1981. *Lectures on Government and Binding.* Dordrecht: Foris.

Clark, Eve V., and Herbert Clark. 1978. When Nouns Surface as Verbs. *Language* 55, no. 4, 767–811.

Coleman, Linda. 1975. The Case of the Vanishing Presupposition. In *Proceedings of the First Annual Meeting of the Berkeley Linguistics Society,* pp. 78–89. Berkeley: Berkeley Linguistics Society.

Coleman, Linda, and Paul Kay. 1981. Prototype Semantics: The English Verb *Lie. Language* 57, no. 1, 26–44.

Craig, Colette, ed. 1986. *Categorization and Noun Classification.* Philadelphia: Benjamins North America.

Cruse, D. A. 1977. The Pragmatics of Lexical Specificity. *Journal of Linguistics* 13:153–64.

Davidson, Donald, and Gilbert Harman, eds. 1972. *Semantics of Natural Language.* Dordrecht: Reidel.

De Sousa, Ronald. 1980. The Rationality of Emotions. In A. O. Rorty, ed., *Explaining Emotions.* Berkeley and Los Angeles: University of California Press.

DeValois, R. L., I. Abramov, and G. H. Jacobs. 1966. Analysis of Response Patterns of LGN Cells. *Journal of the Optical Society of America* 56:966–77.

DeValois, R. L., and G. H. Jacobs. 1968. Primate Color Vision. *Science* 162:533–40.

Denny, J. Peter. 1976. What are Noun Classifiers Good For? In *Papers from the Twelfth Regional Meeting, Chicago Linguistic Society,* pp. 122–32. Chicago: Chicago Linguistic Society.

Dixon, R. M. W. 1968. Noun Classes. *Lingua* 21:104–25.

———. 1977. Semantic neutralization for phonological reasons. *Linguistic Inquiry* 8:599–602.

———. 1982. *Where Have All the Adjectives Gone?* Berlin: Walter de Gruyter.

Dobzhansky, T. 1955. *Evolution, Genetics, and Man.* New York: John Wiley & Sons.

Dougherty, J. W. D. 1978. Salience and Relativity in Classification. *American Ethnologist* 15:66–80. Reprinted in Casson, 1981.

Downing, Pamela. 1977. On the Creation and Use of English Compound Nouns. *Language* 53, no. 4, 810–42.

———. 1984. Japanese Numeral Classifiers: Syntax, Semantics, and Pragmatics. Ph.D. diss., University of California, Berkeley.

Dubois, D., and H. Prade. 1980. *Fuzzy Sets and Systems: Theory and Applications.* New York: Academic Press.

Eklof, P. C. 1976. Whitehead's Problem Is Undecidable. *American Mathematical Monthly* 83, no. 10, 775–87.

Ekman, Paul. 1971. *Universals and Cultural Differences in Facial Expressions of Emotions.* Nebraska Symposium on Motivation series, James K. Cole, ed. Lincoln: University of Nebraska Press.

Ekman, Paul, Wallace V. Friesen, and P. Ellsworth. 1972. *Emotion in the Human Face.* Elmsford, N.Y.: Pergamon Press.

Ekman, Paul, Robert W. Levenson, and Wallace V. Friesen. 1983. Autonomic Nervous System Activity Distinguishes among Emotions. *Science* 221:1208–10.

Emonds, Joseph. 1971. Root and Structure-Preserving Transformations. Ph.D. diss., MIT, Cambridge.

Fauconnier, Gilles. 1985. *Mental Spaces.* Cambridge, Mass.: MIT Press.

Feyerabend, Paul. 1975. *Against Method: Outline of an Anarchistic Theory of Knowledge.* London: NLB.

Fillmore, Charles. 1968. The Case for Case. In E. Bach and R. Harms, eds., *Universals in Linguistic Theory,* pp. 1–90. New York: Holt, Rinehart & Winston.

———. 1975. An Alternative to Checklist Theories of Meaning. In *Proceedings of the*

First Annual Meeting of the Berkeley Linguistics Society, pp. 123–31. Berkeley: Berkeley Linguistics Society.
———. 1976. Topics in Lexical Semantics. In Peter Cole, ed., *Current Issues in Linguistic Theory,* pp. 76–138. Bloomington: Indiana University Press.
———. 1978. The Organization of Semantic Information in the Lexicon. In *Papers from the Parasession on the Lexicon,* pp. 1–11. Chicago: Chicago Linguistic Society.
———. 1982*a.* Towards a Descriptive Framework for Spatial Deixis. In R. J. Jarvella and W. Klein, eds., *Speech, Place, and Action,* pp. 31–59. London: John Wiley.
———. 1982*b.* Frame Semantics. In Linguistic Society of Korea, ed., *Linguistics in the Morning Calm,* pp. 111–38. Seoul: Hanshin.
———. 1985. Frames and the Semantics of Understanding. *Quaderni di Semantica* 6, no. 2, 222–53.
Fillmore, Charles, Paul Kay, and Mary Catherine O'Connor. To appear. Regularity and Idiomaticity in Grammar: The Case of *Let Alone.* Department of Linguistics, University of California, Berkeley.
Fodor, J. A. 1975. *The Language of Thought.* New York: Crowell.
Frege, Gottlob. 1966. On Sense and Reference. In P. Geach and M. Black, eds., *Translation from the Philosophical Writings of Gottlob Frege.* Oxford: Blackwell.
Gazdar, Gerald, Ewan Klein, Geoffrey Pullum, and Ivan Sag. 1985. *Generalized Phrase-Structure Grammar.* Cambridge, Mass.: Harvard University Press.
Geertz, Clifford. 1973. *The Interpretation of Cultures.* New York: Basic Books.
Gensler, Orin. 1977. Non-syntactic Antecedents and Frame Semantics. In *Proceedings of the Third Annual Meeting of the Berkeley Linguistics Society,* pp. 321–34. Berkeley: Berkeley Linguistics Society.
Gentner, Dedre. 1981. Generative Analogies as Mental Models. In *Proceedings of the Third Annual Conference of the Cognitive Science Society,* pp. 97–100. Berkeley: Cognitive Science Society.
Gentner, Dedre, and Donald R. Gentner. 1982. Flowing Waters or Teeming Crowds: Mental Models of Electricity. In D. Gentner and A. L. Stevens, eds., *Mental Models.* Hillsdale, N.J.: Erlbaum.
Gibson, James J. 1979. *The Ecological Approach to Visual Perception.* Boston: Houghton Mifflin.
Gilchrist, Alan, and Irvin Rock. 1981. Rational Processes in Perception. In *Proceedings of the Third Annual Conference of the Cognitive Science Society,* pp. 50–56. Berkeley: Cognitive Science Society.
Gleitman, Lila. 1981. What Some Concepts Might Not Be. Address to Annual Meeting of the Jean Piaget Society. Psychology Department, University of Pennsylvania, Philadelphia.
Goguen, J. A. 1969. The Logic of Inexact Concepts. *Synthese* 19:325–73.
Goodman, Nelson. 1978. *Ways of Worldmaking.* Indianapolis: Hackett.
Gould, Stephen Jay. 1983. *Hen's Teeth and Horse's Toes.* New York: Norton.
Green, Georgia. 1976. Main Clause Phenomena in Subordinate Clauses. *Language* 52, no. 2, 382–97.
Hacking, Ian. 1983. *Representing and Intervening: Introductory Topics in the Philosophy of Natural Science.* Cambridge: Cambridge University Press.
Haiman, John. 1980. The Iconicity of Grammar: Isomorphism and Motivation. *Language* 56, no. 3, 515–40.
Hanson, Norwood R. 1961. *Patterns of Discovery: An Inquiry into the Conceptual Foundations of Science.* Cambridge: Cambridge University Press.

Harris, Zellig. 1957. Co-occurrence and Transformation in Linguistic Structure. *Language* 33, no. 2, 293–340.

Hawkins, Bruce. 1984. The Semantics of English Spatial Prepositions. Ph.D. diss., University of California, San Diego.

Heider, Eleanor (Eleanor Rosch). 1971. "Focal" Color Areas and the Development of Color Names. *Developmental Psychology* 4:447–55.

———. 1972. Universals in Color Naming and Memory. *Journal of Experimental Psychology* 93:10–20.

Heider, Eleanor, and D. Olivier. 1972. The Structure of the Color Space in Naming and Memory for Two Languages. *Cognitive Psychology* 3:337–54.

Hesse, Mary. 1963. *Models and Analogies in Science.* London: Sheed & Ward.

Hinton, Leanne. 1982. How to Cause in Mixtec. In *Proceedings of the Eighth Annual Meeting of the Berkeley Linguistics Society,* pp. 354–63. Berkeley: Berkeley Linguistics Society.

Holland, Dorothy, and Naomi Quinn, eds. 1987. *Cultural Models in Language and Thought.* Cambridge: Cambridge University Press.

Hooper, Joan, and Sandra Thompson. 1973. On the Applicability of Root Transformations. *Linguistic Inquiry* 4:465–98.

Hopper, Paul, and Sandra Thompson. 1984. The Discourse Basis for Lexical Categories in Universal Grammar. *Language* 60, no. 4, 703–52.

Horn, Laurence. 1985. Metalinguistic Negation and Pragmatic Ambiguity. *Language* 61, no. 1, 121–74.

Hull, David L. 1984. Contemporary Systematic Philosophies. In Sober, 1984, pp. 567–602.

Hunn, Eugene S. 1975. A Measure of the Degree of Correspondence of Folk to Scientific Biological Classification. *American Ethnologist* 2, no. 2, 309–27.

———. 1977. *Tzeltal Folk Zoology: The Classification of Discontinuities in Nature.* New York: Academic Press.

Jaeger, Jeri. 1980. Categorization in Phonology: An Experimental Approach. Ph.D. diss., University of California, Berkeley.

Janda, Laura. 1984. A Semantic Analysis of the Russian Verbal Prefixes ZA-, PERE-, DO-, and OT-. Ph.D. diss., University of California, Los Angeles.

———. 1986. Band 192. In *Slavistische Beiträge.* München: Verlag Otto.

Jespersen, Otto. 1909. *A Modern English Grammar on Historical Principles.* 7 vols. London: Allen & Unwin. Reprinted, 1954, by Barnes & Noble, New York.

Johansson, Gunnar. 1950. *Configurations in Event Perception.* Uppsala: Almkvist & Viksell.

Johnson, Mark. 1981. The Preconceptual Basis of Experiential Metaphor. Department of Philosophy, Southern Illinois University, Carbondale.

———. 1983. What Rule Theories of Morality Can't, but Ought to, Do. Department of Philosophy, Southern Illinois University, Carbondale.

———. 1987. *The Body in the Mind: The Bodily Basis of Meaning, Imagination, and Reason.* Chicago: University of Chicago Press.

Katz, Jerrold, and Paul Postal. 1964. *An Integrated Theory of Linguistic Descriptions.* Cambridge: MIT Press.

Kay, Paul. 1979. The Role of Cognitive Schemata in Word Meaning: Hedges Revisited. Department of Linguistics, University of California, Berkeley.

———. 1983*a.* Three Properties of the Ideal Reader. Cognitive Science Report, no. 7. Institute for Cognitive Studies, University of California, Berkeley.

———. 1983*b*. Linguistic Competence and Folk Theories of Language: Two English Hedges. In *Proceedings of the Ninth Annual Meeting of the Berkeley Linguistics Society*, pp. 128–37. Berkeley: Berkeley Linguistics Society.

Kay, Paul, and Willett Kempton. 1984. What Is the Sapir-Whorf Hypothesis? *American Anthropologist* 86, no. 1, 65–79.

Kay, Paul, and Chad McDaniel. 1978. The Linguistic Significance of the Meanings of Basic Color Terms. *Language* 54, no. 3, 610–46.

Keenan, E. L., and A. Faltz. 1987. *Boolean Semantics for Natural Language*. Synthese Language Library Series. Dordrecht: D. Reidel.

Kempton, Willett. 1981. *The Folk Classification of Ceramics: A Study of Cognitive Prototypes*. New York: Academic Press.

Kerr, Nancy H. 1983. The Role of Vision in "Visual Imagery" Experiments: Evidence from the Congenitally Blind. *Journal of Experimental Psychology: General* 112, no. 2, 265–77.

Kimball, John. 1973. The Grammar of Existence. In *Papers from the Ninth Regional Meeting, Chicago Linguistic Society*, pp. 262–70. Chicago: Chicago Linguistic Society.

Kleene, Stephen. 1967. *Mathematical Logic*. New York: John Wiley & Sons.

Kosslyn, Stephen M. 1980. *Image and Mind*. Cambridge, Mass.: Harvard University Press.

———. 1983. *Ghosts in the Mind's Machine*. New York: W. W. Norton.

Kripke, Saul. 1972. Naming and Necessity. In Davidson and Harman, 1972, pp. 253–355.

Kuhn, Thomas. 1970. *The Structure of Scientific Revolutions*. 2d ed. Chicago: University of Chicago Press.

———. 1977. *The Essential Tension*. Chicago: University of Chicago Press.

Kuno, Susumu. 1971. The Position of Locatives in Existential Sentences. *Linguistic Inquiry* 2, no. 3, 333–78.

Labov, William. 1973. The Boundaries of Words and Their Meanings. In Joshua Fishman, ed., *New Ways of Analyzing Variation in English*, pp. 340–73. Washington, D.C.: Georgetown University Press.

Lakatos, Imre. 1976. *Proofs and Refutations*. Cambridge: Cambridge University Press.

Lakoff, George. 1963. Toward Generative Semantics. *Syntax and Semantics*, vol. 7, ed. James D. McCawley. New York: Academic Press, 1976.

———. 1968. Counterparts, or the Problems of Reference in Transformational Grammar. Department of Linguistics, Harvard University.

———. 1970. *Linguistics and Natural Logic*. Studies in Generative Semantics, no. 2. Ann Arbor: University of Michigan Linguistics Department. Reprinted in Davidson and Harman, 1972, pp. 545–665.

———. 1972. Hedges: A Study in Meaning Criteria and the Logic of Fuzzy Concepts. In *Papers from the Eighth Regional Meeting, Chicago Linguistic Society*, pp. 183–228. Chicago: Chicago Linguistic Society. Reprinted in *Journal of Philosophical Logic* 2 (1973): 458–508.

———. 1974. Syntactic Amalgams. In *Papers from the Tenth Regional Meeting, Chicago Linguistic Society*, pp. 321–34. Chicago: Chicago Linguistic Society.

———. 1977. Linguistic Gestalts. In *Papers from the Thirteenth Regional Meeting, Chicago Linguistic Society*, pp. 236–87. Chicago: Chicago Linguistic Society.

———. 1980. Getting the Whole Picture: The Role of Mental Images in Semantics and Pragmatics. In *Proceedings of the Sixth Annual Meeting of the Berkeley Linguistics Society*, pp. 191–95. Berkeley: Berkeley Linguistics Society.

———. 1982*a*. Experiential Factors in Linguistics. In T. Simon and R. Scholes, eds., *Language, Mind, and Brain,* pp. 145–57. Hillsdale, N.J.: Lawrence Erlbaum.

———. 1982*b*. *Categories and Cognitive Models.* Cognitive Science Report, no. 2, Institute for Cognitive Studies, University of California, Berkeley.

———. 1984. *Classifiers as a Reflection of Mind.* Cognitive Science Report, no. 19. Institute for Cognitive Studies, University of California, Berkeley.

Lakoff, George, and Mark Johnson, 1980. *Metaphors We Live By.* Chicago: University of Chicago Press.

Langacker, Ronald. 1981. The Nature of Grammatical Valence. *Linguistic Notes from La Jolla* 10:33–59.

———. 1982. Space Grammar, Analysability, and the English Passive. *Language* 58, no. 1, 22–80.

———. 1983. Remarks on English Aspect. In P. Hopper, ed., *Tense and Aspect: Between Semantics and Pragmatics,* pp. 265–304. Amsterdam: John Benjamins.

———. 1986. *Foundations of Cognitive Grammar,* vol. 1. Stanford: Stanford University Press.

Levy, Robert I. 1973. *Tahitians: Mind and Experience in the Society Islands.* Chicago: University of Chicago Press.

———. 1984. Emotion, Knowing, and Culture. In Richard Shweder and Robert A. LeVine, eds., *Culture Theory: Essays on Mind, Self, and Emotion,* pp. 214–37. Cambridge: Cambridge University Press.

Lewis, David. 1972. General Semantics. In Davidson and Harman 1972, pp. 169–218.

———. 1984. Putnam's Paradox. *Australasian Journal of Philosophy* 62, no. 3, 221–36.

Lewis, Marshall. 1980. Joy in Mudville: A Syncretic Account of There-sentences. Department of Linguistics, Indiana University, Bloomington.

Lindner, Susan. 1981. A Lexico-Semantic Analysis of Verb-Particle Constructions with *Up* and *Out.* Ph.D. diss., University of California, San Diego. Available from the Indiana University Linguistics Club.

———. 1982. What Goes Up Doesn't Necessarily Come Down: The Ins and Outs of Opposites. In *Papers from the Eighteenth Regional Meeting, Chicago Linguistic Society,* pp. 305–23. Chicago: Chicago Linguistic Society.

Lounsbury, Floyd. 1964. A Formal Account of the Crow- and Omaha-Type Kinship Terminologies. In W. H. Goodenough, ed., *Explorations in Cultural Anthropology,* pp. 351–94. New York: McGraw-Hill. Reprinted in Stephen A. Tyler, ed., *Cognitive Anthropology,* pp. 212–54. New York: Holt, Rinehart & Winston, 1969.

Lyons, John. 1968. A Note on Possessive, Existential and Locative Sentences. *Foundations of Language* 3:390–96.

McCawley, James D. 1981. *Everything That Linguists Have Always Wanted to Know about Logic—But Were Ashamed to Ask.* Chicago: University of Chicago Press.

———. N.d. A Selection of *There*-insertion Verbs. Department of Linguistics, University of Chicago.

McCawley, Noriko A. 1973. Boy, Is Syntax Easy! In *Papers from the Ninth Annual Meeting, Chicago Linguistic Society,* pp. 369–77. Chicago: Chicago Linguistic Society.

McCune, Keith Michael. 1983. The Internal Structure of Indonesian Roots. Ph.D. diss., University of Michigan.

Mac Lane, Saunders. 1981. Mathematical Models: A Sketch for the Philosophy of Mathematics. *American Mathematical Monthly,* Aug.–Sept., pp. 462–72.

———. To appear. Mathematics: Form and Function. Mathematics Department, University of Chicago.

MacLaury, Robert. In preparation. Color Categories in Mesoamerica: A Cross-Linguistic Study. Ph.D. diss., University of California, Berkeley.

Malotki, Ekkehart. 1983. *Hopi Time.* Berlin: Mouton.

Marmor, Gloria Strauss, and Larry A. Zaback. 1976. Mental Rotation by the Blind: Does Mental Rotation Depend on Visual Imagery? *Journal of Experimental Psychology: Human Perception and Performance* 2, no. 4, 515–21.

Martin, D. A. and R. M. Solovay. 1970. Internal Cohen Extensions. *Annals of Mathematical Logic* 2:143–78.

Mayr, Ernst. 1963. *Animal Species and Evolution.* Cambridge, Mass.: Belknap Press.

———. 1984*a*. Species Concepts and Their Applications. In Sober, 1984, pp. 531–40.

———. 1984*b*. Biological Classification: Toward a Synthesis of Opposing Methodologies. In Sober, 1984, pp. 646–62.

Merrill, G. H. 1980. The Model-Theoretic Argument against Realism. *Philosophy of Science.* 47:69–81.

Mervis, Carolyn. 1984. Early Lexical Development: The Contributions of Mother and Child. In C. Sophian, ed., *Origins of Cognitive Skills.* Hillsdale, N.J.: Lawrence Erlbaum Associates.

———. 1986. Child-basic Object Categories and Early Lexical Development. In U. Neisser, ed., *Concepts Reconsidered: The Ecological and Intellectual Bases of Categorization.* New York: Cambridge University Press.

Mervis, Carolyn, and Eleanor Rosch. 1981. Categorization of Natural Objects. *Annual Review of Psychology* 32:89–115.

Miller, George, and Philip Johnson-Laird. 1976. *Language and Perception.* Cambridge, Mass.: Harvard University Press.

Milsark, Gary. 1974. Existential Sentences in English. Ph.D. diss., MIT. Available from the Indiana University Linguistics Club.

Minsky, Marvin. 1975. A Framework for Representing Knowledge. In P. H. Winston, ed., *The Psychology of Computer Vision.* New York: McGraw-Hill.

Murphy, Gregory L. 1982. Cue Validity and Levels of Categorization. *Psychological Bulletin* 91, no. 1, 174–77.

Murphy, Gregory L., and Douglas L. Medin. 1984. The Role of Theories in Conceptual Coherence. Psychology Department, Brown University, Providence, Rhode Island.

Nathan, Geoffrey S. 1981. What's These Facts About? *Linguistic Inquiry* 12:151–53.

Newport, Elissa, and Ursula Bellugi. 1978. A Flower Is a Flower Is a Flower. In Rosch and Lloyd, 1978, pp. 49–72.

Osherson, Daniel, and Edward Smith. 1981. On the Adequacy of Prototype Theory as a Theory of Concepts. *Cognition* 9, no. 1, 35–58.

Putnam, Hilary. 1975*a*. *Mind, Language, and Reality. Philosophical Papers,* vol. 2. Cambridge: Cambridge University Press.

———. 1975*b*. The Meaning of "Meaning." In K. Gunderson, ed., *Language, Mind, and Knowledge.* Minnesota Studies in the Philosophy of Science, 7. Minneapolis: University of Minnesota Press. Reprinted in Putnam, 1975*a*, pp. 215–71.

———. 1978. *Meaning and the Moral Sciences.* London: Routledge & Kegan Paul.

———. 1980. Models and Reality. *Journal of Symbolic Logic* 45:464–82.

———. 1981. *Reason, Truth, and History.* Cambridge: Cambridge University Press.

Pylyshyn, Zenon. 1981. The Imagery Debate: Analogue Media versus Tacit Knowledge. *Psychological Review* 87:16–45.

Quine, W. V. O. 1939. A Logistical Approach to the Ontological Problem. In Quine, 1966, pp. 64–69.

———. 1951. On Carnap's Views on Ontology. In Quine, 1966, pp. 126–34.

———. 1966. *The Ways of Paradox and Other Essays.* New York: Random House.

———. 1969. *Ontological Relativity and Other Essays.* New York and London: Columbia University Press.

———. 1983. Ontology and Ideology Revisited. *Journal of Philosophy* 130:499–502.

Quinn, Naomi. 1987. Understanding the Experience of Marriage in Our Culture. In Holland and Quinn, 1987.

Quirk, Randolph, Geoffrey Leech, Sidney Greenbaum, and Jan Svartvik. 1974. *A Grammar of Contemporary English.* London: Longmans.

Rando, Emily, and Donna Jo Napoli. 1978. Definites in There-Sentences. *Language* 54, no. 2, 300–313.

Reddy, Michael. 1979. The Conduit Metaphor. In A. Ortony, ed., *Metaphor and Thought,* pp. 284–324. Cambridge: Cambridge University Press.

Rey, Georges. 1983. Concepts and Stereotypes. *Cognition* 15:237–62.

Rhodes, Richard. 1977. Semantics in Relational Grammar. *Proceedings of the Thirteenth Annual Meeting of the Chicago Linguistic Society.* Chicago: Chicago Linguistic Society.

Rhodes, Richard, and John Lawler. 1981. Athematic Metaphors. *Papers from the Seventeenth Regional Meeting, Chicago Linguistic Society.* Chicago: Chicago Linguistic Society.

Rips, Lance J. 1975. Inductive Judgments about Natural Categories. *Journal of Verbal Learning and Verbal Behavior* 14:665–81.

Rosaldo, Michelle. 1980. *Knowledge and Passion.* Cambridge: Cambridge University Press.

Rosch, Eleanor (Eleanor Heider). 1973. Natural Categories. *Cognitive Psychology* 4:328–50.

———. 1975*a*. Cognitive Reference Points. *Cognitive Psychology* 7:532–47.

———. 1975*b*. Cognitive Representations of Semantic Categories. *Journal of Experimental Psychology: General* 104:192–233.

———. 1977. Human Categorization. In N. Warren, ed., *Studies in Cross-Cultural Psychology.* London: Academic.

———. 1978. Principles of Categorization. In Rosch and Lloyd, 1978, pp. 27–48.

———. 1981. Prototype Classification and Logical Classification: The Two Systems. In E. Scholnick, ed., *New Trends in Cognitive Representation: Challenges to Piaget's Theory,* pp. 73–86. Hillsdale, N.J.: Lawrence Erlbaum Associates, 1983.

———. In press. Coherences and Categorization: A Historical View. In *Festschrift for Roger Brown.* Hillsdale, N.J.: Lawrence Erlbaum Associates.

Rosch, Eleanor, and B. B. Lloyd, eds. 1978. *Cognition and Categorization.* Hillsdale, N.J.: Lawrence Erlbaum Associates.

Rosch, Eleanor, and Carolyn Mervis. 1975. Family Resemblances: Studies in the Internal Structure of Categories. *Cognitive Psychology* 7:573–605.

Rosch, Eleanor, Carolyn Mervis, Wayne Gray, David Johnson, and Penny Boyes-Braem. 1976. Basic Objects in Natural Categories. *Cognitive Psychology* 8:382–439.

Rosch, Eleanor, C. Simpson, and R. S. Miller. 1976. Structural Bases of Typicality Effects. *Journal of Experimental Psychology: Human Perception and Performance* 2:491–502.

Ross, John Robert. 1967. Constraints on Variables in Syntax. Ph.D. diss., MIT. Published as *Infinite Syntax!* Norwood, N.J.: Ablex, 1986.

———. 1972. The Category Squish: Endstation Hauptwort. In *Papers from the Eighth*

Regional Meeting, Chicago Linguistic Society, pp. 316–28. Chicago: Chicago Linguistic Society.

———. 1973*a*. A Fake NP Squish. In C.-J. Bailey and R. Shuy, eds., *New Ways of Analyzing Variation in English,* pp. 96–140. Washington: Georgetown University Press.

———. 1973*b*. Nouniness. In Osamu Fujimura, ed., *Three Dimensions of Linguistic Theory*, pp. 137–258. Tokyo: TEC Corporation.

———. 1974. There, There, (There, (There, (There, . . .))). In *Papers from the Tenth Regional Meeting, Chicago Linguistic Society,* pp. 569–87. Chicago: Chicago Linguistic Society.

———. 1981. Nominal Decay. Department of Linguistics, MIT.

Rudin, M. E. 1969. Souslin's Conjecture. *American Mathematical Monthly* 76:113–19.

Rudzka-Ostyn, Brygida. 1983. Cognitive Grammar and the Structure of Dutch *Uit* and Polish *Wy*. Trier, West Germany: Linguistic Agency, University of Trier.

Rumelhart, David. 1975. Notes on a Schema for Stories. In D. G. Bobrow and A. M. Collins, eds., *Representation and Understanding: Studies in Cognitive Science,* pp. 211–36. New York: Academic Press.

Sadock, Jerrold. 1977. Truth and Approximations. In *Papers from the Third Annual Meeting of the Berkeley Linguistics Society,* pp. 430–39. Berkeley: Berkeley Linguistics Society.

———. 1984. The Poly-Redundant Lexicon. In David Testen, Veena Mishra, and Joseph Drogo, eds., *Papers from the Parasession on Lexical Semantics*. Chicago: Chicago Linguistic Society.

Schachter, S., and J. Singer. 1962. Cognitive, Social, and Physiological Determinants of Emotional States. *Psychological Review* 69:379–99.

Schank, R. C., and R. P. Abelson. 1977. *Scripts, Plans, Goals, and Understanding*. Hillsdale, N.J.: Lawrence Erlbaum Associates.

Schmidt, Annette. 1985. *Young People's Dyirbal.* Cambridge: Cambridge University Press.

Searle, John. 1979. *Expression and Meaning: Studies in the Theory of Speech Acts*. Cambridge: Cambridge University Press.

Shelah, S. 1974. Infinite Abelian Groups—Whitehead's Problem and Some Constructions. *Israeli Journal of Mathematics* 18:243–56.

Shepard, Roger, and Lynn A. Cooper. 1982. *Mental Images and Their Transformations*. Cambridge, Mass.: MIT Press.

Shoenfield, J. R. 1975. Martin's Axiom. *American Mathematical Monthly* 82:610–17.

Smith, Edward E., and Douglas L. Medin. 1981. *Categories and Concepts*. Cambridge, Mass.: Harvard University Press.

Sober, Elliott, ed. 1984. *Conceptual Issues in Evolutionary Biology*. Cambridge, Mass.: MIT Press.

Sokal, Robert, and Theodore J. Crovello. 1984. The Biological Species Concept: A Critical Evaluation. In Sober, 1984, pp. 541–66.

Solovay, R. M., and S. Tennenbaum. 1971. Cohen Extensions and Souslin's Problem. *Annals of Mathematics* 94:201–45.

Sparks, Randall B. 1984. Here's a Few More Facts. *Linguistic Inquiry* 15:179–83.

Stansfield, W. D. 1977. *The Science of Evolution*. New York: Macmillan.

Stross, Brian. 1969. Language Acquisition by Tenejapa Tzeltal Children. Ph.D. diss., University of California, Berkeley.

Sweetser, Eve Eliot. In press. The Definition of *Lie:* An Examination of the Folk Theories Underlying a Semantic Prototype. In Holland and Quinn, in press.

———. 1982. Root and Epistemic Modals: Causality in Two Worlds. In *Proceedings of the Eighth Annual Meeting of the Berkeley Linguistics Society,* pp. 484–507. Berkeley: Berkeley Linguistics Society.

———. 1984. Semantic Structure and Semantic Change. Ph.D. diss., University of California, Berkeley.

Talmy, Leonard. 1972. Semantic Structures in English and Atsugewi. Ph.D. diss., University of California, Berkeley.

———. 1975. Semantics and Syntax of Motion. In J. Kimball, ed., *Syntax and Semantics,* 4:181–238. New York: Academic Press.

———. 1976. Semantic Causative Types. In M. Shibatani, ed., *Syntax and Semantics,* vol. 6: *The Grammar of Causative Constructions,* pp. 43–116. New York: Academic Press.

———. 1978*a*. Relation of Grammar to Cognition. In D. Waltz, ed., *Proceedings of TINLAP-2 (Theoretical Issues in Natural Language Processing).* Champaign, Ill.: Coordinated Science Laboratory, University of Illinois.

———. 1978*b*. Figure and Ground in Complex Sentences. In J. Greenberg, et al., eds., *Universals of Human Language,* vol. 4. Stanford: Stanford University Press.

———. 1981. Force Images. Paper presented at the Conference on Language and Mental Imagery, May 1981, University of California, Berkeley.

———. 1983. How Language Structures Space. In H. Pick and L. Acredolo, eds., *Spatial Orientation: Theory, Research, and Application.* New York: Plenum Press.

———. 1985*a*. Lexicalization Patterns: Semantic Structure in Lexical Forms. In T. Shopen, ed., *Language Typology and Syntactic Description,* vol. 3. Cambridge: Cambridge University Press.

———. 1985*b*. Force Dynamics in Language and Thought. In *Papers from the Parasession on Causatives and Agentivity.* Chicago: Chicago Linguistic Society.

Thorne, James P. 1973. On the Grammar of Existential Sentences. In Patrick Suppes et al., eds., *Studies in Logic and the Foundations of Mathematics,* vol 74: *Logic, Methodology and Philosophy of Science,* 4:863–81. Amsterdam: North Holland.

Tversky, Amos, and I. Gati. 1978. Studies of Similarity. In Rosch and Lloyd, 1978, pp. 79–98.

Tversky, Amos, and Daniel Kahneman. 1983. Probability, Representativeness, and the Conjunction Fallacy. *Psychological Review* 90, no. 4, 293–315.

Tversky, Barbara. 1986. Components and Categorization. In Craig, 1986, pp. 63–76.

Tversky, B., and K. Hemenway. 1984. Objects, Parts, and Categories. *Journal of Experimental Psychology: General* 113:169–93.

Van Oosten, Jeanne. 1977. Subjects and Agenthood in English. In *Papers from the Thirteenth Regional Meeting, Chicago Linguistic Society,* pp. 459–71. Chicago: Chicago Linguistic Society.

———. 1978. Special field examination. Department of Linguistics, University of California, Berkeley.

———. 1984. Subject, Topic, Agent, and Passive. Ph.D. diss., University of California, Berkeley.

Vandeloise, Claude. 1984. The Description of Space in French. Ph.D. diss., University of California, San Diego.

Weschler, Lawrence. 1982. *Seeing Is Forgetting the Name of the Thing One Sees.* Berkeley: University of California Press.

Whorf, Benjamin L. 1956. *Language, Thought, and Reality: Selected Writings of Benjamin Lee Whorf,* ed. John B. Carroll. Cambridge, Mass.: MIT Press.

Wilensky, Robert. 1983. *Planning and Understanding: A Computational Approach to Human Reasoning.* Reading, Mass.: Addison-Wesley.

Wilson, Deirdre. 1975. *Presuppositions and Non-Truth-Conditional Semantics.* New York: Academic Press.

Wittgenstein, Ludwig. 1953. *Philosophical Investigations.* New York: Macmillan.

Zadeh, Lotfi. 1965. Fuzzy Sets. *Information and Control* 8:338–53.

Zimler, Jerome, and Janice M. Keenan. 1983. Imagery in the Congenitally Blind: How Visual are Visual Images? *Journal of Experimental Psychology: Learning, Memory and Cognition* 9, no. 2, 269–82.

Zimmer, Karl. 1971. Some General Observations about Nominal Compounds. *Stanford University Working Papers on Language Universals,* no. 5, C1–C21. Linguistics Department, Stanford University.

Zubin, David, and Klaus-Michael Köpcke. 1986. Gender and Folk Taxonomy: The Indexical Relation between Grammatical and Lexical Categorization. In Craig, 1986, pp. 139–80.

Name Index

Subject Index